New Teacher Education for the Future:
International Perspectives

New Teacher Education for the Future: International Perspectives

Edited by

Yin Cheong CHENG
King Wai CHOW
Kwok Tung TSUI

Contributors

Richard APLIN

Doris Pui Wah
  CHAN-CHENG

Kriengsak
  CHAREONWONGSAK

Sharon Hsiao Lan CHEN

Yin Cheong CHENG

Alice Wai Kwan CHOW

John ELLIOTT

Victor FORRESTER

Ken FOSTER

Maurice GALTON

Andy HARGREAVES

Ruth HAYHOE

Rob de JONG

Michelle Mei Seung LAM

Audrey Swee Eng LIM

María Natividad LÓPEZ
  TINAJERO

Rupert MACLEAN

Magdalena Mo Ching MOK

Paul MORRIS

Angela Hing Man
  MOK-CHEUNG

Alex Mulalo
  MUTSHEKWANE

So Fong NGAN

King Chee PANG

Barbara PRESTON

He-chuan SUN

The Hong Kong Institute of Education
香 港 教 育 學 院

Kluwer Academic Publishers

Co-Published by

≋ **The Hong Kong Institute of Education**
Centre for Research and International Collaboration
10 Lo Ping Road, Tai Po, Hong Kong
Telephone: (852) 2948 7698
Facsimile: (852) 2948 7697
E-mail: cric@cric.ied.edu.hk
Website: http://www.ied.edu.hk/cric/index.htm

✿ **Kluwer Academic Publishers**
P. O. Box 17
3300 AA Dordrecht
The Netherlands
Telephone: (31) 78 639 23 92
Facsimile: (31) 78 639 22 54
E-mail: services@wkap.nl

International Distribution by

✿ **Kluwer Academic Publishers**
P. O. Box 17
3300 AA Dordrecht
The Netherlands
Telephone: (31) 78 639 23 92
Facsimile: (31) 78 639 22 54
E-mail: services@wkap.nl

Greater China Area Distribution by

≋ **The Hong Kong Institute of Education**
Centre for Research and International Collaboration
10 Lo Ping Road, Tai Po, Hong Kong
Telephone: (852) 2948 7698
Facsimile: (852) 2948 7697
E-mail: cric@cric.ied.edu.hk
Website: http://www.ied.edu.hk/cric/index.htm

Permission from the North District Secondary School Headmasters' Conference and Wing Hing Printing Company to adapt their configurative design for developing the book cover of this edited volume is gratefully appreciated.

ISBN 962-949-069-2

*To those dedicated
to education of students and teachers
for the future*

Contents

Preface

In facing up the challenges of globalization, information technology, and transformation towards new knowledge-based economy, there have been numerous diverse reforms and initiatives to change education and teacher education in different parts of the world since the mid-1990s. Particularly at the beginning of the 21st century, how to optimize our efforts to enhance the aims, content, and practice of teacher education for teachers to develop and excel in such a rapidly changing local and global context is an urgent international concern in education reforms.

To address this concern is in essence to develop a new teacher education characterized by effectiveness, quality, and relevance for meeting the challenges to education for our new generations in the new millennium. We are very pleased to report that this edited volume, with 19 chapters prepared by 25 international scholars, is an important outcome of an orchestrated effort to contribute to the search of a new teacher education for the future.

With the staunch support from many internationally renowned scholars, active researchers from different countries, Kluwer Academic Publishers, Hong Kong Institute of Education, and *Asia-Pacific Journal of Teacher Education and Development*, this book can then be published to offer readers new perspectives, insights, experiences, and lessons from different parts of the world, of which, together, form a fruitful basis to support our ongoing efforts to reform and redevelop teacher education.

All the chapters had gone through a rigorous peer review and revision process with the support of numerous anonymous international reviewers. These chapters serve to provide readers with an international understanding of, firstly, how researchers and practitioners in different countries are addressing some essential issues of and/or initiatives in teacher education and development; secondly, what they have found from their basic or applied research; and thirdly, what the implications are, of which are crucial to coping with the challenges, both present and future, from the ongoing developments in teacher education.

We sincerely hope, educators and researchers will find this publication a major source of empirical knowledge, critical ideas, and new perspectives that are essential to facilitating the pursuit of rationalizing, both instrumentally and substantively, teacher education and development in their respective countries.

The preparation and publication of this book would not have been possible without the support and effort of many special people. We would like to thank numerous international scholars, reviewers, and authors who have helped and contributed to the publication at different stages. In particular, we are greatly indebted to Dr. Magdelena Mok for her substantial academic input to our editorial process. Special thanks to Miss Sharon Fan, Mr. Steve Lee, Miss Fanny Liu, Miss Jeannie Tang, Miss Chi Yan Lee, and Miss Emily So for their clerical support to this book project given at various points of time.

Yin Cheong CHENG
King Wai CHOW
Kwok Tung TSUI

The Centre for Research and International Collaboration
The Hong Kong Institute of Education

March 2001

Part I

Introduction

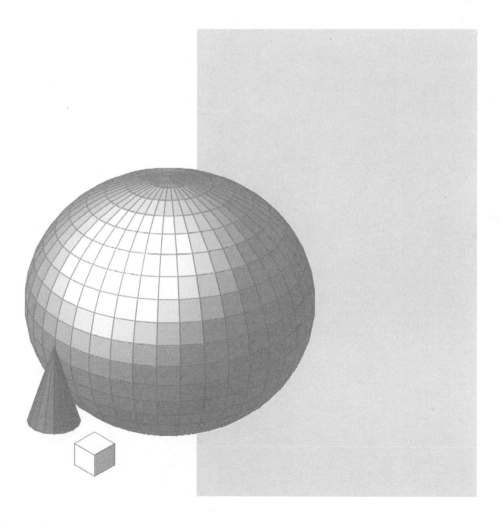

Part 1

Introduction

Chapter 1

In Search of a New Teacher Education: International Perspectives

Yin Cheong CHENG, King Wai CHOW, and Kwok Tung TSUI

Centre for Research and International Collaboration
The Hong Kong Institute of Education, Hong Kong

In the new millennium, one of the core issues in ongoing worldwide educational reforms is the development of a highly qualified and committed teaching force for "the invention of 21st century schools that can educate all children well…" (Darling-Hammond, 1995, p. 9-10; Cheng & Townsend, 2000).

Teacher education, as a field of study, as a professionally educative process, or as an enterprise encompassing all aspects of teacher preparation and development inevitably draws the attention from educators, researchers, policy-makers, and school practitioners in both local and international communities. International sharing of perspectives, ideas, experiences, experimental results, and reform outcomes in this field becomes a necessary to develop a new teacher education and benefit education development in different parts of the world in the new century.

TEACHER EDUCATION AT THE TURN OF THE CENTURY

Unfortunately, in the past decades, when teacher education was placed under the spotlight, critiques often followed, to the extent that such observers as Schnur and Golby (1995) signed: "All is not well with teacher education…" and "… a crisis in teacher education existed" (p. 11). So, is teacher education in crisis?

Teacher Education in the 1980s

Take the United States as an example. Before the early 1980s, negative aspects of schooling had received nation-wide coverage. After the issue of *A Nation at Risk* in 1983, many policy reports that focused on the problems and issues of public education were released. What followed were many national commission reports being released, pointing at the need to redesign or reform teacher preparation (Sikula, 1990).

By then, teachers, school people, and especially teacher educators were being perceived as part of the problem, rather than part of the solution. For example, as the authors of the *A Nation at Risk* (1983) documented, many teachers were "being drawn from the bottom quarter of graduating high school and college students"; many newly employed teachers were not qualified to teach their subjects; the teacher preparation curriculum was "weighted heavily with courses in 'educational methods' at the expense of courses in subjects to be taught" (http://www.ed.gov/pubs/NatAtRisk/findings.html). In view of the hard evidence, some states demanded tougher admission practices and policies for students entering teacher preparation programs and called for "testing to determine the academic fitness of teachers to teach their subject areas" (Schnur & Golby, 1995, p.13), while others even passed legislations to restructure teacher education programs, defining what should be taught and what not (p. 13-14).

England and Wales, on the other side of the Altantic, witnessed the same cynism and drive for radical reform of the structure and content of teacher education. Considering teacher education courses provided by higher education institutions of being non-rational (Young, 1998) or of no practical value (Stones, 1994), different measures were introduced, including specifying teacher competences while, at the same time, giving more responsibilities to teacher of which are "not specifiable in competence terms" (Young, 1998, p. 55); emphasizing quality assessment and inspection (Graham, 1999); and shifting the discipline-based curricula to a classroom problem-based one (Stones, 1994) and from university-based to school-based teacher education (Everton & Younger, 1999). In view of the developments, Young (1998) notes, teacher education in the UK since the early 1980s can be considered "as moving from evolutionary to technocratic modernisation" as the government tried "to make the system more efficient and cost effective" (p. 55).

Teacher Education in the 1990s

Teachers were widely blamed in the 1980s for the failures of schooling, and teacher education was often considered a prime cause for producing under-trained, substandard, or unmotivated teachers. The assault on teacher education continue in the 1990s.

Promoted in the *What Matters Most: Teaching for America's Future* released in September, 1996 by the National Commission on Teaching and America's Future is the proposition that "competent teaching is a new student right" (http://www.tc.columbia.edu/%7Eacademic/ncrest/teachcom/home.htm). Further, underscoring that there are major flaws in teacher preparation programs, the report advocates such broad policy recommendations as setting standards for teachers by "creating performance-based systems of teacher licensing, advanced certification, and education program accreditation that are linked to new student standards, connected to one another, and based on current knowledge about effective teaching"; reinventing teacher preparation and professional development by "creating extended preparation programs that include a year-long internship in a professional development school, ensuring mentoring for beginning teachers, and developing sustained, content-based professional development for veterans"; and fixing teacher recruitment and put qualified teachers in every classroom by streamlining hiring procedures, eliminating barriers to mobility, providing incentives for teaching in shortage areas and fields, and creating high-quality pathways into teaching for mid-career entrants" (ibid.).

The call for serious reforms of teacher education in the United States is echoed in many other countries (see, for example, Bonnet, 1996; Chadbourne, 1997; Dahlstrom, 1999; Elliott, 1999; Hackmann, Tack, & Pokay, 1999; Li, 1999; Ludke, Flavio, & Moreira, 1999; Musonda, 1999; Ruiz & Marcos, 1994; Sachs & Smith, 1999). The reforms tend to revolve around the theme of how to make teacher education "educative," while the measures and initiatives introduced may differ in nature, content, and focus, reflecting the diverse norms and expectations of the society in which teacher education is operating.

In view of the discussion above, how can we turn things around if teacher education is potentially in crisis? Particularly in facing up the numerous challenges to education in a new era of information technology and globalization, how can we improve or reform the existing teacher education and develop a new teacher education for the new millennium?

THE QUEST FOR A NEW TEACHER EDUCATION

This edited volume is to furnish a basis for international readers to appreciate what we know and what we could share and collaboratively do in the quest for a new teacher education for the future. Presented in the book are 19 chapters grouped into three sections: "New Perspectives in Teacher Education and Development"; "Reform and Development of Teacher Education"; and "Innovation and Reflection on Teacher Education Practice." These chapters, prepared by renowned scholars and researchers from different parts of the world with critical insights, offer a variety of approaches and perspectives, as well as findings, that are essential to our efforts in the search for a basis to developing a new teacher education in the new millennium.

New Perspectives in Teacher Education and Development

In the second part of the book, Chapters 2 to 5 reveal the current scholarly urge to reflect on new perspectives in teacher education and development. Cutting across these four chapters are some very fundamental issues and future development trends that deserve serious attention and consideration.

Paradigm Shift
In Chapter 2, Yin Cheong CHENG proposes a paradigm shift for reforming school education and teacher education in the new century. In the proposed new paradigm, long-term relevance, environmental strength, and human initiative are three key elements to support effective education development and teacher education. From these elements, Cheng further proposes that the new education and teacher education for the future should aim to develop student's contextualized multiple intelligences (CMI) such as technological, economic, social, political, cultural, and learning intelligences, through a triplization process that includes globalization, localization, and individualization. Cheng's theory furnishes a basis for explaining why a paradigm shift is necessary and for prescribing the properties of the new paradigm and in turn the appropriate approaches to and measures for formulating education reform and teacher

education change.

According to the new concepts proposed by Cheng, there will be shifts from the traditional paradigm to the triplization paradigm in the aims, curriculum structure, curriculum content, pedagogy, and quality assurance of teacher education. The theories, characteristics, and practices of new teacher education are completely different from the traditional modes. With the paradigm shifts, expectedly, the new school education and new teacher education can support students to become CMI citizens who will engage in lifelong learning and will contribute creatively to building up a CMI society and a CMI global village. And teachers will play a very crucial role in the whole process of triplization in education, and will learn, under the new paradigm, to triplize themselves as triplized CMI teachers, transform their schools into triplized CMI schools, and facilitate students' becoming triplized CMI students.

Overlooking the Fundamental

Maurice GALTON, focuses in Chapter 3 on the consequences of neglecting educational theory in the changes in English teacher education. Galton notes that the 1990s had seen considerable changes in the structure and practice of teacher education in England and Wales. Amid the changes, Galton underscores, these structural reforms fail to acknowledge the major weaknesses of this school-based training in that it is largely atheorectical. Indeed, as Galton points out, "… in all of these changes and confusions, many of the key questions to do with how best to train new teachers and improve older more experienced ones remain unanswered." Moreover, "… at present, there exists no coherent theory of how teachers learn to teach or those who are already teaching learn to do their job better. Without such a developmental approach, it is difficult to provide an agreed common curriculum and also difficult to decide what level of reflection should the teacher undertake at a particular stage."

After presenting, firstly, a review of the definitions of expertise in teaching and of the models of teacher development and, secondly, a diagnosis of the pertinent issues and problems, Galton underscores that existing models of teacher development need be validated, and much work needs be done for constructing the desirable theoretical model of developing expertise. In this context, the basis for such a model, based on the psychology of "expert performance," is outlined in the chapter.

Reinvigorating Teacher Professionalism

In Chapter 4, Andy HARGREAVES reports that "… a number of parallel movements appear to be deprofessionalizing teaching - making it more routinized, less skilled, and not nearly so complex." In view of the current development, the agenda of defining and developing teaching as a profession is an increasingly global issue, even though the agenda seems "confused and contradictory." Noting that various parts of the world have witnessed several stages in the evolution of the idea of professionalism in teaching, Hargreaves identifies four broad historical phases in the changing nature of teachers' professionalism and professional learning. They are the pre-professional age; the age of professional autonomy; the age of the collegial professionalism; and the current postmodern learning stage. Basing on his analysis, Hargreaves recommends: "… if teachers want to become professionally stronger, they must now open themselves up and become more publicly vulnerable and accessible. That is their paradoxical challenge for their professionalism in the postmodern age."

The Self Learning of Teachers

In chapter 5, Magdalena MOK and Yin Cheong CHENG, noting that recent education reforms in many countries have had only modest success, highlight for readers the importance of developing teachers into self learners for successful implementation of education reforms.

They develop in the chapter a theoretical model that encompasses the nature and process of self learning of teachers with the support of a networked human and information technology (IT) environment. The model decomposes a learning episode into a sequence of three components - the mental condition, learner action, and learning outcome. These three components are linked by the processes of planning, monitoring, feedback to mental condition, and feedback to the learning action. The theorizing is grounded on existing literature concerning adult learning and self learning, and on how adult learning is being facilitated by the social and IT environments.

This chapter has raised a number of reflective questions both for policy-makers and for teacher educators concerning how to engender in teachers a culture of self-initiated, self-managed, and self-evaluated lifelong continuous learning in formal, informal, and non-formal learning situations in order that education reform efforts can be successfully implemented and sustained.

Reform and Development of Teacher Education

The theme of the third part of the book concerns the reform and development of teacher education. The section has seven chapters - from 6 to 12 – which invariably focus on various teacher education reform issues at the macro or micro level in the education change contexts of different countries. These chapters furnish a basis for readers to reflect on some profound issues: for example, what are the challenges of education reforms to teacher education and development? How can the nature and essence of teacher development facilitate the ongoing education reform? How do system level factors of respective countries shape and reshape teacher education for the new millennium?

Reforms and Teacher Education
In chapter 5, John ELLIOTT and Paul MORRIS note that the current reforms in Hong Kong have some important implications for teacher education of which must be highlighted and analyzed. For illustration, Elliott and Morris examine a proposal for changing the curriculum, which was released by the Curriculum Development Council in 2000. They then review, among other things, three curriculum elements in the Hong Kong reform context – "what knowledge is most valued; how it should be transmitted; and how it should be assessed." Basing on their analysis, Elliott and Morris, underscoring the centrality of the teacher in the reform process, present 12 implications of the intentions of these reforms for the role of teachers and for schools. They then argue that schools and teachers must receive the needed support from various societal agencies that help define the realities of schooling.

The authors further point out that, in Hong Kong, the teacher education bodies "... have tended to be reactive and to maintain the status quo rather than support change or, more importantly, encourage teachers to act as change agents." Elliott and Morris then review four dimensions of the practice of teacher education "... that are critical to providing trainee teachers with an experience that models the worthwhile images of teaching and learning promoted in the reforms."

Challenges to Teacher Development
King Chee PANG reviews in Chapter 6 the challenges of educational reform to

teacher education in the case of Hong Kong by, first of all, identifying the most critical elements of the reform for success in achieving the objectives, then analyzing their challenges for teachers, and finally examining the implications of these challenges on changes in teacher education in Hong Kong.

Pang's analysis reveals the new teacher competencies for successfully carrying out reforms in the areas of reforming the curricula, improving teaching and learning, and improving student assessment. The identified competencies are important and necessary for facilitating the planning of pre-service and in-service programs, as well as for building up an "In-servic Education Ladder" for teachers' continuous professional development.   Pang then gives recommendations for setting up "parachute teams" to provide schools and teachers with the necessary external expert support for effectively implementing the education changes.

From Government-driven to Market-driven
In Chapter 7, Kriengsak CHAREONWONGSAK focuses on a new alternative for Thailand's in-service teacher development programs, namely marketization. Specifically, Chareonwongsak notes that while significant effort is now being invested into education reform in Thailand, the in-service teacher (INSET) training programs have many problems to be remedied. Consequently, Thai teachers are unable to develop themselves, and in turn students are unable to face the challenges of the new millennium.

To cope with the problems, Chareonwongsak proposes the adoption of a new model which is driven by market mechanisms and directed by teacher choice. To illustrate, Chareonwongsak examines the current INSET development and training processes to identify critical issues and weaknesses that make INSETs inefficient. He further ellaborates on how the new model would effectively address those problems. Finally, implications for research, policy-making, teacher education, developmental practices, pedagogical approaches as a result of such a shift towards marketization, are outlined.

The Complexity of Establishing a Standard
In chapter 8, Barbara PRESTON focuses on the Australian experience in establishing a standard in the domain of profssional preparation of teachers.

Preston reviews the policy development that moved teacher education in Australia from being a two-year course of preparation in dedicated teachers' colleges to fully professional courses conducted in universities where the standard length of preparation is four years. The author also provides a rationale as to why such a standard is important for the teaching profession. Developments in Australia are then placed by Preston in the international context in order to demonstrate the rationale for moving towards a four-year standard.

Finally, Preston highlights for readers some of the pragmatic issues and arguments related to implementation and the quality of pre-service teacher education. To conclude, Preston underscores: "if gains are to be made in improving teacher education, the commitment and leadership of teacher educators are essential; so are the involvement of other stakeholders and a supportive policy environment."

Reforming Initial Teacher Education

In Chapter 9, Richard APLIN reports that initial teacher education in England has become a focus of reform since the early 1980s and that, by late 1990s, much have changed. In providing a detailed description and critical review, Aplin considers the increasing role of the central government over the ensuing 14 years in determining the shape and detail of course structure, content, and management of pre-service training for secondary teachers. Further, Aplin examines the policy dimensions of partnerships between universities and schools. He then considers the development of comparative performance tables, linked to inspection regimes and funding implications.

In conclusion, Aplin records that the system of initial secondary teacher training in England is now highly regulated in three major respects: firstly, the national definition of content and assessment systems of teacher training; secondly, the partnerships between both higher education institutions and schools, in a more or less equal position; and thirdly, the complex system of monitoring established through inspection and financial controls. In sum, initial teacher education in England has changed, both fundamentally and in appearance.

The Constructivist Approach in Teacher Education
In the Chapter 11, Sharon Hsiao Lan CHEN reports that in the current Taiwan reform context, facing the current trend of infusing constructivist perspectives in curriculum design and in classroom teaching, it becomes imperative to make the education of teachers intellectually and experientially more solid about constructivist basis for teaching and learning. But then, it is also important to examine critically about the implications from such an emphasis on recent constructivist thinking hold for teacher education. Thus, Chen conducted a two-year action research (August 1995 – July 1997) to pursue four objectives: to explore the meaning of infusing constructivist perspectives to professional development courses; to understand what the prospective and in-service teachers think about constructivist views on teaching and learning; to evaluate the impacts of the implementation of a constructivist teaching approach on prospective and in-service teachers; and to clarify the embedded factors that may influence prospective and in-service teachers' practice of constructivist teaching approaches.

Chen finds that the implementation of a constructivist approach in professional development courses indeed had impact on prospective and in-service teachers' conceptions of and attitudes toward teaching and learning. However, there were constraints affecting prospective and in-service teachers' practice of constructivist teaching in their classrooms. Further, Chen also addresses these constraints and problems in this chapter.

Developments in the Asia-Pacific
In Chapter 11, Rupert MACLEAN, underscores the need to systematically exploring the various profound issues of teacher education in the Asia-Pacific region so that effective strategies for coping with those issues can be formulated. He briefly reviews the diversity in demography, economy, geography, ecology, and culture within the Region and then highlights that "... teachers are facing major problems that threaten the effectiveness and quality of education systems." Maclean continues his review by examining some common issues and concerns with regard to the changing status and profile of teachers in the Region - recruitment; professional education and development; compensation and reward - as well the challenges stemming from the application of information technologies in education.

After reviewing some programs and activities of UNESCO organized for teachers to enhance professional development, Maclean concludes that the role of teachers has changed dramatically over the years, and more major changes are inevitably to occur. Such an inevitability leads us to pay attention to some critical questions: "What direction should such change take? What innovative changes can we take into the new century with confidence? How can teachers and teacher educators, as well as pre-service and in-service education, adapt to promote effective teacher development suited to the future, its citizens, and the 'brave new world'?"

Innovation and Reflection on Teacher Education Practice

Chapters 13 to 20 are grouped into the fourth part of the book. These chapters, focus on some unique educational experiences or professional practices in teacher education, again, in different countries. The commonalities of the chapters revolves around the themes of reflective practices, optimization of dividends, and innovative experiences for teacher development. These chapters further enrich our knowledge base and draw attention to some obvious, but overlooked, issues that have important implications for teacher education practices.

The Narratives of Influential Teachers

In chapter 13, Ruth HAYHOE furnishes a basis for readers to understand "the role of teachers in modern China through the eyes of individuals who lived out their lives through a tumultuous century of dramatic political and economic change." After reviewing the values of the narrative method in educational research and giving some essential information about the legacy of Chinese education and background knowledge of socio-political changes that occurred in modern China, Hayhoe presents the narratives of the three influential teachers: LI Bingde (a master of Chinese pedagogy), PAN Maoyuan (a pioneer of higher education research in China), and GU Mingyuan (a doyen of comparative education in China).

Hayhoe's objective is to draw some lessons "that we might learn for teacher education and the formation of teachers." And the lessons are indeed educational. For example, the lives of all three of these teachers illustrate "... how important a deep and reflective self-understanding is for the capacity to absorb and apply useful ideas from the international community..." and also reveal "the way in which this kind of understanding can lead one to become a lifelong learner and an educator able to adapt to changing economic and political circumstances, and to inspire and motivate successive generations of students." Another lesson relates to the way in which each of these teachers internalized the Confucian educational progressive elements – "openness to external ideas and a rigorous tradition of self-cultivation that made possible the integration of a wide range of external ideas into the Chinese context." Consider another important lesson: the teachers could develop in the turbulent context of education development in China "an ability to learn in all circumstances and to keep in touch with changing educational circumstances at the grass roots..." and the three teachers genuinely appreciated "the opportunities for practical professional development and for reflection on action and experience."

Stratification of Refresher Courses

In Chapter 14, María Natividad LÓPEZ TINAJERO reports the Japanese experience in providing in-service teacher training. The focus is on the strategies implemented in recent years by the government for the purposes of broadening, systematizing, and rationalizing training for the teachers.

The author firstly presents an overview of Japanese teacher training, with reference to salient issues, including the oversupply of teachers, the necessity of in-service teacher training, and teachers' professional development. After assessing the importance of offering in-service teacher training in Japan's context, particularly focusing on the teaching career stages from the theoretical perspectives, López Tinajero gives an account of courses for experienced teachers according to the length of service of which is organized by the Hiroshima Prefectural Education Center. The author underscores that the stratification of refresher courses according to years of teaching experience is recognized as the most important feature of this program. The rationales, structure, and content are reviewed in light of the theoretical propositions about teaching career stages. The author concludes: "... the stratification of courses according to years of experience can efficiently be put into practice given the standardization of Japanese education .... This organization could represent a good option for teachers' career-long professional development."

Client-based In-service Education

In Chapter 15, Alex Mulalo MUTSHEKWANE focusess on the issues of client-based in-service education and training of teachers in South Africa. In specific, Mutshekwane reviews the education policy development in South Africa in both the pre-apartheid and post-apartheid eras; presents an overview of current teacher education policies; gives a profile of the in-service education of teachers in South Africa; and examines the model of client-based in-service education and training of teachers.

By reviewing the development and operation of two in-service education and training providing institutions in the Northern Province - the Ramaano Mbulaheni Training Centre (RMTC) and the Mathematics, Science, Technology College (MASTEC) - Mutshekwane reveals some qualities of effective and ineffective continuous teacher development practices. With the cases of RMTC and MASTEC, Mutshekwane further underscores 11 critical criteria that affect the effectiveness of client-based in-service teacher education programs.

Belgium and China in Comparison

In Chapter 15, He-chuan SUN and Rob de JONG note that "... to learn more about the necessary conditions for effective schools, international comparative studies are needed." Thus, Sun and Jong conducted a comparative study on secondary education in China and Belgium. In this chapter, they report the findings about secondary education, school effectiveness, and teacher development in China and Belgium, focusing on the differences at both the national level and the school level.

In this chapter, Sun and Jong draw four policy recommendations for Chinese education and teacher education development in China: more funds for Chinese education and equity education; more research on school effectiveness and cost-effectiveness; increased participation in international exchange programs for teacher training and pursuit of teacher training in a more future-oriented and world-oriented way; and reducing the discrepancies between theories and practice of classroom teaching.

Management Training and School Improvement

In Chapter 17, Ken FOSTER, reports the findings of an action research study of the relationship between school management training and school improvement in the context of an innovative management training strategy developed by a large local education authority (LEA) in the North West of England.

Highlighted in the chapter is the application of a flexible and innovative approach to school management training: the Lancashire Education Management Program (LEMP), which was to encourage "a focus on management development in primary and secondary schools based on a series of management standards" and to depart from the traditional path of in-service training by placing an emphasis on school-based activity. Then, Foster discusses the methodological aspects of action research within the Lancashire scheme, including "an assessment of the emergent collaborative structures, linking the contributions of participants who represent the interests of the LEA, the schools, and the university." The chapter ends with Foster's discussion relating to the "future prospects for professional development in relation to changes in the school system and in approaches to school management in particular." Further, "to inform policy on the future professional development of teachers in the field of school management and leadership," Foster presents a total of seven recommendations.

Educator Attachment to School

Chapter 17 is prepared by Angela Hing Man MOK-CHEUNG and Alice Wai Kwan CHOW, reporting the authors' "back-to-school" experience derived from their participating in the Lecturer Attachment Scheme initiated by The Hong Kong Institute of Education. The scheme is for "creating opportunities for ... teaching staff to update their school teaching experience..." while "... school teachers can update their knowledge and reflect upon their practice."

The two authors present details of the attachment arrangement they had made with and in the selected school – a primary school - as well as the problems and challenges they had confronted and experienced. They then give a critical reflection on their experiences with which they underscore that, for example, there are differences in the operational cultures between the primary school and the teacher education institution and that the two authors' perception of learning and homework differs considerably from the teachers'. These differences are also noted in the authors' review of the perceptions of teachers in the school. Mok-Cheung and Chow conclude that the scheme could enhance the professional development of the teacher educators in broadening their knowledge base, bridging the credibility gap of theory and practice, and "validating their knowledge base through reality checks."

Semantic Mapping in Teacher Education

In Chapter 18, the authors, Audrey Swee Eng LIM, Doris Pui Wah CHAN-CHENG, Michelle Mei Seung LAM, and So Fong NGAN, document the findings of an exploratory study applying the use of semantic mapping strategies to facilitate critical and reflective thinking skills in teacher education. In the study, a total of 73 first maps (drawn at the beginning of a series of taught sessions) and 87 second maps (drawn at the end) prepared by 58 Year Two student-teachers from two classess were analyzed for their structural and content complexity. Interviews with nine randomly selected student-teachers were then conducted to provide feedback on the usefulness of semantic mapping strategies in facilitating critical and reflective thinking.

The authors report that the first maps are typically simple in structure, while the second maps are more complex, more integrated, and better presented, reflecting, as documented by the eventual interviews, that semantic maps did help student-teachers understand the different components of the modules taught and that "… semantic mapping facilitated thinking, the organization of key concepts/ideas, brainstorming strategies, convergence of key concepts, and ease of 'reading' and memory." In addition, for example, the semantic mapping strategy also helped student-teachers by facilitating lesson planning as well as curriculum planning.

Student-based Self-research

In Chapter 19, Victor FORRESTER reports a series of student-based self-research tasks in the form of two critiques in order to explore the relationship between pedagogy and tertiary student learning in a teacher education institution. In specific, the first critique considers "a series of student-based research in terms of its results…" and presents a contextual demographic framework to highlight the perceptions held by students moving from secondary school to tertiary teacher education institution, while providing a basis for drawing a number of policy and pedagogy implications that deserve serious attention.

The second critique considers "self-research as a *learning process.*" In this second critique, the pedagogic implications of student-based self-research are considered by Forrester. Forrester concludes that student-based self-research in teacher education, "satisfying the needs of both subject knowledge, 'revolutionary' learning, and the attributes/perceptions of incoming teacher-trainees," serves the combined needs of both policy-makers seeking to implement educational reforms and of pragmatic, conservative students.

IMPLICATIONS FOR THE SEARCH OF A NEW TEACHER EDUCATION

What can we learn from the 19 chapters presented in this edited volume, of which cover a great variey of international perspectives, practices, and issues? Is there now a basis for critical readers to critically reflect on our current values, knowledge, and practices to complete our quest for a new teacher education in the new century? Or will teacher education still be in serious problems and remain a source of frustration and disappointment, a target for political assault, a self-cherishing scapegoat, and an institution relinquishing its prerogative of making a difference in the lives of school teachers and in turn students?

A number of implications for policy formulation and reformulation, for minor improvement or major reconditioning of professional practice, and for advancement of basic and applied research can be drawn from the perspectives, analyses, and findings presented in the chapters. Indeed, many the contributors have explicitly stated or identified for readers those implications in their chapters. Since these chapters are different in their concerns and perspectives, their implications for new teacher education are very fruitful but may be different. The readers would enjoy the detail of these implications in each chapter.

First Order Implications

In addition to the specific implications of each chapter, we can further deduce from the chapters some overall first order implications pertinent to our quest for a new teacher education.

Sophisticated Conceptualization and Formulation

For example, Galton's chapter underscores a fundamental point for insightful readers: too often researchers and teacher educators just take theories at face value without giving it a serious thought on whether or not the "theories" have internal validity and logical consistency, and, when the theories are "borrowed," on whether or not they are applicable in the teaching context due to the unique nature of schooling. Cheng's chapter as another example clearly illustrates that taking a multidisciplinary, multivariate, and multilevel approach (incorporating into it an emphasis on examining the temporal and cross-sectional dimensions of the ever-changing educational phenomena for drawing implications) is imperative to defining the nature, values, and scope of a desirable teacher education in the new century.

Maclean's chapter and the one by Sun and Jong reveal the variety, diversity, and complexity of schooling and teacher education in different countries, compelling readers to recognize that different systems have different issues and problems for different reasons. Then, the chapter by Elliot and Morris illustrates how sophisticated and critical analysis of reform proposals can help delineate a comprehensive picture of interrelatedness of reform measures and needed supporting arrangements for effectuating the reforms. In sum, an important implication from these chapters is to ask for sophisticated conceptualization and formulation in teacher education in the new century.

Systematic Analysis and Strategy

Hargreaves shows to readers how a systematic analysis of the issues of teacher professionalism can yield a systematic basis for understanding the orderly issues of professionalization of teaching and how an un-orderly conclusion (about the paradoxical challenge for teachers) can be drawn. The chapter by Mok and Cheng reveals that a systematic contextualization can provide a basis for constructing a taxonomy of self-learning for the professional development of teachers. Chen's chapter illustrates how a seemingly fussy approach to teacher education can be systematically employed to generate a systematic strategy for systematic implementation that generate pleasant and fruitful outcomes. These chapters urge us to employ more systematic and comprehensive perspectives and analyses in theorizing and reforming teacher education and development towards a new model.

Relevance to the Future Needs

Lopez Tinajro's chapter documents that many existing approaches to designing teacher development program are undesirable and any effective programs must readily accommodate the actual needs of the teacher. Mutshekwane's chapter, highlighting the values and effectiveness of client-based teacher development programs, points to the same: taking appropriate action to directly satisfying the needs of teachers. Cheng's chapter strongly emphasizes the relevance of teacher education to the future needs of developing contextualized multiple intelligence students and teachers and the processes of globalization, localization, and individualization in education. So, one important implication from these chapter is to ensure he relevance to the future needs in the designing and redesigning of teacher education initiatives and practices in an era of rapid globalization, transformation, and information technology.

Innovation in Conception, Policy, and Practice

Foster's chapter, focusing on the application of a flexible and innovative approach to school management training, underscores for readers the values of innovation. Forrester's report of a series of student-based self-research tasks documents how one can creatively function as a self facilitator of tertiary learning while reaping the dividends of student self-research for advancing the knowledge of teaching in teacher education programs. Then, Chareonwongsak's chapter shows that "if we are unable to answer the questions, we might be taking the wrong exam!" The author's creative introduction of a policy option for revitalizing Thailand's in-service teacher development program is indeed refreshing. There are also many examples of new ideas and innovations for teacher education in chapters of this book. Here, one important implication we can immediately draw from the chapters is to pursue innovation in conception, policy, and practice in developing new teacher education and development.

More First Order Implications

With reference to the other chapters - by Hayhoe; Pang; Preston; Aplin; Mok-Cheung and Chow; Lim, Chan-Cheng, Lam, and Ngan – as well as the chapters already referred to, some more first order implications may be drawn (such as "cultural sensitivity" etc.). The essence to be highlighted here is that from their own perspectives, readers can perceptively draw *more their own implications* from these chapters by focusing on the rationales, approaches, methodologies, and principal findings presented, explicitly or implicitly, in these chapters. The first order implications listed above are just some examples to show the insightful fruitfulness of these chapters as a whole to readers when they want to identify the basic implications for their own concerns in teacher education and development. Clearly, readers would look at the specific implications in each chapter.

Second Order Implications

Here, the first order implications together may lead us to consider some direct and overall issues. But at the same time, we need to pay attention to some fundamental contextual and human issues about teacher education. In other words, we have to consider the second order implications for changing contextual constraints and facilitating human initiative in our quest for a new teacher education for the future.

For example, we may have overlooked the cultural, economic, and political contexts in which teachers and teacher educators operate and thus failed to underscore how the contexts shape and reshape the essence and practice of teacher education. The insights of Hayhoe (chapter 13) and of Cheng (chapter 2) draw our attention to the simple fact that teachers and teacher educators are often molded and remolded by the contexts, even though we would strongly encourage breakthroughs to contextual constraints in teacher education. And when Aplin's (chapter 10) and Preston's (chapter 9) sensitivity to politics is blended with the understanding above, we should readily note one fundamental point: some problems teacher educators and teachers are experiencing are inevitable, no matter how hard they try to improve themselves, their work, and professional knowledge, skills, and abilities, because they are often constrained by various types of contextual factors of the contemporary society.

The Contextual Constraints
Politicians often pay lip-service to education reform by failing to rationally formulate feasible and practical policies and programs that can be implemented to produce outcomes which are substantively rational and humanely desirable. Parents often shift their responsibilities to teachers while blaming the teachers for not shouldering those responsibilities (Hargreaves, 1995), and citizens often demand teachers to deliver what cannot be delivered without sufficient support and training. And many teachers and teacher educators themselves may try very hard, often beyond their capacity, to satisfy

the very high demands from society and thus continuously experience frustration while subscribing to the social labeling that there are merely a group of semiprofessionals having limited intelligence to perform equally well as compared with such other sociologically established professionals as medical doctors and lawyers.

More problems and constraints can be added to the list. But it should already be clear enough that the problems of schooling may reflect the problems of social engineering of a society, and thus many of the school education problems require society-wide solutions.

In short, when reforming teacher education for the future, the change of contextual constraints on teachers and teacher educators to encourage professionalization is inevitably necessary.

Human Initiative – Turning Things Around
In view of many of the findings presented in the 19 chapters about the new perspectives, strong commitments, valuable experiences, and innovative practices in the field, we should feel comfortable to assert that the true might of teachers and teacher educators in making a difference in and contribution to the society must not be overlooked. Teachers and teacher educators themselves should realize that they have can achieve perspectives, relevant field experiences, professional competences, and frontier research-based knowledge to play a central role not only in education reform generally but in teacher education in particular.

They can help reconstruct a new teacher education in the new millennium. Such a new teacher education will be characterized by rationality and humanity, building on the premises of what goals teachers and teacher educators can objectively accomplish, of what jobs need to be done and undone if desirable educational goals for school children are to be achieved, and of what concerted social reform efforts must be mobilized to remove the contextual obstacles and cope with the existing problems in teacher education and school education. With these premises, teachers and teacher educators would move away from the old paradigm and become "new" teachers and "new" teacher educators for the new millennium.

The "New" Teachers in Action

In reality, teachers and teacher educators can do a lot to generate real effects even in a changing environment, but only with appropriate support. For example, teachers will have great difficulties to implement the policy of enhancing student-centered learning when they have more than, for instance, in Hong Kong, 40 students in the classroom, while having a unreasonably heavy workload and lacking sufficient administrative supports. By the same token, it will be very unfair for teachers to implement an inclusive education policy, if absence is an array of adequate professional training and supports, particularly for education of both the gifted students and students with special needs.

In facing the challenges of the new century, teachers should be expected to adapt to education changes and pursue lifelong professional development. Their professional knowledge and competencies should be upgraded and further developed to meet the needs of the paradigm shift in curriculum, teaching, and learning in an era of information technology and globalization. This further development process is in fact also a paradigm shift process in teacher education and development. Teachers have to change their existing mind-sets and practicing approaches to teaching from the traditional model to a completely new paradigm. Clearly, it is absolutely not easy. They should be given sufficient time for preparation, as well as support, particularly in form of rationally planned professional development programs that facilitate their changes intellectually, technologically, and professionally towards new teachers for the new century, rather than the ad hoc, piece-meal, and remedial training.

Particularly when teachers are expected to play multi-faceted roles and perform multi-functional services as listed in such mainstream publications as the *International Encyclopedia of Teaching and Teacher Education* (Anderson, 1995), capable of, for example, learning from daily teaching or teaching students with diverse backgrounds as advocated by reformers with visions, such as (Darling-Hammond, 1998), their formal, professional education must be adequately provided for, even if the duration of those educational programs may be as lengthy as, for instance, medicine's.

We hope, teachers can become they really are, "glorious engineers cultivating human souls" (Li, 1999, p. 184), with the extent of their success causally related to the extent of the rationality of education reform policy, as well as the timeliness and sufficiency of the provision of resources and supports needed for the success.

The "New" Teacher Educators in Action

What and how teachers are expected to perform have a direct bearing on what and how teacher educators to perform. Further, the aforementioned issues and problems that teachers confront may be also what teacher educators experience, though not necessarily in appearance. Ultimately, they can scholarly and professionally do what they can do best. That is, basing on their future outlook, international perspectives, field experience, and professional knowledge of schooling, blended with subject knowledge and aided by their critical mind, to perform two critical tasks.

The first is the advancement of pedagogical content knowledge relevant to the future and paradigm shift in education, the turf that no others professional groups can intrude into and the stuff that readily makes teaching a truly unique profession (Turner-Bisset, 1999).

The second task is redesigning the teacher education programs for pre-service an in-service teachers to make them what they are supposed to be – professional, educative, and relevant to the future. Specifically, too often some teacher educators have forgotten the fundamental function of their programs, i.e., influencing teachers' beliefs about the purposes of education, the roles of professional teachers, and the teaching practice (Tatto, 1998): to socialize teachers, pre-service or in-service, to internalize the values of teaching, uphold the oath that teachers vow, and the develop commitment to attain high standard of excellence and to continuous professional development – in short, to make teachers "real teachers," those who would receive intrinsic rewards from making a difference in the lives of students in the new century.

Now, many teacher educators would have to keep expanding the scope and variety of courses to satisfy unlimited externally imposed demands for training of teachers in, for example, collaborative teaching (Yopp & Guillaume, 1999), drug prevention (Harris, 1998), teaching multi-culturally diverse students (Shade, 1995), and legal issues of schooling (Gullatt & Tollett, 1997). Even so, they would consider redesigning the programs to transmit the minimal but necessary informational and operational knowledge and then to send the students through a journey of higher order learning with which they would become self-directed and lifelong learning professionals. They would have the needed intellectual capacity, core knowledge and competence base, and behavioral tendency. And they would be able to efficiently and fruitfully learn, on their own or with inputs from others, what they need to learn and to teach in an ever changing schooling context (Mok & Cheng, Chapter 5). The triplization including globalization, localization, and individualization in teacher education would be an important trend and paradigm for teacher educators to develop new teacher education for the new millennium (Cheng, Chapter 2).

The "New" Researchers in Action

With coordinated specializations, many educators and researchers pursue what ever is relevant and critical to teaching and learning in the new century, particularly education policy and program research so as to further facilitate teachers' work and professional development. More importantly, they help rationalize the education system and its reform measures through their active research.

Some critical research may help adjust the direction or implementation of ongoing education reform. For example, research shows that teacher empowerment is related to improvement in instruction and student learning only when the school policy and culture support a school-wide efforts to improve the learning environment of students (Marks & Louis, 1997). Therefore, the implementation of initiatives on teacher empowerment should be carefully coordinated and supported with other school policies. Research also reveals that what is good for teachers is not necessarily good for students (Levin, 1994) and substantive improvement requires a result-orientation of school people (Hackman, Tack, & Pokay, 1999) as well as fundamental changes in the ethos that underlines schooling (Tabachnick, 1998).

In addition to these research are many other pedagogical research that teacher educators can pursue, of which serves not only improving the practices of teaching and learning at the site level but also contributes to the overall research capacity building, particularly in developing countries (Crossley & Vulliamy, 1996). As shown in the chapters of this edited volume, all these research efforts are important to providing a more comprehensive knowledge base in developing a new teacher education.

While so far many educators and researchers have been making progress in the research arena, many important areas of teacher education have yet to be explored (Cheng, 1998; Ducharme & Ducharme, 1996). But education researchers could in fact be in charge of their research destiny, appreciating the significance of research to teacher education and focusing on important research problems that they would not have in the past. They could have the long due confidence in playing the leadership role in shaping the research agenda that can facilitate paradigm shift in education and benefit teacher education and development in an era of globalization, information technology and knowledge-based society. The chapters in this book have provided numerous implications and significant insights for future research in teacher education.

Most importantly, teacher educators or teachers as researchers would recognize that schooling, reflecting the essence and dynamics of human societies, or even the global ecological system, is inevitably complex, and thus all related educational phenomena and processes, particularly teaching and teacher education, are inevitably characterized by heterogeneity, intricacy, and complexity. As such, educators or other scholars, in pursuing basic or applied research, would consider employing multidisciplinary, multilevel, cross-cultural, or comparative perspectives to address education research problems, while underscoring for stakeholders, particularly policy-makers, that ensuring multifariousness of research in education reform, particularly teacher education reform, is imperative.

CONCLUSION

All in all, this edited volume is to furnish an international basis for readers, firstly, to appreciate what we know and what we could share and collaboratively do in the quest for a new teacher education in the new millennium and, secondly, to experience how we can turn knowledge into intelligence by underscoring some overlooked but fundamental issues and by making the critical analysis of those issues a component of our own automated cognitive system.

With reference to the 19 chapters with international perspectives, both first order and second order implications are drawn to illustrate how and what we can do in our quest for a new teacher education for the future. With the transfer of professional knowledge and international perspectives and experiences into intelligence in developing teacher education, hopefully, all seemingly irresolvable problems or irreconcilable differences can be more efficiently and effectively dealt with in facing the global and local challenges to education and teacher education. It can be done, and it should be done for the future of our students and teachers in a new era of transformation.

REFERENCES

Anderson, L. W. (Ed.), *International encyclopedia of teaching and teacher education.* Cambridge: Pergamon.

Bonnet, G. (1996). The reform of initial teacher training in France. *Journal of Education for Teaching, 22*(3), 249-269.

Chadbourne, R. (1997). Teacher education in Australia: What difference does a new government make? *Journal of Education for Teaching, 23*(1), 7-27.

Cheng, Y. C. (1998). The Pursuit of a new knowledge base for teacher education and development in the new century. *Asia-Pacific Journal of Teacher Education and Development, 1*(1), 1-16.

Cheng, Y. C., & Townsend, T. (2000). Educational change and development in the Asia-Pacific region: Trends and issues. In T. Townsend & Y. C. Cheng (Eds.), *Educational change and development in the Asia-Pacific Region: Challenges for the future* (pp. 317-344). The Netherlands: Swets and Zeitlinger Publisher.

Crossley, M., & Vulliamy, G. (1996). Issues and trends in qualitative research: Potential for developing countries. *International Journal of Educational Development, 16*(4), 439-448.

Dahlstrom, L. O. (1999). Transforming teacher education for a democratic society – the case of namibia. *Teaching and Teacher Education, 15*(2), 143-156.

Darling-Hammond, L. (1995). Changing conceptions of teaching and teacher development. *Teacher Education Quarterly, 22*(4), 9-26.

Darling-Hammond, L. (1998). Teacher learning that supports student learning. *Educational Leadership, 55*(5), 6-11.

Ducharme, M., & Ducharme, E. (1996). A study of teacher educators: Research from the USA. *Journal of Education for Teaching, 22*(1), 57-70.

Elliott, J. (1999). Quality assurance, the educational standards debate, and the commodification of educational research. *Curriculum Journal, 8*(1), 63-83.

Gullatt, D. E., & Tollett, J. R. (1997). Educational law: A requisite course for preservice and inservice teacher education programs. *Journal of Teacher Education,*

48(2), 129-135.

Hackmann, D. G., Tack, M. W., & Pokay, P. A. (1999). Results-oriented school improvement: Lessons from practice. *International Journal of Educational Reform, 8*(1), 8-14.

Hargreaves, A. (1995). Renewal in the age of paradox. *Educational Leadership, 52*(7), 14-19.

Harris, S. (1998). Drugs education for whom? *Journal of Education for Teaching, 24*(3), 273-284.

Levin, B. (1994). Educational reform and the treatment of students in schools. *The Journal of Educational Thought, 28*(1), 88-101.

Li, D. (1999). Modernization and teacher education in China. *Teaching and Teacher Education, 15*(2), 179-192.

Ludke, M., & Moreira, A. F. B. (1999). Recent proposals to reform teacher education in Brazil. *Teaching and Teacher Education, 15*(2), 169-178.

Marks, H. M., & Louis, K. S. (1997). Does teacher empowerment affect the classroom? The implications of teacher empowerment for instructional practice and student academic performance. *Educational Evaluation and Policy Analysis, 19*(3), 245-275.

Musonda, L. W. (1999). Teacher education reform in Zambia...is it a case of a square peg in a round hole? *Teaching and Teacher Education, 15*(2), 157-168.

Ratnavadivel, N. (1999). Teacher education: Interface between practices and policies – the Malaysian experience 1979-1997. *Teaching and Teacher Education, 15*(2), 193-214.

Ruiz, I. G., & Marcos, A. R. (1994). Initial teacher education in Spain: A critical analysis. *Journal of Education for Teaching, 20*(3), 313-323.

Sachs, J., & Smith, S. G. (1999). The changing landscape of teacher education in Australia. *Teaching and Teacher Education, 15*(2), 215-227.

Schnur, J. O., & Golby, M. J. (1995). Teacher education: A university mission. *Journal of Teacher Education, 46*(1), 11-18.

Shade, B. (1995). Developing a multicultural focus in teacher education: One department's story. *Journal of Teacher Education, 46*(5), 375-380.

Sikula, J. (1990). National commission reports of the 1980s. In W. R. Houston, M. Haberman & J. Sikula (Eds.), *Handbook of research on teacher education: A project of the association of teacher educators* (pp. 72-82). New York: Macmillan Publishing Company.

Stones, E. (1994). Reform in teacher education: The power and the pedagogy. *Journal of Teacher Education, 45*(4), 310-318.

Tabachnick, B. R. (1998). Useful educational research in a transforming society. *Journal of Education for Teaching, 24*(2), 101-108.

Tatto, M. T. (1998). The influence of teacher education on teachers' beliefs about purposes of education, roles, and practice. *Journal of Teacher Education, 49*(1), 66-77.

Turner-Bisset, R. (1999). The knowledge bases of the expert teacher. *British Educational Research Journal, 25*(1), 39-56.

Yopp, H. K., & Guillaume, A. M. (1999). Preparing preservice teachers for collaboration. *Teacher Education Quarterly, 26*(1), 5-19.

Young, M. (1998). Rethinking teacher education for a global future: Lessons from the English. *Journal of Education for Teaching, 24*(1), 51-62.

Part II

New Perspectives in Teacher Education and Development

Yin Cheong CHENG
Maurice GALTON
Andy HARGREAVES
Magdalena Mo Ching MOK

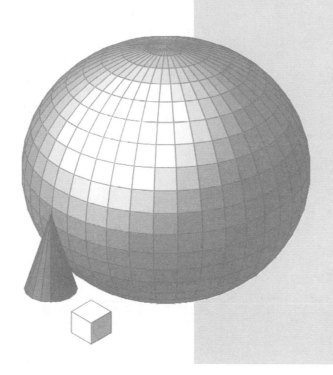

Chapter 2

New Education and New Teacher Education: A Paradigm Shift for the Future[1]

Yin Cheong CHENG

Centre for Research and International Collaboration
The Hong Kong Institute of Education, Hong Kong

INTRODUCTION

Since the 1980s, numerous educational reforms and school restructuring movements have been initiated and implemented to pursue effective education in the Asia-Pacific region and other parts of the world (Cheng & Townsend, 2000). In the process, policy-makers and educators have to seriously consider how to change their schools, reform curriculum and pedagogy, and prepare their young people to more effectively cope with challenges in the new era (Dalin & Rust, 1996; Gardner, 1999).

Then, in approaching the new millennium, the education systems in the world function in a turbulent context, characterized by increasing uncertainties and ambiguities. The rapid globalization, long lasting impacts of information technology, drastic shocks of the 1997 economic downturn in the Asia-Pacific Region, and strong domestic demands for economic and social developments to cope with international competitions have further fueled the flame of reform, accelerating educational changes in the different parts of the world.

In such a context, most policy-makers and educators get confused by numerous novel but conflicting ideas and inevitably lose their directions in the war against mediocrity. It is therefore not a surprise that most of their reform efforts have become reactive, piecemeal, fragmented, or ineffective, notwithstanding their good will, hard work, and substantial investment.

All these are hardly inevitable. The keys are that education reform must be knowledge-based and theory-driven, and that all reform efforts must be rationally orchestrated. To meet these two prescriptions, there must be a general theory to deepen our understanding of the rapid developments and related impacts and to advance significant and relevant implications for reforming school education and teacher education. Such a theory would help describe the essence of education in the age of reason (Handy, 1994), the age of paradox (Handy, 1995), and the age of triplization (Cheng, 2000a). Such an understanding of the essence of education would draw our attention to, firstly, some fundamental misconceptions of school education and, secondly, the demand for a new paradigm for understanding and developing school education and teacher education to meet the challenges in the new millennium, of which is urgently needed in the international community.

The operational assumption here is that the current paradigm is now inappropriate in the 21st century, for many of its premises are no longer valid and its underlying values are becoming incompatible with the peculiar changes taking place on the globe. A paradigm shift is therefore inevitable.[2]

This chapter is to propose a paradigm shift for reforming school education and teacher education in the new century. To substantiate the proposal, a general theory of education in the new millennium, resting on the premises of three key elements drawn from the wisdom of ancient Chinese civilization, on the premises of contextualized multiple intelligences (CMI), and on the premises of triplization, is developed. This theory furnishes a basis for explaining why a paradigm shift is necessary and for prescribing the properties of the new paradigm and in turn the appropriate approaches to and measures for enhancing rationalized education reform.

THE THREE KEY ELEMENTS

The three key elements that can be drawn from the ancient Chinese wisdom include Long-term Relevance, Environmental Strength, and Human Initiative. Particularly relevant to our analysis of the three key elements are the works by Sun Tzu (or Sun Zi).

Sun Tzu (1994) was the most famous martial strategist in ancient China 2,200 years ago. Up to now, his book, *The Art of War*, is still one of the most influential references not only to the military strategists but also to the business, policy, and management strategists operating in the context of contemporary regional and international developments and competitions. Many people in different parts of the world have adopted the insights and thinking from Sun Tzu's strategies and applied them in different types of social, political, and economic activities. The wisdom in Sun Tzu's book is in fact an important part of the deep root of Chinese civilization, reflecting the essence of such important works as *Tao Teh Ching* by Lao Tzu (1991). Based on Sun Tzu's strategies (Sun, 1994), we can identify three key elements for achieving the success of a strategy or a mission: *Tian Shi, Di Li,* and *Ren He.* In the modern language, the meanings of these key elements and their implications for enhancing effective education and teacher education are illustrated in Table 1.

Table 1: *The Three Key Elements for Effective Education and Teacher Education*

The Elements	The Focus	The Essence	The Implications
Tian Shi	Long-term Relevance	• Doing the right things in the right time and in the right direction • Meeting future needs and mega-trends	The aims and content of education should meet the future needs of students and the society and have impacts in the future, such that education can ensure its long term relevance to the developments of the society and its citizens.
Di Li	Environmental Strength	• Taking strengths and advantages from the internal and external environments • Creating and materializing opportunities from the local contexts for completing a task or achieving the mission and enhancing development of the organization	School practices should create and materialize opportunities for teaching, learning, and school development from the internal and external school environments as well as from the local and regional communities.
Ren He	Human Initiative	• Promoting human synergy, and social harmony of an organization • Encouraging initiative, creativity, and staff development	The educational practice and school management should meet the needs of students and teachers, develop their potential, cultivate better social relationship among members, and promote staff development in order to encourage members' commitment, motivation, initiative, and creativity in learning, teaching, and school development.

Tian Shi refers to doing the right things in the right time and in the right direction. This key element prescribes that meeting the needs of the future and mega-trends is critical and necessary so as to ensure the long term development and success of an organization and its mission.

In education, the focus of *Tian Shi* is on the Long-term Relevance of education. In other words, the aims and content of education should meet the future needs of students and the society and have impacts in the future, such that education can ensure its long term relevance to the developments of the society and its citizens.

This concept is inevitably important to the current discussion about effective education or effective school. While effectiveness of any education programs can be subjectively defined by subjectively selected criteria, the application of *Tian Shi* will demystify the subjectivity, as *Tian Shi* underscores the significance of focusing on the interactive relationships among time, space, and the object in operation within the changing temporal and spatial contexts. For example, with reference to *Tian Shi*, one can readily point out that a school is ineffective even when it has been "effectively" and even efficiently providing solid training to students in technical knowledge of and craft in certain manufacturing industries, if in fact the traditional manufacturing industries have already been displaced by the IT intensive industries (Cheng, 1996).

In short, education is a complex process with its outcomes influenced by various factors. In determining effectiveness, the ideas of "doing the right things in the right time and in the right direction," i.e., *Tian Shi*, must be uphold. Consequently, the concept of Long-term Relevance should be a key criterion for defining effective education.

Further, the concept has the same pertinence in the discussion of effective teacher education. Therefore, strengthening the long term relevance of teacher education to educational change and development in the new era must also be a key issue in the quest for a new paradigm for teacher education (Bay & Tozer, 1999; Cheng, 2000c; Griffin, 1999).

Di Li refers to the taking of strengths and advantages from the internal and external environments, by creating and materializing opportunities from the contexts, so as to effectively completing a task or achieving the mission and enhancing development of the organization.

In the education sector, the focus of *Di Li* is on the Environmental Strength for education. In other words, school practices should involve the mobilization of resources available in the internal and external school environments, with the latter broadly defined to include the local and regional communities, so as to create and materialize opportunities for effective teaching, learning, and school development. The typical examples of maximizing the Environmental Strength for effective schooling include the building up of an IT environment and facilities, the consolidation of local support and community linkage, the institutionalization of active parental involvement or home-school cooperation, the effectuation of institutional collaboration, and the routinization of the sharing of educational resources among different interest groups and partners.

With reference to the key element, *Di Li*, the focus is no longer on increasing financial support from funding organizations or the clientele to improve education quality. Instead, the focus is to be on comprehensive review, exploration, redefinition, and reformulation of all resources, processes, and educational know-how so as to reengineer the whole schooling process occurring within the broadly defined school context in such a way that teachers will become high performing teachers and students becoming high achieving students, who together make the school a high achieving school.

Similarly, how to increase Environmental Strength is one of the key concerns for teacher education. Different types of local partnership, networking, internship, and mentorship for upgrading teacher education and the teaching profession are some typical examples of the efforts to creating and maximizing opportunities for teacher learning and development.

Ren He refers to promoting human synergy, initiative, creativity, social harmony, and staff development for completing a task or achieving the mission of an organization. In education, the focus of *Ren He* is on encouraging, promoting, and realizing the Human Initiative in the dynamic educational process. In other words, the educational practices and school management should meet the needs of students and teachers, develop their potential, cultivate better social relationship among members, and promote staff development in order to encourage members' commitment, motivation, initiative, and creativity in learning, teaching, and school development, all in the dynamic educational process that occurs in an interactive and ever changing educational context.

As documented in the literature of educational psychology, educational effectiveness, educational administration or leadership, how to enhance human initiative in education in general or teacher education in particular is often a core issue in the quest for effectiveness of education. Indeed, numerous initiatives in education reforms have been proposed and implemented in the past decades, with an aim to realize students' and teachers' personal growth and development and to promote students' and teachers' commitment and motivation to education. Those initiatives, however, are still insufficient for one very simple reason: the initiatives often narrowly focus on merely the students and/or teachers without taking into account the rapidly changing educational, socio-economic, and political contexts.

It is for this reason that *Ren He* is a very important element in achieving quality education and effective teacher education: it makes reference to the dynamics of the educational process through which Human Initiative can be encouraged, promoted, and realized; it draws our attention to the significance of the contexts in which the educational process occurs, and to the ecological impacts asserted on and implications of the dynamic interactions between the process and contexts.

In sum, the three key elements discussed here focus on how human beings are to be energized and how their potentials can be actualized by prescribing the approaches to achieve a systematic, rational, and balanced development of the educational process through which human growth and development are enhanced, the approaches that take into account the temporal and spatial dimensions of the contexts in which the educational process occurs.

Then, one important point deserving serious attention from educators and policy-makers is that *Tian Shi*, *Di Li*, and *Ren He*, if applied in isolation, cannot guarantee the success of a strategy or the accomplishment of a mission; instead, all of the three elements must be simultaneously considered and systematically integrated to form a more holistic approach to articulating reform efforts to achieve effective education and teacher education. How to formulate and then apply such a holistic approach to maximizing the Long-term Relevance (*Tian Shi*) of educational aims and content, increasing the Environmental Strength (*Di Li*) for learning and teaching, and enhancing Human Initiative (*Ren He*) in the educational process inevitably becomes the key driving issue in the reforms for educational effectiveness. This is particularly so in such a rapidly changing educational environment in the new millennium.

The premises of *Tian Shi*, *Di Li*, and *Ren He* clarify the fundamentals of education reform, broaden the perspectives for educators and policy-makers, prescribe the appropriate approaches to enhancing desirable educational change, and stipulate what and why educators are to generally achieve. These, however, are still insufficient for defining school education and teacher education in the new millennium and for specifying the specific goals, contents, and methods of a new education. The premises of CMI and of triplization must also be taken into consideration.

THE PREMISES OF CONTEXTUALIZED MULTIPLE INTELLIGENCES

As elaborated in my recent work (Cheng, 2000a), the complexities of human nature can be understood in terms of a typology of *Technological Person, Economic Person, Social Person, Political Person, Cultural Person,* and *Learning Person* in a complicated context of the new century. Further, the human intelligence essential to meeting the challenges in the new millennium should be contextualized as *Technological Intelligence, Economic Intelligence, Social Intelligence, Political Intelligence, Cultural Intelligence,* and *Learning Intelligence.*

In order to meet the developmental needs in the technological, economic, social, political, cultural, and learning aspects of individuals and society in the new millennium, school education should be redesigned. The development of students' CMI is the basic condition for the development of individuals, institutions, communities, societies, and international communities in the complex local and global contexts, particularly with reference to the typology of the six important aspects as mentioned (see Table 2). Therefore, school education should be reformed with clear relevance and concrete linkages with the development of CMI. (For a detailed discussion of the premises of CMI, framed as the Pentagon Theory of CMI development, please see Cheng [2000a].)

The new design of education should encourage and facilitate interactions and mutual reinforcements among the CMI. *Intelligence transfer* from one type to other types (e.g., from economic intelligence to political intelligence or social intelligence) should be facilitated in order to achieve a higher level of intelligence or meta-thinking. The transfer itself can represent a type of intelligence creativity and generalization. To accelerate the development of all CMI, the development of learning intelligence can play a central role. Instead

Table 2: *Contextualized Multiple Intelligences*

Human Nature	Contextualized Multiple Intelligences	Definition of the Contextualized Multiple Intelligences
• Learning Person	• Learning Intelligence	• It refers to the ability to learn and think creatively and critically and maximize the use of biological/ physiological abilities
• Technological Person	• Technological Intelligence	• It refers to the ability to think, act, and manage technologically and maximize the use of various types of technology
• Economic Person	• Economic Intelligence	• It refers to the ability to think, act, and manage economically and maximize the use of various resources
• Social Person	• Social Intelligence	• It refers to the ability to think, act, and manage socially and develop harmonious interpersonal relationship
• Political Person	• Political Intelligence	• It refers to the ability to think, act, and manage politically and create win-win situation in competing resources and interests
• Cultural Person	• Cultural Intelligence	• It refers to the ability to think, act, and manage culturally and maximize the use of multi-cultural assets and create new values

of teaching and learning an immerse volume of information and factual materials, the content of curriculum and the process of pedagogy should emphasize on developing students' ability to learn persistently and on how to learn systematically, creatively, and critically.

The successful provision of a CMI education for students depends heavily on the quality of teachers and of the school. Whether teachers themselves own a higher level of CMI and whether the school is a multiple intelligence organization that provides a CMI environment for teaching and learning will affect the design and implementation of a CMI education. Therefore, in the reform of school education, how to develop teachers as *Contextualized Multiple Intelligence Teachers* and schools as *Contextualized Multiple Intelligence Schools* through teacher education and school development inevitably becomes a top priority item on the reform agenda.

In short, through a forward-looking perspective and taking into account the types of major forces operating in the changing socio-economical, political, and technological contexts in which the education system functions, systematic efforts have been expended to construct a typology of six important aspects of the configuration of human nature. With the typology, systematic analysis of most crucial intelligences needed for an individual to effectively grow, develop, survive, and excel in the new millennium has resulted in the identification of CMI, which clearly prescribes the fundamental aims and goals, as well as the content and process, of education in the 21st century.

In order to maximize the opportunities for the development of CMI for students, teachers, and the school, globalization, localization, and individualization in schooling, teaching, and learning are important and necessary to education reforms in the new era. The following paragraphs will highlight their conceptions and use them to propose a paradigm shift for new school education and teacher education.

THE PREMISES OF TRIPLIZATION

Delineated in my recent work (Cheng, 2000b) are the premises of triplization that postulate the consideration of three important processes - globalization, localization, and individualization - in education reform efforts. All of these processes integrated as a whole can be taken as a *Triplization Process* (i.e., triple + izations) that can be used to discuss education reforms and formulate the new pedagogic methods and environment to implement new curriculum for enhancing CMI of students as well as for teacher education.

Globalization refers to the transfer, adaptation, and development of values, knowledge, technology, and behavioral norms across countries and societies in different parts of the world.[3] The typical phenomena and characteristics associated with globalization include growth of global networking (via, for example, the Internet, e-mail, etc.); global transfer and interflow in technological, economic, social and cultural aspects; international alliances and competitions; international collaboration and exchange; global village and multi-cultural integration; and use of international standards and benchmarks.

The most profound implication of globalization for education is the critical need of educators to maximize the global relevance and achieve intellectual assets, resources, and initiatives from different parts of the world for schooling, teaching, and learning (Caldwell & Spinks, 1998; Daun, 1997; Townsend & Otero, 1999). Some examples of globalization in education are Web-based learning; use of the Internet in learning and teaching; international immersion programs; international exchange and visit programs; international partnership in teaching and learning at the group, class, and individual levels; interactions and sharing through video-conferencing across countries, communities, institutions, and individuals; and new curriculum content on globalization in technological, economic, social, political, cultural, and learning aspects.

Localization refers to the transfer, adaptation, and development of related values, knowledge, technology, and behavioral norms from and to the local contexts. Such a concept definition implies that the concept can be applied differently: it can mean the adaptation of all related external values, initiatives, and norms to meet the local needs at the society, community, or site levels; it can also mean the enhancement of local values, norms, concern, relevance, participation, and involvement in the related initiatives and actions.

Some characteristics and examples of localization are as follows: local networking; adaptation of external technological, social, and economic initiatives to local communities; decentralization to the community or site level; development of indigenous culture; meeting community needs and expectations; local involvement, collaboration, and support; local relevance and legitimacy; and concerns for school-based needs and characteristics and for social norms and ethos (Cheng, 1998; Kim, 1999; Tam, Cheng, & Cheung, 1997).

The profound implication of localization to education is the critical need to maximize the relevance, community support, and initiative from the local community in schooling, teaching, and learning. Some examples for practice of localization include community and parental involvement in school education; home-school collaboration; assurance of school accountability; implementation of school-based management, school-based curriculum, and community-related curriculum; and development of new curriculum content related to local developments in technological, economic, social, political, cultural, and learning aspects.

Individualization refers to the transfer, adaptation, and development of related external values, knowledge, technology, and behavioral norms to meet the individual needs and characteristics. The importance of individualization to human development and performance is based on the concerns and theories of human motivation and needs (e.g. Alderfer, 1972; Manz, 1986; Manz & Sims, 1990; Maslow, 1970).

The major implication of individualization in education is the imperative for educators to maximize motivation, initiative, and creativity of students and teachers in teaching and learning through such measures as implementing individualized educational programs; designing and using individualized learning targets, methods, and progress schedules; encouraging students and teachers to be self-learning, self-actualizing, and self-initiating; meeting individual special needs; and developing students' CMI.

Some examples of individualization are provision of individualized services; emphasis of human potentials; promotion of human initiative and creativity; encouragement of self-actualization; self-managing and self-governing; and concern for special needs.

In sum, students, teachers, and schools should be *globalized, localized,* and *individualized* during the process of triplization. Or, simply, they should be *triplized.*

TRIPLIZATION AND THE THREE KEY ELEMENTS

All in all, as mentioned earlier, the premises of *Tian Shi, Di Li,* and *Ren He* furnish a basis for educators and policy-makers to deepen their understanding of the fundamental values of the aims and content of education; of what school practices should be focused on; and of the crucial mission of the educational practice and school management. Stipulating what and why educators are to generally achieve is still insufficient for specifying the specific goals, contents, and methods of a new school education and teacher education in the new millennium. The premises of CMI and of triplization must also be taken into consideration.

In light of the discussion in the preceding sections, the whole picture should now be clear: through the triplization process, the three key elements - Long-term Relevance, Environmental Strength, and Human Initiative - for reform of school education and teacher education can be operationalized and effectuated because globalization ensures Long-term Relevance of education through maximizing the global relevance and drawing upon support, intellectual resources, and initiatives from different parts of the world for schooling, teaching, and learning; because localization achieves Environmental Strength through maximizing the local relevance, community support and initiative in schooling, teaching, and learning; and because individualization enhances Human Initiative through maximizing motivation, initiative, and creativity in schooling, teaching, and learning. (See Table 3 for a summary.)

When all the three premises as discussed are related together, a general theory of education in the new millennium is made available for explaining why education and its reform have been found unsatisfactory: educational reforms without Long-term Relevance, Environmental Strength, and Human Initiative are bounded to be non-rational (if not irrational) and ineffective; educational pursuits without the aims and contents tightly related to achieving CMI of students and teachers are inevitably incomplete and instrumentally deficit; and the goals of enhancing high achieving students, high performing teachers, and high achieving schools cannot be accomplished unless triplization of education occurs.

With reference to the general theory, it should also be clear that, firstly, great impacts from rapid globalization are evident on every aspect of the society in the Asia-Pacific region and other parts of the world (Brown, 1999; Waters, 1995). Inevitably, how education should be responsive to the trends and challenges of globalization has to be a major concern for the long term relevance of education in policy-making in these years (Ayyar, 1996; Brown & Lauder, 1996; Fowler, 1994; Green, 1999; Henry, Lingard, Rizvi, & Taylor, 1999; Jones, 1999; Little, 1996; McGinn, 1996). Moreover, how to meet local needs, how to involve community support, and how to enhance site-level motivation and initiatives are together another key concern in current education reforms (Cheng & Townsend, 2000; Kim, 1999). Thus, localization in education is often assumed to be necessary for building environmental strength for learning and teaching (Cheng, 1998; Cheng & Townsend, 2000; Kim, 1999; Tam, Cheng, & Cheung, 1997).

Furthermore, reform efforts have to meet the needs of students and teachers and to motivate them to be effective in teaching and learning. In other words, individualization in education is crucial to eliciting the necessary human initiative, imagination, and creativity from school members and community

Table 3: *Triplization and The Three Key Elements of Effective Education*

Triplization	Conceptions and Characteristics	Achieving the Three Key Elements of Effective Education
Globalization	Transfer, adaptation, and development of values, knowledge, technology and behavioral norms across countries and societies in different parts of the world: • Global Networking • Technological, Economic, Social, Political, Cultural, and Learning Globalization • Global Growth of the Internet • International Alliances and Competitions • International Collaboration and Exchange • Global Village • Multi-cultural Integration • International Standards and Benchmarks	**To ensure Long-term Relevance of education through maximizing the global relevance and drawing upon support, intellectual resources, and initiatives from different parts of the world for schooling, teaching, and learning: e.g.,** • Web-based Learning • International Visit/Immersion Program • International Exchange Program • Learning from the Internet • International Partnership in Teaching and Learning at group, class, and individual levels • Interactions and Sharing through Video-Conferencing across Countries, Communities, Institutions, and Individuals • Curriculum Content on Globalization in Technological, Economic, Social, Political, Cultural, and Learning Aspects.
Localization	Transfer, adaptation, and development of related values, knowledge, technology, and behavioral norms from/to the local contexts: • Local Networking • Technological, Economic, Social, Political, Cultural, and Learning Localization • Decentralization to the Local Site Level • Indigenous Culture • Community Needs and Expectations • Local Involvement, Collaboration and Support • Local Relevance and Legitimacy • School-based Needs and Characteristics • Social Norms and Ethos	**To achieve Environmental Strength through maximizing the local relevance, community support and initiative in schooling, teaching, and learning: e.g.,** • Community Involvement • Parental Involvement & Education • Home-School Collaboration • School Accountability • School-based Management • School-based Curriculum • Community-related Curriculum • Ability Grouping/ Classroom • Curriculum Content on Local Developments in Technological, Economic, Social, Political, Cultural and Learning Aspects

Table 3: *Triplization and The Three Key Elements of Effective Education* (Continued)

Triplization	Conceptions and Characteristics	Achieving the Three Key Elements of Effective Education
Individualization	Transfer, adaptation, and development of related external values, knowledge, technology, and behavioral norms to meet the individual needs and characteristics: • Individualized Services • Development of Human Potential in Technological, Economic, Social, Political, Cultural and Learning Aspects • Human Initiative and Creativity • Self-actualization • Self-managing and Self-governing • Special Needs	**To enhance Human Initiative through maximizing motivation, initiative, and creativity in schooling, teaching, and learning: e.g.,** • Individualized Educational Programs • Individualized Learning Targets, Methods, and Progress Schedules • Self Life-long Learning, Self-actualizing, and Self-initiative • Self-managing Students, -teachers, and -schools • Meeting Special Needs • Development of Individual's CMI

members for education. In particular, the development of each student's CMI is a core concern in individualization of education. Therefore, globalization, localization, and individualization are all necessary processes to achieve what the three key elements prescribe: Long-term Relevance, Environmental Strength, and Human Initiative.

More importantly, this general theory of the three key elements, CMI, and triplization can be used to propose a paradigm shift for new school education. What we would note is that the assumptions about the future of the world, the human nature, the developments of individuals and the society, the aims of education, the students and learning, the teachers and teaching are contrastingly different between the new paradigm and the traditional paradigm. The new paradigm may also be named as the "New Triplization Paradigm" and the traditional one as "Traditional Site-Bounded Paradigm." (For details, please refer to Cheng [2000a].) The following paragraphs highlight some key features of the paradigm shift in school education that will be helpful to the discussion of paradigm shift in teacher education in the later part of this paper.

PARADIGM SHIFT IN DEVELOPMENT AND EDUCATION AIM

The new triplization paradigm assumes that the world is in multi-dimensional globalization, including technological, economic, social, political, cultural, and learning globalizations. The world is moving very fast to become a global village, in which different parts of the world are rapidly networked and globalized through the Internet and different types of IT, communications, and transportation (Albrow, 1990; Green, 1999; Marginson, 1999; Naisbitt & Aburdence, 1991). All countries and areas have more and more sharing and common concerns. Also, the interactions among nations and among people become boundless, multi-dimensional, multi-level, fast, and frequent. They become more and more mutually dependent with international collaborations, exchanges, and interflows.

In the new paradigm, the human nature in the social context of the new millennium is predictably multi-dimensional as technological person, economic person, social person, political person, cultural person, and learning person in a global village of information, high technology, and multi-cultures. Both individuals and the society need multi-dimensional development in the technological, economic, social, political, cultural, and learning aspects. Life-long learning and learning society (or knowledge society) are necessary to sustain the continuous developments of individuals and the society in a changing new century (Drucker, 1993, 1995).

The new paradigm rests on the premise that the education environment is inevitably characterized by triplization, including globalization, localization, and individualization at the different levels (macro, messo, and micro) and of the different aspects of the education system. The environment is very fast changing and becoming very complicated and full of uncertainties and ambiguities. The boundaries of schools as well as the education system become unclear and disappearing. Students and teachers often interact frequently and intensively with the "real world" in learning and teaching (Caldwell & Spinks, 1998; Townsend, 1999). Continuous educational reforms and developments are inevitable due to various local and global challenges emerging from this changing education environment. In such a context, the aim of education is to support students becoming a CMI citizen who will be engaged in life-long learning and will creatively contribute to building up a multiple intelligence society and a multiple intelligence global village.

The traditional paradigm conceives that the world has limited globalization, mainly in the economic and social aspects. All the nations in different parts of the world are only loosely related. They have serious competitions and conflicts more than sharing and collaboration. There are very limited, loose, and weak interactions among nations and among people. As a whole, they are loosely coupled with some international collaborations and interflows (Beare & Slaughter, 1993; Naisbitt, 1984). The human nature in such a context is mainly assumed as economic person or social person in an industrial or business society. Both individuals and the society pursue narrow developments, mainly on economic, social, or political aspects. School or vocational education is assumed necessary to provide the needed manpower for some specific developments of a society at some stages (Cheng, 1995; Cheng & Ng, 1992). Consequently, the need for life-long learning or learning society may not be so important. The society is an industrial or agricultural society emphasizing on some types of intelligence or knowledge related to the existing stage of development of a society. Individuals are expected to a citizen with bounded types of knowledge or skill that meet the need of society at a certain stage of development.

The traditional paradigm assumes that education environment is mainly characterized by the needs of local community. The environment is rather stable with relatively little uncertainties and complexity. The boundaries of schools and the education system are still stable and clear. Teachers and students rarely interact with the "real world" in their teaching and learning. Students enter the "real world" only after graduation or leaving schools. Educational reforms are often limited and superficial mainly as a reaction to the raised public accountability and local concern. From this paradigmatic perspective, the aim of education is to equip students with the necessary skills and knowledge to survive in a local community or to support the development of a society particularly in the economic and social aspects at a certain stage.

PARADIGM SHIFT IN LEARNING

New Paradigm of Learning

The new paradigm of school education prescribes that students and their learning should be individualized, localized, and globalized (see Table 4). Student is the centre of education. "Individualized Student and Learning" means that students and their learning should be facilitated in a way such that all types of transfer, adaptation, and development of related values, knowledge, technology, and norms during learning process can meet their needs and personal characteristics, and that their potentials, particularly CMI, can be optimally realized.   Different students can learn in different style. Individualized and tailor-made programs (including targets, content, methods, and schedules) for different students is necessary and feasible. Students can be self-motivated and self-learning with appropriate guidance and facilitation. Learning is a process of self-actualizing, discovering, experiencing, and reflecting.   Since the information and knowledge are accumulated in an unbelievable speed but outdated very quickly, it is almost impossible to make any sense if education is mainly to deliver skills and knowledge, particularly when students can find out the knowledge and information easily with the help of IT and the Internet. Therefore, the new century paradigm emphasizes that the focus of learning is on how to learn, think, and create. In order to sustain learning as life long, learning should be facilitated as enjoyable and self-rewarding.

Table 4: *Paradigm Shift in Learning*

New Triplization Paradigm	Traditional Site-Bounded Paradigm
Individualized Student and Learning:	**Reproduced Students and Learning:**
• Student is the centre of education	• Student is the follower of teacher
• Individualized programs	• Standard programs
• Self-learning with appropriate guidance and facilitation	• Absorbing knowledge from their teachers
• Self-actualizing process	• Receiving process
• Focus on how to learn	• Focus on how to gain
• Self-rewarding and enjoyable	• External rewarding and punishment avoiding
Localized and Globalized Students and Learning:	**School-Bounded Learning:**
• Multiple local and global sources of learning	• Teacher-based learning
• Networked learning	• Separated learning
• Life-long and everywhere	• Fixed period and within school
• Unlimited opportunities	• Limited opportunities
• World-class learning	• School bounded learning
• Local and international outlook	• School experiences

Students and their learning should be globalized and localized in such a way that local and global resources, support, and networks can be brought in to create and materialize the opportunities for students' developments during their learning process. Through localization and globalization, students can learn from multiple sources inside and outside their schools, locally and globally, not limited to a small number of teachers in their schools. Participation in local and international learning programs can help them achieve the community experiences and global outlook beyond schools. Also their learning is a type of networked learning. They will be grouped and networked locally and internationally. Learning groups and networks will become a major driving force to sustain the learning climate and multiply the learning effects through mutual sharing and inspiring. We can expect that each student can have a group of life-long partner students in different corners of the world to share their learning experiences.

It is expected that learning happens everywhere and is life long. School education is just the start or preparation for life-long learning. Learning opportunities are unlimited. Students can maximize the opportunities for their learning from local and global exposures through the Internet, Web-based learning, video-conferencing, cross-cultural sharing, and the using of different types of interactive and multi-media materials (Education and Manpower Bureau, 1998). Students can learn from the world-class teachers, experts, peers, and learning materials from different parts of the world. In other words, their learning can be a world-class learning.

Traditional Paradigm of Learning

In the traditional thinking, students and their learning are part of the reproduction and perpetuation process of the existing knowledge and manpower structure to sustain developments of the society, particularly in the social and economic aspects (Blackledge & Hunt, 1985; Cheng & Ng, 1992; Hinchliffe, 1987; McMahon, 1987). It is not a surprise that education is perceived as a process for students and learning being "reproduced" to meet the needs of the society.

In school education, students are the followers of their teacher. Available to students are standard programs of education, in which students can be taught in the same way and same pace even though their ability may be different. Individualized programs seem to be unfeasible. The learning process is characterized by absorbing certain types of knowledge, and students are "students" of their teachers and absorb knowledge from their teachers. Learning is a disciplinary, receiving, and socializing process such that close supervision and control on the learning process are necessary. The focus of learning is on how to gain some knowledge and skills. Learning is often perceived as hard working activities for achieving external rewards and avoiding punishment.

In the traditional paradigm, all learning activities are school-bounded and teacher-based. Students learn from a limited numbers of school teachers and their prepared materials. Therefore, teachers are the major source of knowledge and learning. Students learn the standard curriculum from their textbooks and related materials assigned by their teachers. Students are often arranged to learn in a separated way and are kept responsible for their individual learning outcomes. They have few opportunities to mutually support and learn. Their learning experiences are mainly school experiences alienated from the fast changing local and global communities. Learning happens only in school within a given school time frame. Graduation tends to be the end of students' learning.

PARADIGM SHIFT IN TEACHING

From the paradigm shift in development, education aim, and learning, we can foresee the corresponding paradigm shift in teaching as well as teacher education in the new century. The characteristics (or features) of the paradigm shift are highlighted in Table 5.

New Paradigm of Teaching

From the new paradigmatic perspective teachers and their teaching should also be triplized: individualized, localized, and globalized. Teachers and their teaching are facilitated in an individual way such that their own potentials can be easily realized to facilitate students' learning. Teaching becomes a process to initiate, facilitate, and sustain students' self-learning and self-actualization; therefore, teachers should play a role as a facilitator who support students' learning. The focus of teaching is to arouse students' curiosity and motivation to think, act, and learn. Also, during the process, teaching is to share the joy of learning process and outcomes with students (The Hong Kong Institute of Education, 1998). To teachers themselves, teaching is a life-long learning process involving continuous discovery, experimenting, self-actualization, reflection, and professional development. Teachers should be a multiple-intelligence teacher who can set a model for students in developing their multiple intelligences. Each teacher has his/her own potential and characteristics, and different teachers can teach in different styles to maximize their own contributions. It means that teachers and their teaching are to be individualized.

Table 5: *Paradigm Shift in Teaching*

New Triplization Paradigm	Traditional Site-Bounded Paradigm
Individualized Teacher and Teaching:	**Reproduced Teacher and Teaching:**
• Teacher is the facilitator to support students' learning	• Teacher is the center of education
• Multiple intelligence teacher	• Partially competent teacher
• Individualized teaching style	• Standard teaching style
• Teaching is to arouse curiosity	• Teaching is to transfer knowledge
• Teaching is a process to initiate, facilitate, and sustain students' self-learning and self-actualization	• Teaching is a disciplinary, delivering, training, and socializing process
• Sharing joy with students	• Achieving standards in examinations
• Teaching is a life-long learning process	• Teaching is a transfer and application process
Localized and Globalized Teacher and Teaching:	**School-bounded Teacher and Teaching:**
• Multiple local and global sources of teaching and knowledge	• Teacher as the sole source of teaching and knowledge
• Networked teaching	• Separated teaching
• World-class teaching	• Site-bounded teaching
• Unlimited opportunities for teaching	• Limited opportunities for teaching
• Teacher with local and international outlook	• Teacher with only school experiences
• As a world class and networked teacher	• As a school-bounded and separated teacher

Teachers and their teaching should be globalized and localized in such a way that local and global resources, supports, and networks can be brought to maximize the opportunities for teachers' developments in teaching and their contributions to students' learning. Through localization and globalization, there are multiple sources for teaching inside and outside their schools, locally and globally. Teachers can materialize the opportunities to enhance effectiveness of their teaching from local and global networking and exposure through the Internet, Web-based teaching, video-conferencing, cross-cultural sharing, and the using of different types of interactive and multi-media materials (Education and Manpower Bureau, 1998). With their help, students can learn from the world-class teaching materials, experts, peers, and teachers in different parts of the world such that their teaching can become world-class teaching. Through participation in local and international development programs, teachers can achieve global and regional outlook and experiences beyond schools. Furthermore, their teaching is a type of networked teaching. Teachers are grouped and networked locally and globally to develop and sustain a new professional culture and multiply their teaching effects through mutual sharing and inspiring. They become world-class and networked teachers through localization and globalization. It is hardly surprising that each teacher can have a group of life-long partner teachers in other parts of the world to continuously share and discuss their experiences and ideas of professional practice.

Traditional Paradigm of Teaching

From the perspective of the traditional site-bounded paradigm, teachers and their teaching are often considered part of the reproduction and perpetuation process of the existing knowledge and manpower structure to sustain the developments of the society. Teachers are the center of education. They have some technical, social, and professional competencies to deliver knowledge to students. Teachers teach in some standard styles and patterns to ensure standard knowledge to be taught to students even though teachers' potentials and personal characteristics may be different. Their major task is to transfer to students some knowledge and skills they have previously accumulated and developed; therefore teaching is often a disciplinary, delivery, training, and socializing process. Also, teaching is often perceived as hard working activities undertaken to support students' achieving some external standards in examinations. Teachers and their teaching are bounded within the school. Schools are the major venue for teaching and teachers are the major source of knowledge. Teachers are often arranged to teach in a separated way and are kept responsible for their own teaching outcomes. They have few opportunities to mutually support and learn. Their teaching is bounded such that teachers teach the standard curriculum with textbooks and related materials assigned by their schools and the education authority. The teachers and their teaching are often alienated from the fast changing local communities or international contexts. From this traditional paradigmatic perspective, teachers are clearly school-bounded and separated, and would rarely have any global and regional outlook to develop the world-class education for their students in the new century.

PARADIGM SHIFT IN TEACHER EDUCATION

The above paradigm shift in learning and teaching from the traditional site-bounded paradigm to the new triplization paradigm inevitably signals the necessity of a corresponding paradigm shift in teacher education, particularly if we want to provide a new education for our students to pursue their future in the new millennium. Based on the new paradigm of education, the characteristics of triplized learning and teaching, as well as the developmental need for CMI, the paradigm shift in teacher education, and professional development, are highlighted in the following paragraphs (see Table 6).

Shift in Aims of Teacher Education

Traditionally, teacher education often aims to equip teachers with the necessary competence to deliver knowledge and skills to students such that students can survive in a local community or can meet the manpower needs of a society in the economic and social developments. But in the triplization paradigm, the aims of new teacher education should be developing teachers into triplized life-long learning teachers with CMI who will creatively contribute to students' triplized life-long self-learning and development as CMI citizens of a CMI society and a CMI global village with multi-dimensional developments in technological, economic, social, political, cultural, and learning aspects. They will also help their schools become triplized and turn into CMI schools and learning organizations.

Shift in Curriculum Structure of Teacher Education

In the traditional paradigm, the focus of curriculum is on the content and delivery of subject knowledge. The structure of a curriculum is mainly based on the structure of subject knowledge and the needs for same standard contents and same arrangements for the same subject teacher group. Therefore, the curriculum is often linear, step by step, and subject dependent. Whether the teacher education curriculum is globalized (or world-class), localized, and individualized is not the concern. In contrast, the new paradigm puts the focus of curriculum design on developing teachers' multiple intelligences and ability to enhance triplization in (or of) their own teaching and learning, students' learning and development, and school's development. Therefore, the design and structure of new teacher education are based on the characteristics of CMI development, aiming at creating and materializing opportunities for the development of teachers' learning and teaching through individualization, localization, and globalization. The curriculum structure is often hybrid, integrative, and interactive with the support of IT, networking, local and global exposure, and virtual reality.

Table 6: *Paradigm Shift in Teacher Education*

New Triplization Paradigm for Teacher Education	Traditional Site-Bounded Paradigm for Teacher Education
Aims of the New Teacher Education	**Aims of the Traditional Teacher Education**
To develop teachers as triplized CMI and life-long learning teachers who will creatively contribute	To equip teachers with the necessary competence to deliver knowledge and skills to
• to students' triplized life-long self-learning and development as a CMI citizens of a CMI society and a CMI global village with multi-dimensional developments in technological, economic, social, political, cultural, and learning aspects, and	students such that students can survive a local community or meet the manpower needs of a society in the economic and social developments
• to schools' triplized development as CMI schools and learnig organizations.	
New Teacher Education Curriculum	**Traditional Teacher Education Curriculum**
• **CMI/Triplization-Focused Curriculum:** focused on developing teachers' CMI and ability to make triplization for their own teaching and learning, students' learning and development, and school's development.	• **Subject Focused Curriculum:** focused on the content and delivery of subject knowledge.
• **Triplized Curriculum Structure:** based on characteristics of development of CMI and maximizing development opportunities for teachers' individualized, localized, and globalized learning and teaching, the structure is often hybrid, integrative, and interactive with the support of IT, networking, local and global exposure, and field experience and virtual reality.	• **Standard Subject Curriculum Structure:** mainly based on the structure of subject knowledge and the needs for same standard contents and same arrangements for the same subject teacher group, the structure is often linear, step by step, and subject dependent.
• **World-Class and Globalized Curriculum:** the curriculum content is world-class and globalized, pooling up the world-class materials and designs for learning and teaching and maximizing global relevance and exposure in different development areas; the content is also on technological, economic, social, political, cultural, and learning globalization; whether it is subject-based is not the concern.	• **Subject-Bounded Curriculum:** the curriculum content is mainly based on the subject knowledge and the skill of delivery of this subject, that are assumed to be same of standard for all teachers and be useful to the delivery of the necessary knowledge and skills to all types of students; whether it is globalized (or world-class), localized, and individualized is not the concern.

Table 6: *Paradigm Shift in Teacher Education* (Continued)

New Triplization Paradigm for Teacher Education	Traditional Site-Bounded Paradigm for Teacher Education
• **Localized Curriculum:** the curriculum content includes local resources, materials, and concerns to ensure the local relevance and community involvement to create and materialize opportunities for teachers' localized learning and teaching; school-based/community-based teacher education is one typical practice. • **Individualized Curriculum**: the curriculum is flexible and adaptable and can be indivdualized (in terms of learning targets, content, methods, and schedules) to meet the developmental needs of individual teachers, facilitate their self-learning and self-actualization, and optimize their potentials as a teacher.	
New Teacher Education Pedagogy • **Facilitating Teachers' Life-Long Self-Learning:** pedagogy is to ensure teachers' learning as a self-actualizing, discovery, experiencing, and reflecting process; teacher educators' inspiring and teachers' own motivation and self-rewarding are crucial. • **Multiple Sources of Teacher Learning** • **Globally and Locally Networked Teacher Learning** • **IT Pedagogical Environment including:** − World-wide networking through the Internet − Web-based learning − Interactive self learning − The using of multi-media facilities and learning materials − Video-conferencing for local and international sharing and exposure • **Boundless and Unlimited Opportunities for Learning Inside and Outside Teacher Education Institution**	**Traditional Teacher Education Pedagogy** • **Delivering Knowledge and Skills to Teachers:** pedagogy is to ensure teachers' learning as a disciplinary, receiving, and socializing process; close supervision and control are necessary • **Site-bounded of Teacher Learning** • **Separated Teacher Learning** • **Absence of IT, Classroom-Bounded Pedagogical Environment** • **Limited Opportunities for Learning, Fixed Period, Within Teacher Education Institution**

Table 6: *Paradigm Shift in Teacher Education* (Continued)

New Triplization Paradigm for Teacher Education	Traditional Site-Bounded Paradigm for Teacher Education
• **Pedagogy is Based on the Premises of CMI Development:** – Encouraging CMI interactions – Facilitating intelligence transfer – Learning intelligence at the center: Learning how to learn, think, and create – Teacher educator as a CMI model – Teacher institution and school as CMI pedagogical environment for teacher development – Team/group learning – Open-end project/ Problem-based learning – Case Study – Integrative and thematic learning	• Pedagogy lacks a clear linkage with CMI development, and it is often driven by the delivery of subject knowledge and external standards in examinations
New Quality Assurance of Teacher Education: • How well learning is triplized • How well teachers' learning opportunities are maximized through the IT environment, networking, CMI teacher educators, and CMI teacher education institution and schools • How well teachers' self-learning is facilitated and sustained as potentially life-long • How well teachers' CMI and ability to facilitate students' triplized learning are developed	**Traditional Quality Assurance of Teacher Education:** • How well learning and teaching are organized to deliver knowledge and skills to teachers • How well the delivery of knowledge and skills to teachers can be ensured through the improvement of teaching and learning • How well teacher educators' teaching can be improved and developed in a given time period • How well teachers can arrive at a given standard in teaching examinations

Shift in Curriculum Content of Teacher Education

The curriculum content of teacher education should be world-class and globalized, pooling up the world-class materials for learning and teaching and maximizing global relevance and exposure in different development areas. The content is also related to technological, economic, social, political, cultural, and learning globalization. Whether it is subject-based is not the major concern. The curriculum also includes local resources, materials, and concerns for ensuring local relevance and community involvement in creating and materializing opportunities for teachers' localized learning and teaching.

School-based/community-based teacher education is one typical practice to increase local relevance and support in the field. The curriculum content of teacher education and professional development is flexible and adaptable and can be individualized - in terms of learning targets, content, methods, and schedules - to meet the developmental needs of individual teachers, facilitate their self-learning and actualization, and optimize their potentials as triplized CMI teachers.

Shift in Pedagogy of Teacher Education

The traditional teacher education emphasizes delivering subject knowledge and professional skills to teachers. Inevitably, the pedagogy is mainly to ensure teachers' learning as a disciplinary, receiving, and socializing process, and assumes that close supervision is necessary during the training process. The opportunities for traditional teacher learning are often very limited in a fixed period within an institutional bounded or site-bounded, but IT-absent, environment. Also, the pedagogy has no clear linkage with the CMI development of teachers, and it is often driven by the delivery of subject knowledge and external standards in examinations. Contrastingly different from the traditional paradigm, the new pedagogy has the following characteristics.

Facilitating Teachers' Life-Long Self-Learning
Same as students' self-learning, the new pedagogy is to ensure teachers' learning being a self-actualizing, discovering, experiencing, enjoyable, and reflecting process. Teacher educators' inspiring and teachers' own motivation and self-rewarding are crucial to this self-learning process.

Multiple Sources of Teacher Learning
In addition to the teacher education institution itself, there are multiple sources of teacher learning, inside and outside the institution, locally and globally - for example, self-learning programs and packages, interactive multi-media materials, Web-based learning arrangements, outside experts' support programs, community experimental programs, etc. Through different types of partnership and collaboration, schools, local and overseas organizations, institutions and communities, including those in the sectors of social services, business, and industry, are actively involved in in-service and pre-service teacher education and professional development programs.

Globally and Locally Networked Teacher Learning

Teacher learning is locally and globally networked through, for example, the Internet, e-communications, visiting programs, local and global exchange programs, and sharing by video-conferencing. The networked learning can provide a wide spectrum of learning experiences and maximize opportunities for teachers to benefit from various settings and cultures. With the help of globalized learning, teachers can learn the world-class experiences from different parts of the world and various cultural settings. Therefore, the opportunities for teachers can be optimally created and materialized for enhancing the quality of their learning and teaching from local and global networking and exposure. In the new triplization paradigm, teacher education institutions are conceptualized as world-class and networked learning organizations.

World-wide IT Pedagogical Environment

In order to make triplization of teacher education possible, it is necessary to build up a worldwide IT pedagogical environment for teacher learning. It should include some typical and important components, such as worldwide networking through the Internet, the various programs of Web-based learning and interactive self-learning, the usage of multi-media facilities and learning materials, and video-conferencing for local and international sharing and exposure. Through the help of this environment, boundless and unlimited opportunities can be provided to facilitate teachers' learning and professional development inside and outside teacher education institutions and their schools.

Based on Premises of CMI Development

As for students' development, the pedagogy for teacher education should also be based on the premises of CMI as discussed in the preceding sections. The pedagogy should facilitate intelligence transfer among learning, economic, political, social, cultural, and technological intelligences. Also, developing teachers' learning intelligence should be at the core part of teacher education. Teachers should be facilitated to learn how to learn, think, and create, particularly in the triplization contexts. Teacher educators themselves should set a multiple intelligence model for facilitating and stimulating teachers' self-learning. Teacher education institutions and schools should become a CMI pedagogical environment, in which teachers are immersed and inspired to be self-actualizing and self-developing in CMI. Team/group learning, open-end learning projects, problem-based learning, and integrative and thematic learning are typical examples of the pedagogic approaches in the new teacher education.

Shift in Quality Assurance of Teacher Education

Since the traditional paradigm emphasizes on the delivery of knowledge and skill, the quality assurance of teacher education often focuses on how well learning and teaching are organized to deliver the necessary knowledge and skills to teachers; on how well the delivery of knowledge and skills to teachers can be ensured through the improvement of teaching and learning; on how well teacher educators' teaching can be improved in a given time period; and on how well teachers can arrive at a given standard in teaching examinations. Clearly, the paradigm shift in teacher education towards triplization induces a new conception of quality assurance of teacher education. The new quality assurance can be based on the following major questions:

1. How well teachers' learning is triplized? (This question aims to ensure that teacher learning can be well placed in the globalized, localized, and individualized contexts [or the triplized context].)
2. How well teachers' learning opportunities are optimally created and materialized through the IT environment, networking, CMI teacher educators, and CMI teacher education institution and schools? (This question intends to ensure maximizing opportunities for teachers' learning and development in a triplized CMI environment.)
3. How well teachers' self-learning is facilitated and sustained as potentially life-long? (This question tries to ensure that the maximized opportunities and teachers' self-learning are sustainable to life-long.)
4. How well teachers' CMI and ability to facilitate students' triplized learning are developed? (This question focuses on ensuring the relevance and outcome of teacher learning in terms of multiple intelligences and students' triplized learning.)

In short, from the above discussion, the new paradigm for teacher education is completely different from the traditional paradigm. They can provide a new set of principles and values for reforming teacher education in the Asia-Pacific Region or other parts of the world. With reference to the three key elements of Long-term Relevance, Environmental Strength, and Human Initiative, educators and policy-makers should indeed considered that globalization, localization, individualization and CMI are all necessary in the design of a new teacher education for the new millennium.

CONCLUSION

In facing up the challenges in the new millennium, we need a new paradigm for rethinking and re-engineering our school education and teacher education. If we believe our world in the new millennium is moving towards a multi-dimensional globalization and becoming a global village with boundless interactions among countries and areas in various aspects, we should expect our new generations to be CMI persons capable of meeting the challenges from and making contributions to such a fast changing and interacting global village. The development of the society should be multi-dimensional and geared towards a learning CMI society. The aims of education should be to develop students as CMI citizens who will creatively contribute to the formation of a CMI society and a CMI global village with multiple developments in technological, economic, social, political, cultural, and learning aspects.

With reference to the general theory presented here, we can expect that our schools, teachers, and students will be triplized in the new century. Our learning, teaching, and schooling will be finally globalized, localized, and individualized with the help of IT and the boundless multiple networking. We will have unlimited opportunities and multiple global and local sources for life-long learning and development of both students and teachers. The triplized learning will be interactive, self-actualizing, discovery, enjoyable, and self-rewarding. It is to be a world-class learning. Students can learn from the world-class teachers, experts, peers, and learning materials from different parts of the world in any time frame and get local, regional, and global exposure and outlook as a CMI citizen. We believe, teachers, as the key school actor, will play a very crucial role in the whole process of triplization in education. They will learn to triplize themselves as triplized CMI teachers, transform their schools into triplized CMI schools, and facilitate students' becoming triplized CMI students. Clearly, we need a paradigm shift in teacher education for the future.

We hope, after the great efforts of all of us, all our students will become *triplized CMI students*. They fully enjoy life-long self-learning and actualization and become CMI citizens. All our teachers will become triplized CMI teachers. They share the joy of triplized learning and teaching with their students and pursue life-long learning and professional development. All of our colleagues in teacher education will become triplized CMI teacher educators. And our teacher education institutions will become fully triplized CMI institutions achieving the new vision of teacher education. We hope, all educators will appreciate the significance and values of the new paradigm and will be dedicated to make contribution to the triplization in school education and teacher education and to the creating of unlimited learning opportunities for all teachers and students in the Asia-Pacific Region and other parts of the world in the new century.

NOTES

[1]This chapter is adapted from "New Education and New Teacher Education: A Paradigm Shift for the Future" published in Number 1 of Volume 3 of the *Asia-Pacific Journal of Teacher Education and Development*. For a more detailed discussion on the new paradigm of education, please refer to Cheng (2000a).

[2]In social scientific research, paradigm is often a term loosely used by scholars. Indeed, when one reads Thomas Kuhn's *The Structure of Scientific Revolutions* in which the concept of paradigm is highlighted, one would find that even Kuhn himself causally uses the term in various contexts as theories, models, values, and exemplars (Burns, 1995, p. 96). Inevitably, education researchers have much room in giving their own definitions: for example, Husen (1994) considers it a "cultural artifact" (p. 5051); Miller, Nelson, and Moore (1998) place an equal sign between a paradigm and a framework. Readers would find it equally confusing when "paradigm" is discussed in the literature on teaching and learning. For example, when Evans (1994) calls for a "new paradigm for teaching," no concept clarification is made in the advocacy, except that a paradigm is to serve a function to explain (p. 310), thus making it more or less a "theory." Then, when Aviram (1996) concludes that "... the search for a new paradigm of education has only just begun" (p. 421), readers could merely interpret the argument as one that indicates that certain educational elements, such as aims, contexts, organizational structure, are not clear or operational in such a way that the education system is not functioning properly (p. 427). Thus, one can vaguely define paradigm as just an aggregate of the properties of the education system. Even more interesting is Sweeting's (1996) definition of the concept in his analysis of the issue of globalization of learning: the shifting from micro-analysis of particular educational practices to more macro-level analysis could be considered a paradigm shift (p. 382), thus making "paradigm" merely a perspective or focus more than anything else.

The position here is that the confusion is unnecessary: when we refer to Kuhn's (1970) discussion on paradigm for characterizing the development of disciplinary science and his subsequent further elaboration (Kuhn, 1974), we would realize that he did ambiguously apply the term, but in essence he was defining a paradigm as an infrastructure, i.e., the underlying foundation or basic framework of disciplinary science. When applied in the case education as a discipline, a paradigm is therefore a basic framework for organizing and integrating together the various conceptual frameworks, approaches, perspectives, and theories, as well as all related substantive issues. When applied in the case of education as a sociological system with specific functions, a paradigm is a basic framework prescribing the fundamental values of education as expressed in terms of aims and goals; delineating the parameters, structure, and process of the education system; and specifying the various approaches to understanding and changing the interrelationships among the various properties and processes of education for the purposes of formulating and achieving the aims and goals of education. As such, the call for a paradigm shift here is in essence the call for a modification of the infrastructure of education; as such, the call here differs fundamentally from other researchers' advocacy on paradigm shift, for example, the proposal by Jenkins (1994), which tends to focus on micro-level teaching and learning issues.

[3]Globalization in this chapter is a more broadly defined concept. The concept was originated in the 1980s, referring to "... the accelerated international flows of goods, capital, labour, services and information which have occurred in response to improved transport, the seemingly limitless revolution in communication technologies..." (Green, 1999, p. 57). In the 1990s, globalization refers to the formation of a world system as distinct from "... internationalization of goods and services, money, people and ideas" (Marginson, 1999, p. 19). Such a new world system is a "borderless" world where "... national cultures are transformed by the forces of global communications and cultural commodification" (Green, 1999, p. 57). More importantly, such a new world system creates a new form of marketized and technologized educational provision that result in a new form of inequality (Henry, Lingard, Rizvi, & Taylor, 1999, p. 95), and as such globalization can be understood by some as a product of imperialism in disguise (Hirst & Thompson, 1996).

In this chapter, globalization is more than a process through which economic, political, and cultural activities are being globally undertaken with an osmosis effect by which those individuals, groups (organizations), and nations with might are to dominate. With reference to the Systems Theory (Cibulka, 1994), globalization is defined here as a complex process, characterized by dynamic interactions and cyclical changes, through which the pull and pushes forces are at work, resulting in mutual adaptation, changes, and development that occur in all aspects of human values and activities. That is why globalization is defined here in terms of the transfer, adaptation, and development of values, knowledge, technology, and behavioral norms across countries and societies in different parts of the world.

REFERENCES

Albrow, M. (1990). Introduction. In M. Albrow & E. King (Eds.), *Globalization, knowledge and society*. London: Sage.

Alderfer, C. P. (1972). Existence, relatedness, and growth: Human needs in organizational settings. New York: Free Press.

Aviram, A. (1996). The decline of the modern paradigm in education. *International Review of Education, 42*(5), 421-443.

Ayyar, R. V. V. (1996). Educational policy planning and globalisation. *International Journal of Educational Development, 16*(4), 347-354.

Bay, M., & Tozer, S. E. (1999). Preparing teachers as agents of change. In G. A. Griffin (Ed.), *The education of teachers: Ninety-eighth yearbook of the National Society for the Study of Education* (pp. 18-62). Chicago: University of Chicago Press.

Beare, H., & Slaughter, R. (1993). *Education for the twenty-first century.* New York: Routledge.

Blackledge, D., & Hunt, B. (1985). *Sociological interpretations of education.* Sydney: Croom Helm.

Brown, T. (1999). Challenging globalization as discourse and phenomenon. *International Journal of Lifelong Education, 18*(1), 3-17.

Brown, P., & Lauder, H. (1996). Education, globalization and economic development. *Journal of Education Policy, 11*(1), 1-25.

Burns, R. B. (1995). Paradigms for research on teaching. In L. W. Anderson (Ed.), *International encyclopedia of teaching and teacher education* (pp. 91-96). Cambridge: Pergamon.

Caldwell, B. J., & Spinks, J. M. (1998). *Beyond the self-managing school.* London: Falmer Press.

Cheng, Y. C. (1995). *Function and effectiveness of education* (3rd ed). Hong Kong: Wide Angle Press.

Cheng, Y. C. (1996). School effectiveness and school-based management: A mechanism for development. London, UK: Falmer Press.

Cheng, Y. C. (1998). The knowledge base for re-engineering schools: Multiple functions and internal effectiveness. *International Journal of Educational Management, 12*(5), 203-224.

Cheng, Y. C. (2000a). A CMI-triplization paradigm for reforming education in the new millennium. *International Journal of Educational Management, 14*(4), 156-174.

Cheng, Y. C. (2000b, January 4-8). *Globalization, localization and individualization for effective education.* Keynote speech presented at the 14th International Congress for School Effectiveness and Improvement "Global Networking for Quality Education", Hong Kong.

Cheng, Y. C. (2000c, March 26-30). *Total life-long teacher education driven by triplization: Effectiveness, quality and revelance in the third millennium.* Plenary speech presented at the 2000 International Symposia on Educational Reforms and Teacher Education Innovation for the 21st Century, Tokyo, Japan.

Cheng, Y. C., & Ng, K. H. (1992). Economic considerations in educational policy analysis: A preliminary frame-work. *Primary Education, 3*(1), 55-64.

Cheng, Y. C., & Townsend, T. (2000). Educational change and development in the Asia-

Pacific region: Trends and Issues. In T. Townsend & Y. C. Cheng (Eds.), *Educational change and development in the Asia-Pacific region: Challenges for the future.* (pp. 317-344). The Netherlands: Swets and Zeitlinger.

Cibulka, J. G. (1994). Policy analysis and the study of the politics of education. In *Politics of education association yearbook 1994* (pp. 105-125). Washington, DC: Falmer Press.

Dalin, P., & Rust, V. D. (1996). *Towards schooling for the twenty-first century.* New York: Cassell.

Daun, H. (1997). National forces, globalization and educational restructuring: Some European response patterns. *Compare, 27*(1), 19-41.

Drucker, P. F. (1993). *Post-capitalist society.* New York: Harper Business.

Drucker, P. F. (1995). *Managing in a time of great change.* Oxford: Butterworth Heineman.

Education and Manpower Bureau. (1998, November). Information technology for learning in a new era: Five-year strategy 1998/99 to 2002/03. Hong Kong: Government Printer.

Evans, H. C. (1994). A pedagogy of quality and a new paradigm for teaching. *Journal of Education for Teaching, 20*(3), 301-311.

Fowler, F. C. (1994). The international arena: The global village. *Journal of Education Policy, 9*(5-6), 89-102.

Gardner, H. (1999). The disciplined mind: What all students should understand. New York: Simon and Schuster.

Green, A. (1999). Education and globalization in Europe and East Asia: Convergent and divergent trends. *Journal of Education Policy, 14*(1), 55-71.

Griffin, G. A. (1999). Changes in teacher education: Looking to the future. In G. A. Griffin (Ed.), *The education of teachers: Ninety-eighth yearbook of the National Society for the Study of Education* (pp. 1-17). Chicago: University of Chicago Press.

Handy, C. B. (1994). *The age of paradox.* USA: Harvard Business School Press.

Handy, C. B. (1995). *The age of unreason.* London: Arrow Business Books.

Henry, M., Lingard, B., Rizvi, F., & Taylor, S. (1999). Working with/against globalization in education. *Journal of Education Policy, 14*(1), 85-97.

Hinchliffe, K. (1987). Education and the labor market. In G. Psacharopoulos (Ed.), *Economics of education: Research and studies* (pp. 315-323). Kidlington, Oxford: Pergamon Press.

Hirst, P., & Thompson, G. (1996). *Globalisation in question.* Cambridge: Polity Press.

Husen, T. (1994). Research paradigms in education. In T. Husen & T. N. Postlethwaite (Eds.), *The international encyclopedia of education: Vol. 9* (2nd ed., pp. 5051-5056). England: Pergamon.

Jenkins, J. M. (1994). Old paradigms and new realities. *International Journal of Educational Reform, 3*(2), 216-219.

Jones, P. W. (1999). Globalisation and the UNESCO mandate: Multilateral prospects for educational development. *International Journal of Educational Development, 19*(1),

17-25.

Kim, Y. H. (1999). Recently changes and developments in Korean school education. In T. Townsend & Y. C. Cheng (Eds.), *Educational change and development in the Asia-Pacific region: Challenges for the future* (pp. 87-112). The Netherlands: Swets and Zeitlinger.

Kuhn, T. (1970). *The structure of scientific revolutions*. Chicago, Illinois: University of Chicago Press.

Kuhn, T. (1974). Second thoughts on paradigms. In F. Suppe (Ed.), *The structure of scientific theories*. Urbana, Illinois: University of Illinois Press.

Lao, T. (1991). *Lao-Tzu, tao-te-ching* (L. Wieger, Trans.). Wales, UK: Llanerch.

Little, A. W. (1996). Globalization and educational research: Whose context counts? *International Journal of Educational Development, 16*(4), 427-438.

Manz, C. C. (1986). Self-leadership: Toward an expanded self-influence processes in organizations. *Academy of Management Review, 11*, 585-600.

Manz, C. C., & Sims, H. P. (1990). *Super leadership*. New York: Berkley Book.

Marginson, S. (1999). After globalization: Emerging politics of education. *Journal of Education Policy, 14*(1), 19-31.

Maslow, A. H. (1970). *Motivation and personality* (2nd ed.). New York: Harper and Row.

McGinn, N. F. (1996). Education, democratization, and globalization: A challenge for comparative education. *Comparative Education Review, 40*(4), 341-357.

McMahon, W. W. (1987). Consumption and other benefits of education. In G. Psacharopoulos (Ed.), *Economics of education: Research and studies* (pp. 129-133). Kidlington, Oxford: Pergamon Press.

Miller, S. M., Nelson, M. W., & Moore, M. T. (1998). Caught in the paradigm gap: Qualitative researchers' lived experience and the politics of epistemology. *American Educational Research Journal, 35*(3), 377-416.

Naisbitt, J. (1984). Megatrends: Ten new directions transforming our lives. England, London: MacDonald.

Naisbitt, J., & Aburdence, P. (1991). *Megatrends 2000*. New York: Avon.

Sun, T. (1994). *Art of war.* (R. D. Sawyer & M. L. Sawyer, Trans.). USA: Westview Press.

Sweeting, A. (1996). The globalization of learning: paradigm or paradox? *International Journal of Educational Development, 16*(4), 379-392.

Tam, W. M., Cheng, Y. C., & Cheung, W. M. (1997). A reengineering framework for total home-school partnership. *International Journal of Educational Management, 11*(6), 274-285.

The Hong Kong Institute of Education. (1998). *The vision statement.* Hong Kong: Author.

Townsend, T. (1999). *The third millennium school: Towards a quality education for all students.* (IARTV Seminar Series No. 81). Victoria, Australia: Incorporated Association of Registered Teachers of Victoria

Townsend, T., & Otero, G. (1999). *The global classroom.* Victoria, Australia: Hawker and Brownlow.

Waters, M. (1995). *Globalization.* London: Routledge.

Chapter 3

The Missing Foundation of Teacher Education[1]

Maurice GALTON
Homerton College
University of Cambridge, United Kingdom

In 1979, the Conservative Party, under the leadership of Margaret Thatcher, came to power in Britain and, as part of the new philosophy, began to introduce a "market approach" to public services, including education. At the same time, the policy of devolving management to the smallest units in some areas was confronted by an increase in centralized control in others. In education, schools were made responsible for their own budgets but not for the curriculum. Competition was introduced by allowing schools to recruit pupils from outside their local neighborhood. Widespread testing was introduced and the results published, so those parents could decide which schools were at the top of the table of results. A system of inspection was also set up, and schools that failed this examination could be closed.

In teacher education, it was more difficult to interfere directly, because universities strongly defended their right to academic freedom and had powerful allies among the peers in the upper chamber of the House of Commons, the Lords. The pressure therefore took the form of financial regulation. University departments could resist inspection if they chose, but they would then receive no students and loose their income. At the same time, schools were encouraged to set up their own training schemes, independently of the University, and in direct competition with them. The funds for training courses were taken away from the Higher Education Funding Council and given to a specially constituted Teacher Training Agency (TTA), directly controlled by the government's Department of Education.

The coming of the New Labour government in April 1996 has provided little relief, despite widespread expectations that it would do so. Teacher Training is now even more closely regulated with demands to include additional time for literacy and numeracy, to make all new teachers competent in the new technologies and able to provide courses on citizenship. All these have to be done without additional time or resources. As of 1999, there have been revisions in the role of the TTA so that it now concentrates on initial teacher training with various in-service programs returning to direct government control.

THE CONSEQUENCES OF ATHEORECTICAL APPROACHES TO TEACHER EDUCATION

Meanwhile, in all of these changes and confusions, many of the key questions to do with how best to train new teachers and improve older more experienced ones remain unanswered. In this chapter, I will attempt to set the discussion within a more general international context concerning the debates about teacher education and future research. In particular, I wish to argue the case for an approach to teacher training, based on a theoretical model of developing expertise. The consequence of the absence of such a model has been the lack of coherence in programs of teacher education so that in many countries, such as the USA, the UK, and many of the former British colonies, there are as many different approaches to training as there are institutions. This has allowed governments of all persuasions to step in and impose rationalization and then to institute accountability and inspection procedures designed to ensure institutions conform. Part of this rationalization has been to shift a large part of the training into schools, ostensibly on the grounds that the institutions were preaching outdated practice, but also because it was seen as more cost effective. What is described in the English system has parallels in many others, particularly the USA, Australia, and other parts of continental Europe.

To put the English situation in a wider European context, there are now half a million students undergoing initial teacher training annually in those states belonging to the Council of Europe. This training takes place in 1,000 institutions and involves some 50,000 teacher training staff. As in most advanced countries, teaching is an ageing profession with the majority of teachers now over 40 years of age. Consequently, massive investment has taken place in retraining programs during the last decade. It was estimated that in 1994, the last time figures were prepared by the Council for a meeting of its Education ministers, the equivalent of over five million pounds was being spent each year on inservice training (INSET). Despite this investment, little attempts at systematic evaluation of the effects of these programs has taken place (Vonk, 1994).

In most European Countries, including the UK, there is little attempt to provide adequate induction programs that support the transition from student teacher to self-directing professional. Vonk (1994) describes this as the "greatest omission in Education" (p. 85). However, over the last few years, the growth of school-based initial training has led to increased attention to the role of mentoring, and this has been a major "growth area" in research. Mentoring has begun to include support for beginning teachers as well as novices (Furlong & Maynard, 1995). McNally and Martin (1998) suggest that currently three distinct approaches are being adopted in schools. The first of these, termed *laissez faire,* sees teaching as a natural development so that a mentor's approach varies with a particular student. There is strong emphasis on a counselling role, a reluctance to challenge the novice's practice, and a dislike of competency based approaches.

The second approach is described as *collaborative.* Its main aim is to empower the novice so that the focus is upon managing the training to provide safe relatively non-threatening early experiences. Tutorials and post-lesson feedback sessions tend to address joint agendas, rather than those identified by the student as in the *laissez faire* approach. Consequently, there is an emphasis on action plans, self-reflection, and student goal-setting (ibid., p. 47).

The remaining mentors were said to adopt an *imperial* style. The model was said to be a "deficit" one in which the mentor was a transmitter of expertise. This involved early attempts to challenge the novice's initial practice, establishment of clear lines of authority, and the setting of short and long term targets in accord with the mentor's personal vision of teaching. McNally and Martin (1998, p. 49) are not alone in concluding that few mentors were capable of adopting a collaborative approach in which attempts are made to minimize power imbalances. They see this as important following the recommendations of Daloz's (1986) review of the USA practice that a collaborative framework is an essential pre-requisite for student self-reflection. Zeichner (1991) supports this view, arguing that reflective *teaching* in contrast to reflective *thinking* is a social (and by implication a collegial) activity.

The influence of the above ideas, especially as advocated by such American educators as Zeichner, has been such that nearly all partnership-programs of the kind described by Everton and Younger (1999, see No.2 Issue 2 of

APJTED) take as a primary aim that students will be able to engage in learning to teach through a process of critical reflection. Calderhead (1989), however, has commented that the term, reflection, is often poorly defined. McIntyre (1992) also argues that many writers appear confused about the process of reflecting and its relationship to process of theorizing, and this is borne out by research in many countries (see for example, Chen, 1997). For McIntyre, there are *technical, practical,* and *critical* levels of reflection. Technical reflection has to do with acquiring a repertoire of skills, while in practical reflection the student is engaged in understanding the nature of the subject and its methods of enquiry. In critical reflection, novice teachers begin to contrast theory and practice to gain a better understanding of the influence of school and society on *what* is taught and *how* it is taught. McIntyre, doubting whether a student teacher has time for the kind of reflection advocated by Daloz (1986) and others, argues that there is lack of time during the *practicum,* and that in any case "there is much to be read, discussed and found in the practice of others" (McIntyre, 1992, p. 47). Theorizing is therefore preferable to personal reflection, because it is not limited to one's present practice but "concerns the whole world of possibilities for the future" (ibid., p. 47).

The debate about the role of mentoring in these partnership programs also leads to further questions about the selection and training of mentors and the recruitment of those in universities and colleges of education who also participate in the scheme. Underlying the confusion often surrounding this debate is the failure to distinguish sufficiently between expertise and experience. Even when this is done, there are further problems in determining the relative importance during training of developing expertise in respect of one's subject or discipline and of improving more generic skills to do with helping students to "learn to learn," improving motivation, etc. Neither are the links between these different forms of expertise well understood (Alexander, 1996). As Kennedy (1991) argues, when attempting to map out the key issues which researchers need to investigate if they are to help practitioners become more effective, teachers cannot teach what they do not know. A fundamental research question is how important substantive ideas, embodied in subject knowledge expertise, can be passed on to *diverse* learners? This also requires expertise grounded in general theories of learning as both a cognitive and social process.

The difficulty in reaching a judgement on this issue is that, at present, there exists no coherent theory of how teachers learn to teach or those who are already teaching learn to do their job better. Without such a developmental approach, it is difficult to provide an agreed common curriculum and also difficult to decide what level of reflection should the teacher undertake at a particular stage. In recent years, it would appear that it is the subject knowledge approach which has dictated "best practice." This approach emphasizes the importance of subject expertise whereby, over time, teachers gain what Shulman (1994) defines as *pedagogical content knowledge*. According to Shulman, this term has to do with "aspects of (*subject*) content most germane to its teachability," and includes the "most useful form of representing ideas, the most powerful analogies, illustrations, explanations and demonstrations" (p. 85).

DEFINING EXPERTISE IN TEACHING

In contrast, we have the approach based upon models of expertise developed through studies of artificial intelligence (Ericsson & Charness, 1994). The subject began to appear in major textbooks in cognitive psychology around 1985, according to Glasser and Chi (1988). The motivation for these studies was the failure of researchers in artificial intelligence to construct computer programs that could outperform humans. Chess experts, for example, can retain in the memory a vast array of complicated positions which allows them to select an appropriate move without the need for the kind of elaborate analysis and evaluation required by the computer (Chase & Simon, 1973).

These studies, according to Glasser and Chi (1988), have shown that experts, across a variety of domains, possess similar qualities. Expertise cannot generally be transferred from one domain to another. Chess Grand Masters are not usually Gourmet Chefs. Experts are also quick to recognize meaningful patterns, irrespective of the particular context. As a result, when compared to novices, they usually identify a problem within a broad schema, rather than by listing its individual components. The expert's approach to problem-solving is based first upon trying to understand its nature, rather than in applying a series of routines on a trial-and-error basis. Not surprisingly, experts are much quicker at problem-solving than are novices.

Since about 1985, an increasing number of education studies have taken up these themes in the context of novice-expert teachers. Berliner (1992) lists a number of reasons for this growing interest. First and most important, insight into the cognitive processes associated with the performance of expert teachers could provide a framework for more effective programs of teacher training. Second, there may be policy implications arising from the attempts to introduce merit awards for "good" teaching. And third, greater understanding of the sophisticated repertoire of skills which teachers need to manage successfully the complex environment of the typical classroom could enhance the profession's public image, thereby leading to improved morale.

In his review of the research, Berliner (1992) demonstrates that the general findings on expertise also apply to classroom pedagogy, defined as "knowledge of organisation and management of classrooms, of motivation, teaching methods, discipline and individual differences among students" (p. 223). Pedagogic expertise is often context specific. Expert teachers are unhappy when required to perform in unfamiliar situations, because "they do not know the students" (Berliner et al., 1988, p. 69). Not knowing their students no longer allowed these experts to use the informal methods of classroom control which they generally favored. More importantly, without detailed knowledge of the cognitive abilities of each pupil, they were unable to determine the appropriate level at which to "pitch" the lesson. Novices in contrast were quite happy to use record cards and test scores to sort pupils into groups. Experts preferred to look at a sample of the pupil's work and not just the mark record, because they wished to understand the various approaches that different pupils used while learning. Thus, experts tended to be pupil-focused, while novices tended to be more concerned with their own well-being, complaining for example the amount of time needed to sort the pupils' record cards.

Expert teachers, when viewing slides of classrooms, were quickly able to identify meaningful patterns, unlike novices who tended to concentrate on discrete events (Carter, Cushing, Sabers, Stein, & Berliner, 1988). Novices were often unable to make sense of this data when different events conflicted (e.g., some pupils were on task while others were not). As a result, an expert's representation of a problem was qualitatively different from the novice in that they were able to tackle it on a conceptual level. The novice teacher tended to use strategies designed to deal with each aspect of the problem in turn.

For example, a novice might deduce a failure of pupils to respond to questions as indicating a need for longer wait-times (Budd-Rowe, 1974). If, as a result, noise and disruption increased, this might be attributed to falling off in the pace of the lesson (Kounin, 1970). The novice would find these two conflicting demands difficult to reconcile without abandoning the questioning and resorting to work card assignments. The expert, however, while acknowledging the need to provide pupils with more time to answer difficult questions, would perceive that to do so in an atmosphere where pupils were competing for the right to respond (e.g., by raising hands) could cause difficulties. This would be particularly important when the chosen pupil was still thinking of an answer while others in the class had a correct solution. For such an exercise, the expert might therefore rule out a whole class activity and instead pose the questions to groups of pupils.

A further difference between the expert and the novice teacher is the ability of the former to take into account seemingly unconnected contextual factors in planning and carrying out classroom activity. Thus, rain (indoor playtime) or a report by the dinner lady of a disturbance during lunch may cause the expert teacher either to restructure a practical lesson or to abandon it altogether in favor of a more formal seated activity. Thus, expert teachers are, in Borko and Livingston's (1989) terms, "improvisational performers."

By definition, true experts in any field will be limited in number. Expertise appears to result from a combination of experience and specialized knowledge structures (Glasser & Chi, 1988). Clearly, not all experienced teachers become experts although they have moved considerably beyond the novice stage to where they feel comfortable and "relaxed" in the classroom. Teachers in Nias's (1988) study estimated it took at least five years to reach this point. However, expertise is also time-dependent. What constitutes expertise in one generation may be accepted as standard practice in another as technique improves. In the early 1960s, the ability to run a four minute mile was the mark of an outstanding athlete. Today, with improved training methods, it might not even guarantee a place in an Olympic 1500 meters final. Similarly, some pieces of music written for solo instruments by composers such as Mozart or Beethoven were thought impossible to play except by the most gifted of performers. Today, they are part of the standard concert repertoire. This offers the possibility that with suitable training, the outstanding practice of one generation of teachers may become an accepted part of general competency of future practitioners.

MODELS OF TEACHER DEVELOPMENT

Studies of expert chess players and air pilots have led Dreyfus (1982) and Dreyfus and Dreyfus (1986) to posit the existence of five stages in the transition from novice to expert. They call these stages that of novice, advanced beginner, competent, proficient, and expert. The classification has been used by Benner (1984) in her study of clinical nursing practice. The Dreyfus model is a situational rather than a trait model where the skills or attributes required to progress from one stage to the next can only be acquired by working in real situations and not through principles and theories learned during the course of programs of study.

Applying the model to teaching, novices are students in the initial stage of their training course. To allow them to gain necessary classroom experience, it is argued that they need to be provided with "context free" rules which they can use to guide their performance. Advice on "how to introduce a lesson" and instructions "not to go on talking until you get silence" form part of such general guidance. Part of the dilemma in this approach is that, as Benner (1984) notes, such rules "legislate against successful performance because they (the trainers) cannot tell them (the novices) the most relevant tasks to perform in an actual situation" (p. 21). Novices then come to regard this advice as "too theoretical." Novices, however, are still inclined to believe that there exists somewhere a set of guidelines, or even tips, which will enable them to survive as teachers no matter what the context of their teaching.

At some point, hopefully during their training, but if not then in their induction year, most novices move to the advanced beginner stage. They now can demonstrate marginally acceptable performance and have had sufficient experience to recognize, by themselves, certain regularly occurring features of classroom life or to be able to respond when their mentor points these out. In the Dreyfus (1982) version of the model, these meaningful features are called "aspects of the situation." They might include signs that indicate the pupils are paying attention or indications that the work is pitched at a too difficult level. Thus, beginners learn to judge the moment when the noise level falls and when shoes no longer "scuffle" on the floor as a time to introduce new ideas or issue key instructions.

Advanced beginners thus learn to recognize situations, but they are as yet unable to predict the occurrence of such situations and therefore cannot take anticipatory or avoiding action. They often find it difficult to differentiate between individual pupils so, for example, while they can sense the level of attention in the whole class setting, they find it harder to decide whether a particular pupil is responding positively.

By the time the induction year is complete, a teacher should, typically, be moving into the competent stage. The most important feature of this stage is a teachers' ability to look ahead beyond the immediate situation and therefore to prioritise. Decisions about which task to tackle first, which pupil to deal with, which behavior to comment upon and which to ignore are more easily made. For the first time, the teacher begins to consider problems that may occur in a conscious analytic way. However, unlike experts this problem-solving takes place within the context of very explicit pre-planning. The structure which such a "deliberative planned approach" provides helps the competent teacher to achieve satisfactory levels of efficiency and organization and generates the feeling of being able to cope with a variety of contexts.

Such an approach tends to be inflexible and somewhat slow, because the competent teacher has to refer each "aspect of the situation" to the plan. Proficient teachers, however, learn through experience the main constituents of any situation and to judge the most salient events. They are thus in a position to recognize when "the normal picture does not materialise" (Benner, 1984, p. 28) and to take appropriate action accordingly. This "holistic" view increases the rapidity of decision-making. Principles, or in Benner's words, "maxims," are then employed to solve the particular problem.

An example of this approach would be the softer versions of the "don't smile until Christmas" maxim. When taking a new class, most teachers believe that they should be firm at first, setting out the rules and routines that govern behavior in their classroom (stage one). Only when pupils perform these routines with a degree of automicity does the teacher begin to develop a more relaxed atmosphere (stage two). For example, primary pupils may be allowed to talk quietly when working on certain practical tasks, such as making a model or sewing. Because proficient teachers, unlike competent ones, have the ability to detect what Benner (1984, p. 100) calls the "early warning signal," indicating deterioration in the situation, they are very quick to deal with any problem. However, they tend to do so in accordance with their previously formulated principle. Thus, if the class was perceived to be getting unsettled, the teacher would re-introduce a period of greater firmness over implementation of previously stated rules and routines. The set of principles or "maxims" that provide the guidelines for the proficient teacher's practice is termed by Dreyfus and Dreyfus (1986) a perspective.

Unlike the proficient teacher, an overall perspective of this kind does not dictate the expert's practice. If they adhere to any kind of maxim, it is that "circumstances alter cases." Because, as Berliner (1992) points out, the actions of expert teachers appear to be strongly influenced by a "respect for their students": they are more concerned with understanding the reasons for the pupils' behavior, rather than applying well tried routines to eliminate or suppress it. Carter et al. (1988) describe one illustration of this skill. Experts and novices were asked to comment on a series of slides, in some of which a girl was seen to be crying. The use of a wide-angled lens to shoot the slides made it difficult to see her tears, but one expert was able to pick up this detail while others sensed that something "was wrong with the girl." Furthermore, experts, because of this pupil-centered perspective, often attribute failure to learn on the nature of instruction in contrast to numerous studies which show teachers usually attribute pupil failure to factors outside of their immediate control (Beckmann, 1976). Thus, such causes as "lacking concentration" or "poor home background" will often be cited to explain a pupil's poor performance. Expert teachers, however, were often critical of instructional practices when viewing a series of videotaped extracts of a science lesson simultaneously on three separate monitors (Sabers, Cushing, & Berliner, 1991), because, as with teachers in Calderhead's (1987) study, they started with a view that all pupils would respond to good teaching.

In summary, while the focus of the novice and advanced beginner is on their personal concerns (of being able to cope), this gradually diminishes during the competency and proficiency stages where the emphasis shifts to ways of performing the task as efficiently as possible. Direct instruction is often used, because this ensures teacher control over the implementation of the task and production of suitable products indicative that pupils have accomplished something. Experts, however, being pupil-focused, will give priority to inculcating "conceptual" rather than "procedural" knowledge in their pupils (Borko et al., 1992). This distinction refers to "teaching for understanding" in contrast to teaching rules and algorithms for problem-solving.

EXPERTISE IN TEACHING: ISSUES AND PROBLEMS

The above account, although building on Berliner's and other studies of novices and experts, is somewhat speculative, particularly in setting out the characteristics of the competent and proficient stages of teacher development. The data on which these speculations are based comes from the descriptions and interviews with clinical nurses described by Benner (1984) on the assumption that training to teach and training to be a nurse have certain similarities, an assumption shared by those educationalists in the UK who have recently advocated the setting up of teaching "hospital" schools (Hargreaves, 1996).

However, a number of problems remain concerning the above stage' model. First, the parallels between nursing and teaching are not exact, and in one respect there is an important difference. Only a very few of those who enter nurse training have participated in the life of a hospital as patients, whereas all entrants into teaching have been pupils at one time. The perceptions they bring with them and the interpretations they make of what they see must be formed, in part, from this previous experience. We know little about how this past history contributes to a teacher's development (Goodson, 1994; Grundy & Hatton, 1998).

Second, it is not clear whether expert teachers are a very distinct group as Berliner's own studies suggests or whether they constitute the "best" examples of experienced proficient teachers. This is because the way that expertise is defined has varied from study to study. Berliner, for example, took ratings of head teachers and advisers followed by three rounds of observation before selecting seven teachers from the original "nominated" pool of 55 (Sabers et al., 1991). Others, for example, Housner and Griffey (1985) in their study of physical education teachers, used experience as the main criteria. In those studies where ratings of "excellence" without observation have been used to make the selection, there is a danger that the selection will be biased because raters have preferences for a particular teaching style.

There is therefore a need to set up clearer criteria that distinguish each stage of teaching development. Such criteria must not be circular in execution as, for example, classifying teachers as experts because they used less direct methods of instruction. A finding that such teachers were more pupil-focused would then be a consequence of the selection procedure, rather than an observed difference between expert and proficient teachers. As far as possible, the criteria should relate to observable aspects of superior performance, such as more pupil involvement, higher levels of motivation or achievement that demonstrates understanding. One important source of such evidence is the pupils' own evaluations of the teaching that apart from one reported study (Sabers et al., 1991) appear to have been largely ignored.

The third problematic issue concerns the degree to which expertise is transferable. The model proposed by Dreyfus and Dreyfus (1986) postulates that expertise is confined to specific domains. Thus, a teacher who is expert in art will not necessarily be an expert in science. Yet, common sense would suggest that the pedagogic skills which experts are said to possess and to do with methods of classroom control and the means of motivating pupils should have implications for the way a class functions, irrespective of subject content.

There is therefore, as indicated earlier, a potential conflict between those researchers, such as Grossman (1990) who study subject matter growth in teachers and those who study the development of pedagogic expertise. As Borko and Livingston (1989) argue it may be a mistake for policy-makers to assume that the teaching of mathematics and other core disciplines will automatically improve as a result of increased content knowledge. The interaction of subject matter knowledge, content pedagogy, and the more general aspects of pedagogy as discussed in the chapter are still not clear. Subject matter knowledge may be a necessary criterion for effective teaching, but common sense would suggest it is not a sufficient one. Part of the cause for the present confusion arises from the way in which the terminology is used in different contexts. As Reynolds (1992) demonstrates in her review, the various authors all define content specific pedagogy differently; and, in a similar review, Alexander, Schallert, and Hare (1991) conclude that there is a similar degree of ambiguity in the terminology used to develop a typology of knowledge demanded by various forms of subject content.

TEACHER TRAINING AND DEVELOPMENTAL TEACHING MODELS

The type of development model outlined in the previous sections has important implications for teacher training, both at the initial and in-service levels. In particular, it can offer some guidance about the choice of suitable mentors and also indicates the most suitable form that training should take at a particular stage of a teacher's development. A developmental model based on the notion of expertise suggests that contrary to the accepted belief, mentors should not be drawn from groups of teachers who are regarded as experts. Not only is this because they may be more usefully employed in the same way as music experts give Master classes, helping proficient teachers improve their skills. It is also because, although capable of recreating the world of the classroom in ways that accommodated the limited schema available to the novice and beginning teacher, it is not their normal way of articulating pedagogic decisions. More often, when experts are asked to give reasons for their decisions about classroom practice, they reply, as did Benner's (1984) expert nurses: "I did it because it just felt right" (p. 30).

Competent teachers, possibly moving into the proficient stage, would appear to be ideal mentors. They have the confidence to cope with most situations and to plan meticulously, and they have the capacity to detect "early warning signs" of trouble. They have clear perspectives that provide a rationale for most of their decision-making. They therefore offer an analytic framework within which novices can confront and discuss problems.

An objection to this approach is that it emphasizes training rather than education. Allowing a novice to develop skills from the perspective of a particular mentor is a strategy which is likely to prove restrictive to future growth since, once the novice has found something which "works," he or she is unlikely to consider alternative teaching approaches. It is argued that, to overcome such problems, student teachers, from the beginning, need to reflect upon their observations and experiences so that, in developing their own personal "craft theory" of teaching, they can, unlike the merely competent teacher, examine and test out a number of explanations for any difficulties or successes that may occur in their classroom.

As mentioned earlier, Calderhead (1989) has pointed out that the concept of the "reflective teacher" is highly problematic. Reflection can mean, according to Schwab (1970), consideration of what is known of the strength and weaknesses of a given practice in the light of personal observation. Thus, armed with a knowledge about the effects of short wait-times on the capacity of slow learners to answer cognitively demanding questions, novices might observe a mentor's lesson or watch a videotape of themselves in action. Reflection, as advocated by Pollard and Tann (1987), however, requires novices to derive their own theories from action (Schon, 1983) so that they learn to become teacher-researchers in the manner proposed by Stenhouse (1975). It is doubtful, however, given the characteristics of novice teachers portrayed by the research, whether student teachers have sufficient experience or knowledge of routines to operate in this reflective way. This view is taken by both Berliner (1992) and Reynolds (1992) and lends support for McIntyre's (1992) conclusion discussed previously.

Clearly, any program of training should involve carefully chosen teams of mentors so that students experience a variety of perspectives. But the clear articulation of a developmental model based on stages would go a long way to overcome some of the problems identified in the previous paragraphs. Such a model would create an expectation of further progress throughout the first five years of teaching. Models of "bureaucratic" classroom control would gradually be superseded by more humanistic approaches. Clear transitions would be delineated whereby students learned the skills of direct instruction before moving to more complex arrangements involving, for example, various forms of collaborative grouping. These transitions could provide the framework for individual student teacher's "action plans" (Tomley, 1992), as suggested in the model of collaborative mentoring discussed earlier.

The forms of training required to move teachers from one point in their development to the next differ considerably. Benner (1984), for example, argues that, at the proficiency stage, case studies presenting teaching dilemmas are highly appropriate. Yet, the general practice of all forms of INSET is to offer the same treatment to all participants, irrespective of the developmental stage they have reached. In school-based INSET programs, for example, coordinators more often act as supply teachers, either replacing the class teacher or teaming up with him/her to divide the class into two smaller units (Alexander, 1992). In summary, therefore, those responsible for organizing both initial and in-service programs need to plan the curriculum and choose the methods of delivery so that they match the needs of teachers at their particular stage of professional development. The five-stage model, adapted by Berliner (1992), charting the transition from novice to expert, at least provides one basis for such a program.

FUTURE DIRECTIONS IN RESEARCH

A number of important themes, in relation to teacher development and training, suggest themselves for a possible future research agenda. First, there is a need to validate existing models of teacher development, particularly those which emphasize developing expertise in a similar manner to that carried out by Benner (1984). So far, as we have seen, research has almost entirely been devoted to contrasting behavior of novice and expert teachers with little attention given to possible intervening stages. Replication of some of the existing studies, for example, that of Sabers et al. (1991) in which simultaneous videotapes were observed by teachers and their observations and comments recorded, would provide opportunities to extend the present analysis to include differences between experienced proficient teachers and experts. The study might then be repeated in different contexts, for example, with pupils from different age range or with different subject content. An interesting variant in such analysis would be to take expert teachers who are deemed to be experts from one domain and to confront them with the analysis of what, for them, are novel situations. Classifications of teachers, based upon this analysis, as either competent, proficient or expert, would then need to be correlated with observed classroom behavior (using both systematic and participant observation techniques as appropriate). When identifying expertise, more emphasis needs to be given to pupils' evaluation of teachers.

Existing studies of teacher expertise have tended to concentrate on an analysis of teachers' cognitions. From the reviews of such research (Clarke & Peterson, 1986; Floden & Klinzing 1990; Lampert & Clarke, 1990; Reynolds, 1992) have emerged serious criticisms of the research methodology. Currently, the field is characterized by a tendency to use small samples in a variety of unconnected contexts, over dependence on interview methods for analysis with only rare attempts to incorporate "between methods" triangulation procedures and few follow-up studies which look for correspondence between cognition and behavior. Some studies, for example, Peterson, Fennema, Carpenter, and Loef (1989) and Smith and Neal (1989), have used multiple methods, including questionnaires, which allow a wider sample of teachers to be studied but, as Alexander et al. (1991) have observed, such studies at present lack coherence because of the variety of paradigms used to classify knowledge growth in teachers. Developing a framework for knowledge terminology into which the analysis of the various forms of data can be classified appears to be an important priority within the research agenda.

Alternative views of professional growth in teaching, as we have seen, reject Berliner's (1992) argument that novice teachers should not be asked to engage in reflection during their initial teacher training. Grossman (1992), for example, reviewing studies of growth in teachers' subject matter knowledge, reports that novices spend considerable amounts of time questioning the purposes of teaching their subject well before they develop established classroom routines (Grossman & Richert, 1988). Such criticism, however, seems misplaced in that Berliner's argument concerning reflective teaching relates, in particular, to tactical elements of classroom practice and not strategic considerations, based essentially on an analysis of the situation prior to teaching. Strategic analysis is highly dependent on initial aims, objectives, and personal philosophy; and novice teachers, as a result of their academic training, should be perfectly capable of engaging in the kind of philosophic enquiry, relating to the nature of knowledge. This is akin to what McIntyre (1992) calls reflection at a practical level, and seems similar to the examples cited by Grossman (1992) as evidence of the novices' capacity for theorizing. However, studies of classrooms, for example, Galton, Hargreaves, Comber, and Wall (1999), have frequently demonstrated the mismatch between teaching strategies and tactics. For example, teachers claiming to help pupils 'think for themselves' (the strategic aim) often end up using a guided discovery approach that enables pupils to guess what is in the teacher's mind because of the way questions are posed and suggestions made (on-going tactics). There is a clear need for those who advocate models of professional growth in teaching, based upon a developing knowledge base, to link such analysis with observed practice in the manner of Borko et al. (1992), who have observed the first attempts of mathematics students to teach their subject.

GENERAL CONCLUSION

I have attempted to argue that much of the current thinking about the most effective approach to educating future teachers suffers from the failure to ground recommended practice on adequate theoretical models of how teachers learn to teach and improve over time. While such models need to be concerned with the development of subject expertise, there is an even greater urgency to engage in research that focuses on the way that generic teaching expertise can best be developed.

For professional development of this kind to work, it will be necessary to ensure that a teacher's career is clearly signposted by a number of carefully defined stages, the passage through which (determined, in part, through peer review) leads to further rewards. Such a system is very different from that currently proposed in the UK based largely on "payment by results." Lacking any theory of how one learns "to teach better" as one's career develops, there is little incentive, at present, for a teacher to change his or her practice, unless one's present methods result in a drastic breakdown in discipline or there is abundant evidence that pupils are failing to learn. Lacking a coherent theory of pedagogy, it is all too easy, in such cases, to attribute such failures to factors outside the teacher's control, such as a pupil's home circumstances. Even when colleagues succeed in overcoming similar problems, this can be put down to their having outstanding personal qualities which enable them to forge special relationships with difficult children.

If such a notion of professional development were to become a central feature of teachers' culture, I believe it would have immediate and important consequences beyond improved pedagogy. To give one example, it would force a re-evaluation of the content of training courses. If student teachers entered a profession, whose culture regarded what was taught on the course as only a first stage, then there would no longer be a need to cover a wide range of teaching methods. Instead, we might concentrate on getting students to do a few things well so that, as Gage (1985) suggests, "within the art form called classroom teaching" we could explore "the infinite variations within this stable art form ... that make the difference between superb, average and atrocious' classroom teaching" (p. 49).

NOTES

[1]This chapter is adapted from "Two Decades of Change in English Teacher Education: The Consequences of Neglecting Educational Theory" published in Issue 2 of Volume II of the *Asia-Pacific Journal of Teacher Education and Development*.

REFERENCES

Alexander, P. (1996). Stages and phases of domain learning: The dynamics of subject matter knowledge, strategy knowledge and motivation. In C. Weinstein & B. McCombs (Eds.), *Strategic learning: Skill, will and self-regulation*. Hillsdale, NJ: Lawrence Erlbaum.

Alexander, P., Schallert, D., & Hare, V. (1991). Coming to terms: How researchers in learning and literacy talk about knowledge. *Review of Educational Research,*

61(3), 315-344.

Alexander, R. (1992). *Policy and practice in primary education.* London: Routledge.

Beckmann, L. (1976). Casual attributions of teachers and parents regarding children's performance. *Psychology in Schools, 13,* 212-218.

Benner, P. (1984). *From novice to expert: Excellence and power in clinical nursing practice.* Reading, Massachusetts: Addison-Wesley.

Berliner, D. (1992). Some characteristics in experts in the pedagogical domain. In F. Oser, A. Dick & J. Patry (Eds.), *Effective and responsible teaching: The new synthesis* (p. 223). San Francisco: Jossey-Bass Press.

Berliner, D., Stein, P., Sabers, D., Clarridge, P., Cushing, K., & Pinnegar, S. (1988). Implications of research on pedagogical expertise and experience for mathematics teaching. In D. Grouws & T. Cooney (Eds.), *Perspectives on research on effective mathematics teaching* (p. 67). Reston, Virginia: National Council of Teachers of Mathematics.

Borko, H., & Livingstone, C. (1989). Cognition and improvisation: Differences in mathematics instruction by expert and novice teachers. *American Educational Research Journal, 26*(4), 473-498.

Borko, H., Eisenhart, M., Brown, C., Underhill, R., Jones, D., & Agard, P. (1992). Learning to teach hard mathematics. *Journal of Research in Mathematics Education, 23*(3), 194-222.

Budd-Rowe, M. (1974). Wait time and rewards as instructional variables, their influence on language, logic and fate control. *Journal of Research in Science Teaching, 11,* 81-94.

Calderhead, J. (Ed.). (1987). *Exploring teachers thinking.* London: Cassell.

Calderhead, J. (1989). Reflective teaching and teacher education. *Teaching and Teacher Education, 5*(1) 43-51.

Carter, K., Cushing, K., Sabers, D., Stein, P., & Berliner, D. (1988). Expert-novice differences in perceiving and processing visual information. *Journal of Teacher Education, 39,* 25-31.

Chase, W., & Simon, H. (1973). Perception in chess. *Cognitive Psychology, 4,* 55-81.

Chen A. Y. (1997). Experienced and student teachers' reflection on classroom practice. In J. Tan, S. Gopinathan & W. K. Ho (Eds.), *Education in Singapore.* Singapore: Prentice Hall.

Clarke, C., & Peterson, P. (1986). Teachers' thought processes. In M. Wittrock (Ed.), *Handbook of research on teaching* (3rd ed., p. 225). New York: MacMillan.

Daloz, L. (1986). *Effective teaching and mentoring.* San Francisco: Jossey Bass.

Dreyfus, H., & Dreyfus, S. (1986). *Mind over machine.* New York: Free Press.

Dreyfus, S. (1982). Formal models vs. human situational understanding: Inherent limitations on the modeling of business expertise. *Office Technology and People, 1,* 133-155.

Ericsson, K., & Charness, N. (1994). Expert performance. *American Psychologist, 49*(8), 725-747.

Everton, T., & Younger, M. (1999). The changing nature of secondary its partnership in England and Wales in the 1990s. *Asia-Pacific Journal of Teacher Education and Development, 2*(2), 3-40.

Floden, R., & Klinzing, H. (1990). What can research on teaching contribute to teacher preparation? A second opinion. *Educational Researcher, 19*(4), 15-20.

Furlong, J., & Maynard, T. (1995). *Mentoring student teachers.* London: Routledge.

Gage, N. (1985). *Hard gains in the soft sciences: The case for pedagogy* (CEOR Monograph). CEDR and its Bloomington, Indiana: Phi Delta Kappa.

Galton, M., Hargreaves, L., Comber, C., & Wall, D. (1999). *Inside the primary classroom: 20 years on.* London: Routledge.

Glasser, R., & Chi, M. (1988). The nature of expertise: An overview. In M. Chi et al. (Eds.), *The nature of expertise* (p. xv). New York: Lawrence Erlbaum.

Goodson, I. (1994). Studying the teacher's life and work. *Teaching and Teacher Education, 10*(1), 29-37.

Grossman, P. (1990). *The making of a teacher: Teacher knowledge and teacher education.* New York: Teachers College Press.

Grossman, P. (1992). Why models matter: An alternative view on professional growth in teaching. *Review of Educational Research, 62*(2), 171-180.

Grossman, P., & Richert, A. (1988). Unacknowledged knowledge growth: A re-examination of the effects of teacher education. *Teaching and Teacher Education, 4,* 53-62.

Grundy, S., & Hatton, E. (1998). Teacher education, student teachers and biographical influences; implications for teacher education. *Asia-Pacific Journal of Teacher Education, 26*(2), 121-138.

Hargreaves, D. (1996). *Teaching as a research-based profession: Possibilities and prospects* (Teacher Training Agency 1996 Annual Lecture). London: TTA.

Housner, L., & Griffey, D. (1985). Teacher cognition: Differences in planning and decision making between experienced and inexperienced teachers. *Research Quarterly for Exercise and Sport, 56,* 44-53.

Kennedy, M. (1991). *An agenda for research on teacher learning* (Special Report for the National Council for Research on Teacher Learning). East Lancing: Michigan State University.

Kounin, J. (1970). *Discipline and group management in classrooms.* New York: Holt, Rinehart and Winston.

Lampert, M., & Clarke, C. (1990). Expert knowledge and expert thinking in teaching: A response to Floden and Klinzing. *Educational Researcher, 19*(5), 21-23.

McIntyre, D. (1992). Theory, theorising and reflection in teacher education. In J. Calderhead & P. Gates (Eds.), *Conceptualising reflection in teacher education.* London: Falmer Press.

McNally, P., & Martin, S. (1998). Support and challenge in learning to teach: The role of the mentor. *Asia-Pacific Journal of Teacher Education, 26*(1), 39-50.

Nias, J. (1988). Informal education in action: Teachers' accounts. In A. Blyth (Ed.),

Informal primary education today. London: Falmer Press.

Peterson, P., Fennema, E., Carpenter, T., & Loef, M. (1989). Teachers' content pedagogical beliefs in mathematics. *Cognition and Instruction, 6*(1), 1-40.

Pollard, A., & Tann, S. (1987). *Reflective teaching in the primary classroom.* London: Cassell.

Reynolds, A. (1992). What is competent beginning teaching? A review of the literature. *Review of Educational Research, 62*(1), 1-36.

Sabers, D., Cushing, K., & Berliner, D. (1991). Differences among teachers in tasks characterised by simultaneity, multidimensionality and immediacy. *American Educational Research Journal, 28*(1), 63-88.

Schon, D. (1983). *The reflective practitioner.* London: Temple Smith.

Schwab, J. (1970). *The practical: A language for curriculum.* Washington, DC: National Education Association Centre for the Study of Instruction.

Shulman, L. (1994). Those who understand: Knowledge growth in teaching. In B. Moon & A. Mayers (Eds.), *Teaching and learning in the secondary school* (p. 125). London; New York: Routledge. (Reprinted from *Educational Researcher, 15*(2), 4-21, 1986)

Smith, D., & Neal, D. (1989). The construction of subject matter knowledge in primary science teaching. *Teaching and Teacher Education, 5*(1), 1-20.

Stenhouse, L. (1975). *An introduction to curriculum research and development.* London: Heinemann.

Tomley, D. (1992). *First annual report. Leicester University, School of Education. Action Planning in Teacher Training Project.* Sheffield: Department of Employment.

Vonk, J. (1994). Teacher induction: The great omission in education. In M. Galton & B. Moon (Eds.), *Handbook of teacher training in Europe* (p. 85). London: David Fulton.

Zeichner, K. (1991). *Conceptions of reflective teaching in contemporary US teacher education programs.* Paper presented at the AERA Annual Meeting, Chicago, IL

Chapter 4

The Changing Nature of Teachers' Professionalism in a Changing World[1]

Andy HARGREAVES
Ontario Institute for Studies in Education
University of Toronto

INTRODUCTION

All professional work is complex and demanding. Poor professional judgment can mean that patients die, buildings fall down, or innocent people go to jail. While teachers still have high status and are accorded great respect in many countries, teaching as a profession is rarely viewed as being as complex or as crucial as architecture, law, or medicine. Yet, poor teaching can mean lost opportunities, spoiled life chances, and people's giving up on their own life-long learning. Its consequences may not be so immediately dramatic as collapsed buildings or dead bodies, but its long term effects for people's lives can be just as damaging. It is easier, indeed, to reconstruct a building than it is to rebuild someone's life.

If anything, teaching is becoming more demonstrably complex than it has ever been. In many places, teachers today are having to learn to teach in ways they themselves were not taught (McLaughlin, 1997). Teaching today means responding more sensitively to increasing cultural diversity in places like Ireland, Hong Kong, Japan, and Chile as well as most of mainland Europe. It means accommodating new technology and incorporating teaching strategies that will help individuals and economies invent and apply knowledge, rather than merely memorize it. Schooling systems that excessively emphasize basic skills, memorization, and recall of factual knowledge cannot develop the capacities for creation and innovation that are essential to live and work successfully within informational societies (Schlechty, 1990). New sources of teaching are therefore beginning to work their way on to the agenda of educational reform around the world. Constructivism, metacognition, cooperative learning, authentic assessment, and many other strategies are now challenging the work of teaching. So too are movements for teachers to respond to increasing parental demands, to work closely with colleagues to implement an accelerating pace of reform, and to integrate the learning requirements of special needs students within their classrooms. Being a teacher today means working effectively and openly with adults, as well as directing the classroom learning of students.

Using quantitative indicators to compare the knowledge, skills, and tasks of teaching to those employed in other professions, Rowan (1994) concludes that "teaching is a highly complex form of work" (p. 10). Moreover, given that the data on which he draws were collected in the early 1980s, it is possible that some areas of work which received relatively low ratings then, such as coordination, negotiation, and collective decision-making, exhibit greater complexity today. These findings are important, Rowan argues, because increases in work complexity appear to help shape increases in professional prestige and occupational earnings.

At the same time, a number of parallel movements appear to be deprofessionalizing teaching - making it more routinized, less skilled, and not nearly so complex. In a number of American states (and imminently in my own Canadian province of Ontario), teachers have been compelled to take written tests of basic competency and recertification in order to retain their qualifications to teach. Elsewhere, while movements towards more site-based management in many school systems may have involved teachers more in school development planning and collective decision-making, this has often been in a context where overall budgets have been reduced ("we give you less; you allocate it"), where many of the major areas of decision-making in terms of curriculum outcomes and testing requirements have been arrogated to the center ("we set the ends: you deliver the means"), and where what schools and teachers are required to manage is downloaded administrativia rather than issues of fundamental purpose and direction ("we control; you manage") (Robertson, 1993). As Darling-Hammond (1993) has noted, "[W]e see states passing laws that pay lip service to teacher professionalism while, with the other hand, they erect greater restraints on curricula, textbooks, tests and teaching methods" (p. 60). Paradoxically, some of the jurisdictions that have been most proactive on teacher professionalization issues are the selfsame ones that have capped teachers' salaries (e.g., Ontario, Canada), made sweeping job cuts (e.g., Victoria, Australia), or made teachers spend more of their professional time in the classroom.

The agenda of teacher professionalization therefore seems confused and contradictory. Teacher professionalization appears to be advancing in some respects, retreating in others. What is clear across all these trends is that the agenda of defining and developing teaching as a profession is an increasingly global issue - a central topic for educational debate even in countries where it has been accorded no traditional importance in the past. Even in many Asian countries, for example, where teaching and the status of and respect for teachers have been defined by history, culture, and tradition, what it means to be a teacher and to have the authority to teach is becoming increasingly problematic as the tacit agreement on learning goals that existed between homes and schools in pedagogically simpler times is collapsing. As the explosion in pedagogical science impacts more and more on schools, parents in all societies are becoming and will become increasingly bewildered by these developments, especially if teachers use the language of *classical professionalism.* to defend and distance their expertise in relation to the ordinary language and understandings of parents (Hargreaves & Goodson, 1996; Nespor, 1997).

For generations, many Asian parents have effectively been their school's and its teachers' *silent partners.* Some attribute this support-at-a-distance to the historical influence of the Confucian tradition in many Asian contexts. The opening sentence of the *Analects of Confucius* (Confucius, 1929), for example, ask rhetorically "[I]s it not pleasant to learn with a constant perseverance and application?" As Wing O. Lee (1996) summarizes the issue, "the concept that everyone is educable, everyone can become a sage and everyone is perfectible, forms the basic optimism and dynamism towards education in the Confucian tradition" (p. 30). This Confucian tradition, alongside the economic and educational competitiveness of post-war modernization in Japan and other Asian societies, has led to the belief (in families as in schools) that achievement is primarily the result of effort, not ability (Biggs, 1996). Where the goals of learning are shared between home and school, and where the technology of teaching is relatively straightforward and familiar (in terms of whole class teaching, seatwork, and question-an answer routines), then parents become the teacher's ideal silent partn pushing the student to work harder at home, while maintaining a res distance from the teacher and his or her expertise at school (Shim Sakai, 1995).

In most places new, even in Asian countries, the conditions f partnerships between home and school apply less and less.   The goals of learning are becoming disputed, and the pedagogies of schooling are no longer straightforward or uncontroversial.   What children need to learn and teachers must teach is changing.   Subject partnerships and remote professionalism which says that teachers always know best are no longer sustainable when the goals of learning and strategies of teaching take dramatically new directions.   Teaching and the profession of teaching are therefore very much at a crossroad, not just in the West, but in many other parts of the world as well.

The concepts of *professionalism* - usually referring to the quality and character of what teachers do - and *professionalization* - more often concerned with the status and standing of an occupation - are "essentially contested," as philosophers say.   Outside education, professions have been represented theoretically in the image of those who belong to them and advance their interests, as having a strong technical culture with a specialized knowledge base and shared standards of practice, a service ethic where there is a commitment to client needs, a firm monopoly over service, long periods of training, and high degrees of autonomy (see, e.g., Etzioni, 1969).   Larson (1977) identifies the criterion of autonomy as a crucial one that helps distinguish professional from proletarianized work.   Johnson (1972), however, takes many of these classical criteria of professionalism to represent ideologies of self-promotion rather than realities of practice where professionals' self-interest are often privileged over those of their clients. Friedson (1994) argues that common-sense discourses of professionalism and behaving like a professional have been captured by managerialism as a way to control white-collar workers.   Meanwhile, Schön (1987) has recast professional action as comprising distinctive, reflective, and practical judgments, rather than esoteric knowledge.

In addition to the impact of these wider debates about the professions, teacher professionalism in particular has taken on very different meanings over the past century· or so (Murray, 1992).   Many parts of the world have witnessed veral stages in the evolution of the idea of professionalism in teaching, each ze carrying significant residues and traces from the last.

of and ideas about teacher professionalism and even about the nature g itself linger on from other agendas and other times - remaining as to be reckoned with in the imaginations and assumptions of policymakers, the public, and many parts of the teaching profession itself. Teaching is not what it was; nor is the professional learning required to become a teacher and improve as a teacher over time. This chapter identifies four broad historical phases in the changing nature of teachers' professionalism and professional learning.

These phases are not universal, but are relatively common across Anglophone cultures, though there are differences even there. For example, teaching is far from being an all graduate profession in New Zealand. The phases are ones with which many other nations are now engaging, however, although not necessarily in the same order. For example, Chile is trying to move more towards being an all-graduate profession (a characteristic of the second age of professionalism below), while at the same time experiencing more school-based staff development (a third age phenomenon).[2] The ages should therefore be seen as a contingent history of Anglophone nations that now contributes a collage of opportunities with which other cultures engage, rather than being viewed as discrete stages with an evolutionary necessity that all other cultures must follow.

THE PRE-PROFESSIONAL AGE

Teaching has always been *demanding,* but it has not always been technically *difficult.* Even in the earliest days of mass education, teachers struggled alone in their own classrooms to cover content with large groups of often reluctant learners, with few textbooks or resources to help them, and with little reward or recognition. Teaching and learning could never be pursued without reference to the necessities of classroom control, and teachers' success and survival depended on their ability to balance the two.

What has come to be regarded as "real school" to many people, as the seemingly normal, natural, and given way to organize teaching and curriculum, is therefore a highly specific socio-historical invention, rooted in the needs and concerns of generations past (Cuban, 1984; Hamilton, 1989; Metz, 1991; Meyer & Rowan, 1978; Tyack & Tobin, 1994). At the heart of this historical legacy is a particular set of practices that for decades defined the essence of teaching itself.

The basic teaching methods of mass public education were most commonly ones of recitation or lecturing, along with note-taking, question-and-answer, and seatwork (Cuban, 1984). These enabled teachers working with large groups, small resources, and students' whose motivation was often in question to meet four fundamental demands of the classroom: maintaining student attention, securing coverage of content, bringing about some degree of motivation, and achieving some degree of mastery (Abrahamson, 1974; Hoetker & Ahlbrand, 1969; Westbury, 1973).

In his classic text on the *Sociology of Teaching*, Willard Waller (1932) memorably depicted the school as "a despotism in a state of perilous equilibrium ... capable of being overturned in a moment" (p. 10). The successful teacher in this setting, he said, was "one who knows how to get on and off his high horse rapidly" (p. 385). Traditional patterns of teaching were understandable coping or survival strategies for teachers in the first six decades of this century, given the purposes, constraints, and demands that teachers had to meet (Hargreaves, 1977, 1978, 1979; Pollard, 1982; Scarth, 1987; Woods, 1977).

For a century or so, transmission teaching formed the accepted and largely unquestioned wisdom of what teaching really was. In this pre-professional view, teaching was technically simple. Once you had learned to master it, you needed no more help after that point. Schools where teachers continue to believe teaching is basically easy and where the pre-professional view persists are ones that Rosenholtz (1989) has described as "learning impoverished." With teachers who feel there is little else to learn in teaching, they achieve poorer results in basic skills achievements than their more professionally-oriented counterparts.

In this context of pedagogical certainty, professional learning for new teachers was largely seen as a matter of apprenticing oneself as a novice to someone who was skilled and experienced in the craft. In reality, much of that apprenticeship was served in the thousands of hours observing one's own teachers while being in their classes as a student (Lortie, 1975). To this experience was usually added a period of teaching practice or practicum, served at the side of an experienced cooperating teacher (as they later came to be called) as part of a wider program of teacher preparation (D. Hargreaves, 1994).

Practice made practice (Britzman, 1991). The unquestioned grammar of teaching was passed on from experienced teachers to novice ones. And once they had served their brief apprenticeship, experienced teachers saw no more of their colleagues in the classroom, received no feedback on their practice, and changed and improved mainly by trial-and-error in their own isolated classes. This individual, intuitive, and incremental approach to improvement and professional development confined teachers in the pre-professional age to what Hoyle (1974) calls "restricted professionalism" - scarcely a form of professionalism at all.

In the pre-professional age, the "good" teacher was the "true teacher" who "devoted herself to her craft," demonstrated loyalty and gained personal reward through service, "whatever the costs." In this age, teachers were virtually amateurs: they "only needed to carry out the directives of their more knowledgeable superiors" (Murray, 1992, p. 495).

These pre-professional images and discourses of teaching and teacher development are not just items of historical curiosity. They persist, for example, in pockets of the profession today especially among teachers in later career who started their work in the pre-professional age (Huberman, 1993; Sugrue, 1996; Weber & Mitchell, 1996). As McCulloch (1997) has shown in Britain, pre-professional images are also highly influential among many Ministers or Secretaries of State for Education, who tend to draw on their own biographical (and sometimes sentimental) memories of schooling as children, instead of referring to broader histories of education as a public project, as they go about the business of formulating educational policy. Pre-professional images also figure prominently in public perceptions of teaching among adults whose own schooling and experiences of teachers took place in the pre-professional age, and whose nostalgia-tinted ideas about teaching often remain rooted there (Hargreaves & Fullan, 1998).

Lastly, pre-professional images of teaching continue to be dominant in many East Asian countries, partly because of the constraints of class sizes and other factors mentioned earlier, but also because of the cultural importance of Confucian conceptions of teaching and authority within schools and families. In these contexts, the designation "pre-professional" may be a derogatory misnomer, since certain Asian whole-class teaching methods, such as "sticky probing" (questioning an individual's understanding at some length in front of the rest of the class), are often explicitly refined and reflected upon by educators themselves (Watkins & Biggs, 1996).

Elsewhere, in the still pervasive and influential pre-professional view, teachers are (at best) enthusiastic people, who know their subject matter, know how to "get it across," and can keep order in their classes. They learn to teach by watching others do it, first as a student, then as a student teacher. After that, barring a few refinements gained through trial-and-error, they know how to teach and they are on their own! If one holds to a simple, pre-professional image of teaching, teachers need little training or on-going professional learning, preparation time is relatively expendable (since the demands of preparation are not so great), and budget restrictions that limit contact with colleagues outside the classroom are seen as having little impact on the quality of what goes on within it (because it is assumed that teachers control everything within their individual classroom domain and keep all their work confined to it). If the task of teaching is seen as basically simple, why do we need to invest in continuous professional learning beyond a few in-service sessions connected to the government's latest policies?

Given the growing diversity of our classrooms and of students' learning needs within them as well as the challenging expectations we have for learning today, it is important to confront these images and discourses of professionalism which deny the difficulty of teaching. Combating the pre-professional view of teaching means challenging the nostalgia that many policy-makers, members of the public and teachers themselves have for "real teaching" and "real schools!" As the novels of Gabriel Garcia Marquez (e.g., 1982) portray so superbly, a strong dose of reality can be a powerful cure for nostalgia - whether this involves exiles returning to their actual homeland, or adults being led through focus group discussions to remember the gritty details (and not merely the ideal images) of their own schooling. Against this, policy-makers and the public need to be persuaded of how complex and difficult teaching is today in an age of cultural diversity and new technology, why teaching needs to become more sophisticated still, and what kinds of supports and learning opportunities teachers need to improve their work even further.

THE AGE OF THE AUTONOMOUS PROFESSIONAL

From the 1960s onwards, the status and standing of teachers in many countries improved significantly, compared to the pre-professional age. In this period, the words "professional" and "autonomy" became increasingly inseparable among educators. In what Hobsbawm (1994) calls the "golden age" of history in the 20th century (at least in the industrialized North and West), full employment, futures for school leavers to go to, the favorable demographics of a baby-boom expansion in the school population, and the belief that an expanding economy provided the wherewithal to treat education as an investment in human capital, all helped relieve teachers from external pressures on their pedagogical freedom. So teachers in many places were granted a measure of trust, material reward, occupational security, and professional dignity, as well as discretion in exchange for broadly fulfilling the mandates the state expected of them (Helsby & McCulloch, 1997).

How teachers taught now was no longer beyond question. From the 1960s onwards, classroom pedagogy started to become an ideological battleground between child-centered and subject-centered education, open-classrooms and closed classrooms, and traditional methods and progressive ones (Silberman, 1970). The child-centered, developmentalist theories increasingly espoused in faculties of education were now extending their influence into the world of educational practice. Pedagogical expertise could no longer be passed on as an assumed tradition from expert to novice. For more and more teachers, pedagogy was becoming an ideological decision. Unquestioned routines and traditions were being replaced by an ideological conflict between two great meta-narratives of traditionalism and progressivism.

In reality, the claims of open education (as of innovative curriculum projects) were often exaggerated. In practice, there was little evidence of discovery learning or cooperative groupwork (Galton et al., 1980), and basic skills continued to receive exceptionally high emphasis (Bassey, 1978). The reason was teacher individualism (D. Hargreaves, 1980). Most teachers taught in a box. They instructed their classes in isolation, separated from their colleagues (Rosenholtz, 1989; Zielinski & Hoy, 1983). When teachers did interact, this tended to be around materials, discipline, and individual student problems rather than about curriculum goals, teaching behavior, or classroom learning (Little, 1990; Lortie, 1975). The consequences of this individualism were extensive and disturbing.

While professional autonomy enhanced the status of teaching as the amount of teacher preparation was lengthened and salaries rose, it also inhibited innovation. Few innovations moved beyond adoption to successful implementation (Fullan & Stiegelbauer, 1991). The benefits of in-service education seldom became integrated into classroom practice, as individual course-goers returned to schools of unenthusiastic colleagues who had not shared the learning with them (Little, 1993). And pedagogy stagnated as teachers were reluctant or unable to stand out from their colleagues. Induction and mentoring programs did begin to be introduced in a profession that was now acknowledged as being more difficult, but the surrounding culture of individualism meant that helping relationships in a school were confined to new mentoring (Hargreaves & Fullan, in press). The message was that only novices or incompetents needed help. The rest of the teaching staff could manage just fine by themselves. Not surprisingly, when help was associated with weakness, new teachers sought to extricate themselves from it as fast as they could (Little, 1990).

Important legacies of the age of professional autonomy are ones of status, reward, and relative independence from bureaucratic control. In many developing countries, these are unfulfilled legacies. When teaching is so poorly paid that teachers must hold down two or three jobs to make a living - a situation that World Bank investment refuses to make an intervention priority - any professional development and upgrading efforts designed to help teachers develop learners for the knowledge society are destined to be unsuccessful. Meanwhile, pay restrictions in many more developed countries along with increasing bureaucratic controls over the details of teacher judgement, including mandated pedagogical approaches to literacy in England, for example, make teaching an increasingly unattractive profession for potential new entrants and an increasingly demoralizing one for those who remain within it. Status, standing, and quality of training are legacies of professional autonomy worth protecting. But the legacy of autonomy, which makes teaching professionally exclusive and self-interested so that teachers are placed on pedestals above parents and students, is a problematic one. In this sense, the age of professional autonomy has provided teachers with poor preparation for coping with the dramatic changes headed their way and against which their classroom doors have offered little protection.

THE AGE OF THE COLLEGIAL PROFESSIONAL

By the mid-1980s, individual teacher autonomy was becoming unsustainable as a way of responding to the increased complexities of schooling; yet, the persistence of individualism in teaching meant that teachers' responses to the challenges they faced were ad hoc, uncoordinated with the efforts of their colleagues, and based on rates of the development in their own personal knowledge and skill that just could not keep pace with constantly changing demands they had to meet.

At the same time, there was growing pressure to create collaborative cultures due to the knowledge explosion, the widening of curriculum demands, the increasing range of special education students in ordinary classes, and the accelerating pace of change. Teaching was becoming even more difficult and complex. In the age of collegial professionalism, there are increasing efforts to build strong professional cultures of collaboration in order to develop common purpose, cope with uncertainty and complexity, respond to rapid· change, create a climate of risk-taking and continuous improvement, develop stronger senses of teacher efficacy, and create ongoing learning cultures for teachers that replace patterns of staff development which are individualized, episodic, and weakly connected to the priorities of the school (Ashton & Webb, 1986; Fullan & Hargreaves, 1996; McLaughlin, 1997; Newman & Wehlage, 1995; Rosenholtz, 1989; Ross, 1995; Talbert & McLaughlin, 1994).

In this age, the implications for initial teacher education, ongoing professional learning, and mentoring in particular include the following:

- teachers must learn to teach in ways they have not been taught;

- professional learning is seen as a continuous process grappling with complex and evolving issues;

- continuous learning is both an individual responsibility and an institutional obligation;

- professional learning is not to be found in a choice between school-based and course-based modes of provision, but in an active integration of and synergy between the two;

- collegial professionalism means working with, learning from, and teaching colleagues; and

- teaching must be framed and informed by professional standards of practice that define what good teachers should know and be able to do (and, we would add, what qualities and dispositions they should possess and display to care for and connect with their students).

Professionalism here is "new," rather than "old" (D. Hargreaves, 1994) and collegial and collective, rather than autonomous and individual (Hargreaves & Goodson, 1996). However, if collegiality is "forced" or "imposed," teachers can quickly come to resent and resist it (Grimmett & Crehan, 1992; Hargreaves, 1994).   Also, the flattened management structures that are sometimes represented as empowerment can easily turn into using collaboration as a form of exploitation and enslavement (Renihan & Renihan, 1992).   In England, for example, while implementation of the National Curriculum initially created more teacher consultation and collaboration, "the deluge of directives" which fell upon teachers reduced much of this collaboration to technical tasks of coordination, rather than working together for fundamental change (Helsby, 1995; Webb & Vulliamy, 1993).   Not surprisingly, collaboration of this sort began to be abandoned once the urgency of implementation had passed (Helsby, 1999). All too often, teachers find themselves in circumstances where they are losing possession of their purposes to central governments and other outside interest groups, while being offered the carrot (or is it the stick?) of professional collaboration to determine the means of delivering these purposes (Smyth, 1995).   Moreover, collaboration is often encouraged in working conditions which provide teachers with little time to meet each other in the school day - and in some cases, what little time teachers already have is targeted for cutbacks and economies (Hargreaves, 1998).

In contexts of large-scale educational reform, professional collaboration can help teachers marshall their resources, conserve their energy, and sift their way through the plethora of requirements and demands; or it can be a strategy to get teachers to steer themselves towards implementing the dubious policy ends of others, sacrificing their ideals and their energy as they do so and dulling the profession's critical edge.   The challenge, in the age of collegial professionalism, is how to build strong professional communities in teaching without using collaboration to overload teachers or steer unpalatable policies through them (Smyth, 1995).

THE FOURTH PROFESSIONAL AGE

As we enter the turn of the new century, the world in which we live is undergoing profound social, economic, political, and cultural transformations. The social geography of postmodernity is one where the boundaries between institutions are dissolving, where roles are becoming less segregated and where borders are becoming increasingly irrelevant. What is "out there" in the world beyond schools is now right "in here" in the lives and dispositions of the children teachers teach, and this has fundamental implications for the roles of teachers and administrators (Hargreaves & Fullan, 1998). Teachers are having to learn to work with more diverse communities, to see parents as sources of learning and support, rather than interference, to work more with other social agencies, and so on.

Not only are the social geographies of schooling changing in ways that blur the boundaries between schools and the world outside, but the social geographies of professional learning are also changing. There is much more access to networks of professional learning. In many contexts, the content of professional learning now needs to become wider and deeper to encompass working with parents, becoming assessment literate in relation to standards and data about student learning, keeping up with scientific breakthroughs in the pedagogy of learning that derive from brain research and cognitive psychology, rekindling the purpose, passion, and emotional intelligence of teaching, and working with others to bring about positive reforms in education. All of these is occurring in the midst of intense pressure and contradictory trends of centralization and school-based management.

Whether this age will see exciting and positive new partnerships being created with groups and institutions beyond the school, as well as teachers learning to work effectively, openly, and authoritatively with those partner, or whether it will witness the deprofessionalization of teaching, as teachers crumble under multiple pressures, intensified work demands, and reduced opportunities to learn from colleagues, is something that remains to be seen.

Moving towards a more principled postmodern professionalism means teachers protecting themselves against the forces of deprofessionalization - protecting salaries and standards, agitating for conditions that attract high caliber people to the profession, pushing for the leadership and opportunities that promote collegiality, countering the pre-professional prejudice that teaching is technically easy, and ensuring that teachers retain discretionary judgment over the details of how to teach their own classes.

At the same time, connecting with the community "out there" beyond the school, in relation to a practice that is becoming more complex, means developing different relationships with parents and other adults; and with that, a less insular and self-protective view of what professional autonomy and identity involves.

The literature on parent-teacher relations suggests that considerable strides have yet to be made beyond parent-teacher relationships, which sustain teachers' senses of professional superiority (parents as supporters or learners), to ones of genuine partnership where relationships between teachers and parents are both open and authoritative (Hargreaves & Goodson, 1996) and where, in Vincent's (1996) terms, they are relationships of reciprocal learning.

In a more principled postmodern professionalism, teachers should try to learn from parents as well as having parents learn from them. There are many ways to do this, including two-way student reports (Earl & LeMahieu, 1997), having students run interviews with their parents on parents' night in relation to portfolios of work they have accumulated - rather than teachers trying to run and control all the communication themselves (Hargreaves, 1997) - setting homework assignments to be shared with a family member (Epstein, 1995), and setting up focus groups of parents to talk about their concerns where the role of teachers in each group is primarily to listen and learn, and not to argue or defend (Beresford, 1996).

Paradoxically, this greater openness will provide teachers with more support from parents, not less. The public is yet to be convinced that teachers need more time to work with each other, and not just their students. It has, in large part, yet to understand how and why teaching and the students that teachers teach have changed since the time most parents were themselves at school. It is not yet persuaded to commit to the kind of tax increases that would benefit the public education system and the quality of those who teach in it. It is therefore vital that the teaching profession now works in partnership with the public, to become a vigorous *social movement* of acting subjects rather than fragmented individuals (Touraine, 1995), who work together to improve the quality and the professionalism of teaching. This is what the fourth age of professionalism promises most of all.

CONCLUSION

The forces of deprofessionalization in teaching have cut deep, and in many places teaching has not even approached becoming a profession, by any definition of the term. But the prospects for building or reinvigorating

Press; Toronto: University of Toronto Press.

Hargreaves, A. (1997). Rethinking educational change. In A. Hargreaves (Ed.), *Rethinking educational change with heart and mind* (The 1997 ASCD Yearbook) (pp. 1-26). Alexandria, VA: Association for Supervision and Curriculum Development.

Hargreaves, A. (1998). Teachers role in renewal. *Orbit, 129*(1), 10-13.

Hargreaves, A., & Goodson. I. (1996). Teachers professional lives: Aspirations and actualities. In I. Goodson & A. Hargreaves (Eds.), *Teachers' professional lives* (pp. 1-27). London: Falmer Press.

Hargreaves, A., & Fullan, M. (1997). *Mentoring in the new millennium. Theory into practice.*

Hargreaves, A., & Fullan, M. (1998*). What's worth fighting for out there?* Buckingham: Open University Press; New York: Teachers' College Press; Toronto: Elementary Teachers Federation of Ontario.

Hargreaves, D. (1980). The occupational culture of teaching. In P. Woods (Ed.), *Teacher strategies* (pp. 125-148). London: Croom Helm.

Hargreaves, D. (1994). The new professionalism: The synthesis of professional and institutional development. *Teaching and Teacher Education, 10*(4), 423-438.

Helsby, G. (1995). Teachers' construction of professionalism in England in the 1990s. *Journal of Education for Teaching, 21*(3), 317-332.

Helsby, G. (1999). *Changing teachers' work and culture.* Buckingham: Open University Press.

Helsby, G., & McCulloch, G. (Eds.). (1997). *Teachers and the national curriculum.* London: Cassell.

Hobsbawm, E. (1994). *Age of extremes.* London: Abacus Press.

Hoetker, J., & Ahlbrand, W. P. (1969). The persistence of the recitation. *American Educational Research Journal, 6.*

Hoyle, E. (1974). Professionality, professionalism and control in teaching. *London Educational Review, 3,* 13-19.

Huberman, M. (1993). *The lives of teacher.* London: Cassell.

Johnson, T. (1972). *Professions and power.* London: Macmillan.

Larson, M. S. (1977). *The rise of professionalism.* Berkeley: University of California Press.

Lee, W. O. (1996). The cultural context for Chinese learners: Conceptions of learning in the Confucian tradition. In D. A. Watkins & J. B. Biggs (Eds.), *The Chinese learner: Cultural, psychological and contextual influences* (pp. 25-41). Hong Kong: Comparative Education Research Centre; Melbourne: Australian Council for Educational Research.

Little, J. W. (1990). The persistence of privacy: Autonomy and initiative in teachers' professional relations. *Teachers' College Record, 91*(4), 509-536.

Little, J. W. (1993). Teachers' professional development in a climate of educational reform. *Educational Evaluation and Policy Analysis, 15*(2), 129-151.

Lortie, D. (1975). *Schoolteacher: A sociological study.* Chicago: University of Chicago Press.

Marquez, G. G. (1982). *One hundred years of solitude.* New York: Penguin Books.

McCulloch, G. (1997). Marketing the millennium: Education for the twenty-first century. In A. Hargreaves & R. Evans (Eds.), *Beyond educational reform: Bringing teachers back in* (pp. 19-28). Buckingham: Open University Press.

McLaughlin, M. W. (1997). Rebuilding teacher professionalism in the United States. In A. Hargreaves & R. Evans (Eds.), *Buying teachers back* (pp. 77-93). Buckingham: Open University Press.

Metz, M. (1991). Real school: A universal drama amid disparate experience. In D. E. Mitchell & M. E. Gnesta (Eds.), *Education politics for the new century: The twentieth anniversary yearbook of the Politics of Education Association* (pp. 75-91). Philadelphia: Falmer Press.

Meyer, J. W., & Rowan, B. (1978). The structure of educational organizations. In M. W. Meyer & Associates (Eds.), *Environments and organizations* (pp. 78-109). San Francisco: Jossey-Bass.

Murray, C. E. (1992, Winter). Teaching as a profession: The Rochester Case in historical perspective. *Harvard Educational Review, 62*(4), 494-519.

Nespor, J. (1997). *Tangled up in school: Politics, space, bodies and signs in the educational process.* New Jersey: Lawrence Erlbaum Associates.

Newmann, F., & Wehlage, G. (1995). *Successful school restructuring.* Madison, WI: Center on Organization and Restructuring Schools.

Pollard, A. (1982). A model of coping strategies. *British Journal of Sociology of Education, 3*(1), 19-37.

Renihan, F. I., & Renihan, P. (1992, Spring). Educational leadership: A renaissance metaphor. *Education Canada, 32*(1), 11.

Robertson, S. L. (1993). The politics of devolution, self-management and post-Fordism in schools. In J. Smyth (Ed.), *A socially critical view of the self-managing school* (pp. 117-136). London; New York: Falmer Press.

Rosenholtz, S. (1989). *Teachers' workplace.* New York: Longman.

Ross, J. A. (1995). Strategies for enhancing teachers' beliefs in their effectiveness: Research on a school improvement hypothesis. *Teachers' College Record, 97*(2), 227-251.

Rowan, B. (1994). Comparing teachers' work with work in other occupations: Notes on the professional status of teaching. *Educational Researcher, 23*(6), 4-17.

Scarth, J. (1987). Teacher strategies: A review and critique. *British Journal of Sociology of Education, 8*(3), 245-262.

Schlechty, P. (1990). *Schools for the twenty-first century: Leadership imperatives for educational reform.* San Francisco, CA: Jossey-Bass.

Schön, D. (1987). *Educating the reflective practitioner.* San Francisco: Jossey-Bass.

Shimahara, K., & Sakai, A. (1995*). Learning to teach in two cultures: Japan and the United States.* New York: Galard Publishing.

Silberman, C. E. (1970). *Crisis in the classroom: The revaluing of American education.* New York: Random House.

Smyth, J. (Ed.). (1995). *Critical discourses in teacher development.* London: Cassell.

Sugrue, C. (1996). Student teachers' lay theories: Implications for professional development. In I. Goodson & A. Hargreaves (Eds.), *Teachers' professional lives* (pp. 154-177). London; New York: Falmer Press.

Talbert, J., & McLaughlin, M. (1994). Teacher professionalism in local school contexts. *American Journal of Education, 102,* 123-153.

Touraine, A. (1995). *Critique of modernity.* Oxford: Blackwell.

Tyack, D., & Tobin, W. (1994, Fall). The grammar of schooling: Why has it been so hard to change? *American Educational Research Journal, 31*(3), 453-480.

Vincent, C. (1996). *Parents and teachers: Power and participation.* London; Washington, DC: Falmer Press.

Waller, W. (1932). *The sociology of teaching.* New York: Wiley.

Watkins, D. A., & Biggs, J. B. (Eds.). (1996*). The Chinese learner: Cultural, psychological and contextual influences.* Hong Kong: Comparative Education Research Centre.

Webb, R., & Vulliamy, G. (1993). A deluge of directives: Conflict between collegiality and managerialism in the post ERA primary school. *British Education Research Journal, 22*(4), 441-58.

Weber, S., & Mitchell, C. (1996). Using drawings to interrogate professional identity and the popular culture of teaching. In I. F. Goodson & A. Hargreaves (Eds.), *Teachers' professional lives* (pp. 109-126). Washington, DC: Falmer Press.

Westbury, I. (1973). Conventional classrooms, open classrooms, and the teachnology of teaching. *Journal of Curriculum Studies, 5*(2), 99-121.

Woods, P. (1977). Teaching for survival. In P. Woods & M. Hammersley (Eds.), *School experience: Explorations in the sociology of education* (pp. 271-293) London: Croom Helm.

Zielinski , A. K., & Hoy, W. K. (1983). Isolation and alienation in the elementary schools. *Education Administration Quarterly, 19*(2), 27-45.

Chapter 5

Teacher Self Learning in a Networked Environment[1]

Magdalena Mo Ching MOK and Yin Cheong CHENG

Centre for Research and International Collaboration
The Hong Kong Institute of Education, Hong Kong

Education reform is an international trend and in the past three decades there have been numerous good ideas, experiments, and reform efforts, both major and minor, in many education systems around the world (Cheng & Townsend, 2000). Most of these reform endeavors, however, have yielded only moderate success on school improvement (Angus & Louden, 1998; Carpenter, 2000; Fullan, 1998a; Hopkins, 2000; Pipho, 2000). The policy reforms launched in the 1970s and early 1980s, typically concerned with curriculum reform and organizational restructure (Fullan, 1998b), did not yield promised advancements in student achievement. Later movements in the 1980s and 1990s including site-based management (Cheng, 1996; David, 1994; Fullan, 1995), total quality education (English & Hill, 1994; Herman & Herman, 1994), competence-based assessment (Darling-Hammond, 1995), which has support in education ideology and methods from high profile educators as well as in handsome financial terms from the government, also failed to deliver the expected improvement in student learning (Fullan, 1998a; Hopkins, 2000).

Many reasons have been offered to explain the failure of the reforms (e.g., Fullan, 1998a; Hopkins, 2000; Pipho, 2000), but several reports highlight the inadequate preparation and involvement of teachers for the implementation of these reforms as being the key attribute (Darling-Hammond, 1999; Fullan, 1998a, 1998b; Futrell, 1994; Sergiovani, 2000). That teachers have a critical role in the successful implementation of reform is not a new concept; it has been identified, amongst others, in the Holmes Group (a national consortium comprising about 100 American research universities advocating for reform in teacher education) report *Tomorrow's Teachers* (1986) and the Carnegie Report *A Nation Prepared: Teachers for the 21st Century* (1986), and emphasized by such researchers as Cheng (1996); Fullan (1996); Hopkins (1994); Hopkins and Stern (1996); Lieberman (1995); Lieberman and Miller (1999); and Tsui and Cheng (1999, 1997). These authors provide evidence that unless teachers change the ways they teach, students cannot become effective learners. Further, research suggests that professional development empower teachers to initiate changes in their classrooms; changes that are sustained by favorable school environment (Cheng, 1996; Hopkins, 2000). Thus, the link between teaching and learning is enhanced and school improvement eventuated.

Nevertheless, two issues still need to be resolved. First, in which direction should teachers change and, second, who is to initiate the change? Answer to the first question is being informed by the explosive innovations in information technology (IT) and the recent developments in learning theory. IT development not only has revolutionized the speed and form at which we communicate with each other but also has redefined learning, curriculum, pedagogy, and the function of schools (Cheng, 1999). Recent literature on learning theory is being dominated by constructivism (Phillips, 1995; von Glaserfeld, 1995), which asserts that knowledge is being constructed by the practitioners being involved in the action. From a constructivist perspective, teachers need to be involved in order for them to develop ownership of the reform. Foundation of the reform takes root in teachers' interpretation and internalization of reform policies and their operationalization in classroom situations. Teachers need to be able to make sense of the reform within the reality of their classrooms. Borrowing from the language of constructivists (e.g., Driver, Asoko, Leach, Morfimer, & Scott 1994), teachers construct their own understanding concerning the reform. That is, teachers have to be self-directed learners (Mok & Cheng, 2000c). Moreover, for the reform to be sustained, teachers have to create new knowledge (Cheng, 1999) through the applications of knowledge generated in their specific teaching and learning contexts in themselves and in their students, based on their prior experiences and with their understanding of the reform.

Research into self learning is a fast growing industry since the end of the last century but most studies are concerned with school children. Much is yet to be learned in the area of adults' self learning. Under-researched are such important questions as what motivates the adult learner in the first instance in an IT rich environment, how this motivation is sustained, what the drawbacks are if IT is over emphasized, how important is a networked social human environment with other adult learners to self learning at both individual and group levels, and how the networked IT environment and the networked human environment can work together to initiate and maintain a culture of self learning and facilitate each adult learner's persistent learning in both local and global contexts. Without a comprehensive theory to address these questions in the context where the adult learner is a teacher, the efforts of education reforms could become ineffective and fail, if not causing greater problems and disasters to students, teachers, and schools. As such, there is an urgent need to develop a theory of self learning for teachers in a context of networked human and IT environment.

The discussion of self learning in a human and IT environment may be related to the following clusters of literature: the literature on adult learning (e.g., Caffarella, 1993; Flannery, 1993; Merriam & Caffarella, 1999); the literature on learning psychology or motivation psychology (e.g., Schunk, 1996); the literature on self-directed learning or self-regulated learning at a separated individual level from a psychology perspective (e.g., Boekaerts, Pintrick, & Zeidner, 2000; Brockett & Hiemstra, 1991; Caffarella, 1993; MacKeracher, 1996; Schunk & Zimmerman, 1998;); the literature on learning environment (e.g., Cheng, 1994; Tam & Cheng, 1995); the literature on collaboration and networking in learning (Cowie & van der Aalsvoort, 2000; DuFour, 1999; Fullan, 1997; Lieberman, 1996; Saltiel, 1998; Saltiel, Sgroi, & Brockett, 1998); the literature on information and communication technology in education (e.g., Basto, 1999; Bennett, 1999; Burbules & Callister, 1999; Chung & Baker, 1997; Lu, Wan, & Liu, 1999), and the literature on lifelong learning and learning society (e.g., Knasel, Meed, & Rossetti, 2000).

From these clusters of literature, the following observations can be identified:

a. There is substantial advancement of knowledge in each of the related areas in these years. It can be used to understand some key aspects of self learning of teachers.

b. The literature on self-directed/self-regulated learning is growing up quickly. Most of the literature focuses on separated individual learners from a psychological perspective or a micro perspective. It is rare to link the self learning process with a larger social context beyond individual, classroom, or school levels. How the sustainability of self learning is related to networked learning environment in a global context is often ignored particularly for teachers.

c. There is lack of literature that can integrate the advances in these different areas to provide a comprehensive model or theory to explain the nature and possibility of self learning of teachers in a networked human and IT environment.

In responding to the above knowledge gap in current education reforms, this chapter aims to develop a theoretical model for understanding and enhancing effective teacher self-learning in a networked human and IT environment. Based on the integration of the existing literature, this model can be used to deepen the understanding of the nature and process of self learning and to facilitate teachers becoming a highly motivated and effective self learner with the support of a networked human and IT environment. In this chapter, some implications will be drawn from the theory to inform the paradigm shift, policy formulation, and innovation of education in current worldwide education reforms.

TEACHERS AS ADULT LEARNERS

Before the discussion of teacher self learning theory, the understanding of teachers being adult learners should be important and necessary. Although there has been much attention to adult learning during the last three decades, a single unifying theory on how adults learn has yet to be developed (Brookfield, 1994; Merriam & Caffarella, 1999). Instead, there has been a plethora of philosophies, theories, and models, each attempting to describe some aspects of adult learning as distinguished from learning in general.

Each adult learner is idiosyncratic in terms of their learning style, learning goal, and prior experiences, as well as the life stage – early adulthood, middle adulthood, and late adulthood – of the learner at the time of learning. For instance, Cross (1981) highlighted, amongst other goals, intrinsic knowledge, personal fulfillment, community service, religious well-being, social relationships, and novelty as the learning goals of adults. Each of these goals calls for a different level of commitment, which in turn may have affected the level of perseverance and success of the learning. The multiplicity of learning goals is one of the distinguishing features between adults and children or adolescent learners. Boorkfield (1994, p. 36) maintains that adults, more so than children or adolescents, are driven by affective goals and served by self-mediated, conscious learning plans.

Further, the life role expectations of the adult change, depending on the life and career stage the adult is at, and these expectations would have different implications for the adult learner. For instance, the learning demands on the teacher as a panel chairperson pose quite a different set of issues than those to be handled by a teacher facing induced early retirement. Similarly, senior teachers differentiate from junior teachers in their professional role, and hence the type of learning, expected of them. For example, while younger teachers may be concerned with further development in subject knowledge and classroom management, senior teachers are expected to learn more about recruitment and corporate management skills. More importantly, adult learners distinguish themselves from younger learners as having to satisfy multiple life roles and professional roles which not only affect the motivation to learn but also the content of learning as well as the success or otherwise of their learning endeavor. The interaction between multiple life roles and professional roles can be illustrated by a beginning teacher having to resolve issues in relation to new parenthood and induction to the new job at the same time. A balance between these simultaneous demands of life roles and professional roles may not be taught in a formal teacher education program, and hence the capacity of self learning beyond formal institutional situations cannot be over emphasized.

In addition to the complexity of multiple goals and multiple roles, physiological developments (such as changes in long- and short-term memory) and cognitive developments (such as the development of dialectical thinking in adulthood) when the adult learner gets older have significant implications for the learning process. A number of researchers (e.g., Kegan, 1994; Kramer, 1989; Kramer & Bacelar, 1994; Merriam & Caffarella, 1999; Riegel, 1973, 1975, 1976) highlighted the interaction of maturation and environmental factors as contributing to the cognitive development of adults in general and teachers in particular. The concept of dialectical thinking is one of the key perspectives put forward by these researchers in adult cognitive development.

Dialectical thinking refers to the ability to handle in one's thought processes contradictions, disparities, and paradoxes that are inherent in our daily world. Examples of such contradictions include some government emphasizes learner-control learning, but imposes externally mandated public examination for all learners; a teacher practices inclusive education on humanistic grounds, but his class is continuously disrupted by students with severe behavioral problems; we spend more time at work to achieve short-term "value-added" in the workforce, only to discover that the social costs in the form of broken families and associated social problems in the long run are high. Dialectical thinking is developed in response to these contradictions. Although dialectical thinking does not confined to adulthood (Brookfield, 1994; Kramer, 1989; Riegel, 1973), several researchers (e.g., Kegan, 1994; Kramer, 1989; Kramer and Bacelar, 1994) consider dialectical thinking to characterize mature adult thinking. Some researchers maintain that dialectical thinking can be taught (Brookfield, 1994), and teacher education programs should include the development of dialectical thinking in teachers.

In the myriad of adult learning theories, of particular relevance to the development of teacher self learning theory is Malcolm Knowles' assumption concerning the adult as a self-directed learner, in which he states: "As a person matures, his or her self-concept moves from that of a dependent personality toward one of a self-directing human being" (Knowles, 1980, p. 44). Under this assumption, teachers as adult learners have tendencies toward self-directedness and they tend to resent learning imposed upon them or threatens their sense of autonomy (Knowles, 1983, p. 56). Although this assumption has been challenged by many researchers (e.g., Brookfield, 1994) who find that adults differ in their readiness and competence as self-directed learners, the concept of self-direction does offer a lens for studying teacher self learning.

Self-directed learning refers to "a self-initiated process" whereby the learner takes primary responsibility in planning, implementing, and evaluation of his or her own learning (Caffarella, 1993, p. 25-26). Greater learner autonomy is the hallmark of self-directed learning. Based on extensive literature review, Danis (1992, p. 56-59) developed a model of the self-directed learning process comprising five key components:

- Strategies: they refer to the approaches to learning and the learner's awareness of these approaches.
- Phases: they refer to six recursive stages of learning activities, including reacting to a trigger event; identifying knowledge to be learned and relevant resources; organizing strategies and knowledge to be acquired; acquiring the new knowledge; and evaluating the quality of learning and applying the new knowledge.
- Content: it refers to the type and level of complexity of new knowledge acquired by the learner within the framework of prior knowledge.
- Learner: the concept of learner can refer to an individual learner or a

group of learners.
- Context: it refers to the environment surrounding the learning process including the social structure within which learning takes place as well as the resource materials available to the learner.

Although Danis' model remains hypothetical as no study has been found using it (Merriam & Caffarella, 1999, p. 300), the comprehensive nature of the model provides a good reference for conceptualizing the process of teacher self learning.

TEACHER SELF LEARNING CYCLE

The concept of self learning is not a new one. Knowles (1975) stated that it is but a "basic human competence – the ability to learn on one's own." Based on the above discussion of adult learning as well as the concepts of action learning (Argyris, Putnam, & Smith, 1985; Argyris & Schon, 1974;Yuen & Cheng, 1997, 2000), the process of teacher self learning can be conceptualized as a cyclic process as shown in Figure 1. It subdivides a learning episode of a teacher into a sequence of three components such as mental condition (mind-set), action, and outcome, linked by four processes including planning, monitoring, feedback to mental condition and feedback to action. As a learner, teacher's mental condition (mind-set) includes his or her pre-existing conditions of motivation, cognition, and volition to learning. It will determine the process of planning learning activities as well as the content of action in learning. Action refers to the intended activities and behaviors demonstrated by teachers in their self learning. Monitoring refers to the process of detecting any mismatch between the teacher's intended targets and action and the outcomes of learning process. Outcomes refers to the results or consequences from the learning activities, including positive and negative, overt and subtle learning experiences during the teacher self learning process.

There are two types of feedback from the monitoring process and outcomes to the teacher in self learning: one to the mind-set and the other one directly to action. The feedback to mind-set will help the teacher reflect on and change his or her own mental models including meta-cognition, thinking methods, meta-volition, and knowledge and then to change the planning process as well as the action of learning. The learning associated with change in teacher's mental-set or mental models is often referred to as the second order learning or double-loop learning (Argyris & Schon, 1974). Particularly, the cognitive side of learning with change in mental condition is well recognized as change in schemes (Piaget, 1962), schemata (Schmidt, 1975), images (Denis, 1991), repertoires (Schön, 1987), or theories-in-use (Argyris & Schön, 1974).

Figure 1: *A Self Learning Cycle in a Networked Human and IT environment*

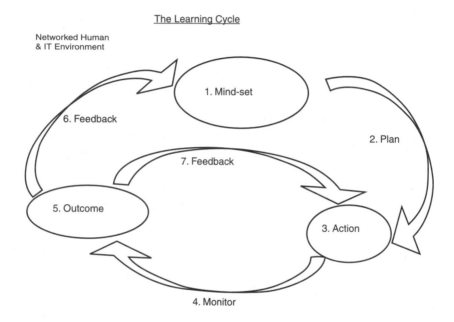

The feedback directly to action of learning will help the teacher adapt his or her learning behaviors. The learning associated with change in behaviors or actions is often referred to as the first order of learning or the single loop learning. Since this type of learning may not have changed the mental conditions of the teacher, it may not produce long lasting learning effects at a higher level.

In the model, relationships between components may be reciprocal, even though there are one-way arrows used to show the major features of the learning process in the diagram. For instance, a certain mental condition impacts upon the learning action which subsequently produces outcome and feedback to impact upon the mental condition of the teacher. The cyclic nature of self learning reflects that learning may go through many such experience cycles before mastery of a higher level thinking or a lower level skill to be learned. The self learning is also layered because after completing a cycle, the knowledge level of the learner concerning the learning task, the strategies, and the context will advance to a higher level.

How to sustain the cyclic process of self learning by the teachers themselves continuously throughout their life span is really the core issue of current education reforms. Particularly, how the human and IT environment can be designed, developed, and used to facilitate such a continuous lifelong self learning for teachers inevitably becomes an important question to guide the development of the teacher self learning theory.

The theory of teacher self learning in a networked human and IT environment is proposed, developed, and elaborated in following sections.

IT ENVIRONMENT

Teacher self learning occurs in a context. Whether the learning context facilitates or hinders continuous learning by teachers themselves has to be considered and redesigned in teacher education or education reforms. According to the literature of learning environment, both human environment and technological environment are important to facilitating and sustaining self learning (Garrison, 1997; Henderson & Cunningham, 1994). Due to the tremendous developments in IT, the Internet, and global networking, recently a great demand for developing an IT environment to support paradigm shift in learning and teaching. Computer technology makes it possible for multiple teachers to be networked and participate in the learning task, thus greatly enhancing the social interactions, sharing of learning experiences and resources in a very convenient way. IT can also facilitate and accelerate the monitoring, assessment, and feedback processes during self learning in a very fast and efficient way (Embretson & Hershberger, 1999).

In education reforms or teacher education, there may be four important aspects in which new technology can contribute to the development of a powerful IT environment that can facilitate the teachers' self learning cycle:

1. The computer technology revolutionalized both the speed and access to information (Hallinger, 1998). Information is interpreted in its broadest sense, including resource materials for the teacher as well as feedback

concerning how well the teacher has learned. With the help of the Internet, learners can access the best quality of web-based learning materials in different parts of the world. Also, because of the high speed of information technology, feedback can be immediately generated for each step of learning tasks and activities as well as for the overall proficiency of learning. The fast feedback to teacher's mental conditions and learning behaviors in fact accelerates the speed of learning, including cognitive changes and behavioral changes of the teacher.

2.   Developments in IT make it possible for the application of measurement theory to assessment tasks during the teacher self learning process no matter in formal teacher education programs or not. Technology is now available for real-time scoring (Herl, Baker, & Niemi, 1996), computer adaptive testing (CAT), automated data logging (Chung & Baker, 1997), and computer item construction (Bennett, 1999). The advanced assessment methods can greatly improve the quality and accuracy of monitoring and feedback such that the quality and opportunity of learning can be ensured. Since assessment is an integral part of learning, teacher education programs can ideally expose teachers to new approaches to assessment, including new computer aided assessment methods.

3.   Developments in IT enable learning to move away from the paper-pencil format to rich imagery multimedia task presentation and submission (Bennett, 1999; Chung & Baker, 1997) that can capture richly contextualized performance in learning process (Bennett, 1999; Chung and Baker, 1997). The information would be powerful to understanding the complex nature of learning process and improving learning strategies, activities, and outcomes.

4.   And IT environment breaks down distance barriers of access to education and creates connectivity amongst teachers as learners (Mok & Cheng, 2000a). When teachers, mentors, peers, resource people, and other related experts can be networked through IT, it will create more opportunities for social interactions, experience sharing, and information flow. With this, a networked human environment can be created to sustain and support self learning of individual teachers.

NETWORKED HUMAN ENVIRONMENT

It is easy to misinterpret a self-directed learner to be an isolated learner (Brockett, 1994). Learning has inevitably to be pursued by the individual: the learner has to make sense of the new learning and integrates the new learning with existing knowledge. As well, the learner has to engage in individual reflection. Notwithstanding, social interaction gives room for new insights and synergy. The importance of the social milieu to teacher self learning is acknowledged by such researchers as Garrison (1997), taking a "collaborative constructivist" perspective. The meaningfulness of teacher self learning should be constructed within a human environment that comprises the teacher as learner, peer teachers, the mentor or facilitator (if any), and such other people as the principal or even students. The human environment plays a significant role in all aspects – pedagogical, psychological, and behavioral – of self learning (Schunk, 1998). Particularly, Zimmerman (2000) highlight the interdependent role of social, environmental, and self and their bi-directional influences in self learning.

In a formal learning situation, such as that presented by a teacher education program, the human environment of learning tends to be constant and well defined. The actors in this human environment comprises the lecturers, fellow in-service or pre-service student teachers in the program, and the principal, staff, and students in the school for teaching practice. Nevertheless, formal learning situations available to teachers are rare rather than frequent, unless there is a change in government teacher development policies. In addition, whereas teachers may engage in continuing education for interest or knowledge motives, we have now come to an age of lifelong learning and learning throughout the life span is mandatory. The explosive development of IT and knowledge economy meant that many people would take up jobs that do not exist when they were at schools. Continuous engagement in informal or non-formal education is therefore a way of life in this century. Consequently, teachers must affiliate themselves to favorable human environment in order to facilitate their self learning no matter in formal, informal, or non-formal learning situations.

The human environment can be designed in the learning endeavor as an important resource. The mentor, often perceived as an experienced peer or expert in the human environment of learning, can help the teacher learner develop attitudes and skills for goal-setting, self-management, self-monitoring, and self-evaluation which are essential to the success of self learning. For example, in this IT age, there is no short of information, but the teacher needs to make judgment about the information. Consequently, the teacher has to develop critical thinking skills to validate and authenticate the quality of instructional materials, such as those downloadable from the web. Further, the mentor as a proficient professional provides appropriate learning references or guides the teacher to these materials. Winne and Perry (2000) identified the unique position held by mentors in judging the quality of the learner's self learning and provide guidance where appropriate. The teacher also learns from peers and other experts by observation and emulation (Schunk, 1987; as cited in Schunk, 1998).

The mentor and the teacher learner assume shared control of the learning endeavor, including the decisions on the "what" and "how" of learning. The balance of control between the mentor and the teacher learner may shift during the course of learning, with the mentor taking a greater share of responsibility at the beginning of the learning, and gradually "fade out" of the controlling role to give the teacher learner more autonomy as the teacher learner has acquired more professional skills, is more familiar with the subject matter and has gained more confidence in their own learning (Brookfield, 1994; Slusarski, 1994).

Teacher self learning is a complex process and the endeavor can result in non-accomplishment, frustration, or even failure. In such instances, the empathy and social support from the mentor and peers acts as an emotional safety net for the teacher . A strong social climate gives strength to the teacher in self learning to continue engagement in the task, analyze strategies, and manage the failure and frustration in a positive way. A collaborative human environment is particularly important for adult self-directed learning. Pascual-Leone and Irwin (1998), referring to such research findings as reported by Brookfield (1991), Deshler and Hegan (1989), and Knowles (1980), conclude that motivational, affective and self-developmental factors are even more crucial for the adult learner than for younger learners. It is very threatening to the self-esteem of the adult learner, who is a school teacher and already has acquired professional success and social status, if he or she fails to submit on time an assignment for an in-service course, or has difficulties in performing a task on a self-instruction computer package. The adult learner has more stake in self-esteem than has the younger learner if the adult learner's otherwise established success in their professional role cannot be transferred directly to the new learning task (Brookfield, 1994). The mentor of the teacher learner therefore has to move beyond the cognitive realm in order to take up an expanded, humanistic role and to provide emotional support to the teacher (Slusarski, 1994). Hiemstra and Sisco (1990, p. 61; quoted in Slusarski, 1994, p. 73) refer to the multitude roles assumed by mentors of adult learners, including, "facilitator, manager, resource guide, expert, friend, advocate, authority, coach, mentor" and Slusarski (1994, p. 73) conceptualized mentors of adult learners as co-learners.

In education reforms, it is now possible, with development in IT, to network the teacher learner with the mentor, peers, and other professionals in the community such that influence of the human environment on teacher self learning can be maximized (Mok & Cheng, 2000a).

When individual teachers are networked with the support of IT, as shown in figures 2 and 3, there may be multiplying effect on the amount of available information as well as human touches and interactions that will become fruitful stimulus to teacher's self learning. The networked individual teacher learners, mentors, peers, and other professionals may form a learning system to support teachers' continuous self learning. In a learning school, each teacher is self-motivated and generates a learning cycle of self learning and self evaluation. Teacher learners, mentors, and peers are networked to form a learning group; learning groups are networked to form a learning community; learning groups and learning communities are networked to form a learning society; learning societies are networked across nations (Mok & Cheng, 2000b). IT speeds up the process of providing social messages and informative feedback to the teacher learners and members in the learning system. This speed, coupled with the massive amount of information available via the informative network, not only means that this will be the information-rich era, but also, it implies that a closely networked social environment needs to be in place for promoting and supporting self learning of individual learners. Teacher self learning is no longer the acquisition of information of individual teachers in an isolated context. Instead, effective teacher self learning occurs in the human environment that can facilitate higher level of intelligence and motivation of teachers as well as other members in the human network in the selection, management, transfer, creation, and extension of knowledge (Mok & Cheng, 2000a).

Figure 2: *Networked Human Environment: Networked Teacher Self Learners and Learning Groups*

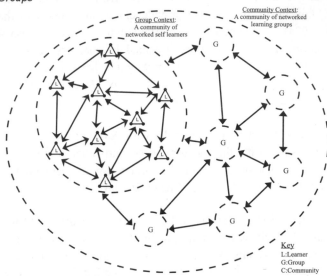

Figure 3: *Networked Human Environment: Networked Learning Groups, Communities, and Nations*

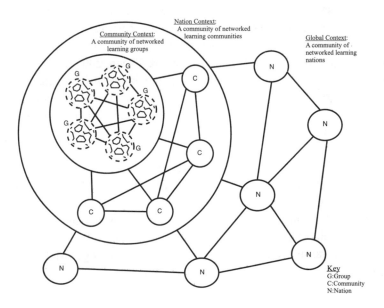

FACILITATING TEACHER SELF LEARNING CYCLE

Building up a strong and direct linkage between each stage of teacher self learning cycle and networked learning environment should be an important issue in teacher education and development. From the above nature of learning cycle and networked human and IT environment, we may consider how each stage of teacher self learning cycle can be initiated and sustained continuously to achieve effective learning with the support of a networked human and IT environment.

Stage 1: Initiating Learning from Mind-set

In the first stage of the learning cycle, how the teacher's mental condition or mind-set can be ready for initiating learning is a major concern. Three elements of the teacher's mental condition are crucial to initiating self learning including their motivation, meta-cognition, and meta-volition. How the human and IT environment can facilitate the mental condition to start self learning activities is summarized in Table 1.

Motivation
For self learning to take place, the teacher learner has to be motivated to initiate the learning task and engage in it. Many models of motivation for self learning have been offered in the literature (e.g., Rheinberg, Vollmeyer, & Rollett, 2000). The commonality among them in describing the characteristics of a self-initiated learner points to two key factors: expectancy – the learner has to believe that the learning activity has a positive effect on the learning outcome – and value – the learner considers the learning outcome to be of personal importance. Motivation is of particular importance to the teacher learners because of the demand on their time and attention by their social and professional roles. Knowles (1980) and others (e.g., MacKeracher, 1996; Merriam & Caffarella, 1999) highlighted the importance of matching the learning tasks with the teacher's social roles. In addition, teachers as adult learners are motivated by an immediacy of solutions to practical situations. Relevance of teacher education programs to classroom situations is therefore of importance.

Motivation is inspired and sustained by the human environment, comprising the teacher, mentor, peers, and significant others. These social actors can motivate learning by inspiring the teacher learner to establish the link between

Table 1. *Teacher's Mental Condition Facilitated by Networked Human and IT Environment*

A teacher's mental condition	Facilitated by networked human environment	Facilitated by IT environment
• Motivation: The teacher learner is motivated to initiate the learning activity and prepared to engage in it.	• Inspiring: Mentor and peers provoke learning needs through challenges or identification of gap in knowledge or skill. • Sustaining: supportive social environment to sustain motivation.	• Stimulation: IT provides information rich and stimulating environment to instill learning desire. • Facilitation: IT facilitates speedy and frequent correspondence between teacher learner, mentor, and peer.
• Meta-cognition: The teacher learner has a clear idea of one's own prior knowledge and the learning activities to be engaged in.	• Cognitive capacity building through social support: Mentor and peers help the teacher learner develop: - clear expectation of learning outcomes. - understanding about the teacher learner's level of rior knowledge. - understanding on the amount of learning effort to be spent to achieve expected outcomes.	• Information generation: IT provides information that facilities the teacher learner to establish understanding: - information on prior achievement recorded and stored using IT helps teacher learner develop a realistic expectation of learning outcomes. - the teacher learner's level of knowledge can be established through self-administered tests and checklists on the web.
• Meta-volition: The teacher learner is willing to engage in learning activities and make good use of all available resources.	• Engendering volition: Mentor cultivates amongst teacher learners a collaborative learning culture in order to: - enhance the teacher learner's willingness to engage in the learning activities. - increase the teacher learner's confidence in the mentor and peers as resource people to support learning.	• Supporting volition: User-friendly and enticing learning environment enhances volition: - well designed teach-ware can reduce resistance and fear in using technology to support learning, which in turn enhance willingness of the teacher learner to participate. - IT increases the frequency of group communication, thus help build rapport amongst learners for further collaboration.

effort and outcome, affirm the importance of the learning outcome or identify gaps in the teacher's knowledge base. A supportive social environment helps sustain teacher motivation.

Motivation can be stimulated and facilitated by the technology environment that determines to a certain extent the composition and nature of the social environment. For instance, who can participate in the learning experience as "peers," whether it is someone in the same school or in a distant geographical location; whether the interaction and feedback among peers is instantaneous or delayed; whether the interaction is one-to-one, many-to-one, or simultaneous; whether the exchange is frequent or sparse. As such, IT has a facilitating role in motivating the teacher learner. Further, capacity of the technology also sets the parameter for the amount, form, presentation, and accessibility of learning resources for the teacher. If designed properly, IT can provide information rich and stimulating environment to instill learning desire in teachers.

Meta-cognition

Three levels of cognition are relevant to the teacher self learner: the pedagogical level, the sociological level, and the psychological. Pedagogical cognition concerns the teacher learner's awareness and understanding about own level of prior knowledge, learning style, nature of the learning task involved, learning strategies to be used, learning outcomes, and attribution of learning outcome. Sociological cognition concerns the teacher's level of awareness and understanding of the social context, including its network composition, operation, rules and regulations of interaction, social climate, and relevance of elements in the human context, as well as skills to maximally benefit from the social resources. Psychological cognition refers to the teacher's level of awareness and understanding of own affective aspects in relation to the learning task, including the learning goal, expected outcomes, and the motivation and value espoused by the teacher learner concerning the learning outcome.

The teacher learner's understanding concerning his or her own level of prior knowledge affects his or her motivation in a number of ways. First, if the level is too low for the current learning, then the demand on the teacher will be very great, but if the level is too high, then the challenge may not be enough to sustain motivation. Similarly, level of pedagogical cognition affects the teacher's learners commitment to the learning and decisions concerning learning action. The teacher learner's level of sociological cognition affects the degree to which he or she can benefit from the social context.

A skilful teacher self learner is high in her or his pedagogical, social, and psychological cognitive levels. The roles of the mentors, facilitators, and peers are to support the teacher learner to develop the meta-cognition skills and to enhance the teacher learner's meta-cognitive level through systematic mentoring, as well as group discussion and group reflection on relevant documents including the learner's record of prior achievement. In this sense, the human context facilitates teacher self learning by cognitive capacity building.

In education reforms, IT environment should be designed to facilitate meta-cognitive development not only by providing a forum for social interaction but also by providing a medium for storage of large volume of pedagogical information concerning the teacher learner's previous learning episodes. In this sense, technology environment supports teacher self learning through information generation.

Meta-volition
Meta-volition involves the teacher learner's willingness to engage in learning activities and regulation of the willingness. It also includes the teacher learner's willingness and regulation in making good use of all available resources and persevering with the learning activity, as well as the teacher learner's preparedness to change learning behavior to conform to plans.

The mentor may facilitate the teacher self learner by engendering volition through the cultivation of a collaborative learning climate amongst peers and the creation of a safe environment for the teacher to explore and experiment. A strong rapport in the group increases the teacher's willingness and confidence in mentors, facilitators, and peers as resource people for learning.

A user-friendly and enticing technology environment enhances volition. Well-designed teach-ware can reduce resistance and fear in using technology to support learning, which in turn can enhance willingness of teacher learner to participate. Further, IT increases the frequency and speed of group communication, thus help build rapport.

Stage 2. Planning for Learning Action

Planning refers to the analysis, strategies, and behavior of the teacher self learner in preparing for the learning action to achieve his or her learning goals. It takes the form of environmental analysis, preparation, and affiliation (see Table 2). Environmental analysis is undertaken to establish understanding of the learning environment and self in terms of strengths, weaknesses, opportunities, and threats. It also includes the analysis of the conditions and resources available in the networked human and technology environment. Preparation and affiliation include analyzing the learning task, setting learning goals, selecting and organizing learning strategies, social network building, establishing group interaction protocol and etiquette, and engendering group loyalty. An important component in planning for learning action is the establishment of strategies for self-monitoring and resolving conflicts between plan and action, as well as management strategies to handle failure.

A skilful teacher self learner has a clear idea of the learning environment and of the learning task, sets hierarchical goals, links goals to action plans (Ford, 1995), and is more likely to commit to goals (Gollwitz, 1996). The mentor and peers contribute to planning by perspective building, fostering supportive social environment, maximizing learning opportunities, and empowering the teacher learner. The mentor as a knowledgeable informant helps the teacher learner put the task in perspective by supporting him or her in analyzing the task difficulty, relevance, and links with prior learning. A mentor can also support the teacher learner by breaking down a difficult goal into smaller, hierarchical, and more achievable goals. The mentor's input at the planning stage also includes group building in order to foster a strong team spirit in support of later learning. Mentor support in developing self learning skills, self-monitoring skills, and stress management skills empowers the teacher learner. Research (e.g., Gollwitzer, 1996; Zimmerman, 1994) has identified supporting evidence that enhanced self-confidence of the learner and optimistic view of goal achievement increases chances of goal commitment. Consequently, to develop a high quality human environment is essential to the success of the teacher self learner.

In education reform or teacher education, the quality of human environment can be facilitated by developing favorable technology environment. IT greatly expands the options as well as the type and sources of information available

Table 2: *Planning for Action Facilitated by Networked Human and IT Environment*

A teacher's planning for action	Facilitated by networked human environment	Facilitated by IT environment
• Environmental analysis: An assessment of the learning environment and self strengths and weaknesses.	• Capacity building: Mentor and group help the teacher learner analyze:	• Resources expansion: IT greatly expands:
	- cognitive resources, social resources, psychological resources, and educational resources to facilitate learning task. - self learning style, readiness to learn own strengths and weaknesses.	- options and resources available to the learner such that the learner is accessible to multiple sources and multiple types of resources. - possibilities and methods of building an imagery of the learner.
• Planning and affiliating: The teacher learner analyzes task, and sets goals and strategic plan.	• Perspective building: Mentor as a knowledgeable informant help the teacher learner put the learning task in perspective by: - pursuing task analysis. - setting achievable and realistic goals.	• Judicial use of IT: Mentor as a knowledgeable informant help the teacher learner use IT judiciously.
	• Fostering supportive social environment: Instill in group a culture of sharing, trust, and affiliation.	• Enabling supportive social environment: Social interaction facilitated by IT.
	• Maximizing learning opportunity: Mentor creates learning environment that provides multiple learning opportunities for the learner.	• Enabling maximal learning opportunity: Maximal learning opportunity made facilitated by IT.
	• Empowering: Mentor systematically develops in learners skills for self-motivating, self-learning, and self-monitoring.	• Broadening: Enabling complex multifaceted and multidimensional perceptual generation; Versatility of IT enables multiple learning approaches to suit learners of different learning styles.

for planning. IT is particularly important if planning involves complex perception. Social interaction is also facilitated during the planning phase of learning. It is possible for the mentor to guide the setting of group goals. At the planning phase, judicious use of IT is an important skill to be established.

Stage 3. Learning Action

In this stage, implementation of learning action as planned involves control, task enactment, and appreciation components. How these components can be facilitated in a networked human and IT environment should be an important issue in supporting teacher self learning (see Table 3).

Table 3: *Learning Action Facilitated by Networked Human and IT Environment*

A teacher's learning action	Facilitated by networked human environment	Facilitated by IT environment
• Control: The teacher learner chooses the best course of action, exercises self-control in continual engagement in the learning activities, and regulates learning strategies to achieve learning goal.	• Expert support: Networked mentor provides expert advice on possible learning paths and scaffolding to the teacher learner and facilitates him or her to focus on learning task.	• Knowledge accumulation: IT helps keep track of learning path, attempts, success, and failures such that learning is focused and grounded on knowledge accumulated.
• Task engagement: Accretion of knowledge through a series of learning activities, including assimilation, accommodation, integration, extrapolation, and origination.	• Discourse on new knowledge: Mentor facilitates and promotes discourse about the learning experience among networked teacher learners such that learning of an individual learner can have a multiplicative effect on other learners through observation and emulation.	• Plurality of learning experience: Through IT, a dialogue on the learning experiences can be shared easily, thus enabling plurality of learning experience. Accumulation of knowledge is enabled through documentation in e-format for later learners.
• Appreciation: The teacher learner appreciates the new knowledge gained and is further motivated to continue engagement in the learning task.	• Emotional safety net: Networked mentor and peers share the joy of achievement and display empathy in case of failure, thus providing a safe environment for the teacher learner to experiment with learning.	• Positioning against internal and external frame of reference: IT facilitates voluminous storage and speedy retrieval of previous achievement records made by this and other teacher learners such that the learner appreciates where he or she is.

Control

Control refers to the process that the teacher learner chooses the best course of action in engaging in learning to achieve the goals of learning. It means that the teacher self learner believes in a causal relationship between action and outcome. By implementing the planned learning action, the teacher learner accepts the responsibility for the outcome (Zimmerman, 1994). Kuhl and Goschke (1994) identified four types of control during self learning action: attention and intention control, meaning focusing selectively on task and relevant information; emotion and motivation control, meaning avoiding emotional states that may inhibit task accomplishment and focusing on emotions that are aligned with intention; action control, meaning keeping away from counter-intentional impulses; and volitional control, meaning wilfulness in goal maintenance.

The networked mentor can facilitate teacher learners' implementation of learning action by providing expert support and scaffolding to them in exercising control in learning process. IT facilitates control through knowledge accumulation in the form of keeping track of the learning path, attempts, success, and failure such that learning is focused and grounded on knowledge accumulated.

Task Engagement

Task engagement involves the implementation of learning plan. New knowledge is being acquired through assimilation, accommodation, integration, extrapolation, and origination, resulting in an accretion of knowledge. Skilful teacher self learner intentionally uses such learning strategies as repetition, elaboration, and reorganization (Weinstein, Husman, & Dierking, 2000) to promote achievement of learning goal.

There is empirical evidence that learning strategies can be learned and modified (Weinstein, 1978; as cited in Weinstein, Husman, & Dierking, 2000). In addition, these learning strategies can be developed through observation and emulation of proficient models (Bielaczyc, Pirolli, & Brown, 1995; as cited in Weinstein, Husman, & Dierking, 2000). As such, the role of the mentor, peers, and significant others in facilitating the learning enactment is to encourage and maintain active knowledge discourse about the learning experience among group members such that experience of an individual learner can have a multiplicative effect on other learners through observation and emulation. Further, while the teacher learner appreciates new knowledge gained and become further motivated on the task, through sharing the joy of achievement and displaying empathy towards failure, the social environment provides a safety buffer for the teacher learner to experiment with learning.

IT facilitates the enactment of learning activity in two aspects: informative and technological. IT enables voluminous storage and speedy retrieval of information with regard to previous achievement of this and other teacher learners such that the teacher learner can position himself or herself against internal and external frames of reference. Accumulation of knowledge about activities, strategies, pitfalls, and merits can be documented in e-format for later learners. IT expedites dialogue on individual learning experience, thus enabling plurality of learning experience of all teacher learners.

Stage 4. Monitoring and Evaluation

Meta-cognitive monitoring is a key construct in teacher self learning. The teacher learner perceives the learning task and monitors progress of action plans. Attribution of action to goal and of activity to outcome impact upon learner's decision upon revising, maintaining, and abandoning of learning plan and strategies. Based on the appraisal, the teacher learner may modify learning goal or strategies midcourse (see Table 4).

In teacher education or education reform, a networked human environment can be built up in such a way that the networked mentor, the teacher learner, and peers help monitor learner progress and provide input concerning the judgment and decision on modification of learning goal, activities, and strategies. The mentor may also establish group monitoring protocols such that transfer of learning from successes and mistakes of other teacher learners can be maximized through discussion and sharing.

IT facilitates self-directed learning by its reduction on cognitive demand for progress monitoring. IT not only facilitates evaluation of current effort by charting personal achievement, it also allows recording of group achievement of and achievement of other teacher learners, as well as strategies used, thus reducing cognitive load on the teacher learner. In addition, features can be built in, with the support of technology, to support learner edit, fine-tune, or restructure learning activities and strategies midcourse. IT enables speedy feedback that permits the teacher learner to modify action immediately before discrepancy between target and achievement is too irrecoverable.

Table 4: *Monitoring Facilitated by Networked Human and IT Environment*

A teacher's monitoring	Facilitated by networked human environment	Facilitated by IT environment
• Meta-cognitive monitoring: The teacher learner perceives learning activities, learning strategies, and outcome of effort. Based on appraisal of these elements, the teacher learner may modify learning goal or strategies midcourse.	• Expert monitoring: Networked mentor or peers may help monitor teacher learner progress and provide input concerning the judgment and decision on modification of learning goal, activities, and strategies. • Maximal transfer learning from successes and mistakes: Networked mentor may establish group monitoring protocols such that transfer of learning from successes and mistakes of other teacher learners can be maximized through discussion and sharing.	• Reduction on cognitive demand for progress monitoring: IT facilitates evaluation and allows recording of achievement (learner, group, and other learners), strategies thus reducing cognitive demand on the teacher learner. • Enabling editing features: IT features can be built in that support learner edit, fine-tune, or restructure learning activities and strategies midcourse.

Stage 5. Outcomes

Outcome can have different facets. A successful outcome is goal realization where the teacher learner develops mastery or has changed in the knowledge, skills, and disposition relating to the task or the learning strategies used. How teacher learner perceives the outcomes of learning depends on the outcome expectation at the planning phase, personal importance of the outcome, amount of effort, attribution of effort to outcome, and the valence of the consequence. The consequence from the teacher learner's perception can be satisfaction, pride, or disappointment.

In a networked human environment, the teacher learner, the mentor, peers, and other social actors can play an important role at the outcome stage. Acknowledgement and reward from the mentor, peers, and significant others can affirm achievement made by the teacher learner. The networked members can support the teacher learner in undertaking attribution analysis on the outcome. In cases where there is a group structure, group reflection, and concrete suggestions with regard to action in the next learning cycle, as well as empathy towards the teacher learner, can have significant impact on the teacher learner. In evaluating outcome, either social reference norm or individual reference norm can be used.

Stage 6. Feedback to induce Changes in the Teacher Mind-set

Feedback on learning outcome can have impact on the teacher learner's motivation, meta-cognition, and meta-volition. The role of human and IT environment to be developed in education reforms is crucial to facilitating feedback to induce changes in teacher learner's mind-set (see Table 5).

Change in Motivation

On the basis of feedback, if the outcome is perceived to be controllable by the teacher learner, then there is likely to be higher self-motivation (or intrinsic motivation) for the teacher learner to engage in the next learning episode. Positive feedback boost learner confidence in using the learning strategies.

Actors in the human environment, particularly mentors, facilitators, peers, and significant others, support the teacher learners in assessing the meaning and validity of feedback and further develop them by highlighting next target, potentials, and possibilities. On the other hand, whilst networked mentor and peers may contribute to teacher learner edification, eventually the teacher learner has to integrate external feedback with existing schema to construct meaning. Internalization of feedback affects entry motivation for further learning. The role of IT in providing feedback concerns extension. Versatility of IT extends the learning horizon beyond the current achievement. Feedback with regard to the next milestones and pathways to reach them can be accessed easily using IT.

Change in Meta-cognition

Feedback of the previous learning cycle heightens teacher learner's awareness and knowledge. The teacher learner has a better idea of how much is known and not known about the content domain, the specific learning task, and the strategies to perform the task. The teacher learner is also more knowledgeable in self-management skills, self-monitoring skills, self-instruction skills, and networking skills.

The teacher learner, mentor, and networked group together reflect upon the activities, strategies, and achievement involved in the previous learning cycle,

Table 5: *Feedback to Induce Changes in the Teacher Mind-set*

A teacher's learning from feedback	Facilitated by networked human environment	Facilitated IT environment
• Change in motivation: Feedback on outcome changes teacher learner's motivation and aspiration.	• Transfer to intrinsic motivation: Networked mentor and peers together analyze attribution of achievement to self and strategies to facilitate internalization of motivation. • Edification: Networked mentor further develops the teacher learner by highlighting next target, potentials, and possibilities.	• Support internalization of motivation: IT enables detailed record of complex learning processes, thus providing evidence on causal relations between effort, strategies, and outcomes. Records of group members provide multiple cases. If congruent, multiple cases triangulate teacher learner's experience. • Extension: Versatility of IT extends the learning horizon beyond the current achievement. The next milestones and pathways to reach them can be accessed easily with the help of IT.
• Change in meta-cognition: Feedback of the previous learning cycle heightens learner awareness. The learner is also more knowledgeable in self-management skills, self-monitoring skills, self-instruction skills, and networking skills.	• Further building meta-cognitive skills: The teacher learner, mentor, and networked group together reflect upon the activities, strategies, and achievement involved in the previous learning cycle, and build up skills based on the experience.	• Reduce cognitive load: Self-management, self-instruction, and self-monitoring are complex and cognitively demanding activities. Memory available by IT reduces cognitive load.
• Change in meta-volition: Informed decision and self-determination to engage in further learning activities grounded on prior positive academic and social experience.	• Building meta-volition: The teacher learner, mentor, and networked group together reflect upon the learning experience to have a better imagery of self efficacy and goal orientation for purposeful commitment.	• Enhancing confidence in making commitments: Experience with IT in the previous learning cycle enhances confidence in the capabilities and drawbacks of IT, thus enhancing confidence of volition.

and further build up their meta-cognitive skills based on the experience. Self-management, self-instruction, and self-monitoring are complex and cognitively demanding activities. Memory available by IT reduces cognitive load.

Change in meta-volition

With feedback on the outcome, the teacher learner is able to make informed decision and self-determination to engage in next cycle of learning activities grounded on prior positive academic and social experiences.

The teacher learner is supported by networked mentor and group in building meta-volition through discourse and group reflection in order to have a better imagery of self-efficacy and goal orientation for purposeful commitment.

It should be noted that experience with IT in the previous learning cycle enhances confidence in the capabilities and drawbacks of IT, thus enhancing confidence of volition.

Stage 7. Feedback to induce Changes in Learning Action

Feedback affects the learning action both in terms of a change in the teacher learner's skill level and strategies with regard to learning action. As similar in the changes in teacher mind-set, how the feedback can be facilitated to induce changes in learning behavior or action is also an important question in designing the networked human and IT environment in teacher education and development.

Changes in Skills and Action

Inevitably, after one learning episode, the teacher learner becomes more skillful and purposeful in self learning strategies, monitoring self-progress, skills in the attribution of outcomes to strategies, changing strategies, or adjusting goals based on feedback.

Learning engagement tends to be more focused on performance and parsimonious in information processing. Goal setting may be more refined and hierarchical.

An important change to be induced by the teacher learner with support from networked mentor, peers, and significant others is the shifting of learning control and learning responsibility to the teacher learner. With more experience, the teacher learner has to take more ownership of the learning activities, including the planning, enactment, monitoring, and response to feedback. Mentors, facilitators, peers, and significant others step back and regulate scaffolding and supportive according to learner readiness, complexity of task, and prior outcome: In designing the human and IT environment, the attention should be paid to facilitating feedback from learning cycle and inducing changes in both the mind-set and behavior of teacher learners.

CONCLUSION

From the above model of teacher self learning in a networked human and IT environment, the sustainability and effectiveness of self learning of teachers is related to four key elements such as cognition, control, commitment, and context in the self learning process.

Cognition refers to the teacher learner's understanding of the self, the learning task, and the contextual factors. A skilful teacher self learner has a clear awareness and understanding of his or her own knowledge (domain and task), goal orientation, efficacy, learning style, level of commitment, and skill level in self-management of the learning (Garrison, 1997). Awareness and understanding of the learning task, including its level of difficulty, complexity, links with prior learning, and possible outcomes are also essential (Biemiller, Shany, Inglis, & Meichenbaum, 1998). The teacher self learner also needs to have a good cognition of the contextual factors, comprising both the human and technology resources and their constraints on the learning task. Much of the cognition is built up by the teacher self learner's continual monitoring of task, action, context, and progress (Butler & Winne, 1995; Zimmerman, 1998).

Control refers to the teacher self learner's regulation of the learning engagement, including the effort devoted to the learning task, the learning strategies used, proactively seeking feedback, and strategic modifications of goal and action based on feedback (Kuhl & Goschke, 1994). The teacher learner has to control both the self and the contextual factors. Controlling self involves the volition to pursue task, self-instruction, and self-monitoring (Zimmerman & Kitsantas, 1996); and controlling contextual factors means selecting, and making use of, best resources in the networked human and technology environments to facilitate learning.

Commitment, or motivation (Garrison, 1997; Meece, 1994; Schunk, 1998), refers to the teacher learner's sustained motivation and perseverance in the engagement in learning in spite of difficulties and set back.

Context means the networked human environment (Garrison, 1997; Henderson & Cunningham, 1994) within which the teacher's learning takes place. Networked human environment can provide enhanced human resources including the networked mentors, facilitators, peers, and other significant figures, group intelligence, social interaction, and social support essential for maintaining a psychological balance and zest for continual commitment to the learning. IT environment includes three aspects of IT. First, IT can be a powerful learning tool. Second, it is a medium enabling speedy feedback on multiple dimensions to the teacher learner, who upon the feedback readjusts approaches for subsequent learning. And third, IT facilitates simultaneous interaction and mutual support among networked group members during the learning process.

The theory of teacher self learning in a networked human and IT environment as well as these four key elements can provide an important base for discussion and formulation of teacher education and education reforms that strongly believe in the importance of learner-centered education and lifelong self learning to the development of professional teachers in the new millennium. As discussed above, there are numerous implications and suggestions from the theory proposed in this chapter for re-designing learning environment for teacher education and development in order to promote effective self learning at each stage of the learning cycle or continuously, no matter in formal teacher education program or not. The major implications drawn for teacher education and education reforms can be summarized and driven by the following questions:

1. How much the current and coming reforms and initiatives in educational context for teacher education are relevant to the enhancement of teachers' self learning cycle to be more effective and sustainable to lifelong?

2. Particularly how the reforms and initiatives are related to facilitating the four key elements – cognition, control, commitment, and context – in the teacher self learning process, such that teachers can initiate, maintain, and enjoy self learning and benefit from it?

3. How can the human environment in schools or in teacher education

contexts be well organized and networked to facilitate teachers' effective self learning in a larger social context, within and beyond schools, locally and globally, as described by the theory proposed by this chapter?

4. How can the IT environment in schools or in teacher education programs support the development of networked human environment and facilitate each stage of self learning cycle of teachers, as proposed by this theory?

5. How can the government establish infrastructures to enable supportive human and IT environments to facilitate in-service teachers' lifelong self learning in both informal and non-formal education?

Addressing these questions are in fact addressing the key issues of barriers to the initiatives in teacher education and education reforms from a new perspective. The issues concern how to empower teachers through a paradigm shift towards learner-centered education and lifelong self learning. Without a comprehensive understanding of how effective self learning of teachers can be facilitated in a networked human and IT environment, all initiatives to support teacher education and education reform may result in frustration and failure, if not disastrous to students, teachers, and schools. It is hoped that the proposed model of teacher self learning can benefit ongoing efforts on teacher education and reforms in different parts of the world.

NOTES

[1]This chapter is adapted from a paper presented at the European Conference on Educational Research (ECER 2000) held in 20-23 September 2000, Edinburgh, Scotland.

REFERENCES

Angus, M., & Louden, W. (1998). Systemic reform in a federal system: The national schools project. In A. Hargreaves, A. Lieberman, M. Fullan & D. Hopkins (Eds.), *International handbook of educational change* (Part Two, pp. 831-854). Boston: Kluwer.

Argyris, C., & Schön, D. A. (1974). *Theory in practice: Increasing professional effectiveness*. San Francisco: Jossey-Bass.

Argyris, C., Putnam, R., & Smith, D. M. (1985). *Action science*. San Francisco: Jossey-Bass.

Basto, J. (1999). Learning in the digital era. *Educational Media International, 36*(1), 74-76.

Bennett, R. E. (1999). Using new technology to improve assessment. *Educational Measurement, 18*(3), 5-12.

Biemiller, A., Shany, M., Inglis, A., & Meichenbaum, D. (1998). Factors influencing children's acquisition and demonstration of self-regulation on academic tasks. In D. H. Schunk & B. J. Zimmerman (Eds.), *Self-regulated learning: From teaching to self-reflective practice*. New York, London: The Guilford Press.

Boekaerts, M., Pintrich, P. R., & Zeidner, M. (Eds.). (2000). *Handbook of self-regulation*. San Diego, California: Academic Press.

Brockett, R. G. (1994). Resistance to self-direction in adult learning: Myths and misunderstandings. In R. Hiemstra & R. G. Brockett (Eds.), *Overcoming resistnace to self-direction in adult learning*. San Francisco: Jossey-Bass.

Brockett, R. G., & Hiemstra, R. (1991). *Self-direction in adult learning*. London: Routledge.

Brookfield, S. D. (1994). *Understanding and facilitating adult learning: A comprehensive analysis of principles and effective practices*. Milton Keynes: Open University Press.

Burbules, N. C., & Callister, T. A. Jr. (1999). The risky promises and promising risks of new information technologies for education. *Bulletin of Science, Technology & Society, 19*(2), 105-112.

Butler, D. L., & Winne, P. H. (1995). Feedback and self-regulated learning: A theoretical synthesis. *Review of Educational Research, 65*(3), 245-281.

Caffarella, R. S. (1993). Self-directed learning. In S. B. Merriam (Ed.), *An update on adult learning theory.* (New directions for adult and continuing education No. 57) San Francisco: Jossey-Bass.

Carnegie Forum on Education and the Economy. (1996 May). *A nation prepared: Teachers for the 21st century: The report of the Task Force on Teaching as a Profession.* Washington, D.C.: The Forum.

Carpenter, W. A. (2000). Ten years of silver bullets: Dissenting thoughts on education reform. *Phi delta kappan, 81*(5), 383-389.

Cheng, Y. C. (1999). *Curriculum and pedagogy in the new Century: Globalization, localization and individualization for multiple intelligence.* Keynote Speech presented at the 5th UNESCO-ACEID International Conference "Reforming Learning, Curriculum and Pedagogy: Innovative Visions for the New Century." The Imperial Queens Park Hotel, Bangkok, Thailand, December 13-16.

Cheng, Y. C. (1996). *School effectiveness and school-based management: A mechanism for development*. London, Washington, D.C.: Falmer Press.

Cheng, Y. C. (1994). Classroom Environment and Student Affective Performance: An Effective Profile. *Journal of Experimental Education, 62*(3), 221-239.

Cheng, Y. C., & Townsend, T. (2000). Educational change and development in the Asia-Pacific region: Trends and issues, In T. Townsend & Y. C. Cheng (Eds.), *Educational Change and Development in the Asia-Pacific Region: Challenges for the Future* (pp.317-344). The Netherlands: Swets and Zeitlinger.

Chung, G. K. W. K., & Baker, E. L. (1997). Year 1 technology studies: Implications for technology in assessment. (ERIC Document Reproduction Services ED 418 099)

Cowie, H., & van der Aalsvoort, G. (Eds.). (2000). *Social interaction in learning and instruction: The meaning of discourse for the construction of knowledge.* New York: Pergamon.

Cross, K. P. (1981). *Adults as learners: Increasing participation and facilitating learning.* New York: Jossey-Bass.

Darling-Hammond, L., Ancess, J., & Falk, B. (1995). *Authentic assessment in action: Studies of schools and students at work.* New York: Teachers College Press.

Darling-Hammond, L., Wise, A. E., & Klein, S. P. (1999). *A license to teach: Raising standards for teaching.* San Francisco, Calif.: Jossey-Bass.

Danis, C. (1992). A unifying framework for date-based research into adult self-directed learning. In H. B. Long & others (Eds.), *Self-directed learning: Application and research.* Norman: Oklahoma Research Center for Continuing Professional and Higher Education, University of Oklahoma.

David, J. (1994). School-based decision-making: Kentucky's test of decentralized decision-making. *Phi Delta Kappan, 75*(9), 706-712.

Denis, M. (1991). *Image & Cognition.* Hertfordshire: Harvester Wheatsheaf.

Driver, R., Asoko, H., Leach, J., Mortimer, E., & Scott, P. (1994). Constructing scientific knowledge in the classroom. *Educational researcher, 23*(7), 5-12.

DuFour, R. P. (1999). Help Wanted: Principals Who Can Lead Professional Learning Communities. *NASSP Bulletin, 83(614),* 12-17.

Embertson, S. E., & Hershberger, S. L. (1999). *The new rules of measurement: What every psychologist and educator should know.* Mahwah, New Jersey: Lawrence Erlbaum Associates.

English, F. W., & Hill, J. C. (1994). *Total quality education: Transforming schools into learning places.* Thousand Oaks, Calif.: Corwin Press.

Flannery, D. D. (Ed.). (1993). *Applying cognitive learning theory to adult learning.* (New directions for adult and continuing education No. 59). San Francisco: Jossey-Bass.

Ford, M. E. (1995). Intelligence and personality in social behavior. In D. H. Saklofske & M. Zeidner (Eds.), *International handbook of personality and intelligence.* New York: Plenum.

Fullan, M. (1998a). The rise and stall of teacher education reform. (ERIC Document Services ED 415 201)

Fullan, M. (1998b). Education reform: Are we on the right track? *Education Canada, 38*(2), 4-7.

Fullan, M. (1997). (Ed.). The challenge of school change. Arlington Heights, IL: IRI/SkyLight Training and Publishing.

Fullan, M. (1996). Professional culture and educational change. *School psychology review, 25*(4), 496-500.

Fullan, M. (1995). The school as learning organization: Distant dreams. *Theory and practice, 34*(4), 230-235.

Futrell, M. H. (1994). Empowering teachers as learners and leaders. In D. R. Walling (Ed.), *Teachers as leaders* (pp. 119-135). Bloomington, Indiana: Phi Delta Kappa Educational Foundation.

Garrison, D. R. (1997). Self-directed learning: Toward a comprehensive model. *Adult Education Quarterly, 48*(1), 18-30.

Gollwitzer, P. M. (1996). The volitional benefits of planning. In P. M. Gollwitzer & J. A. Bargh (Eds.), *The psychology of action: Linking cognition and motivation to behavior.* New York: Guilford.

Hallinger, P. (1998). Educational change in Southeast Asia: The challenge of creating learning systems. *Journal of Educational Administration, 36*(5), 492-509.

Henderson, R. W., & Cunningham, L. (1994). Creating interactive sociocultural environments for self-regulated learning. In D. H. Schunk & B. J. Zimmerman (Eds.), *Self-regulation of learning and performance.* Hillsdale, NJ: Lawrence Erlbaum Associates.

Herl, H. E., Baker, E. L., & Niemi, D. (1996). Construct validatoin of an approach to modelling cognitive structure of U.S. history knowledge. *Journal of Educational Research, 89,* 206-218.

Herman, J. J., & Herman, J. L. (1994). *Education quality management: Effective schools through systemic change.* Lancaster, Pa.: Technomic.

Hopkins, D. (2000). Powerful learning, powerful teachers and powerful schools. *Journal of educational change, 1,* 135-154.

Hopkins, D. (1994). *School Improvement and Cultural Change: An Interim Account of the "Improving the Quality of Education for All" (IQEA) Project.* Paper presented at the Annual Meeting of the American Educational Research Association, New Orleans, LA, April 4-8, 1994. (ERIC Document Services Number ED 377 541)

Hopkins, D., & Stern, D. (1996). Quality Teachers, Quality Schools: International Perspectives and Policy Implications. *Teaching and teacher education, 12*(5), 501-517.

Kegan, R. (1994). *In over our heads: The mental demands of modern life.* Cambridge, Mass.: Harvard University Press.

Knasel, E., Meed, J., & Rossetti, A. (2000). *Learn for your life: A blueprint for continuous learning.* London: Pearson.

Knowles, M. S. (1975). *Self-directed learning.* New York: Association Press.

Knowles, M. S. (1980). *The modern practice of adult education: From pedagogy to androgogy.* New York: Cambridge University Press.

Knowles, M. S. (1983). Andragogy: An emerging technology for adult learning. In M. Tight (Ed.), *Adult learning and education.* Beckenham: Croom Helm.

Kramer, D. A. (1989). Development of an awareness of contradiction across the life span and the question of postformal operations. In M. L. Commons, J. D., Sinnott, F. A. Richards, & C. Armon (Eds.), *Adult development: Comparisons and applications of development models.* New York: Praeger.

Kramer, D. A., & Bacelar, W. T. (1994). The educated adult in today's world: Wisdom and the mature learner. In J. D. Sinnott (Ed.), *Interdisciplinary handbook of adult lifespan learning.* Westport, Conn.: Greenwood Press.

Kuhl, J., & Goschke, T. (1994). A theory of action control: Mental subsystems, models of control, and volitional conflict-resolution strategies. In J. Kuhl & J. Beckman (Eds.), *Volition and personality: Action versus state orientation.* Gottingen, Germany: Hogrefe & Huber.

Lieberman, A. (1996). Creating intentional learning communities. *Educational Leadership, 54(3),* 51-55.

Lieberman, A. (Ed.). (1995). *The work of restructuring schools: Building from the ground up.* New York: Teachers College Press, Teachers College, Columbia University.

Lieberman, A., & Miller, L. (1999). Teachers: Transforming their world and their work. New York: Teachers College Press.

Lu, G., Wan, H., & Liu, S. (1999). Hypermedia and its application in education. *Educational Media International, 36*(1), 41-45.

MacKeracher, D. (1996). *Making sense of adult learning.* Toronto, Canada: Culture Concepts.

Meece, J. L. (1994). The role of motivation in self-regulated learning. In D. H. Schunk & B. J. Zimmerman (Eds.), *Self-regulated learning and performance.* Hillsdale, N.J.: Lawrence Earlbaum Associates.

Merriam, S. B., & Caffarella, R. S. (1999). *Learning in Adulthood: A comprehensive guide* (2nd ed.). San Francisco: Jossey-Bass.

Mok, M., & Cheng, Y. C. (2000a). *Self-learning driven assessment: A new framework for assessment and evaluation.* Paper presented to the 13th International Congress for School Effectiveness and Improvement (ICSEI 2000), The Hong Kong Institute of Education, Hong Kong, January 4-8.

Mok, M., & Cheng, Y. C. (2000b). *Global knowledge, intelligence and education for a learning society.* Keynote Speech presented at the 6th UNESCO-ACEID International Conference "Information Technologies in Educational Innovation for Development: Interfacing Global and Indigenous Knowledge". The Imperial Queens Park Hotel, Bangkok, Thailand, December 12-15.

Mok, M., & Cheng, Y.C. (2000c). *Self-directed learning in a human and technological environment.* Paper presented to European Conference on Educational Research (ECER 2000) University of Edinburgh, Edinburgh, Scotland, September 20-23.

Pascual-Leone, J., & Irwin, R. R. (1998). Abstraction, the will, the self and modes of learning in adulthood. In M. C. Smith & T. Pourchot (Eds.), *Adult learning and development: Perspectives from educational psychology.* Mahwah, New Jersey: Lawrence Erlbaum Associates.

Phillips, D. C. (1995). The good, the bad and the ugly: The many faces of constructivism. *Educational researcher, 24*(7), 5-12.

Piaget, J. (1962). *Play, Dreams and Imitation.* New York: Norton.

Pipho, C. (2000). A new reform model for teachers and teaching. *Phi Delta Kappan, 81*(6), 421-422.

Rheinberg, F., Vollmeyer, R., & Rollett, W. (2000). Motivation and action in self-regulated learning. In M. Boekaerts, P. R. Pintrich & M. Zeidner (Eds.), *Handbook of self-regulation.* San Diego, California: Academic Press.

Riegel, K. F. (1973). Dialectic operations: The final period of cognitive development. *Human development, 16*, 346-370.

Riegel, K. F. (1975). Adult life crises: A dialectical interpretation of development. In N. Datan & L. H. Ginsberg (Eds.), *Life-span developmental psychology: Normative life crises.* Orlando, Fla.: Academic Press.

Riegel, K. F. (1976). The dialectics of human development. *American Psychologist, 31*, 689-700.

Saltiel, I. M., Sgroi, A., & Brockett, R. G. (Eds.). (1998). *The power and potential of collaborative learning partnerships.* San Francisco: Jossey-Bass.

Saltiel, I. M. (1998). Adult students as partners in formal study. In I. M. Saltiel, A. Sgroi, & R. G. Brockett (Eds.), *The power and potential of collaborative learning partnerships* (pp. 13-22). San Francisco: Jossey-Bass.

Schmidt, R. A. (1975). A Schema Theory of Discrete Motor Skill Learning. *Psychological Review, 82*, 225-260.

Schön, D. A. (1987). *Education the Reflective Practitioner: Toward a New Design for Teaching and Learning in the Professions.* San Francisco: Jossey-Bass.

Schunk, D. H. (1998). Teaching elementary students to self-regulate practice of mathematical skills with modeling. In D. H. Schunk & B. J. Zimmerman (Eds.), *Self-regulated learning and performance.* Hillsdale, N.J.: Lawrence Earlbaum Associates.

Schunk, D. H. (1996). *Learning theories* (2nd ed.). New Jersey: Prentice Hall.

Schunk, D. H., & Zimmerman, B. J. (Eds.). (1998). *Self-regulated learning and performance.* Hillsdale, N.J.: Lawrence Earlbaum Associates.

Sergiovanni, T. J. (2000). *The lifeworld of leadership: Creating culture, community, and personal meaning in our schools.* San Francisco: Jossey-Bass.

Slusarski, S. B. (1994). Enhancing self-direction in the adult learner: Instructional techniques for teachers and trainers. In R. Hiemstra, & R. G. Brockett (Eds.). *Overcoming resistance to self-direction in adult learning.* San Francisco: Jossey-Bass.

Tam, W. M. & Cheng, Y. C. (1995). School Environment and Student Performance: A Multi-level Analysis, *Educational Research Journal, 10*(1), 5-21.

Tomorrow's teachers: A report of the Holmes Group. (1986). East Lansing, MI : Holmes Group.

Tsui, K. T., & Cheng, Y. C. (1999). School organizational health and teacher commitment: A contingency study with multi-level analysis. *Educational Research and Evaluation (An International Journal on Theory and Practice), 5*(3), 249-68.

Tsui, K. T., & Cheng, Y. C. (1997). *Total teacher effectiveness: Implication for curriculum change (TOC) in Hong Kong.* Paper presented at the Annual Meeting of the American Educational Research Association, Chicago, IL, March 24-28, 1997. (ERIC Document Services ED 418 085)

von Glaserfeld, E. (1995). Sensory experience, abstraction, and teaching. In L. P. Steffe & J. Gale (Eds.), *Constructivism in education.* Hillsdale, N.J.: Erlbaum.

Weinstein, C. E., Husman, J., & Dierking, D. R. (2000). Self-regulation interventions with a focus on learning strategies. In M. Boekaerts, P. R. Pintrich, & M. Zeidner (Eds.), *Handbook of self-regulation.* San Diego, California: Academic Press.

Winne, P. H., & Perry, N. E. (2000). Measuring self-regulated learning. In M. Boekaerts, P.R. Pintrich & M. Zeidner (Eds.), *Handbook of self-regulation.* San Diego, California: Academic Press.

Yuen, P. Y., & Cheng, Y. C. (2000). Leadership for teachers' action learning. *International Journal of Educational Management*, 14(5), 198-209.

Yuen, P. Y., & Cheng, Y. C. (1997). *The action learning leadership for pursuing education quality in the 21ˢᵗ century.* Paper presented at the Fifth International Conference on Chinese Education Towards the 21ˢᵗ Century: Key Issues on the Research Agenda, Hong Kong.

Zimmerman, B. J. (2000). Attaining self-regulation: A social cognitive perspective. In M. Boekaerts, P. R. Pintrich & M. Zeidner (Eds.), *Handbook of self-regulation.* San Diego, California: Academic Press.

Zimmerman, B. J. (1998). Developing self-fulfilling cycles of academic regulation: An analysis of exemplary instructional models. In D. H. Schunk & B. J. Zimmerman (Eds.), *Self-regulated learning and performance.* Hillsdale, N.J.: Lawrence Earlbaum Associates.

Zimmerman, B. J. (1994). Dimensions of academic self-regulation: A conceptual framework for education. In D. H. Schunk & B. J. Zimmerman (Eds.), *Self-regulated learning and performance.* Hillsdale, N.J.: Lawrence Earlbaum Associates.

Zimmerman, B. J., & Kitsantas, A. (1996). Self-regulated learning of a motoric skill: The role of goal setting and self-monitoring. *Journal of Applied Sport Psychology, 8*, 60-75.

Part III

Reform and Development of Teacher Education

Richard APLIN
Kriengsak CHAREONWONGSAK
Sharon Hsiao Lan CHEN
John ELLIOTT
Rupert MACLEAN
Paul MORRIS
King Chee PANG
Barbara PRESTON

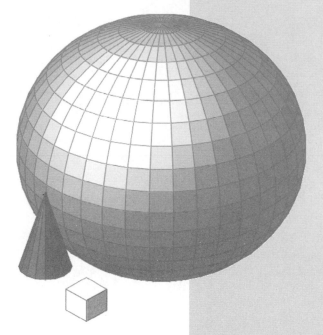

Chapter 6

Educational Reform, Schooling, and Teacher Education in Hong Kong

John ELLIOTT
School of Education and Professional Development
University of East Anglia, United Kingdom

Paul MORRIS
Office of the Directorate
The Hong Kong Institute of Education, Hong Kong

The Government of the Hong Kong Special Administrative Region is currently engaged in promoting a wide range of educational reforms in an attempt to improve the quality of schooling and enhance the future competitiveness of the economy. These reforms will face a number of hurdles, some of which will arise from the nature and process of policy-making, whilst others will arise from the contexts within which reforms are implemented. Our concern in this chapter is to analyze some of the implications of the reforms for teacher education. However, this task first requires an analysis of the nature of education and schooling that the reforms are trying to achieve.

Accordingly, we begin by identifying the main features of the reforms and, in section two, we consider the nature of the support that schools will require if change is to occur. Subsequently, in the third section, we focus on teacher education and discuss how its structures and curriculum can support change in schools. Our analysis is based on two self-evident, but frequently ignored, assumptions:

1. *That changes in the quality of students' engagement with learning is ultimately dependent on how teachers structure and manage that engagement.*

   In other words, the quality of learning is dependent on what teachers *do* in the classroom. Changing the *curriculum in action* is rarely a straightforward matter of implementing a centrally designed blue-print, for it inevitably has to accommodate the complex configurations of factors that shape what teachers do in particular classrooms and school contexts. Curriculum change has to be pedagogically constructed by teachers within particular *teaching-learning milieu* (Parlett & Hamilton, 1976).

Consequently, the problem of change is not that of securing compliance to external prescription, but of enhancing teachers' capacities for discernment, discrimination, and judgement in relation to the particular contexts in which they are expected to effect change. Such a pragmatic perspective inevitably implies continuities as well as discontinuities. In this respect, it differs from the Utopian perspective on change which implies a radical discontinuity with existing practice.

2. *If teachers are to change the curriculum in action in their classrooms and schools, they require consistent support over a long period of time from a variety of sources, including policy-makers and government officials, school principals, parents, and teacher trainers.*

The actions of all these parties influence and shape what teachers do with students in their classrooms. Support implies *trust* in and *respect* for the professionalism of teachers, and may be contrasted with the exhortation, derision, and high levels of external surveillance associated with a *compliance model* of curriculum change. In this respect, our conception of curriculum improvement would not be consistent with a reliance on policy actions that revolve around "quick fixes": for example, the testing of teachers through benchmarking as the means for creating change.

These assumptions relate primarily to the strategies or policy actions employed to bring about change rather than the intentions of policy *per se.* This distinction is important as the history of educational reforms in Hong Kong has been one in which worthwhile policy intents have failed to change the deep structures of schooling, because the actions designed to move the policy into the schools have violated the two assumptions outlined above (Adamson et al., 2000). In our discussion below, we focus on the intentions of the reform and suspend judgement on the associated policy actions, the proposed time scale for change, and the sheer range or scale of reform. It is these elements that will eventually determine whether the reform has a significant impact on improving the quality of teaching and learning. Unfortunately, the omens are ominous as the current indications are that the quest is for rapid, radical change of all aspects of schooling using policy actions that replicate the worst features of previous reform cycles (Morris, Lo, & Adamson, 2000).

EDUCATIONAL REFORM IN HONG KONG

A range of official documents (e.g., Education Commission, 2000) has recently been published, explaining the goals of the reform exercise. We do not describe these in detail, but rather attempt to identify the broad intentions that the proposals are attempting to achieve. This task requires going beyond recounting the rhetoric of policy, which has to date dominated the consultation process.

The proposals for educational reform include a proposal for changing the curriculum (See Curriculum Development Council, 2000). This does not prescribe syllabi that list in detail the knowledge content to be covered at various stages of education for the purposes of examinations. Nor does it specify a curriculum in the form of a program of learning tasks and teaching-learning activities. Instead it provides a holistic and open framework to guide and support the development of specific curricula and appropriate forms of assessment at the school level. The framework is based on a set of aims for education during the 21st century, and specifies principles for selecting worthwhile learning experiences that are consistent with these aims. It is presented as an open framework in two senses. First, it is open to continuous revision in the light of experience; and second, it is flexible inasmuch as it can be adapted by schools and teachers to suit the particular needs of their students.

> The school curriculum should provide all students with essential life-long learning experiences for whole person development in the domains of ethics, intellect, physical development, social skills and aesthetics, according to individual potentials, so that all students could become active, responsible, and contributing members of society, the nation and the world.

> The school curriculum should help students to learn how to learn through cultivating positive values, attitudes, and a commitment to life-long learning, develop generic skills to acquire and construct knowledge, which are essential for whole-person development to cope with challenges of the 21st century.

> A quality curriculum for the 21st century should therefore set the directories

for teaching/learning through a coherent and flexible framework which could be adaptable to changes and different needs of students and schools. (CDC, 2000, p. 17)

The intention of the curriculum framework that is being proposed is clearly consistent with the view of curriculum change outlined in the introduction. Underpinning it are the beliefs that curriculum change has in the final analysis to be pedagogically constructed by teachers at the level of the classroom and school, and that the role of a central curriculum framework is to orientate and support *pedagogically-driven* curriculum change.

Overall, the planned reforms are attempting to reduce the strong boundaries that currently surround what Bernstein (1971) describes as the three basic message systems of the school curriculum: what knowledge is most valued, how it should be transmitted; and how it should be assessed. We focus on these curriculum elements.

The Nature of Knowledge and Understanding

The fundamental question here is this: how are the reforms trying to redefine the nature of the knowledge that is valued and which pupils are expected to learn in schools? Overall, the goal is to weaken the boundaries between the traditional school subjects in terms of which propositional knowledge has been classified for the purposes of systematic transmission in schools.

The reorganization of subject matter around eight Key Learning Areas (KLAs) allows for a new synthesis of knowledge content organized around overarching themes, issues, ideas, and values. It can, of course, be justified as a solution to the problem of an overcrowded curriculum, in terms of a more economical and efficient use of time and other scarce resources. However, its justification consists in more than this and fundamentally resides in a reiteration of a long standing holistic vision of the aims of education as *the development of understanding* (see Elliott, 1973; Elliott, 1988; Sankey, 2000) or what R. S. Peters (1966, 1973) called a *cognitive perspective*. From this standpoint, the learning of specific bodies of knowledge and skills is educationally worthwhile if it permeates and transforms pupils general outlook on life. For pupils to acquire knowledge and skills *with understanding* is to be able to connect their knowledge to its wider meaning and significance within a coherent pattern of life. In this sense, the *development of understanding* engages pupils in the *personal construction* of meanings and implies an active rather than passive learning process directed towards the *integration* of parts into wholes. The objects of learning are not simply facts to be memorized and recalled, or skills to be practiced, but patterns to be discerned, issues to be explored, ideas to be explored, and values to be interpreted. Knowledge of specific facts and the acquisition of specific skills are educationally important as resources for learners in developing *a personal synoptic understanding* of the world, and themselves as part of it (see Sankey, 2000).

The Consultative Documents on the curriculum reforms (CDC, 2000) clearly envisages the re-organization of the school curriculum around KLAs as the provision of *contexts* to facilitate the *development of understanding* as the major aim of schooling for all students. This aim is also evident in other elements of the proposed curriculum framework that may be regarded as principles for constructing learning experiences for pupils which are consistent with the aim. They include the following:

The Provision of Learning Experiences for Whole Person Development

This principle highlights the importance of schooling as an agent of personal transformation. Learning experiences should be designed to *educate* pupils rather than simply fill them with "knowledge," and this implies engaging them with learning that transforms their general outlook on life. Although such an outlook may be described in terms of a *cognitive perspective*, this does not exclude a concern for pupil's values and emotional attitudes. At the core of peoples' moral and emotional responses to situations are beliefs that shape the way they see things and events. Changes in their responses imply changes in their cognitive perspective.

This explains why the concept of "multiple intelligences" is figuring so centrally in the curriculum discourse surrounding the proposed reforms. It refers to the variety of human capacities, such as "emotional" and "ecological" intelligence, which pupils need to exercise in developing a *cognitive perspective* which, in the words of R. S. Peters (1973), transforms "mere living into a quality of life."

The Provision of a Broad and Balanced Set of Learning Experiences
for All Students at All Stages of Schooling and thereby the
Avoidance of Early Specialization

The central concept here is the "common curriculum." The original 1999 Consultative document expresses a concern (also neglected in the later documents) to avoid separate curriculum pathways for different groups of pupils (e.g., vocational studies, sciences, technology, humanities, and art) although some allowance for a degree of specialization is recommended at senior secondary level. This is consistent with the development of *understanding* or a *cognitive perspective* as the major aim of education. A deep but circumscribed and disconnected knowledge of a limited range of activities is no basis for the development of a coherent outlook on life, which depends on seeing connections across a range of different contexts of experience. However, as Peters (1973) pointed out, the educational desirability of avoiding narrow specialization is clearer than what this means in terms of specific curriculum arrangements and requirements. There is certainly room for public debate over the delineation and number of KLAs for the curriculum framework. For example, Chinese and English could be viewed as included within a single KLA concerned with languages.

Nevertheless, we recognize that the development of *understanding* or *cognitive perspective* as the over-riding aim of schooling suggests that there are no absolute categories for organizing educational experiences which can be regarded as universally valid. Human consciousness is *historically conditioned* inasmuch as it is situated in place and time. Many societies at the present time are experiencing the impact of the globalization of the forces of production and economic markets, which has been made possible by scientific and technological developments. The economies of countries are increasingly dependent on the supply of appropriate "knowledge skills" and, as Sachs (2000) has argued, this has created an intractable division between nations based on their access to technology. Around 15 percent of the world's population provide nearly 100 percent of technological innovations; around 50 percent are involved in adopting these technologies in production and consumption; and the remainder are technologically disconnected and excluded. What is notable is that the technological innovators are located primarily in English speaking societies. It is hardly surprising that this has resulted in the prioritizing of science and technology in the curriculum and a continued emphasis on the language of technological innovation – especially in societies, such as Hong Kong, which are technological adopters.

In parallel with these global influences, there has been a desire to strengthen local and national identities (See Gray, 1998). This has placed a priority on including bodies of knowledge and a language that incorporates that identity. The potential for tension between these broader trends is clearly manifested in the competition for space between subjects and specifically the ongoing conflict between the role of and relationship between Chinese history and history in the school curriculum. The proposed delineation of KLAs for the curriculum framework reflects the tension between these global trends and search for local identities in the structuring of the school curriculum. However, it also reflects the fact that the impact of globalization on the curriculum in particular societies differs. In this respect it is interesting to note that the global trends cited are not demarcated from others in terms of a core compulsory curriculum as they are in some other countries, including the UK. Other KLAs, such as personal, social and humanities education, the arts, and physical education, are intended to carry equal weight as essential elements in the curriculum. The consultation document clearly expects connections to be made across these elements. For example, scientific and technological development is accompanied by the growth of *risks* and *hazards* to health and the natural environment which impinge on the quality of peoples lives and are unequally distributed (see Beck, 1992) within and across societies.

The proposed curriculum framework for Hong Kong tacitly acknowledges the significance of the intersection of *time* and *place* for the development of *understanding* or *cognitive perspective*. This significance is particularly acknowledged in the delineation of "Personal, Social Education & the Humanities" and "the Arts" as KLAs and the proposals that the learning of Putonghua be incorporated into the Chinese language KLA, and that in the longer term Putonghua become the medium of instruction for this KLA. All these proposed changes in the organization of the curriculum can be connected to the search for a cultural identity in the particular context of Hong Kong. It has been shaped by the change over from a British Colony to a Special Administrative Region of the People's Republic of China over a period that coincided with the Far Eastern economic crisis, a marked decline in the quality of the environment and the emergence of a stronger *self-reflexive* dimension within the society.

This emerging self-reflexivity is evidenced in the proposal to develop a holistic framework for personal, social and humanities education aimed at "the strengthening of students' personal and social developments." This would include a "fact-slimmed" General Studies curriculum at the primary level aimed at strengthening "the development of personal and social values/attitudes through contexts pertaining to civic, moral, sex, environmental, consumer education and other cross-curricular areas." There are also proposals to develop a modularized "issues-focused" and "inquiry-based" course at the junior secondary level and an integrated humanities foundation course for the senior secondary level. At the latter level, the proposals allow for a degree of specialization but the expectation is that students specializing in science subjects undertake a humanities course and those specializing in humanities and arts subjects undertake a general science course.

Such proposals are indicative of the importance attributed to values in the Hong Kong context, as are the proposals for strengthening the learning of Chinese culture as a source of value. They express a concern to provide curriculum experiences that are "relevant to daily life" inasmuch as they enable students to construct a coherent outlook on their lives in a particular place at a time when the forces of production and consumption are becoming increasingly globalized.

The Weakening of the Boundaries between the Formal Curriculum and Informal and Non-formal Learning Environments

The 1999 and 2000 Consultation Documents propose greater links between the classroom as a learning environment and the learning that takes place in extra-curricular settings, in the home and the community. They aspire to the construction of learning experiences that bridge schooling and life and incorporate classroom learning into a more comprehensive *learnscape*. The reasons cited are "providing more curriculum space, enhancing vocational skills and making learning more relevant to life." All are entirely consistent with the shift from *knowledge acquisition* to the development of *understanding* or *broad cognitive perspective* as the primary aim of schooling. The latter is powerfully shaped by learning experiences that currently are largely disconnected from students' experience of the formal curriculum in classrooms. If knowledge is to become a resource for students in constructing a personal and holistic understanding of the things that matter in life, including "the world of work," then the curriculum needs to be conceived as the bridge between schooling and life.

This carries important implications for the process of school-based curriculum development. It suggests that responsibilities for organizing extra-curricular activities should not be segregated in schools if the *informal curriculum* is to be aligned with the *formal curriculum*. It also suggests that teachers will need to collaborate more with parents, employers, and others in their communities when constructing worthwhile learning experiences for students that bridge *formal* and *non-formal* settings.

The Provision across all KLAs and throughout All Stages of Schooling for the Development of Generic Elements for Life-long Learning

These elements include the values and attitudes governing personal morality, participation in civil society, and the relationship between human beings and the natural environment. They also include interpersonal skills, study skills, information technology skills, critical thinking skills, and creative thinking skills. All these elements are regarded by the 1999 Consultation Document "as paramount for life-long learning in a world where knowledge is ever changing." Again this proposal is consistent with the fundamental shift of aim we have described. It recognizes that the development of *a cognitive perspective* is a life-long process and has no predictable outcome or end-point. As R. S. Peters (1965) remarked "to be educated is not to have arrived at a destination; it is to travel with a different view. What is required is not feverish preparation for something that lies ahead, but to work with precision, passion, and taste at worthwhile things that lie to hand." (p. 110) The generic elements set out in the reform proposals are not values, attitudes, and skills to be learned in preparation for some predictable future tasks but elements inherent in what is conceived as a personal engagement in a life-long process of deepening and widening ones understanding and sensitivity. The reform proposals recognize that life-long learning of this kind involves the formation of values and attitudes as well as the acquisition of knowledge. In doing so, it acknowledges that we live in an age in which it has become increasingly difficult to sustain the view that what count as facts about the world can be demarcated from value positions and commitments.

The rhetoric of life-long learning is now in wide circulation and is associated with the emergence of increasingly unstable, fluid, and dynamic labor markets in advanced industrial societies. Its meaning and significance as a guide to policy-making may, however, vary between such societies. Some may emphasize it as an aspect of an educational process aimed at the development of the individual as a whole person. Others may link it primarily to the economic function of schooling and emphasize its significance as a solution to the problem of predicting the *commodity value* of learning for the labor market. Whilst the curriculum reforms emphasize the first aspect, other developments suggest that the latter interpretation is the motive behind the reforms or at least their implementation. For example, the attempt to construct indices of the "value added" by schools, and to partly fund universities based on the starting salary of their graduates are both crude attempts to portray education as a commodity.

The future *commodity value* for the labor market of particular learning outcomes, in the form of specific knowledge and skills, is increasingly difficult for societies to predict. One of the traditional functions of schooling, that of categorizing, sorting, and credentialing their students for the purpose of allocating them to jobs in life, appears to be breaking down. Confidence in the ability to predict the future needs of the labour market varies from one society to another. The degree of importance attributed to life-long learning might be viewed as a *confidence indicator*, inasmuch as it refers to generic dispositions and capacities which enable people to respond constructively to changing and unpredictable circumstances in their lives, and thereby take responsibility for constructing their own futures. An educational system designed to make serious provision for life-long learning will tend to possess a relatively low amount of confidence in its ability to predict the commodity value of achievements in particular school subjects. Those countries that demarcate *a core curriculum* in their national curriculum frameworks might be said to be specifying the limits of their confidence to predict the commodity value of schooling. However, this apparent expression of confidence may be merely a politically symbolic gesture for the purpose of winning votes at election time, and mask a very real anxiety and uncertainty. In this light one can interpret the demarcation of a core curriculum, such as the one obtaining in the UK, as an obstinate 'last stand' on the part of educational policy-makers to demonstrate the commodity value of traditional schooling to their citizenry.

Viewed as a whole, the aspirations of the curriculum reform proposals refrain from the neo-liberal tendency, manifested in many contemporary policy-contexts, to subordinate schooling to the production of predictable commodity value for the labor market. In emphasizing the generic elements of life-long learning as aspects of whole person development across all KLAs, they aspire to resolve a long-standing dichotomy between the intrinsic *aims of education* and the economic functions of schooling. The impetus resides in the erosion, in the Hong Kong context, of the myth that there exists a straightforward causal relationship between the measurable attainment of specific subject knowledge and skills and sustainable economic growth (Morris & Sweeting, 1995). It has been suggested that the difference between the proposed curriculum framework and more neo-liberal proposals is not that it gives a lesser place to the economic functions of schooling, but conceptualizes them differently. Rather than constituting a design for "engineering" the commodity value of schooling for the labor market, the Hong Kong framework embodies a Darwinian perspective on the relationship between education and the economy. It is the task of education to establish the conditions under which a diversity of human capacities, talents, and skills can be developed within and between individuals. These conditions alone will enable the society as a whole to sustain itself through an ever changing economic environment. What is being evoked here analogously is the Darwinian notion of "natural selection."

How Knowledge Should Be Transmitted

The main changes proposed for pedagogy arise directly from the view of worthwhile knowledge outlined above. The proposals for the personal, social and humanities curriculum view learning as an active process of inquiry rather than a passive process of reception. The Consultation Document refers to the development of students thinking and problem-solving skills, and creativity, as an integral part of their personal and social development. However, it does not view KLAs as tightly bounded categories of knowledge. They are not conceived as *new curriculum subjects* for the purpose of transmitting inert bodies of knowledge but as *broad contexts of human inquiry* where emerging understandings and insights inform each other and can be integrated into a holistic outlook on life. *Inquiry Learning* is therefore seen as a cross-curricular pedagogical orientation that applies to all KLAs. As such, it should not be confused with particular teaching methods. Whether a particular "method" is appropriate will depend upon the extent to which it is consistent with the values and principles of inquiry in a particular learning context. For example, it does not rule out "whole class instruction" in contexts where either the teacher cannot use it effectively to facilitate learning or where students express a need to know something before they can proceed to discuss an issue or problem. Nor does it proclaim the superiority of discussions "in groups" over whole class discussions (Mok & Morris, forthcoming). In this respect the proposed curriculum framework invokes a consideration and explication of its pedagogical implications, conceived as generic principles of human inquiry, which orient teaching and learning but do not prescribe specific "methods" (See CDC, 2000, Learning to Learn, Chap. 4). Peters (1973, pp. 21-24) argued that such pedagogical principles are often clustered around broad statements about the aims of education, such as "the self-realization of the individual," which function to "draw attention to a class of *procedures*" of education rather than prescribe any particular direction or content for it. They draw attention, he claims, to the claims of individual students with respect to their learning that education should provide them with space for discretion, autonomy, and self-origination.

If, as the proposals suggest, knowledge is to be seen as provisional, open to question and therefore a resource for developing a personal understanding of the world rather than a fixed and certain body of established information, and if students are to learn how to learn, then the pedagogic role of the teacher shifts from that of a transmitter of knowledge to a facilitator of inquiry (See Stenhouse, 1975, Chap. 6-7). This implies providing students with opportunities for collaboration with others, critical thinking, reflection, action learning, and creativity as vital elements of the learning process. Essentially, the goal is to reduce the strong barriers that exist between teachers and pupils, which arise when the teacher is defined as an expert and pupils are empty vessels to be filled with knowledge. This has, as we elaborate below, important implications for teacher education, for if we expect teachers to be active and collaborative learners, then schools and teacher education curricula need to support this goal.

How Knowledge Should Be Assessed

The goals here are to reduce the strong boundaries that currently exist between assessment, teaching, and learning and, in so doing, to shift the function of assessment away from a wholly selective to a more formative one, in which constructive feedback to pupils is viewed as a critical influence on learning.

Thus, the intentions are that high stakes selective assessment exercises prior to the end of secondary schooling are to be abandoned; greater emphasis is to be placed on assessing the process of learning; teachers are to play a more central role in assessment exercises; and tertiary entrance criteria are to be broadened to include competencies that are not readily examined. These shifts go along with a package of planned structural changes designed to reduce the elitist features of the school system which in the past involved extensive assessment for selective purposes. Thus, the matriculation course (Forms 6 and 7) is to be abandoned and most/all pupils are expected to stay on a school until the end of the new Form 6, rather than leave at the end of Form 5 as at present. Most pupils are also expected to proceed from primary school to their local secondary school without any stratification or selection based on assessment of their academic aptitude.

The nature of these reforms is neither novel nor unique to Hong Kong. They reiterate some of the features of previous innovations, such as the Target Oriented Curriculum (TOC), and bear many similarities to what has been described as the "third wave" of education reforms, which advocate a comprehensive or systemic restructuring of schooling. More specifically, the images of schools (as learning organizations), of curriculum development (as a partnership between various stakeholders), and of teachers (as researchers in their own classrooms) have close parallels to those which have guided reform initiatives elsewhere – especially the USA, UK, Australia, and Canada (see Elliott, 2000).

SCHOOLS AND TEACHERS

The implications of these reforms for schools and teachers are legion, and it is axiomatic that any change – let alone a shift towards the implementation of the reforms – will require recognition of the centrality of the teacher. Ironically, as noted earlier, many reform exercises have been premised on a heavy-duty critique of schools and teachers, which is often accompanied by a process of "naming and shaming." Inevitably, this has served to undermine teachers' professionalism, reinforced resistance to change, and contributed to the very pessimistic portrayals of the overall extent of the impact of reforms on their ultimate goal namely, the quality of teaching and learning.

Before proceeding, we highlight below what we view as some of the major implications of the intentions of these reforms for the role of teachers and for the organizations that establish the framework and structures in which teachers operate – schools.

Teachers will need to:

- move from stressing pupils' compliance to an established body of knowledge and towards stressing its importance as a resource for pupils' construction of personal and synoptic meaning;

- develop classroom environments in which the key indicators of effectiveness are not compliance with rules (and silence) but evidence of understanding, thinking, discussion, collaboration, and problem-solving;

- provide feedback that supports and encourages all pupils to improve their learning (This is in contrast to the present focus on feedback that highlights error recognition and failure.); and

- develop the skills to operate in classrooms that are made up of pupils with a very diverse range of abilities.

In parallel, schools will need to:

- see teachers as professional partners who have a role in decision-making and in changing the curriculum to meet the needs of all pupils;

- unfreeze the boundaries which demarcate formal learning in the classroom and informal/non-formal learning through extra-curriculum activities and the activities students participate in within the home and the community (This will necessitate new forms of educational partnerships and collaborative curriculum decision-making with parents, employers and others, who will not simply be viewed as the passive consumers of schooling.);

- reward and celebrate both the diversity of achievement and success of pupils, rather than stressing compliance and obedience;

- encourage pupils to make choices and involve them in the process of decision making (This will be in marked contrast to the prevailing situation in Hong Kong where schools tend to view pupils as unable to make decisions until after they leave.);

- view knowledge as a resource for thinking and action in the real world

(The unfreezing of its boundaries with that world will involve schools transforming themselves, from being mere transmitters of passively received knowledge into agencies for the creation of locally useful knowledge.);

- provide flexible arrangements that cater for the diverse needs of pupils and that encourage pupils to learn though a variety of means;

- encourage and support teachers' collaboration and to engage in the ongoing process of curriculum improvement; and

- support the ongoing evaluation and improvement of teaching, and reward teachers in ways that recognize the inherently moral nature of the teacher's role.

The above will remain a "wish list" unless schools and teachers are provided with support by the range of societal agencies that help define the realities of schooling. These include the universities, which define what is valued at the end of secondary schooling; the public examination agencies, which operationalize assessment; the government, which provides resources and defines what society values in schools; and the teacher education bodies, which define what competencies a qualified teacher requires.

In the past many well-intentioned reforms in Hong Kong have simply failed to have a significant impact on schools because their goals have not been matched by consequent changes in the priorities and policy actions of the other agencies. The universities have simultaneously criticized schools and effectively encouraged them to maintain a narrow and specialized academic curriculum; and the examinations' authority has focused on assessing propositional knowledge, which can be more "objectively" measured. The government has lacked commitment and its agencies have not shared a common purpose. It has focused on symbolic actions, failed to provide resources, expected radical changes to occur overnight, and blamed others (especially teachers, schools and teacher education bodies) for its failures. The teacher education bodies have tended to be reactive and to maintain the status quo rather than support change or, more importantly, encourage teachers to act as change agents. Below we focus on the role of the teacher education bodies.

TEACHER EDUCATION: STRUCTURES AND CURRICULA

This section takes as axiomatic that it is the responsibility of teacher education agencies to model the structures and processes of the reform agenda that they view as worthwhile. Essentially, all of the implications that we identified above for schools and teachers are equally applicable to teacher education organizations and teacher educators. We focus below on four dimensions of the practice of teacher education that are critical to providing trainee teachers with an experience that models the worthwhile images of teaching and learning promoted in the reforms. These relate to the relationships between:

a. the organizational culture of teacher education institutions and the teacher education curriculum,

b. pedagogy and the assessment of teacher professional development,

c. research and practice,

d. their role as both agencies designed to support policy and as critical commentators on policy.

The teacher education curriculum will need to be reconstructed to prepare student teachers to handle the realities and complexities of multi-level change in classrooms and schools, rather than simply preparing them to either fit into a presumed status quo, or to adopt idealized models of good practice that neglect the contexts of practice.

Such a reconstruction would place the study of the central questions that professional teachers grapple with as they strive to help pupils learn and the study of educational change - namely, teaching and learning - at the heart of the professional studies strand in the curriculum. This is not simply a matter of studying different theories of pedagogy and change and the relevant research. The aims and principles which under-pin the proposed curriculum framework for schools have to be realized in particular contexts of action. Their realization will depend on the extent to which teachers are able to understand the ways in which factors operating in their particular situation interact to shape the curriculum-in-action at the level of the classroom and school. Here, a knowledge of relevant theories of pedagogy and change may prove to be a useful resource for thinking about how to change the curriculum-in-action in a particular context. As such, they are a source of hypotheses for the student teacher to test, explore, and refine in relation to his or her own practical situation.

This is in marked contrast to the situation where student teachers constantly face a massive disjuncture between the ideals they have learnt and the reality of schooling. The end result is all too often the adoption of a cynicism that involves a combination of the "small potato" syndrome and that theory has no link to practice. Using research means doing research in the context of teacher preparation for participation in curriculum change. This has profound pedagogical implications for tutors in the teacher education institutions involving a shift into an "inquiry" mode of learning, which is focused on problems and issues that arise from real settings in classrooms and schools that students face. The professional knowledge components of the professional studies curriculum will need to be re-organized as resources to support school-based action inquiry.

This interaction between theory and practice implies that teacher education institutions move away from a combination of a subject-based and theory-into-practice model of curriculum organization in which "research" is seen as a distinct rather than integrated component of the curriculum. They will also need to unfreeze the boundaries between both the in-house course organization and the school context for the practicum. This will imply changing the organizational structures which shape the way courses are developed to make them more responsive to the key issues and change contexts in which student teachers will have to operate in schools. The professional studies components may need to be organized around broad learning areas that reflect both the key issues and change themes in the proposed reforms. Examples of key issues include the following: How do pupils learn? How can teachers support diversity? How can pupils be provided with positive feedback? What forms of explanation and classroom organization support effective learning? Themes relevant to change might include "designing curricula at the classroom and school level," "transforming the culture of teaching and learning," "designing curriculum experiences for life-long learning," "the implications of multiple intelligence theory for curriculum organization and development," etc, etc. This will require a shift away from the highly specialized educational subjects demarcated by the organization's existing departmental structures and on curriculum design sometimes primarily motivated by the quest for territory and resources.

Just as the school curriculum reforms are asking subjects to consider how they contribute to developing a pupil's understanding, so the partnership schools will need to become more involved in the planning of the professional studies components since they will involve a holistic process of using theory and research into teaching and learning, schooling, and educational change to improve the curriculum-in-action in particular practice settings. The staff of partnership schools will need to help support student teachers undertaking case-study-based action research and to collaborate with them and their tutors in a research-based process of classroom and school focused curriculum development. In this way, pre-service and in-service teacher professional development for educational change could be integrated through the same programs which incorporate differentiation of levels: from Bachelor to Masters level, for example.

All these will have profound implications for the assessment of student-teachers. The action-research-based process of professional development suggests a shift away from the assessment of student-teachers' knowledge of theory in ways that resemble the tendency of school examinations to focus on propositional knowledge. It implies a greater concern for the assessment of how they are able to link theory and practice. It also implies a move towards student-teachers having a greater say in assessing their achievements and progress as beginning teachers and in developing a personal cognitive perspective on what it means to be and become a teacher in the 21st century. At a more mundane level, this could be expressed as a move away from assessing whether student-teachers were able to reproduce at the end of the course the "information" distributed in course handouts by lecturers, and towards an assessment of their ability to undertake tasks that require them to reflect on their practice, use the library and technological resources, and to revise their work in the light of feedback. Portfolio records of case evidence gathered in researching practice with the aim of improving it should form a basis for analytic and formative self-assessments, which are externally audited on the basis of observations of experienced teachers and tutors. Self-assessment would proceed in the context of a dialogue with such observers. As for summative assessment this would ideally be an outcome of such dialogue at the end of the program of teacher preparation.

Finally, there is an ongoing tension between the role of teacher education agencies and teacher educators as supporters of curriculum change and as independent critical analysts. Their role is not to automatically respond to government policy initiatives and accept them as fiats that require unquestioning obedience and compliance. To merely respond to policy initiatives in this technical way would serve to undermine the rationale that informed the recommendation of Education Commission Report No. 5 (Education Commission, 1992) to disestablish the colleges of education and create the Hong Kong Institute of Education. That rationale was based on the premise that the previous status of the colleges, as part of the Education Department, did not encourage the development of scholarship, which includes the capacity to engage in critical enquiry and to develop curricula based on principle, not expediency. Just as teacher educators are endeavoring to produce teachers who are able to engage in (and encourage their pupils to engage in) critical and independent enquiry, so teacher educators must themselves engage in critical enquiry and be seen to make decisions on principle rather than in response to the perennial shifts in government policy (or in the quest to maintain or extend departmental territories). In simple terms, the tensions could be expressed thus: we cannot expect student teachers to operate as critical, independent thinkers who make decisions on the basis of what is best for their pupils if teacher educators fail to display the capacity for critical and independent thinking, and if their curricula are devoid of any principles beyond that of territorial self-interest.

In the ways outlined above, teacher education institutions would begin to model many of the precepts that underlie their curriculum and thus serve to reduce the gap between what is preached and how it is experienced. It would also serve to support the worthwhile aspirations of the curriculum reforms proposed for Hong Kong.

REFERENCES

Adamson, et al. (2000). *Changing the curriculum: The impact of reform on primary schooling in Hong Kong.* Hong Kong: Hong Kong University Press.

Beck, U. (1992). *Risk society: Towards a new modernity.* London: Sage.

Bernstein, B. (1971). On the classification and framing of educational knowledge. In M. F. D. Young (Ed.), *Knowledge and control: New directions for the sociology of education.* London: Collier-Macmillan.

Curriculum Development Council (CDC). (2000, November). *Learning to learn: The way forward in curriculum development. Consultation document.* Hong Kong:

Author.

Education Commission. (1992). *Education commission report No. 5.* Hong Kong: Government Printer.

Education Commission. (2000, September). *Learning for life, learning through life.* Hong Kong: Government Printer.

Elliott, J. (1988). The state v education: The challenge for teachers. *The National Curriculum.* British Educational Research Association.

Elliot, J. (2000). Revising the national curriculum: A comment on the Secretary of State's proposals. *Education Policy, 15*(2), 247-255.

Elliot, J. (in press). Characteristics of performative cultures: Their central paradoxes and limitations as resources for educational reform. In C. Husbands (Ed.), *The Performing School.* Falmer Press.

Elliott, J. (2000). Revising the national curriculum: A comment on the Secretary of State's proposals. *J. Education Policy, 15*(2).

Elliott, R. (1973). Education and human being 1. In S. Brown (Ed.), *Philosophers Discuss Education.*

Gray, J. (1998). *False dawn: The delusions of global cagoitalism.* London: Ganta Books.

Mok, I., & Morris, P. (Forthcoming). The metamorphosis of the virtuoso. *Teaching and Teacher Education.*

Morris, P., & Sweeting, A. (Eds.). (1995). *Education and Development in East Asia.* New York: Garland.

Morris, P., Lo, M. L., & Adamson, B. (forthcoming). Improving schools in Hong Kong - Lessons for the future. In B. Adamson et al. (Eds.), *Changing the Curriculum.* Hong Kong: Hong Kong University Press.

Parlett, M., & Hamilton, D. (1976). Evaluation as illumination. In D. Tawney (Ed.), *Curriculum Evaluation Today: Trends and Implications.* London: Macmillan Education.

Peters, R. S. (1965). Education as initiation. In R. D. Archambault (Ed.), *Philosophical Analysis and Education.* New York: Humanities Press.

Peters, R. S. (1966). *Ethics and Education.* London: George Allen & Unwin.

Peters. R. S. (1973). Aims of education - A conceptual inquiry. In R. S. Peters (Ed.), *The Philosophy of Education.* Oxford: Oxford University Press.

Stenhouse, L. (1975). *An Introduction to curriculum research and development.* London: Heinemann Educational.

Sachs, J. (2000, June 24-30). A new map of the world. *The Economist,* 113-115.

Sankey, D. (2000). *Prioritising personal synoptic understanding in education.* Unpublished Ph.D. thesis, University of London, Institute of Education, London.

Chapter 7

Challenges of Contemporary Educational Reforms to Teacher Education: The Case of Hong Kong

King Chee PANG

The Office of the Directorate
The Hong Kong Institute of Education, Hong Kong

As the Government of the Hong Kong Special Administrative Region (HKSAR) considers education vital to the strategic development of HKSAR and the growth and development of its citizenry (HKSAR, 1997a, 1997b, 1998, 1999a, 1999b, and 2000), the last few years witnessed rapid changes in Hong Kong's education. Initiatives introduced by the Education Department and Education and Manpower Bureau, such as school-based management, leadership education, school-based curriculum tailoring, use of information technology (IT), quality assurance inspections, and language benchmarks, all aim at improving the quality of education in Hong Kong (see, for example, Education Department, 1997, 1998a, 1998b, 1999b; Education and Manpower Bureau, 1998a, 1998b, 1998c, 1998d). At the same time, the Board of Education, Curriculum Development Council and the Education Commission (Pang, 1999; The Board of Education, 1997; Education Commission, 2000a) have also been actively conducting reviews and making recommendations for improvements, as are evident in their various reports and consultation documents. Among all these efforts, the review conducted by the Education Commission in the last two years with final recommendations for reforming education in Hong Kong released in May 2000 (Education Commission, 2000a) is the largest and most influential, and is the most representative educational reform of the new century. This chapter will identify the critical elements of the proposed reform, analyze their challenges for teachers, and consequently examine their implications on changes in teacher education in Hong Kong. It is hoped that the case of Hong Kong will also benefit the ongoing education reforms in different parts of the world.

THE MAJOR REFORM IN EDUCATION FOR THE NEW CENTURY

After more than two years of work with two rounds of earlier consultation, the Education Commission has finalized its comprehensive reform proposal in May 2000 for final public consultation (Education Commission, 2000a). The proposal includes new aims for education in Hong Kong, and an education blueprint for the 21st century.[1]

The blueprint maps out exciting plans to improve the quality of education in Hong Kong. Emphasizing a student-centered approach and a concept of whole-person development through life-long learning, the Commission recommends a wide range of reform initiatives to create space for facilitating the teaching profession to achieve excellence and to develop students who will enjoy learning, be effective in communications, have a strong sense of commitment, and be creative in thought, expression, and action - the so-called "ECCC" as the four key strategic aims for the new century (Enjoyment of learning, Communicative abilities, Commitment and Creativity). Developing life-long learning is also a key goal.

New Aims of Education for Hong Kong

Specifically, the overall aims of education for the 21st century drawn up by the Education Commission are as follows:

> To enable every person to attain holistic and individual development in the domains of ethics, intellect, physique, social skills and aesthetics, so that he/she is capable of life-long learning, critical and exploratory thinking, innovating and adapting to changes in life; filled with self-confidence and team spirit; willing to strive incessantly for the prosperity, progress, freedom an democracy of the society, and for the future well-being of the nation and the world at large.[2]

Key Components of the Reform

To achieve the new aims of education, numerous specific reform initiatives are being drawn up. They mainly fall into six different categories referred to as six key components of the reform. The key features of each are briefly summarized, as shown in Table 1.

Table 1: *Key Components of the Reform*

Categories	Key Features
1. Reforming the curricula	• towards all-round development for lifelong learning School-based curriculum development • providing comprehensive and balanced learning experiences
2. Improving the assessment mechanism	• enhancing teaching and learning through assessment and introducing core-competency assessments • improving public examinations: contents, modes, and assessment methods
3. Removing obstacles to learning in the system	• allowing for through-road progress in basic education • reforming primary one admission and reducing drilling • reforming secondary school places allocation and eliminating the Academic Aptitude tests and the banding system to eliminate drilling and labeling
4. Removing the university admission system	• reforming the criteria for admission for positive effects to secondary education • urging universities not to over-emphasize public examinations results and considering students' overall performance
5. Increasing post-secondary learning opportunities	• increasing post-secondary learning opportunities in line with the knowledge-based society • developing a diversified education system for more generalists & specialists
6. Formulating resource strategies	• towards more effective use of resources: making better use of existing resources and identifying new resources

Key Reform Proposals for the Different Levels of School Education

Specific reform proposals are developed by the Commission for each level of education, from early childhood to higher education and continuing education. Key proposals affecting school education that have implications for the education of teachers are as shown in Table 2:

Table 2: *Key Proposals Affecting School Education*

Level/Domain of Education	Key Proposals
1. Early Childhood Education	• enhancing the professional competence of principals and teachers • improving the quality assurance mechanism • enhancing the interface between kindergarten and primary education • reforming the monitoring mechanism • promoting parent education and participation
2. Nine-year Basic Education	• reforming the school curriculum and enhancing the teaching methods for all-round, balanced, inspiring and interesting learning experiences, to cultivate basic skills and a sense of integrity and civic-mindedness (key tasks: promoting moral and civic education, reading culture, project learning and use of IT) • reforming the Primary One Admission: 85% by vicinity allocation according to school nets and parental choice (school's own selection drops from 65% to 15%) • abolishing the Academic Aptitude Tests and reducing the number of bands during the Secondary School Places Allocation • establishment of basic competency assessments in Chinese, English, and Mathematics and enhancing remedial and enhancement measures
3. Senior Secondary Education	• curriculum to provide five types of learning experiences to construct a wide knowledge base whilst allowing to choose different combinations of subjects • reviewing the desirability of moving from a "5+2" to a "3+3" secondary structure • reforming public examinations in terms of content, modes, and marking system and extending the teacher assessment scheme to other subjects, encouraging independent thinking and creativity. A core competency approach will be introduced.
4. Higher Education (reforms related to school education)	• reform of university admission to play down the emphasis on public examinations, and due consideration to be given to students' all-round performance in setting admission criteria.
5. Catering for students' diverse abilities and learning needs	• At the school level: clear policies and measures for catering for students' diverse abilities and learning needs • Promotion of integrated education • Promotion of gifted education

WHAT ARE THE MOST CRITICAL ELEMENTS OF THE REFORM?

Of the various reform initiatives in the six categories and across the various education levels described in the last section, which of them will be most critical for achieving the fundamental aims of the reform (i.e., achieving the aims of developing ECCC in students and developing a habit of life-long learning)?

In reviewing the reform initiatives in the six categories, it is obvious that many of them are related to changes in structures and systems (e.g., moving from a "5+2" secondary structure to a "3+3" structure, vicinity allocation of students to primary schools, abolishing the Academic Aptitude Test and reducing the number of bands in Secondary School Places Allocation, through-road progress in basic education and reforming university admissions. These are important for creating spaces for schools and teachers, to make it more likely for reforms in curriculum and teaching to take place effectively. However, though important and necessary, and though having become hot topics in public discussions, these are not as critical as those reform initiatives that will have direct impact on students' learning for achieving the new aims, when real impacts in classrooms and schools are considered.

Thus, from the perspective of initiatives that are critical for achieving real changes and impact in classrooms and in schools (so that students' learning are enhanced to achieve the new aims of education), reform initiatives which are directly linked to classroom and school processes are most important. An analysis of the various proposed initiatives reveals that the most critical reform initiatives for direct impact in the classroom to achieve the fundamental aims of developing ECCC and life-long learning in students mainly lie in three main areas: Reforming the Curricula; Improving Teaching and Learning; and Improving Student Assessment.

Regarding Reforming the Curricula, the essence has to do with refocusing the aims (ECCC, all round-development, and life-long learning), re-conceptualizing contents into eight new Key Learning Areas, introducing nine generic skills, focusing on developing values and attitudes, as well as emphasizing on curriculum integration (Curriculum Development Council, 2000). Regarding Improving Teaching and Learning, the essence is placing an emphasis on providing suitable learning experiences for students and on using contemporary and interactive methods. Regarding Improving Student Assessment, the focuses are on introducing core competency assessment for better understanding of the achievement of students at different levels and stages, emphasizing on the use of assessment results in improving learning of students (Assessment-based Improvement), and improving public examinations for more comprehensive and balanced assessment of students' varied achievements.

NEW CHALLENGES FOR TEACHERS

As teachers are the persons directly implementing these reforms in schools and classrooms, whether these critical reform initiatives are to be successful or not will therefore very much depend on the teachers' success in implementing the various initiatives effectively. The special requirements of the reform in the curriculum, teaching, and learning as well as assessment areas described above involve a shift in the philosophy of and attitudes towards teaching and learning, and demand special competencies. As a result, they present new challenges for teachers.[3]

Thus, for effective implementation of the reform, it will be necessary to ensure that adequate in-service education support are offered for teachers, to facilitate their understanding of the new philosophy, and development of the new attitudes, as well as mastery of the special competencies required for implementing changes in these important reform areas. Similarly, adjustment will also need to be made to the pre-service teacher education programs, so that student teachers will be adequately prepared with the special knowledge, attitudes and competencies before they join the profession. In sum, suitable teacher education for teachers on the reform from the pre-service to the in-service stages therefore becomes a most crucial factor for the success of the reform.

Apart from helping teachers appreciate the new philosophy and develop new attitudes, supporting them to develop the essential competencies is an important focus of teacher education. In order to identify the competencies required for effective implementation of the proposals in the critical reform areas of curriculum, teaching, and learning as well as assessment, an analysis of the requirements of the various reform initiatives on teachers was conducted. Then, when the key reform initiatives are classified in terms of

Reforming the Curricula, Improvement in Teaching and Learning, and Improvement in Assessment, the competencies that teachers should possess can be highlighted.

The key reform initiatives within the category of Reforming the Curricula include refocusing the aims towards ECCC, all round-development, and life-long learning; re-conceptualizing the curriculum into a new framework comprising eight new Key Learning Areas (KLAs), nine generic skills, and a focus on development of values and attitudes; emphasizing curriculum integration; flexible arrangement of time-table and learning time; and promoting school-based curriculum development to improve the design of the school curriculum. The corresponding competencies that teachers should have are in the domains of all-round development of students and balanced education (e.g., knowledge of multiple intelligences), school-based curriculum development, and understanding of the new curriculum (KLAs, generic skills, and values and moral education) and curriculum integration.

The key initiatives within the category of *improvement in teaching and learning* include promoting a new culture in teaching and learning; emphasizing the providing of suitable learning experiences for students; emphasizing the using of contemporary and interactive methods of teaching; emphasizing the use of diversified teaching and learning materials; better use of the resources in the school library and public libraries as well as the mass media including the Internet; learning beyond the confines of the classroom; developing the independent learning skills of students and encouraging sharing with peers; use of project learning; and strengthened use of IT to enhance teaching and learning effectiveness. The competency requirements of teachers identified by the author's analysis include organization of learning experiences; contemporary and interactive methods of learning and teaching; catering for diversified learning needs and mixed-ability teaching, inclusive education; preparation and use of diversified teaching and learning materials; effective use of library and community resources; teacher-parent interactions; use of IT in education; learning skills for students; and project learning.

The key initiatives within the category of improvement in assessment include introducing core competency assessment; emphasizing the use of assessment results in improving learning of students; improving public examinations for more comprehensive and balanced assessment, including extension of the teacher assessment scheme to more subjects; and adopting a diversified assessment model in school (e.g., flexible formative assessment). The corresponding competencies that teachers should have include assessment literacy, effective use of formative assessment in improving teaching and learning, and school-based teacher assessment.

Table 3 depicts the competency requirements of teachers identified by the analysis, against a summary of the key reform initiatives.

The competencies identified provide a useful list of needs of teachers which adequate teacher education support should be provided for successful implementation of the reform. They will therefore be useful for the planning of suitable in-service provisions for teachers, as well as for reviewing pre-service teacher education curricula for ensuring their essential coverage during pre-service education.

THE NEW TEACHER EDUCATION AND THE HONG KONG INSTITUTE OF EDUCATION

It is common knowledge in the field that "[W]e cannot improve the quality of education in our schools without improving the quality of the teachers in them" (The Holmes Group, 1986, p. 23) and that "[T]he quality of teachers will not be improved unless we improve the quality of their education" (p. 23). Such wisdom also applies in the case of Hong Kong. Thus, in the context of the current reform, it is particularly important for teacher education providers to offer the needed teacher education support so that the reform proposals put forward by the Education Commission can be effectuated.

Like all other universities in Hong Kong offering teacher education programs, the Hong Kong Institute of Education also has an important role and responsibility in this regard. The Institute is a tertiary institution established in 1994 under The Hong Kong Institute of Education ordinance (Cap. 444), by amalgamating and upgrading the former Northcote College of Education, Grantham College of Education, Sir Robert Black College of Education, the Hong Kong Technical Teachers' College and the Institute of Language in Education, as recommended by the Education Commission (1992). Apart from supporting the reform in various ways including participation in the relevant sub-committees for developing the reform proposals, conducting relevant researches, and participating in the reform discussions, a major role of the Institute, as a key teacher education provider, is to ensure that the pre-

Table 3: *A Summary of the Key Initiatives*

Reform initiatives	Competencies required
Reforming the Curricula Refocusing the aims towards ECCC, all round-development and life-long learning; re-conceptualizing the curriculum into a new framework comprising eight new KLAs (Key Learning Areas), nine generic skills, and a focus on development of values and attitudes; emphasizing curriculum integration; flexible arrangement of time-table and learning time; promoting school-based curriculum development to improve the design of the school curriculum	• All-round development of students and balanced education (e.g., knowledge of multiple intelligences) • School-based curriculum development • Understanding of the new curriculum (including eight KLAs, nine generic skills, and a focus on developing values and attitudes) and Curriculum integration
Improvement in Teaching and Learning Promoting a new culture in teaching and learning: emphasizing the providing of suitable learning experiences for students; emphasizing the using of contemporary and interactive methods of teaching; emphasizing the use of diversified teaching and learning materials; better use of the resources in the school library and public libraries as well as the mass media including the Internet; learning beyond the confines of the classroom; developing the independent learning skills of students and encouraging sharing with peers; use of project learning; strengthened use of IT to enhance teaching and learning effectiveness	• Organization of learning experiences • Contemporary and interactive methods of learning and teaching • Catering for diversified learning needs and mixed-ability teaching, inclusive education • Preparation and use of diversified teaching and learning materials • Effective use of library and community resources • Teacher-parent interactions • Use of IT in Education • Learning skills for students • Project learning
Improvement in Assessment Introducing core competency assessment; emphasizing the use of assessment results in improving learning of students; improving public examinations for more comprehensive and balanced assessment, including extension of the teacher assessment scheme to more subjects; adopting a diversified assessment model in school (e.g., flexible formative assessment)	• Assessment literacy • Effective use of formative assessment in improving teaching and learning • School-based teacher assessment

service teacher education programs will be fully meeting the requirements of the reform for teacher attitudes and competencies. In addition, the Institute is to offer also in-service courses covering the needs identified above so as to support serving teachers in their corresponding attitudes and competencies development.

In this regard, in the last two years, concurrent with the work of the Education Commission in developing the reform blueprint, the Institute has established its new Vision and has developed a Strategic Plan (Strategy 2000) (The Hong Kong Institute of Education, 1999) to guide the Institute in achieving the Vision in a systematic and coordinated way across all levels. It is very encouraging to note that, coincidentally, the directions of the Institute's Vision are very much in line with the key directions of the Education Commission's reform blueprint, and that three of the seven Key Results Areas of the Strategic Plan will be directly supportive of the reform.

A comparison of the key aims for education in Hong Kong put forward by the Education Commission and the key features of the Institute's Vision Statement reveals a high degree of compatibility: the key aims for education put forward by the Education Commission focus on developing enjoyment in learning, effectiveness in communications, a sense of commitment, and creativity; the Institute's Vision emphasizes "optimizing each child's potential through the shared joy of learning and teaching."

Recorded in Table 4 is a list of the strategic objectives of the seven key result areas of the Institute's Strategic Plan. It can be seen that the strategic objectives of the Key Result Areas of "Students", "Programmes," and "Scholarship" are particularly relevant to supporting the implementation of the reform.

Given the reform, the Institute will further fine-tune and align its strategies in the appropriate key result areas, especially those related to "students" and "programmes," so that the Institute will in ways that are in line with advanced practices as reported by various scholars (e.g., Bartell, 1998; Brunetti, 1998; Chin & Russell, 1996; Darling-Hammond, 1995, 1996, 1998; Jones, 1998; Knowles, 1998; Strawderman & Lindsey, 1995; Young, 1998), develop teachers who will be fully capable of implementing the new aims of ECCC and life-long learning in schools, and meeting the challenges and new demands in curriculum, teaching and learning, and assessment as identified in the last section of this chapter. In addition, through fine-tuning strategies

Table 4: *The Strategic Objectives of the Seven Key Result Areas of the Institute's Strategic Plan*

Key Result Area	Strategic Objective
Students	To develop students as knowledgeable, caring and responsible teachers committed to ongoing professional development, who are able to excite the interest of each and every one of their students and optimize their students' potential through the shared joy of learning and teaching
Programs	To upgrade all programs to university-level, to enhance their professional relevance to meet the contemporary needs of school education, and to introduce new quality programs in areas of demand unique to the position and expertise of the Institute.
Staff profile and quality	To enhance staff expertise, qualifications, skills and leadership, and to develop shared commitment and enthusiasm to achieve the vision
Scholarship	To undertake applied research and scholarship development (including teaching) to develop "research-based scholarship," especially in areas of the Institute's unique expertise and to contribute to teacher, school, and policy development in order to raise the status and quality of education in Hong Kong.
Culture	To develop an organizational environment in which students and staff exhibit a shared vision of the future, high morale, harmonious working relationship, and responsiveness to change; and to develop a quality culture and a culture of life-long learning and innovation among staff and students.
Global relationship and partnership	To develop effective partnership with schools and institutions in the HKSAR, in mainland China and in other parts of the world, blending elements of Chinese heritage with ideas and practices at the international cutting-edge to create unique expertise and an ethos that would lead to the best practices in Hong Kong.
Governance and administration	To achieve efficiency, effectiveness, quality, and equity in governance, as well as in the use of all resources employed, including manpower, financial, and physical resources, towards achieving the Institute's vision as a university-level institution.

in the "Scholarship" KRA, the Institute will also focus research on issues related to the reform and developing research-based scholarship in relevant areas for supporting the reform.

In developing the new initial teacher education degree and postgraduate diploma programs in the last two years, guided by the vision, the Institute has indeed been including elements in the new programs that are in line with the reform, and hence a review of the new programs shows that actually they have been covering the special competencies required by the reform described in the earlier section well: for example, multiple intelligences, constructivism, motivation theories, curriculum design and development (including school-based models, thematic approaches, interactive methods), supporting pupils with special needs in the regular classroom, inclusive education, personal and social education, IT in Education, and assessment and reporting of student learning (including the use of portfolio in assessment, project-learning, home-school cooperation) are all standard elements in the new programs. A systematic field experience program emphasizing on reflections and integration of theory and practice is a coherent feature of all programs to ensure effective development of competencies, an integral component well appreciated in the teacher education enterprise (Smith & Souviney, 1997; Upitis, 1999). Hence, the new pre-service teacher education programs should play a useful role in supporting the implementation of the reform through the preparation of teachers with the potentials of taking up the challenges of the reform as beginning teachers.

In the in-service area, the Institute is fully prepared to take up commissions to offer additional in-service courses on the new competencies required to support teachers in implementing the reform.

THE WAY FORWARD

In addition to the efforts of the Institute in supporting the reform, various means and strategies of support as described in the reform document are essential for success. Out of the various measures, two measures regarding teacher education will be particularly important and are discussed below.

Integrating the New In-service Needs into the In-service Ladder for the Professional Development of Teachers

As discussed earlier, a crucial factor for the success of the reform is the provision of suitable teacher education support. Whilst pre-service education could be duly aligned and fine-tuned to ensure suitably preparing teachers to acquire the fundamental competencies before entering the profession as exemplified by the case of the Institute's pre-service work above, a major task is to ensure that the large number of teachers in the profession are given due support to master the new competencies and to develop the new culture and attitudes through appropriate in-service education, with both being considered fundamentally important in the field (Arnstine, 1998; Darling-Hammond, 1996; Tatto, 1998).

In this regard, an important first step will be to integrate the new in-service education needs into the "In-service Ladder" framework (Pang, 2000) which maps out the in-service needs of teachers during the various stages of their professional career following entry, so that the needs will be appropriately covered and provided for as in-service provisions are being planned and funded.

The In-service ladder framework, which is also proposed by the author in a separate piece of work, is a two-dimensional framework that classifies teachers' in-service needs into four main types across different stages of their career. The four main types of needs are as follows:

- Induction needs: adjustment and socialization needs of beginning teachers on entry to the profession
- Updating and retraining needs: needs of teachers to be kept up-to-date with professional knowledge and skills, and to be able to implement innovations and reforms successfully
- Extension needs: needs of teachers to develop further professional competence in broadening the scope of work and contributions
- Conversion needs: new needs of teachers when taking up duties at a higher rank or of a different nature

The competencies required by the reform described in the earlier section should therefore be integrated into the "updating and retraining needs" component of the framework. These elements that should be added include the following:

- All-round development of students (e.g., knowledge of multiple intelligences and moral, values, and civic education)
- School-based curriculum development
- Key learning areas and curriculum integration

- Organizing learning experiences
- Contemporary and interactive methods
- Diversified learning needs and inclusive education
- Preparation of diversified teaching and learning materials
- Using library and community resources
- Teacher-parent interactions
- Use of IT in education
- Learning skills for students
- Project learning
- Assessment literacy
- Effective use of formative assessment for improving teaching
- School-based teacher assessment.

Supporting Teachers in Effective Implementation at the School Level: Setting up "Parachute Teams"

Though suitable pre-service and in-service education provisions are crucial to the success of implementation of changes, simply providing off-site provisions and courses are not adequate. Some recent work have shown that for reforms to be successful and effective at the school and classroom level, close and regular support to schools and teachers in the form of expert teams visiting schools on a regular basis for a long enough period of time (say one term or a year), working jointly with teachers in planning, implementing, reflecting on, and systematically improving their work will be critical (Pang, 1999). These so called "parachute teams" normally consist of curriculum development and teacher education experts, together with some experienced school teachers or principals. Apart from providing on-site collaborative and expert support, these teams can enrich the teachers' work through action research and promoting sharing of experiences among schools.

The idea of the parachute teams arises from one of the recommendations from a report on support services for schools with Academically Low Achievers (ALA) (Education Department, 1993). In this report, "Central Curriculum Development Support Teams" (the so-called "Parachute Teams") are being recommended to be set up to support these schools. These are teams of six experts including teachers of different subject background experienced in curriculum development and experts of school-based guidance and counseling set up by the Curriculum Development Institute (CDI) of the Education Department. These teams go around visiting schools on a regular basis, providing on-site support to schools in their course of tailoring the school curriculum to suit the needs of the ALA and assisting teachers to tackle problems related to guidance and counseling. Apart from working together with school teachers to provide expert support in curriculum development, these teams also provide school-based in-service education for the teachers on areas directly relevant to their identified needs. Drawing upon their experiences in working with teachers, these teams also develop curriculum models, exemplar tailored curriculum materials, diagnostic tests for students and guidelines on curriculum tailoring for distribution to other schools, as well as organize sharing functions and activities among schools with ALA. Since 1994, these teams have now served over 100 schools in Hong Kong with ALA, and have demonstrated that this kind of external expert support to schools offering direct and close curriculum development and in-service education support is a very effective form of support to ensure successful implementation of reforms. Through this work, students' learning has been improved, and they have become more active in their learning. Apart from improvements in students' learning, improvements in teachers' knowledge and skills in curriculum tailoring, resource design, teaching strategies, and teaching skills were also observed in the teachers. The teachers have also found to be more reflective in their teaching.

Educational changes and reforms could never be considered successful unless they can result in direct impact at the school and classroom level consistent with their intentions. In the past two or three decades, numerous reforms have failed to achieve their intended impacts, though significant resources have been invested. Often they fail because the reforms are too remote to the teachers, and inadequate attention has been paid to ensuring that teachers fully understand the reforms, and are supported to develop the essential knowledge, skills, and motivation for implementing them. The "Parachute Teams" of external expert support have been shown by the Hong Kong experience as serving an important function to fill this gap. Through directly working with teachers on their reform on-site, these experts not only provide direct support to teachers in their curriculum development, teaching and assessment work, but also provide a close and direct source of school-based in-service education for teachers to provide them with the necessary knowledge, skills, and motivation in carrying out the reforms. Hence, by combining curriculum development and in-service education support, these teams have shown to produce a strong effect in facilitating successful implementation of the reform.

Generalizing from the experiences and effectiveness of these "Parachute Teams", it is highly recommended that *expert consultancy support teams* are centrally set up to support schools and teachers in implementing the present educational reform.   Ideally, these teams should consist of experts in curriculum development and in-service education, plus other personnel as appropriate such as experienced teachers with experience in the area, and experts in the relevant fields.   These teams can be located in The Hong Kong Institute of Education or Faculties of Education of tertiary institutions, which can combine their work with and enhance them by relevant research.   Though these teams originate from the need to support teachers and schools in reforms related to curriculum tailoring, it is believed that such kind of close, regular on-site curriculum development and in-service education support should play a very useful role in supporting the kind of overall curriculum reform highlighted in this chapter.   It is trusted that the availability of these teams will be a critical factor for success, as teachers and schools are no longer left on their own, but are professionally supported and networked by such teams.

CONCLUDING REMARKS

Focusing on the Education Commission's reform blueprint as the key reform which will affect education in Hong Kong in the new century, this chapter has analyzed the implications of this reform on teacher education in Hong Kong, through first clarifying the most critical elements of the reform for impact in the classroom, then identifying the challenges for and consequently the new competencies required of teachers for the reform, and finally highlighting the importance of comprehensive coverage of these in pre-service and in-service provisions.   Lastly, the importance of including the new in-service needs in the "In-service ladder," as well as the importance of setting up "parachute teams," to support schools in the reform apart from adequate teacher education provisions are brought out.

The two key concepts of the present reform blueprint as advocated by the Education Commission are "creating spaces and aspiring for excellence."[4] The various structural and system reforms put forward by the Commission will hopefully create the necessary spaces for schools, students, and teachers for quality enhancement work.   Nevertheless, these efforts mainly provide a suitable context, and real quality enhancement will have to rely on the success of teachers in carrying out the reform.   In this regard, appropriate teacher education support will be the key to support teachers in their important mission of "aspiring for excellence." This case of Hong Kong that is experiencing various challenges of education reforms to teacher education would provide some insights for educators and policy-makers in different parts of the world to reshape their teacher education in the new century.

NOTES

[1]The Education Commission (2000b) eventually submitted on 28 September 2000 to the Honourable Mr. Tung Chee Hwa, Chief Executive of the HKSAR, the report on "Reform Proposals for the Education System in Hong Kong" (hereafter referred to as the Reform Proposal). The final report presents more detailed information about proposed reforms while the essence and spirit of the final report and the proposal drafted for public consultation are remarkably similar.

[2]Modified in the Reform Proposal (Education Commission, 2000b) is mainly the first clause of the overall aims of education: "To enable every person to attain all-round development in the domains of ethics, intellect, physique, social skills and aesthetics according to his/her own attributes so that he/she is capable of life-long learning, critical and exploratory thinking, innovating and adapting to change; filled with self-confidence and a team spirit; willing to put forward continuing effort for the prosperity, progress, freedom and democracy of their society, and contribute to the future well-being of the nation and the world at large" (p. 4). [Emphasis original] Moreover, the Reform Proposal also states clear the priority of the reform: "Our priority should be to enable our students to enjoy learning, enhance their effectiveness in communication and develop their creativity and sense of commitment" (p. 4). Furthermore, the Proposal delineates in detail the vision of the proposed reforms, as follows:

To achieve the aims of education for the 21st Century, the education reform must be backed up by comprehensive planning, multi-faceted coordination and participation by the whole society. We aim to realize the following vision:

- **To build a lifelong learning society:** to develop Hong Kong into a society that values lifelong learning, so that everyone enjoys learning, has the attitude and ability for lifelong learning, and has access to diverse channels and opportunities for learning.
- **To raise the overall quality of students:** to improve the overall quality of our society through upgrading the knowledge, ability and attitude of all students.
- **To construct a diverse school system:** to inject diversity in education ideologies, modes of financing and focus of curriculum, so that learners have more choices and multi-faceted talents will be nurtured.
- **To create an inspiring learning environment:** to build a learning environment

that is inspiring and conducive to the creative and exploratory spirit.

- **To acknowledge the importance of moral education:** to provide students with structured learning experiences in the areas of moral, emotional and spiritual education.
- **To develop an education system that is rich in tradition but cosmopolitan and culturally diverse:** to help students develop an international outlook so that they can learn, work and live in different cultural environments. (p. 5) [Emphasis original]

[3]Indeed, when one refers to the Reform Proposal (Education Commission, 2000b), one could note that as the Education Commission now places a premium on helping students develop all-round abilities and positive attitudes in preparation for lifelong learning: "We must provide them with comprehensive and balanced learning experiences. We propose to provide five important learning experiences, namely intellectual development, life experiences, job-related experiences, community service as well as physical and aesthetic development through reforming the curricula"; students are therefore to be provided with "comprehensive and balanced learning experiences" (p. 45). [Emphasis original]

[4]These two concepts remain the key building blocks of the Education Commission's (2000b) *Reform proposals for the education system in Hong Kong.*

REFERENCES

Arnstine, D. (1998). Two points of debate in teacher education. *Teacher Education Quarterly, 25*(4), 76-80.

Bartell, C. A. (1998). A normative vision of teacher as professional. *Teacher Education Quarterly, 25*(4), 24-30.

Brunetti, G. J. (1998). Teacher education: A look at its future. *Teacher Education Quarterly, 25*(4), 59-64.

Chin, P., & Russell, T. (1996). Reforming teacher education: Making sense of our past to inform our future. *Teacher Education Quarterly, 23*(3), 55-68.

Curriculum Development Council (2000). *Learning To Learn: The way forward in curriculum development (Consultation Document).* Hong Kong: Author.

Darling-Hammond, L. (1995). Changing conceptions of teaching and teacher development. *Teacher Education Quarterly, 22*(4), 9-26.

Darling-Hammond, L. (1996). The quiet revolution: Rethinking teacher development. *Educational Leadership, 53*(6), 4-11.

Darling-Hammond, L. (1998). Teacher learning that supports student learning. *Educational Leadership, 55*(5), 6-11.

Education and Manpower Bureau. (1998a, November). *Establishment of a general teaching council,* [Online]. Available: http://www.info.gov.hk/emb/eng/new/ gtc_table.html [2000, January 20].

Education and Manpower Bureau. (1998b, November). *Information technology for learning in a new era: Five-year strategy 1998/99 to 2002/03,* [Online]. Available: http://www.info.gov.hk/emb/eng/new/it_table.html [2000, August 14].

Education and Manpower Bureau. (1998c, July). *Outstanding teacher and school awards,* [Online]. Available: http://www.info.gov.hk/emb/eng/new/out_table.html [2000, May 15].

Education and Manpower Bureau. (1998d, May). *Review of the education-related executive and advisory bodies (consultation document),* [Online]. Available: http://www.info.gov.hk/emb/general/recent/0513.htm [2000, January 13].

Education Commission. (1992, June). *The Education Commission report no. 5,* [Online]. Available: http://www.info.gov.hk/ed/english/resource/education_ documents/download/ecr5_e.PDF [2000, October 26].

Education Commission. (2000a, May). *Education blueprint for the 21st century - review of education system: Reform proposal* [Online]. Available: http://www.e-c.edu.hk/eng/aims/index5.html [2000, October 26].

Education Commission. (2000b, September). *Reform proposals for the education system in Hong Kong* [Online]. Available: http://www.e-c.edu.hk/eng/aims/ report.html [2000, October 26].

Education Department. (1993). *Final report of the working group on support services for schools with band 5 students.* Hong Kong: Author.

Education Department. (1997, December). *Implementation of the medium of instruction policy* [Online]. Available: http://www.info.gov.hk/ed/english/school/ medium_instruction/index.htm [2000, October 26].

Education Department. (1998a, November). *An investigation into the development and implementation of the TOC initiative with special reference to professional competencies, professional devleopment and resources: Executive summary.* Hong Kong: Author.

Education Department. (1998b). *Quality assurance in school education: Performance indicators for primary school* (1st ed.). Hong Kong: Government Printer.

Education Department. (1999a, January). *An investigation into the development and implementation of the TOC initiative with special reference to professional competencies, professional devleopment and resources: Final report.* Hong Kong: Author.

Education Department. (1999b, July). *Leadership training program for principals* (consultation paper), [Online]. Available: http://www.info.gov.hk/ed/ english/resource/consultation_paper/download/prtrng_e.PDF [2000, October 26].

HKSAR. (1997a, October). *Policy address of the SAR Chief Executive* [Online]. Available: http://www.info.gov.hk/pa97/english/paindex.htm [2000, September 28].

HKSAR. (1997b, July 1). *Inaugural speech of the SAR Chief Executive* [Online]. Available: http://www.info.gov.hk/isd/speech/0701cein.htm [2000, June 10].

HKSAR. (1998, October). *Policy address of the SAR Chief Executive* [Online]. Available: http://www.info.gov.hk/pa98/english/index.htm [2000, September 28].

HKSAR. (1999a, October). *Policy address of the SAR Chief Executive* [Online]. Available: http://www.info.gov.hk/pa99/eindex.htm [2000, September 28].

HKSAR. (1999b, April). *Global tertiary education development* [Online]. Available: http://www.info.gov.hk/gia/general/199904/19/0419057.htm [2000, June 10].

HKSAR.. (2000, October). *Policy address of the SAR Chief Executive* [Online]. Available: http://www.info.gov.hk/pa00/eindex.htm [2000, October 26].

Jones, A. H. (1998). Ten points of debate in teacher education: Looking for answers to guide our future. *Teacher Education Quarterly, 25*(4), 9-15.

Knowles, J. G. (1998). Theory and practice: Expressing a seamless assumption in teacher education. *Teacher Education Quarterly, 25*(4),31-36.

Pang, K. C. (1999, December 13-16). *Challenges and strategies for effective reforms in learning, curriculum and pedagogy for the new century: A Hong Kong case.* Paper presented at the First UNESCO-ACEID International Conference, Bangkok.

Pang, K. C. (2000, 4-8 January). *In-service education ladder for teachers for the new millenium.* Paper presented at the 13th International Congress for School Effectiveness and Improvement (ICSEI 2000), Hong Kong.

Smith, J., & Souviney, R. (1997). The internship in teacher education. *Teacher Education Quarterly, 24*(2), 5-19.

Strawderman, C., & Lindsey, P. (1995). Keeping up with the times: Reform in teacher education. *Journal of Teacher Education, 46*(2), 95-100.

Tatto, M. T. (1998). The influence of teacher education on teachers' beliefs about purposes of education, roles, and practice. *Journal of Teacher Education, 49*(1), 66-77.

The Board of Education. (1997, October). *Report on review of 9-year compulsory education: Sub-committee on review of school education,* [Online]. Available: http://www.info.gov.hk/ed/english/resource/consultation_paper/index.htm [2000, October 26].

The Holmes Group. (1986). *Tomorrow's teachers.* East Lansing, MI: The Holmes Group, Inc.

The Hong Kong Institute of Education. (1999, December). *Strategy 2000: Strategic Plan for 1999-2004.* Hong Kong: Author.

Upitis, R. (1999). Teacher education reform: Putting experience first. *Teacher Education Quarterly, 26*(2), 11-20.

Young, M. (1998). Rethinking teacher education for a global future: Lessons from the English. *Journal of Education for Teaching, 24*(1), 51-62.

Chapter 8

From Government-controlled to Market-driven: The Case of Thailand's In-service Teacher Development

Kriengsak CHAREONWONGSAK

Institute of Future Studies for Development, Thailand

INTRODUCTION

Education in Thailand has a history of more than 700 years. Between 1220 and 1868, the responsibility for educating the population, from the King downwards, was the duty of the parents and monks (and for girls, their mothers and grandmothers). The year 1868 marked the ascension of King Rama V, also known as King Chulalongkorn, who initiated great reforms, including the introduction of Western-style formal education. Between 1868-1932, during the reigns of King Chulalongkorn and his successor, King Rama VI, Thailand's formal education system was founded. After that, between 1932 and 1997, Thai education moved into its modernization period (Office of the National Education Commission [ONEC], 1999a, pp. 19-24).

The year 2000 brought increased calls to transform institutions, structures, values, and relationships. Some calls promoted world-wide information technology, knowledge-based societies, democracy and human rights, advanced technology, trade liberalization, and a new economic order. Others focused on specific local demands for environmental preservation, cultural diversification and sovereignty, or equity in the work place (Chareonwongsak, 1998a, pp. 1-15). Thailand is now confronting the most drastic social changes from within and from without: the interconnectedness and complexity of the new world are rapidly changing Thailand's education system.

Thailand has realized that it is not exempt from the winds of change. Instead of being passively swept along, Thailand must respond to increasingly dominant globalization by reforming its education system (as it is broadly defined) so that its people will be able to wisely manage the changes in which they find themselves willing or unwilling participants.

Although significant effort is now being invested into educational reform, Thailand faces major problems in its in-service teacher (INSET) training programs. Thai teachers are unable to develop themselves, resulting in students who are unable to face the challenges of the new millennium. To deal with this deficiency, a more suitable INSET training and development program is required. This chapter proposes a radical shift in INSET models – from a government-initiated, government-enforced model to one which is market-initiated and directed by teacher choice – as the solution for the identified weaknesses. Using market mechanisms in teacher development processes will help prepare in-service Thai teachers for the 21st century.

A Brief History of INSET in Thailand

INSET in Thailand can be classified into five eras (Pitiyanuwat, 2000, pp. 5-7). At first, in the informal teacher education era (1857-1891), teachers were trained in the palace and the temples. There was no formal teacher education institution or curriculum. The people who taught were the parents, the monks, and the king. In this second era, teacher education focused on national reformation (1891-1912). During this period, the foundations of Thailand's earliest formal teacher educational institutions were established in Bangkok and other major cities. Teacher education for rural development was the third era (1913-1945). Between these years, teachers were trained so they could be sent to the rural areas. The next period was the teacher education for the modernization era (1945-1973) which was directly influenced by the stream of western ideologies. Between 1974-1987, the fifth era, teacher education focused on national identity formation, which later because the foundation for the education reform movement.

A significant change occurred in 1978 when the focus of Thailand's education system changed (United Nations Educational, Scientific and Cultural Organization [UNESCO], 1992, pp. 38-40). At the time, a major focus on INSET development programs was made:

- Provision of continuous in-service programs to assist teachers to identify teaching-learning problems in their own classrooms and to train them to search for solutions.
- Provision of education service centers to help teachers update themselves with the latest developments in teaching-learning practices. Resources and different kinds of activities were provided at these

centers for professional growth and to raise teacher competencies.

Current INSET Administrative Structure in Thailand

Thailand does have an extensive and often complex system of INSET training. The country has approximately 600,000 teachers, or about 1% of Thailand's population. The number and percentage of teaching staff in the 1996 academic year can be seen in Table 1.

Ninety-six percent of all teachers in Thailand are employed at the primary and secondary levels. The Ministry of Education (MOE) is the main organization overseeing the majority of INSET training and development programs. Major institutions that regulate and implement INSET training in Thailand are under the Ministry of Education.[1] The Ministry of Interior oversees educational institutes at the local level and works with the Bangkok Metropolitan Administration and the Office of the Local Education Administration (Office of the National Education Commission [ONEC], 1999a, pp. 46-50).

As well, the National Teacher Education Reform Office (TERO) was set up in 1996 to initiate non-bureaucratic teacher reform measures (TERO, 1996). TERO's projects include the National Teacher Awards, which are the highest honours awarded to teachers in Thailand, and the Master Teacher Award, which aims to encourage proficient teachers to train other teachers in their field.

However, Thailand's INSET training and development programs must be reformed. The need for a highly efficient means of nation building has brought INSET training within Thailand to the forefront of educational, political, and even economic agendas.

CRITICAL ISSUES OF THAILAND'S INSET PROGRAMS

A report released by the Ministry of Education (1996, pp. 23-24) indicates that INSET training and development programs in Thailand are neither seriously nor consistently implemented. Four years later, the Office of the National Education Commission (ONEC) released a report that concurred with the previous report: Thailand's INSET development programs were severely troubled (Pitiyanuwat, Boon-nim, Chu-cheep, Panapoonnung & Sansakorn, 1999, pp. 12-14). Both reports stated that Thai INSETs tend to have lower

Table 1: *Number and Percentage of Teaching Staff in Thailand (1996)*

Institutions	Number	%
In state-owned institutions	549,595	86.96
1. Ministry of Education	*504,834*	*79.88*
1.1 National Office of Primary Education	356,867	56.47
1.2 Department of General Education	117,545	18.60
1.3 Department of Fine Arts	1,059	0.17
1.4 Department Vocational Education	17,587	2.78
1.5 Department of Physical Education	701	0.11
1.6 The Office of Rajabhat Institutes	6,751	1.07
1.7 The Office Rajamangkala Institute of Technology	4,324	0.68
2. Ministry of Interior	*26,128*	*4.13*
2.1 Office of Education, Bangkok Metropolitan Administration (BMA)	13,065	2.07
2.2 Office of the Local Education Administration	13,063	2.07
3. Ministry of University Affairs	*18,633*	*2.95*
3.1 Universities with limited admission	17,119	2.71
3.2 Universities with unlimited admission	1,359	0.22
3.3 Universities under supervision	155	0.02
In privately-owned institutions	82,384	13.04
1. Ministry of Education	*76,267*	*12.07*
Office of Private Education		
• Secondary Education	61,826	9.78
• Vocational Education	14,441	2.29
2. Ministry of University Affairs	*6,117*	*0.97*
Private Universities	6,117	0.97
Grand total	**631,979**	**100.00**

Source: Office of Educational Policy and Planning Developing Educational System and Macro-level Planning, *Report on Educational Department (fiscal year 1996)* (Bangkok: Office of the National Education Commission, 1996). Accessed on the Internet http://tero.infonews.co.th/tre/html/body_estat11.html [November 2000].

academic competence, weaker knowledge transmission skills, and less of a sense of professionalism than teachers in other countries. Even though the Eighth National Education Development Plan (1997-2001) (ONEC, 1997) and the Master Plan for Teacher Education Reform and Educational Personnel Development (ONEC, 1995) contain policies to guide INSET training and development in Thailand, reform of teacher education and training is progressing slowly and is still far from being fully realized.

Few Incentives for Teacher Self-Development

Even though Thailand's INSET training mechanism has been in place for a number of years, it is ineffective as it fails to provide incentive for teachers to develop their abilities. Extremely low salaries in the teaching profession of Thailand cause teachers to take more interest in finding outside jobs as tutors or direct sales agents than in improving their teaching skills (Suwannavela, 1991; TERO, 1998a, pp. 61-62). For example, teachers in public schools start on a salary of 6,360 baht per month, while an engineer gets 12,000-20,000 baht, a computer engineer 11,000-18,000, and a business administrator 8,000-11,000 baht. Thai teachers do not willingly spend their time attending additional self-development programs because they do not offer direct financial benefit. Furthermore, school administrative systems do not encourage teachers to develop themselves. School administrators rarely stress the importance of training programs. They do not consider extra training in salary and promotion reviews (TERO, 1997b, p. 38; 1998a, p. 59). These conditions cause most teachers to ignore self-development and rob them of their motivation to engage in additional learning.

No Continuity

Polls conducted by ONEC and Suan-Dusit in 1997 surveyed the quality of Thai teachers and found that only 47.0% of teachers upgraded their knowledge and skills through extra training programs (Suan-Dusit Poll, 1997). These results are consistent with research conducted in 1998 by the Teacher Education Reform Office (TERO, 1998b). Results indicate that between 1995-1997, only 63.4% of the nation's 63,605 high-school teachers received extra training. If we compare this figure to the education reform guidelines published by the Ministry of Education (1995) which state that each teacher should receive additional training at least once every two years, we notice most Thai teachers lack any sort of consistent training. The main reason is due to limited funds for INSET training. During the period of the Seventh National Education Development Plan (1992-1996), the budget for INSET training amounted to only 0.2% of the total education budget or 0.02% of total teacher salaries in the national budget. This is quite low and insufficient when compared to other nations such as Denmark, which allots 2% of its budget for INSET training programs (Birkvad, 1997, pp. 611-614). Thus, in Thailand, very few training programs for INSETs are available.

Poor Quality

Thailand's INSET development programs fail to transfer the knowledge and abilities that Thai teachers require in order to participate in nation building through their teaching efforts. One critical problem in the teacher development system is the mismatch between INSET development programs and teacher needs (Pitiyanuwat, 2000, p. 10). Teacher-training curricula is noticeably irrelevant to the challenges and demands faced by INSETs. The INSET development system and methods are obsolete, inconsistent with new knowledge and teachers' real needs. Training agencies usually survey training needs by asking educational institution administrators or executives, rather than directly ask teachers who are actually doing the teaching. Moreover, it places too much emphasis on theory rather than practice (Chulawattanatol, 2000, pp. 107-108; TERO, 1998a, p. 5). The result is that the content of any training program cannot be fully applied in real working conditions. Training programs thus cause very little improvement in classroom practices. Another point is that teachers who attend development programs generally have the wrong motivation for participation. The Committee of Teacher and Educational Personnel (1990) states that most teachers engaging in INSET training do so because they want to upgrade their job ranking rather than to increase their work competencies. TERO (1997b, p. 38) indicates that some teachers attend short-term training courses offered by government organizations out of obligation rather than willingness to gain new knowledge and practices. Hence, many teachers pay little attention to INSET training programs. This causes the training programs to be ineffective.

Insufficient Evaluation of Results

TERO has identified the lack of appropriate evaluation of training programs (TERO, 1998a, p. 59). A study of secondary and high school INSET training development programs between 1978-1991 revealed that the people responsible for the programs did most of the evaluation of INSET development programs themselves (Northeast Teachers Union Commission Office, 1993). Most evaluation is pre- and post-training comparisons, showing better post-training scores. However, this method of evaluation is not beneficial because it is normal for those receiving training to have an increased amount of knowledge. Rather, the trainees' post-training classroom behavior should be monitored as the basis for judging whether the teachers profited from the training. Thailand lacks a continuous follow-up system for evaluating INSET training, especially in terms of evaluating teaching behavior in the workplace (Chulawattanatol, 2000, pp. 109-110).

Inequity

Training courses are the main format of INSET development program in Thailand. These cause teachers to take leave from their daily work for several days or several weeks at a time. However, these courses are usually feasible for only those teachers who are not actively teaching, normally teachers at the administrative level (Chulawattanatol, 2000, p. 106-107). Urban teachers, moreover, generally have better opportunities to receive INSET training than rural teachers who form the majority of Thailand's teaching force. Usually, small-school teachers have fewer opportunities to develop themselves than those from larger schools who have access to more learning materials and larger budgets. Large-school teachers find it easier to apply for study leave because of a sufficient source of substitute teachers in the cities (Boonyanan, 1996, pp. 5-6). Teachers in remote areas have fewer opportunities to upgrade their knowledge because of insufficient sources of extra training in their localities. They require longer leave periods and higher expenses to go to another city for extra studies (Tangkietwong, 1997, p. 24).

Monopoly by the Government

The major organizations which provide INSET training and development in Thailand are the Department of General Education, the Office of the Private Education Commission, the Office of the National Primary Education Commission, the Institute of Science and Technology Teaching Promotion, and the Teachers Council of Thailand Secretarial Office (ONEC, 1992). Thus, most of Thailand's INSET training is facilitated through government agencies. Private sector organizations and non-governmental organizations (NGOs) rarely contribute to teacher development. This monopoly by Thailand's bureaucracy means INSET training programs lack the competitive and quality development aspects necessary to deliver excellent INSET training. This is a critical problem that contributes to the inefficiency and ineffectiveness of INSET development in Thailand. Disadvantages of the present government-controlled teacher-training system are as follows:

- The present bureaucratic system has never implemented a serious performance review of its training staff members. Thus, there is no motivation for officials in charge of the training programs to produce excellent programs. Work by these agencies is sluggish, doing little to promote the development of INSETs.

- For the most part, teacher development policies are formulated by central government organizations without the collaboration of INSETs who understand the demands of delivering quality education. As a result, teacher development programs are unable to meet the real needs of teachers. In addition, most curricula focus on theory rather than on modifying teaching behavior through practical strategies and skills.
- The lack of competition for government monopolies controlling INSET training causes the quality of training programs to fall. Teacher development programs lack innovation and sufficient information of modern pedagogical methodology. Thus, INSET development programs are often out of date, uninspiring and irrelevant.
- Teachers have few choices for development programs. Most of the curricula are designed by teacher development organizations and lack practical value.

The monopoly condition of Thailand's INSET development programs is the major problem that induces other subsequent problems. Though Thailand has various problems in its INSET development programs, the best strategy is to cope with the main problem that directly determines the quality of INSET development programs. This paper proposes reforming present INSET training and development by introducing a proper market mechanism within Thailand's INSET training structures. It focuses on how to inject the competitive spirit into conditions of a monopoly INSET training market. The next step is to illustrate the mechanism that would achieve the essential reform required.

REPLACING MONOPOLY WITH FREE COMPETITION

Consequences of Having a Monopoly in INSET Development Programs

Monopolistic markets theoretically have a cost advantage because of the economies of scale (savings gained by producing a large amount of product) and the economies of scope (savings gained through the simultaneous production of a limited number of products and the avoidance of redundancy). However, they are inefficient for government agencies because they do not promote innovation and do not stimulate government agencies to enthusiastically seek cost-cutting measures. In the case of Thailand's INSET development, INSETs, who are the consumers of INSET training programs, have no choice of training programs and the suppliers, who are the government departments involved in INSET training services, are not motivated to develop their training programs (Baumol & Blinder, 1982, pp. 497-515; Kohler, 1992, pp. 715-739). Moreover, monopolies may result in misallocation of resources because the decisions are constrained by government considerations of the benefits and costs of INSET training to society as a whole. At times, unwise decisions may still be taken even though the benefits are less than the costs, especially if those who benefit are more politically powerful than those who pay the costs of wrong decisions and misallocation (Froyen & Greer, 1989, pp. 100-101; pp. 514-518). When this happens, an insufficient diversity of INSET opportunities and out-dated INSET development programs cannot be avoided.

This chapter regards the government-controlled teacher development program, which presently monopolizes Thailand's INSET training services, as a major hindrance to the development of competent Thai teachers. Under a monopoly, the teacher development process encounters many problems, as follows: (1) most curricula do not meet the requirements of INSETs; (2) curricula are out-dated and out of touch with current world developments; (3) teacher development lacks innovation; (4) the present training system does not offer equal opportunities for all INSETs to develop themselves; (5) officials in charge of these programs do not take their responsibilities seriously because of the bureaucratic culture; and (6) all training programs lack efficient evaluation mechanisms. Therefore, the government agencies associated with INSET training should evaluate their performance and responsibilities and decide which aspects of their involvement with INSET training should be performed on their own and which responsibilities should be given to the private sector, NGOs or to the public. Government should, by principle, be responsible for the areas for which the private sector is not interested.

Injecting Competition to Re-engineer the Government Structure

Osborne and Gaebler (1993) conclude that one of the best ways to "reinvent" the government is to inject competition into the delivery of public services. They indicate that competition causes government service providers to (1) increase efficiency in their performance by lowering costs, (2) respond rapidly to the changing demands of consumers, (3) seek new methods of satisfying their customers, and (4) try to be innovative in the way they meet customers' demands in order to gain more market share – the end-result being creative products and high-quality services. This concept can be highly useful in solving Thailand's problems in its INSET training structures. Competition could be fostered among government training institutes (for better outcomes and tighter fiscal budgets), between government and private institutes (for higher quality government administrators who can develop themselves and programs that can compete with the private sector), or even among private institutes (for more highly relevant, creative, and innovative programs).

One research report of TERO concludes that future teachers need the ability to adapt themselves to change; thus, Thailand's teacher training system must be tailored to each teacher's need. To ensure that INSETs are well prepared, any attempt to put all teachers in one standard training program, without considering the unique needs of each teacher, under a monopolistic bureaucracy could be ineffective and inefficient. The government must inject competition into INSET training programs by privatizing teacher training programs and increasing the role taken by non-government agencies. This would allow teachers more choices that would correspond to their needs. The government should allow such private training companies, NGOS, and religious organizations to administrate some INSET training. Some overseas governments have already done this by contracting teacher development projects to large private companies, religious organizations, NGOs or even to individuals (TERO, 1997a, pp. 28-29). Thailand's government must pass legislation to allow the private sector and NGOs sector to participate in development programs for INSETs. The more people who participate, the more competition there would be, and the greatest overall benefit to the teachers - the consumers.

The Functioning of Market Mechanism

The severity of problems besetting the current INSET development programs significantly hinders Thailand from producing the calibre of teachers able to carry Thailand into the next century. All policies and processes governing INSET training services must be reformed. Thus, the author proposes the introduction of market mechanisms into the present INSET training and development programs conducted by government organizations. The author projects this innovation would be fruitful: increased opportunities for teachers to gain through continuous self-development programs; an ongoing mechanism to motivate INSETs to develop themselves; more competition amongst INSET training programs, causing these programs to become more appropriate to the real needs of the teachers and to incorporate more creative innovations; and more efficient training, evaluation and development systems. The proposed market mechanism in this chapter attempts to embody these attributes.

The objective of injecting market mechanisms must involve, on the primary level, building competition into Thailand's INSET training system. This would eliminate existing monopolies in each government department that currently give teachers few INSET training program alternatives. This chapter applies an economic model to Thailand's INSET training system in which the training courses may be equated to products while each INSET may be seen as a consumer or buyer. The training provider units in each department may be compared to vendors in the marketplace.

Competition occurs when the consumers (in this context, the INSETs) are given the freedom to choose their own products (in this case, the training courses) from many vendors (in this case, the training units). This means that each INSET is given the right to study any course in which he or she is interested. Teachers can choose from any training unit, inside or outside their department, if they have enough money to pay the course fee. Another factor in the equation, the training units, will determine the courses they will offer (similar to determining which products will be sold) and the price for each course. At the same time, training units in each ministry would be required to allow teachers from other ministries to take their courses as well. When the consumers are given such complete purchasing power, this will cause each vendor to compete with the others so that the most number of clients will purchase their own products. This means that if any training units want more clients, they would have to upgrade the quality of their courses.

Applying market mechanisms to Thailand's INSET development programs according to this framework will cause the INSET training market to become more dynamic. Such dynamism can be explained by the laws of demand and supply as follows:

According to demand's law for normal goods, the demand for each type of product will have inverse relationship with the price of that product. If the price of the training course increases, the demand for that course decreases. On the other hand, if the price is lowered, this will automatically increase the demand for that training course. According to the law of supply, the quantity of a training course has a direct relationship with its price. If the course price that may be charged increases, the training units will tend to open more courses. So, the number of training courses will increase. But if the price that may be charged decreases, the quantity of courses will also decrease. Demand and supply will determine appropriate prices and quantity of training. The market equilibrium point then is the point where both demand and supply are equal. This point will not be changed until factors affecting the demand or the supply changes.

If there are any changes in market demand or market supply, market mechanisms will adjust automatically to produce a new equilibrium price and quantity of training. We can say that, if any course is needed by the market, this will cause a shift to increase demand. But if the training units cannot increase their quantity on time, market mechanisms will push prices upwards. In this case, training units can reap greater returns. Naturally, an increase in demand motivates the training units to offer more units of that training course. Then, the market supply will increase automatically. When supply increases in line with market demand, prices will not increase too much. But if the supply cannot keep up with the increase in demand, prices will increase too much and may cause INSETs to think it is not worth taking. INSETs will tend not to choose that course, thus causing the demand for that course to decrease. This will bring the price down to a suitable level.

It is obvious that market mechanisms could produce more effective and efficient management of INSET training. Any course that is not in demand will have a low price. If the training units decide that they cannot cover the costs of that training course, that training unit will automatically close the course until a new demand for it arises. Thus, training courses are offered according to real needs of INSETs and could prevent training units from offering unnecessary courses which may waste the nation's resources. This mechanism will also cause each training unit to conform its curricula and courses to modern standards and the needs of teachers. At the same time, if any course is in high demand, its price will increase. This can motivate training units to open more courses of similar nature. This then will provide more alternatives for INSETs.

Applying the market mechanism to Thailand's INSET training constitutes a shift in paradigm, from the present monopoly by authorized agencies to competition amongst the various training units. Changes to Thailand's INSET training programs as proposed by this chapter are summarized in Figure 1.

Figure 1: *A Paradigm Shift in INSET Training Program*

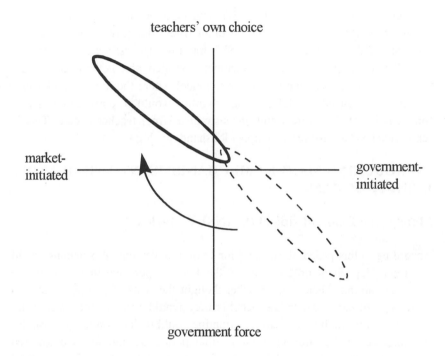

Figure 1 illustrates a paradigm shift in Thailand's INSET training programs. First, the starting point is represented on the *x axis*. At the far right – representing the present paradigm – is the "government-initiated" extreme. Here, programs desired, course content, and procedures chosen, as well as the teachers to receive INSET training, are selected by government agencies. At the extreme left – representing the proposed paradigm – is the situation where curriculum, pedagogy, participants, and other factors of learning are determined mainly by market mechanisms. The *y axis* represents the agent who drives INSET development program, whether it be official and government agencies represented by the lowermost extreme or by the teachers themselves at the uppermost extreme. "Teachers' own choice" denotes the freedom teachers have to select the topics, programs, contents, and procedures that are interesting and appropriate to themselves and their own classroom situation.

The state of Thailand's current INSET development programs is denoted by the ellipse in the lower right-hand quadrant where the government is the sole initiator and dominant force over INSET training. It is estimated that 95% of INSET training programs are government-initiated and government-driven. However, this chapter proposes a mirror model where the initiator and driver are reversed. Instead, INSET training programs would be powered by market forces as initiated by direct and unconstrained (free) teacher choice. This is represented by the ellipse in the upper left-hand quadrant.

INTRODUCING MARKET MECHANISMS INTO THAILAND'S INSET PROGRAMS

Manage the Demand-side of the INSET Market

According to this proposal, demand for INSET development programs would be largely dependent on the benefits the INSETs perceive they would gain from the training. Then, if the teacher thought the costs of gaining additional training were excessive to the benefits they would receive, they would not want the extra training. The costs of training could include travelling costs for training, lodging fee during training, time period of training, and lowered chances of promotion at work because of necessity to take leave for additional training, while the benefits include new knowledge and skills, salary and other compensations, guarantee of certificate or degree, and an opportunity for advancement in work responsibilities and remuneration.

The strategy to induce demand for INSET training is to increase the benefits gained from attending INSET development programs, while decreasing cost they have to pay. Thailand's government must enact regulations that would ensure satisfactory compensation for teachers who want to develop themselves, as explained in the following paragraphs.

Allow INSETs to Choose Training Courses by Themselves
Novick (1996) makes a strong case that professional development must not be top down but "tied directly to the daily life of classroom and grounded in the

questions and concerns of teachers." In competitive market conditions, the people who set up INSET training course content, methodologies, and duration would no longer be government officials as in the past. Instead, this responsibility would be transferred to INSETs. Under normal market conditions, the consumers – in this case, the teachers – must be given the freedom of choice. At the same time, teachers must be given the power to choose which INSET training programs they will attend.

The basic assumption held in our understanding of market mechanisms is that consumers display rational behavior: that is, they usually choose the goods and services that will give them the most satisfaction for the lowest price. INSETs will choose the courses that benefit them most and fall within their personal budget (this budget will be discussed later). Allowing INSETs to choose training courses by themselves means each teacher can study the INSET training subjects in which he/she is interested in. As a result, INSET training courses offered would more closely match each teacher's real need. This condition would cause INSETs to be eager to learn rather than being forced to learn as they presently are. Enthusiastic learners who are given interesting and relevant materials are more likely to apply what they have learned into their workplace, in this case, the classroom. Moreover, programs not chosen by teachers would not receive financial support, meaning those programs will not satisfy teacher needs. Any attempt to preserve a poorly attended INSET training program or to keep it running would be a waste of resources. Thus, it should be reasonable to cancel it. The demand-side of the market mechanism automatically identifies these programs as explained in the previous section. Introducing such consumer choice mechanisms into the INSET development paradigm would automatically introduce higher quality and better economic value for the services provided.

Pay Remuneration Based on Work Performance
Thailand's system of evaluating teacher performance must be changed. At present, teachers are ranked into nine levels. Teachers who want to be promoted must publish an academic paper. This stipulation causes many teachers to place their priorities on publishing an academic paper instead of developing their teaching competencies. Moreover, such a criterion does not guarantee that the teachers with the highest rank are the best. There is also no motivation in such a system for top-level teachers to further develop their abilities and skills. So, awarding extra financial compensation to teachers on the basis of overall competency and work performance would encourage them

to perform well after their INSET training program has finished. Because teachers attending effective training programs will likely be more competent and able to have a better performance, such an evaluation system could increase the demand for INSET development programs. Remuneration based on competency and work performance could motivate INSETs to develop themselves continuously because the more they develop, the better performance they will have at work, and the more compensation they would earn.

Establish Criteria for Work Performance

In this model, each teacher's work performance review would be used as a guideline for each INSET to select training courses that would be advantageous for his career development. Criteria for work performance is defined as the criteria used to rate each teacher's job position ranking at each level (primary, secondary, and vocational level). This set of criteria would fully encompass all dimensions related to the teaching profession. It should include knowledge criteria for both the teaching profession in general and in the specific field they teach, criteria judging their teaching skills, criteria evaluating their character, and criteria that would rate their morals and ethics.

This set of work performance criteria would differ at each level (primary, secondary, etc.) and for different teaching subject areas. Teachers in primary and secondary school would have some different criteria; as well, teachers in urban and rural areas should have a different rating scale since, in Thailand, the mission and focus of each group is certainly not the same. As well, within each level of education, there should be a number of ranks, with each level representing a stage of the teacher's professional development. Each level would be given a different remuneration package in order to motivate the individual to develop themselves in such a way that they could progress to a higher level. These criteria should be reviewed and improved every three to five years, depending on the degree of change that occurs in the working conditions and environment. Such a system would automatically force INSETs to continually develop themselves and their skills.

These criteria would function as a self-enforcing mechanism for INSET because teachers would have to choose the proper kind of INSET training courses required to meet the pre-determined criteria set by this ranking system. The ranking system would clearly outline which skills and abilities they would need at each level of the ranking system, and they could choose the appropriate courses that would enable them to gain the required skills and abilities. In other words, Thailand's INSETs would clearly know which course should be chosen to improve their skills and abilities in order to meet the pre-established standards. If any INSET is unable to meet the criteria, they would not need a supervisor to identify which areas they must develop. They would automatically know which areas were lacking, be able to search for the appropriate course to strengthen that area and, in this way, they would be able to control their own career path. So, this framework of standards and ranks would function as a framework for selecting the appropriate training course. Moreover, these criteria would also provide a guide for each teacher's career development since they could know in advance which criteria are required to gain a higher position. This would benefit INSETs, as they would know exactly which courses to take in order to gain a higher job ranking.

This measure would be even more effective if it is combined with a system of administering teaching licenses. In Thailand presently, teachers are not required to earn teaching licenses. Thus, it is difficult to control the quality of teacher performance. If teaching licenses were to be issued, we could more specifically define the standards of teacher professionalism, competency, and merit. It would also be necessary to maintain a system of continual evaluation and give provision for revoking the licenses of sub-standard teachers. The result is that there would be a demand for INSET training programs, because teachers would need to maintain a continual process of self-development in order to maintain their professional accreditation. Though the government has already taken one step towards reforming Thailand's education system by ratifying its 1999 National Education Act, implementing teaching licenses – as identified in section 53 of the Act – is still in process (ONEC, 1999b, p. 22; Pitiyanuwat, Boon-nim, Chu-cheep, Panapoonnung & Sansakorn, 1999, Chap. 4).

Conduct an Appraisal to Measure the Status of Each INSET

Though each of the INSETs may be aware of the criteria for their particular job position, they may not be able to choose courses that are suitable if they do not know their own strengths and weaknesses in relation to the criteria. Hence, in the author's INSET paradigm, each INSET would submit to a test in order to evaluate themselves. This test, which would evaluate the various criteria mentioned above, would be a useful tool in helping the teacher gain a clear, unbiased appraisal of the stage at which their teaching abilities lie. The test must conform to the normal standards of validity, reliability, and objectivity in order to determine the true current status of the INSET test takers. It would help INSETs figure out their strengths and weaknesses as well as things that they need to develop. The evaluation process should involve various participants, including INSET supervisors, subordinates, colleagues, and the teacher themselves. By doing this, the evaluation process would be more likely to reflect the exact condition of the teacher.

Conducting this self-test would help INSET know themselves better. The test would establish which information, skills, capabilities, attitudes, values, or character traits they have or lack. INSET could compare test results with the job criteria mentioned above, and know exactly "who they are" and "who they should be." Moreover, this type of test helps promote continuous development of each INSET. Each authorized agency would test their teachers on an annual basis and store the results systematically in a database. In this way, each authorized agency can monitor and evaluate each teacher's progress on a continuing basis. For better effectiveness, the test results should complement the remuneration system based on work performance, as mentioned earlier.

Allocate a Training Allowance for Each INSET
This proposed measure offers benefits to each INSET in Thailand's present education system. All INSETs who attend training courses would not pay their way, but the proposed system would see the allocation of a training budget to each teacher. Reasons for this proposal is that in Thailand's present system, some INSETs have unequal opportunities to attend development programs, especially if they have not been selected by their supervisors or their authorized agency. The author's proposed new system would ensure equity for each INSET, as each INSET would be given a sufficient personal budget to attend training courses. This budget would be granted on an annual basis and could not be redeemed for other purposes aside from training purposes.

However, in reality, Thailand's education budget is limited and different INSETs have different training needs. Hence, each teacher would require a different personal training budget in order to meet his or her individual needs. A report on INSET programs, published by the Department of General Education, discovered that the average per capita expenditure for INSET training was around 1,180 baht per annum between 1992-1996. This amount increased to 3,136 baht in 1997. However, the average of cost of an INSET training project conducted by the Office of the Private Commission between 1996 and 1997 was 1,872 baht per person. Furthermore, the average per person cost of INSET training under the Office of Secretary of the Teachers Council of Thailand in 1997 was 6,820 baht (Chulawattanatol, 2000, pp. 99-106). As a result, determining the amount of training allowance to be given to each INSET requires proper analysis and calculation of all related factors. Factors used to determine a particular INSET's training allowance must include the nation's annual education budget, the monthly salary of the teacher, the nature of their current work responsibilities, the location of their jobs and the training course as well as the cost for travelling to and from the training program.

Each INSET would be expected to use their training allowance in the most judicious way they could. They would decide which courses they wish to attend under the constraints of the allowance they receive. The INSET's decision should result from a careful consideration of both the work performance they wish to reach and their present status. If they chose to study expensive courses, they would have less training allowance to pay for other programs.

Training allowances would not be disbursed as cash in order to prevent leakage and abuse of the system. Instead, they would be given as training vouchers or an approval form which is approved by the principal or director of that teacher's school. In this way, the training units would collect their tuition fees directly from the teacher's authorized institution. Training allowances would come from the *Fund for Promotion and Development of Teachers, Faculty Staff and Educational Personal* as identified in Section 55 of the *1999 National Education Act* (ONEC, 1999b, p. 23). The fund would be earmarked specifically for INSET development, with current expenditures limited to interest earned by the fund. The fund would remain under the jurisdiction of the government although the private sector could contribute towards it. There should be a variety of endowment funds, each having a specific purpose: for example, a fund for rural teachers, a fund for teachers who work with the poor, etc.

Managing the Supply-side of INSET Market

Under normal market conditions, gaining a profit is the primary motivation for any entrepreneur. Thus, by introducing market conditions into the INSET environment, decisions made by INSET training institutes would be based on how much economic compensation they would gain at the end. INSET training institutes should thus be allowed to set their prices according to the rate of return they can get for their courses. Entrepreneurs offering INSET training would need to study consumer demand (the needs of the teachers) and extend or alter their products and services accordingly. Allowing for a larger number of INSET training providers could increase competition and result in a broader range of programs. This market mechanism could filter out ineffective training providers whose services are non-competitive. The main measures used are as follows.

Foster Healthy Competition among INSET Training Units

Training service providers would still be the existing training unit of the various government departments. Each unit would offer training courses suited to market demand. But as a change from present practices, INSETs would not be forced to receive training from their own authorized department. Teachers could select any training course in which they were interested from any department or government ministry. This would benefit the teachers as they could take courses according to their personal interests rather than according to the particular set of courses offered by their own educational authority. This would also boost efficiency as training courses in very low demand would be closed. Under the proposed new INSET training paradigm, teachers could take the courses offered by other departments if they felt that they were more beneficial to their professional development.

This system would automatically introduce competition into the INSET system through market mechanisms. When training units provide high quality, interesting courses, qualified guest lecturers, practical training methods for special classroom conditions, etc., this would attract many INSETs from other departments. And the more attendees at such courses means the more revenue a training unit would gain (details to be discussed later below). This condition would force training units in each department to compete with each other. Such competition would bring high benefits to INSETs because every training unit would be forced to improve their training content, teaching methods, and quality of their guest lecturers in order to attract more attendees. At the same time, INSETs can select the highest quality courses. Specialized courses, for example, classes on teaching techniques for science and technology, may be exceptions since it is difficult for other units without experts in that specific area to offer such Specialized courses. At the very minimum, however, this proposal would yield better results than Thailand's present monopoly system that fails to motivate the development and improvement of INSET training programs.

Also, the government must allow the private sector and non-governmental sector to participate in the INSET training market. Some business training companies, research institutes, and non-governmental organizations could potentially conduct good training programs using high-tech equipment that would greatly aid INSETs gain advanced knowledge in some specific areas of study. Moreover, the more participants in the market, the greater the competition, and the more market mechanisms will function properly.

Separate Training Units

The various units in each department must be allowed to work autonomously in order to give them more flexibility to compete. However, all must still remain a part of the government apparatus and receive an operating budget from the government. Yet, current budget levels would be reduced, so that the training units would be weaned away from their reliance on the national annual budget and instead forced to rely on income from training courses. These autonomous training units must have a management system that is not handicapped by bureaucratic procedures and regulations, particularly for their financial management. Training unit must not be required to send all of their income back to the government's Budget Bureau as they currently do. Revenue from the courses could be divided into three parts. The first part would be sent back to the Budget Bureau. This amount would be equivalent to the budget monies it had received from the government.

The residue would be divided into two parts. One part would be given to the training unit's authorized agencies and be saved in the form of a *Human Resource Development Fund* for that Department. This fund would be used for other personnel development activities for that department. This fund would motivate the government department over each training unit to support other training units as it would contribute some benefit to the department. This fund could not be redeemed for other purposes except for developing the department personnel. The amount should be determined in specific proportion, such as 20–30% of the income left after the first portion had been sent back to the Budget Bureau. The other part of the residue would be used for operating expenses for conducting training courses by the training units themselves. Since the training unit could earn and manage their own income, this would motivate training units to improve their courses in order to compete in the market. The reason is that, if it could provide better training programs, more INSETs would attend the classes, meaning a higher income for that unit.

Managing Competitive INSET Programs

This proposal for introducing market mechanisms into Thailand's INSET training market is based on the assumption that the consumers have the ability to make correct decisions and to correctly judge what is best for themselves. This rational decision would occur only when INSETs have adequate supplies of valid information. However, this assumption potentially weakens this model, especially if the consumers – the teachers – have faulty information causing them to make wrong decisions (Baumol & Blinder, 1982, p. 546). Therefore, to prevent the market failure caused by potential imperfect information dissemination, if market mechanisms are introduced, Thailand's government must assume the role of providing information to INSETs, for example, giving them lists of licensed training institutes, certified training programs and average prices of INSET programs. These details would help teachers make informed decisions.

Establish a Central Unit to Collect and Distribute Information
Before distributing information, some unit must be made responsible for collecting all information about INSET training courses that are being offered in Thailand. This process should start by commissioning a central information agency, probably the Ministry of Education, which functions as a center for collecting and organising information about every training course available being offered by each training unit. Whenever any training units offer new courses or change their curriculum, the training units would be required to send all details to the central agency. In this way, this agency could distribute up-to-date information to INSETs throughout the country and thereby help them select appropriate courses. Necessary information should be included as follows:

- name of available courses;
- name of training units who provide the service;
- course objectives;
- general content and curriculum of the course;
- target group for the course;
- training period and the dates;
- teaching methods;
- application period;
- course load limit; and
- charges and other fees

Distribute Information to INSETs

Besides the duty of collecting all information on training programs, central unit should also distribute this information to INSET. Distribution could be done on the Internet or in a newsletter. Regarding the former, the reason is that this is a cheap and efficient way to communicate to many people. Moreover, is it easy to update the information as well. So, the central information agency would have to open a website to disseminate information about courses being offered by each government, private, and non-government training unit. Each web site would include all information as mentioned in the preceding paragraph.

Regarding the latter for the teachers who live in rural areas where Internet service is not available, the central information agency should provide a newsletter to communicate detailed information about training programs and any changes in training activities, such as courses which are available or cancelled each month. Details in this newsletter would be the same as offered on the website. At the very least, these newsletters would be distributed to each administrative unit so that INSETs in each locality would be able to access that information easily.

Evaluate the Quality of Each Course

The central information agency would also evaluate the quality of each course in order to help INSETs choose the best course and stimulate the improvement of each training unit. Evaluation would be elicited from INSETs who had previously taken that course. The evaluation would be structured as follows:

- **Ranking:** Each course would be ranked according to specific criteria, for example, the quality of the course, the popularity of the course, etc. A composite index would be used to measure standards in each course and to compare the results with other courses.
- **Rating:** This would be used to evaluate the standard for each course. The results could be in the form of A, B, or C grades.
- **Evaluation materials:** Central information agency must evaluate each course by itself. The results of the evaluation process could be skewed if the training units were allowed to evaluate courses by themselves. The responsibility of the central unit is to develop evaluation materials and distribute its findings to INSETs.

Results from this evaluation would be made available on the website and newsletters.

Issuing Licenses to INSET Training Institutes
While the INSET market was being liberalized, the original government organizations controlling INSET programs must still monitor quality and strictly enforce training standards on a continuing basis. They must oversee the licensing of private and non-government institutes that want to provide INSET training and prevent below-par institutes from entering the market.

In this way, the government would assume the roles of evaluating and monitoring the performances of private training institutes and form policy for INSET programs.

All recommendations in this part are relevant to the problems of present INSET training system as discussed in the first part of the chapter.

DISCUSSION

A recapitulation of the current issues of INSET training programs as well as the recommended solutions presented in the preceding sections is presented in table 2.

The proposal to move INSET training towards greater teacher choice constitutes a radical shift in the provision of INSET training in Thailand. Other nations are recognizing the crucial role of teachers in ensuring a nation's long-term viability and comprehensive and continuous professional development – these areas are being seen as desperately required.

For example, Rönnerman (1996) discusses how the decentralization of the Swedish school system has placed a greater emphasis on teacher choice and initiative in developing INSET. In Singapore's public school system, Toh, Diong, Boo, and Chia (1996) discovered that academic qualifications and teaching experience were not interrelated with teacher professionalism, while professional development was an important determinant of teacher professionalism.

Table 2: *Current Issues of INSET Training and Recommended Solutions.*

Issues of INSET training programs	Recommended solutions Presented in this chapter
A lack of incentives for teacher self-development	• Establishing criteria for teacher's work performance • Awarding remuneration based on competency and work performance • Conducting appraisal tests to measure the status of each INSET
A lack of continuous development programs for INSETs	• Setting criteria for teacher performance • Awarding remuneration based on- competency and work performance • Conducting appraisal tests to measure the status of each INSET • Giving each INSET a training allowance
A mismatch between INSET development programs and teacher needs	• Allow INSETs to choose training courses by themselves. • Setting of criteria for teacher's work performance • Conducting the appraisal test to measure each individual INSET status • Building competition among training units
Wrong motives for participation	• Setting criteria for teacher performance • Awarding remuneration based on competency and work performance
Poor quality INSET training and development systems and methods	• Building competition among training units • Evaluating the quality of each course
Insufficient evaluation of training results	• Setting criteria for teacher performance • Conducting appraisal tests to measure the status of each INSET • Evaluating the quality of each course
Unequal opportunities to attend development programs	• Allowing INSETs to choose training courses by themselves • Allocating training allowances to each INSET
Most curricula do not meet the needs of INSETs	• Allowing INSETs to choose training courses by themselves. • Evaluating the quality of each course
Curricula are out-dated and out of touch with current world developments	• Allowing INSETs to choose training courses by themselves • Building competition among training units • Evaluating the quality of each course

On the one hand, advancing information structures demands leap across strategies in education (Chareonwongsak, 2000, p. 4). On the other hand, the realities of a flood of competitors in a liberalized market as well as the increasing gap between the "haves" and "have-nots" make the hope of catching up seem like a dream. Panic about these changes has set in as governments and educators alike recognize the importance of adapting to and indeed fully embracing the changes that are sweeping the world. In this sense, great hopes are being pinned on teachers as being key agents of the requisite changes. Governments, education systems, teachers, parents, and students will have to accommodate great change. Implications of shifting to a greater teacher-initiated and market driven INSET configuration include the following paragraphs.

Implications for Research

Much more effort would have to be invested to determine the specific mechanisms required to shift a heavily government controlled INSET training system into a teacher-choice and market-driven one. The key agenda should focus on the critical measures mentioned above, including the level of personnel development allowance given to each INSET in different positions and areas; appropriate criteria to evaluate work performance for each position; the amount of national budget allocated to each training unit; and the percentage of income that should be deposited into the Human Resource Development Fund of each ministry. As well, more research would be required on how to effectively monitor such a system and how to assign value to the knowledge and skills gained by INSET training.

Implications for Policy-making

In many countries, including Thailand, such a shift in that nation's INSET training and development system represents the equivalent of a night to day change. Policies would have to be completely reformed, not just readjusted, restored, or re-invented (Chareonwongsak, 1998b). Major shifts in policy must proceed along four initial lines. First, strong and specific policy would be required at the national level for such radical shift, in order that the necessary changes in personnel, administrative structures, and function would be achieved. Second, policy at the level of the Ministry of Education would be required to link teacher remuneration to their work performance and to skills they would gain via INSET training. Third, the departmental level would require strong policies that would guide the establishment of evaluations schemes for merit for teaching performance, merit for attending INSET training, and merit for demonstrating new knowledge and skills gained from the training program. Fourth, at the school district level, policies would have to be implemented that would create the specific mechanisms required to enable teachers in that district to have sufficient access to INSET training. For example, schools districts in the rural areas would require policies that would allow per diems for INSET training in distant locations plus provision for substitute teachers. Policy would have to be passed of which creates time for teachers to access INSET development program on a monthly, quarterly, and yearly basis. Finally, policy would have to be set on the national level that would encourage the private sector to initiate and develop appropriate INSET development programs. Policy would have to be created that would allow the creation of an ordered and progressive ranking of desired skills needed for teachers and a means of evaluating the implementation of them.

Implications for INSET Personnel Management

Remuneration and the image of teachers would change, from being underpaid civil servants to being highly educated and qualified trainers of Thailand's youth. Within Thailand, this means the governments must be prepared to triple to quadruple teacher wages within a five to ten-year span. The remuneration system would reward competent teachers with salaries commensurate with other professionals with similar professional preparation periods and responsibilities. In turn, teachers would be held fully responsible for teaching outcomes, student results on tests, school rankings in national evaluations, etc. The teaching profession would become a feasible profession for intelligent, promising students. Education faculties could rival the medical, business, and law faculties for the brightest students.

Limitations of this Model

Even though such a market mechanism would provide many benefits, there would be some shortcomings as well. For example, the products and services provided by market mechanisms might not sufficiently provide for all sectors of the market. As well, introducing competition into the market for INSET training programs may not continue to provide adequate resources in the future (Baumol & Blinder, 1982, pp. 532-548). So even though a market mechanism were to be adopted, the government would still have to play an active role in monitoring the system to ensure equity among teachers.

This model is based on three fairly substantial assumptions. First, that the government must be willing and able to display a substantially higher financial commitment to the education sector. The money the government would save in not having to directly provide INSET training would probably not cover the extra costs of creating the framework for this model: that is, significantly higher base salaries for teachers; and rewards for teachers who take advantage of INSET development program. Civil servants who are now responsible for designing and administering INSET training would presumably be needed to monitor and evaluate INSET programs and teacher performance under the new model. If the savings created by privatizing INSET would not cover provision of the second phase of this model, governments would have to be willing to provide the extra money. As is common in every country, politicians pay lip service to the centrality of education within the nation's economic welfare and future viability, but are unwilling to give education a more prominent position within the national budget. This model, however, would be unsuccessful without accompanying strong financial backing of the government.

Second, the advantage of this model is that applying market mechanisms would ensure fair reward of those who work the hardest and were most committed to embracing change. As the market system is applied to the INSET training system in Thailand, free choice, and free exchange of value-holding entities, in the case of this model – excellent teaching skills – ensure that the most worthy and most motivated teachers would be rewarded accordingly. However, despite the equity a system such as this theoretically promises, there would always be gaps, meaning some individuals would suffer injustice. For example, the growth of independent INSET providers would naturally flourish much faster within cities. Would this mean that rural teachers would be doomed to lower salaries just because they must make greater sacrifices of time and effort to attend INSET training in further away locations? As well, would such a system require older teachers to adjust to the new system as quickly as the younger teachers? Would the salaries of the older teachers suddenly be reduced because they had less stamina to attend night classes and over-the-weekend seminars? Many other issues are bound to arise through the five to ten years required to apply such a model.

Third, in many developing nations, the market mechanisms are substantially influenced by the so-called "under the table" tactics, such as bribing, offering "tea money", etc. Although corruption does exist in every nation, education in some countries is especially prone to outside influence from socially or politically powerful sources. Thus, in such countries, including Thailand, where social values turn a blind eye to such practices, applying this model would be especially tricky. This model is based on equitable evaluation of teacher performance and equitable disbursement of financial rewards. Thus, this model is driven by the assumption that teacher performance would be evaluated impartially. In countries where traditional practice would dictate otherwise, many safeguards would have to be implemented to assure teachers that this model would indeed be fair and to their best advantage. The degree to which the market system prescribed by this model is corrupted by non-market forces equals the degree to which this model would be weakened and rendered ineffective in promoting quality INSET training.

CONCLUSION

Just as societies, political systems, ways of doing business are being redefined and radically reshaped, so too education will be molded by the geothermic pressures of globalization and market liberalization. Market liberalization will inevitably have a permanent and fundamental effect on INSET training in every nation of the world.

The fact that the teaching profession was the only profession mentioned specifically in Thailand's 1997 Constitution only highlights its importance. There is recognition that the teaching profession is key to the long-term viability of the nation. This chapter proposes a way of reforming INSET development programs by introducing market mechanisms into existing government INSET programs. The author submits the idea of opening the INSET market to qualified non-government and private interests. Within the context of Thailand, the resulting increased sense of competition would help delimit and solve problems currently paralyzing efforts to develop teachers. As the 1999 National Education Act emphasizes, reforming Thailand's education system – including its INSET programs – is not an option.

NOTES

[1]They are the Department of General Education, the Office of the Private Education Commission, the Office of the National Primary Education Commission, the Teachers Council of Thailand Secretarial Office, the Department of Vocational Education, the

Office of Rajabhat Institutes, and the Office Rajamangkala Institute of Technology.

REFERENCES

Baumol, W. J., & Blinder, A. S. (1982). *Economics: Principles and Policy*. New York: Harcourt Brace Jovanovich.

Birkvad, B. (1997). Teacher professional development in Denmark. *Phi Delta Kappan, 78*(8), 611-614.

Boonyanan, C. (1996, October). *Prasittiphab krue nai prated thai: korranee suksa krue radab mattayom suksa torn plai* [Efficiency in Thai teachers: A case study of secondary teachers]. Paper presented at academic seminar on Strategic Teacher Development for the Future of Thailand. (in Thai)

Chareonwongsak, K. (1998a). *Anakot prated Thai: Moom mong darn settakit, sungkom, garnmueng* [The future of Thailand: The economic, political and social perspectives]. Lecture notes for Thai Economic, Social and Political Systems course, Siam University, Bangkok. (in Thai)

Chareonwongsak, K. (1998b, September 24-30). How should Thai people solve their problems: Restoration, reinvention, revolution or reform? *The Asian Tribune*, 7.

Chareonwongsak, K. (2000, February 15). Thai Tong Chai Yudhasart Kaokradod Song Kon Taktuang Kwamru Koo Anakot Chart [Leapacross strategy: Sending People to Gain Knowledge for the Strengthening of the Nation in the Future]. *Siamrath Newspaper*, 4. (in Thai).

Chulawattanatol, M. (2000). *Raiyngan garn weejai ekkasarn rueng nayobaiy garn phaleit lae pattana krue* [Documentary Research Report: Teacher Production and Development Policy]. Bangkok, Thailand: Office of the National Education Commission. (in Thai)

Froyen, R. T., & Greer, D. F. (1989). *Principles of Economics*. New York: Macmillan.

Kohler, H. (1992). *Economics*. Massachusetts: D.C. Health.

Ministry of Education. (1995). *Naiw tang garn phatealoop garn suksah kong krasueng suksah thee garn* [Educational Reform Guidelines of the Ministry of Education]. Bangkok: Ministry of Education. (in Thai)

Ministry of Education. (1996). *Development of education*. Paper taken from a national report presented at the 45th session of the International Conference on Education in Geneva, Bangkok.

Northeast Teacher Union Commission Office. (1993). *Garn sungkroh raiyngan garn weejai darn garn fukhua* [The Synthesis of Teacher Education Research Paper]. Khon Kan, Thailand: Department of Teacher Education. (in Thai)

Novick, R. (1996, August 27). Actual schools, possible practices: New directions in professional development. *Education Policy Analysis Archive 4*(14) [on-line],. Available: http://olam.ed.asu.edu/epaa/v4n14.html [March 2000].

Office of Educational Policy and Planning Developing Educational System and Macro-level Planning. (1996). *Report on Educational Department (fiscal year 1996)* [online]. Available: http://tero.infonews.co.th/tre/html/body_estat11.html [November 2000].

ONEC. (1992). *Phan pattana karn suksa hang chard chabab tee jed 2535-2539* [The Seventh National Education Plan 1992-1996]. Bangkok: Office of the Prime Minister. (in Thai)

ONEC. (1995). *Phan lakkarn patiroop karn fukhad krue patana krue lae bukkalakorn tang karn suksa* [The Master Plan for Teacher Education Reform and Educational Personnel Development]. Bangkok: Office of the Prime Minister. (in Thai)

ONEC. (1997). *Phan pattana karn suksa hang chard chabab tee pad 2540-2544* [The Eighth National Education Plan 1997-2001]. Bangkok: Office of the Prime Minister. (in Thai)

ONEC. (1998). *Krue naiw mai pee 2541* [New-Trend Teachers 1998]. Bangkok: Office of the Prime Minister. (in Thai)

ONEC. (1999a). *Education in Thailand 1999.* Bangkok: Office of the Prime Minister.

ONEC. (1999b). *National Education Act of B.E. 2542 (1999).* Bangkok: Seven Printing Group.

Osborne, D., & Gaebler, T. (1993). *Reinventing Government: How the Entrepreneurial Spirit is Transforming the Public Sector.* Reading, MA: Perseus.

Pitiyanuwat, S. (2000). *Kor saner cherng nayobai karn palid lae karn patana krue* [Policy Recommendation for Teacher Education and Development]. Bangkok: Office of the National Education Commission. (in Thai)

Pitiyanuwat, S., Boon-nim N., Chu-cheep, K., Panapoonnung, W., & Sansakorn, N. (1999). *Raiyngan garn veejai ekkasarn rueng baiannuyart prakorn weechacheep krue* [Documentary Research Report: Teacher Licensing]. Bangkok, Thailand: Office of the National Education Commission. (in Thai)

Rönnerman, K. (1996). Relying on teachers: A new Swedish in-service method for school development. *School Finance* [On-line]. *22*(2). Available: http://www.triangle.co.uk/bji/bji-22_2.htm#jg [March 2000].

Suan-Dusit Poll. (1997). *Garn sunruad tadsanah kathee phier raiyngan garn suksah pee 2540* [An Attitude Survey for the 1997 Education Report]. Bangkok: Rajabhat Suan-Dusit Institute. (in Thai)

Suwannavela, C. (1991). *Leur prap rabop chulalongkorn maha wittayalai?* [Reengineering Chulalongkorn University?]. Bangkok: Chulalongkorn University Press. (in Thai)

Tangkietwong, R. (1997, January 10-16). Raingan pee set jark rhonglien sue rattasapa nai tar nah tour tann prachachon. [A special report: from school to parliament as the representative]. *Nation Weekly, 240,* 24. (in Thai)

Teacher Education Reform Office. [TERO]. (1996). *Garn phateeloop garn fukhud krue: ruam kan kid bang kan tam* [Teacher education reform: Think together, do together]. Bangkok: Office of the National Education Commission. (in Thai)

TERO. (1997a). *Garn phateeloop garn fukhud krue nai tang pratedd pajjuban lae anakot: pon garn wijai jark laeng kormoon internet* [Teacher Education Reform in

Overseas Countries in the Present and the Future: A research report from the internet]. Bangkok: Office of the National Education Commission. (in Thai)

TERO. (1997b, February 20). *Raiyngan peeset jark rhonglien suerattasapa nai tarnah tourtann prachachon.* [Report from the consultative meeting to determine the Co-operation in Teacher Education Reform]. Bangkok: Office of the National Education Commission. (in Thai)

TERO. (1998a). *Khru Hang Chat 2541* [National Teacher Awards 1998]. Bangkok: Office of the National Education Commission. (in Thai)

TERO. (1998b). *Lai ngan prajumpee 2541.* [The 1998 Annual Performance Report]. Bangkok: Office of the National Education Commission. (in Thai)

TERO. (1998c). *Raiy nyan pon garn sumruad kwam thong garn garnfuk aob romm kong kru poosorn ladab mattayom ma suksah.* [Training Needs of Secondary-School Teacher in Thailand]. (survey report). Bangkok: Office of the National Education Commission. (in Thai)

The Committee of Teacher and Educational Personnel. (1990). *Ngiern kai pajjuban punha lae korsaner naie sumlab kru lae bookkalagorn tang garn suksah.* [Present Condition, Problems and Recommendation for Teacher and Education Personal]. Bangkok: Ministry of Education. (in Thai)

Toh, K., Diong, C., Boo, H., & Chia, S. (1996). Determinants of Teacher Professionalism. *School Finance,* [Online], *22*(2), Available: http://www.triangle.co.uk/bji/bji-22_2.htm#jg [March 2000].

UNESCO. (1992). *Towards Developing New Teacher Competencies in Response to Mega-Trends in Curriculum Reforms.* Bangkok: UNESCO Principal Regional Office for Asia and the Pacific.

Chapter 9

The Professional Preparation of Teachers: The Australian Experience in Establishing a Standard[1]

Barbara PRESTON[2]
Australian Council of Deans of Education
Canberra, Australian Capital Territory, Australia

In Australia in the late 1960s and early 1970s, the standard for concurrent (single award) initial teacher education moved from two years to three years for both primary and secondary teachers. There had been for a long time the pattern of a one-year graduate Diploma in Education following a relevant first degree from a university for secondary teachers and a very small number of primary teachers, but the bulk of teacher education was carried out in single purpose teachers' colleges. In 1972, the former teachers' colleges became multi-purpose Colleges of Advanced Education (CAE), a status they had generally maintained until the creation of the "unified national system of higher education" in 1989, when CAEs amalgamated with or were designated as universities.

During the 1970s the fourth year in-service Bachelor of Education (BEd) award was established, and the *ideal* standard became a three year pre-service program, followed by a period of teaching experience, then the fourth year course, usually taken on a part time basis over two or more years. This was the "3 + e + 1" model. That model is of four years in total, not three years. *In practice,* many teachers did not enroll in the fourth year course until well into their teaching careers, if at all.

Over the past two decades, the professional debate in Australia has been between the educational virtues of the "3 + e + 1" model and a four year pre-service model. At the Federal government policy level, the matter of cost has often been decisive. A failure to account for the fourth year in the "3 + e + 1" model, combined with misleading statistics on enrollments in teacher education, have often led to gross over-estimations of the cost to the government of moving to a four year pre-service standard.

This chapter will review the developments that have taken place in Australia since the 1970s to establish four years as the standard for initial teacher education and provide a rationale as to why such a standard is important for the teaching profession.

REPORTS THAT FELL ON STONY GROUND

In the mid to late 1970s, a growing interest in and concern with teacher education led to the establishment of a number of state inquiries into teacher education and the National Inquiry into Teacher Education (NITE) (Auchmuty, 1980). The inquiries were concerned with many and diverse aspects of initial teacher education and the continuing professional education of teachers. Their recommendations regarding duration were for either four years pre-service or the "3 + e + 1" model. While a minority report which supported the "3 + e + 1" model was included in the NITE report, the (majority) recommendation of the NITE report was that all pre-service courses should become four years in length (Auchmuty, 1980, p. 139).

The recommendation arose explicitly out of a consideration of "the kinds of knowledge and understanding which beginning teachers require" (p. 137), and the report went on:

> The majority of the Committee feels there is a compelling case for four years of initial education and training for *teachers of younger children*, if that period of preparation is required for prospective secondary teachers. The intellectual and other demands on teachers of younger children unquestionably are as great as those laid upon teachers of adolescents. This implies an overall consistency of approach, but not uniformity of practice in course design, provision and teaching (p. 138). (Emphasis original)

The recommendations of the State reports were mixed. Those supporting a minimum of four years pre-service education included the Victorian Asche (1980) report and the report of the South Australian Enquiry into Teacher Education (Gilding 1980).

Other reports, such as the earlier Queensland Bassett (1978) and the NSW Correy (1980) reports, supported the "3 + e + 1" model. The support was often argued cogently - for example, in the Bassett (1978) report:

> The case for requiring the student to gain teaching experience before

undertaking the final year of the course we regard as compelling. While we recognize that much can be done during a course of teacher education to encourage students to relate practice and theory, we believe that it is when they come to grips with the practical problems of teaching as teachers that they can gain most from pedagogical theory and the background disciplines on which it rests. From the examination that we have made of existing three-year courses, it is clear that these courses attempt to do too much, and would be even more overloaded if they attempted to cover the broader range of general and professional knowledge that teachers now need, as well as giving them a reasonably comprehensive grasp of basic pedagogical skills.

It is for these reasons that we consider that the fourth year leading to degree level should be a requirement for all as an integral part of a teacher's preparation. We have recommended accordingly.

We stress, however, that we do not wish to see the diploma course extended by a year before the teacher is employed, since clearly there are diminished returns if a course of teacher education is lengthened without the benefit of professional experience [of at least one year]. (p. 29)

These issues of the relationships between "theory and practice" and the "overloading" of the pre-service program will be returned to later.

While teacher education institutions took up many of the matters discussed and recommended on in the 1978 - 81 reports, there was little happening at the Federal government policy level. As the Federal government controlled the funding, structure, and length of initial teacher education, it was able to ensure that few graduates of three year programs could proceed directly to a fourth year and that new four year programs were very difficult to introduce. Certainly there was no support for movement towards a general four-year pre-service standard or for other recommendations which required Federal government decision and financial support.

The re-allocation of higher education resources *away* from teacher education was a major aspect of the Federal government's higher education policy in the early 1980s. The October 1979 brief to councils of the Tertiary Education Commission (TEC) had included the requirement regarding teacher education that funding be reduced by 1984 to "approximately 30% below the provided in 1978" (TEC, 1981, p. 3). Amendments to the States Grants (Tertiary Education Assistance) Amendment Act (No. 2) in 1979 provided the TEC with the discretion to "disapprove" (thus denying Federal funds) certain "new teaching developments," including "The lengthening of a course leading to a professional/vocational qualification" (TEC, 1981, p. 7-8). The February 1981 *Report for the 1982 - 84 Triennium* of TEC included as Appendix H "The Commission's Response to the National Inquiry into Teacher Education" (TEC, 1981, p. 102-109). It had been forwarded to the Minister in December 1980 and was unequivocal in rejecting the NITE recommendation for four years of pre-service teacher education, based largely on cost considerations (TEC, 1981, p. 105).

The tone of the whole eight page TEC response to NITE was of weary dismissiveness. NITE was also an obstacle in the way of the TEC's preferred directions for higher education. In its main report, the TEC (1981) commented:

> The Commission is . . . concerned that the [NITE] Report may encourage State
> authorities and other interested parties to plead for delay in implementing plans
> for the reallocation of resources in higher education from teacher education to
> such fields as commerce, computing, applied science and technology. (p. 24)

The Federal government's Review of Commonwealth Functions (RCF) reported in April 1981. To support the policy of moving resources out of teacher education, it proposed the closure or amalgamation of all 30 CAEs that were primarily concerned with teacher education. Such a move was given support by a teacher surplus in the early 1980s after the severe shortages of the early and mid-1970s. The surplus was a result of a complex conjunction of factors, many associated with the economic slowdown of the time - in particular a sharp reduction in the rate of improvement in pupil-teacher ratios in schools, and a sharp reduction in teacher resignation rates. The number of commencing students in initial teacher education had already begun reducing by the late 1970s (Preston, 1997, p. 11-12).

The NITE and State reports' positive enthusiasm for improvements and innovation in teacher education fell on the barren ground of Federal policy of retrenchment in teacher education.

HIATUS AND RECONSIDERATION

In 1983 the Federal Minister for Education requested the Commonwealth Schools Commission and the Commonwealth TEC to jointly review the Commonwealth's roles and responsibilities in teacher education. The Schools

Commission began a substantial, consultative review of in-service education. The TEC did little about pre-service. After an interim report released in early 1985, a Joint Committee was set up in March 1985 to move the project along with better consultation between the two commissions. The commissions reported in August 1986 in *Improving Teacher Education: Report of the Joint Review of Teacher Education* (Commonwealth Tertiary Education Commission and Commonwealth Schools Commission [CTEC/CSE], 1986).

Improving Teacher Education discussed the length and structure of initial teacher education. It recommended the continuation of the "3 + e + 1" model for primary teacher education. The reasons given were contradictory. On the one hand, it was argued that the model was educationally superior to a four-year course while, on the other hand, it was argued that the model was cheaper for the Commonwealth than a four year course. Yet, they were adamant that the fourth year should be completed "without undue delay" (CTEC/CSC, 1986, p. 31).

The recommended "3 + e + 1" is only cheaper to any significant extent if a high proportion of graduates of the initial three year course never enroll in the fourth year. If that is the case, the claimed educational advantage cannot be realized. This failure to account for the fourth year BEd when considering the cost implications of options for length and structure of initial teacher education has been common in the Australian education policy debate.

The Board of Teacher Education in Queensland drew on the Bassett report (1978) and *Improving Teacher Education* in its consideration of length and structure of initial teacher education in its report, *Project 21: Teachers for the Twenty-first Century* (Queensland Board of Teacher Education, 1987). The Board noted that it "... holds firmly the view that the minimum period of tertiary study included in the initial professional preparation of teachers should be at least four years" but it did not support a fourth year of pre-service education. (Queensland Board of Teacher Education, 1987, p. 108).

In the late 1980s, length of programs had become a sensitive matter at the Federal level as the government maintained its policy position of no increase in length on the ground of cost – grounds which were to over-ride other considerations.

The 1988/89 Discipline Review of Teacher Education in Mathematics and

Science (Speedy 1989) worked within the three year limit for early childhood and primary pre-service teacher education. However, the recommendations for minimum allocations of time to mathematics and science in early childhood and primary teacher education programs (Speedy, 1989, p. 19, 22-23, 38-39) were difficult to meet within a three year program unless other important aspects of courses are eliminated.

The Schools Council (1989) was carrying out at the same time a consultative study into "teacher quality." The report of the early stages of that study, *Teacher Quality: An Issues Paper,* indicated that "the Schools Council believed that sooner or later four-year training must be a necessary minimum for the great majority of teachers" (p. 21). However, in the preceding paragraph, the cost of moving to a four year standard for all initial teacher education had been over-estimated by a factor of about ten. The estimated cost was about $105 million, compared with the $14 million indicated by the Australian Education Council working party on teacher education, chaired by Dr. Fred Ebbeck (National Board of Employment, Education and Training [NBEET], 1990a, p. 47), as well as a similar estimate made independently at about the same time by the Australian Teachers (now Education) Union (Australian Teachers Union 1990). It appears that the Schools Council counted as three year Diploma in Teaching (or equivalent) commencing students all students commencing diploma or bachelor courses in Education (including four year concurrent courses and the in-service fourth year BEd), and did not take into account the cost of the fourth year of the "3 + e + 1" model. The Council suggested that "more data be gathered on the costs of moving to four year training for all teachers and on a scaled implementation related to the supply and demand situation" (NBEET, 1990a, p. x). There was discussion in the chapter of the issues of improvement of the school-based aspects of initial teacher education through internships, and the importance of collaboration between stakeholders in teacher education.

The Australian Education Council working party on teacher education took up a very broad brief of initial and in-service teacher education and national recognition of teacher qualifications in its consultations and deliberations in late 1989 and early 1990. The working party developed a preferred model for initial teacher education which involved a three year course followed by a two year part time course during which the student/beginning teacher would be on a 0.5 teaching load (NBEET, 1990a). The model was controversial and received little support. Those who did support it generally recognized its practical difficulties, but emphasized the value of its principles of partnerships between the stakeholders in initial teacher education and substantial school-based teacher education.

In 1990 the National Board of Employment Education and Training (NBEET) prepared an analysis and synthesis of the Schools Council's *Teacher Quality*, the report of the Discipline Review of Teacher Education in Mathematics and Science and the report of the AEC working party on teacher education. That report, *The Shape of Teacher Education: Some Proposals* (NBEET, 1990b), considered the issues of the quality of pre-service education and its relation to length and content, the structure of pre-service education, financing practicum supervision, induction, a national professional body for teachers, in-service education, and co-operative arrangements. The report outlined some positions in relation to length, including the following claim:

> There is little, if any, demonstrable benefit to be gained from four years of pre-service training, especially if it is more of the same; an appropriate range of diversity exists at present to cater for different needs; and present arrangements are proving to be reasonably cost effective. (NBEET, 1990b, p. 5)

The "proposals" relating to length were as follows:

1. Minimum length of basic preparation be at least a three-year degree meeting the agreed national criteria for such awards.

2. That a degree or other qualification acceptable to any State or Territory . . . be acceptable in any other State or Territory.

3. Extensions of basic preparation be undertaken on the basis of an agreement between the higher education institution, the employing authority/ies, the Commonwealth and other appropriate parties, such as the teachers professional body or union.

4. These extensions should be through integrated programs of employment, study and structured training designed jointly by higher education institutions and the employing authority/ies.

5. Higher education institutions and employers should improve the quality of teacher education courses in the areas of content, prerequisites, course standards and employer involvement in course delivery.

6. Employers to indicate to higher education institutions any perceived difficulties to their courses of teacher training. (NBEET, 1990b, p. 6-7)

In the late 1980s, the Higher Education Council of the National Board of Employment, Education and Training was investigating course length and nomenclature in higher education courses. One of the controversial areas was course length of pre-service teacher education. The Council suggested in its discussion paper, *Course Length and Nomenclature* (Higher Education Council, 1989), that a three year degree (not diploma) be the standard award for primary and early childhood education, rejecting any move to a four year program as too expensive (p. 7-8). The Council apparently did not consider the fourth year of the "3 + e + 1" model as part of the "standard" or as a factor in the estimation of cost. "For the sake of consistency," the Council suggested that the four year BEd for preparing secondary teachers be replaced by a three year BTeach followed by a diploma in a subject area (p. 8). The Council, reflecting the Government's view, was concerned that an increase in length on one professional field may "flow-on" to other fields. In response, the Australian Teachers Union and others pointed out that for teachers the standard was a four year program - either four years pre-service or the "3 + e + 1" model - and thus there would not be a logic of "flow-on" if the final year of the latter model was brought forward to pre-service.

THE END OF TIGHT FEDERAL GOVERNMENT CONTROL

The Higher Education Council's final report on the issues of course length and nomenclature (and incorporating investigations into graduate studies), entitled *Higher Education Courses and Graduate Studies* (Higher Education Council, 1990), was less specific on most matters than the discussion paper. There was a general statement of reluctance to support any lengthening of professional courses on the grounds of cost and "flow-on" (p. 12), suggesting that any lengthening should only occur with the agreement of all stakeholders (Higher Education Council, 1990, p. 14).

The change between the discussion paper and the final report in part reflected a change in the administration of Federal funding of universities. In 1989, single line operating grants for universities were introduced, and the Federal government no longer had a direct input regarding such matters as the length of pre-service professional programs. Such matters were now to be broadly discussed during the annual "profiles rounds" negotiations between universities, government officers and the Higher Education Council. This general regime of Federal funding of universities has continued in operation, allowing changes in course length and structure to be negotiated (within institutions, as well as between institutions and the government). Lengthening of pre-service teacher education courses has often occurred with a reduction in intakes, so that the total student load of the four year program would approximate that of the three year program. The fourth year BEd has often not entered the equation and has continued as an in-service program. Lengthening of courses has not involved paid "employment" or "professional work" as recommended in *The Shape of Teacher Education (NBEET, 1990b)* and *Higher Education Courses and Graduate Studies* (Higher Education Council, 1990, p. 14) respectively. However, the longer courses often allow time for more extended field experience and, in some cases, this has been associated with formal agreements between universities, school authorities, and teacher unions covering such matters as supervision and the responsibilities of student teachers.

In the early 1990s, around two third of students commencing initial primary and early childhood teacher education throughout Australia were enrolled in three year programs, though many would continue on to a fourth year BEd program on completion of the three year program.

By the mid-1990s, it was clear that four years was developing as the almost universal standard for initial teacher education. Yet, in its 1996 report, *Professional Education and Credentialism*, the Higher Education Council (1996) appeared to repeat the errors of the Schools Council in its costings for "moving to the new models" of pre-service teacher education. The cost of moving to a four year undergraduate pre-service teacher education model was calculated to be $42.8 million (p. 49), based on the assumption that "[T]he current intakes and total enrollment in undergraduate teaching courses are 14,758 and 35,909 EFTSU respectively" (Higher Education Council, 1996, p. 49). Yet, at the time there would have been fewer than 5,000 students commencing three year programs in Australia, many of whom would proceed directly to a fourth year (estimated from Table 1, Preston, 1994, p. 8), and in total there were about 14,000 students commencing all initial teacher education courses including graduate Diploma in Education, and not double counting three year BTeach commencements and one year BEd commencements. The Higher Education Council apparently used flawed government statistics, and included many one year, fourth year BEd courses, as well as some Diploma in

Education courses, as "undergraduate teaching courses," and did not take account of existing four year programs. On the Higher Education Council's assumptions, but with more accurate mid-1990s enrollment data, the cost estimate would be in the order of $3 million.

Thus, in 1996, while in practice four year (minimum) pre-service programs were becoming almost universal, the policy debate within the Federal government assumed it was a long and expensive way off.

AUSTRALIAN DEVELOPMENTS IN AN INTERNATIONAL CONTEXT

Teacher education has been fairly high on the international policy agenda since the mid-1980s as debates around the "quality of teachers/teaching" and "teacher professionalism" developed. Australia has been influenced by, and in turn has sometimes influenced, international developments in teacher education.

In the early 1980s in the USA, the focus was on school reform concerned with standardization and testing. Yet the debate changed in the mid 1980s, with a series of reports which focused on the quality of teaching and teacher education. The most significant of these were the National Commission for Excellence in Teacher Education (1985), the Holmes Group (1986), and the Carnegie Forum on Education and the Economy Task Force on Teaching as a Profession (1986).

The National Commission for Excellence in Teacher Education, which was sponsored by the American Association of Colleges of Teacher Education and with members from school authorities, state and national government, school boards, universities/ colleges, and teacher unions, included detailed consideration of many qualitative aspects of initial teacher education. Regarding length, the unanimous Commission position was for at least a (four year) bachelor's degree, with strong support for at least an additional year. A group of nine of the 17 commissioners were less equivocal, stating the following:

> We believe that the kind of teacher education program proposed by the Commission cannot take place within the usual four year baccalaureate. A minimum of four years should be devoted to the liberal arts component; a minimum of five years to the total program. (National Commission for

Excellence in Teacher Education, 1985, p. 15)

The Holmes Group (1986) was also unequivocal at the time in their advocacy of a five year initial teacher education standard for "Professional Teachers" (p. 75). In the following years, however, problems in moving to five year programs (from four year programs) became apparent, and this reform lost priority (Fullan et al., 1998, p. 50).

Initial teacher education in the USA was, and continues to be, generally of at least four years duration, and carried out in universities or colleges with formal approval from the states. The exceptions are emergency licensing in various forms in response to teacher shortages.

The Organization for Economic Co-operation and Development (OECD) Education Committee Working Party on "The Condition of Teaching" was established in 1986, and its work culminated in the report, *The Teacher Today* (OECD, 1990). That report noted the move in many OECD countries from two to three years of initial primary teacher education in the 1970s and early 1980s. The discussion in the report implied that at least four years of initial teacher education study might be necessary. The importance of a substantial grounding in "content" and the practical/pedagogical/professional aspects of teaching was noted, "[T]eachers need a repertoire of teaching strategies that are embedded deeply in content areas" (p. 83). There was also an indication that the specialist skills of primary teachers are equivalent to those of secondary teachers. In more recent OECD education reports (*Quality in Teaching* [OECD, 1994] and *Educational Research and Development: Trends, Issues and Challenges* [OECD, 1995]) arguments and recommendations have a bearing on the length and structure of initial teacher education, and they are considered later in this chapter.

The 1994 edition of the *International Encyclopaedia of Education* noted that "[T]he worldwide trend is towards requiring a minimum of a bachelor's degree for programs to prepare teachers," and that in 1988 Taiwan increased its minimum requirement for primary teachers from two to four years (Gimmestad & Hall, 1994, p. 5997). In 1989, France undertook a restructuring of initial teacher education with prospective teachers completing an undergraduate degree then undertaking a "highly selective" two year graduate program (National Commission on Teaching and America's Future [NCTAF], 1996, p. 33). Five years of pre-service teacher education is required of German primary school teachers (Teaching and teacher development abroad, 1998). A survey of Asia-Pacific Economic Cooperation members (Cobb et al., 1995) found a "common trend . . . toward more extensive preparation for teachers - especially elementary teachers."

WHY IS THE LENGTH OF PREPARATION SO CRUCIAL? SOME PERSPECTIVES FROM RESEARCH

There is scant Australian empirical research comparing the outcomes of pre-service teacher education programs of varying length. There has been research in Australia on issues such as beginning teachers' views about their pre-service teacher education. However, even though respondents often included a mix of those who had completed three year and four year programs (e.g., the often-cited Batten et al., 1991), those results have seldom been reported. Findings of a survey involving 1,322 teachers in their second year of teaching in New South Wales were reported in Hatton et al. (1991). Of the primary teachers who had undertaken a four year, integrated program, 80 per cent saw themselves as "fairly" or "very well" prepared for their initial appointment (mostly in difficult-to-staff schools) by their pre-service teacher education course. Only 65 per cent of those who had undertaken a three year course so considered themselves. The score for one year graduate Diploma Education was much lower. The findings for secondary teachers with three compared with four years of pre-service teacher education were not reported though there were substantial numbers involved. Hatton et al. (1991) concluded:

> The ratings indicate that a four year degree program, with carefully sequenced experience spread over a long period of time, is judged a more adequate preparation. There are also more opportunities for growth, integration, and reflection upon experience than can be incorporated into [a shorter course]. (p. 4)

The relevant research from the USA generally compares four year graduates (who have completed an undergraduate teacher education program) with graduates of five year programs. It also compares teachers without some key aspect of initial teacher education with those fully eligible for a teaching license (four or more year qualification). For example, Fullan et al. (1998) note that "[T]here is evidence of the benefits of extended programs in terms of placement and retention of new teachers, as well as teaching performance and professional commitment as perceived by graduates, principals and supervisors" (p. 14-15).

The National Commission on Teaching and America's Future, in *Doing What Matters Most* (NCTAF, 1997), reports:

> Research confirms that teacher knowledge of subject matter, student learning and development, and teaching methods are all important elements of teacher effectiveness. Reviews of more than two hundred studies contradict the long-standing myths that "anyone can teach" and that "teachers are born and not made." This research also makes it clear that teachers need to know much more than the subject matter they teach. Teacher education, it turns out, matters a great deal. In fields ranging from mathematics and science to early childhood, elementary, vocational and gifted education, teachers who are fully prepared and certified in both their discipline and in education are more highly rated and are more successful with students than are teachers without preparation, and those with greater training in learning, child development, teaching methods, and curriculum are found to be more effective than those with less.

> Not only does teacher education matter, but more teacher education appears to be better than less - particularly when in includes carefully planned clinical experiences that are interwoven with coursework on learning and teaching. Recent studies of redesigned teacher education programs - those that offer a five-year program including an extended internship - find their graduates are more successful and more likely to enter and remain in teaching than graduates of traditional undergraduate programs. (p. 10)

The report provides extensive data and references to support it conclusions.

Mark Fetler (1997) reviewed the literature and carried out empirical research in California on the correlations between initial teacher education (generally bachelor's only, compared with a full five year program) and student drop-outs (early school leavers), teacher resignations, and other factors. He referred to findings that "[T]eachers with regular state certification receive higher supervisor ratings and student achievement than teachers who do not meet standards [are not fully qualified]. Teachers without preparation have trouble anticipating and overcoming barriers to student learning, and are likely to have low expectations for low-income children" (p. 4-5). Moreover, Fetler found from his own research that "[T]he smaller the percent [in a school] of teachers with only a bachelor's degree, the lower the dropout rate. This influence appears to hold independently of poverty, and school size, and location" (p. 10).

The brief account of some research findings and authoritative reviews indicates that the length of initial teacher education can make a significant difference.

TEACHERS' WORK

In the following section of this chapter, an analysis of what is expected of teachers will be followed by a consideration of the implications of this for the length and structure of initial teacher education, taking account of common and alternative practices in the deployment of beginning teachers.

What Is Expected of Teachers

The effective work of teachers is deeply professional in that it requires constant situational judgements which draw on high level competencies - complex and dynamic combinations of knowledge, values, and skills, as well as personal dispositions, sensitivities, and capabilities (Preston & Kennedy, 1995, p. 39). It is collective and strategic professional work in the sense that the core outcome - the education of students - occurs through the work of many teachers (and others) over many years, and optimal outcomes require complementarity of the work of those teachers (and others) over time and space. This is very different from some other professional work where the core activity is a discrete interaction between the professional and client.

Quality teachers' work in schools has always been thus - to some degree. But there have been developments in recent years, which add to the complexity and responsibility of teachers' work. These developments cover *who* should be taught, *what* should be taught, and *how* teaching is best done.

The change in the dominant thinking about *who* should be taught was discussed in the Schools Council's (1990) *Australia's Teachers: Agenda for the Next Decade*, where it was put simply as an "increasing tendency for the teaching workforce to become teachers of all rather than instructors of the able" (p. 29). This focus on teachers' professional responsibility to all students, not just the "already taught" or "easily teachable," places *teaching* at the center of teachers' professional work. It means that teaching must vary according to particular students in particular circumstances, rather than expecting students to respond to a standardized presentation of content. Thus, a responsibility for all students implies an on-going need for high level professional judgements, rather than the routine application of methods and materials developed elsewhere. It requires deep knowledge of learners: background knowledge about learning differences, difficulties and disabilities and about cultures and communities, It requires the capacity to learn about the individual students and their communities in every new situation. And it requires the "pedagogical content knowledge" to transform and adapt content knowledge to each particular student or group of students. Being "teachers of all" also implies a responsibility and a consistent and ethical commitment to all students and their communities.

Changes in *what* should be taught are most striking in the incorporation of the "key competencies" (or similar) into the school curriculum. The key competencies highlighted in recent Australian literature are seven: collecting, analyzing and organizing information; communicating ideas and information; planning and organizing activities; working with others and in teams; using mathematical ideas and techniques; solving problems; and using technology.

Some of these may have been part of the curriculum in some way for a long time. What is new is the explicit, integrated approach, which is having an effect across the curriculum at all levels.

Changes in *what* is being taught also include an emphasis on content, which differs from that of the past. All teachers, at the secondary as well as primary level, have a responsibility to teach literacy and numeracy - to all students. All teachers also have responsibilities in areas such as Indigenous education - teaching Indigenous students, and teaching all students Indigenous studies. Primary teachers have responsibilities, which they cannot evade, across the key learning areas, though provision of specialist teachers differs between schools and systems.

The nature of the key competencies is such that central attention must be given to *how* teaching is done, and the appropriate pedagogy may be very different from traditional practices. Teachers need to work together in flexible new ways. The responsibility to teach all students means that pedagogy needs to be sensitive and responsive to individual needs. New technology can significantly change many aspects of teachers' work. Teachers not only need to know how to use the technology in their teaching and other professional work, but be able to make the judgements about its optimal use - how and when it should be used. They also need to be able to teach students its optimal use. The teachers and their students also need the understanding and skills to take advantage of other new or advanced technology as it becomes available.

Structure of Initial Teacher Education

The previous sections of this chapter have put the argument for substantial initial preparation of teachers based on the knowledge and capabilities required for effective beginning teaching and a potentially successful teaching career. Much of this was agreed by the advocates of the "3 + e + 1" model of initial teacher education in the late 1970s and 1980s. Certainly the case for even more substantial initial teacher education is stronger now, but the arguments for "3 + e + 1" still need to be addressed because of the influence they have held in policy circles.

There are two pragmatic issues, and the substantive, pedagogical comparison between the ideal "3 + e + 1" model and four years of pre-service teacher education. The pragmatic issues are, first, whether the "3 + e + 1" model ever existed in practice for substantial numbers of students/teachers and, second, the effect on the quality of education for school students of the "3 + e + 1" model as compared with the effect of a four year pre-service model.

In practice, it appears that the ideal "3 + e + 1" model usually ends up as a simple three year initial teacher education model. There is much evidence for this. Firstly, it appears that many teachers with three year qualifications have not enrolled in the fourth year program. Commencing student numbers in the fourth year BEd appear to have been less than half the commencing numbers in three year programs some years earlier (poor DEET [1991; 1992]/ DEETYA [1997] statistics make only rough estimates possible). Secondly, ending (or lowering) the "three year barrier," which prevented movement to the top of the salary incremental scale and promotion for teachers with only three year qualifications, was a major industrial issue for teachers in most jurisdictions in the late 1980s and early 1990s. Thirdly, if the fourth year is taken up, it is usually quite a few years after the pre-service program. Enrolment statistics for 1990 support this. In that year, more than 70 per cent of students commencing a three year pre-service primary teacher education program were under 20 years of age (through the 1980s it is likely that a higher proportion of commencing students were under 20), while almost half of those commencing a "post-initial" bachelor's in primary education were 30 or over, and many of the younger ones may have enrolled in the course directly after completing the three year program. Finally, the *in-service* fourth year BEd has been seldom systematically related to an initial three year program or the early period of the teachers' professional practice - it has been a genuine continuing professional education program involving updating, enriching, and further developing professional knowledge and competence, rather than a completion of the initial phase of professional preparation. In short, all this is evidence that, while "3 + e + 1" was a serious contender in the policy debates, it has not really existed in practice.

The second pragmatic matter is the quality of education provided to school students by the "3 + e + 1" model, even assuming that the program does exist in the ideal form of completion of the fourth year within about five years of initial employment as a teacher. Current practices of teacher employment around Australia (and internationally) tend to place beginning teachers in difficult and demanding situations - often casual or short term employment, or in the hard-to-staff schools which experienced teachers do not find desirable because of geographic remoteness, the inherent difficulty, or low status of teaching in such schools. These beginning teachers tend to seek, and obtain, transfers out of these schools after several years - before they would be expected to have completed the fourth year of an ideal "3 + e + 1" model. Students who are disadvantaged in the schooling system in various ways - low income communities and low resource schools, geographic isolation, and so on - are disproportionately taught by beginning teachers in these harder-to-staff schools. The schools of the educationally and socially advantaged (such as high fee nongovernment schools) tend to employ teachers with proven experience and full qualifications. Thus, the competence of teachers during the "experience" period of the "3 + e + 1" model is crucial in terms of the quality of teaching for those students who are already likely to be disadvantaged; yet, by definition, the teachers are not fully prepared because they have not completed the final phase of their initial teacher education. The likely much lower quality of education for any school students taught by teachers before they have completed the fourth year is a major argument against the "3 + e + 1" or any three year pre-service model. While there is always room for improvement in the deployment, support and supervision of beginning teachers, it is administratively very difficult to ensure that school students are in no way disadvantaged by a "3 + e + 1" or other three year pre-service model of initial teacher education.

The substantive arguments related to the quality of initial teacher education for and against "3 + e + 1" as compared with four years pre-service must take account of the assumed, existing, and possible pedagogical and curriculum practices in initial teacher education programs, as well as the intended outcomes of those programs. In brief, supporters of "3 + e + 1" generally believe that there are marginal diminishing returns in adding more content to courses - the three year courses are already "overloaded" with content which the students have difficulty coming to grips with in the absence of sustained practical experience. There is also the argument that much of the content considered necessary at one time would be redundant and replaced with new knowledge or issues in the future. From this perspective, the curriculum in the first higher education phase of the course is an aggregation of units or subjects, with no particular coherence or deep structure. In particular, most of the units are not integrated with the practical field experience, and have a traditional "academic," unpractical and "theoretical" orientation. Field experience in this pre-service phase is primarily to ensure survival in the early period of teaching, providing only "basic pedagogical skills." It is the comprehensive teaching experience of the beginning teacher that would provide the basis for the "fusion of context and content." After a year or more teaching, the fourth year program would bring it all together. In the traditional "3 + e + 1" model, the three phases of the program are distinctly serial, discrete in time.

The next step then is to bring the fourth year into the initial sustained experience period, but not changing the first three years. As noted earlier, this is the proposal of the 1986 *Improving Teacher Education Report*, and there are similarities with the preferred option of the 1990 Australian Education Council working party on teacher education (NBEET, 1990a). A further step is to connect the fourth year to the pre-service program (to consider it a "course lengthening"), putting a condition on such course lengthening that it could only occur if there is "an integrated program of professional work and further study" developed within the framework of a partnership between universities, school authorities, and the teaching profession (e.g., Higher Education Council, 1990; NBEET, 1990b). This model still leaves the first three years of the program untouched.

Some of those developing and implementing initial teacher education programs through the period to the early 1990s (for example, drawing from Dewey [1916]) did seek coherence and integration. However, in the early 1990s, the principles of coherence and integration, especially the deep integration of "theory" and "practice" and integration of generic understandings and specific instances, have become widespread and explicit. The basis of that coherence and integration is a vision of teachers as committed, effective practitioners (as highly professional in the sorts of ways outlined earlier), not individuals who "know" an aggregation of matters, and have a collection of skills not particularly connected with the more significant things that they "know." The new course objectives tend to focus on the development of effective practitioners, deriving the curriculum and pedagogy of the course explicitly from a practical understanding of how that development could best be achieved in the context of the university, the student teachers, and the situations in which the graduates are likely to find themselves as beginning teachers. This contrasts with the older models of course objectives which listed specific material to be covered - almost as an end in itself. There is also the application of constructivist or similar learning theories. In the new courses there is a range of perspectives or philosophies involved, incorporating notions and practices of active learning, contextual learning, group learning, inquiry and reflection and, in some cases, the application of professional competency standards or problem-based approaches (see, e.g., Beattie, 1997; Crawford & Deer, 1993; Hager, 1996; Marland, 1993; Preston & Kennedy, 1995). The overall model for such courses is developmentally integrated. For example, Hager (1996) describes a three level course structure where "Each of the levels is to be thought of as *nested in*, and as a prerequisite for, the next level" (p. 241). (Emphasis added) "Nested in" implies a different relationship between elements than the strictly serial structure of the "3 + e + 1" model and its successors.

The integration of specific instances (such as understanding the circumstances and learning needs and styles of students from a particular recent refugee ethnic group) with generic understandings (notions of diversity of students and their communities) in the context of generic capabilities (developing relationships with students and parents) helps overcome the problem of the "overloaded curriculum." Understanding and being able to take action in relation to specific cases is part of developing the broader understandings and capabilities, which are necessary for effectively responding to new specific instances in the future.

Coherence and integration, especially in the context of the common practices of deployment of beginning teachers in Australia, entail the completion of the initial pre-service program before commencing responsible professional practice. It has now been generally accepted, at least by the profession, that at least four academic years is necessary for an adequate preparation for employment as a teacher. Quality induction, support, and continuing professional education are still necessary for the novice beginning practitioner, however well prepared, to develop full professional expertise, but that is another issue.

CONCLUSION

Pre-service teacher education has moved to a general (but not yet universal) four year standard in the face of indifference, even hostility, from successive Federal governments and authorities and some school authorities. Yet, it is clear from international benchmarks, research outcomes, the changing nature of teachers' work, and developments in the pedagogy and curriculum of initial professional education that this is the preferred direction. The report of the federally-funded, collaborative project, the National Standards and Guidelines for Initial Teacher Education (Adey, 1998), provides a comprehensive set of recommendations that could see national accreditation and standards as a key platform for developments in the future. While it has not received sustained attention, the report remains a potentially valuable resource for Australia and elsewhere. The lessons from the review outlined here are clear: if gains are to be made in improving teacher education, the commitment and leadership of teacher educators are essential; so are the involvement of other stakeholders and a supportive policy environment.

NOTES

[1]This chapter is adapted from "How Long Does It Take for the Professional Preparation of a Teacher? The Australian Experience in Establishing a Standard" published in Issue 2 of Volume I of the *Asia-Pacific Journal of Teacher Education and Development*.

[2]Barbara Preston is a private educational consultant who is also the Executive Officer of the Australian Council of Deans of Education. She has worked on in the areas of teacher competencies and teacher supply and demand in recent times and is a regular contributor to academic debates concerned with teacher education in Australia.

REFERENCES

Adey, K. L. (Chair). (1998). *Preparing a profession* (Report of the National Standards and Guidelines for Initial Teacher Education Project). Canberra: Australian Council of Deans of Education.

Asche, A. (Chair). (1980). *Teacher education in Victoria*. Melbourne: Victorian

Government Printer.

Auchmuty, J. J. (Chair). (1980). *Report of the National Inquiry into Teacher Education.* Canberra: AGPS.

Australian Teachers Union. (1990). *Response to the Higher Education Council discussion paper, 'Course length and nomenclature'.* Melbourne: Author.

Bassett, G. W. (Chair). (1978). *Teacher education in Queensland* (Report of the Committee appointed by the Board of Advanced Education and the Board of Teacher Education to advise on desirable developments in teacher education in Queensland). Brisbane: BTE.

Batten, M. et al. (1991). *Recently recruited teachers: Their views and experiences of preservice education, professional development and teaching.* Canberra: AGPS.

Beattie, M. (1997). Fostering reflective practice in teacher education: Inquiry as a framework for the construction of a professional knowledge in teaching. *Asia-Pacific Journal of Teacher Education, 25*(2), 111-128.

Carnegie Forum on Education and the Economy Task Force on Teaching as a Profession. (1986). *A nation prepared: Teachers for the twenty-first century.* New York: Carnegie Commission on the Improvement of Teaching.

Cobb, V. L. et al. (1995). Teacher preparation and professional development in APEC members: A comparative study. *APEC Education Forum* [On-line]. Avaliable: http://inet.ed.gov/offices/OUS/ APEC/ef9.html [Accessed 1998, April 13].

Commonwealth Tertiary Education Commission and Commonwealth Schools Commission (CTEC/CSC). (1986). *Improving teacher education: Report of the Joint Review of Teacher Education.* Canberra: AGPS.

Correy, P. M. (Chair). (1980). *Teachers for tomorrow* (Report of the Committee to Examine Teacher Education in NSW). Sydney: NSW Government Printer.

Crawford, K., & Deer, C. E. (1993). Do we practice what we preach?: Putting policy into practice in teacher education. *South Pacific Journal of Teacher Education, 21*(3), 109-121.

DEET. (1991). *Selected higher education statistics 1991.* Canberra: Author.

DEET. (1992). *Departmental discussion paper on teacher education.* Canberra: Author.

DEETYA. (1997). *Selected higher education student statistics 1991.* Canberra: Author.

Dewey, J. (1916). *Democracy and education.* New York: Macmillan.

Fetler, M. (1997). Staffing up and dropping out: Unintended consequences of high demand for teachers. *Education Policy Analysis Archives* [On-line serial], *5*(16). Available: http://olam.ed.asu.edu/epaa/

Fullan, M., Galluzzo, Morris, & Watson, N. (1998). *The rise and stall of teacher education reform.* Washington: American Association of Colleges for Teacher Education.

Gilding, K. R. (Chair). (1980). *Report of the South Australian Enquiry into Teacher Education.* Adelaide: South Australian Government Printer.

Gimmestad, M. J., & Hall, G. E. (1994). Teacher education programs: Structure. In T. Husen & T. N. Postlethwaite (Eds.), *The international encyclopaedia of education* (2nd ed.). Oxford: Pergamon.

Hager, P. (1996). Professional practice in education: research and issues. *Australian Journal of Education, 40*(3), 235-248.

Hatton, N. G. et al. (1991). School staffing and the quality of education: Teacher stability and mobility. *Teaching and Teacher Education, 7*(3), 279-293.

Higher Education Council (1996) *Professional education and credentialism*. Canberra: AGPS.

Higher Education Council. (1989). *Course length and nomenclature: A discussion paper*. Canberra: AGPS.

Higher Education Council. (1990). *Higher education courses and graduate studies*. Canberra: AGPS.

Holmes Group. (1986). *Tomorrow's teachers: A report of the Holmes Group East Lansing*. Michigan: Author.

Marland, P. W. (1993). Review of the literature on implications of teacher thinking research for preservice teacher education. *South Pacific Journal of Teacher Education, 21*(1), 51-63.

NBEET. (1990a). *Teacher education in Australia* (Commissioned Report No. 6). Canberra: AGPS.

NBEET. (1990b). *The shape of teacher education: Some proposals*. Canberra: AGPS.

National Commission for Excellence in Teacher Education. (1985). *A call for change in teacher education*. Washington, DC: American Association of Colleges of Teacher Education.

NCTAF. (1996). *What matters most: Teaching for America's future*. New York: Author.

NCTAF. (1997). *Doing what matters most: Investing in quality teaching*. New York: Author.

OECD. (1990). *The teacher today: Tasks, conditions, policies*. Paris: Author.

OECD. (1994). *Quality in teaching*. Paris: Author.

OECD. (1995). *Educational research and development: Trends, issues and challenges*. Paris: Author.

Preston, B. (1994). *Length of initial teacher education: The debate and the reality* (A report to the Australian Council of Deans of Education). Canberra: Australian Council of Deans of Education.

Preston, B. (1997). *Teacher supply and demand to 2003: Projections, implications and issues*. Canberra: Australian Council of Deans of Education.

Preston, B., & Kennedy, K. (1995). The national competency framework for beginning teaching: A radical approach to initial teacher education?. *The Australian Educational Researcher, 22*(2), 27-62.

Queensland Board of Teacher Education. (1987). *Project 21: Teachers for the twenty-first century*. Brisbane: Board of Teacher Education.

Report of the Review of Commonwealth Functions (RCF). (1981). Canberra: AGPS.

Schools Council. (1989). *Teacher quality: An issues paper*. Canberra: AGPS.

Schools Council. (1990). *Australia's teachers: An agenda for the next decade*. Paper prepared by the Schools Council for the National Board of Employment, Education and Training. Canberra: AGPS.

Speedy, G. (Chair). (1989). *Discipline review of teacher education in mathematics and science* (Report). Canberra: AGPS.

Teaching and teacher development abroad. (1998). In *National Commission on Teaching and America's Future* [On-line]. Avaliable: http://www.tc.columbia.edu/%7Eacademic/ncrest/teachcom/home.htm [Accessed

1998, April 9].

Tertiary Education Commission. (1981). *Report for the 1982 - 84 triennium*. Canberra: AGPS.

Chapter 10

The Changing Face of Initial Secondary Teacher Education in England (1984-1998)[1]

Richard APLIN
School of Education
University of Leicester, United Kingdom

The established picture of initial secondary teacher education until 1984 in England (Scotland, Wales and Northern Ireland are outside the purview of this account) was straightforward and apparently secure. Qualification was open only to graduates, and most entrants chose to follow a route which involved the study of a specialist subject at the degree level, usually BA or BSc, followed by a one-year teacher training course leading to the award of the Postgraduate Certificate of Education (PGCE). A substantial minority entered the training system to work for a four-year graduate qualification (BEd) which combined study of one or more specialist subjects with concurrent work on pedagogy and educational studies. Training took place in universities, polytechnics, colleges of education, or institutes of higher education, with block periods of teaching practice located in schools which had a connection with the higher education establishment. In both cases, the standards of entry and exit to courses, the content and mode of provision and the arrangements for practical work in schools were within the power of the universities or the Council for National Academic Awards (CNAA) which awarded or validated the certification. Qualified Teacher Status was awarded by the Secretary of State to all those who had been certificated at the completion of their training. Apart from an insistence that all entrants had to hold GCE Ordinary level passes in English Language and Mathematics, and an overall control of numbers of students recruited by the calculation of student quotas, there was little overt interference in the operation of the system from the central government. Her Majesty's Inspectors (HMI) could visit and inspect public sector institutions, but the results of such visits were not available to others. HMI could only visit universities by invitation.

When the Conservative government led by Margaret Thatcher was first elected in 1979, it became clear that it intended to recast radically the role of the public services, specifically with regard to the notion of "value for money," and opening them up to market forces. By the period of its second term, it was experienced, and successful, in taking on what it saw as powerful interests and, in retrospect it is hardly surprising that the turn of teacher training was to come. What is curious is that the world of higher education seemed to be taken by surprise. Yet, there had been no shortage of debate about the perceived shortcomings of the existing provision. There had been four publications from the Department of Education and Science (DES) alone in the years leading up to 1984, which alluded to problems of content and approach (DES, 1980, 1981, 1982, 1983).

CIRCULAR 3/84: ESTABLISHING A NATIONAL MODEL

Nevertheless, when in 1984, Circular 3/84 was published (Department of Education and Science/Welsh Office [DES/WO], 1984), it was as if the extension on centralized power it heralded was an intolerable and unwarranted invasion of higher education autonomy. With the advantage of hindsight, the requirements it laid down seem fairly mild - certainly in comparison to the regimentation incorporated in the Education Reform Act of 1988, which laid down the schools' National Curriculum, or to the later circulars which are referred to below. But the shock to the higher education world reverberated much more deeply than the detail of its content perhaps warranted.

The Circular announced the setting up of a single council - the Council for the Accreditation of Teacher Education (CATE) - to advise on the approval of teacher education courses in both the university and public sectors. CATE had, as its first task, to review all existing approved courses and then to scrutinize proposals for new ones. Training courses were to be reassessed at regular intervals. This marks the beginning of a national systematic review process whereby training for teaching was to be subject to a more overt level of government supervision, albeit through a quango.

The membership of CATE was to be representative of "experienced professionals with a broad knowledge of the best practice in teacher education" (DES/WO, 1984, para. 5). These would be mainly practicing school teachers, teacher trainers and elected members and officers of local education authorities, who would be personally invited to serve by the Secretary of State, Sir Keith (later Lord) Joseph, a right-wing member of the cabinet and strong proponent of the market. The voice of the wider educational world (both practitioners and employing bodies) was thereby to be heard within any advice which was to be given to the government about pre-service teacher training. But in practice, the membership did not represent any of the professional bodies which would have been able to speak authoritatively about teacher education (Edwards, 1992).

In addition to their usual and continuing program of visits to teacher training institutions (and still, in the case of universities, by invitation), HMI would make available to CATE their knowledge of the institutions. The significance of this was to make more overt the role of the inspectorate in the process of systematic review.

Each course had to have the support of a local committee, which again would have representation from local education authorities, practicing teachers, and individuals outside the education service.

Such a neutral description of the new regime created under CATE existence should not obscure the assault on freedom which was felt by universities, despite its first chairman, Sir William Taylor, having had a distinguished history within university education departments. "CATE was an instrument of government interference in the erstwhile autonomy of university departments" (Pring, 1996, p. 13). What was happening was that the radical Conservative policy of breaking down consensus, and replacing it with specific agenda-driven policies and formalized bodies to implement, monitor, and report was beginning to hit teacher education (and thus university autonomy) as it had already in other areas of public expenditure (Broadfoot, 1986).

It was the introduction of explicit criteria for course approval, which had the most radical effect on the teacher training community, as the specification annexed to Circular 3/84, now seen as relatively benign in comparison with the detail of later circulars' demands, established the precedent of an overt set of factors which would dominate much of the development in teacher education over the following 14 years. The interference with autonomy which Pring (1996) had noted could also be claimed to be an instrument in guaranteeing quality. This is how the government preferred to portray it, and their perspective also reflected the desire to see "value for money." By laying down basic criteria, it would be possible to make judgements about how courses conformed with them, and to identify and investigate any apparent shortcomings.

There were a number of structural requirements. PGCE courses would have to be no shorter than 36 weeks in duration. Courses would have to "be developed and run in close working partnership with ... schools." Experienced teachers from schools should have "an influential role in the assessment of students' practical assessment," and should be "involved in the training of the students within the institutions. The staff of training institutions who are concerned with pedagogy should have school teaching experience ... [and] should have enjoyed recent success as teachers of the age range to which their training courses [were] directed and should maintain regular and frequent experience of classroom teaching" (DES/WO, 1984, annex). There were specifications of minimum periods of time to be devoted to subject studies in the case of BEd courses. Institutions were exhorted to relate the degree content of PGCE students to the school curriculum. Emphasis was to be placed on practical experience of teaching methodologies. There was advice about the required procedures for recruiting to courses. This list is by no means exhaustive, but is indicative of the style of content and approach of the Circular's demands.

Many aspects of the criteria were uncontroversial. Some had fundamental implications for the way in which courses operated. Although these features might not have been prominent in the wording or even implementation of Circular 3/84, they were to be built upon in the later circulars. Thus, the notion of working in partnership with schools and the involvement of HMI in a systematic review of courses would become key features of developments in the 1990s.

Institutions had of course been working with schools, since there had been pre-service teacher education which involved placements in schools. But the nature of such working arrangements was locally determined, and the extent to which consultation took place between the partners varied widely. In many cases, the contact was purely administrative, relating to the logistical arrangements about placements. Anything beyond that was generally of an informal nature, and was determined by the working practice of individual tutors rather than a systematized institutional policy. There already existed some more developed forms of partnership between the higher education institution and schools. Leicester, Oxford, and Sussex Universities, among others, had schemes whose features fitted in part or in whole the new exhortation.

But in most cases, the new requirement that practicing teachers in secondary schools were to make a contribution to selection, training, and assessment was a major and significant move away from a situation in which they were participating recipients of guidance from the training institutions. The use of the word "partnership" was problematic, as there was a wide range of interpretations of the term, which gave rise to a similarly wide range of potential misunderstandings. A similar set of ambiguities was to arise later by the use in different educational contexts of the word "standards."

Some saw the new prescription to be an opportunity for developing a more far-reaching model than the government had probably intended, and in which the profession (both at higher education level and in the schools) could retain the initiative. The Oxford Internship scheme (Benton, 1990) is such a response. Harry Judge, the then Director of the Department of Educational Studies at Oxford, grasped the opportunity to set in place a school-based training scheme, operated in full partnership between skilled practitioners in schools and university tutors, but fully grounded in a long and considered history of research into teacher education with an international dimension (Judge, 1990; Judge, Lemosse, Paine, & Sedlak, 1994). At Leicester, a team of tutors and teachers formulated a more equal partnership between the university and schools, with the particular objective of there being benefits to both (Everton & White, 1992).

One of the aspects of CATE's operation was the publication of CATENOTEs which gave guidance to teacher training institutions about how the criteria listed in the annex to Circular 3/84 were to be implemented. CATENOTE 4, for example, focused on the setting up of partnerships, and the opportunities which would be necessary for trainers to have recent and relevant teaching experience. The content indicates that some fairly fundamental change was sought in some institutions:

> Students' teaching practice and school experience are likely to be less valuable where a tutor in charge of school practice does little more than to write to a number of schools asking how many students they will take and in what subjects, and where the schools selected receive students mainly because they have expressed willingness - or it is their turn - to do so.... The material provided for schools ... needs thorough discussion in advance with those teachers who will be working with the students. (CATE, 1986, para. 8)

Paragraph 16 of the same document refers to the different roles of the partners, identifying "a spirit of partnership through which both trainers and teachers can make their own contributions towards a shared professional objective" (CATE, 1986).

One effect of the move to partnerships as defined in Circular 3/84, and as required for course approval, was a debate both locally and nationally about such shared objectives and about the roles and responsibilities which contributing members of partnerships should exercise. A substantial literature has since evolved in which the nature of partnership in teacher education is explored, and which has tended to reflect the specific pressures from the centre experienced by institutions at any one time (inter alia, Barker, Brooks, March, & Swatton, 1994; Benton, 1990; Bines & Welton, 1995; Everton & White, 1992; Furlong, Hirst, Pocklington, & Miles, 1988; Griffiths & Owen, 1995; McCulloch & Fidler, 1994; Williams, 1994, 1995).

Because of the practical focus, which was required under the new criteria, training institutions found it difficult to retain in their pre-service programs coverage of the foundation subjects of history, philosophy, sociology and psychology. The 1980s saw these disciplines broadly fall out of the initial teacher training curriculum.

Thus, by 1991 (halfway through the time-span which is the subject of this review), the picture of pre-service secondary teacher education had moved quite substantially from that which obtained in 1984. All approved courses had to be provided through higher education-school partnerships; serving practitioners from schools were involved in a number of different ways with the provision of the training; the bias of the work was quite firmly towards a practical, subject methodology orientation; and the sector was, grudgingly perhaps in some cases, becoming attuned to a regime of review which also included the participation of HMI on a systematic basis. Despite the extent of the changes, teacher training was still relatively stable as a field of activity and, although the character of course provision had altered, there were few who argued against the broad direction of the developments.

CIRCULAR 9/92: A STRONGER DIRECTION FROM THE CENTER

The period of 1992 to 1998 was very different since the publication of Circular 9/92. Wilkin (1999) has described Circular 3/84 as "mild-mannered ... with relatively cautious aims" (p. 9). By 1999, however, in view of the implementation of Circular 9/92, she asserts that the government, "[I]n the tradition of its predecessors, is maintaining a seriously repressive regime." How does this apparent contradiction occur?

Some of the answers can be found in the second stage of the implementation of the Conservatives' radical agenda. Market forces cannot be said to have figured very strongly in Circular 3/84. In Circular 9/92 (Department for Education/Welsh Office [DfE/WO], 1992), they substantially change the nature of relationships within partnerships and between institutions. This was not a document which reflected a professional agenda, but was clearly heavily influenced by the right-wing groupings which had been stridently stating their agenda through a series of pamphlets and an effective lobbying of the mass media.

As an example of the stance taken by such groups, such statements as "[D]espite the intentions of government reforms, the training discourages good candidates from entering the profession and undermines the standards of those who do" (Lawlor, 1990, p. 7), "[T]eaching theory has subverted teaching practice" (DfE/WO, 1992, p. 22) and "[T]he bright graduate ... will be put off teaching by the emphases on the psychological and sociological side issues" (DfE/WO, 1992, p. 40) typify the slant which was used to attack teacher training, as well as the inaccurate basis for the attack. After all, side issues or not, the possibility of encountering psychology or sociology as part of teacher training had all but disappeared by 1990. The power of such attacks and the ascendancy of the new right in much of the government's policy-making cannot be overstated, although many of the claims were based entirely on ignorance. One of the calls was for "on the job training." Lawlor claims that it "would improve the quality of applicant teachers and encourage good qualified graduates to enter the profession" (DfE/WO, 1992, p. 38).

Indeed, two "on the job" routeways towards QTS had been announced in 1989. One was the Licensed Teacher Scheme, by which a person could be employed as a teacher, and with an individually designed two-year training program, could be licensed to teach while being trained, and paid a salary on the unqualified teacher scale. The other was the Articled Teacher Scheme, by which the trainee would not be employed, but would work in a school for two years and be in receipt of a bursary, and would undergo a training program. Schools were able to buy training from higher education institutions to supplement their own training of the licensees or articled teachers.

The number of takers was never high for these two schemes, which tended to respond to the needs of mature students who were unable, for financial or residential reasons, to enrol on a full-time course, and were more attractive to schools in such areas as London where recruitment to teaching was traditionally problematic. In the first year of operation, 175 secondary schools were involved in the Licensed Teacher Scheme (Barrett & Galvin, 1993). By July 1992, about 500 had obtained qualified status through this route, although this figure includes both primary and secondary phases (Office for Standards in Education [Ofsted], 1993).

The principal routeway for secondary teachers remained the PGCE. HMI reported in 1991 that, although the schools' participation in training could, in the right circumstances, be beneficial to teachers and students, there were certain practical problems to be overcome before there could be a general increase in the involvement of schools. These related to resourcing, training for the trainers, selection of trainers and of suitable schools, and a recognition that the prime purpose of schools is to teach pupils (DES/WO, 1991).

ORGANIZATIONAL IMPLICATIONS OF CIRCULAR 9/92

The principal differences introduced by Circular 9/92 which affected the climate within which partnerships operated were the issue of resources and the specification of the balance between institutions. The introduction to the Circular was quite clear about the principles which led the new criteria and procedures:

1. schools should play a much larger part in ITT as full partners of higher education institutions (HEIs);

2. the accreditation criteria for ITT courses should require HEIs, schools and students to focus on the competencies of teaching; and

3. institutions, rather than individual courses, should be accredited for ITT. (DfE/WO, 1992, p. 1)

The right-wing fantasy of higher education institutions being repositories of impractical theorists undermining graduates' determination to teach had found a ready ear. The reforms of 1984 were clearly too soft and ineffective. Even CATE was seen to be too closely connected to the tainted providers, although it was by no means independent of political influence before then (Landman & Ozga, 1995). Circular 9/92 tightened its terms of references and methods of working. There would be the possibility of suspension or withdrawal of accreditation from institutions which did not conform to the new criteria. The requirement for local committees was withdrawn.

The language and tone of Circular 9/92 were markedly different from those of Circular 3/84. As Landman and Ozga (1995) note, "[A]t this time the Secretary of State was a high-profile politician who had already taken on the health service professions" (p. 34). The new document was much more detailed and resembled more a manual of instructions than a general policy directive.

Within partnerships, "[S]chools will have a leading responsibility for training students to teach their specialist subjects, to assess pupils and to manage classes; and for supervising students and assessing their competence in these respects." Moreover, "HEIs will be responsible for ensuring that courses meet the requirements for academic validation, presenting courses for accreditation, awarding qualifications to successful students, and arranging student placements in more than one school" (ibid., para. 14). To ensure that there was no evasion of this specified nature of the partnerships, the minimum time that students would spend in schools was laid down as 24 weeks. No argument was advanced for this number, just as the 36 week total in Circular 3/84 was specified without supporting argument, but the neatness of a 60%-40% split was doubtless very attractive to those calculating proportional responsibility.

The assessment of candidates for qualified teacher status was to be based on a set of "competencies" specified in the Circular. The nature of these was sometimes practical: for example, "[N]ewly qualified teachers should be able to employ a range of teaching strategies appropriate to the age, ability and attainment level of pupils" (ibid., annex A). The nature was sometimes broader: for example, "[N]ewly qualified teachers should have acquired in initial training the necessary foundation to develop an understanding of the school as an institution and its place within the community" (ibid., annex A). The Circular was careful to state that the competencies were not a statement of a syllabus. Yet, it was clear that the first moves towards a nationally imposed program of content were in place.

The resources issue was the one which caused the most overt problems over the next few years. HMI had already noted that, if schools were to offer more, they should be properly resourced (DES/WO, 1991). The government's adoption of market forces as being a determining factor in the success of public ventures as well as commercial ones - for example, the internal market within the National Health Service - and its belief in the merits of the enterprise culture and competition as the prime factor in raising standards of all kinds were clearly important factors in the notion underlying the way in which resourcing of schools' work in teacher training was to be handled. HEIs were to transfer resources to schools for their contribution to the partnerships, but "[A]ccording to the local situation and existing arrangements, transfers should therefore be negotiated locally, on the basis of clear statements of the new roles and responsibilities of schools" (DfE/WO, 1992, para. 15). This statement was followed by a clear example of the stance to be taken by central government over the next few years in many of the decisions they took which fundamentally affected and, in some cases, placed in jeopardy the operation of institutions: "The Secretary of State does not intend to intervene in the event of disagreements about the financial arrangements between HEIs and individual schools, but the costs to schools and the resources transferred to them will be monitored closely" (ibid., para. 15).

In order to carry out this monitoring and to gather more broadly the information about institutions which would inform CATE in its new role, HMIs would carry out full inspections of the initial teacher training at all HEIs. There was no longer any pretence at their being invited to universities. Although independent of CATE, the inspectorate was clearly a crucial element in the accreditation process.

The higher education institutions then were faced with a much less friendly regime than before. They would be subject to a regular inspection and accreditation process conducted from outside the institution. They were required to pass considerable sums of money to their partner schools. Whatever developments in course restructuring and creating partnerships had taken place in response to Circular 3/84 now had to be further revised to comply with the new demands (Aplin, 1994). If one part of their provision failed to comply with the requirements, HEIs were prone to lose their entire accreditation on a temporary or permanent basis.

There was a period when the local negotiations about the transfer of resources to schools in some cases led to unseemly striking of bargains and open competition between institutions for placements in schools, especially where a number of HEIs worked in close proximity. Some head teachers, already well versed in the financial management they were exercising through the Local Management of Schools, were ready to see the possibility of extra income for their establishments, and were less than sympathetic to higher education departments whose funding had to allow for contributions to institution-wide overheads. The guidance offered to head teachers by one professional organization called on HEIs to stop making such contributions, and estimated a minimum figure which should be transferred to schools, despite the circular's desire for local negotiation in the light of varying partnership patterns (Secondary Heads Association[SHA], 1993). Any attempts at co-operation between institutions at this stage were fragile and largely deemed to be unwise. A period of serious instability followed, with a great deal of effort and attention being paid to the design and negotiation of contracts, financial agreements and delineation of roles and responsibilities. This unsettled period was made more urgent as the Circular clearly stated a desire to increase the pace of change, setting 1994 as the year by which all courses should comply with the new requirements. This demand for rapid compliance was to be a major feature in the further changes introduced later in the 1990s.

How had existing courses responded to the onset of Circular 9/92? Much depended on the level of resource which was enjoyed by the course. It became clear, although by no means transparently so, that courses were run on quite different financial lines. This was determined to some extent by the level of block grant provided by the government and to some extent by the financial and accounting regime which operated in the higher education institution. Whereas this might have been less important while transfer of resources was not involved, the circular's insistence on schools' receipt of funds led to considerable problems for some courses, as the varied constraints on course providers pulled in opposing directions and as schools, in some areas, lobbied for their share. In terms of course design, the main principles lying behind the Circular were followed, and the balance of time and responsibilities within the training changed. Higher education institutions considerably reduced its participation in teaching and assessment, but retained all the responsibility for quality and administration. With less direct control over what the trainees were doing and with a largely reducing staff to deal with these issues, this change in role created its own problems. In some universities, it was quickly evident that the implications on the shape of the department's work were of major significance. The structural effect of the moves took longer to show themselves in other universities. The strains of adequately staffing the higher education portion began to show themselves in the late 1990s as, faced with such other pressures as the universities' Research Assessment Exercise, some institutions, for example, Liverpool and Nottingham, responded by seeking Teacher Fellows to provide teaching on training courses, rather than lecturers on established academic grades.

THE TEACHER TRAINING AGENCY: A NEW CENTRAL STRUCTURE

Further reform was on the way. CATE was replaced by the Teacher Training Agency (TTA), which had a central role of funding the whole of the initial teacher training field in England, as well as monitoring the field and advising the government. This was part of a drive to, firstly, pursue what were seen as higher standards and to develop "... a wider range of courses so that new teachers are not only competent professionals but have particular combinations of knowledge and skills to meet the increasingly diverse needs of schools" and to, secondly, ensure that "[S]chools should not only act as full partners with higher education institutions but should also be able, if they wish, to play the leading role in planning and providing courses" (DfE/WO, 1993).

Competition was not only to be between courses offered by higher education institutions in partnership with schools, a new route for initial training also appeared, in which higher education was to play a minor or indeed no part at all. One of the notions of the right-wing attack had been to insist on the value of on-the-job training, with the assertion that it was in the classroom that all that was needed for a teacher would be found.

The introduction of what was termed School-Centred Teacher Training (SCITT), as opposed to the existing partnerships' School-Based Teacher Training, demonstrated a willingness on the part of politicians to remove pre-service training from the clutches of higher education. The first six consortia of schools were approved to begin courses in September 1993. The 1997 Handbook of the Graduate Teacher Training Registry, through which all applications have to be lodged, lists ten SCITT consortia in the secondary phase. The main focus was on shortage subjects, and there was in each case only a small target quota of trainees. The significance of the SCITT initiative was that, for the first time, an approved full-time initial training course could lead to Qualified Teacher Status without any participation by a higher education establishment. This was to set a precedent for another, later, development. In fact, in most cases, the courses were advertised as being provided in conjunction with or accredited by a higher education institution. Despite the pressures from the right-wing think tanks, the development of SCITTs has been slow, and the numbers of participants have remained low. The problems of running a SCITT for establishments whose prime purpose is to teach pupils cannot be overstated, as they are subject to all the constraints and regulations which touch on what might be called mainstream teacher training. In their inspection of the first year's cohort in SCITTs, HMI noted that "[F]urther improvement will depend on schools having sufficient time to plan and prepare the training programme" (Ofsted, 1995).

SCITTs remain a routeway available in areas where there are few opportunities for attendance at a higher education institution and where schools find a difficulty in recruiting staff (Anderson, 1995).

The TTA's control of the central government financing of teacher education resulted in a transparent separation of funding sources and accounting within the higher education sector. The adoption of an agency structure with separate offices and staffing, as well as a wider brief, led to a more pro-active stance and the growth of an individual culture. The funding issue was clearly crucial, and there was much discussion about the most appropriate methodology to be adopted (TTA, 1996). At the consultation stage of certain measures, the TTA was sometimes to take a different stance from that of Ofsted or even of the Department for Education and Employment (DfEE). Institutions had to learn how to interpret the messages differently from before, and it was not always clear in the early years how to be certain that the reading of a situation was accurate, especially as some of the advice emanating from the TTA was clearly based on little direct experience of the operation of teacher education.

It was determined that, in order to inform TTA of the quality of provision, Ofsted should conduct inspections of all initial teacher training courses on a regular cycle. The reports would be published, and the grading arrived at would inform the subsequent decisions about funding and target numbers. Unlike the inspections for schools, which were carried out by privatized teams on the basis of tenders, the inspections of teacher education were staffed by a specialist HMI team. Thus, a clear connection between a published inspection framework (Office for Standards in Education/Teacher Training Agency, n.d.), an inspection process and centralized funding decisions was established and set in train. The first three year cycle began in 1996.

The effect of the inspection findings was to be more brutal than simple publication in documents. Already, schools were subject to the annual publication of performance tables related to their test and examination results, and these were rapidly subverted by the press into league tables. The same was now to apply to teacher training institutions, with the results of their inspections (although not all on the same basis or of the same cohorts) translated into comparative tabular form encouraging the illusion that this was useful to potential trainees.

After its first 15 months of existence, the TTA was able to set out a series of objectives and targets relating to its vision of teaching as "a high quality profession" (TTA, 1996, p. 11). As part of these, there was a proposal to offer advice in May 1997 to the Secretary of State "on the implications for qualified teacher status of the draft national standards for newly qualified teachers" (ibid., p. 19) within an overall framework which would "promote well-targeted, effective and co-ordinated continuing professional development" (ibid., p. 12).

CIRCULARS 10/97 AND 4/98: FROM COMPETENCIES TO STANDARDS

On 1 May 1997, a Labour government was elected, with the principal shibboleth "Education, Education, Education." Not only was the advice duly delivered in May but in the enthusiasm of the new dawn, it was issued in the form of Circular 10/97, to be implemented with immediate effect (DfEE, 1997).

In place of the competences of Circular 9/92, the world of initial teacher training was faced with a complex and lengthy set of "standards" which would be the basis of qualification. Instead of having time for planning and implementation (fairly leisurely under 3/84, more demanding under 9/92), no time allowance was to be made for the complexities of implementing the intricacies of a new system. Less than 12 months later, further sets of requirements in trainees' knowledge and skill levels in Information and Communications Technology and for incorporation from September

1999, content specifications for secondary trainees in English, Mathematics and Science were laid down in Circular 4/98 (DfEE, 1998).

Despite the rhetoric and the hard-sell approach (Circulars 10/97 and 4/98 are headed "Teaching: High Status, High Standards"), numbers applying for PGCE continued to decline during the 1990s, most seriously in subjects which were already designated as shortage subjects. Various financial incentives were offered to potential students in the shortage areas, but with little conclusive evidence that they had any long-term effect.

By 1997, the TTA was exploring alternative routes. The Articled and Licensed Teacher Schemes had come to an end and the SCITT development was modest in its overall numbers. A new route, for those already employed as teachers was opened to graduates - the Graduate Teacher Programme. Subject to the standards contained with Circular 10/97, graduate untrained teachers already employed in schools as unqualified instructors could work towards qualification with training funded by the TTA. This could be a useful route for those whose personal circumstances prevented full-time training or who were working in subjects for which there was no training locally available. By 1998, there were a small number of schemes in operation, but the numbers of individuals involved were low.

CONCLUSION

The picture of initial secondary teacher training in England in 1998 is generally far removed from its 1984 predecessor. Clearly, there are recognizable elements, but much has changed, both fundamentally and in appearance.

The system is now highly regulated in three major respects, which are significant shifts away from the previous model which was dominated by the universities. First, there is a national definition of content and assessment systems. This has focused especially on the practical rather than the theoretical, with the identification of competences and subsequently standards. Secondly, course provision has to be through partnerships which involve both higher education institutions and schools, in a more or less equal position of influence. Thirdly, a complex system of monitoring has been established through inspection and financial controls, to ensure that as standard a national pattern as possible is adhered to, and this has fundamentally altered the relationship between universities and central government.

Yet, despite this increased level of demand on providers of training in organizational and managerial aspects, the overall resource base has remained broadly similar. The move towards a national pattern has developed at the same time as a shift away from a relatively small number of providers to a large number of schools, combined with a consequent shift of resources, which has fragmented the solidity and led to wide variety. The transfer of resources away from universities has led some of them to reconsider their role in initial teacher education. Some have developed other activities in order to re-orientate themselves; others have seriously thought of withdrawing from initial training altogether.

At the central level, a continued concern over quality has led to further tightening of the entry, course and exit requirements. For example, from 1998, all entrants to teacher training courses have to undertake a year's induction after their initial training, success in which is to be required if their QTS is to be confirmed. Plans are in train to introduce tests in numeracy, literacy and Information and Communications Technology for all training teachers from 1999.

Yet, the issues of quantity are also to the fore, as recruitment to initial teacher training shows little sign of improvement. So, once again, contradictory measures are in place. Those elements which seek to improve quality of entrants and the training they receive are counterbalanced by moves to increase the numbers of entrants through proposals for modular routeways and the urgent need to fill teaching posts in areas of growing recruitment difficulties. It remains to be seen if the demands to meet every criterion of quality are compatible with strategies to meet the serious shortages of teachers, especially in secondary education, and if the traditional players are able to exercise a full role, pressurized as they are to satisfy not only the quality demands from central government for teacher training, but also the persistent and increasing demands from university managers to perform at a high level in obtaining research funding and producing publications. The changes of the last 15 years have not produced a secure model which can be relied upon to remain for the next 15.

NOTES

[1]This chapter is adapted from "The Changing Face of Initial Teacher Education in England (1984-1998)" published in Issue 2 of Volume II of the *Asia-Pacific Journal of Teacher Education and Development*.

REFERENCES

Anderson, L. (1995). Conceptions of partnership in school-centred initial teacher training. In H. Bines & J. M. Welton (Eds.), *Managing partnership in teacher training and development* (pp. 80-90). London: Routledge.

Aplin, R. (1994). Partnership: The Leicester experience. In A. Williams (Ed.), *Perspectives on partnership: Secondary initial teacher training* (pp. 47-62). London: Falmer Press.

Barker, S., Brooks. V., March, K., & Swatton, P. (1994). *Initial teacher education in secondary schools: A study of the tangible and intangible costs and benefits of initial teacher education in secondary schools*. London: Association of Teachers and Lecturers.

Barrett, E., & Galvin, C. (1993). *The licensed teacher*. London: Modes of Teacher Education Project.

Benton, P. (Ed.). (1990). *The Oxford Internship Scheme: Integration + partnership in initial teacher education*. London: Calouste Gulbenkian Foundation.

Bines, H., & Welton, J. M. (Eds.). (1995). *Managing partnership in teacher training and development*. London: Routledge.

Broadfoot, P. (1986). Power relations and English education: The changing role of central government. *Journal of Education Policy, 1*(1), 53-62.

CATE. (1986, January). Links between initial teacher training institutions and schools. *Catenote, 4*.

DfEE. (1997). *Requirements for courses of initial teacher training* (Circular 10/97). London: Author.

DfEE. (1998). *Requirements for courses of initial teacher training* (Circular 4/98). London: Author.

DfE/WO. (1992). *Initial teacher training (Secondary phase)* (Circular 9/92 [DfE] 35/92 [WO]). London: Department for Education.

DfE/WO. (1993). *The government's proposals for the reform of initial teacher training*. London: Department for Education.

DES. (1980). *PGCE in the public sector*. London: Author.

DES. (1981). *Teacher training and the secondary school*. London: Author.

DES. (1982). *The new teacher in school*. London: HMSO.

DES. (1983). *Teaching quality* (White Paper, Cmnd 8836). London: HMSO.

DES/WO. (1984). *Initial teacher training: Approval of courses* (Circular 3/84 [DES] 21/84 [WO]). London: Department of Education and Science.

DES/WO. (1991). *School-based initial teacher training in England and Wales: A report by HM inspectorate.* London: HMSO.

Edwards, T. (1992). Issues and challenges in initial teacher education. *Cambridge Journal of Education, 22*(3), 283-291.

Everton, T., & White, S. (1992). Partnership in training: The University of Leicester's new model of school-based teacher education. *Cambridge Journal of Education, 22*(2), 143-155.

Furlong, V. J., Hirst, P. H., Pocklington, K., & Miles, S. (1988). *Initial teacher training and the role of the school.* Milton Keynes: Open University Press.

Griffiths, V., & Owen, P. (Eds.). (1995). *Schools in partnership.* London: Paul Chapman.

Judge, H. (1990). The reform of teacher education. In P. Benton (Ed.), *The Oxford Internship Scheme: Integration + partnership in initial teacher education* (pp. 1-16). London: Calouste Gulbenkian Foundation.

Judge, H., Lemosse, M., Paine, L., & Sedlak, M. (1994). The university and the teachers. *Oxford Studies in Comparative Education, 4*(1/2).

Landman, M., & Ozga, J. (1995). *Teacher education policy in England.* In M. Ginsburg & B. Lindsay (Eds.), *The political dimension in teacher education: Comparative perspectives on policy formation, socialization and society* (pp. 23-39). London: Falmer Press.

Lawlor, S. (1990). *Teachers mistaught: Training in theories or education in subjects?* London: Centre for Policy Studies.

McCulloch, M., & Fidler, B. (Eds.). (1994). *Improving initial teacher training? New roles for teachers, schools and higher education.* Harlow: Longman.

Ofsted. (1993). *The Licensed Teacher Scheme September 1990 - July 1992.* London: HMSO.

Ofsted. (1995). *School-centred initial teacher training 1993-1994.* London: HMSO.

Ofsted/TTA. (n.d.). *Framework for the assessment of quality and standards in initial teacher training 1997/1998.* London: Author.

Pring, R. (1996). Just desert. In J. Furlong & R. Smith (Eds.), *The role of higher education in initial teacher training* (pp. 8-22). London: Kogan Page.

(SHA. (1993, October). *Teacher training: Further advice* (SHA Information Sheet). Leicester: Author.

TTA. (1996). *Promoting excellence in teaching: Corporate plan 1996.* London: Author.

Wilkin, M. (1999). *The role of higher education in initial teacher education* (Occasional Paper No. 12). London: Universities Council for the Education of Teachers.

Williams, A. (Ed.). (1994). *Perspectives on partnership: Secondary initial teacher training.* London: Falmer Press.

Williams, A. (Ed.). (1995). *Partnership in secondary initial teacher education.* London: David Fulton Publishers.

Chapter 11

Constructing a Constructivist Teacher Education: A Taiwan Experience

Sharon Hsiao Lan CHEN

Office of Research and Development
National Taiwan Normal University, Taiwan

In Taiwan, there have been numerous educational reforms introduced in the past decade. One of the most challenging tasks was the enactment of new curriculum standards for school education.[1] The "New Curriculum Standards for Elementary Schools" was promulgated in 1993 and put into practice nation-wide in the 1996 school year (Ministry of Education, 1993). Based on the goals of engaging students in problematic situations that matters to them and of encouraging students to learn more at higher levels of understanding, the new curriculum standards for elementary education have adopted a lot of constructivist views on the teaching and learning (Taiwan Provincial Institute for Elementary School Teachers' In-service Education, 1995). In order to prepare elementary teachers for the teaching of the new curriculum, it is necessary for teacher education in Taiwan to provide opportunities for pre-service teachers as well as in-service teachers to learn and to experience more about constructivist views of teaching and learning. Thus, employing an action research approach, I conducted a two-year study (August 1995 – July 1997), to explore the meaning and the possibilities of implementing a constructivist teaching approach to professional development courses for teacher education in Taiwan.

The main purposes of the study are four: first, to explore the meaning of infusing constructivist perspectives to professional development courses; second, to understand what the prospective and in-service teachers think about constructivist views on teaching and learning; third to evaluate the impacts of the implementation of a constructivist teaching approach on prospective and in-service teachers, in terms of the impacts on their professional growth and their pedagogical practices; and fourth, to clarify the embedded factors that may influence prospective and in-service teachers' practice of constructivist teaching approaches in elementary classrooms. I hope that this Taiwan experience will present an insightful case to international audience and educators who are interested to enhance or reform the teaching approach to teacher education.

THEORETICAL BASELINE

Constructivism is a theory of knowledge and knowing (Bodner, 1986; Von Glasersfeld, 1995). Although not until recent year has constructivism received a great deal of attention in education, it surely is not a new idea. We may find the roots of constructivism in the writings of Dewey, Piaget, Bruner, and Vygotsky (Richardson, 1997). We may even trace its origin far back to the philosophical thoughts of Vico and Kant in the 18th century (Von Glasersfeld, 1984). Combing philosophical, sociological, and psychological thoughts, constructivism provides an alternative epistemology to think about the formation of knowledge and understanding and to provide different perspectives on teaching and learning. Though there are different versions of constructivism and various theoretical approaches to constructivism (e.g., the Piagetian, situated cognition, sociocultural, and emancipatory approaches), it is generally based on the assumption that knowledge is constructed by learners as they attempt to make sense of their experiences.

There are two major approaches applied in educational studies, which are radical constructivism and social constructivism (Phillips, 2000; Steff & Gale, 1995). While radical constructivism focuses on the individual meaning-making process of knowledge construction, social constructivism places emphasis on the shared cultural meaning-making process in social interaction of knowledge construction (Richardson, 1997). However, to enhance knowledge construction, it is necessary to infuse these two in teaching practice (Kroll & Black, 1993). On one hand, the teacher facilitates the cognitive alteration through designing tasks that create dilemmas for students and, on the other hand, the teacher also pays attention to the importance of social elements of learning, and on the power relationships among the teacher, students, and formal knowledge.

Basically, constructivists believe that learners approach learning tasks with a set of personal beliefs, motivations, and conceptions about knowledge itself. When learners are taught, they construct individual meanings from the material by relating it to their existing conceptions and frameworks of knowledge. As Kroll and Black (1993) pointed out, an important component of constructivism is the recursive nature of learning that new knowledge is acquired by consolidating old knowledge through practice and extending that knowledge to new situations. Also, new knowledge can be created in social interactions, from imitations of others and rewards by others. Thus, unlike traditional teaching dealing with the transmission of static knowledge, constructivist teaching requires that teachers extend freedom of choice to students and create the climate where students may feel free to raise their own questions and spur their own development. In Burbules' (2000) words, "[T]he principles of constructivist pedagogy – encouraging collaboration, promoting activity and exploration, respecting multiple points of view, emphasizing "authentic" problem-solving – have a number of benefits, and among these may be that these approaches do facilitate a more creative synthetic attitude toward learning" (p. 328).

To conduct such a constructivist pedagogy, teachers must possess a sense of agency and must be able to recognize that meaning and reality are socially constructed and capable of transformation. Consequently, teachers are able to, as Vadeboncoeur (1997) suggested, develop a pedagogy that is "inclusive of both students' voices and experiences and aimed at exposing, examining and reducing the constraints of the traditional transmission model of pedagogy" (p. 30). In other words, in a constructivist classroom, the teacher becomes a coach, analyzer, and facilitator of the strategies used in the process of teaching and learning that would lead to empower students in knowledge construction. However, to encourage these constructivist ideas in the real teaching world, it is so important that we do not neglect the support that teachers need in their try-out efforts. Vadeboncoeur (1997) put it very well:

> The ability of teachers to become agents of change and to empower their students is dependent on support; teachers need to learn how to do this. If we engage pre-service [and in-service] teachers in processes of emancipatory knowledge construction, we have an obligation to prepare them to work toward the political changes necessary to allow them to incorporate these practices in their (future) classrooms. (p. 30)

It is believed that most of the problems associated with implementing a constructivist approach to teaching could be overcome if teachers are willing to rethink not only what it means to know subject matter, but also what it takes to foster this sort of understanding in students. Then, it is important to encourage constructivist teaching practice by modeling it in the teacher education classroom (e.g., Loughran & Russell, 1997; Meyer-Smith & Mitchell, 1997; Peterman, 1997). In his remarks on the education of elementary teachers, Bauersfeld (1998) criticizes the dominant model of teacher education: "What is taught at universities about the realities and conditions of teaching is based more on "knowledge" and skills than on the spin-off of participation in a process of teaching which provides for a genuine approximation with the teacher's (future) practice in a classroom setting" (p. 216).

In order to emphasize the development of an attitude through participation, rather than the oft-mentioned pedagogical techniques going under the heading of collaborative learning or constructivist teaching, teacher education programs are responsible for "enculturation" of a type that is appropriate with respect to the teacher's role in the classroom. As Black & Ammon (1992) suggested, we need to find a way in teacher education to demonstrate that a constructivist perspective on learning is perhaps uniquely suited to serve as core knowledge for teaching, since it is comprehensive enough to guide elementary school pedagogy and teacher education. Just as a craftsman would not teach an apprentice using prepared scripts, programs for teacher education should focus on realistic approaches to solving real-world problems constructively.

Furthermore, teachers' teaching practices are influenced and directed by their beliefs (Clandinin, 1986; Clark & Peterson, 1986; Glasson & Lalik, 1993). Teachers need to learn to examine their beliefs about knowing, teaching, and learning and to reflect on their teaching practice (Schon, 1991; Zeichner & Tabachnick, 1991) in order to change their "culturally constructed ideological systems." By doing so, they may become productive constructivist teachers. In this regard, Fosnot (1996) looked into the thing needed to occur in teacher preparation programs to enable beliefs to shift and the process of constructing constructivism. Regarding the facilitating shifts in beliefs, he underscores constructing pedagogy from an analysis of one's own learning; constructing pedagogy from an analysis of children's thinking; cooperative field work in the sites; integrative field experience; and developing teachers as change agents. Fosnot (1996) also makes the claim as follows:

> If understanding the teaching/learning process from a constructivist view is itself constructed, and if teachers tend to teach as they were taught, rather than as they were taught to teach, then teacher education needs to begin with …

traditional beliefs and subsequently challenge them through activity, reflection, and discourse ... throughout the duration of the program. Most importantly, participants need experiences as learners that confront traditional views of teaching and learning in order to enable them to construct a pedagogy that stands in contrast to older, more traditionally held views. (p. 206)

Indeed, the crux of implementing a constructivist perspective in pedagogical practice lies in the fundamental changes that must be brought about in teacher's attitudes and beliefs. Teacher education programs based on a constructivist view of teaching and learning need to do more than offering a constructivist perspective in a course or two. Prospective and in-service teachers need to have the opportunities to express and to reconstruct their beliefs privately and publicly. As Fosnot (1996) suggested, "[T]eacher's beliefs need to be illuminated, discussed, and challenged" (p. 216). Further, "[T]eachers need to be engaged in learning experiences that confront traditional beliefs... Only through such extensive questioning, reflecting, and constructing will the paradigm shift in education – constructivism – occur" (p. 216).

COURSE DESIGN AND INSTRUCTIONAL STRATEGIES

One of the most important missions of institutions for teacher preparation in Taiwan (nine teachers colleges and three normal universities) is to promote the professional growth of prospective teachers as well as of in-service teachers.[2] At teachers colleges, for example, there are three sorts of courses offered to help preparing elementary school teachers. They are general courses (to increase general understanding of liberal arts), specialized courses (to enhance deeper understanding of content knowledge based on students' chosen discipline area); and professional courses (to build comprehensive understanding of educational foundations and to cultivate educational professional knowledge and skills). The courses applied a constructivist approach for this study were the required core of professional development courses that I taught at the National Chiayi Teachers College – "Fundamentals of Instruction and Assessment" and "Instructional Theory." "Fundamentals of Instruction and Assessment" was a teacher preparation course for prospective teachers, being scheduled for two hours per week and for 17 weeks (28 February 1996 – 26 June 1996). "Instructional Theory" was an in-service teacher training course offered in summer, being scheduled for four hours per week and for eight weeks (4 July 1996 – 22 August 1996).

Altogether, there were 30 prospective teachers and 46 in-service teachers involved in my experimental constructivist course design.

Since constructivism is a theory of knowledge and knowing, my claim is that constructivism in education is neither "the teaching method" nor "a set of formulaic teaching procedure" for teachers to follow. Rather, it is an alternative pedagogical paradigm, providing different perspectives about teaching and learning that may help teachers carry out ways of teaching that will encourage students' active participation in knowledge construction. To help teachers get more familiar with and be more skillful in constructivist teaching approaches, it is necessary for them to have personal constructivist teaching and learning experience first. My assumption is that based on their personal cooperative experiences in knowledge construction, they may reach the core of constructivism in education better and then may carry out constructivist teaching practices more adequately.

Basically, the constructivist approach used in these two courses attempted to build a student-centered, inquiry-oriented collaborative learning environment to help students actively engage in personal instructional theory building. The general model for the development of the two courses is given in Figure 1 (ideas gained from Driver and Oldham's constructivist model for curriculum development [1986, p. 113]), which indicates that the actual course design is in an on-going circulating/feedback mode. However, for prospective teachers, the course design placed more emphases on discussion of principles, methods, and strategies. But for in-service teachers, the emphases were on re-examination of theories into practices.

Most learning activities and tasks in both courses were designed to get prospective teachers and in-service teachers involved in group discussions and collaborations and engaged in self-reflection and examination of personal instructional theory and practical models of teaching. In other words, both courses were designed with the attempt to stimulate inquiry, reflection, and the construction and restructuring of prospective and in-service teachers' knowledge base on teaching. Following different topics of the lessons, students were provided with a variety of learning opportunities to participate in simulations, debates, problem-posing and -solving, critiques, and instructional design projects related to elementary schooling in contemporary setting. In terms of evaluation, it was conducted through alternative approaches, including learning journals, instructional design projects, involvement in group discussions, oral presentations, self-evaluation reports, and the final examination.

In terms of the instructional design for the professional development courses I taught, I also found Driver and Oldham's constructivist teaching sequence model (1986, p. 119) very helpful (see figure 2). Basically the overall guidelines and instructional strategies applied in the courses are as follows:

Figure 1: *Constructivist Curriculum Development Model for Professional Course Design*

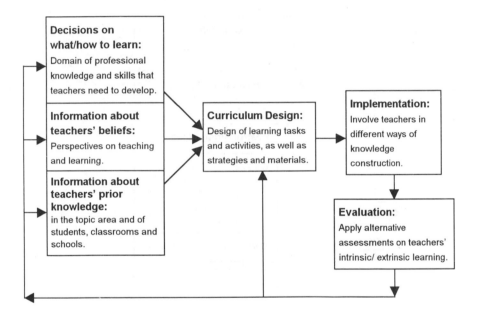

1. to actively involve every learner in the construction of knowledge;
2. to make the classroom for teaching and learning having a sense of belonging and psychological safety;
3. to make the focus of instruction on learning tasks inherently meaningful to learners;
4. to emphasize teacher-student and student-student interaction and collaboration;
5. to demonstrate and to use knowledge of learners' culture, prior understandings, misconceptions, beliefs, values, and so on in planning learning activities;
6. not only to demonstrate technical competence in planning, implementing,

and organizing instruction and classroom management, but also to organize and manage the classroom teaching in ways that foster learners' self-reflection;

7. to demonstrate in-depth understanding of content as well as the ability and skills to create conceptual links across subject areas; and

8. to provide an informed rationale for instruction decisions.

Figure 2: *A constructivist teaching sequence (Driver & Oldham, 1986, p. 119)*

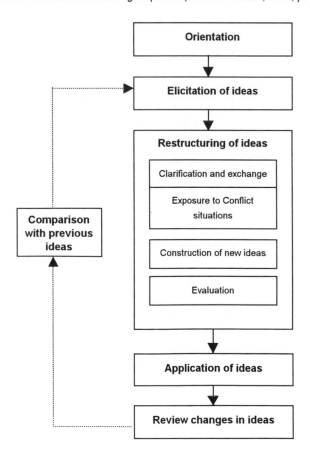

It was hoped that through individual thought process, group deliberation process, dialectic discourses, and alternative assessments, prospective teachers and in-service teachers would have chances to experience different ways of knowing and to experience in-person and in-practice constructivist teaching approach. Based on their real personal experience in such constructivist course designs, prospective teachers as well as in-service teachers would grasp the meaning of constructivist teaching better and would be willing to try it out in their own teaching practice.

As I made the claim earlier, constructivist teaching is not a set of fixed teaching procedures for teachers to follow. Rather, it provides different perspectives on pedagogical practice that encourage teachers to apply multiple ways of teaching to invite students' active participation in knowledge construction. To help prospective and in-service teachers get prepared for constructivist teaching, it is important to change their beliefs about teaching and learning and to equip them with the knowledge of *what* and knowledge of *how* for constructivist teaching. Basically, I believe that only through the personal engagement in constructivist learning experiences that confront the traditional beliefs can prospective and in-service teacher learn about constructivist teaching. Based on this assumption, I designed the professional development courses I taught as small-scale experiments offering flexibility and opportunities through various collaborative learning tasks for involvement by, and change in, the individual prospective or in-service teacher. It is to the process and results of my investigation of implementing a constructivist approach in my own classes that I now turn to.

RESEARCH METHODS AND PROCEDURES

To achieve the research goals, a two-year longitudinal research design (August 1995 – July 1997) was conducted for this study. During the first year of my study, I first generated suggestions from literature review in order to gain ideas for the design and implementation of a constructivist teaching approach to the professional courses for teacher education. Then, I conducted an action inquiry approach, employing qualitative research methods, to examine my experimental constructivist teaching experience with an attempt to develop applicable constructivist teaching approaches and/or models for teacher education in Taiwan.

Since there were two courses involved in this study and the content design and the characteristics of teachers in those two courses were different, the actual research procedures took in two classes were slightly different accordingly. For example, because prospective teachers have no teaching experience, the course design for "Fundamentals of Instruction and Assessment" – a teacher preparation course – stresses more on constructing pedagogy from collaborative explorations of instructional theories and techniques. The investigation in this class was then focused more on the concept-building of prospective teachers as well as their personal growth in professionalism. Because in-service teachers have their own teaching experiences and personal beliefs of and attitudes toward teaching and learning, the course design for "Instructional Theory" – an in-service training course – placed more emphasis on critical examination of theories and critical reflection on ideologies. In consequence, the explorative efforts in this class were more on tracing the changes of in-service teachers' beliefs and attitudes.

Methods employed for data collection at this stage included participant observations, focus group interview, and document analysis of learning journals and self-evaluation reports. Starting from the first day of both classes till the end of the course, there had always been a research assistant in the classroom conducting observation and taking field-notes. Meanwhile, videotaping and tape-recording techniques were also conducted in order to keep detailed data for analysis. In general, the foci of observations were on classroom interactions, collaborative relationships and patterns, and the situations or conditions that promoted or limited the social construction of knowledge. After class, the research assistant would conduct focus group interviews with different groups of members – one group a time; there were six groups for prospective teachers and 8 groups for in-service teachers – to record their responses to and attitudes toward constructivist learning experience. Learning journals and self-evaluation reports were collected at the end of the course, which led to better understanding of the changes in students' beliefs and attitudes.

For the second year of my study, it was basically a qualitative follow-up investigation on how well prospective teachers and in-service teachers carried out constructivist perspectives in their teaching practice and what factors might influence their perceptions on and practices of constructivist teaching. Since I continued teaching the practicum course of teaching practice of the prospective teachers, I got wonderful chance to trace the professional growth of those prospective teachers. For them, everyone was required to write learning journals and field logs of their teaching practices. Each student was scheduled for being observed at least once in teaching practice for the sake of the course design. But, for the sake of this study, four prospective teachers, who were willing to try out constructivist approaches in their teaching practice, were selected for in-depth investigation.

For in-service teachers, there was a monthly professional growth group meeting holding for them on voluntary basis. There were eight to ten in-service teachers attending the monthly meetings in average. They were not required to keep logs or journals of their teaching, but were invited to share their experiences and to reflect upon the issues and problems they were facing at the meetings. Also, there were four in-service teachers, who were willing to open their classrooms for observations, engaged in-depth exploration of constructivist teaching practice. Methods applied for data collection at this stage included classroom observation, in-depth personal interview, and tape-recording and memo of every monthly professional growth group meeting for in-service teachers, and document analysis of learning journals and field logs for prospective teachers.

In addition, throughout the whole study, I not only met with my research assistants to have reflective discussion on a regular basis, but also kept my personal notes summarized observations, reflections, and related issues which served as important guidelines for data analysis. Basically, in this study data collection and analysis was simultaneously conducted in the field. Using multiple sources of data and applying constant comparison techniques, the validation process of this study was practiced in a reflective dialogical manner suggested by Chen (1997). And, applying the idea of building a "grounded theory" (Strauss & Corbin, 1990), the framework for data stories of this study was based on the "emerging themes" generated in the process of data analysis.

FINDINGS AND DISCUSSION

The results of the first year of study were very encouraging, which I found a great deal of promises of implementing a constructivist approach to professional courses for teacher education. Through the implementation of a constructivist approach to the courses, most prospective teachers as well as in-service were in favor of constructivist teaching practices and there were obvious "growth" and conceptual changes among them.

The Growth of Prospective Teachers

Generally, prospective teachers were quite open to constructivist views, and were willing to try out new ideas. The influences of the constructivist professional course design on prospective teachers were shown in five aspects as follow:

Acquiring Positive Learning Behaviors and Attitudes

Based on reflective notes in prospective teachers' learning journals, I found evidences showing that many prospective teachers were turning from passive information receivers to active knowledge inquirers, from a perfunctory attitude to a more serious attitude toward learning. Many of them expressed that they extended their discussions after class quite often and would actively search for supportive materials or information for the completion of learning tasks. One of the groups even agreed to devote an hour per day to work together on their instructional design project co-operatively. As they said, the time, energy, and intellect they spent for the group tasks almost "took up their leisure time for personal life." Though I seldom had roll call in the class, the attendance rate was very good because they were afraid that they (and their group) would miss a lot if they did not show up. Some of them reflected in their self-evaluation that "[B]eing in the college for two years, this is the only course that I've never ever skip once," and that "[T]hough I thought about skipping the class, I finally keep the 100% attendance rate."

Development of Collaborative and Active Learning Habits

In classroom activities prospective teachers were encouraged not only to acquire knowledge independently but also to create knowledge collaboratively. Infused with a constructivist perspective, the inquiry-oriented collaborative learning tasks applied in the course did challenge prospective teachers' learning habits. At the beginning, many of them were not used to so many group discussions and critiques in class but later on they all started to enjoy the collaborative efforts of knowledge building. The group dynamics and social interactions became more vital and more active. As several of them pointed out in their learning journals that the enthusiasm in expressing personal ideas could not be seen in other courses. From sharing with each other, they had not only appreciated the joy of "Aha!" from listening to other's ideas, but also experienced the fact that "two hands are better than one." One student expressed his thoughts about collaborative learning experience in class:

> This kind of learning keep my brain functioning actively and coming up with
> ideas and concepts. It makes me try hard to sort things out and to find the

most satisfactory answer... I can clarify my own understanding and share other persons' unique ideas that I never have thought about. The collaborative process stimulates one another's thoughts.

Establishment of a Supportive Climate for Collaborative Learning

The design of the learning activities for the course was aiming at helping prospective teachers having the sense of fellowship and learning community, and being willing to respect and help each other. Through a variety of collaborative group processes, prospective teachers learned to appreciate different ways of thinking and knowing, and learned to see things through different angles and to accept differences. They also learned to recognize the importance of questioning, dialectical argumentation, and critical reflection in knowledge construction. As a prospective teacher wrote:

> As all thoughts contend for attention, though sometimes it goes no where, lots of time we would come up with a unique theory that belongs to our own." Describing how they felt about group work, another prospective teacher wrote, "as a team, we need to work together to complement our project, and this has helped us to learn how to get alone. We are much closer now. Due to different personality, some members in the group were more industrious but some were lazier, however, we all learned to encourage and to push one another to do our best for completing our assignments in a most satisfactory way. And, it was a wonderful feeling.

Because of this, flowers of collaborative learning bloomed in their friendship and in their collaborative works, and in the cultivation of democratic spirits in knowledge building.

Advancement of Pedagogical Knowledge and Skills

The constructivist approach applied in the course not only helped shape prospective teachers' knowledge about teaching and learning, but also helped increase their understanding of what would promote effective teaching and productive learning. Through simulations and instructional project design and presentation, prospective teachers got chances to practically apply the concepts, methods, and strategies learned in class. Many of them realized the following, a prospective teacher's assertion:

> The most important of lesson plan is not the writing-up but the thinking process – think about how to teach, think about the materials, and think about the foci of the instruction, objectives, activities, evaluation, and so forth. Of

course it would be better for a novice teacher to write up their lesson plan, because then it can serve as a reference source for instruction, reflection, and for improvement as well.

Also, the prospective teachers had wonderful opportunities to test their concept maps of teaching and instructional plans in public. Though some of the shy prospective teachers were not comfortable to state their points of views or present their lesson plans in public, as they were "forced" to challenge their fears, they started to rediscover their potential. Many of them shared that such "terrible" but "terrific" experiences had gradually helped them build their confidence in teaching.

Enhancement of Capability and Sensitivity in Reflection
It is important to prepare prospective teachers to be more critical about taken-for-granted situations and thoughts. Through dialogical learning processes, prospective teachers were getting more able to questioning critically on theories, educational problems, pedagogical issues, and textbooks. In their writing of learning journals, they also realized the importance of critical self-reflection in professional development. They felt that only through critical reflection together with thoughtful planning could a teacher find better ways of teaching. A prospective teacher wrote: "A good teacher should be able to self-reflect a lot.... Self-reflection is rational, is not a reaction out of personal emotion." Another wrote: "Teaching requires constant critical reflection and creative thinking; then, there are possibilities to create effective teaching approaches that are helpful to students' learning."

The Changes of In-service Teachers

Since in-service teachers already had teaching experience for years, most of them had already formed their personal teaching beliefs and had their own teaching styles. The analysis of the course impacts on in-service teachers was on their attitudes toward constructivist teaching and changes in beliefs about teaching and learning.

Views on Constructivist Teaching Approach
Most in-service teachers described the constructivist teaching approach they had experienced in the course was student-centered, flexible, dynamic, challenging, but less tidy. "It invites participation, but also creates pressure." In-service teachers' views on constructivist teaching were varied. Most of

them could well recognize the key characteristics of constructivist teaching. They reflected what they thought about constructivist teaching to me that "[I]t is different from the traditional approach. It provides two-way communication ... gives students opportunities to discuss, to analyze ideas, to conclude thoughts. It is a process that belongs to the critical one." Some of them even believed that it would go well with the idea of "open-education." But, some of them, though recognizing that it was a kind of "higher level teaching," still preferred to "teach/tell" them more (transmit more knowledge to them). They felt if they teach/tell them more about the new concepts, they would learn more. Also, there were few in-service teachers feeling frustrated, being "not sure about what the teacher wants," as I talked less and teaching seemed become less tidy. A teacher told me: "I am not used to this kind of new teaching approach. It's just too open that I can hardly catch it or adjust to it."

Attitudes toward Constructivist Teaching Approach

Generally speaking, most in-service teachers were actively participating in learning, and were willing to reflect upon personal teaching practice and willing to try it out in their own teaching practice. Their attitudes toward constructivist teaching were positive, although they were not as excited about it as prospective teachers were. Based on their own constructivist learning experiences, most in-service teachers felt that it indeed had a great impact on them. The constructivist teaching practices in classroom had helped them enhance further understanding of teaching and learning. An in-service teacher said: "The tasks in class made me think seriously about my daily teaching practice, re-examine own instructional designs and the pedagogical world that I am in, as well as get inspired with new insights and new thoughts for educational practice." Quite often they would apply the constructivist perspective to reflect upon their own teaching practice. They started to think about what they would do when they go back to school. Some of them were concerned more about "practical issues" in the implementation of a constructivist approach. Thus, they hesitated to make a change to break through the socio-cultural values on traditional teaching. But some of them would like – according to their journal writing, some of them were determined – to give up the old thinking and practice and to try out the new one, though they felt "[I]t's painful to get rid of the old..." as they just have to start all over, to spend time to think of the new direction." They believed that "[I]f the techniques of constructivist teaching can be successfully implemented in real teaching, the classroom learning would be more vital and inspiring, and the teaching would be more effective."

Changes among In-service Teachers

Tracing the reflective notes in in-service teachers' learning journals, the typical changes among in-service teachers were from uneasiness to awareness, adjustment, reflection, and self-growth. From the beginning to the end of the course, changes of in-service teachers can be sorted into three stages. At the first stage, many in-service teachers were not comfortable about the newly experienced constructivist teaching and learning. Some teachers felt they were under great pressure because of the course design, some were with a great deal of expectations for the "new experiences." An in-service teacher expressed that "thought it's scary, it actually challenging. It provides me an opportunity for change, adjustment and for breaking through." At the second stage, some began to become aware of the strength of constructivist teaching and enjoy collaborative learning, but some felt sharking about the break-through of old beliefs in teaching and learning and did not know what to do about it. An in-service teacher described it very well that "[T]he process is hard and painful though, it is rewarding!" Then, at the final stage, almost all of them would start to self-reflect, but some accepted the constructivist perspective, some still struggled at the crossroads between the ideal and the reality. As a teacher said, "[W]hen I go back to school, though I won't apply the whole set of ideas to my teaching, I cannot deny that it indeed has some effects on me already. If I don't try out something, I won't be able to comfort my own educational conscientiousness."

Factors Influencing the Practice of a Constructivist Approach in Professional Courses

As I trace back reflectively, there were five factors that influenced the practice of a constructivist approach in the two professional courses. They are instructional activities, situated learning tasks, supportive feedback and encouragement, the climate in peer interactions, and degree of openness toward new things/ideas. The actual effects depended on which way each factor went, to the positive or the negative. Basically, most prospective and in-service teachers were fond of the versatile and challenging activities and learning tasks provided in class and were pleased with the supportive feedback, encouragement, and inspiration they gained in classroom discussion. For these teachers, they all held their positive attitudes toward constructivist teaching and believed that teaching and learning were more effective and productive by engaging students in knowledge construction. However, there were also teachers feeling frustrated in self-revelation as well as in group dynamics and therefore reserved their faith in constructivist teaching. For these teachers, their frustrations were mainly caused by the somewhat negating factors in collaborative group learning processes, such as lacking strong leadership in the group, completing learning tasks in a rush, loosing focus and getting into tedious or trivial talks, or having someone with strong personality dominating the group discussion. A teacher reflected:

> A lot of times, while we were discussing target issues we were oriented toward completing the tasks assigned by the teacher as soon as possible, without concerning the quality of our rationale. Quite often, we did not have thorough understanding of the theories but came up with our own explanatory guesses. Also, because there was no one really in charge of our group discussion, we all often talked in confusion. As we offered different opinions, it was so easy for us to be off the track. In consequence, the effects out of our group discussions were not good. These are the shortcomings of our group and we need to work hard for the improvement.

Another teacher expressed the following:

> It was easy to have a chat with classmates. But, when having a discussion on a certain issue with them, I found that there was always someone dominating the group discussion. If she favored an idea she would support it with a firm mind without going for any further discussion. If she did not like certain ideas she would grab for every possibility to fight for her own opinions. Then, the group climate would drop on to complaint. She would never quite until everybody was against her ideas. I really felt frustrated to have discussions with this kind of person. Sometimes I even questioned myself if I was so incapable.

In my own experimental constructivist teaching process, I learned that when implementing a constructivist approach in teaching, learning tasks cannot be too challenging at the beginning, questions for critical thinking cannot be too many at a time, and there are always needs for clear communications and explanations of learning tasks. I also learned that a constructivist teacher needs to prepare students with adequate communication skills as well as proper manner in questioning and attitude toward differences, to try every possibility to help students appreciate each other. A constructivist teacher needs to be very supportive and thoughtful in many ways.

It was encouraging that the implementation of a constructivist approach in professional development courses indeed had impacts on prospective and in-service teachers' conceptions of and attitudes toward teaching and learning. However, the results of the follow-up study in the second year turned out to be not so excited due to the constraints that affect prospective and in-service teachers' practice of constructivist teaching in their classrooms. Though there was a practicum course or a professional growth group to backup participant teachers' practices of constructivist teaching, the supports were in fact limited. They needed more help to solve the problems they had in trying out a constructivist approach in their teaching practice.

Problems Found in Prospective Teachers' Teaching

The four prospective teachers involved in the second year of study were in the field to do student teaching practice for one month. They all had strong desire to carry out constructivist ideals in their teaching. Since they did not have their own class, their mentor teachers actually would influence the way they conducted teaching. Sometimes they could not try alternative teaching approaches freely. A prospective teacher told me:

> Because we were there for just one month, I did not think it would be a good idea to create too many changes in the class, which might result in chaotic situations for the mentor teacher. I would feel embarrassed and guilty if the mentor teacher was not able to restore the class back to normal order. In fact, we were there only for a month but the mentor teacher was there for a long time. So, I felt it was better for me not to make too many changes. If I did make changes, they should be limited to a certain frame. Of course, we all expected ourselves to conduct good teaching. During this period of student teaching practice, because it was somebody else's class, we were not able to implement our ideas fully.

Another prospective teacher said:

> I knew that my mentor teacher would sit on the back watching my teaching and commenting on my teaching procedures and strategies. She would question why I bothered to conduct activities that were meaningless and wasting time. She suggested me that I should tell students directly, not to ask them to figure out on their own, because she thought students were not able to figure out the answer if I did not teach them first. These were the problems I had. At that moment, should I be honest to my belief? Or should I listen to her and follow her suggestions to go with her ways of teaching?

Because they were novice teachers, their professional knowledge base was not profound enough to cope with real life teaching, not to mention to practice a constructivist approach. In consequence, they were not thoughtful enough in instructional design, and had problems in time management and classroom management. Basically, they were able to reduce lecturing and to increase questioning and to provide opportunities for students to have group discussion. However, there were too many competitions in their so-called collaborative group activities and quite often they wasted too much time in "running activities" that they could not catch up their pre-scheduled lesson plan. One of them reflected that because of their limited pedagogical synthetic knowledge, they were short of flexibility and guiding ability in leading the group discussion constructively and productively. She said:

> I realize that I cannot allow my students to have too many discussions because sometimes I have problems in summing up – leading them back to the track. In many cases, though I posed the questions, I had problems to get them back to the main point because there were just too many answers. Especially when some students were intentionally making troubles, I just could not handle the situations well enough to carry on the teaching. Because I did not know how to make the ending, of course the discussion would turn into circling around without any progress. As a result, my teaching was far behind the schedule.

When prospective teachers were compared with in-service teachers, they were more creative in task design. Yet, in-service teachers performed better in keeping the interactive flow of knowledge construction than pre-service teachers. As a matter of fact, the learning tasks designed by prospective teachers were so creative that quite often they were not necessarily relevant to the content or the concepts desired to be taught. Since content knowledge makes a great different in constructivist teaching, how well the participant teachers knew about the content would have impacts on task design and on guiding students' discussions and directing the flow of learning activities. Particularly, they were not mature enough to make proper decisions in the process. Sometimes right after they posed problems for students to work on, they realized that their questions were just too dull for the students to try out any constructive collaborative effort. Also, there were times they felt the needs to provide guided instructions in their teaching, but they had difficulties to do so because they "had no idea about the students' thought process, cognitive development, and life experience in real." More seriously, one of the prospective teachers had false understanding of constructivist teaching, which made the case even worse. All these personal factors would cause problems in their teaching and affect the way they practice constructivist teaching and learning. No wonder one of the prospective teachers reported honestly the following:

> I don't think constructivist teaching is applicable for every teacher. It has put into consideration of individual teacher's characteristics. Some teachers are good at leading discussions then they probably are more adequate to implementing a constructivist approach. For me, I am not good at posing questions or leading discussions. I just feel I'd better try not to ruin the class. I think if I don't try out any constructivist approach I can handle my teaching better and at least I will not misleading my students to do harm to them. Indeed, I need to examine myself to see if I am capable to apply this approach in teaching.

From the problems found in prospective teachers' teaching practice, I realize that most participant prospective teachers were lack of autonomy, ownership, pedagogical judgement, and professional confidence as they first got into the teaching field. Although they were equipped with new perspectives and were willing to try out new approaches, they were not mature enough to handle the constraints or to overcome their limitations to apply the constructivist approach in a proper way.

As I reflected upon the course design I had for prospective teachers in the first year, I realized that I might have not provided enough simulated experiences for them to construct the pedagogical knowledge they needed for professional judgement in the field. Nor had I created opportunities to test or to understand if they did build the professional confidence for being a constructivist teacher. Although I provided the theory, the methods, and skills, as well as the constructivist learning experiences in the professional development course, the course by itself did not provide for "enculturation" of a type, as mentioned by Bauersfeld (1998), that is appropriate with respect to a (constructivist) teacher's role in the classroom. When the prospective teachers got into the field and provided their individual efforts, of course, they would become frustrated and confused.

Indeed, the training model of teacher education, even the professional development course I implemented with a new approach, often ignored the curriculum structure and the social and political contexts that the prospective students would be confronted with in a real school setting. It is important for me, as a teacher educator, to reexamine what needs to be included in teacher preparation programs to enable prospective teachers be mature and confident enough for their teaching profession.

Problems Reflected in In-service Teachers' Teaching

For the participant in-service teachers, they were so used to the traditional way of knowledge transmission that it was so difficult for them to turn over to the constructivist approach right away. As they reflected that they were "used to follow the steps/preplanned procedures in teaching," they had to try hard to conduct different ways of teaching, including waiting for and dealing with students' alternative ideas. Only two of the participant in-service teachers were able to slow down their pace and to appreciate the time spent for creating interactive environment for constructive learning. As they realized that providing students opportunities to think and to express themselves was very helpful for their students to become active learners, they thought it was worthy trying. For other participant in-service teachers, although they were eager to make a change too, lots of times they were just so tired of spending so much time to re-design their course plan and to prepare the materials and the environment for constructivist teaching and learning. A lot of times they felt frustrated that there were just too many administrative chores taking up their time and they were not able to spend more time on thinking and planning. A teacher reflected:

> To conduct a constructivist approach well, the teacher needs to be well prepared for the whole unit. It involves a series of thorough deliberation. It requires teacher to think ahead about many questions and alternatives. It is time consuming. I don't have that much time. There are so many affairs involved in leading a class. Truly, often times I feel I don't have the energy.

Struggling between the ideal and the reality, they sometimes felt they "bite off more than they can chew." As an in-service teacher pointed out that there was no way for them to apply what they learned from the theories into teaching practice right away. In other words, they needed time "to learn the 'how to' by actually doing it." They said: "We are actually adjusting ourselves gradually in our real teaching." Since participant in-service teachers were not used to the new teaching approach, quite often they would slip back to their old way of teaching, consciously or unconsciously. Particularly, they were not patient enough in waiting for students' construction of knowledge. They would pop out the "correct answer" to assist students, to make the flow of learning go smoothly. One of them reported:

> To let students discuss and report their findings one group after another, it just wastes too much time. I have to move fast in order to catch up the schedule. Because of the unified monthly joint exam scheduled by the school, I have to concern what needs to be covered in my teaching. Though constructivist teaching allows students to construct their own knowledge, it wastes more time than traditional teaching in clarifying students' misconceptions.

Although all the participant in-service teachers recognized the advantages of applying a constructivist approach in their teaching, all these mentioned practical concerns would more or less decreased the power of constructivist approach to knowledge building of their students. One in-service teacher told me that since she was the only one in her school to try out constructivist teaching, she could hardly find someone to share experience and exchange ideas. She urged that "If there are more teachers doing it together or there is someone else to support you, things will be much easier. The atmosphere will be changed gradually for the encouragement of implementing new ideas in teaching. Then, it would be easier for the adoption of constructivist teaching methods."

Indeed, we cannot clap with one hand. When there are more than one teacher trying out new ideas together in a school, it would have a better chance to see the effective change happening in teaching and learning. For the implementation of a constructivist teaching approach, no teacher can do it alone. It is important for teachers to find a critical friend and to form a supportive team as they strive for the betterment of (constructivist) teaching and learning. From the problems reflected in in-service teachers' teaching, I realize they need stronger will to confront traditional views of efficient/effective teaching and learning as well as to transcend old/familiar ways of educational practices. They also need more commitment to the constructivist pedagogy that stands in contrast to the more traditionally held "authoritarian" forms of pedagogy. I think the professional development course designed for in-service teachers should have engaged them more in reflective learning experiences that confront traditional beliefs and practices. Also, it would be better to include opportunities for in-service teachers to see "teacher as a researcher" and to be able to practice action inquiry in their own classroom setting to construct their personal theories. I believe in-service teachers need to be empowered with a better sense of professional autonomy that they are able to decide about how to teach what should be taught in what pace.

Contextual/External Problems for Both Prospective and In-service Teachers

Students' Ability and Motivation

As mentioned earlier, students' ability and skills in expressing self and in communication, as well as the classroom/group climate, would have effects on the practice of constructivist teaching and learning. In-service teachers also doubted if the constructivist approach was appropriate to all students and all subject matters. Particularly, for low achievement students and low motivation students, some teachers expressed that they would be glad to help but cannot through a constructivist approach which, they believed, was more helpful for medial or high achievement students. A third-grade teacher noted:

> Constructivist teaching encourages students to construct their own knowledge based upon their prior knowledge foundation. But how about a student with very low degree of knowledge of a subject? How do we help such a student to construct knowledge? Build upon what? Or how about if a student has no motivation at all? How do we help such a student to learn actively through a constructive approach?

School Culture that Treasures "Quietness"

Participant teachers reflected that it is hardly to change students' learning habits, to make them talk, and to know what they are thinking. However, applying constructivist teaching causes more problems for classroom management than traditional teaching approach. An in-service teacher pointed out:

> I had difficulties in managing my class when I applied a constructivist approach. When the class was so easy to be out of control and the students were so easy to get into chattering around. I was so afraid that if they got used to talking in the class, they would not learn to keep quiet when they are supposed to. This disturbs me a lot.

Indeed, due to the low tolerance of the noise and the pressure from the competition for "classroom order," many teachers would quite often quit group discussions and went back to lecturing as they felt the discussions were somewhat "clamorous." In an oriental culture that treasures "quietness" with sayings like "silence is gold" and "a child should have ears to hear, but not a mouth to chatter," the applications of constructivism in Taiwan education maybe is good for individual construction but not so good for social construction. However, the issue of culture as a powerful factor that may promote or constrain constructivist views and practices is still under debate.

Unified Curricular Plan and Assessment

Also, there were more serious contextual problems concerned by both prospective and in-service teachers. They expressed that the school-wide unified progress plan for content coverage in teaching and the calendar-based monthly unified examinations were their major concerns as they were struggling between if they should implement the constructivist approach in their teaching or not. Although many of them had experienced the advantages of the constructivist approach in terms of "encouraging students' participation," "promoting intrinsic learning motivation," "enhancing meaningful knowledge construction," and "creating enjoyable learning experiences," they still withdrew from being a constructivist teacher. It was just because they had to deal with the pressure and requirement from the fixed curriculum schedule of the school. Sometimes, the parents even put more pressure on teachers than the administrators by requiring teachers to cover or to teach everything shows in the textbooks and to prepare their kids to get better grades. As the teachers put it, "[P]arents are more difficult to communicate with the new ideas and are harder to persuade to give up the old practices."

Large Classroom Size with Insufficient Teaching Supplies

Large number of students (average around 35-40 students per class) and insufficient teaching supplies were the other common factors that always cause problems in implementing a constructivist approach in teaching. For example, the participant teachers told me that "[I]t is very difficult for me to do the grouping with limited classroom space for over 35 students," and "[I]t is quite challenging for me to trace and utilize so many students' prior knowledge and to conduct an open-ended constructivist instruction." Also, they complained that "[A]lthough the instructional materials and teaching supplies are much improved and well equipped in every school nowadays, the demands of better and more teaching supplies in a constructivist classroom are greater than the traditional one." Therefore, many participant teachers felt that implementing a constructivist teaching approach in their classroom was not easy. They could hardly take their mind off figuring out some alternative ways to solve such practical problems beyond planning for the learning tasks.

All these external contextual problems are very troublesome for both participant prospective and in-service teachers, as well as for other teachers in general. "Unless these problems be solved, they would remain as nightmares, practically and psychologically," said by one of the in-service teachers. From the responses I got from other teachers in the professional growth group, these contextual problems and barriers contributed to their being reluctant in trying out constructivist teaching. However, I believe removing any of the above contextual problems and barriers is by no means an easy task, because they all call for reason and argument, reforming effort, and ideological breakthrough. Since most schools in Taiwan are overwhelmingly dominated by didactic, content-oriented, and test-driven methods and most teachers believe transmitting "correct knowledge" is what a "good" teacher should do, it is hard for them to believe that constructivist perspectives could provide a set of resources for these challenging educational tasks in Taiwan.

To create a better context for encouraging constructivist teaching and learning, there must be collective efforts from teachers, administrators, educational policy-makers, and so forth. It is a fact that many of the contextual problems must be resolved by administrative, social, or even political efforts. However, teacher education programs still can do something to contribute to develop teachers as change agents and to equip teachers with the ability to adopt and adapt multiple approaches to deal with various learning styles and degrees of motivation found among students. Through providing an alternative approach to professional development courses – a constructivist approach – to help teachers "be free of bureaucratic and discipline-based structures so they can determine curriculum activities themselves ... both teachers and students ought to be more creative and experimental..." (McCarty & Schwandt, 2000, pp. 81-82).

CONCLUSION

As teacher educators, we face the challenge of helping our students create classroom contexts and instructional strategies that demonstrate a constructivist perspective on teaching and learning. There are more and more teacher educators beginning to report on efforts to accomplish this goal (e.g.,

Black & Ammon, 1992; Kroll & Black, 1993; Fosnot, 1996; Richardson, 1997). As findings of this study show, while lots of the outcomes are very encouraging and educationally helpful, there are still problems that need to be solved and barriers that need to be overcome. We need to encourage more thoughtful programs that emphasize reflection and inquiry on the part of teachers and help them "identify and defend their own perspectives" in their practical, constructivist endeavor.

Fosnot (1996) suggest that teacher education programs based on a constructivist view of learning need to do more than offering a constructivist perspective in a course or two. Indeed, the power and effects of one or two professional development courses are just too limited. To make the paradigm shift in education happen, teachers need to be engaged in learning experiences that challenge them to keep questioning, reflecting, and constructing. Professional development courses for teacher education can be organized and designed to provide constructivist learning experiences that promote necessary changes in teachers' basic orientations and routines toward pedagogical practices. Another illuminating idea out of this study is that running a professional growth group, which provides constant support for in-service teachers' professional development, can be considered as one of the applicable alternatives with great potentials to encourage the implementation of a constructivist approach or any other new perspectives in teaching.

A constructivist approach requires that teachers build, or restructure, their knowledge about teaching so that it makes sense to them. No matter which approach we choose to encourage constructivist thinking and practices, we should recognize and invite critical inquiry into attitudes and beliefs about teaching. We also need to prepare teachers with sound rationales for teaching if their views about what to teach and how to teach are tested. Yet, at the same time, we have to understand and help teachers understand that constructivism is not the panacea for all of the instructional problems in education. It is quite true that constructivism is just like many other theories and technologies are – all are designed to make learning a more realistic and meaningful process.

As Richardson (1997) reminds, we should not oversimplify or romanticize about the benefits of adopting a constructivist approach. In fact, questions remain that the constructivist teaching practice can be applied to all students and all curricular practices. No constructivist shall try to offer monolithic pictures of teaching and learning. As many educational researchers and teacher educators are exploring the effects and constraints of implementing constructivist perspectives in educational praxis, Phillips (2000), in the Ninety-ninth yearbook of the NSSE, provides his opinions to warn us that we should not be beguiled by the currently "fashionable magic word – constructivism." Burbules (2000), in the same volume, encourages theorists, researchers, and educators to move beyond the impasse of current philosophical and pedagogical debates on constructivism. He makes his point clear:

> Teaching and learning in a constructivist manner force us to narrow in on understanding the practices and procedures by which human actors in specific social contexts generate hypotheses, assess them, compare them with others, adjudicate disagreements or controversies over methods of inquiry, and so on. The irony is that debates over constructivist theory quickly lose sight of these factors and get embroiled in disputes that are almost entirely generated at an abstract level (p. 329).

Like many scholars has done in the volume – rethinking constructivism in education and providing opinions on related controversial issues – we teacher educators should also be cautious and be critical about what we are advocating. We also need to be willing, as Phillips (2000) suggests, "… to probe beneath the surface, to attempt to tease out what is important and good, what is important but mistaken, and what is not important at all in the various schools of thought that have appropriated the constructivist label in one or other of its various manifestations" (p. 2).

Last but not least, due to the socio-cultural background and the educational values and traditions in Taiwan as many other oriental countries, I believe, we need to pay more attention to the culture differences may effect the outcomes of implementing constructivist thinking and practices "imported" from the west. Yes, "constructivism" may embodies a thesis about the bodies of knowledge that "have been built up during the course of human history" (Phillips, 2000, p. 6). Yet, in terms of its implications and implementations in education, there should not be "universalized" approaches or procedures. Educational practices are culture- and context-bounded. The politics, ideologies, values, beliefs, traditions, and so forth are all at play. As it shows in the findings, there are implementing problems that are uniquely situated in the educational context in Taiwan. As we realize that the constructivist approach in teaching and learning capitalizes on context a lot, how can we not to pay attention to the issue of contextualization in the implementation of a constructivist approach. In order to search for the possibilities of transcending contextual constraints along instrumental and practical lines, of course, there is an imperative need to call for the contextualized transformation of constructive approaches that will be culturally relevant to the unique educational context in Taiwan, so as of teacher education programs.

NOTES

[1] The Task Force Committee for the revision of curriculum standards was formed in December 1988 and it took four years to complete the task. Comparing to the old curriculum standards (of the 1975 version), the new curriculum standards (of the 1993 version) has infused with a lot of new concepts, characteristics, and elements. Teachers not only have to change their perceptions about teaching and learning but also have to change their teaching practices. With such a background, this study also set its goal to prepare pre-service and in-service teachers to cope with the enactment of new curriculum standards. However, there are currently other new curriculum policies as well as reform efforts for the implementation of newly promulgated Curriculum Guidelines for Compulsory Education (1-9) (the 1998 version, which will be put into practice in the school year of 2001).

[2] Before 1995, the teaching training education programs were only provided at teachers colleges (preparing elementary and kindergarten teachers) and normal universities (training teachers for the secondary level). All of them are four-year programs. After the Teacher Education Law was promulgated and enacted in 1995, public and private colleges and universities are also eligible to provide teacher education programs to train teachers (40 credit hours for elementary teachers and 26 credit hours for subject teachers at secondary level).

REFERENCES

Bauersfeld, H. (1998). Remarks on the education of elementary teachers. In M. Larochelle, N. Bednarz & J. Garrison (Eds.). *Constructivism and Education.* (pp. 213-232). Cambridge, UK: Cambridge University Press.

Black, A., & Ammon P. (1992). A developmental-constructivist approach to teacher education. *Journal of Teacher Education, 43*(5), 323-335.

Bodner, G. M. (1986). Constructivism: A theory of knowledge. *Journal of Chemical Education, 63*(10), 873-878.

Burbules, N. C. (2000). Moving beyond the impasse. In D. C. Phillips (Ed.). *Constructivism in education: Opinions and second opinions on controversial issues* (pp.308-330). Chicago, IL: NSSE.

Chen, H. L. S. (1997). Toward a re-constituted action inquiry for educational studies. *Proceedings of the National Science Council, ROC, Part C: Humanities and Social Sciences, 7*(2), 167-180.

Clandinin, D. J. (1986). *Classroom practice: Teacher images in actions.* London: Falmer Press.

Clark, C. M., & Peterson, P. L. (1986). Teachers' thought processes. In M. C. Wittrock (Ed.), *Handbook of research on teaching* (3rd ed.), 256-296. NY: Macmillan.

Driver, R., & Oldham, V. (1986). A constructivist approach to curriculum development in science. *Studies in Science Education, 13,* 105-122.

Fosnot, C. T. (1996). Teachers construct constructivism: The center for constructivist teaching/teacher preparation project. In C. T. (ed.). *Constructivism: Theory, perspectives, and practice* (pp. 205-216). New York: Teachers College Press.

Glasson, G. E., & Lalik, R. V. (1993). Reinterpreting the learning cycle from a social constructivist perspective: A qualitative study of teachers' belief and practices. *Journal of Research in Science Teaching, 30*(2), 187-207.

Kroll, L., & Black, A. (1993). Developmental theory and teaching methods: A pilot study of a teacher education program. *The Elementary School Journal, 93*(4), 417-441.

Loughran, J. & Russell, T. (1997). Meeting student teachers on their own terms: Experience precedes understanding. In V. Richardson (Ed.). *Constructivist teacher education: Building a world of new understandings* (pp. 164-181). London: Falmer Press.

Meyer-Smith, J. A. & Mitchell, I. J. (1997). Teaching about constructivism: Using approaches informed by Constructivism. In V. Richardson (Ed.). *Constructivist teacher education: Building a world of new understandings* (pp. 129-153). London: Falmer Press.

McCarty L. P. & Schwandt, T. A. (2000). Seductive illusions: Von Glasersfeld and Gergen on epistemology and education. In D. C. Phillips (Ed.). *Constructivism in education: Opinions and second opinions on controversial issues* (pp.41-85). Chicago, IL: NSSE.

Ministry of Education (1998). *Curriculum Guidelines for Compulsory Education (1-9).* Taipei: Author.

Ministry of Education (1993). *New Curriculum Standards for Elementary Schools.* Taipei: Author.

Peterman, F. (1997). The lived curriculum of constructivist teacher education. In V. Richardson (Ed.). *Constructivist teacher education: Building a world of new understandings* (pp. 154-163). London: Falmer Press.

Phillips, D. C. (2000). An opinionated account of the constructivist landscape. In D. C. Phillips (Ed.). *Constructivism in education: Opinions and second opinions on controversial issues* (pp.1-16). Chicago, IL: NSSE.

Richardson, V. (1997). Constructivist teaching and teacher education: Theory and practice. In V. Richardson (Ed.). *Constructivist teacher education: Building a world of new understandings* (pp. 3-14). London: The Falmer Press.

Schon, D. A. (1991). The reflective turn: Case studies in and on educational practice. New York: Teachers College Press.

Steffe, L.P., & Gale, J. (Eds.). (1995). *Constructivism in education*. Hillsdale, NJ: Lawrence Erlbaum.

Strauss, A., & Corbin, J. (1990). Basics of qualitative research: Grounded theory procedures and techniques. Newbury Park, CA: SAGE.

Taiwan Provincial Institute for Elementary School Teachers' In-service Education [TPIESTIE] (Ed.). (1995). *The spirit and characteristics of new curriculum standards*. Taipei: Author.

Vadeboncoeur, J. A. (1997). Child development and the purpose of education: A historical context for constructivism in teacher education. In V. Richardson (Ed.). *Constructivist teacher education: Building a world of new understandings* (pp. 15-37). London: Falmer Press.

Von Glasersfeld, E. (1984). An introduction to radical constructivism. In P. Watzlawick (Ed.), *The invented reality* (pp. 17–40). New York: Norton.

Von Glasersfeld, E. (1995). A constructivist approach to teaching. In L. P. Steffe & J. Gale (Eds.), *Constructivism in Education* (pp. 3–15). Hillsdale, NJ: Lawrence Erlbaum Associates.

Zeichner, K. M., & Tabachnick, B. R. (1991). Reflections on reflective teaching. In B. R. Tabachnick & K. M. Zeichner, (Eds.), *Issues and practices in inquiry-oriented teacher education.* (pp. 1-21). London; New York: Falmer Press.

Chapter 12

Developments in Teacher Education in the Asia-Pacific: Issues and Prospects towards the 21st Century[1]

Rupert MACLEAN

UNESCO International Centre for
Technical and Vocational Education and Training, Paris

INTRODUCTION

While the present century draws to a close, education has emerged at the forefront of the world's concerns over its own future. The challenges of the new century to eliminate poverty, achieve equity and justice, and ensure sustainable development and lasting peace will fall to today's young people, and so educating the young to meet these challenges has become a priority objective for every society. In this regard, the teacher is seen as being the cornerstone of education development. The Delors Report (1996) has observed that in the coming century "[M]uch will be expected, and much demanded of teachers" (p. 141). This is hardly an overstatement in the case of Asia-Pacific.

Given the significance, yet increasingly demanding, role played by teachers, development in teacher education in Asia and the Pacific must be reviewed for systematically exploring the various critical issues so that effective strategies for coping with those issues can be formulated. Nevertheless, it is worth pondering for a moment the characteristics of the Asia-Pacific region in order to establish an appropriate context for examining teachers and teacher development.

The region, being home of 63% of the world's population of almost 6 billion, is outstanding for the vast range of diversities which encompass almost all aspects of life, whether it be geographical, socio-economic, cultural, political, or developmental.

There are in the region countries of vast land masses - Australia, China, and India - and also island countries lying in vast ocean areas - the Maldives and Pacific Islands. Countries with the largest populations - China (1.2 billion) and India (973 million) - and the most rapidly growing mega-cities are to be found in the region, as are countries with relatively small populations - Bhutan (600,000) and Niue (1,800). The levels of economic development also vary widely, with some of the richest countries, such as Japan, and some of the poorest countries on Earth, such as Bangladesh.

The region also faces some of the major problems that mankind at the current time must tackle. For instance, there are estimated to be currently a total of 625 million illiterates in Asia-Pacific, i.e., 71% of the world's total, of whom 64% are women and girls. It is estimated that by 2000 there will be 74 million out-of-school children in the 6-11 years age group in developing countries in the region. Some of the wide disparities that exist in Asia are particularly disturbing. For instance, the literacy rate in South Asia is 42%, compared to 72% in East and South East Asia; further, life expectancy in South Asia is 10 years lower than for those living in East and South East Asia.

This diversity in demography, economy, geography, ecology, and culture within the region presents challenges for international aid agencies, such as United Nations Educational, Scientific and Cultural Organization (UNESCO).[2]

Despite such mammoth problems and such diversity, there is still a *common thread* in that all countries in the region. In order to achieve poverty eradication, sustainable human development, and equity in all respects, there is a need to make greater efforts to improve the *quality, effectiveness,* and *relevance* of education and schooling. It follows that improving teacher capability in this increasingly demanding context is imperative.

IMPORTANCE OF TEACHERS

The Teaching Force

In terms of their sheer numbers, teachers are an important occupational group that warrants our attention. For example, there are currently 57 million teachers in the world's formal education systems, while 30 years ago there were 16 million; and in a majority of countries, school teachers are the largest single category of public sector employees, and the largest group of people engaged in professional and technical occupations (UNESCO, 1998c, p. 22).

Then, one out of every two teachers in the world today lives in the Asia-Pacific. Of these teachers, 64% are in less developed countries; 23% in more developed countries; and 13% in countries in rapid transition, such as the five Central Asian Republics, Vietnam, and Mongolia. In fact, a growing percentage of the world's teachers are employed in the world's less developed countries, as these countries pursue a policy of expanding the teaching service to achieve the goals of education for all, the universalization of primary education, and universal literacy.

Further, despite their importance worldwide, teachers are facing major problems that threaten the effectiveness and quality of education systems.

Professional Importance into the Future

Many variables, as we well know, influence the effectiveness of a nation's school system: adequate school buildings and classrooms; a relevant curriculum; high quality and affordable teaching and learning materials, such as textbooks, writing materials, and laboratory equipment; and an accurate system for monitoring education outcomes. All these are important.

Then, there is clear evidence showing that the bottom line is that the quality of any education system ultimately depends on the knowledge, skills, and commitment of teachers. In the words of the Delors Report (1996), *"Good schools require good teachers."* It is therefore essential that the most capable and appropriate people are recruited into the occupation, and are provided with career-long professional development to ensure they continuously update their capability to do the very best job possible in the school and classroom. And so, the matters of the status of teachers, teacher recruitment, pre-service teacher education, the professional career-long development of teachers, and the provision of suitable financial and other rewards to attract and retain suitable individuals in the occupation of teaching are receiving great attention from policy-makers and policy implementors in countries throughout the region, and indeed throughout the world.

There is currently considerable worldwide apprehension about both the present and future situation regarding the place of teachers in a changing world. Even more will be expected of teachers in the future in providing pupils with ethical training, training for tolerance, citizenship, creative thinking, and the ability to manage uncertainty. Yet, as the Delors Report (1996) suggests, at a time when the expectations for teachers have never been greater, in terms of the increasingly diverse nature of the teachers' role, as well as the economic and social status of teachers, in many parts of the world, including the Asia-Pacific, teacher status is in severe decline. Indeed, informally informed observers (see, e.g., World Education Report, 1998c) believe that the *status of teachers* has in fact declined over the past 30 years, and continues to decline in every region and most countries. Indeed, some have argued that it is because of the large number of personnel involved that it is difficult to give teachers a status similar to smaller technical and professional groups, such as doctors, lawyers, and engineers. Through this perspective, it is understandable that, in many of the countries in the region, teachers have a *semi-professional* rather than a full professional status.

Teachers have a major role to play in the process of educational reform and educational change. If the educational reforms initiated by governments to achieve "education for all" and to confront the challenges of the future, such as the effective use of new educational technologies, are to be effective, they must be systematically and effectively be implemented at the school level and in the classroom, implying that teachers are to play a key role in the process of transforming education, and that it is not possible to effectively reform education systems without taking teachers into greater consideration (Ordonez & Maclean, 1997).

Clearly, therefore, one of the major education challenges facing countries currently is to attract and then retain the most able people in the teaching service. Meeting this challenge requires great attention to finding ways to increase the status of teachers, improve their working conditions, and provide appropriate salary levels. These should reflect the important role that teachers play in social, economic, cultural, and technological development. It is now widely recognized by most governments in the Asia-Pacific region that if that children are to have the high quality education, which they and their countries deserve, teachers must receive greater attention (UNESCO, 1999).

CHANGING STATUS AND PROFILE OF TEACHERS: SOME COMMON ISSUES AND CONCERNS

UNESCO has written a number of reports and held several regional meetings at which countries in the Asia-Pacific region have reported upon current issues and concerns with regard to teacher recruitment and teacher education. In terms of the less developed countries in the region in particular, the following are the issues and concerns that have been most frequently identified as being of special importance.

Recruitment

Traditionally, in many less developed countries in the Asia-Pacific, teaching (especially at the post-primary school level) has been a high status occupation, which has attracted well-qualified and committed recruits. In Buddhist countries, for example, teachers have traditionally been revered along with the Monk and parents, for their vitally important work in educating the young to take their place in society. One of the unfortunate developments in many countries is that teaching no longer has the same high status as was the case in the past, when the occupation of teaching was one which would attract some of the best-qualified members of society. In virtually all countries in this region, the status of teachers is on the decline.

Teaching is also a relatively low-status occupation, in that it does not attract the same financial rewards as do many other occupations, particularly those in the private sector. Partly as a result, it is now a second or third choice occupation for many potentially qualified candidates, and there are inevitably major problems in attracting well-qualified recruits into the occupation. Thus, a vicious cycle develops, whereby because many recruits to the occupation are not well qualified, this further lowers the status of the occupation and the bargaining power of teachers to obtain salary increases.

Professional Education and Development

In many countries, recruits to the occupation of teaching commence work with little or no pre-service teacher training. Partly as a result, recruits are socialized on the job by those already employed as teachers, and into what is often a conservative occupational culture which stresses "chalk and talk," the dominance of rote-learning as a teaching technique, and a passive model of student learning. This makes it very difficult for the teachers involved to play a decisive and important role in the process of educational reform.

In many countries, whatever training new recruits to the occupation receive is their "one shot of training," there being few teacher induction programs and very limited facilities to enable in-service training and the career-long professional development of teachers. Partly as a result, it is very difficult to change teacher behavior over time and to bring teachers up to date with latest developments as to how they can be most effective in their work.

Given that UNESCO statistics show that one-third of the 50 million teachers in the world have no formal educational qualifications and another 40% have received inadequate training, the critical importance of in-service teacher education becomes even more evident (International Bureau of Education, 1995).

Reward Structures in the Occupation

The matter of teachers' career and promotion patterns has received considerable attention from researchers (see, e.g., Maclean, 1992). In many countries, difficulty is experienced in keeping well-qualified teachers in the occupation. Particularly in less developed countries that are going through rapid economic transition, such as Vietnam and the Central Asian Republics, employment opportunities available in the expanding economies in such areas as tourism, the hospitality industry, and the development of private sector firms make it difficult to recruit well-qualified candidates into teaching. The salaries of teachers in these countries are well below those offered for equivalently qualified employees in some other occupations, and so there is a "brain drain" of potential (and existing) teachers into these more lucrative occupations.

Indeed, teacher *attrition rates* - that is, the percentage of teachers who leave the profession each year, excluding retirees - continue to be high in all regions and most countries, when compared to those in occupations with comparable levels of qualifications. Then, with regard to the characteristics of teachers, the percentage of teachers who are *females* continues to rise in all regions, including Asia, while the percentage of teachers in Asia who have received at least a secondary education has consistently risen.

In some countries, as already suggested, so much is expected of teachers; yet, they are paid very low salaries. For example, teachers in Cambodia have recently been on strike in order to press for higher salaries: the current salary of a classroom teacher in that country being US$20 per month while that for a backbencher in parliament is US$1,000 or 50 times more. Then, it is interesting to note that the teachers on strike have received substantial backing from students and their parents in their claim for a major salary increase.

In addition, teaching in many countries does not offer a sufficiently attractive reward structure in terms of opportunities for promotion; and when promotion is available, it is generally only available to those who are willing to leave the classroom to take on administrative-type positions. Many countries have not as yet successfully grappled with the matter of how to keep good and effective teachers in the classroom by offering them promotion and increasing their salaries as they deserve.

In looking at the change in status and profile of teachers, the 1998 *World Education Report*, published by UNESCO and on "Teachers and Teaching in a Changing World," indicates that only in a relatively small minority of countries do teachers have reasonably comfortable *incomes* and *conditions* of employment. In the majority of countries, this is certainly not the case: teachers salaries and working conditions are inferior to those of employees with equivalent qualifications entering other occupations.

Because of the low level of salaries, many teachers in the less developed countries are virtually forced into a situation where they have to "moonlight" in order to earn enough to feed, clothe, and house their families. It is not uncommon for teachers to have one or two other jobs, in addition to that of being a teacher. In some countries, individuals subcontract their work as teachers out to other less qualified individuals, where the person to whom the work is sub-contracted receives, for example, 40% of the full salary, while the qualified teacher receives the other 60% of the salary, being at the same time able to engage in a second job.

TEACHERS, TEACHER EDUCATION, AND THE NEW INFORMATION TECHNOLOGIES

For UNESCO and many countries in the region, the new information technologies deserve special mention with regard to their potential impact on teachers and teacher education, particularly as the new millennium approaches (see, e.g., Birch & Maclean, 1998).

The new technologies refer mainly to the computer and related communication equipment and software that enable one computer to "network" with other computers. It also refers to innovative forms of TV satellite communications, such as interactive TV - indeed all interactive media. Emerging challenges for teachers, teaching, and teacher education are posed by the introduction into education of new information and communication technologies.

What have these new information technologies to offer for those living and working in the large and diverse Asia-Pacific region? Are these technologies just as useful and appropriate for those living in the poorest countries in the region as they are for those living in the richest countries? What impact can and will these technologies have on helping achieve greater equity, poverty eradication, and sustainable development in the region? And what is the potential impact of the new information technologies in helping improve the quality, effectiveness, and relevance of education and schooling, in poor and rich countries alike?

One possible but undesirable impact of these technologies is that they might contribute to a widening of the gap between and within countries, between rich and poor, the haves and the have-nots, and between the empowered and those who are marginalized. In reality, there are many possibilities of harnessing information and communication technologies for the achievement of the "education for all" goal, and other aspects of education and schooling. Indeed, there are signs that these technologies could eventually have radical implications for conventional teaching and learning processes, and therefore for the work of teachers and teacher education.

However, according to the 1998 *World Education Report* (UNESCO, 1998c, p. 78), the educational potential of these new information and communication technologies has, as yet, barely been tapped. What is clear is that, as is the case with other sectors of the wider economy and society, education (and in particular teachers) will need to come to terms with the new technologies, in not just the less developed but the more developed countries as well. Special attention and assistance in this regard are required for countries to ensure that the poorest countries do not fall further behind or that the rich-poor gap between developed and developing countries would not widen.

Some examples of the ways in which the new information technologies are being harnessed in less developed countries include the following:

- In Bangladesh, the UNICEF Resident Representative aims to put Internet into every school that has electricity as the planners think this is the most effective way of improving the quality and effectiveness of schooling and for enhancing in-service teacher education programs.

- In India, a pilot study is under way on expanding the use of computers and the Internet in primary and secondary schools and in rural communities.

- In Bhutan, China, and Vietnam, there is widespread use of satellite communications for in-service teacher development courses.

- And in remote parts of China, Cambodia, Pakistan, and India, there is widespread development of literacy programs at the village level using satellite TV with particular reference to adult literacy programs.

Although much more needs to be learned about the educational potential of the new technologies, it is clear that they are likely to have major implications for teachers and teaching. For example, with regard to teaching and learning materials, available evidence (see, e.g., Birch & Maclean, 1998) suggest that books will be increasingly complimented by multi-media software and that there will be greater use of computers in classrooms. However, a major constraint remains cost. Moreover, there is a problem with regard to the production of software, both in terms of who should produce what software and how much to be produced to meet the demand for it; there is also an issue of local development as against that which is imported (especially from the U.S.A.). Furthermore, there is the problem of the access to new technologies of the poorer countries and poorer communities within countries.

With regard to teaching methods and approaches, many existing school buildings and classrooms were not designed to accommodate the use of the new technologies, which often require using available classroom space in a very different way. For example, it is no longer appropriate to have a classroom design where the teacher is always out front, as occurs in conventional classrooms, for given the ways in which the new technologies are being used, the role of the teacher in the classroom changes to that of a "learning coach" or "facilitator."

Over the years, there have been some who have believed that, with the advent of increasingly sophisticated technology, machines can replace the teacher. Teaching machines were all the range in some countries back in the 1960s, the view being that students could most effectively be taught by machines, rather than by teachers, while the teacher would be a technician programming the machines. With the advent of computers and the Internet, as well as their increasingly widespread use in classrooms, there has been further speculation that they may eventually replace the teacher.

Despite such speculation about the use of machines and other educational technologies in classrooms, evidence (see, e.g., Birch & Maclean, 1998; UNESCO, 1998c) suggests that while technology will have an increasingly important role to play in schooling, it is unlikely to replace the teacher. Rather, the teacher will draw upon a wider repertoire of technology when going about her or his work, while maintaining a central role as facilitator and co-ordinator in the educational environment. Hence, teachers need to learn how to use the new information technologies in order to utilize these technologies to improve the effectiveness of their own teaching. They should also assist their students in the use of these new technologies, where the latter have not already in possession of such competencies.

SOME UNESCO ACTIVITIES WITH REGARD TO TEACHERS AND TEACHER DEVELOPMENT

In all of UNESCO's program areas in the Asia-Pacific region, a common theme which has been emphasized is that of strengthening the role of teachers and teacher education in a changing world, particularly in less developed countries in the region.

For example, in the Delors Report (1996), the teacher is seen as the key to the education reform process with regard to implementing the four pillars of learning: *learning to know*; *learning to be*; *learning to do*; and *learning to live together in peace and harmony*. In this regard, the authors of the Report note that "much will be expected, and much demanded, of teachers." They go on to say:

> Our vision of the coming century is of one in which the pursuit of learning is valued by individuals and by authorities all over the world not only as a means to an end, but also as an end in itself. Each person will be encouraged and enabled to take up learning opportunities throughout life. Hence, much will be expected, and much demanded, of teachers, for it largely depends on them whether this vision can come true. Teachers have crucial roles to play in preparing young people not only to face the future with confidence but also to build it with purpose and responsibility. The new challenges facing education - to contribute to development, to help people understand and to some extent come to terms with the phenomenon of globalization, and to foster social cohesion - must be met from primary and secondary school onwards.

> The importance of the role of the teacher as an agent of change, promoting understanding and tolerance, has never been more obvious than today. It is likely to become even more critical in the twenty-first century. The need for change, from narrow nationalism to universalism, from ethnic and cultural prejudice to tolerance, understanding and pluralism, from autocracy to democracy in its various manifestations, and from a technologically divided world where high technology is the privilege of the few to a technologically united world, places enormous responsibilities on teachers who participate in the moulding of the characters and minds of the new generation. (p. 141-142)

This interest of UNESCO in key concerns, such as teacher recruitment, teacher education, teacher effectiveness, and the crucially important role of teachers in educational development, is not just of recent interest and concern. Indeed, 33 years ago, in 1966, UNESCO and ILO (the International Labour Organisation) developed the UNESCO/ILO *Recommendation Concerning the Status of Teachers* (UNESCO/ILO, 1988), which was adopted by a special intergovernmental conference convened by UNESCO and ILO and has been ratified by countries on a regular basis.

This UNESCO/ILO document, which is just as relevant today as when it was first written, provides guidelines for countries to follow in regard to the professional preparation, employment, and conditions of service of teachers, with the focus of the Report being on teachers in the formal school system. One of the important points made in the "recommendations" is that the status of teachers depends on the status of education, and vice versa, as the authors of the Report put it:

If education does not command the respect and support of the entire community, teachers will not command that respect and support. Teachers are those who do the educating in the schools. Other institutions play co-ordinate roles: the family, the media, cultural institutions and others. Schools serve at the very core in the efforts to provide the common basis of learning skills, knowledge, culture, respect for constructive achievement and adherence to common codes of behaviour which are essential to economic, social and cultural progress in society.

When a society fails to recognize that this role must be played by organized education in the schools and under-values its educational system, the status accorded those responsible for the direct day-to-day performance of the educational function is necessarily reduced. It is, of course, teachers who occupy this position in the schools.

The converse is also evident: as teachers are regarded, so are education and the schools. Respect for teachers engenders respect for the function they perform. When teaching as a profession is ill regarded in a society that ill-regard reflects itself on the entire system of organized education.

We believe it to be true that the status of teachers and the status of education are so inter-twined that whatever produces changes in the one will normally produce changes in the same direction in the other. (paras. 13 to 17)

Although the UNESCO/ILO *Recommendation Concerning the Status of Teachers* sets out standards for their working conditions, salaries, training, and career opportunities, the situation has steadily deteriorated in many developing countries.

Then, because of its concern with the declining status of teachers, UNESCO inaugurated *World Teachers' Day* in 1993, which is celebrated on 5 October each year. Since 1996, UNESCO has teamed up with Education International (EI), the world's largest teachers' union, to mark World Teachers' Day in close partnership with teachers themselves. World Teachers' Day is dedicated to correcting the adverse status situation faced by many teachers and to recognizing the significant role played by these men and women.

While the issue of status is to the fore, it is also important to remember that many teachers work under very difficult conditions in remote areas of the country where there are few creature comforts, such as electricity. Given the level of civil unrest that is occurring in many countries at the current time around the world, teachers are also often working under dangerous circumstances, such as in areas where there is armed conflict. In order to help publicize the work of such teachers working in difficult circumstances, UNESCO has recently produced a booklet, *Portraits in Courage* (UNESCO, 1998a). It portrays the courage of teachers who, day in day out, give children an education despite poverty, crisis, and violence. It is also a tribute to their integrity, dedication, and commitment beyond the call of duty. The moving account of these teachers bring their situations to life: confronting violence in school, dealing with pupils who have serious physical, psychological, and learning handicaps, or improvising in large classes under conditions of extreme deprivation without the basic tools for teaching and learning.

Other recent examples of the activities of UNESCO to increase awareness about teachers as an important occupational group in society and to provide guidelines for policy-makers in this area are at least three:

- in 1995 the Annual UNESCO-ACEID (Asia-Pacific Centre of Educational Innovation for Development) International Conference on Education, which had some 500 participants from 32 countries in the Asia-Pacific region, was on the topic of "Partnerships in Teacher Development for a New Asia";

- the 45th Conference of the UNESCO International Bureau of Education in Geneva, which was held in 1996 and attended by over 2,000 participants, was on the topic of "Strengthening the Role of Teachers in a Changing World"; and

- The 1999 UNESCO-ACEID International Conference on Education, held in Bangkok on 13-16 December, was on the topic "Reforming Learning, Curriculum and Pedagogy: Innovative Visions for the New Century."

UNESCO is also involved in providing support and assistance for teacher development in numerous other ways, such as through the UNESCO Teacher Education Resource Pack, which includes a wide range of professional development materials that are particularly relevant for teachers working in the less developed countries; the publications on research for teachers which seek to put the best possible latest educational research into the hands of teacher educators and classroom teachers in an accessible form, and the activities of the 198 ACEID Associated Centres in the Asia-Pacific region, many of which are lighthouse institutions concerned with developing and implementing innovative approaches to improving various areas of education and schooling which impact on teacher education and teacher effectiveness.

Attention may also be drawn to two current projects in ACEID - one ongoing (in the area of environmental education) and the other, which has just been launched (concerned with values education) - both of which are of particular interest, value, and importance at the current time.

The Innovations in Teacher Education through Environmental Education and Education for Sustainable Development Project is a joint undertaking of UNESCO's ACEID and Griffith University, Brisbane, Australia. The project, which has been operating for over four years, has received combined resources of half a million dollars from the Australian Government, the Japanese National Institute for Educational Research, and from UNESCO-ACEID itself. The project is now entering its third stage which focuses on region-wide implementation.

The purpose of the project is to expand the range of innovative practices used in teacher education programs in the Asia-Pacific region by introducing teachers and teachers in training to the curriculum planning skills and teaching methodologies of environmental education and education for a sustainable future. This is being done through the establishment of a professional development network for teacher educators. The network is a voluntary group of teacher educators who are sharing in the development of carefully researched and evaluated (and culturally sensitive) workshop modules for use in both pre-service and in-service teacher education programs. In this way, the project is providing professional development opportunities for teacher educators by engaging them in a process of sharing, evaluating, and further developing the innovative approaches and materials they are using to promote environmental education. The nine teaching and learning modules developed as part of the project are now being widely used (generally in national languages) in teacher education institutions throughout Asia-Pacific.

The Teacher Education for Peace and International Understanding Project is a joint project between the Flinders University's Institute of International Education (Australia) and ACEID. This project, which was launched in 1998, aims to promote teaching for peace through strengthening the cultural identify of teacher educators and teacher trainees; enhancing the cross-cultural understanding and tolerance of teacher educators and teacher trainees; and enabling teacher trainees, on completion of their studies, to facilitate the development of cultural identity and of cross-cultural understanding and tolerance among the students they teach. This project is being funded by Japan, Australia, and UNESCO-ACEID in Bangkok. Like the teacher education for environmental education project referred to earlier, after identifying a core curriculum that is acceptable to a range of countries in the region, teaching and learning modules will be commissioned and, after trailing in various countries in the region, these will be translated into national languages for use in teacher education institutions throughout the region.

CONCLUSION

In entering the new century, it is important that we do so positively in the belief that the future is there to be shaped, if we have the will to do so. The task will not be easy, as there are a number of tensions to be resolved. The Delors Report (1996) categorized these as tensions between:

- the global and the local;
- the universal and the individual;
- tradition and modernity;
- long-term and short-term considerations;
- competition and equal opportunity;
- the knowledge expansion and the capacity to assimilate it; and
- the spiritual and the material to which one could add "conflict and peace." (p. 16-18)

In our profiling of the future, we need to identify what the citizen of the new age will look like and the competencies we, our children, and their children are going to need to become effective citizens of the new age.

Next, we have to determine what should be taught best to provide these competencies. If the three "Rs" have been battered and buffeted by winds of change, such that those who entered this century would barely recognize them now, what will the next century bring? How is the information explosion to be managed? And what of technological change? How is what that is indigenous to be safeguarded? How is conflict to be resolved peacefully? These and other questions will need to be addressed in determining the curriculum for the future.

The bottom line will be the teachers and the pedagogy. Many have seen the role of the teacher change dramatically over the years. More major change is inevitable. What direction should such change take? What innovative changes can we take into the new century with confidence? How can teachers and teacher educators, as well as pre-service and in-service education, adapt to promote effective teacher development suited to the future, its citizens, and the "brave new world"?

To grapple with these critical issues, it is essential to underscore the fact that teachers and teacher educators are the key to effective education into the future.

NOTES

[1]This chapter is adapted from "Development in Teacher Education in Asia and The Pacific: Issues and Prospects towards the Twenty-First Century" published in Issue 1 of Volume II of the *Asia-Pacific Journal of Teacher Education and Development* of which was an edited version of the Keynote Address on "Teaching Effectiveness and Teacher Development in the New Century," presented at the International Conference on Teacher Education held at The Hong Kong Institute of Education on 22-24 February 1999.

[2]UNESCO's mission statement for the region encapsulates this development-disparity duality: "UNESCO is committed to consolidating the economic growth the region has (until recently) experienced over the past three decades, but it recognizes its ethical mission to complement this growth by addressing the threats to the peace, security and equitable development of this region. There is a widening disparity of opportunity, wealth and empowerment, between and within nations leading to social injustice, discrimination and deprivation of human rights, and an alarming reduction in the quality of individual lives, of communities and societies and of natural environments in many areas of the region" (UNESCO, 1997, p.1). This mission statement helps establish the context within which the matter of teacher education and development in the Asia-Pacific region will be examined in this paper.

REFERENCES

Birch, I., & Maclean, R. (1998). Information and communication technologies for teacher development in the Asia-Pacific region: Issues and challenges. *Asia-Pacific Journal of Teacher Education and Development, 1*(2), 41-52.

Delors Report. (1996). *Learning: The treasure within. Report of the international commission on education for the twenty-first century.* Paris: UNESCO.

International Bureau of Education. (1995). *Educational reform and educational research: New challenges in linking research, information and decision-making.* Geneva: IBE.

Lortie, D. (1975). *School teachers: A sociological study.* Chicago: University of Chicago Press.

Maclean, R. (1992). *Teachers career and promotion pattern: A sociological analysis.* UK: Falmer Press.

Ordonez, V., & Maclean, R. (1997). Impact of research on education policy and practice in Asia-Pacific. *Prospects, 27*(4), 701-712.

UNESCO. (1996a). *Asia-Pacific regional meeting in preparation for the international conference on education.* Bangkok: Author.

UNESCO. (1996b). *Partnerships in teacher development for a new Asia. Report of the first UNESCO-ACEID international conference.* Bangkok: Author.

UNESCO. (1996c). *Strengthening the role of teachers in a changing world: An Asia-Pacific perspective.* Bangkok: UNESCO-ACEID.

UNESCO. (1997). *UNESCO principal regional office for Asia and the Pacific.* Bangkok: Author.

UNESCO/ILO. (1988). *Recommendation concerning the status of teachers.* Paris: Author.

UNESCO. (1998a). *Portraits in courage.* Paris: Author.

UNESCO. (1998b). *Statistical yearbook.* Paris: Author.

UNESCO. (1998c). *World education report.* Paris: Author.

UNESCO. (1999). *Second meeting of the intergovernmental regional committee on education in Asia and the Pacific (EDCOM).* Bangkok: Author.

Part IV

Innovation and Reflection on Teacher Education Practice

Doris Pui Wah CHAN-CHENG
Alice Wai Kwan CHOW
Victor FORRESTER
Ken FOSTER
Ruth HAYHOE
Rob de JONG
Michelle Mei Seung LAM
Audrey Swee Eng LIM
Maria Natividad LÓPEZ TINAJERO
Angela Hing Man MOK-CHEUNG
Alex Mulalo MUTSHEKWANE
So Fong NGAN
He`-chuan SUN

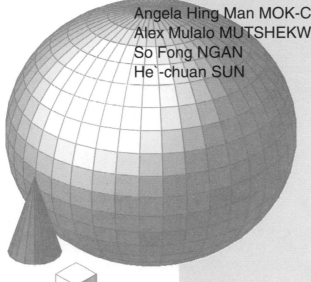

Chapter 13

The Teacher in Chinese Culture: Learning from the Narratives of Influential Teachers

Ruth HAYHOE

Office of the Directorate
The Hong Kong Institute of Education, Hong Kong

This chapter focuses on the role of the teacher within Chinese culture. It is an experimental effort to understand the role of teachers in modern China through the eyes of individuals who lived out their lives through a tumultuous century of dramatic political and economic change. The three teachers whose life stories are shared here began their interest in education through an initial experience as a primary school teacher, which ignited a lifelong commitment to teaching. The eldest was born in 1912, a year after the revolution which ended the last imperial dynasty. The second was born in 1920, a year after the May Fourth Movement, often described as China's enlightenment, a turning point from the constraints of Confucian orthodoxy to democracy and science. The third was born in 1929, a year after the Nationalist regime managed to establish the first unified republican government. They thus lived through great movements of change, each at a different age and in a different stage of their career development.

The chapter begins with a brief exploration of narrative method as a way of understanding educational development and the role of the teacher. It then considers the traditions of the teacher in Chinese culture, identifying opposite poles in an educational context which was conservative, yet characterized by certain progressive features. Next, a brief overview of the century of change highlights the regime changes, revolutionary movements and the changing kaleidoscope of external influences that formed the context of these three lives. The three narratives of influential teachers, and the lessons they derived from the experience of their own professional lives, make up the main body of the chapter. The conclusion seeks to draw lessons for teachers and teacher education in Asia today.

NARRATIVE METHOD IN EDUCATIONAL RESEARCH

A few references from the burgeoning literature on narrative method in educational research may serve to illustrate the features that narrative work introduces to the understanding of education. Ivor Goodson, one of the pioneers of this type of research, makes the following point: "The project I am recommending is essentially one of reconceptualizing educational research so as to assure that the teachers' 'voice' is heard, heard loudly, heard articulately" (Goodson, 1991b, p. 139). Farady and Plummer comment from their experience with narrative research that "[W]hen one conducts a life history interview, the findings become alive in terms of historical process and structural constraints. People do not wander around the world in a timeless and structureless limbo..." (as quoted in Goodson, 1991a, p. 133).

In the case of teachers in China, the weight of history and constraint of structure is particularly great. Thus, the voice of the teacher, speaking from inner experience acquired over a long period of time, is particularly fascinating. The following quotation from Marx may shed light on the reasons why Marxist ideas were so appealing to young Chinese seeking a way out of their historical dilemma early in the century: "Men make their own history, but not in any way they please: they make it under circumstances not chosen by themselves but ... given and transmitted from the past. The tradition of dead generations weighs like a nightmare on the brain of the living" (Marx, 1969, p. 369).

In addition to the weight of tradition, there have also been great constraints upon Chinese teachers arising from the intense series of political movements they have lived through since 1949. Many political struggles targeted teachers, for their conservatism, and so one could not expect them to speak openly and freely about their thoughts and experiences, especially with outsiders. For this reason, narratives of living individuals have seldom been included in research carried out on Chinese education after 1949. Only in the greater openness that has emerged in the 1980s and 1990s has it become possible for an outsider to pursue research which focuses on the experience of individual teachers and their own personal accounts of how they built up the field of education in modern China. A quote from Bertaux (1981) points to this element in the literature on narrative: "What is really at stake is the relationship between the sociologist and the people ... accepting to be interviewed on their life experience" (p. 9).

OPPOSITE POLES IN THE CHINESE TRADITION OF THE TEACHER

For nearly two millennia, Chinese education was dominated by civil service examinations which provided the apex of the education system. The system itself had often been described as an examination ladder, that began at the county level, operated at prefectural, provincial, and capital levels, and opened the door for the few successful candidates into the imperial palace itself. The Emperor Zhen Zong wrote a poem which described the system with great vividness (as quoted in Henze, 1984, p.94):

> *To enrich your family, no need to buy good land;*
> *Books hold a thousand measures of grain.*
> *For an easy life, no need to build a mansion:*
> *In books are found houses of gold.*
> *Going out, be not vexed at absence of followers:*
> *In books, carriages and horses form a crowd.*
> *Marrying, be not vexed by lack of a good go-between:*
> *In books there are girls with faces of jade.*
> *A boy who wants to become a somebody*
> *Devotes himself to the classics, faces the window and reads.*

The ideal teacher was one who had himself succeeded in climbing this ladder, and then come back in an official capacity to administer and supervise the examinations which allowed the next generation to cross the same narrow path into power and wealth. Relations were formal, involving the memorization of a large number of texts and the monitoring of intense competition. In one form or another, this examination ladder has haunted East Asia ever since, and its patterns can be seen up to the present in the kinds of pressures facing students and teachers in Hong Kong's schools. One of the best depictions of the system was written by a Japanese scholar, seeking to understand a set of patterns that has also exerted a strong influence on modern Japanese education: *China's Examination Hell* by Miyazaki (1977).

While this model has tended to dominate the imagination when thinking of classical China, there are also progressive traditions of the teacher and settings in which teachers were able to interact in less formal ways with their students. The model associated with the traditional academy or *shuyuan* is a particularly attractive example of the progressive tradition of the teacher in Chinese culture (Hayhoe, 1996, pp. 3-5). The *shuyuan* was an institution that emerged during the Tang dynasty (628-907 C.E.), a period when China's civil service examination system was being consolidated. Opposite in many ways to the official institutions associated with the imperial examination system, it was a local institution, often established by a scholar out of favour with officialdom, sometimes in association with local gentry and at times with Buddhist temples. Ownership of land and its rental for agricultural purposes was what made academies financially independent, while the library and provision for wide-ranging scholarly research attracted students of all ages.

Activities of the *shuyuan* included lectures, essay contests, and self-study in a quiet environment, with each student developing a close relationship with the master or *shanzhang* (Meskill, 1982). During the Song dynasty (960-1279 C.E.), academies conformed more and more to the dominant Confucian ideology in the content of knowledge dealt with; yet, this apparent conformity led to a constant questioning and re-thinking of Confucian orthodoxy, as ideas from Buddhist, Daoist, and other sources were introduced (De Bary and Chaffee, 1989). This openness to external influence stood in contrast to the canonical approach to knowledge of the institutions associated with the imperial examination system. The *shuyuan* was thus an important institution in Chinese educational tradition, a main point of intellectual innovation and progressive thought within an imperial system where knowledge was effectively tied to the maintenance of power (Ding and Liu, 1992). The informal character of teaching and learning it encouraged was one of its notable features. There was also the sense of a scholarly community committed to critical reflection and debate over all areas of knowledge and their relation to society and polity in a dialectic that challenged and transformed official canons of knowledge. Furthermore, there was a connectedness to local issues and concerns, that made it a vital and dynamic institution (Keenan, 1994).

A CENTURY OF CHANGE AND REVOLUTION IN CHINESE EDUCATION

The 20th century has been a period of dramatic change for China, including a number of regime changes, from the last Manchu dynasty, through the Nationalist period to the establishment of the People's Republic in 1949, and a series of revolutionary upheavals after 1949, most notably the Great Leap Forward of 1958 and the Cultural Revolution of 1966. Each change had tremendous consequences for education, and in each period a different foreign model for educational reform was emulated. The main periods of political and social change over the 20th century will be sketched out briefly, to give a framework of the tumultuous times the three teachers have lived through.

At the opening of the century, a certain number of Chinese reformers were looking to Japan as a model for a kind of constitutional monarchy, which could maintain Confucian social values while bringing China into the modern world. A very large number of young Chinese studied in Japan over this period, most of them being prospective teachers, and the first modern system of education, established in 1902-03 was modelled very closely on Japan (Abe, 1987). In fact, many of the young people studying in Japan were influenced by currents of radical thought and contributed on return to the movements that overthrew the last dynasty in 1911, and opened the way for a whole new phase.

In the next phase, European influences were quite strong, due to the fact that the first minister of education in the new republic, Cai Yuanpei, had spent many years of study in France and Germany. New legislation explicitly supported education for republicanism, and new structures for primary and secondary education followed more closely European than Japanese models. The greatest difficulty of this period was the failure to establish republican political institutions and the near re-establishment of an imperial dynasty under Yuan Shikai in 1917, creating a very unstable situation for modern educational development. The May 4th movement of 1919 was a kind of clarion call among students and intellectuals to embrace science and democracy, and turn away once and for all from the kinds of traditional social and familial values that had supported the imperial system (Chow, 1960). John Dewey arrived for a two year visit at the time of the May 4th movement, and the subsequent period of educational development was greatly influenced by a younger generation of Chinese scholars who had studied in America (Keenan, 1977). Educational legislation passed in 1922 and 1924 supported the decentralization of school management and a philosophy of education that encouraged problem-solving and social responsibility (Yin, 1924).

With the establishment of the Nationalist regime in 1928, there was greater and greater concern for the regularization of the modern education system, to ensure consistent academic standards across various levels and regions and to instil patriotism and an understanding of Sun Yat Sen's "three principles of the people" which were meant to underlie the new regime. European models appealed to the new leaders, because of their greater centralization and capacity for control, and a European delegation under the League of Nations was invited to review the education system and give suggestions for improvement in 1931 (Hayhoe, 1984, pp.

35-42). With the outbreak of the Sino-Japanese War in 1937, followed by the Second World War, then the Civil War between Nationalist and Communist forces in China, from 1945 to 1949, a prolonged period of suffering and disruption occurred for all Chinese people and particularly for teachers. Many schools moved inland as the Japanese invaded and took control over large parts of the coastal area, and there are many stories of heroism among teachers and students who tried to continue their educational work under extremely difficult circumstances (Freyn, 1940). There were also difficult choices between education and direct involvement in the political struggles of the time, and in the anti-Japanese war effort. A whole alternative approach to education was developed in Yanan under the Communist party, which came to be known as the Yanan model of education, and emphasized linking theory to practice and relating education to political change (Wang, 1975).

With the victory of the Communist forces in 1949 and the establishment of the People's Republic, a completely new era began for education. The new leaders felt a strong sense of urgency to achieve "socialist construction" as quickly as possible, after the years of warfare, and they were convinced that the Soviet model of education would be most suited to this. Therefore, Soviet patterns were adopted at all levels of the system, and Soviet experts assisted in the re-education of teachers and teacher educators for this new model. A textbook on pedagogy, edited by the then Soviet minister of Education, I. A. Kairov, became the standard text in all normal universities (Price, 1987). Although much was achieved under this period of intense Soviet influence, there was also considerable discontent with the constrictions of a highly academic and highly centralised model, having features that were reminiscent of certain aspects of the European influence of the 1930s (Orleans, 1987). While the Great Leap Forward of 1958 was largely inspired by Maoist politics, there was some genuine concern for a more indigenous approach to education that reflected China's own values, and for wider accessibility to education in hinterland and rural areas (Pepper, 1987, 1996). The new higher institutions established at this time reflected some of these values, and helped ensure a kind of indigenization of aspects of the Soviet model (Hayhoe, 1999, pp. 94-96). By contrast, the Cultural Revolution, which started with an all out attack on "Soviet revisionism" was almost entirely destructive, leaving the legacy of a ten year gap in education for a large part of the population.

When Deng Xiaoping came to power in 1978, he gave education an important role in his new policy of "four modernizations," setting its direction as "facing modernization, the world and the future" (Epstein, 1991; Hayhoe, 1992; Pepper, 1990). An unprecedented number and range of interactions with other countries in education emerged, including North America, Europe, Japan, Russia, and Australia. For the first time in the century, a range of eclectic influences were brought to bear on the educational reform process. Under rhetoric such as "socialism with Chinese characteristics" or "Chinese-style modernization," there was a genuine attempt to think through patterns/ approaches to education that combined China's own traditions and historical experience with new ideas drawn from external models (Henze, 1992).

NARRATIVES OF THREE INFLUENTIAL TEACHERS

All three of the teachers whose stories will be told here regard the period after Deng Xiaoping came to power as the time they were finally able to fulfil their life mission as teachers, after decades of turbulence. The eldest was 66, the second 58, and the third 49 in 1978. They all came from impoverished families, and all began their interest in teaching through an early experience as a primary school teacher. Each lived through the turbulent events of the century at a different age and phase in their career, and each contributed to a different region - the Northwest, the Southeast, and Beijing. Furthermore, each was exposed to a different set of external influences. The eldest spent a period of time in Switzerland and other parts of Europe during the late 1940s; the second had no opportunity for study abroad; the third grew up in an era that made possible five years of educational study in the Soviet Union during the 1950s. Each became known as a pioneer in a distinctive area of education: pedagogy, higher education, and comparative education, respectively.

Li Bingde: Master of Chinese Pedagogy[1]

Li Bingde was born in 1912, in the city of Luoyang, Henan province. His father had had a few years of education in a traditional *sishu* or private school and, on having to go out to work as an accountant, he put all his books in one place and cried at not being able to continue to study. Li was the oldest of five brothers, and from a very early age he felt responsible for his brothers' education, as well as his own, due to his father's uncertain employment and the family's poverty. He started school in 1919, the year of the May 4th movement, and before long the traditional private school where he was enrolled became a government primary school. When he reached lower secondary school, there was so much disruption to his school due to warlord fighting in the Henan area that he often had to spend long periods at home, times when he and his brothers were instructed by their father in the Four Books and Five Classics of the traditional curriculum. At age 16, he succeeded in getting a scholarship to attend an upper secondary school attached to Henan University in the provincial capital of Kaifeng. During his years of study there, he taught English in a private secondary school in order to be able to send money home for the education of his younger brothers.

After two years of upper secondary education, he was accepted into Henan University and chose English as his major. Within a year, he decided to change to education as a major, being deeply affected by a generation of American returned scholars in the university, who believed education was the only way China could be "saved" from the desperate situation it was in. His most intense memories are of Dr. Tai Shuangqiu, who held a PhD from Columbia University under John Dewey's supervision. Dr. Tai had chosen to wear traditional Chinese attire on return from America and gave impassioned lectures, often interrupted by tears, on "a way out for China through education."

On graduation in 1934, Li found a job in a rural primary school, leading the work of an experimental project developed by his professor, Li Lianfang, to help children master reading and mathematics in an accelerated way, following methods of the Belgian educator Decroly. This early experience resulted in a lifelong commitment to teaching and a lifelong interest in educational experimentation. In 1936, he was awarded a scholarship for graduate study at Yanjing University in Beijing, but the second year was interrupted by the outbreak of the Sino-Japanese war in 1937. On his return to Henan, he visited three of the most important experimental sites in education - Liang Shuming's rural education experiment in Zouping, Shandong province; Jimmy Yan Yangchu's Ding County experiment in Hebei; and Tao Xingzhi's Xiaozhuang school in Jiangsu. Overall, he felt Tao achieved the best integration of Chinese and Western thinking, in contrast to Liang's traditionalism, and Yan's Western orientation. During the Sino-Japanese War, Li worked for a provincial normal college, until he was appointed associate professor at Henan University in 1941. He took his young family and followed the university to its remote rural campus in Song county, four days travel through difficult countryside from Luoyang. His fourth child and only son was born in a tiny hamlet on the way. After the war, Li was one of only 100 scholars in the whole of China to gain a full scholarship from the Nationalist government for study abroad. He spent several years in Switzerland and France, studying under Jean Piaget and travelling to visit different sites of educational experimentation.

His return to China in November of 1949, one month after the establishment of the

People's Republic, was never in question, though many others stayed abroad. Both his family and his country called, and he did not hesitate to offer his services to the new regime. He spent nine months at People's University, undergoing courses in Marxism Leninism taught by experts from the Soviet Union, along with many other educators and senior officials of the former Nationalist regime. Then in June of 1950 he was posted to Northwest Normal University in Lanzhou, where he was made full professor and provost immediately. In the anti-Rightist movement of 1957, he was attacked and had a reduction in salary, but was able to keep his professorial title. In 1966, with the Cultural Revolution, he was subjected to even more severe attack and was sent to teach in the primary school attached to the university for a number of years. He regarded this as a welcome opportunity to return to primary school teaching and carry out further experimentation in the teaching of mathematics and Chinese to young children. His son remembers the enthusiasm and energy in teaching preparation he demonstrated during this difficult period.

While Li had published some works before 1949, and a certain number relating to language and literacy teaching in the 1960s, it was really only after 1978, that he was able to bring together a lifetime of educational research and experimentation into a number of important texts which are widely used in normal universities: Research Methodology in Educational Science (*Jiaoyu kexue yanjiu fangfa*); The Theory of Teaching and Learning (*Jiaoxuelun*), and Primary School Language Teaching Methodology (*Xiaoxue Yuwen Jiaoxuefa*). He has also been able to train a new generation of educators at the masters and doctoral level, many of whom are serving in Northwest Normal or other parts of the Northwest, and others in Beijing and Shanghai. He takes great pride in their achievements and keeps in close touch with them.

How did he maintain and build his unwavering commitment to education and teaching through such tumultuous times? How did he cope with the interruptions that came from war before 1949 and political movements after? Li explained that fundamental to everything in his life was the Confucian morality he had been taught in his father's home. Its special feature lies in the fact that it rejects nothing and absorbs all things unto itself, including elements of Daoism and Buddhism that nurture the spirit and support quiet reflection. At the heart of Confucianism is the practice of self-examination, three times each day, questioning one's inner integrity and the direction of one's life.

For the future, Li sees the development of human talent, as envisaged in the concept of "quality education" (*suzhi jiaoyu*) as the key. This concept is now being widely explored in China, and Li feels it has great depth and is closely linked to China's national character (*guoqing*). Only with a full development of human talent can the issues of energy, environment, population, political culture, ethnic conflict, and the regional distribution of economic good be effectively addressed. He also feels that now, more than ever before, the concept that once attracted so many talented people to education in the 1920s, education to save the country, has a new resonance.

In the past, Li believes, both Western and Soviet ideas were introduced to bring about change, but they did not take root, and were not effectively integrated into the Chinese context. There was always a lack of balance, a tendency to lean too far toward external solutions, and a resultant inability to absorb what was introduced from outside. Only with the rise of Deng Xiaoping to power, and the reforms he introduced, was it possible for socialism to be opened up for discussion and debate and to be seen as a way of liberating the mind and seeking practical solutions to real problems. Somehow Li found the strength in his own traditions and in his personal experience of educational experimentation to make a contribution to education that has national significance and has been particularly important to the Northwest region of China.

Pan Maoyuan: Pioneer of Higher Education Research in China[2]

Pan Maoyuan was born in 1920, a year after the May 4th movement, in the city of Shantou, on the northeast coast of Guangdong province, near Fujian. His family was extremely poor, having neither land nor profession, and only three of ten children survived to adulthood. Taught to read by his father and an older brother, because they could not afford to send him to school, he was finally able to enter a local primary school at age eight, where the main content of the curriculum was still traditional classical texts, beginning with the *Three Character Classic*. On finishing primary school, he was needed at home to help his father grind rice and make rice flour and cakes. Fortunately, however, one of his teachers who had a *juren* (second level) qualification from the traditional civil service examinations had noted his flair for writing Chinese, and found him a place where he could be exempt from fees in a Confucian school for lower secondary studies in Shantou. He graduated at age fifteen and was asked to teach primary school for a few months. This experience turned out to be a definitive turning point, as he gained a sense of how significant a teacher's work could be and of all that he would need to learn, in order to pursue teaching as a profession.

The following year he entered an upper secondary school for the training of primary teachers, Haibin secondary school in Shantou, and supported his studies through teaching evening classes. On graduation in 1937, he threw himself into primary school teaching with great enthusiasm, while also contributing to the anti-Japanese war effort, doing organizational and propaganda work in association with the underground work of the Communist Party. His interest in teaching was intense, and outshone a budding interest in literature and the writing of short stories, where he had also been quite successful. Thus in 1940 he decided to take entry examinations to the Faculty of Education of Xiamen University, in spite of the difficult war-time conditions. A year later he managed to enter, and spent the period from 1941 to 1945 in the Faculty of Education at the university's remote location in Changting county, in Fujian province near the border with Jiangxi province.

Most of the professors at that time were American returned scholars, and the department chair, Li Peiyou, had translated a number of Dewey's works into Chinese. Pan was very attracted by their progressive ideas on teaching and learning, which he not only studied, but attempted to put into practice in the teaching he did in both primary and secondary schools as a way of supporting himself through his university study. In his final year, he was head of the teaching affairs section of the county middle school.

On graduation in 1945, Pan taught briefly in county schools in Jiangxi, then moved back to Xiamen in 1946 to take up the position of principal of the attached primary school at Xiamen University and teaching assistant in the faculty of education. In this work, he was most helped by the writings of Tao Xingzhi, who had done much to integrate progressive ideas learned under Dewey with China's own progressive traditions, particularly those of Wang Yangming and Ming neo-Confucianism. Like Li Bingde, he felt that Tao had done most to develop a modern pedagogy rooted in China's own traditions. After 1949, Pan was invited to join the Teaching Affairs office at Xiamen University, and in 1951 he was sent to Beijing for a period of postgraduate study, first at People's University and then at Beijing Normal University, where Russian specialists gave courses on Marxism-Leninism, political economy and educational theory. He was impressed by the thoroughness and attention to academic quality that characterized the Soviet approach to education; he felt that these patterns were particularly suited to China's needs in the 1950s when large numbers of professionals in engineering and other sciences were being trained to make possible the rapid development of a planned socialist economy.

In 1952 he was called back to Xiamen University by the president, and given the task of helping to write the new teaching plans for all subjects, as section chief of the curriculum section in the teaching affairs office. When the Soviet-inspired reorganization of the whole higher education system reached Xiamen University in 1954, the faculty of education was moved to Fujian Normal College in Fuzhou, and Pan had wished to go with it and pursue his interest in the history of education. However, the president requested him to stay and offer education courses in such subjects as biology, physics, and mathematics to students who were likely to become upper secondary school teachers and would need such courses.

With these dual responsibilities, teaching courses in education and developing new teaching plans for both sciences and humanities courses, Pan was in an ideal position to reflect on the field of higher education over the 1950s. In 1956, at the age of 36, he came to a realization that was to shape his subsequent career. Most of what he had studied in education was relevant only to primary and second schooling, and there was a need for a different approach to educational theory and thought in higher education. In 1957 he published an article concerning the importance of higher education problems in educational theory in Xiamen University's journal, *Scholarly Forum*, and subsequently he edited a book on the same theme, with contributions from several colleagues. This was the first scholarly book on higher education in China after the revolution, and it stirred considerable interest.

In 1964, Pan was invited to Beijing to work with several other influential scholars in writing articles critical of Soviet educational ideas and influences, but the group was dissolved within a year. Pan stayed on in Beijing for the opening period of the Cultural Revolution, and for this reason escaped some of the worst excesses of the revolutionary activists on his campus. Overall he felt deeply upset during the Cultural Revolution decade, as all of the achievements of the 1950s were criticized as Soviet revisionism, and nothing else was able to fill the lacuna this left. For him, it seemed to be a total reversal that made nonsense of all the efforts of the past decade.

In 1978, after Deng Xiaoping had opened up the new era of modernization, Pan was able to fulfil the dream he had nurtured since 1956, the establishment of China's first Institute for Higher Education Research. Several years later, in 1984, his book on *The Study of Higher Education* was published by People's Education Press and Fujian Education Press. In subsequent years, he educated a large number of masters and doctoral students in the field of higher education, and the publications of his Institute have led the field. His contribution has thus been a national one, though it has also been a matter of pride for Xiamen University in the southeast, where he has spent his entire career. He has offered important opportunities for graduate studies to young people from provincial or hinterland universities, whose choices are more limited than those of students in major centers such as Beijing and Shanghai.

When I visited the university in December of 1997, in order to carry out the interviews on which this study is based, I was fortunate to be invited to the "salon" he helds every Saturday evening, in his house high up on a hill within the Xiamen University campus. His large and spartan study, on the second floor of the house, was lined with bookcases, and furnished with a sofa and extra chairs brought in for the occasion. About 12 graduate students, from different regions of China, including Xiangtan University in a rural part of Hunan, Yantai Normal College in Shandong, and Hebei University two hours south of Beijing, had gathered for an exciting evening of debate and discussion. The focus on this particular evening was on an article, written by one of the graduate students present, critically attacking a sociological perspective on education put forth by a leading scholar in Nanjing, because its premises totally excluded the functions of higher education as a field. This student was preparing a response to the published comments made by the Nanjing scholar on her critique. Hours passed in passionate and lively arguments put forward by various students, with an occasional interjection by Professor Pan, bringing everyone back to the core issue that had started the evening's discussion.

What had sustained Professor Pan in his devotion to students and education through so many tumultuous changes? Where had he gained the strength to create a whole new field of study and lead its development? Like Li Bingde, his original inspiration had come from an early experience teaching primary school, one of the few possibilities for employment open to him, and an experience that made him immediately aware of how complex and fascinating is the process of education.

In commenting on his own educational philosophy, he took up with humor and irony the nihilism of the Cultural Revolution, which had repudiated Chinese feudalism (*feng*), Western capitalism (*zi*), and Soviet revisionism (*xiu*). By contrast, he said, all three ideologies had been highly significant in his own development. From his early studies of Chinese classical literature, he gained a basic moral orientation and a strong sense of Confucianism as a philosophical tradition that could adapt to every age. From all that he had learned about American pragmatism in education, he gained many useful ideas for school improvement, for more lively teaching methods and for curricular reform. From his extensive experience with Soviet patterns in the 1950s he had come to appreciate the value of well structured teaching materials, unified standards across the country, and thoroughness in teaching preparation and presentation. In the final analysis, he felt Soviet teaching materials and approaches were more suited to China's traditions of centralization in education and the realities of China's development needs than American patterns.

For Pan, the period since 1978 has been the most productive in his life, and he takes great pride in the leading position of his center for higher education research, the first of only four throughout China that are able to confer doctoral degrees. The greatest challenge in contemporary higher education, he believes, is the need to emphasize students' ability and bring about reforms in teaching that give greater support to the full development of students' talent. Pan feels the focus of reform should be on teaching quality and support for the further development of university teachers, not only on changing the management structure and bringing about a redistribution of power, issues that are closely linked to overall reforms in the political system. He believes that Chinese higher education will follow world trends more and more closely in the future. There will be an emphasis on breadth of knowledge and adaptability and also on the overall intellectual and moral quality of graduates. The concept of lifelong education will become more and more important in China, as people recognize the need to constantly upgrade their own knowledge in order to keep abreast of the rapid changes in society, and higher education must adapt to this.

Pan was able to adapt to the different opportunities of different periods, and to bring out the strengths of American patterns in the period before 1949 and Soviet patterns in the 1950s. Through his dedicated lifelong service in one institution, he gained the stature and credibility that enabled him to launch a whole new field in the 1980s, and weave together a range of external influences into the new tapestry of higher education emerging in the reform period. All of this began in a primary classroom, where a 15 year old boy from a very poor family had his first experience of teaching!

Gu Mingyuan: Doyen of Comparative Education in China[3]

Gu Mingyuan was born in 1929 in the town of Jiangying near Wuxi, Jiangsu province. He grew up with his mother and grandparents, poor farmers who did not own their own land. His father, a primary school teacher, had abandoned the family and remarried, after returning from a brief period of study in Japan in 1930. Gu was able to attend the local primary school from 1935 to 1937, but then it closed with the outbreak of the Sino-Japanese war. In the next year or two he went to a traditional private school or *sishu* and studied the Four Books and Five Classics. Subsequently he attended several different primary schools.

In 1942, while the war was still raging, he managed to enter Nanqing secondary school, a former *shuyuan* which had very good academic standards. Although his grandparents and mother were very poor, they valued education and managed to support him through lower and upper secondary schooling in this school. The period spanned the last three years of the Second World War, 1942-45 and the first three of the Civil War, 1945-48, an extremely difficult time. Nevertheless, the teachers at Nanqing were excellent, reflecting the strong scholarly traditions of the region, and Gu was particularly inspired by many of the older students who were actively involved in revolutionary projects. Some had joined the Communist underground at major universities where they were studying and others had gone to the liberated areas. During the summer they returned and organised drama groups, literacy work and various types of propaganda work which he joined with enthusiasm. Generally he found his learning experience to be enlivening and exciting throughout secondary school, due to the combination of good teaching and an atmosphere of concern and commitment among students. Upon graduation in 1948, Gu took university entrance examinations, in hope of a scholarship. His family were so poor that they had not even been able to buy uniforms for high school activities, so this was his only hope. He tried for civil engineering at Qinghua University and Railway management at Jiaotong University, also biology at Nanjing University, thinking these were promising practical areas for career development. However, he failed to get into any of these universities. As a result, he went to Shanghai and sought a primary school teaching job, as seemed the only possibility for him to make a living. To his surprise, he discovered a delight in seeing children learn during this year in a primary school, and the future direction of his life became clear.

With the establishment of the People's Republic in 1949, a whole new set of opportunities opened up for a young person of his background, and he applied both to Beijing Normal University and Fudan University in Shanghai. He was accepted by both, but received the acceptance from Beijing Normal first, and so he travelled to Beijing to start classes in September of 1949. On October 1st he stood on Tiananmen Square for the celebration of the new People's Republic. After two years at Beijing Normal he was sent to Moscow in 1951 for five years of study at the Lenin Normal College.

This period was a kind of high tide of the Soviet revolution and he found life in Moscow very stimulating, in terms of cultural as well as educational opportunities. He found the atmosphere extremely friendly, and enjoyed the opportunity to see films and participate in many cultural activities. The main focus of his study was on pedagogy and the psychology of education, and around 30% percent of his time was taken up with reading classics of Marxism Leninism in Russian. In retrospect, he feels this was the most important and valuable aspect of his study, giving him a deep understanding of issues of social and economic change from a Marxist perspective; he also values the strong links with primary schools and the extensive periods of time spent in observation and teaching practice in schools as part of the program.

In 1956, Gu returned to Beijing and took up a position as teaching assistant in the department of education at Beijing Normal University. In 1957 he worked in an experimental centre for training primary school teachers attached to the university, while also lecturing in the department of education. In 1958 he was invited to teach in Beijing Normal's attached secondary school in an inner city neighbourhood and he was to teach there for four years, up till 1962. Wang Huanxun, an old professor who had been in Yanan, was made principal of the school during these years, and he asked Gu to join him in teaching there. He thus gained a lot of practical classroom experience. This was the time of the Great Leap Forward, also called the Great Educational Revolution (*Jiaoyu dageming*) of 1958, which emphasised practice, and efforts to develop an indigenous Chinese model of education rather than relying too closely on Russian models.

In 1962 he went back to the department of education and participated in the attempts of this period to strengthen teaching and research quality, after some of the excesses associated with the education revolution. By 1965 he was vice-dean of the department and head of a newly established foreign education research centre, which had been approved by the Central Ministry of Propaganda. With the Cultural Revolution looming, once again there was pressure to develop strong links with practice, and he established a branch campus in Linfen, a poor county in northern Shaanxi province, where students were sent for their first year of study in 1965. With the outbreak of the Cultural Revolution in 1966, he was strongly criticised, due to his interest in foreign education, and he spent the next four years working in agricultural labour and in factories. In 1970 he went to Linfen for two years, and in 1972 returned to Beijing to become principal of the second attached secondary school of Beijing Normal University for three years.

While the Great Leap Forward had seen some revolutionary extremism there were also concrete achievements in education and in other significant development areas, Gu felt. In education, there was a genuine attempt to encourage local self-reliance and greatly broaden access to secondary and tertiary education. There was also a widely felt sense of pride in some of the major projects which China carried out on its own, without Soviet help, including the Miyun Reservoir, designed by Qinghua professors, the Great Hall of the People, the Beijing Railway Station, and the Minorities Palace. By contrast the Cultural Revolution was a time of destruction and retrogression in education. No new students were recruited to Beijing Normal until 1973, due to the fact that Mao had spoken only of science and engineering universities when he called for a reopening of universities in 1971.

In 1974, Gu was the only scholar of education included in a high level Chinese official delegation to Paris, to attend the 18th meeting of the United Nations Education Science and Culture Organization (UNESCO). He remembers how all of the others in this delegation were officials, absorbed in the rhetoric of opposing imperialism and resisting revisionism which prevailed in China at the time. This was his first opportunity for exposure to the outside world, since the years in Moscow in the 1950s, after many years of isolation and the interruption of political movements. He was deeply impressed by the meetings and by all that he observed over a period of seven weeks living in Paris. On return to Beijing Normal University, he took up the post of section head for all humanities programs in the university. At this time People's University had not yet been reopened, so its students in philosophy, economics, and party history were also enrolled at Beijing Normal.

In 1979 Gu returned to the Department of Education as Department head, and re-established the centre for foreign education, which he had set up in 1965. In 1980 he invited Professor Hu Changtu of Columbia University to Beijing to teach a three month course in Comparative Education, and invited senior scholars of education and younger teachers from 11 universities in different parts of the country to attend the course. Out of this course the first book on comparative education since 1948 was developed, with Wang Chengxu, Zhu Bo and Gu Mingyuan as editors. Entitled *Comparative Education (Bijiao jiaoyu)*, it was first published by People's Education Press in Beijing in 1982. Meanwhile, in 1978 the first national meeting to discuss foreign education had been convened by Gu at Beijing Normal University, and this was followed by a second meeting at South China Normal University in 1979, when the Chinese Comparative Education Society was founded.

In the 20 years since that time Gu Mingyuan has led the field of comparative education, with 13 books and 208 scholarly articles in his most recent list of publications, including a 12 volume educational dictionary, many works on comparative and foreign education, and a significant contribution to the cultural history of Chinese education. All of this has been done on top of an active teaching role, a lengthy period of leadership as vice-president of Beijing Normal University, and dean of the graduate school, also considerable travel within China and internationally.

A number of things seem to have sustained him through the difficult years up to 1978, and enabled him to make this 50 years long contribution to education in China. First, his work was always rooted in practice, beginning with the experience of a year teaching in primary school in Shanghai. During the late 1950s fifties and early 1960s he spent considerable time in Beijing Normal's first attached secondary school. Later, during the Cultural Revolution, he established an educational program in the countryside, and after returning to Beijing, he spent a further period of time as principal of Beijing Normal's second attached secondary school.

Secondly, his experience of Soviet education in the 1950s was profound and thorough, leaving him with a grasp of Marxist thought and analysis which, paradoxically, proved extremely helpful when he set himself to explain the relation between education and economic development after Deng Xiaoping declared an opening up to "modernization, the world and the future." At that time he published an influential lecture which drew heavily on chapter 13 of Marx's classic, *Das Kapital*, emphasizing the need for workers to adjust to the changing demands of modern production and to adopt patterns of continuing education. This lecture was given on 40 different occasions all over the country and was published in the authoritative Party journal *Red Flag* (*Hong Qi*) in 1980. He felt it was important in contributing to the shift of emphasis from class struggle to economic development in the early 1980s. His experience of Soviet education had left him with a critical and analytical ability to appreciate what he had learned, and adapt it to China's situation.

A third factor in Gu's lifelong commitment to teaching may have been the strong foundation he had gained in Chinese classical knowledge at the excellent secondary school he attended for six years in the 1940s. His early school experiences during the difficult days of the Sino-Japanese war and the civil war gave him a firm grounding in China's cultural traditions, and in their relevance to the struggle for national survival at that time. His later work in developing comparative education benefited from these strong roots in China's own traditions, and his thorough understanding of the Soviet patterns that had been so influential in establishing the new system put in place in the 1950s.

LESSONS FROM INFLUENTIAL CHINESE TEACHERS

In this concluding section of the chapter, I would like to reflect on lessons that we might learn for teacher education and the formation of teachers in Hong Kong and more generally in the Asia-Pacific, from these narratives of influential teachers in China. One might feel that times have changed to a degree that it is difficult for us even to imagine some of the challenges they faced, coming from homes that were poverty-stricken and growing up in times of war and revolution. Nevertheless, I believe there are enduring aspects of their experience, related to their roots in Chinese civilization and their lifelong efforts to integrate what they learned in a wide range of international experiences to the needs of their own society as it went through a rapid series of changes.

The first and most striking point is the way in which each of these teachers viewed the Confucian educational heritage, learned in their family and early schooling. In each case, they felt it provided an important moral foundation for their lives and their professional development as teachers. In spite of the conservatism associated with state Confucianism and the imperial examination system, which has been sketched out earlier in this chapter, they found patterns of openness to external ideas and a rigorous tradition of self-cultivation that made possible the integration of a wide range of external ideas into the Chinese context. Progressive elements in this tradition, which have also been described earlier, seemed to provide fertile ground for them to engage in active educational experimentation and to draw upon the best of what they could learn from American pragmatism, Soviet academic rigor, and European rationalism and empiricism. There was thus a clear connection between their ability to draw effectively on external ideas and their degree of rootedness in their own culture.

It is clearly of great value for young people to be exposed to literature and research at the international cutting-edge as they prepare to be teachers in Hong Kong today, but they also need to know themselves and to be given exposure to Chinese educational literature and traditions, which are an important part of their heritage. Self-understanding would also involve knowing the history of education in Hong Kong, and the particular ways in which British patterns and ideas of education became integrated into this environment. It might also call for an understanding of cultural and religious traditions shared with other parts of East Asia, such as Buddhism, Islam and Asian Christianity. The lives of all three of these teachers illustrate how important a deep and reflective self-understanding is for the capacity to absorb and apply useful ideas from the international community. They also demonstrate the way in which this kind of understanding can lead one to become a lifelong learner and an educator able to adapt to changing economic and political circumstances, and to inspire and motivate successive generations of students. Gu Mingyuan's ability to use fundamental Marxist ideas, learned in the Soviet Union, to help open up people's thinking to the concept of human capital and the needs of "market socialism" in the early 1980s is a striking example of the application of ideas learned abroad to a situation never anticipated by his Russian teachers.

A second element in their life histories that stands out is the valuing of practice and practical professional experience, that may have deep roots in an epistemology of knowledge and action going back to scholars such as the 17th century neo-Confucian, Wang Yangming, and earlier. Even though the experiences of return to the primary and secondary classroom took place largely under the harsh circumstances of a series of political movements, they were valued for the opportunities they provided for practical professional development and for reflection on action and experience. Paradoxically, the storms brought into their lives by unwelcome political movements may have stimulated an ability to learn in all circumstances and to keep in touch with changing educational circumstances at the grass roots. This has ensured a rich professional and practical thread running their scholarly writing. Li Bingde's enthusiastic embrace of innovative methods in the teaching of primary school mathematics during the Cultural Revolution made a real difference to his works on pedagogy which became standard texts after 1978.

Finally, each has developed intensely personal relationships with a wide range of students over the years, whose mentoring involved academic knowledge, professional and personal morality, and an unwavering commitment to China's educational and social development. The vignette depicting Pan Maoyuan's students engaged in lively and critical discussion during the Saturday evening salon in his home on campus illustrates the way in which the spirit of the traditional *shuyuan* has continued to inform relations between teachers and students in modern China. One can also see here the encouragement of critical thinking and of a spirit that challenges academic authority, which may owe something to progressive influences Pan acknowledged in the heritage of his American trained teachers during the

1930s.

All three teachers began their careers in primary schools, under circumstances that were limited both by the scope and possibilities of their own education and the political and economic circumstances that shaped their schools. Yet, all three showed a determination to pursue every avenue available to them to expand their own knowledge and understanding, through further formal education and through professional experience. At the same time, they dedicated themselves to serve where they were needed most. Their lives demonstrate the immense possibilities that may lie before primary teachers who adopt principles of lifelong learning and are passionately committed to their calling as educators.

NOTES

[1]Interviews with Li Bingde conducted in Lanzhou on May 8th and 12th, 1998.
[2]Interviews with Pan Maoyuan conducted in Xiamen on December 6th and 8th, 1997.
[3]Interviews with Gu Mingyuan conducted in Beijing on October 28th, 1998 and in Hong Kong on December 11th, 1998.

REFERENCES

Abe, H. (1987). Borrowing from Japan: China's first modern education system. In R. Hayhoe & M. Bastid (Eds.), *China's education and the industrialised world: Studies in cultural transfer* (pp. 57-80). New York: M. E. Sharpe.

Bertaux, D. (1981). *Biography and society: The life history approach in the social sciences.* London: Sage.

Chow, T. T. (1960). *The May fourth movement.* Stanford, CA: Stanford University Press.

De Bary, W. T., & Chaffee, J. (Eds.). (1989). *Neo-Confucian education: The formative stage.* Berkeley: University of California Press.

Ding, G., & Liu, Q. (1992). *Shuyuan yu Zhongguo wenhua* [Academies and Chinese culture]. Shanghai: Shanghai jiaoyu chubanshe.

Epstein, I. (Ed.). (1991). *Chinese Education: Problems, Policies and Prospects.* New York: Garland.

Freyn, H. (1940). *Chinese education in the war.* Shanghai: Kelly and Walsh.

Goodson, I. F. (1991a). History, Context and Qualitative Methods. In I.F. Goodson & R. Walker (Eds.) *Biography, identity and schooling: Episodes in educational research* (pp. 114-136). New York: Falmer Press.

Goodson, I. F. (1991b). Teachers' Lives and Educational Research. In I.F. Goodson & R. Walker (Eds.) *Biography, identity and schooling: Episodes in educational research* (pp. 137-149). New York: Falmer Press.

Hayhoe, R. (1984). The evolution of modern educational institutions. In R. Hayhoe (Ed.), *Contemporary Chinese education* (pp. 26-46). London: Croom Helm.

Hayhoe, R. (Ed.). (1992). *Education and modernization: The Chinese experience.* Oxford: Pergamon Press.

Hayhoe, R. (1996). Introduction: The Context of the Dialogue. In R. Hayhoe & J. Pan (Eds.). *East-West dialogue in knowledge and higher education* (pp 3-14). Armonk, N. Y.: M. E. Sharpe.

Hayhoe, R. (1999). *China's universities 1895-1995: A century of cultural conflict.* Hong Kong: Comparative Education Research Centre, The University of Hong Kong. (First published in 1996 by Garland Publishing, Inc., New York)

Henze, J. (1992). The formal education system and modernization: An analysis of developments since 1978. In R. Hayhoe (Ed.), *Education and modernization: The Chinese experience* (pp. 103-140). Oxford: Pergamon.

Henze, J. (1984). Higher Education: The Tension between Quality and Equality. In R. Hayhoe (Ed.), *Contemporary Chinese Education* (pp. 93-152). London: Croom Helm.

Keenan, B. (1977). *The Dewey experiment in China.* Cambridge, MA: Harvard University Press.

Keenan, B. (1994). *Academy revival and the management of China's education in the lower Yangtze region 1865-1911.* Berkeley: Institute of East Asian Studies, the University of California.

Marx, K. (1969). The eighteenth brumaire of Louis Napoleon. In K. Marx & F. Engels (Eds.), *Selected works.* Moscow: Progress Publishers.

Meskill, J. T. (Ed.). (1982). *Academies in the Ming Dynasty: A historical essay.* Tuscon, AZ: University of Arizona Press.

Miyazaki, I. (1977). *China's examination hell: The civil service examinations of imperial China.* New York: Weatherhill.

Orleans, L. (1987). Soviet influence on China's higher education. In R. Hayhoe & M. Bastid (Eds.), *China's education and the industrialized world.* New York: M. E. Sharpe.

Pepper, S. (1987). New Directions in Education. In R. MacFarquhar & J. Fairbank (Eds.), *The Cambridge History of China,* (Vol. 14, pp. 398-431). Cambridge: Cambridge University Press.

Pepper, S. (1990). *China's Education Reform in the 1980s: Policies, Issues and Historical Perspectives.* Berkeley: Institute of East Asia Studies, the University of California.

Pepper, S. (1996). *Radicalism and Education Reform in 20th-Century China: The Search for an Ideal Development Model.* Cambridge: Cambridge University Press.

Price, R. (1987). Convergence or copying: China and the Soviet Union. In R. Hayhoe & M. Bastid (Eds.), *China's education and the industrialized world.* New York: M. E. Sharpe.

Wang, H. (1975). *Chinese communist education: The Yenan period.* Taiwan: Institute of International Relations.

Yin, C. (1924). *The reconstruction of modern educational organisations in China.* Shanghai: Commercial Press.

Chapter 14

Rationalizing the Japanese In-service Teacher Training: A Case of Effective Strategy Formulation and Implementation

María Natividad LÓPEZ TINAJERO

Graduate School of Education
Hiroshima University, Japan

Many factors, including the aging of the population, the improvement of the level of people's income, and an increase in leisure time, have brought about changes in today's living environment in Japan. Along with these changes, people's aspirations for learning have been heightened. The advancement of science and technology, the development of an information-oriented society, and "internationalization" have also made it imperative to acquire new knowledge and technology. All these developments have made it increasingly important for the Japanese to engage in lifelong learning (Ministry of Education, Science, and Culture of the Government of Japan [MONBUSHO], 1994). In this context, career-long in-service training for teachers has become a high priority in Japanese education.

In Japan, schools increasingly play a dominant role in children's lives, as we witness a noticeable decline in the educational functions traditionally assigned to family and community. Accordingly, teachers are expected to play a central role in children's education (White, 1987). Teaching is considered a respected profession, a lifetime commitment, and a much sought-after occupation. Teachers are well paid, and there are many more well qualified candidates than posts. The growing reduction of enrollment rates in elementary and lower secondary schools has provoked a drastic reduction in the demand for teachers, and new graduates face serious difficulties for obtaining a teaching post. In 1996, of the 135,956 candidates that took the prefectural recruitment examination, only 14,607 were appointed as teachers (Shimizu, 1998).

There is presently some concern that the current recruitment and training systems in Japan are not producing teachers with sufficient vocational commitment and practical skills (Organisation for Economic Co-operation and Development [OECD], 1998). Nevertheless, in-service teacher training (INSET) has been a long-standing feature of Japanese education. There is a conception that teachers must constantly devote themselves to study and self-cultivation in order to fulfill their educational duties. In order to support the professional development of teacher, there has been established a coherent and comprehensive system of teacher training centers. At the prefectural level, the Educational Centers play a key role in offering in-service courses for teachers.

This chapter focuses on the strategies implemented in recent years by the Japanese Ministry of Education in order to broaden and systematize training opportunities for in-service teachers. It concentrates on a long-range INSET program for the long-term education of in-service teachers. The stratification of refresher courses according to years of teaching experience is recognized as the most important feature of this program, and is analyzed in detail in this chapter. Particular attention is given to the role played by the Hiroshima Prefectural Education Center in the development of such a program. It is hoped that this stratification case in Japan will provide same important experiences and insights to benefit the improvement and innovation in teacher education.

THE JAPANESE TEACHER TRAINING

As long as it has existed, the Japanese system of teacher training has undergone three major transformations. The first was the establishment of the normal school, under the Educational Decree in 1872; the second was the decree of normal education of 1886 in which a normal school was founded in each prefecture; and the third was the abolition of the normal education system due to the establishment of a new educational system after World War II. After the war, a drastic reform of the teacher training system was instituted. Normal schools were reorganized into four-year teacher training universities and, in addition, faculties of education and colleges of liberal arts and sciences aimed at teacher training were established in national universities.

Today, institutions of higher education in Japan include universities, colleges of technology, and junior colleges. Future teachers are educated in these institutions of higher education, especially in universities and junior colleges. Not only universities of education and faculties of education are allowed to conduct teacher education programs, there are as well many institutions authorized by the Ministry of Education to confer teaching certificates (open system). By 1995, there were 1,192 higher education institutions, including universities, junior colleges, and graduate schools, offering teacher training programs (Shimizu, et al., 1998).

Those graduates who obtained teaching certificates at universities or colleges apply through universities or individually to prefectural boards of education for the issuance of certificates. Certificates are valid nationwide and for life. Graduates who are certified and want to become teachers of public or secondary schools must take the prefectural recruitment examinations.

The existing teacher training in Japan is therefore characterized by the following three points: it is based on certification system; it is carried out only in institutions of higher education; and it is an open system.

Oversupply of Teachers

In Japan teaching has traditionally been a respected profession. Teachers are well paid and there are many more well qualified candidates than available posts. In addition, the continued reduction of enrollment rates in elementary and lower secondary schools, brought about by the marked decline in the birth rate, has provoked a dramatic reduction in demand for teachers. New graduates face serious difficulties for getting a teaching post.

In 1974, during the process of accelerated economic growth, the Law Governing Special Measures for Securing of Capable Educational Personnel in Compulsory Education Schools for Maintenance and Enhancement of School Education Standards was promulgated. According to this Law, teachers' salaries were augmented 25% with respect to other public servants. After this measure, the number of candidates to the teaching profession notably increased. In 1996, of the 135,956 candidates (45,241; 53,052; and 37,663 in elementary, lower secondary and upper secondary schools, respectively) that took the examination, only 14,607 (5,392; 5,676; and 3,539, respectively) were appointed as teachers (Shimizu et al., 1998). Looking at the educational background of these candidates, we found that 24.0% came from universities of education; 56.7% came from general universities; 14.0% are graduates from junior colleges; and 5.3 % came from graduate schools.[1]

Furthermore, the examination carried out at the prefectural level became more competitive. In 1997, for example, the examination, for elementary school teachers in the Hiroshima Prefecture was divided into two stages. The first stage included a written test on general education, professional education subjects, and teaching subjects, as well as a personal interview. The second stage included composition, group interview, physical examination, aptitude examination, and a practical skill examination, which includes swimming, physical education, and music. Some prefectures, such as Tottori and Okinawa, require all the aforementioned examinations during the first stage; in addition, they require computer skills in the second stage.

Necessity of In-service Training for Teachers

Looking at the above-mentioned data, one may conclude that teachers in Japan possess a wide educational background and that only the best candidates are selected to become teachers. However, there is some concern that the current recruitment and training systems in Japan are not producing teachers with sufficient vocational commitment and practical skills (OECD, 1998). In addition, Japanese education is presently facing large-scale pathological problems, such as bullying and school refusal. Moreover, advances in science and technology have produced significant changes in the every day life of Japanese, demanding corresponding shifts in the traditional teaching-learning methods at schools. All these circumstances demand that teachers be prepared not only at the initial stage of their career, but in every stage of their professional lives. In this context, INSET becomes an indispensable means for keeping teachers abreast to date of new developments in education.

INSET has been a long-standing feature of Japanese education. Teacher development has long been considered the key element to achieve educational improvement. Its importance as a tool of democratic education was particularly stressed after the World War II. There is a conception that teachers must constantly devote themselves to study and self-cultivation in order to fulfill their educational duties.

Teachers' participation in in-service programs does not result in an increase in salary. The training of teachers is based on "self-study," which means constant research and cultivation by teachers themselves. In these circumstances, the biggest issue concerning in-service education is how to assure the willingness of the teachers to participate in training programs.

In 1996, the Minister of Education asked the council of Educational Personnel

Training to investigate improvements in teacher education for the 21st century. The council's recommendations were as follows:

> With regard to in-service training, there is a need for systematic provision of many different kinds of training opportunities. In this context, with a view to broadening the professional education given in university graduate schools and the social perspective of teachers, we feel there is a need to promote more long-term, systematic training that makes use of such facilities as private-sector firms, adult education facilities and social welfare facilities. Furthermore, reflecting the need for even greater emphasis to be put on caring for the hearts of children so as to enable them, for example, to cope with the problem of bullying, we feel there is a need to strengthen the development of basic counseling ability in all teachers and with particular reference to nursing teachers, to strengthen their training at the time of their employment and at all subsequent stages of their career. Moreover, in order to ensure smoother and more effective enhancement of the qualities and abilities of teachers throughout every stage of their initial teacher education, appointment and in-service training, an indispensable requirement is that there should be closer liaison and cooperation between those concerned with teacher education in universities on the one hand and those in boards of education and elsewhere concerned with appointment of teachers and in-service training on the other. (MONBUSHO, 1997)

According to these recommendations, there is now a general tendency to diversify in-service training and professional development, which are more directly oriented towards the improvement of schools. The Ministry of Education is the apex of a centralized and hierarchical educational system. It is responsible for the coherence of the system overall, for defining strategies for the implementation of central government policies, and for forward planning and quality control. It is aided in this by a number of central institutions, notably the National Education Centre, which acts as a staff college for the teaching profession and as a focal point for the dissemination of new policies and information. Schools are administered by the 47 prefectures, which have devolved powers within the prefectural system (OECD, 1998). At the prefectural level, the education centers play a key role in offering courses for in-service teachers. There exists a coherent and comprehensive system of teacher centers.

Teachers' Professional Development and Opportunities for In-service Training

Because the Law for Special Regulations Concerning Educational Public Service Personnel (Arts. 19 and 20) requires teachers to pursue continuous in-service training, various systematic programs are conducted at national, prefectural, municipal, and school levels.

At the National Level

At the national level, MONBUSHO holds "central workshops" (offered at the National Education Centre) for the in-service training of principals, vice-principals, and teachers who play leading coordination and advising roles at the prefectural level. The Ministry also gives grants for in-service training which is administered by prefectural boards of education and teacher training organizations.

At the Prefectural Level

Prefectural boards of education are required by law to be responsible for planning and encouraging daily in-service training in local public schools. Prefectural education centers, which have lodging facilities, educational equipment and apparatus, and professional staff, play an important role in offering training courses.

A system of induction training for beginning teachers was created in the school year 1989 by the Law for Special Regulation Concerning Educational Public Service Personnel. It is conducted for all new teachers for one year after their appointment in national and public schools. This induction-training program is spread out over the school year for a total of at least 90 days. Sixty days or more of training are school-based during which new teachers receive instruction from their advising teacher. Not less than 30 days are spent attending lectures, seminars, and various practical training sessions that include five-day workshops held in education centers or other institutions outside of school (MONBUSHO, 1994).

Prefectural boards of education also dispatch teachers to universities, research institutes, private firms, and other institutions for long-term training. Following the amendment of the National School Establishment Law, Hyogo University of Teacher Education, Joetsu University of Education, and Naruto University of Education were founded in October 1978 as universities devoted mainly to in-service teacher education, with an equal emphasis on theory and practice. The main objective of the Graduate Schools of Education (Master Course) is to help in-service teachers and recent university graduates to improve their competence in research, teaching, and student guidance. About two-thirds of the 300 graduate students admitted each year in graduate schools are in-service teachers who have at least three years of teaching experience, and who are given leave of absence on full pay for two years to undertake their studies.

National universities are also allowed to receive schoolteachers in their graduate schools. However, the number of teachers studying there is notably lower than the aforementioned universities. In 1999, for instance, Hiroshima University accepted only three schoolteachers in the Graduate School of Education, and 12 in the Graduate School of School Education. These numbers represent only 2.6% and 8% of the total enrollment, respectively.[2]

Prefectural boards also conduct periodic in-service training at different stages of a teacher's career, for example, after 5 years, 10 years, and 20 years of service. Another type of in-service training is directed toward meeting the educational needs of teachers in various positions such as principals, vice-principals, and coordinating and advising teachers.

Along with these training programs offered by prefectural boards of education, various lectures and workshops are held by municipalities and educational organizations as well.

At the School Level

The school-based in-service training is one of the main features of Japanese education. This kind of training has been well popularized among teachers. Through the school-based in-service training, teachers work together to improve their skills and carry out group research projects. At the beginning of the year, a meeting takes place where they decide specifically the topic of study of each individual. Local educational authorities determine and coordinate which school will show to the rest of the schools its research results, the specific year the members will share their new concepts, and so forth. Once the school is chosen, the members organize a presentation on their research process and offer public classes so that invited teachers can observe them. In addition, there are panels of discussion where teachers from different institutions can debate and exchange their views and concerns. Once the school year ends, the hosting school publishes the results of its research. According to Maki (1996), during 1994-95, 98.8% of the Japanese primary school teachers participated in school-based in-service training.

IMPORTANCE OF OFFERING PERMANENT IN-SERVICE TEACHER TRAINING

Before analyzing the program developed by the Hiroshima Prefectural Education Center, it is paramount to take a look at the importance of offering permanent in-service teacher training.

Since the 1980s, there has been an emphasis on improving the quality of education throughout the world. This tendency has recognized the value of the teachers, their educational process, and the importance of their permanent education. In fact, the importance of permanent teacher education has undergone the most radical transformations in history (Hargreaves, 1999).

Particularly, during the last two decades we have seen significant research progress centered around this topic. Repeatedly, we are reminded that the teacher steady improvement, renovation, and progress are extremely important. And what is even more important, we are often told, is the continuous training not only to guarantee a higher academic standard on the part of the student, but also to fulfill the teacher's sense of development and professionalism (Burden, 1980; Fessler, 1995; Glickman, 1990; Hargreaves, 1999).

In recent years, United Nations Preparatory Educational, Scientific, and Cultural Commission (UNESCO) (1998) has been involved in the career-long professional development of teachers. The organization has been promoting meetings where both local and international educational authorities and experts have gathered in order to analyze strategies to improve and expand the possibilities of better teacher training.

Professional development in education is considered a process of change in the teachers' mental models, in their believes, and in their perceptions; and this very process is intimately related to the children mentality and learning as well (Mevarech, 1995). Any activity, regardless of its nature, but as long as it improves the teacher skills and enriches his/her knowledge as a teacher, is valid. For example, "passive" activities that makes the teacher think and reflect on different topics and ideas as well as formal courses taken by the professional (OECD, 1998). Based on the above, teacher training plays an integral part in the educator professional development. Needless to say, educational researchers constantly discover new aspects about teaching and learning. These new aspects are expanded day by day so what becomes imperative is that teachers – of all levels – must learn and control what they have just learned. In other words, teachers could be like those who exercise other professions, they learn something new, get ready to use the new knowledge, and prepare themselves to use their conceptual and practical abilities.

Traditionally, teacher training programs were designed using this criteria: they were created taking only into account the technical improvement of the educator. The reason behind this was the fact that the teacher would be able to teach more effectively. However, there are programs that are more progressive and that have gone beyond. The latter include in their courses topics of general interest and contemporary theory so that the teacher is challenged intellectually and is not only centered and reduced to technical topics. Even though both types of courses are valid because they target different groups of educators, there are several complains on behalf of the teachers. They often say that the programs of professional development are repetitive and that they have very little to do with their actual classroom practice. As a result, according to the teachers, the courses do not help improve their teaching ability and, in fact, theoretical concepts have very little to do with the reality experienced in the classroom on a daily basis (Monk et al., 1999).

Generally, when there are training sessions or courses on new concepts and skills, teachers either reject them or are unwilling participate. Those who participate only select carefully material that is related to their specific necessities. Others do not participate and wait until a fresh innovation comes to light (Hargreaves, 1995). It is clear that when attendance is not mandatory only a small group of teachers participate, and it is not unusual to see only the youngest enthusiastic educators.

In order to promote a more active participation, it is necessary to make the following changes. It is important that the programs are intimately related to the teachers practice so that teachers are more positive about the system. In addition, it is paramount to diversify the teacher professional development and training opportunities so not only the student receives the benefit. Undoubtedly, the programs must pay attention to the interests, necessities, and concerns of the teacher so he or she can benefit as well.

One can say that a good professional development program has been successful when the teachers develop innovative teaching methods, apply them, and see a positive outcome. This is particularly evident when the teacher sees that during the learning process the student is modifying his or her believes, attitudes and ways of understanding reality. When this happens, the programs contribute to the professional development of the educators and indeed serve their purpose which is to improve the quality of education. In order to create a successful course that truly improves the professional development of the teacher it is imperative that the content of such is related to his or her interests and necessities. And, if this is the case, the condition is that first there must be an in-depth study of the different stages of the teacher in his or her professional life. This is the only way the courses will meet the necessities of the professional.

The Teacher Career Stages

There are few studies related to the teacher career stages. Frances Fuller (1969), Unrud and Turner (1970), Katz (1972), and Gregorc (1973) have developed interesting research in this field. However, a major limitation of these studies is that they tend to "lump" all experienced teachers together without further differentiation. The view that experienced, mature teachers continue to grow and change was not emphasized in the works of these early theorists (Fessler, 1995).

In recent years, Vonk (1989), Maki (1990a, 1990b, 1990c), Fessler and Christensen (1992), Fessler (1995), and Huberman (1995) have developed more detailed models for understanding the dynamics of the teaching career cycle. Vonk's model of teachers' professional development is based on a review of the literature and on his own studies of teachers' professional development. His framework provides for the following stages: pre-professional phase; threshold phase; the phase of growing·into the profession; the first professional phase; phase of reorientation to oneself and the profession; the second professional phase; and the phase of running down.

Fessler and Christensen (1992) consider that the career cycle corresponds to conditions found in the teacher's personal environment, as well as the environment of the organization. To Them, "[A] supportive, nurturing, reinforcing environment can assist a teacher in the pursuit of a rewarding, positive career progression. Environmental interference and pressures, on the other hand, can impact negatively on the career cycle" (Fessler, 1995, p. 179).

In their Teacher Career Cycle Model, these authors include the following stages: preservice; induction; competence building; enthusiastic and growing; career frustration; career stability; career wind-down; and career exit.

In addition, Fessler (1995) offers a theoretical model for studying the phases of a teacher's career. The model first concentrates on an analysis of the "real world" which includes literature reviews, observation in natural settings, interviews, and emerging problems. It is a cyclical model, through which the study of the professional development stages generates both educational research and guidelines for action. Subsequent data gathered should be cycled back into the model to make modifications and refinements. The product of such modifications and refinements becomes, in turn, the basis for new studies.

Huberman (1995) synthesizes the work of other scholars and presents his Modal Sequences of the Teacher Career Cycle, in which the teaching career is divided into five phases according to years of experience: career entry (survival and discovery – one to three years); stabilization (four to six years); experimentation/diversification (7 to 18 years); serenity (19 to 30 years); and disengagement (31 to 40 years). Huberman (1995) adds two alternative phases - stock-taking/interrogations and conservatism – to experimentation/ diversification and to serenity, respectively. This demonstrates the way in which his model offers more than one possibility in a teacher's career sequence. In short, not all teachers necessarily pass through the aforementioned five phases at the same rate. On the contrary, each teacher develops a personal and some times discontinuous career trajectory.

Huberman (1995) points out that these phases should not be seen as progressive and lineal models, since "[a] large part of development is neither externally programmed nor personally engineered but rather discontinuous, that is, lacking in continuity and order, and sometimes downright random" (p. 195).

He states that studies of the teaching career that look for a discernible sequence of phases are vulnerable to many of the criticisms leveled at stage theorists working with ontogenetic models of development, in which chronological age is the key variable.

> First, most of this work is resolutely biological or psychological when transferred to teaching, [SIC] it tends to underestimate the importance of social and historical factors. Second, stage theory tends to view individual development as "teleological," that is, individuals observe and plan out the sequences through which they pass, and can thereby influence or even determine the nature or the succession of stages in their career. (Huberman, 1995, pp. 194-195)

Huberman (1995) does not deny the importance that stage theory has in the design of ad hoc programs for in-service teachers. However, he proposes an "Open" Collective Cycle in which a group of teachers coming from several schools share a subject matter, discipline, grade level, problem, or activity they would like to work on. Instead of having a consultant or specialist, the group members manage the cycle. Specialists are called in at various times, depending upon the kind of issues with which the group is concerned at that moment.

In Huberman's (1995) words,

> This is a forum for everyone. The novice discusses, debates, experiments with more experienced peers, and profits accordingly. "Stabilized" teachers extend their repertoires, both conceptually and practically, and better consolidate the passage from subject-matter mastery to its didactic transposition in class. Teachers in the "diversification" phase will be stretching themselves collaboratively. In other words, a heterogeneous group reflecting, conversing, debating, and experimenting together is a powerful device for intimacy, mutuality, mastery, and, in the best cases, a resocialization or rebonding to their professional guild. (pp. 218-219)

At the end of the 1980s, Maki (1990) developed an extensive study about the interests and needs of Japanese teachers in each stage of their professional career. In his study, Maki associates teachers' professional life with their chronological age, and divides a teacher's professional career into four stages: the 20s, the 30s, the 40s and the 50s.

In Maki's (1990a) research on the teacher career cycle, he includes a study of teachers' self-perceptions, the biological life stages, expectations for teachers inside and outside the school, problems that teachers face in each stage, and opportunities for teachers' self-development.

Maki's (1990a, 1990b, 1990c) study demonstrated that the needs and interests of teachers vary throughout each stage and, as time elapses, teachers acquire more experience and are expected to assume more responsibility inside the school. Maki suggests that in order to promote teachers' self-development, a variety of courses responding to teachers' needs should be offered throughout the teaching career, and that it is important to provide teacher with the necessary information concerning available resources.

The Hiroshima Prefectural Education Center has utilized Maki's classification system, but in recent years, rather than dividing the teacher career cycle according to chronological age, the Center emphasizes years of teaching experience, as Huberman suggests in his model. Taking into account this method of classification, the Center has structured training programs that endeavor to respond to teachers needs and interests in each stage. Even though this has been a practical classification that corresponds primarily to the reality of Japanese teachers, it is my opinion that this model can be used in the reorganization of programs to focus on the professional development of teachers in other contexts. It can help us rethink professional development in fundamental terms, because it considers basic issues about the growth and learning of teachers as professionals over time.

COURSES FOR EXPERIENCED TEACHERS ACCORDING TO LENGTH OF SERVICE

Even though school-based teachers training is one of the most successful programs since they have a very high participation percentage, off-site teacher centers still play a crucial role. There is an educational center in each prefecture and all major cities have a center each. There is one center at the Hiroshima City (for the City exclusively) and another for the prefecture. Here, we will focus on the Hiroshima Prefectural Education Center.

There are in the Hiroshima Prefecture 667 elementary schools, 284 lower secondary schools, and 143 upper secondary schools. The number of teachers is 10,506, 6,425, and 6,977 in each level, respectively. As stated above, there are many opportunities for in-service teachers training. At the prefectural level, the institution in charge of offering in-service training seminars and workshops is the Hiroshima Prefectural Education Center. This Center was the result of a fusion of three institutions: Hiroshima Education Research Institute (established in 1950), the Science Education Center, and the Commerce Education Center. In 1972 the Institute was moved to Higashi Hiroshima, changing its official name to the Hiroshima Prefectural Education Center.

Organization

The Center is organized into five divisions – General Affairs Division, Planning Division, Curriculum Program Division, Education for the Disabled and Educational Guidance Division, and the Computer Information Division – and each of them is responsible for organizing and carrying out a certain number of in-service training programs and special research projects.

The Center conducts a wide range of in-service education/training programs for teachers and school administrative officers. Courses are offered to teachers who work in kindergartens, elementary schools, lower and upper secondary schools and special education institutions located in Hiroshima prefecture. National, prefectural, municipal and private school teachers are allowed to participate. All the courses are free including accommodations when necessary.

In 1985, the Provisional Education Council (*rinji kyouiku shingikai*) recommended the systematization of training courses for in-service teachers. Two years later, the in-service Teachers' Education Council (*kyoiku shokuin yousei shingikai*) published a report, entitled "Strategies for improving teachers' quality." In that report, the revitalization of school-based teacher training and the assurance of training opportunities for teachers throughout their career (specifically at five, ten, and twenty years of teaching experience) were recommended.

Taking into account such recommendations as well as the study carried out by Maki, the Center has organized four wide training programs: Basic Training Program; Practical Training Program; Special Issues Training program; and Integrated Issues Training Program (see Table 1).

These programs are arranged according to degrees of difficulty and each of them contains several short-term courses. The courses refer to a great diversity of themes such as international education, subject-matter (Mathematics, Japanese Language, etc.), moral education, computer literacy, etc.

Most of courses offered at the Center are short-term courses organized in one or two-day sessions. The Center also conducts long-term training programs lasting either six months or one year.

Teachers participate voluntarily in the courses, but newly appointed teachers, as well as those six-year and eleven-year experienced teachers, are encouraged to participate in the Initial Training Program, Practical Training Program, and Special Issues Training Program, respectively. For this reason, the first, sixth, and eleventh years of teaching experience are emphasized in Figure 1. In addition, newly appointed vice-principals must participate in the School Management Program.

In-service Training Programs and the Teacher Career Stages

As Figure 1 shows, the Center has divided the teacher professional career in four stages. Each stage coincides with one of the training programs designed by the Center itself. The first stage is concomitant with the Basic Training Program; the second, with the Practical Training Program; the Special Issues Training Program corresponds to the third phase; and the fourth deals with a the Integrated Issues Training Program. In general, the phases established by the Center are concomitant to those established by Maki, as the top of Figure 1 shows.

First Stage (0-5 years): Induction Training Program and Basic Training Program
The first stage includes newly appointed teachers and those with few years of teaching experience (0-5 years). During this period new teachers learn from their experienced colleagues. They need to receive basic knowledge and skills to improve their teaching ability. During the first year, teachers participate in the induction-training program, which is spread out over the school year for a total of at least 90 days. Sixty days or more of training are school-based during which new teachers receive instruction from their advising teacher. Not less than 30 days are spent attending lectures, seminars, and various practical training sessions that include five-day workshops held in education centers. The Hiroshima Prefectural Education Center offers these courses for beginning teachers.

Second Stage (6-10 years): Practical Training Program
Includes teachers with between 6 and 10 years of experience. Most trainees in

Table 1: *Classification of Training Programs*

Program (objective)	Characteristics	Sess-ion	Number of courses (1997)	Number of Participants	Profile
Basic Training Program (To develop fundamental skills necessary for teachers)	• Production of new teaching methods for each subject • Gaining experience based on fieldwork and practical skills. • Fundamental teaching skills	1 day	24	546	Offered mainly to teachers with 1 to 6 years of teaching experience
Practical Training Program (To improve practical teaching skills through learning from various techniques)	• To focus in depth on a topic using discussion based on concrete reports and lectures • There are two kind of courses: Course (A) includes areas common to any teacher, and course (B) applies to the teaching of specific subjects	2 days	47	1,433	Offered mainly to teachers with 6 to 10 years of teaching experience
Special Issues Training Program (To improve task solving ability by learning a systematic approach)	• Teachers develop a research project in their own school and receive periodic feedback from the Center; they give a report of their research results upon completion of the program • There are two kind of courses: Course (A) includes areas common to any teacher, and course (B) applies to the teaching of specific subjects	1 to 6 days	42	1,394	Offered mainly to teachers with 11 to 20 years of teaching experience
Integrated Issues Training Program (To improve teachers' comprehensive leadership qualities)	• Teachers engage in training to improve their comprehensive leadership qualities, emphasizing an understanding of education through a wide and diversified perspective	1 to 2 days	12	428	Offered to teachers with over 20 years of teaching experience

the Center belong in this stage. During this period, teachers are considered to acquire self-confidence in their teaching ability, but they still have some difficulty in facing certain educational issues. This group of teachers is also considered to lack experience in the use of audiovisual media and computer. Teachers under its sixth year of teaching experience are encouraged to participate in this program.

These two first stages coincide with Maki's first stage of teachers in their 20s. According to Maki, teachers at this stage act as pupils' friends and have an idealistic understanding of school, instruction, and pupils. They have a good disposition for learning.

Third Stage (11 to 20 years): Special Issues Training Program

Teachers between 11 and 20 years of experience are expected to act as leaders. They are required to design and carry out educational projects as well as to be able to construct their own educational theories based on their own experiences. During this stage many teachers are elected as leaders (*shunin*) of particular school duties in terms of both instructional managerial matter under educational matters as working out and implementing education plans, making overall adjustments of the timetable, and handling textbooks and teaching materials. Another *shunin* who is in charge of a particular grade level deals with establishing the grade's management policy, planning and implementing the grade's activities. In addition, there is a *shunin* in charge of guidance about pupils' lives. Another is in charge of providing students with guidance on their future courses. They all play important roles in school management (National Institute for Educational Research of Japan, 1992).

During this stage, teachers feel great self-confidence in teaching and are able to teach without preparing their lessons beforehand. For this reason, according to the Center, training offered to teachers must provide an opportunity to reflect upon their own limitations, and must include discussion and analyses of current educational issues. Through the Special Issues Training Program, the Center promotes five one-day courses for teachers under this stage. Each participant must have his or her own research theme. The school year is divided into four or five periods, and at the end of each period teachers receive feedback from the Center. At the end of the program teachers are required to present the results of their research. The Center began to offer long-term courses in 1972. Both the prefectural and national governments support these

Figure 1: *In-service Training Programs and the Teaching Career Stages*

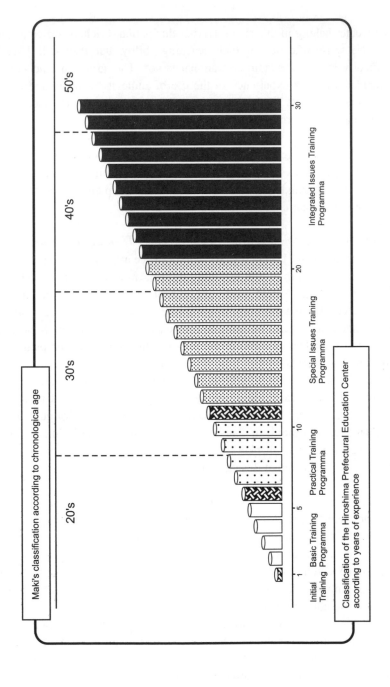

long-term programs. Local authorities try to diversify the research themes and provide schools with equal opportunities to participate. In 1998, 31 teachers participated in this program; nine of them developed a one-year research project.

Authors with successful research projects are called to participate as lecturers in the Center in future courses. In this way, the Center promotes the dissemination of research results, and allows schoolteachers the opportunity to instruct other teachers on a topic of a specialized nature.

Teachers under 11 year of teaching experience are encouraged to participate in this program.

According to Maki, during this stage (the 30s), teachers assume an important role in school management. They leave their role of pupils' friend and become more interested in school management. But at the same time, they are expected to become the model for younger teachers and good collaborators with senior teachers. On one hand, they are expected to act as leaders among their colleagues and, on the other hand, they are expected to gain pupils' confidence.

Fourth Stage (21-years): Integrated Issues Training Program
Teachers at this stage have a wide knowledge about the internal organization of the school. In Japan, this is the period in which teachers move toward administrative positions. Many teachers during this period become head teachers of the school-based in-service training or newly appointed teachers' advisors. Consequently, they need to possess knowledge about the school and its relationships with community and other organizations. School legislation, school management, and mental health courses seem to be of important interest to them.

This stage coincides with Maki's age-40s stage. At this stage, teachers broaden their abilities for planning, acquire a practical ability for leadership, and develop the ability to promote human relationships. Teachers at this stage have a more comprehensive idea about education and usually act as head teachers. This is the most important stage in a teacher's career.

SUMMARY AND DISCUSSION

A number of general observations can be derived from this study. First, Maki's classification supposes a linear progression from one stage to the next, as well as a progressive process in the acquisition of new knowledge and new experiences. Maki's rationale for associating evolutionary development with years of experience is directly related to the fact that experience is greatly emphasized in Japanese organizational culture. Within this dynamic it is expected that school teachers will complete their initial education at the age of 22, will be appointed as teachers at 22~23, and upon gaining several years of experience, are expected to become head teachers during their 30s. An experienced teacher (*senpai*) becomes the model for younger colleagues (*kohai*) and acquires the moral responsibility of being more knowledgeable than his juniors. It is not coincidental that Maki considers the 40s (the stage prior to retirement), the most important phase in a teacher's life. This social dynamic occurs differently in Western societies where accredited academic knowledge and personal leadership abilities of an individual are valued regardless the age and the experience.

The philosophy of Hiroshima Prefectural Education Center is similar to that of Maki. In that the organization of training programs according to degree of difficulty assumes that the experienced teacher is more knowledgeable than the less experienced one. Figure 1 represents this progression in an ascending format. Upon analysis of Huberman's (1995) research, we can conjecture that the Japanese model could be improved by taking into account periods of inactivity common among senior teachers and by incorporating other paths in the teachers' professional life cycle.

The incorporation of a pre-professional phase as an integral part of teacher professional development is a valuable contribution of Vonk (1989) and Fessler and Christensen (1992). In recent years, there has been an ongoing debate about the theoretical links between preservice and in-service teacher education. If we contend that the initial education of teachers strongly influences their professional performance, we need to look more closely at the relationship between preservice and in-service education.

The stages constituting a teacher's career cycle, as described by the authors and the literature from the Hiroshima Prefectural Education Center, both coincide closely to years of experience. However, the importance of the Center's classification lies in its organization of training programs, with the objective of offering special courses to teachers based upon their own needs, interests, and situations.

Looking at the organization, classification, and content of training programs, we can see that most courses offered at the Center are short-term courses. In 1997, the Center offered 123 short-term courses in which 3,580 teachers participated. In addition, 16 long-term courses were organized with the participation of 221 teachers. In other words, during 1997, 23.5% of all teachers in the Hiroshima Prefecture participated in the courses offered by the Center. Despite the fact that the Center offers the courses for all schoolteachers in Hiroshima Prefecture, the participation of national and private school teachers within the prefecture is very low. In the same year, only seven of these teachers participated in the courses. Incidentally, there are very few courses specifically offered to kindergarten and special education teachers. As Figure 1 shows, most of these participants were enrolled in the Practical Training and Special Issue Training Programs. Based on this data, we can conclude that in terms of training, the most active teachers in Japan have between six and twenty years of teaching experience.

Most of the teachers participating in the programs are primary school teachers (33.1% of the total), followed by lower secondary school teachers (20.9%) and upper secondary school teachers (17.7%). There exists a marked difference between the Center's resources available to accommodate teachers and the number of teachers who register as participants. In 1997, although the Center invited a total of 5,000 teachers and school administrators, the actual number of participants was less than 4,000. Those who are not taking advantage of the courses tend to be secondary school teachers. Consequently, it is necessary to examine the reasons behind this relatively low rate of participation among secondary school teachers in INSET. One reason may be the heavy work schedule of Japanese secondary school teachers. According to the data mentioned above, the majority of newly appointed teachers tend to be secondary school teachers. Most of these teachers come from general academic universities, and consequently have little background in teaching methodology, and have not taken coursework dealing with the issues affecting school education. Moreover, the highest percentages of school bullying and school refusal, two of the most serious current pathological problems affecting Japanese education, are found at the secondary school level. According to an article in the *Mainichi* Newspaper, in 1997 there were 18,209 reported cases of school bullying in lower secondary, and 4,108 cases in upper secondary schools.[3] Therefore, it seems apparent that lower and upper secondary school teachers need more intensive training to enhance their teaching competence, but also to be able to handle the current multitude of problems facing education in Japan. The Center needs to find ways to promote more active participation of these teachers in the training programs.

Looking at the content of the courses, there is a noticeable preponderance of courses related to school subjects (62 courses), followed by moral education (18 courses), computer literacy (18 courses), and counseling and guidance (17 courses). This data illustrates that INSET is mainly oriented toward teaching methodologies, and focuses on how to produce new teaching methods and materials. The Center also emphasizes topics related to social problems affecting Japanese education. In fact, it can be argued that the Center is contributing, to a certain degree, to the solution of those problems. Unfortunately, the short duration of courses does not allow teachers to engage in an in-depth study of those issues.

One of the unique features of these courses is that they are mainly designed by topic, so that teachers of all school levels are able to participate. For example, there is a course, entitled "Classroom Management: How to Foster Human Relations." The Center offered this course to 15 elementary, 10 lower secondary, and 10 upper secondary school teachers. In the author's opinion, this kind of organization could contribute to broadening the teachers' conceptions about educational issues, since teachers have the opportunity to exchange opinions not only with teachers of different schools but also with teachers of different levels of schooling. For this reason, it is perhaps necessary to promote the debate and discussion of themes within study sessions at the Center.

As it was stated in "The Model for Japanese Education in the Perspective of the 21st Century," there is a lack of coordination among the different agencies in charge of teacher education. Many university professors, including those at Hiroshima University, are invited by the Center to conduct lectures and workshops. However, there is not a specific program of collaboration between the various universities and the Center. On the other hand, local boards of education, which are responsible for the development of school-based in-service training, have not established effective relationships with the center, the universities, and other institutions. Such relationships are essential to solicit the cooperation of these institutions in order to improve the school-based in-service training. The establishment of cooperation among different institutions could be a valuable resource in the Japanese educational system. New educational projects such as the American Professional Development Schools could represent an effective model for a Japanese program.

Most schoolteachers in Japan are full-time staff. Teachers work at least eight hours each weekday, and two Saturdays every month. Consequently, their opportunities for self-development are limited by their heavy work schedule. It is not a coincidence that school-based in-service training tends to be very popular in Japan. However, there exists a lack of theoretical support for the research that is done under the rubric of school-based training. The revitalization of school-based in-service training is, therefore, of great importance. It may also be beneficial if this training were connected with the programs offered by the Education Center. Teachers require the theoretical background to develop their research projects, and the Center has the staff and resources for providing this assistance. Specifically, the Special Issue Training Program (which consists in developing a research project throughout the school years under the advice of the Education Center) could very well serve as a bridge between the Center and in-service training held at the school level.

Finally, it is important to note that the stratification of courses according to years of experience can efficiently be put into practice given the standardization of Japanese education, and its teachers' seniority-based promotion system. Japanese school teachers are expected to enter into the system at the age of 22-24, to become head teachers during their 30s-40s, to become principals in their 40s-50s, and retire sometime in their 60s. The system does not allow teachers to transfer between school levels, and once appointed, they have few opportunities to enroll in graduate schools in order to obtain a better position. Under these circumstances, such stratification of courses corresponds only to the Japanese situation. Nonetheless, we can consider that this kind of stratified organization of courses, if modified to suit local needs and realities, has possibilities for implementation in other countries. This organization could represent a good option for teachers' career-long professional development.

NOTES

[1]Percentages including the number of candidates looking for a post in special

education, whose number of candidate was 10,976.

[2]Data obtained from the files of Hiroshima University's Graduate School of Education and Graduate School of School Education.

[3]*Mainichi Shinbun* (Daily Newspaper). 12A. No. 41699, 19 December, 1998, p. 1.

REFERENCES

Burden, P. (1980). *Teacher's perceptions of the characteristics and influences on their personal and professional development.* (Eric Document No. ED 198087)

Fessler, R. (1995). Dynamics of teacher career stages. In Guskey & Huberman (Eds.). *Professional development in education* (pp. 171-192). Columbia: New Paradigms & Practices. Teachers College, Columbia University.

Fessler, R., & Christensen, J. (1992). *The teacher career cycle: Understanding and guiding the professional development of teachers.* Boston: Allyn & Bacon.

Fuller, F. (1969). Concerns of teachers: A developmental perspective. *American Educational Research Journal, 6,* 207-226.

Glickman, C. (1990). *Supervision of instruction: A developmental approach*, Boston: Allyn & Bacon.

Gregorc, A. F. (1973). Developing plans for professional growth. *NASSP Bulletin, 57,* 1-8. (Cited by Fessler [1995])

Hargreaves, A. (1995). Development and desire. A postmodern perspective. In T. R. Guskey & M. Huberman (Eds.), *Professional development in education: New paradigms and practices* (pp. 9-34). New York: Teachers College Press.

Hargreaves, A. (1999). *Reinventing professionalism. Teacher education and teacher development for a changing world.* Paper presented at the International Conference on Teacher Education: Teaching Effectiveness and Teacher Development in the New Century, The Hong Kong Institute of Education, Hong Kong, February 1999.

Huberman, M. (1995). Professional careers and professional development: Some intersections. In T. R. Guskey & M. Huberman (Eds.), *Professional development in education: New paradigms and practices* (pp. 193-224). New York: Teachers College Press.

Katz, L. G. (1972). Development stages of preschool teachers. *Elementary School Journal, 3,* 50-54. (ERIC Document No. EJ 064759)

Maki, M. (1990a). *20 dai. Kyoushi no jikokeihatsu-kenshu. 20 dai kyoushi wa naniwo benkyoushitara yoika.* [Study about teachers self-development. What is good for teachers to study during their 20's?]. Japan: Gyosei.

Maki, M. (1990b). *30 dai. Kyoushi no jikokeihatsu-kenshu. 30 dai kyoushi wa naniwo benkyoushitara yoika.* [Study about teachers self-development. What is good for teachers to study during their 30's?]. Japan: Gyosei.

Maki, M. (1990c). *40 dai. Kyoushi no jikokeihatsu-kenshu. 40 dai kyoushi wa naniwo benkyoushitara yoika.* [Study about teachers self-development. What is good for teachers to study during their 40's?]. Japan: Gyosei.

Maki, M. (1996). *Kyoin kenshu. jikokeihatsu katsudo ni kansuru jittai chosa kenkyu saigo hokokusho* [Inservice teacher training. Teachers self professional development. Study about the real situation. Final report]. Tokyo: kuritsu Kyoiku Kenkyu-jo.

Mevarech, Z. R. (1995). Teachers' paths on the way to and from the professional development forum. In T. R. Guskey & M. Huberman (Eds.), *Professional development in education: New paradigms and practices* (pp. 151-170). New York: Teachers College Press.

MONBUSHO. (1994). *Education in Japan 1994. A graphic presentation.* Japan: Gyosei Corporation.

MONBUSHO. (1997). Kyoiku Shokuin Yosei Shingikai. Aratana Jidai ni Muketa Kyoin Yosei no Kaizen Hosaku nitsuite [First Report on Strategies to Improve Teacher Education in a New Age]. *Dai Ichiji Toshin.* Tokyo: Author.

Monk, M. et. al. (1999 February). *Teacher development and change in Asia and Africa: An evolutionary perspective.* Paper presented at International Conference on Teacher Education: Teaching Effectiveness and Teacher Development in the New Century, The Hong Kong Institute of Education, Hong Kong.

NIER. (1992). *School teachers in Japan.* Occasional Paper 01/1992. Japan: Author.

OECD. Centre for Educational Research and Innovation. (1998). *Staying ahead. Inservice training and teacher professional development.* France: Author.

Shimuzu, K. (1998). *Kyoiku dataland. A data-book of educational statistics 1998-1999.* Japan: Jiji Tsushinsha.

United Nations Preparatory Educational, Scientific, and Cultural Commission. (1998). *World education report 1998 - Teachers and teaching in a changing world.* Paris: Author.

Unruh. A., & Turner, H. E. (1970). *Supervision for change and innovation,* Boston: Houghton Mifflin.

Vonk, J. H. C. (1989). *Becoming a teacher, brace yourself.* Unpublished paper. Vrije University, Amsterdam.

White, M. (1987). *The Japanese educational challenge.* USA: Free Press.

Chapter 15

Client-based In-service Education and Training: From South Africa with Lessons

Alex Mulalo MUTSHEKWANE

Association For Research Advancement, Republic of South Africa.

Prior to 1994, South Africa never had a coherent policy for teacher development and governance. Policies were scattered and divided among the 19 apartheid different education departments classified according to racial and ethnic groups. This was the era of apartheid or separate development. Consequently, the new democratic government of South Africa inherited in 1994 a total of 19 employing authorities for teachers and a range of institutions and procedures to manage them (McFarlane, 1996). The new government has completed the process of restructuring and transforming education in general and teacher education specifically, resulting in several policies which serve to realign the education system of South Africa.

The White Paper on Education and Training captured the dichotomy of educational control as follows:

> The national and provincial Ministries of Education are dealing daily with the legacy of South Africa's historically separate education and training systems … Until recently, all these separate systems have operated more or less in isolation from each other, except at the level of top management. Mutual ignorance has therefore been the norm, even between teachers and administrators working virtually side by side in neighbouring systems. (Department of Education, 1995, p. 18.)

The restructuring, reorganization, and transformation of education resulted in the country having one National Department of Education responsible for National Education policy and nine Provincial Education departments overseeing the implementation of National Education policy. The nine provinces are Northern Province; Mpumalanga; Gauteng; Northern Cape; North-West; Western Cape; Eastern Cape; Free State; and KwaZulu-Natal. Some of these provinces are more rural than others and are more resourced than others. The Northern Province, KwaZulu-Natal, and the Eastern Cape Province are considered to be more rural, less developed and requiring assistance from National government and Donor agencies (Integrated Sustainable Rural Development Strategy, 2000).

In the policy arena, the new democratic government of South Africa has embraced the vision for systemic educational change, and has made significant progress in establishing a number of key policy instruments in a number of areas, as follows:

1. Constitutional rights. The new constitution establishes basic education and equal educational access to educational institution as the right of all citizens (Government of South Africa, 1996).

2. Qualifications. The South African Qualifications Authority (SAQA) Act (Government of South Africa, 1995) is the first step towards establishing a coherent framework for the recognition of all education qualifications.

3. School governance. The South African Schools Act makes provision for the establishment of school governing bodies through which parents will exercise considerable authority and responsibility in the governance of schools.

4. Curriculum 2005. The Policy Document for the Foundation Phase (Department of Education, 1997).

5. Assessment. The Assessment policy in General Education and Training Phase (Department of Education, 1998d)

6. Gender. The Report of the Gender Equity Task Team makes recommendations for the establishment of gender equity measures throughout the education system.

7. *The Education White Paper 3: a Program for the Transformation of Higher Education* and the *Higher Education Act, Act 101 of 1977* provides the policy and legislative framework for the transformation of the higher education system (Burger, 2000 p. 436). The Higher Education system is made out of universities, Technikons, and colleges of education.

8. Teacher management. Four instruments -- Norms and Standards for Educators (Department of Education, 1998a), Employment of Educators Act (Department of Education, 1998b), Manual for the Developmental Appraisal of Educators (Department of Education, 1998b), Duties and Responsibilities of Educators (Department of Education, 1998c), and Norms and Standards for Educators (Department of Education, 2000a) – aim to align regulations governing teacher qualifications, certifications, and management, and to make provision for establishing a system of performance management for teachers.

From the above legal frameworks, it can be deduced that the key policy instruments that impact heavily on teacher education, including those in the domains of higher education and teacher management. Colleges of education are now part of the Higher Education System. Norms and standards for teachers have been formulated and all these must be communicated with teachers, parents, and other stakeholders who will then assist with monitoring of the performance of schools and the education system as a whole.

Taken together, the aforementioned documents represent an impressively coherent vision for the fundamental transformation of the South African schooling system. These policy documents pave the way of the task of building the human and systemic capacity, which form the foundation on which innovation relies (Taylor & Vinjevold, 1999).

The Ministry of Education considers in the White Paper on Education and Training "... teacher education as one of the central pillars of national human resource strategy, and the growth of professional expertise and self-confidence ... the key to teacher development" (Department of Education, 1995, p. 29).

Programs of professional development and capacity-building of educators nationally and in the Northern Province are important for improving the quality of education. These are necessary and important in the light of curriculum changes coming about because of the new political dispensation in South Africa. The continuing professional development of teachers is increasingly regarded as critical if national targets of creating more effective schools and raising standards of pupil achievement are to be realized (O'Brien & MacBeath, 1999).

This chapter reviews education policy development in South Africa, current teacher education policies, and existing In-service Education and Training (INSET) providing institutions in the Northern Province in order to recommend improvements in the planning and organization of INSET programs. It focuses on the contribution of courses to teacher development and teacher upgrading. For a client-based INSET program to emerge, partnerships between stakeholders (teachers, principals, lecturers at INSET institutes, subject advisers, and inspectors) and higher education institutions need to be formed in order to satisfy the needs of educators and the system of education (Mutshekwane, 1995). Some of the difficulties experienced by INSET providing centers and staff can be overcome by inter-institutional co-operation where bilateral links are established between universities and schools (Cross & Sehoole, 1996). This form of co-operation entails a process of working together to achieve mutual benefits in the form of quality service and the promotion of access to already stretched resources. The experiences from this client-based INSET Program in South Africa may contribute to the ongoing efforts for teacher education and development in different parts of the world.

AN OVERVIEW OF TEACHER EDUCATION IN SOUTH AFRICA

Teacher education and training is the largest single field of study in South Africa's higher education and is offered by a large range of institutions including universities, technikons, colleges of education, private and public colleges, non-governmental organizations and provincial education departments (Department of Education, 1996a). This sector includes pre-service education, induction of educators, and on-the job training and professional development of teachers. According to the *National Teacher Education Audit* (Department of Education, 1996a) report, there were 281 institutions offering pre- and in-service teacher education programs in South Africa. The teacher education field is large, fragmented, and diverse. The quality of teacher education was generally poor, despite pockets of excellence and innovation; the system was inefficient as a result of the high matriculation failure rate (pass rate of 31.8% was for November 1997). In November 2000, the pass rate had improved significantly from 48.9% in 1999 to 57.9% nationally (Asmal, 2000b). Moreover, most students enroll for teacher education programs, because there are no other alternative fields of study exposed to them. Others do so with no intention of teaching, but to obtain a tertiary education qualification. Most of the teachers who were forced by conditions to do a teachers' course end up joining the teaching profession without being dedicated to teach.

The quality of teaching has been an important area of focus since 1994. Given the poor quality of teacher training in the past and the magnitude of change in the education sector, the issues of teacher morale and professional development continue to be critical focus areas (Department of Education, 2000c). It is for this reason that this chapter is being written.

INSET refers to the whole range of activities by which serving teachers and other categories of educationalists within formal school systems may extend and develop their personal qualities, professional competence, and general understanding of the role which schools are expected to play in changing societies (Chilana, 1972; Thompson, 1982). INSET includes the means whereby a teacher's personal needs and aspirations may be met as well as those of the system in which he or she serves. It further includes the promotion of innovation in response to educational problems (Eraut, 1972).

INSET is conveniently defined by Bolam (as quoted in Husen & Postlethwaite, 1995) as "[T]hose education and training activities engaged in by primary and secondary school teachers and principals, following their initial professional certification, and intended mainly or exclusively to improve their professional knowledge, skills, and attitudes in order that they can educate children more effectively" (p. 3).

INSET is taken to include all those courses and activities in which a serving teacher may participate for the purpose of extending his or her professional knowledge, interest, or skill. Preparation for a degree, diploma, or other qualification is included within this definition (Cane, 1971; Department of Education and Science [DES], 1972).

The Bulletin of the International Bureau of Education (1981) defines INSET to designate "the sum of diverse processes in which the practical specialist becomes the object of the educational process." The various aspects of the process are described using terms such as perfecting, raising qualifications, further education, post-diploma and post-graduate studies, and others. Important in the present context is the relation of the in-service education of teachers to their initial or pre-service training and to their teaching performance.

From these definitions, it can be deduced that INSET plays a role in satisfying the needs of teachers, the system of education he or she serves, and the society served by schools.

Millar (1980) argues that "[O]ne is trained to carry out pre-defined tasks to pre-defined specifications. One is educated to respond creatively and with judgement to situations and in ways that are unpredictable" (Millar, 1980, p. 5). The distinction between the two concepts training and education is, however, a theoretical one (as cited in Hartshorne, 1992, p. 257).

Hartshorne (1992, p. 258) is of the opinion that INSET has to do with "bringing about teachers' professional, academic and personal development through the provision of a whole series of study experiences and activities of which training should be rated as but one aspect" (Morant, 1981, p. 3), and that INSET is "a crucial variable in the process of improving the quality of children's learning in the classroom" (Greenland, 1983, p. 5).

Hartshorne (1992, p. 25) advances the notion that INSET cannot be considered in isolation from other aspects of teacher education, and that it should be seen as part of a continuum concerned with integrated, continuing academic, professional, and personal development of the teacher. INSET should not be considered in isolation from the conditions under which the teacher works; the nature and quality of the education system around and within which INSET programs and strategies have to work; and the total social, economic, and political context within which schools and education takes place.

Oldroyd and Hall (1991) state that INSET refers to "[P]lanned activities practiced both within and outside schools primarily to develop the professional knowledge, skills, attitudes and performance of professional staff in schools" (P.7) in order to influence student performance. The focus here is on activities that will enhance the performance of students.

INSET IN SOUTH AFRICA

The education system of South Africa (including its nine Provinces) is faced with numerous problems one of which is the shortage of skilled, motivated teachers who can perform as dedicated professionals. The demand for effective INSET to improve the quality of teaching and learning, to empower unmotivated teachers, and to assist in the broad transformation process is a *sine qua non.*

The South African Democratic Teachers' Union (SADTU) has made a proposal for the professional development of educators. This has been entrenched in regulations. It specifies that each educator must complete 80 hours per year participating in in-service training activities. Funds have been secured to upgrade the skills of under-qualified educators. A comprehensive skills development plan will be introduced over the next two years (Department of Education, 2000c)

The process of reform in teacher education and the rationalization and re-deployment of educators is complete or at an advanced phase in South African Provinces. The process requires imagination, resourcefulness, and co-operation from parties involved. It is meant to be collaborative, interactive, and a partnership between the Government, teacher unions, social forces, and relevant stakeholders are to drive the process of education transformation. The INSET process can also play a major role in the re-orientation of those affected by the rationalization and re-deployment process provided they accept the challenge.

Hofmeyr and Jaff (1992, p. 169) have argued that separate and unequal system of apartheid education gave rise to the current situation where the majority of African teachers have received less training and endure worse working conditions than their White counterparts. They further indicate that the quality of education is declining resulting in the learning environment that has collapsed in most provincial schools of South Africa and the Northern Province in particular. The time is ripe for a democratic non-racial, non-sexist government to take charge of this sorry state of education and to finalize the restructuring process so that citizens of South Africa can benefit.

It is against this background that INSET can be considered as the prime strategy which can be implemented to further the academic and professional development of teachers, accelerate the achievement of equal education for all children, and prepare all teachers to participate in the actual transformation of education and society.

Bagwandeen and Louw (1993, p. 59) indicated that literature on INSET in the South African context is limited. The most comprehensive survey in South Africa according to Hofmeyr (1988) is the report written by Hartshorne (1985) for submission to the INSET sub-committee of the Human Sciences Research Council (HSRC). Other reports on INSET were those by Jane Hofmeyr (1988) for the Mobil Foundation of South Africa, a doctorial dissertation by Murphy (1985) on the Teacher Opportunity Program; Mkhize's (1989) dissertation on the professional and academic upgrading of black teachers in Kwazulu-Natal; Hofmeyr's (1992) dissertation on INSET, and Mutshekwane's (1992) dissertation on In-service training of teachers in Venda. These and other works have made an important, critical, and analytical study of INSET in South Africa.

Researchers on INSET in South Africa (Bot, 1986; Hartshorne, 1985; Hartshorne, 1992; Hofmeyr, 1992; Mutshekwane, 1992; National Education Policy Initiative [NEPI], 1992) have indicated the need for a coherent policy for INSET in South Africa. The absence of such a policy is the main reason why INSET provision by the public sector is ineffective, ad-hoc, and under-funded. Most attempts at formulating INSET policies were scattered among the 19 "apartheid" education departments and attempts to centralize such efforts are still pending in the new education dispensation. The climate is conducive for a fresh look into this important facet of teacher education because a new education dispensation for a democratic South Africa is being implemented. INSET can contribute meaningfully towards the reconstruction and development of education and training because of its merits.

Curriculum change is a *sine qua non* now that a democratic South Africa is in place. In order to effectively retrain teachers and update them in the much needed and relevant subject matter, teaching skills, and attitudes which may render South African learners to be worthy of being world citizens, there is a need to embark on a massive INSET program which will incorporate the needs, aspirations, and interests of all stake-holders of INSET. Curriculum 2005 is being implemented and its successful implementation will depend on a clearly defined and implemented INSET strategy.

The demand for the establishment of a single education department in South Africa has been met, but this strategy alone will not prove to be an answer to problems surrounding the South African teacher education system if proper plans are not put in place to improve the provision of quality education. INSET can prove to be a critical catalyst and a factor in removing knowledge gaps created by apartheid education. There is thus a need for a sincere commitment to a policy of in-service education and training of teachers in order to rectify a history of neglect in this area (Bagwandeen & Louw, 1993, p. 16).

The Education Renewal Strategy (ERS) (Department of Education and Training, 1992) scantily entrenched INSET as an essential organ of addressing some of the ills of Apartheid pre-service education, with the exception of a brief mention of its role in the qualification structure and its link with distance education. This side stepping of on-the-job training is dangerous because INSET is an important strategy for the reconstruction and development of education. The teachers' role as agents of change cannot be ignored. Teacher INSET must thus entrench the change mindset in teachers so that they can assist in the mammoth task of re-directing and re-engineer education in South Africa.

The author's involvement with INSET planning and delivery of INSET programs from 1982 to 1992 unfolded to him the necessity and value of INSET as a contributor to education transformation. An appropriate INSET policy statement by the country's National Education Department can promote funding windows of teacher education by the private sector and overseas donors in order that the knowledge, skills, and competencies of teachers can be upgraded and improved. Funds may also be available for the improvement of teacher education in general (initial, induction, and INSET). Teacher education must train for employment rather than qualifications (Monobe, 1995). If on-the-job effectiveness is the focus of teacher upgrading courses then teachers may benefit by attending INSET courses.

The Northern Province has a high rate of unemployed teachers which stood at over 20,000 since 1997. Both the National Education Department and the Northern Province's Department of Education have taken bold steps of substantially reducing the number of teacher training colleges thereby reducing the intake of prospective teacher-trainees. The Province has a population of over 5,337 million and 60,000 teachers (Burger, 2000, p. 19). INSET can play a role in improving the quality of teaching and learning.

The challenge faced by INSET is to address the problem of the current teaching corps' capacity to render service of the highest quality (NEPI, 1992, p. 32). This can be achieved through a well planned needs-based and client-based INSET. INSET referred to here has to do with assisting teachers to grow, learn, improve, enjoy, think, and work diligently, with an emphasis on improving staff performance (Bagwandeen & Louw, 1993). There is a need for each subject area to have specially designed INSET programs which will meet identified needs of clients and to improve teachers' performance. The Ministry of National Education under Professor Bengu was concerned with the upgrading of under- and unqualified teachers, most of whom teach in the rural schools. Professor Bengu, former Minister of Education, was of the opinion that the quality of school teaching and teacher education must be given serious attention (Campbell, 1996). The successful implementation of the new curriculum for South Africa, Curriculum 2005, would depend on well planned and well executed INSET for Curriculum 2005 programs. The current Minister of Education, Professor Kader Asmal, is implementing and improving on the foundation laid by his predecessor. Signs of hope are showing and the Department of Education's communication is informing the majority of South Africans about changes being introduced to our education system, for example, the review of Curriculum 2005 which has yielded Curriculum for the 21st Century.

As South Africa enters the new millennium, it is clear that its education, training, and development system will evolve in relation to changing economic, political, social, technical, and global trends. It is crucial that teacher education qualifications should not be rigid or static, but flexible and able to adapt in response to global trends. We are in the era of the information society where the Internet and e-mail are revolutionizing all sectors of life. Education will not be left alone. It has to adapt to global trends. For this to happen, comprehensive in-depth analyses of occupational roles and requirements, both academic and professional, are required.

The occupational roles of and academic requirements for teachers to meet are likely to change dramatically as South Africa implements an outcomes-based life-long learning system that seeks to become a player in the global economy (Department of Education, 1997).

Prior to 1994, there were strong boundaries between pre-service education and training (PRESET) and INSET, and between universities and technikons and colleges of education. These boundaries have been weakened by policy changes that seek to have teacher education as part of the Higher Education System for better control and financing purposes. This paves the way for INSET and PRESET to relate better to each other as part of the PRESET-INSET continuum. Teacher education is a component of higher education, and higher education is an exclusive national competence.

In the case of school teachers, INSET was largely seen to be a provincial competence: for example, the Department of Education's Teacher Policy Support Program has developed policies for INSET programs in 1997. Under the new dispensation, all PRESET qualifications will be part of higher education and will be a national competence. INSET, by contrast, will be both a provincial and national competence, because what happens in schools and classrooms falls under the provinces and clearly. Provinces will continue to engage in various kinds of INSET programs, but INSET programs that lead to accredited qualifications are to be part of higher education and are therefore, a national competence.

A Teacher Development Center (TDC) of the National Department of Education, through which provinces are represented, could play a crucial role in coordinating provincial non-qualification INSET programs for school educators. TDC would include the responsibility of co-coordinating national and provincial policy on and support of PRESET and INSET (Department of Education, 1997).

A further development is that a Teacher Development Directorate has recently been established in the National Department of Education. The Department of Education (1999) is in the process of institutionalizing and systematizing the field of teacher development driven by the following imperatives: the agreement on 80 hours per annum INSET for each teacher; the development of new norms and standards for educators; the establishment of a Standards Generating Body (SGB) for the Schooling sub-field under the South African Qualification Authority framework (SAQA); and the establishment of a Sectoral Education ad Training Authority (SETA) for Education.

The Ministry of Education recently announced an *"Implementation plan for Tirisano January 2000 – December 2004"* with tight target dates to round off the policy development process. Examples of key teacher development target dates are: development of a policy framework for educator development (February 2000); white Paper on educator development (April 2000); upgrading of unqualified and under-qualified educators (ongoing starting March 2000); educators trained to implement curriculum 2005 (ongoing); policy on the role of the South African Council of Educators (SACE) (February 2000); and all school management teams attend training programs

(April 2000); and all new school principals attend induction programs (March 2000) (Department of Education, 2000b). These target dates will ensure a programmatic implementation of changes in teacher education.

The future of teachers colleges, which are still under provincial control, has been subject to a protracted process of investigation and planning. In 1994, approximately 150 institutions provided teacher education to about 200,000 students, of whom about 80,000 where enrolled in colleges of education. Most of the colleges of education were established by the apartheid government, homeland governments and independent states without consideration of cost, need, quality, and availability of teacher's posts. By the year 2000, the number of teachers' colleges has been reduced to 50, with 20,000 students, out of a total of 82 public institutions offering teacher education to 115,000 students. Of these, 20,000 are to be enrolled in pre-service programs and 95,000 in in-service programs. By the end of provincial rationalization process, 25 contact colleges of education will have about 15,000 students, and two distance education colleges will enroll another 5,000, measured as full-time equivalents (Asmal, 2000a). Further, all colleges surviving rationalization will be incorporated into universities and Technikons, respectively.

In summary, teacher policy development is currently at an advanced stage and implementation has started. It is, however, one good thing to have good policies, but another story to have that policy interpreted accurately, communicated to all stakeholders, and implemented at provincial and local school levels. Provinces and their Regional structures experience acute capacity shortages. There is a need for capacity building programs to strengthen administrative capacities, the capacity to plan, to manage, to teach, and to perform other essential tasks required by the education system.

There are two types of INSET that are predominant in South Africa: INSET for higher qualifications and INSET focuses on school competence and improvement. INSET for upgrading and further qualifications constitute a huge industry with state colleges, private colleges, universities, non-governmental-organizations (NGO), and technikons as main providers. The majority of teachers engaged in this type of INSET are un- or under-qualified. In 1994, more than 124,000 teachers were enrolled with service providers for this form of INSET (Hoffmeyr & Hall, 1995)

The second type of professional development is INSET for school competence.

In 1995, 239,000 teachers participated in curriculum related courses and management training without any formal accreditation. The State provides this form of INSET through its centers, teacher centers, and NGOs. This type of INSET consists of short courses, seminars, and workshops, and the impact of this on teaching and learning is limited (Hoffmeyr & Hall, 1995).

Universities throughout the world are increasingly entering into partnerships to promote collaboration between themselves and with colleges and schools. Such partnerships deal with research and academic issues, administrative issues, community outreach, and consultation. Teacher in-service training can also form a basis of sustainable partnerships between higher education sector and INSET providing agencies. Such links can be vertical with schools and NGOs, and horizontal with other institutions of higher learning (colleges, technikons, and universities) (Cross & Sehoole, 1996).

CLIENT-BASED INSET OF TEACHERS

The effect of general INSET on teaching practice seems to be very limited and, for this reason, client-based INSET can play a pivotal role in bridging the gap between theory and practice.

INSET propagated in this chapter is confined to learning area-oriented guidance aimed at developing teachers' working knowledge of a school subject. The emphasis here is on "client-based" dedicated INSET of teachers. Capacity-building of teachers to concentrate on a school phase or grade and specific learning area content (in at least two or three subjects) should be the target of INSET programs. The real needs of teachers who are the main clients must be met. This form of INSET cannot be offered in isolation, but should take into account the context of education, especially in a country like South Africa where all was not well until 1994 when a democratic South Africa was ushered. Partnerships between INSET offering institutions, teacher unions, and higher education institutions (universities and technikons) should be fostered. These institutions should most importantly share experiences, human resources, and physical facilities while implementing client-based teacher empowering programs.

There has been moves towards more school-based in-service and self-help programs, reflecting moves from traditional INSET to staff development and, subsequently, to the concept of professional development (Hargreaves, 1994).

Fullan (1991) describes professional development as follows: "Continuous development of all teachers is the cornerstone for meaning, improvement and reform. Professional development and school development are inextricably linked" (p. 123).

Staff development has been variously defined or described, for example, as follows:

> In-service training should begin in the schools. It is here that learning and teaching take place, curriculum and techniques are developed and needs and deficiencies revealed. Every school should regard the continued training of its teachers as an essential part of its task, for which all members of staff share responsibility. An active school is constantly reviewing and reassuring its effectiveness and ready to consider new methods, new forms of organizational and new ways of dealing with the problems that arise (DES, 1972).

Staff development embraces not only individual education and training, individual appraisal, and careers enhancement, but also whole-staff development as part of a dynamic and changing organization. Staff development includes all-round development of the individual and the inter-relationships of teachers' different subject areas and levels of responsibility.

Purposes of staff development include motivation and communication; review and improvement of professional performance; staff development; and career review (O'Brien & MacBeath, 1999). Key principles of staff development according to the Scottish National Guidelines for Staff Development and Appraisal (Scottish Education Department, 1990) are identified as, first, all staff to be consulted in the development and implementation of a staff development appraisal policy and procedures; second, staff development and appraisal arrangements to be systematic, clearly defined, and embedded in a school's overall policies and procedures; third, policies and procedures to be regularly monitored and subject to review; fourth, an annual program of staff development to be planned and provided, reflecting the schools' identified priorities and individual professional needs; fifth, such programs to include a range of activities indicating that staff development involves more than in-service courses; and sixth, prioritization of needs to provide opportunities for individuals, schools, and local authorities, and the ability to control the pace of change.

The client-centered INSET program envisaged concentrates on practical and useful teaching strategies for the working situation of the client, that is, the teacher's classroom. Two important principles to be considered are the development of pupil-ready teaching materials for classroom use and the engagement of all stakeholders involved in the didactic situation. This ensures that interventions made at classroom level will have a direct impact on the quality of education provided resulting in whole-school development. MacBeath and Mortimore (1997) argue that closing the gap between the real and desired situation is clearly one important factor in improving school effectiveness. There needs to be clarity of vision of what staff development is, what it can accomplish, and how it may be facilitated for it to succeed.

This kind of INSET is a practically oriented teacher upliftment program that focuses on the classroom as a hive of activities. It has implications for certification, accreditation, and curriculum renewal and design. This calls for partnerships between certificating bodies (National Qualification Framework & the South African Qualification Authority [SAQA]) and INSET providing institutions, between accrediting institutions and INSET clients, and lastly, between curriculum designers and those who will implement curricula changes, namely, teachers. Emphasis is now on delivery – that is, the ability to do the job – rather than paper qualifications.

Subject-oriented INSET emphasizes the development of professionalism in a learning area. Teachers must know both the learning area content and the learners they teach. The justification for subject-oriented INSET is to be found in the demand for change and relevancy made by the public. The high failure rate of candidates at grade 12 level (standard 10) calls for more emphasis to be placed on subject-oriented INSET. Curricular changes introduced to schools in provincial education departments of the new South Africa since 1998 brought about new emphasis on client-based and subject-oriented INSET as well as innovative approaches of imparting knowledge. To ensure successful implementation of new curricula, INSET courses must be intensified.

Huang (1993, p. 177) argues that good teaching includes teaching learners how to learn, how to remember, how to think, and how to motivate them. Helping learners develop effective ways of handling the barrage of information coming from the environment, as well as their own thinking process is a major goal of our educational system today. The use of particular learning and teaching strategies can affect the encoding process, which in turn affects the learning outcome and performance. However, the learner needs to be the center of teaching and learning activities. Maximum learner participation must be encouraged to promote effective learning. Client-based INSET can contribute in making educators realize that they have an important role to play in guiding learners to be active candidates.

INSET PROVIDING INSTITUTIONS IN THE NORTHERN PROVINCE

Prior to 1994, INSET in the Northern Province was provided by the Limburg In-service Training Center in the former Lebowa; Giyani Science Center in the former Gazankulu and the former Venda In-service Training Center renamed Ramaano Mbulaheni Training Center (RMTC) in Venda. Various education circuit office inspectors of schools used primary school halls for INSET and induction of new teachers and new principals. Some teachers had to travel long distances (400km) from the Northern Province to Pretoria (Mamelodi Teacher In-Service Center and later to Soshanguve Transvaal Training College and its In-Service component).

In this chapter, INSET at RMTC and the Mathematics, Science, Technology College (MASTEC) has been reviewed because of their distinguishing characteristics as outlined in Table 1. The two institutions were established as teacher development centers in different time periods, 1979 and 1996, respectively. The purpose of choosing the two INSET providing centers is to demonstrate that INSET or professional development for teachers is not a new phenomenon. The process is as old as the teaching profession. There has been name changes to the process from in-service teacher training to in-service teacher education. Other related terms used include staff development, professional development of teachers, professional development of educators and continued professional development of educators. Further, the first college was selected because of historical reasons: that is, it started offering teacher in-service development courses in 1979 and PRESET in 1984. The second, MASTEC, opened its doors for PRESET and INSET in 1996, specializing in Mathematics, Science, and Technology. Both centers are found in the Northern Province and are still operational at different venues: RMTC is still conducting courses for teachers, whereas MASTEC was transferred to the Mokopane College and subsequently to the University of the North in Sovenga. This was done in order to offer courses accredited by a University because all teacher training institutions belong to higher education.

Table 1 outlines a comparative analysis of the two case studies. The purpose of including the two case studies is to demonstrate what was done in the past so that lessons of experience can be drawn to assist in the design and planning of better centers and to document best practice experiences. A distinguishing characteristic of the two centers is that they are situated in the rural province of the North, in South Africa. Both of them where established by education authorities in the Province during two different time periods, one during "apartheid" and the second during the democratic era, that is, post-1994.

Table 1: *Justification for the Selection of the Two Cases*

	RMTC (1979 – to date)	MASTEC (1995 – to date)
1	Established in 1979 by the Department of Education of the Venda Government	Established in 1996 by the Northern Province Department of Education after the 1994 democratic election of South Africa.
2	It was a regional departmental institution (Region 3)	It was meant to be a provincial departmental institution.
3	Currently located 200 km away from Ministry of Provincial Education	Located close (10 km) to the Ministry of Provincial Education – moved to Mokopane, which is 55 km from the Ministry and subsequently transferred to the University of the North (30 km) from the Ministry.
4	Situated in a rural setting (Tshakhuma)	Situated in an urban setting (Pietersburg)
5	Radius served is about 120 km	Radius is about 240 km
6	Funding: Departmental budget	Departmental funds are topped up by donor funds – Open Society Foundation of South Africa; Overseas Development agency (Department for International Development), and Northern Province Education Development Trust)
7	Teacher population served 7,000	Serves over 60,000 teachers (Decentralization is recommended)
8	Facilities: Need upgrading	Relatively modern and appropriate
9	Established as a teacher development center dedicated to INSET. PRESET courses added are Mathematics; Home Economics; Technical drawing; Computer Studies; Engineering directions (civil, mechanical, and electrical); Pre-school education or Early Childhood Education.	Established through the assistance of donor funds as a teacher development center specializing in the training of Mathematics; Science, and Technology pre-service teacher training over a four-year period. A component dealing with INSET is also attached to the college.

The two case studies serve to demonstrate how teacher development programs evolved over the past two to three decades, from apartheid teacher education to democratic teacher education.

MRTC: A CASE STUDY

MRTC was established in 1979 to upgrade both the methods of teaching and subject content of various primary and secondary school teachers. The aim of establishing the Center was to improve the quality of teaching and learning through the provision of INSET courses (Mutshekwane, 1992. p.40).

The departmental policy stated the aims of the INSET as follows: "(1) To upgrade both method and content of all school subjects in primary and secondary schools and to raise the standard of teaching; (2) To contribute to curriculum development; (3) To provide educational management training as identified by the Department of Education and culture " (Mutshekwane, 1992. p.47). Although the above aims and objectives were ambitious, they served to provide direction to staff so that they can contribute unselfishly towards teacher development or continued professional development of teachers.

Many in-service training courses for teachers have been criticized because they focused on narrow aspects of teachers' activities, namely, simple presentation of subject matter, without adequately addressing teaching techniques, or vice versa. A useful framework for teacher knowledge that includes three major domains was suggested for consideration. The three domains are content knowledge (mastery of specific content being taught); pedagogical knowledge (understanding the theories and principles of teaching and learning, understanding the learner, and knowledge of theories and principles of classroom behavior and management); and pedagogical content knowledge (ability to blend technique and content, including understanding how the given topics are related and how they are most effectively organized and presented in the classroom) (Schulman, 1987).

INSET courses planned and implemented at MRTC satisfied the aforementioned criteria. INSET courses were planned for the pre-primary, primary, and secondary school curriculum subjects to upgrade teachers' qualifications, competence, and confidence. Competence is the extent of knowledge, skill, ability, and prior experience to perform a particular task and confidence being the degree of self-assurance, willingness, motivation, interest, or enthusiasm to become engaged in the task (Barak & Waks, 1997)

INSET Sessions

INSET courses consisted of morning sessions with an average duration of four to six hours. The sessions consisted of lectures (information exchange) interjected by questions and discussions. The majority of secondary school teachers preferred to be given course notes, prepared weekly and monthly tests, previous examination question papers and memoranda, syllabi, work programs, subject policies, and teaching media. The reason for this was that most of the teachers attending INSET courses were under-qualified in the subjects they taught and this also reflects on the inadequacy of pre-service courses to equip teachers for life long learning. Some of the teachers came from isolated and neglected rural schools, which did not have any facilities that could facilitate meaningful teaching and learning.

An INSET day was subdivided into the following sessions: a lecture by an expert in the subject matter for a grade, e.g., Grade 11 or 12 (standard 9 or standard 10); a didactically oriented session covering teaching methods or didactic issues; and sample test questions and answers. Teaching media were also prepared so that teachers would take them with for use in their schools.

Funding and Staffing

Regarding funding, the Venda homeland government funded the INSET. Teachers were not charged for the services rendered.

Then, experienced personnel drawn from schools staffed the INSET. The staff was responsible for planning, preparing, and conducting INSET courses at pre-primary, primary, and secondary school levels. In certain courses the tutors would be assisted by experienced subject teachers, lecturers from the University of the North near Pietersburg or the University of Venda, subject didactic lecturers from neighbouring colleges of education (Tshisimani & Venda colleges), and book publishers. Partnerships were developed between the INSET participants and these institutions. The benefit of this link was the expertise that could be drawn from universities to bridge the gaps between theory and practice. Participating academics exchanged their views and shared their experiences with practising teachers.

Popular and Effective INSET Courses

INSET courses, which involved a variety of experts, especially those who were involved in teaching subjects like geography, mathematics, and biology, were very popular than those, which were only presented by the INSET course tutors. Other popular courses were those conducted by National external examiners in subjects such as biology, mathematics, physical science, geography, history, English, agricultural science, and luvenda. Book publishers and book suppliers sponsored some courses in order to promote their textbooks. The advantage of this approach was that publishers had contact with reputable academics and subject specialists who made valuable inputs during courses.

Timing of Courses

Observations made at the time indicate that courses conducted early in the year proved to be less popular than courses conducted during the second half of the year, particularly towards the final external public examinations. This reflects the emphasis placed on public examinations. Subject courses also focused on areas in which teachers felt were difficult to teach, that is, problem areas (Mutshekwane, 1984). Limited revision courses involving matriculants (grade 12) were also conducted with learners to improve the quality of final examination results. These were held at education circuit centers, at secondary schools, and at the RMTC. Although these courses were examination-focused, they assisted candidates and teachers who aimed at getting better subject symbols in the final examinations.

INSET Course Evaluation

All course participants were required to complete standard evaluation questionnaires to assess the impact of course content, methods of presentation, and presenters. In-service courses involved continuous interaction between the instructor and participants ranging from a few hours to several days. Participants differed from regular students in that they were adults who brought particular vocational experience and skills to the in-service training site, which was shared with other teachers (Townsend & Moore, 1994).

It might be expected that such groups would be more exacting in their evaluation of professional in-service courses for two reasons: firstly, their skills and experience in the relevant subject area makes them more able to comment critically on the content and significance of the course; and secondly, they are keenly aware of the importance of making good use of their time away from work.

Further Education RMTC for Teachers at RMTC

Teachers who attended INSET courses at RMTC were encouraged to enroll for the Higher Diploma in Education (HDE) program offered using a combination of contact and distance methods. A co-operation agreement was signed with the University of Venda in Thohoyandou (Mutshekwane, 1992). The aim of the upgrading course was to improve the quality of education, school efficiency, and teacher effectiveness. The course was available to teachers working at pre-primary, primary, or secondary schools. The HDE course enabled teachers to accumulate five to six university accredited courses. Teachers who had passed teaching courses from the University of South Africa, a distance learning and teaching internationally renown institution, had them transferred and were accredited for academic degree purposes. This scheme/project encouraged teachers to be involved in life long learning and continued professional enrichment leading them to complete academic degrees, which are status symbols.

Other higher education institutions contributing meaningfully towards the upgrading of teachers in the Northern Province are the University of South Africa, which has a campus in the Northern Province (Pietersburg); Vista University (Distance Education Campus); South African College of Education (a distance education institution); Success correspondence college in association with the University of Pretoria; Randse Afrikaans University offering teacher upgrading courses using a mixture of distance and contact teaching on Saturdays; Technikon Pretoria; Technikon RSA; and Potchefstroom University which has also opened satellite campuses in the province where teachers can enroll for upgrading courses.

The new South Africa and the education dispensation have opened the way for new partnerships to promote the portability of courses. Doors are also open for international universities, which are also assisting by offering opportunities for upgrading of teachers' academic and professional qualifications on condition that the institutions register with the National Department of Education.

At RMTC, the Higher Diploma in Education diploma offered by the center in association with the University of Venda was renamed Diploma in Primary Education Upgrading. The aim of the upgrading course is to improve the quality of education, school efficiency, and teacher effectiveness. The course is offered using a combination of distance education approaches mixed with contact teaching during vacations. The HDE course is being used to upgrade primary school teachers.

All in all, the RMTC case study reveals that, firstly, courses presented by experts were often excellent from an academic point of view, but were frequently of little practical use to teachers in their daily routine. By the time teachers went back to their respective schools, they resorted to their usual teaching methods, i.e., textbook reading and chalk-talk methods.

Secondly, although a different lecturer presented each lecture, the teachers' needs were rarely taken into consideration during the planning of courses, especially with regard to the level of content or subject matter.

Thirdly, subject content offered sometimes covered sections already done in schools.

Fourthly, teachers were not differentiated according to experience and qualifications (professional or academic, well qualified, qualified, unqualified, or under-qualified);

Fifthly, as a result of an examination-focused type of education system that prevailed, most of the teachers were only interested in examination-oriented guidance (courses conducted by examiners were very popular and attendance was very good);

Finally, teachers enjoyed sessions handled by their colleagues; participation increased during such sessions.

THE CASE OF MASTEC

Nieuwenhuis and Mamabolo (1995) in a study of rationalizing colleges in the Northern Province recommended that in-service training, teacher upgrading, and retraining of teachers in the hardcore subjects (mathematics, physical science, and biology) be a priority for the short to medium term (five – ten years). They recommended that an existing college be developed into an in-service teacher education center to offer programs on a distance education basis combined with limited content teaching (Nieuwenhuis & Mamabolo, 1995). At the time of making this recommendation, little did they know that what they were recommending has already been implemented in part at RMTC in the same province. MASTEC was then started to implement the recommendations of the study.

In 1996, the Northern Province Government established a unique Mathematics, Science and Technology Education College, the MASTEC, to provide pre-service and in-service training for whole school development in subject areas with few qualified teachers in the Province. The college received financial and institutional support from the Northern Province Department of Education, the Northern Province Education Development Trust, The Open Society Foundation, and The UK Department for International Development. Specialist international advisers and local lecturing staff were seconded to the project and were operating from the college precinct at Seshego (Kwena Moloto College of Education) in the Northern Province. The college was transferred to Mokopane College of education (1999) in Potgietersrus and has since been incorporated into the University of the North in 2001.

The PRESET component enrolled 160 students for a four-year diploma in Mathematics, Science, and Technology. At the beginning of 1997, 88% of them had managed to pass and proceed to their second year.

Thirty schools were selected to participate so that pre-service student teachers can find schools to do their teaching practice and the staff from these schools were targeted for INSET and the supply of various teaching and learning aids depending on the security prevailing in the school.

The college has as yet to demonstrate its ability to upgrade the quality of teaching in the science subjects in order to improve teacher effectiveness in a Province with the lowest grade 12 pass rate in South Africa. Initial indications are that it is an expensive project benefiting few educators. There is a need for some of its advantages to be decentralized to other regions of the Province in order that the majority of teachers and pupils can benefit from the work of the college's contribution.

Policy Framework and Goal Statement

The INSET policy has been spelt out by different political and administration officials of the department in different meetings addressed by senior departmental staff. Emphasis was placed on INSET for transformation where Mathematics, Science, Biology, Technology, English, and Management sciences are emphasized by curricula and receive priority attention.

Regarding the goal statement of the project, the purpose statement was as follows: "MASTEC/PRESET model incorporated into the Northern Province Department of education programs and effectively used to improve Mathematics, science and Technology."

MASTEC in collaboration with the Provincial Education Directorate of Teacher Education came up with the following initiatives: INSET division; establishment of links with other colleges of education; establishment of international links for Aid in human resource capacity development; materials development, equipment and books; and seeking funds to expand the college.

Other Noteworthy INSET Initiatives

The sub-directorate In-Service Training set in motion the following programs:

1. Capacity Extension Program for Science, Mathematics and English teachers (CEPSMET). The program ran in 120 schools for grade 3, 7, and 10 teachers.

2. Mathematics, Science and English Teacher Upgrading Program (MSETUP). The Program targets unqualified and under-qualified teachers at grade 11 and 12 levels in Mathematics, Science and English. Funding was sought from the Open society Foundation of South Africa. A train–a–trainer approach is followed and several service providers assisted.

3. Telkom, Mathematics, Science and Technology Project (TELMAST). This project targets primary and secondary school teachers in two regions (3 and 6).

4. INSET for Curriculum 2005. The department offers in-service training sessions to teachers so that outcomes-based education, part of a new

curriculum for South Africa, can be introduced in schools.

5. Other programs running are the Primary Science Program; Science Education Program; and Schoolnet – Internet project (Mukhavhuli, 1998).

The impact of most of the above INSET programs is yet to be felt in the education system of the province. The conclusion one can draw is that for these programs to be effective and sustainable, they should be implemented province-wide; otherwise the province is not going to move beyond piloting or experimenting. Similarly, the MASTEC type of programs can yield better results if it is spread throughout the province. Education planners and subject specialists should take into consideration the considerable cost of setting up such ventures.

Problems and Issues

Although it is early to assess this project, there are some positive indications of achievements associated with the INSET strategies; positive attitudinal and cognitive changes at school level and commitment revealed by teachers and learners. There are professional achievements in the college curriculum development, professional development, introduction of computerized accounting system, and school cluster strategies.

There is overall a human capacity problem in the Province, a lack of critical mass of appropriately trained personnel, and a perennial budgetary/financial crisis (Harrison, 1998). The appointment of a capable superintendent-general of education in the Northern Province in 1999 has helped stabilize the education environment, and significant improvements are becoming visible after three years. The senior certificate examination results improved from a pass rate of 37,5% in 1999 to 51,4% in November 2000 (Asmal, 2000b). This is attributable to the total quality management being implemented throughout the education system with the support of teacher unions, principals' associations, positive learner attitudes cultivated, and support provided by school governing bodies to schools.

Regarding evaluation, an independent consultant was commissioned by the Department for International Development (1998) to "evaluate teaching and learning within the Mathematics, Science and technology College of South Africa" as part of a larger evaluation of teacher training and development program. While the evaluation was based on the PRESET component, its findings shed some light on INSET planning, implementation, and evaluation. Hereunder follow some important findings.

First, the MASTEC program is an exciting and ambitious initiative with a major role to play in the development of an outcomes-based approach to education in South Africa. The production of a new curriculum for 2005 will depend for its success in schools on there being sufficient well-trained teachers who understand and are able to implement the approaches to teaching and learning. The fact that MASTEC focuses on areas of the curriculum in which standards of achievement must be raised in order to secure the future competitiveness and prosperity of the country adds to the importance and potential of this initiative.

Second, evidence of progress show that the MASTEC project has made a big impact over a relatively short period of time.

Third, staff at the college was found to be committed to the aims of MASTEC. INSET together with practical demonstration, paired teaching, and feedback from lesson observation indicate that improvements are possible.

Fourth, the move to an outcomes-based education system will depend as much on effective in-service training as on pre-service training if the targets set are to be met. An evaluation of INSET funded by the Open Society Foundation of South Africa is being conducted and results are expected soon.

Fifth, providing further INSET to MASTEC staff and teachers from participating schools to develop pedagogical knowledge and skills (general and subject-specific) is necessary to enable staff to consolidate their knowledge and understanding of a range of teaching approaches.

Sixth, there is a need to develop greater integration between the work of INSET tutors and PRESET tutors.

Seventh, when teaching staff is absent from College, e.g., attending INSET, procedures should be in place to ensure that their classes are taught so that students' education is not unduly disrupted.

And eighth, the Department of Education in the Northern Province of South

Africa should monitor and support the MASTEC program in order to gain from this development of an outcomes-based teacher training curriculum; an integrated approach to PRESET and INSET; a definition of the pedagogical knowledge and skills expected of mathematics, science, and technology teachers on entering the profession (Harrison, 1998).

DISCUSSION

In light of the findings reported in the preceding sections, some criteria ensuring effective and successful INSET courses that can be deduced from case studies are the following. First, a needs assessment should be made so that teachers can articulate sections of subject curriculum problematic to them. Interventions could then be planned carefully based on researched needs and areas identified as being difficult to teach.

Second, experienced teachers who were asked to prepare and present lectures on topics perceived by teachers to be difficult to teach helped generate participation from teachers. The involvement of other subject and methodology experts is necessary to sustain the interest of teachers.

Third, copies of subject syllabi, work scheme, work programs, subject policies, previous examination papers, and memoranda issued to teachers for use in their schools and classrooms were well received. It should be noted that some teachers are from remote rural areas where there are no facilities. Whatever printed material teachers may get from a teacher's center may be handy when he or she is alone in a deep rural school without a telephone nor electricity.

Fourth, subject committees were elected to assist with the identification of problem areas (needs assessment), to review and recommend textbooks or learning support materials for use by pupils, and to set trial examination questions and develop memoranda.

Fifth, teachers were also encouraged to integrate local content in preparation and presentation of lessons.

Sixth, teachers preferred to be supplied with teaching media because most of them taught in rural schools with no facilities. Monobe's (1995) recommendation that there is a need for the INSET of teachers in media so that they can integrate their teaching with carefully selected teaching media

(Monobe, 1995).

Seventh, selected information adapted to teachers' daily tasks is essential and necessary. The learning material or information should be relevant to teachers' needs and the needs of pupils, i.e., materials (subject content and media) that could be used in the classroom;

And eighth, examination oriented courses stimulated interest. Tours or excursions enabled teachers to experience and learn how to plan and organize them for pupils were found to be enriching to teachers. Teachers sometimes need a break from demotivating sites and appreciate out of school venues for courses.

The contribution of 20 colleges of the Northern Province towards PRESET and INSET is acknowledged. Fifteen of the colleges have been rationalized because of over-producing teachers who cannot be absorbed by the market due to budgetary constraints and products irrelevantly qualified in respect of the needs of the education system. The following colleges of education are to be rationalized or redirected to offer other courses: Dr C.N Phatudi; Sekhukhune; Shingwedzi; Tivumbeni; Venda college; Tshisimani; Bochum; Sekgosese; Modjadji; Lemana; Thaba-Moopo; Napuno; Mmamokgalake Chuene, and Setotolwane. Some of the rationalized colleges of education are community colleges while others are specialized high schools. All these colleges have in one way or another assisted teachers in surrounding schools by offering venues for INSET activities and have also provided educators who guided teachers in various teaching subjects.

The remaining colleges, viz. Makhado, Mapulaneng, Giyani, and Mokopane (MASTEC), are being encouraged to link up with the two universities in the province, the University of the North and University of Venda, for accreditation purposes.

The Provincial Department of Education has accepted a proposal that MASTEC be incorporated into the Mokopane College of education, which is to be affiliated to the University of the North. This proposal makes academic, professional, and financial sense in terms of promoting the PRESET-INSET continuum and to redirect programs to be based on the needs of the community and the province at large. Similarly, the Mapulaneng College is also to be incorporated into the University of the North (Northern Province Department of Education, 2000).

Colleges of Education of Makhado and Giyani are to be incorporated into the University of Venda for Science and Technology while Mapulaneng, Mokopane and MASTEC are declared as subdivisions of the University of the North (Department of Education, 2000d). This move will allow for the streamlining of teacher education and professional development programs.

The above proposals will redirect teacher education to benefit participants and the department of education while sacrificing some of the long serving administrative, academic, and professional staff who may be absorbed by subject advisory services, schools, public sector, and private sector.

The two case studies provide the historical context of INSET over the past three decades. Developments in PRESET-INSET intensified over the past five years when the policy framework for a democratic South Africa started falling into place.

Some of the shortcomings emanating from the two case studies are these: a lack of a coherent policy on INSET is still a problem (this issue has not been sufficiently resolved at both national and provincial level); a lack of capacity-building of INSET providers so that the real needs of teachers in schools can be addressed; too much emphasis is being placed the institution rather than what happens in it; a lack of comprehensive research and evaluation studies of INSET programs; a lack of research into teaching and learning to enrich INSET planning and provision; INSET offered by some providers not being recognized for further qualification purposes except in cases of university courses where there are associations or memoranda of understanding; and removing teachers from their classrooms and training them at sites away from their schools creates problems for learners who are left unattended.

The lack of follow-up of INSET and other capacity-building activities can be identified as a major shortcoming. INSET courses require follow-up; otherwise, the effect could be disastrous because the motivation and stimulus the participants gained could soon have been negated by the confusion and frustration they would have suffered in trying to apply all that they have learned within the parameters of syllabus guidelines, examinations, learning and teaching support materials, official expectations, time, and class size. Extreme care must be taken because what tutors say will not necessarily be what participants hear or remember later. INSET courses sometimes have effects quite unanticipated by instructors.

Barak and Waks (1997) are against the presence of a stranger in a classroom. They argue that the presence of an external body in the school, or in the classroom, is liable to rouse distrust or antagonism on the part of the teacher who may perceive the presence as a threat to the teacher's autonomy. This is true of the majority of teachers in the Northern Province. Effective and successful INSET courses are those designed co-operatively with teachers to address specific school related problems, teacher concerns and frustrations. Top-down courses should be used sparingly.

While it is reasonable to promote professional development of teachers, it is also logical to give attention to capacity development of educational managers and support staff. One factor influencing teacher education reform is the capacity of managers and educators at all levels of the system. In 1994, new leaders capable of leading dramatic processes of organizational change were sought but were hard to come by. There is the lack of appropriate skills, knowledge, and overall poor management capacity on the one hand and, on the other, imperfect delivery systems that are critical in re-engineering the education system so that it can meet critical challenges facing South Africa in the 21st Century. This is also true for managers who are required to drive INSET processes. There is a need for managers having INSET as a line function to be exposed to change management, people-centered service delivery, business planning, systems engineering, total quality management, balanced scorecard approaches, information management, planning, budgeting, financial management, project management, monitoring, and evaluation.

Educator development is also addressed in the Northern Province through the implementation of the Development Appraisal System, which has an instrument to identify personal and professional needs of serving teachers. Such information is used to plan and provide relevant INSET programs in order to enhance learner achievements.

RECOMMENDATIONS

The following recommendations are made from the review provided in this chapter as well as conclusions drawn after discussions with teachers and education officials from the Northern Province:

1. *One Stop Service Centers for Teachers*: Given the wide area covered by Northern Province and the number of schools and teachers served by the provincial education department (over 4,000 schools with approximately 60,000 teachers in 1999), a network of teacher in-service centers should be established in central schools or rationalized colleges of education which has adequate facilities or colleges in order to assist teachers by facilitating the exchange of valuable knowledge and experiences. A partnership needs to develop between INSET planners, subject experts, and higher education institutions in the Northern province so that institutions can share human and physical resources. The One Stop Service Centers for Teachers must be well equipped with the latest technological gadgets (Computers with Internet access and E-mail), laboratory equipment, library facilities (books, journals, CD-ROM, CD-players, video players, video tapes, video camera, and air photographs; photo copiers and other printing facilities; stereoscopes; weather station; topographical maps; survey equipment; and others which may be required by teachers and learners). Such a service center can be a meeting place for teachers who would like to develop themselves in order to assist their learners obtain better marks. It is proposed that INTERNET Cafes, Science center functions, computer laboratory, and user-friendly libraries be part of the one-stop service centers for teachers.

   Sites of rationalized colleges of education such as Hoxani college, Venda College, Dr C.N. Phatudi college, Tivumbeni could be turned into One stop service centers for teachers with a Science center, Computer Laboratory, INTERNET Café, a Continuous Professional Development Center for educators specializing in teaching Mathematics, science, Technology, and other subjects (Muswana, 2000). Learners, teachers, and communities surrounding these centers can benefit from their existence.

2. Institutions of higher learning involved with teacher education must strengthen horizontal and vertical links between themselves, schools, and NGOs in order to offer quality teacher support programs. Institutions of higher learning are encouraged to establish Institutes of Education that can take charge of the new function of continued professional development of teachers or teacher development. The University of Venda for Science and Technology and the University of the North are least prepared to take up the extra burden of incorporating professional development of teachers into their schools or faculties of education. There is a need for capacity

development of staff in order to strengthen them to accept new challenges presented by the new leadership roles they are expected to execute in transforming teacher education and continuous professional development of educators specifically.

3. Proper needs assessment to address the real needs of stakeholders should be conducted. Curriculum 2005 and globalization brought new subject area terminology and by itself is a sufficient justification for the massification of INSET in the Northern Province and in other Provinces of South Africa.

4. INSET courses conducted through distance education need to be explored, researched, planned, and tested in order to minimize disruptions in schools. INSET programs need to combine distance tuition with contact sessions. With the convergence of technologies, tele-tuition or tele-education can be harnessed to contribute meaningfully to continued professional development of educators. Staff responsible for INSET will have to demonstrate their ability to keep up with developments in technology. Technology is here to stay; the Northern Province education Department must not allow developments in other sector overtake it. The Education Department assisted by schools of education of universities has a mammoth task of championing technological developments in the Northern Province.

5. Teachers, lecturers, and INSET providers should ensure that the content of subjects taught remain relevant in practice over a medium to long time period. Continued professional development of educators is there to support this vision.

6. Research, learning, and study strategies should be taught to students and teachers to promote the culture of research, learning, and teaching.

7. Teacher Unions are encouraged to contribute towards the continued professional development of their members in order to protect them against burn-out in the information age.

School-based and client-based programs for teacher development can work in the Northern Province and in South Africa if designed to be appropriate for the environment and circumstances of the country, taking into account the resources available (financial, time, and human), the existing infrastructure, the culture of learning and teaching in schools, and if they have one objective – the development of teachers themselves as learners. Uncritical transfer of models from other countries to South Africa and uninformed assumptions leading to the adoption of school-based training models are unlikely to be successful.

CONCLUSION

This chapter has presented some perspectives on how a client-based INSET program can be designed and implemented. The shortcomings identified in the case studies can be overcome by offering on-site school-based continued professional development of teachers provided that adequate resources and trained personnel are available to work alongside teachers. The successful implementation of the program also depends on proper planning of interventions; proper needs assessment, proper implementation of INSET plans; partnerships that can be established between INSET centers and teachers as clients; and amalgamation of INSET centers with tertiary education institutions from which subject specialists come. The design of academic plans for continued professional development supported by mentoring programs for staff who will embark on professional development activities will ensure the success of INSET as an important equal partner of teacher education.

There is a need to conduct research in the field of INSET to develop lessons of best practice and have the lessons emerged with a theoretical framework that guide the implementation of planned interventions. For effective INSET to be realized, solutions to pitfalls identified must be provided for, namely, follow-up after an INSET program. Client-based INSET can make a significant contribution to changing and improving the culture of teaching and learning.

REFERENCES

Asmal, K. (2000a). *Education budget vote 2000/2001*. Parliament, Cape Town: National Council of Provinces.

Asmal, K. (2000b). *Statement on the 2000 Senior Certificate Examinations*. Paper presented to the Media on the release of Senior certificate examination results, Goodhope Auditorium, Parliament, Cape Town.

Bagwandeen, D. R., & Louw, W. J. (1993). *Theory and practice of in-service training for teachers in South Africa*. Pretoria: J.L van Schaik Academic.

Barak, M., & Waks, S. (1997). An Israeli study of longitudinal in-service training of mathematics; science and technology teachers. *Journal of Education and Teaching*, 23(2), 179-190.

Bot, M. (1986). *An overview of Teacher In-service Education and Training (INSET)*

Programs in South Africa. South Africa: SA Indicator Project, University of Natal, Durban, for the Urban Foundation.

Burger, D. (Ed.). (2000). *South Africa Yearbook 2000/01.* Pretoria: Government Communication and Information System.

Campbell, E. (1996, January 12). Matric results show teachers need to do their homework. *Business Day*, 6.

Cane, B. (1971). In-service education for teachers. In T. W. Tibble, *The future of teacher education.* London: Routledge and Kegan Paul.

Chilana, M. R. (1972). *In-service education of elementary school teachers.* New Delhi: Indian Association of Teacher Educator.

Cross, M., & Sehoole, T. (1996). Rethinking the future of teacher education in South Africa: The role of partnerships. In J. V. der Vyver (Ed.), *Conference on Teacher Education Towards 2000* (pp. 1-18). Johannesburg: Southern African Society for Education.

Department of Education. (1995). White Paper on Education and Training. *Government Gazette, 357(*16312). Pretoria: Government Printer.

Department of Education. (1996a). *Green paper on higher education transformation.* Pretoria: Department of Education.

Department of Education. (1997, March). *An agenda of possibilities. National policy on teacher supply, utilisation and development. A stakeholder's response.* Pretoria: Department of Education.

Department of Education. (1998a). *National norms and standards for educators.* Pretoria: Department of Education.

Department of Education. (1998b). *Employment of Educators Act, Act 1245 of 1998.* Pretoria: Government Printers.

Department of Education. (1998c). *Duties and responsibilities of educators.* Pretoria: Department of Education.

Department of Education. (1999). *Status report for the Minister of Education.* Pretoria: Department of Education.

Department of Education. (2000a). Norms and standards for educators. *Government Gazette 415*(20844). Pretoria: Government Printer.

Department of Education. (2000b, January). Quality education for all: Statement of public service commitment. TIRISANO: Working together to build a South African education and training system for the 21st Century. Pretoria: Department of Education.

Department of Education. (2000c, November 27-30). *Education in a global era. challenges to equity, opportunities for diversity. Globalisation, values, and HIV/AIDS.* Paper presented at the Fourteenth Conference of Commonwealth Education Ministers, Halifax, Nova Scotia, Canada.

Department of Education. (2000d, December 15). Declaration of colleges of education as subdivisions of universities and technikons. *Government Gazette no. 21913.* Pretoria: Government Printer.

Department of Education and Science [DES]. (1972). *Teacher education and training (James Report)*. London: HMSO.

Department of Education and Training. (1992). *The education renewal strategy*. Pretoria: Author.

Eraut, M. (1972). *In-service education for innovation*. London: Council for Educational Technology.

Eraut, M. (1995). Teacher education: Inservice. In T. Husen & T. N. Postlethwaite (Eds.), *The international encyclopedia of education* (2nd ed., Vol. 10) (5966-5973). Oxford: Pergamon Press.

Fullan, M. C. (1991). *The new meaning of educational change*. New York: Teachers' College Press.

Government of South Africa. (1995). *The South African Qualification Act No. of 1995*. Pretoria: Author.

Government of South Africa. (1996). *Constitution of the Republic of South Africa. Act No. 108 of 1996*. Pretoria: Government Printers.

Greenland, J. (Ed.). (1983). *The in-service training of primary school teachers in English-speaking Africa*. London: Macmillan Education.

Harrison, S. (1998). *Evaluation report on teaching and learning within the Mastec College* (Under assignment from the Department for International Development). Pietersburg: Department of Education.

Hargreaves, D. H. (1994). Devolved school management: The "new deal". *Scottish Education Journal of Education policy, 9*, 129-140.

Hartshorne, K. (1985). The state of education in South Africa: Some indicators. *South African Journal of Science, 18*, 158-51.

Hartshorne, K. (1992). *Crisis and challenge: Black education 1910 – 1990*. Cape Town: Oxford University Press.

Hofmeyr, J. M. (1988). *Policy issues in INSET. International and South African perspectives*. Johannesburg: Mobil Foundation of South Africa.

Hofmeyr, J. (1992). *Policy change in South African education: The roles of the public and private sectors in in-service teacher education*. Unpublished PhD thesis, University of the Witwatersrand, Johannesburg.

Hofmeyr, J., & Hall, G. (1995). *The national teacher education audit. A synthesis report*. Pretoria: Department of Education.

Hofmeyr, J., & Jaff, R. (1992). The challenges of INSET in the 1990s. In R. McGregor & A. McGregor (Eds.), *McGregor's education alternatives (chap. 7)*. Kenwyn: Juta & Company.

Huang, J. H. (1993). *The learning strategies of first year university students in South Africa and the Republic of China - A comparative study*. Unpublished doctoral dissertation, Rand Afrikaans University, Johannesburg, South Africa.

Integrated Sustainable Rural Development Strategy [ISRDS]. (2000, March). *The development of an integrated sustainable rural development strategy for South Africa. Report by the ISRDS Secretariat to the Core Group of Ministers*. Pretoria:

Government of South Africa.

Macbeath, J., & Mortimore, P. (1997, January). *Effective schools – are they improving?* Paper delivered to Tenth International Congress on School Effectiveness and improvement, Memphis.

McFarlane. (1996). *An address during a graduation ceremony for UNISA students.* Pietersburg.

Mkhize, M. G. (1989). *The professional and academic upgrading of black teachers in Natal and KwaZulu.* Unpublished master's thesis, University of Durba-Westville, Durban.

Monobe, R. J. (1995, July). *Media training of teachers in the Northern Province.* Paper presented at the World Meeting of Educational Media, La Coruna, Spain.

Morant, R. W. (1981*). In-service education within the school.* London: George Allen & Unwin.

Mukhavhuli, S. (1998). *Programs of the Department of Education, Northern Province. Presentation during a Communication Carnival.* Bepha la Mukondeni, Mukondeni: Government Communication.

Murphy, J. G. (1985). *The evaluation of an in-service training project for Black primary school teachers in South Africa in the early 1980s.* Unpublished doctoral dissertation, University of Cape Town, Cape Town.

Muswana, E. (2000, February 25). Speech by Mr Edgar Mushwana, Northern Province Member of the Executive Council For Education on the occasion of the 10th anniversary celebration of the Giyani Science Center, Giyani, Northern Province.

Mutshekwane, M. A. (1984). Problem areas in the teaching of geography in secondary schools in Venda. *Venda Education Journal, 1*(2).

Mutshekwane, M. A. (1992). *In-service training of teachers in Venda.* Unpublished master's thesis, Rand Afrikaans University, Johannesburg, South Africa.

Mutshekwane, M. A. (1995). In-service training of teachers in Venda. *South African Journal of Higher Education, 9*(2).

Naama Sabar & Ayelet HaShahar-Francis (1999). School-focussed in-service training: Key to restructuring schools. *Journal of In-service Education, 25(2), 1999.*

National Education Policy Initiative [NEPI]. (1992). *Teacher education.* Cape Town: Oxford University press/NECC.

Nieuwenhuis, F. J., & Mamabolo, M. Z. (1995). *The rationalisation of teacher training in the Northern Province.* Pretoria: Human science Research Council.

Northern Province Department of Education. (2000). *Provincial status report on the incorporation of colleges of education into higher education sector.* Pietersburg: Directorate Teacher Development.

O'Brien, J., & MacBeal, J. (1999). Co-ordinating staff development: The training and development of staff development co-ordinators. *Journal of In-service Education, 25*(1), 1999.

Oldroyd, D., & Hall, V. (1991). *Managing staff development. A handbook for secondary schools.* London: Paul Chapman Publishing LTD.

Schulman, L. S. (1987). Knowledge and teaching: Foundation of the new reform. *Harvard Educational Review, 57,* 1-22.

Scottish Education Department [SED]. (1990). *The Scottish National Guidelines for staff development and appraisal.* Edinburgh: Scottish Education Department.

Taylor, N., & Vinjevold, P. (Eds.). (1999). *Getting learning right. Report of the President's Education Initiative Research Project.* Wits University: Joint Education Trust.

Thompson, A. R. (Ed.). (1982). *In-service education of teachers in the Commonwealth.* London: Commonwealth Secretariat.

Townsend, M. A. R., & Moore, D. W. (1994). Cooperative group versus individual evaluation in professional in-service training. *Australian Journal of Education, 30*(20), 139 –147.

Chapter 16

Secondary Education, School Effectiveness, and Teacher Development: China and Belgium in Comparison

He-Chuan SUN and Rob de JONG
Groningen Institute for Educational Research
University of Groningen, The Netherlands

Within the system of formal education, secondary education plays an important and multifaceted role. On the one hand, it is not only a key link between primary school education and higher education, but also a crucial stage at which young people learn to exercise their critical judgment and decide their own futures according to their own tastes and aptitudes. On the other hand, the fast economic growth requires that a large proportion of the population receive secondary education. Taken worldwide, in terms of enrolment ratios, secondary education is the fastest-expanding sector of formal education (Delors, 1996). Undoubtedly, secondary education has played a pivotal role in the paths of individual learning and in the development of societies.

Making secondary schools more effective remains one of the greatest challenges of the new millennium. However, this is not only a task for schools. Educational systems can create positive and encouraging conditions for the functioning of schools. However, in school effectiveness research, the varied contexts within which schooling occurs have been ignored. In order to learn more about the necessary conditions for effective schools, international comparative studies are needed.

Heynemann and Loxley (1983) carried out a research which compared 16 developing and 13 developed countries. Their findings show that, in developing countries, the block of school factor variables, covering such factors as textbook availability, teachers' own educational achievement, and the length of the instructional program, can explain 26% of the variance in achievement which is rather high as compared to the influence of family background factors (on average 5%). Reynolds (2000) also points out that the developing country studies suggest a need to measure more resource based variables, such as financial resources, equipment, and the like. The factors that are associated with student's achievement in developing countries are interestingly different to those within the Western research paradigm. Maclean (1999) has the same point of view. He argues that adequate school buildings and classrooms; a relevant curriculum; high quality affordable teaching and learning materials, such as textbooks, writing materials, and laboratory equipment; and an accurate system for monitoring education outcomes are important variables which influence the effectiveness of a nation's school system.

Therefore, the message is clear: financial resources are important for educational achievement in developing countries, probably not as a direct influence but as a means to increase relevant school effectiveness factors.

The development of a nation depends upon education. The development of education depends upon teachers. Thus, teachers' knowledge, skills, devotion, and commitment play a decisive role in raising the quality of any education system. Essentially, it is teachers who make educational policies, reforms, and curriculums work. It is impossible to make good and effective schools without serious consideration of teachers. Given these, "[T]he status of teachers, teacher recruitment, pre-service teacher education, the professional career-long development, and the provision of suitable financial and other rewards to attract and retain suitable individuals in the occupation of teaching are receiving great attention from policy-makers and policy implementers in countries throughout the world" (Maclean, 1999, p. 88).

Based on the above statement, this chapter explores secondary education, school effectiveness, and teacher development in two countries: China and Belgium. It focuses on the national contextual level and the school level. It starts from the national level and then goes downwards to the school level. At the national level, we focus on financial resources and in-service teacher training. At the school level, we present a case study by describing the school climate and school culture of a Flemish school, the "Sancta Mariainstituut" (SM), in Leuven, Belgium. Obviously, we cannot discuss the whole field of secondary education in China and Belgium. In addition, not all information related to key factors are available or totally comparable in these two countries. Nevertheless, we hope that this chapter can serve as a small window allowing some glances of secondary education, school effectiveness, and teacher development in both China and Belgium, especially the Flemish part of Belgium. Some preliminary

implications can be drawn from comparison for teacher education and development in China or other developing countries.

MACRO-ANALYSIS AT THE NATIONAL CONTEXT LEVEL

The National Contexts in China and Belgium

Education is always embedded in a specific socio-cultural context, such as the people, the political system (centralized system or decentralized system), the economic conditions, and so on.

With a land area of 9,572,900 km², China is a vast country with the largest population in the world. It is 17.6 times as large as France. In the year 1995 China's population was up to 1,206,600,000, with approximately 27.7% being children under 15, that is 334,228,200 (Edwards, 1996, pp. 563-585) which is over 30 times the total population of Belgium. The population is heterogeneous, embracing 56 ethnic "groups" with different cultures, histories, and lifestyles. Economic and cultural backgrounds and development differ between areas because of varying natural conditions and historical reasons.

China is a highly centralized country. China's educational system is centrally organized. For example, primary and secondary schools are obliged to use the uni-edited textbooks, which must be examined and approved by the National School Textbooks Examination and Approval Committee before publication. According to the Educational Law of the People's Republic of China (China State Education Commission [CSEC], 1995), the following components are controlled by the State and the governments: a national education examination system; a system of education certificates; a system of academic degrees; enrolments and the distribution of students; an educational inspection system and evaluation system; and a system of qualifying, posting, recruiting, and appointing teachers.

Belgium, with a surface area of 30,518 km², is relatively small. Nevertheless, it has a population of 10,064,000 and, as a result is, one of the most densely populated countries in the world, among which children under 15 years old is 18.1% of the population (Edwards, 1996, pp. 563-585). Further, 20% of the school population in full-time education are in nursery school (kindergarten); 32.3% are in primary education; and 35.3% are in secondary education. Higher education accounts for 12.4% of the school population.

Belgium is a federal constitutional monarchy country with three communities: Dutch-speaking Flanders as the northern half, French-speaking Wallonia as the southern half, and a German-speaking minority in the East. Of Belgium ten million inhabitants, about 9% are of foreign nationality. Of the other 9.1 million, about 1% are German speakers; 38% are French-speaking; and 61% Dutch-speaking (Goethals, 1997). The determinant constituent element of a community is its culture and language. Belgium is a country with a decentralized system. In this decentralized system, "[T]here are three levels of decision-making with their respective structures of legislative and executive power: the Central State, the Communities and the Regions" (Ministerie van de Vlaamse Gemeenschap, 1991, p. 12). In 1983, the Compulsory School Attendance Act obliges parents to have their children attend school for 12 years, that is, from 6 to 18 years of age. If parents fail to send their children to schools for compulsory education, the policemen can put those parents in prison. In Belgium, compulsory education has been achieved.

Economically speaking, China is a fast developing country; it is an "emerging power," although it still belongs to the Third World. According to statistics in the *World Development Report 1995* (The World Bank, 1995, pp. 162-180), among 132 countries in the world, China's GNP was approximately US$490 per inhabitant. The compulsory education in China is *not free of charge.*

In comparison, Belgium is a highly industrialized country; its GNP is approximately US$21,650 per inhabitant, which places Belgium in among the top ten richest countries in the world (The World Bank, 1995, pp. 162-180). It is able to provide *free* primary and secondary school education to all children in Belgium.

Table 1 basing on data from the *World Development Report 1995* presents the population, GNP, and adult illiteracy of China, Belgium, and the whole world. (The World Bank, 1995, p. 162)

The Funds put into Education in China and Belgium

As we have stated before, the funds put into education is one of our focuses in this chapter. The quality of education, to a considerable degree, is dependent on finances put into pre-service and in-service teacher training and put into teachers' working conditions. Teachers need the appropriate knowledge and skills, personal characteristics, professional prospects, and motivation if they

Table 1: *The Population, GNP, and the Adult Illiteracy of China and Belgium*

	Population (in millions) 1993	GNP per capital*		Adult illiteracy Total 1990 %
		In dollars 1993	Average annual growth in % (1980-1993)	
China	1,178.4	490**	8.2	27
Belgium	10.0	21,650	1.9	<5***
The World	5,501.5	4,420	1.2	33

Note:
* GNP per capita figures in US dollars are calculated according to the World Bank Atlas method.
** Preliminary estimate, see the technical note to Table I of the Report.
*** According to UNESCO, illiteracy is less than 5 percent.

are to meet the expectations placed upon them. Further, to improve the quality of education, a powerful learning environment must be build up for students, with rich resources and learning materials offering opportunities for social interaction. In this respect, Chinese schools have a long way to go. Take computer-assisted learning as an example: at the end of the 1980s, all secondary schools in Belgium were already provided with computers. When students enter secondary education, schools start to teach them how to operate a computer, to use computers to do their homework, to use the Internet to search for information, to use e-mail, and even to create their own website and communicate with foreign schools. Before they enter university, most Belgian students are able to use e-mail and the Internet and write their papers on computers. At present, a project termed "PC-KD" funded by Flemish Ministry of Education is being carried out in Belgium of which will last for 4 years. It aims to increase *computer literacy*. Every year Flemish schools receive 1,500 Belgian francs ($40) per student from this project; schools can get 6,000 Belgian francs per student to realize the goal of having at least one computer for every 10 students within 4 years. Moreover, 1,560 schools have been given fast Internet-lines, and 200 schools have accepted the offer of Telenet for free access. Furthermore, 30 schools have been selected for the European Network for Innovative Schools (ENIS). The goal of ENIS is to have a network covering 500 schools in Europe by co-operating, giving examples of good practices, testing educational software and technology, and giving advice and information about information and communication technologies (ICT) (http://www.ond.vlaanderen.be/ict, 2000). Chinese secondary schools are lagging far behind this level, which of course requires money and funding. What follows is a comparison of how much money both countries put into education.

China

According to the statistics in the *1991 World Development Report* (The World Bank, 1995, pp. 162-180), China's GNP growth rate was the world highest in the 1980s. However, the proportion of funds spent on education constantly hovered below 2.5% of the GNP. It was lower than the averages for low-income countries (2.6%), middle-income countries (4.4%), and high-income countries (5.7%). Moreover, it ranked one of the lowest in the world, even lower than the proportion spent in India, which also had a large population. "The Chinese government has spent more money on defense than on education during the last ten years. China spends even less on education than other developing countries in its neighbourhood region" (Luyn, 2000, p. 5). To clarify this further, a typical example follows. In the 1989 national-wide budget of China, 50.4 *yuan* (about US$9) would be spent on each secondary student, and 13.49 *yuan* (about US$2.5) on each primary student. At the provincial level, the province that spent the least expenditure per head for secondary schools was only 24.27 *yuan* (about US$4.5), and only 3.24 *yuan* (about US$0.60) for primary schools (Zhou, 1995, p. 278). If the teachers' salaries were excluded, "the average annual expenditure per student in middle school for pedagogical purposes (including equipment) was only 5 *yuan*" (*Zhongguo Jiaoyu Bao*, 1988, p. 4).

Low expenditure on education undoubtedly resulted in a low salary for teachers. In many places, teachers' salaries were the lowest of the 12 main categories of employment, especially the salaries of the *minban* (village-run) school teachers. Here we need to explain a little bit more about this situation. There were two types of teachers in China: the first one was *gongban* (state-hired) teachers, and the other was *minban* (village-run) school teachers. The *minban* teachers' salary was extremely low. The Gansu Provincial Education Commission estimated that a *minban* teacher earned only one half or even 1/3 of what the state-hired teachers did. As for the health care and retirement benefits, *minban* teachers had to manage by themselves; no funds were available (Sun, 1997). It was no wonder that 300,000 primary and middle school teachers were reported to have quitted their jobs in 1988 due to the low wage issue (Thogersen, 1990).

Low expenditure on education undoubtedly results in unequal funds for urban and rural schools. The urban schools, in particular, the key schools, receive considerable state support. On the contrary, almost all rural schools are funded by the local peasant community (Thogersen, 1990). Brown (1981) unfolds this problem:

> It costs 6,900 yuan to educate an average urban child, usually from kindergarten through lower secondary school, and an additional 6,000-7,000 yuan to put him/her through a regular tertiary education programme. By contrast, the average expenditure for the entire education of a rural child, usually including up to five years of primary schooling and three years of lower secondary, is about 1,600 yuan. The difference can be traced to poorer salaries, facilities, and educational materials in the countryside, in addition to the low educational attainments of rural youths. (p. 171)

Since China adopts the policy of national entrance examinations for higher education and the policy of children attending schools in their own neighborhood (according to their registered permanent residences), children in urban schools have much better human and material resources and, consequently, have more opportunities to receive further education. Children in rural areas have fewer opportunities to advance themselves educationally from the start. Opportunities for further education are denied by the poorer educational quality they receive and by the unfair competition from the very beginning.

Belgium
In the same period, the funds put into education in Belgium (the Flemish community) were much higher. According to Ministerie van de Vlaamse Gemeenschap (1991, pp. 362-368), in the year 1989 and 1990, the overall spending by the national authorities and the Flemish community on education was up to 324 billion Belgian francs and 322.6 billion Belgian francs, respectively, which account for 15.3% and 15% of its public expenditure in 1989 and 1990. The average public spending per pupil at the primary level was 67,400 Belgian francs. The average public spending per secondary education student was about 168,200 Belgian francs (approximately 42,000 *yuan*), which was about 340 times higher than that in China. Although living costs in China are much cheaper, at about 10% of that in Belgium, the Flemish average subsidy per student was still 34 times higher than that of China. In other

words, if the Flemish government offers one loaf of bread to every student in secondary education, Chinese government could only offer one loaf of bread for 34 students in secondary education to share. The situation for Chinese primary education is even worse: if the Flemish government offers one loaf of bread to every pupil, the Chinese government can offer only one loaf of bread for 100 pupils to share (Sun, 1997).

In Belgium, the government pays all teachers' salaries, no matter whether they are in official schools or free (including private) schools. The basic monthly salaries for middle school teachers (graduates of teacher training college) range from 66,339 Belgian francs (about US$1,840) to 115,538 Belgian francs (about US$3,300) (45% of which should be subtracted for income taxes). The basic salaries for higher secondary teachers (graduates of university) range from 83,085 Belgian francs to 146,514 Belgian francs (US$2,370-US$4,180) (45% should be subtracted for income taxes) (Ministerie van Onderwijs, 1997). Although the living cost in China is much cheaper, the salaries of the Belgium teachers are, at least, 4 or 5 times higher than that of the *gongban* teachers and at least 8 to 10 times higher than that of the *minban* teachers in China.

The System of Secondary Education in China and Belgium

The system here refers to the numbers of secondary schools, the school types and tracks, schooling, the syllabi within the curriculum, the Psychological, Medical and Social Guidance Centre (PMS) system, the inspector system and the in-service teacher training system.

The Numbers, Schooling, and Types of Secondary Schools
In 1995, China had 82,795 secondary schools, 3,167,000 secondary school teachers, and 47,391,000 students (age 13-17). The student/teacher ratio was 15 to 1. In addition, China had 13,945 secondary specialized schools (such as vocational schools), 501,000 vocational school teachers, and 6,446,000 students. This student/teacher ratio was 12.9 to 1 (Edwards, 1996, p. 585).

In 1995, Belgium had 1,962 secondary schools, 110,599 secondary school teachers, and 790, 377 (age 12-18) students. Its student/teacher ratio was 6.9 to 1. Moreover, it also had 304 vocational and teacher training schools, which had 14,548 teachers and 155,192 students. Its student/teacher ratio was about 10.7 to 1 (Edwards, 1996, p. 563). About 4% of the overall school population attends special education.

In China, three systems co-exist for primary and lower secondary education: the "6 (primary education) +3 (lower secondary)" system, the "5+4" system and the "nine-year" system, with the 6+3 system predominating in most areas. For secondary specialized schools, there are two possibilities. For schools that enroll lower secondary school graduates, the length of schooling is four years. For schools that enroll upper secondary school graduates, the length of schooling is usually three years and for upper secondary vocational schools, two or three years (UNESCO, 2000. p. 34).

At the lower secondary schools, all students learn the same courses. When they finish lower secondary school, they have to choose whether to go to upper secondary school which mainly trains candidates for colleges and universities or to go to *zhiyezhongxue* (vocational schools), *jixiao* (technical schools), *shifan* (normal schools), *nongxiao* (agricultural schools), or *weixiao* (nursery schools) in order to start working earlier.

For those who attend upper secondary schools, divergence starts, mostly, in the final year when students start to move down a *wenke* (liberal arts) or a *like* (science) track, paralleling the two specializations tested by the national entrance examination for higher education. If the students fail the national entrance examinations for higher education, they cannot find a job. They have to attend the various vocational schools again. The school year of lower secondary schools comprises 39 weeks of teaching sessions with an additional week in reserve and 12 weeks for holidays and vacations. The school year of upper secondary schools comprises 40 weeks of teaching sessions with one or two weeks in reserve and 10 to 11 weeks for holidays and vacations (CSEC, 1997).

In Belgium, the unified system of secondary education, introduced in 1989/90, comprises six years of study divided into three grades of two years each. The major difference is the first year of secondary education in Belgium which is divided into A and B. A is for normal students, and B is for at-risk students since Belgium has no selective examinations for entering secondary schools. In the 1st year A, at least 27 of the 32 weekly periods are spent on basic education. In the 2nd year, at least 14 of the 24 periods are spent on basic training. The 1st year B is designed for students with learning arrears or those who are less suited to attend predominantly academic education. For these students, this year is a transitional year between primary and secondary education. Afterwards, they can go on either to the 2nd year of prevocational education or to the 1st year A. From the third year on, students start to choose a certain line of study from general secondary education, technical secondary education, artistic secondary education, or vocational secondary education (Ministerie van de Vlaamse Gemeenschap, 1991).

In sum, the differences between the types and schooling of Chinese and Belgian secondary education are as follows. Firstly, the student/teacher ratio is 8.1 higher in Chinese secondary schools than that in Belgium.

Secondly, there are no unified selective examinations when Belgian students finish their primary and first three years of secondary education. Instead, the 1st year B in Belgian secondary schools serves as the remedial year for at-risk students. Chinese students are selected by the unified entrance examinations organized by the local level authorities (e.g., the county/city educational committee) for entering the secondary education and organized at the district/provincial level when students want to attend one of the various upper secondary schools.

Thirdly, the track system starts much earlier in Belgian schools (from the third year on in lower secondary school) than in China.

And fourthly, although the goal in Chinese compulsory education is nine years, as compulsory education is not free and parents have to pay the tuition fees and the other costs, many low income families are unable to send all their children, especially girls, to schools. Given the fact that children in Belgium are obliged to attend school from 6-18 years old, the education level of the population as a whole is higher than that of China.

Syllabi within the Curriculum
After passing into law the nine-year compulsory education statute, CSEC (1986) published in October 1986 the draft "Teaching Plan for Full-time Primary School and Secondary School Compulsory Education" which partially included 13 subjects (see Appendix One). In the autumn of 1993, a decentralization occurred. Subjects were divided into two categories, state-arranged subjects and locally-arranged subjects, with the latter determined by the authorities of provincial-level governments in light of local realities and needs. For example, rural schools are allowed to delete foreign languages if

they do not have the teachers with the needed competence. In minor subjects, nationally defined content occupies 80 per cent of the time and the remaining 20 per cent is left for local decisions.

We have the syllabi for junior and senior secondary education in China (see Appendix One); unfortunately, the only available Flemish syllabus we have is the "syllabus of the first year 'A'" in secondary schools (see Appendix Two). Having compared the two syllabi, we found the following:

a. The total time scheduled for learning during the first year of secondary schools is comparable between the two countries.
b. The school year in China is longer (39 weeks) than that of Belgium (32 weeks) and therefore has more scheduled teaching time.
c. Chinese schools spend more time on native language, foreign language learning, biology, geography, and history while the Flemish schools spend more time on physical education.
d. The four other courses in the Flemish syllabus (third language, technology, Latin, complementary activities) are not found in the Chinese syllabus. This indicates that within the comparable time (30 periods per week), Chinese schools focus on less targets (subjects). This also means that Flemish students have a more diverse education (e.g., technology and two more foreign languages) upon entering secondary school.

A Student Caring System

The PMS system in Belgium deserves special mentioning, since no such system exists in the Chinese educational system. However, Chinese schools need such a system. Every year in some Chinese schools, a few students commit suicide.

> Chinese newspapers report about students abusing parents, teachers or themselves because they cannot cope with the workload and the competition at schools. A student commits suicide because he cannot compete with his classmates. A student kills his mother because she kept complaining about his low marks and punished him. A mother killed her child because of too low marks. Especially in the cities parents suffer from a huge compensation complex and put all their hopes and expectations on their child who is often the only one they have. Parents believe that only a university study can offer their child a future. These extreme examples even shocked China's president Jiang Zemin. He raised the question whether the Chinese education system puts sufficient attention to the whole development of the child. (Luyn, 2000, p. 5)

If Chinese schools had a PMS-type system, it could provide the opportunities for those students to talk, to relieve their stress and pressure, at least, it might partially solve their problems. According to many Belgian students we contacted, they could tell more to PMS workers than to their parents, teachers, and friends. In addition, PMS also provides the students with information or advice concerning opportunities in studies, training, and employment. Then, what is PMS?

PMS stands for the Psychological, Medical and Social Guidance Centre. Each PMS center works for one network only, usually serving at least 2,500 pupils. They operate independently from schools. PMS centers play a complementary role in counseling, study, and career guidance of the youngsters attending schools. The centers operate in a multi-disciplinary way. They consist of psychologists, educationists, social workers, physicians, and paramedics. The principles of PMS centers are to develop the potential human capabilities; to participate in the concrete realization of these capabilities; to remove obstacles to this realization; and to remedy such handicaps (Ministerie van Onderwijs, 1988, p. 48).

PMS centers collect data from each pupil as he or she enters the kindergarten up to he/she starts higher education. They analyze and assess these data. The data consist of a series of psycho-medico-social elements which are regularly updated, discussed with the pupil, and compared with the observations of the teachers, the pupil's family, and other circles. PMS is a helpful students caring system.

The Inspectorate System
Chinese education uses the national entrance examinations to supervise and test the quality of schools while Belgium education has neither national entrance examinations nor national standardized examinations. Instead, it applies a system of inspectors. First and foremost, the inspectors are given the tasks of supervising educational quality and recognizing the educational institutions and guidance centers. They also examine whether the determined attainment targets or developmental objectives are being effectively realized. The responsibility of the inspectors extends to all education levels from nursery school to higher education. The inspectors are not subject-oriented nor meant to check on individual teachers. They aim at examining the whole school (Ministerie van de Vlaamse Gemeenschap.1996, p.7-9). Nowadays, they come into schools as a group. It will usually take them about two or three

weeks per school. This new method of inspection will also evaluate the teacher training colleges. Schools have to prepare an enormous mass of paperwork before the inspectors come along. After the visit, the inspectors write a report and visit the school again a week later and talk to the director and give remarks. When the judgment of the inspectors is (partly) negative, the inspectors suggest improvements and visit the school again within a year to see if the school has taken any action to carry out any reforms. In a worst case scenario, the inspectors can inform the Education Minister about the school refusing to take any action to improve its quality. Then, the Minister has the power to mete out financial penalties. In the near future, inspectors will review schools according to the CIPO Model (Bhesena & Edelenbos, forthcoming). In CIPO model, "C" stands for Context, "I" stands for Input, "P" stands for Process and "O" stands for Output. Essentially, CIPO Model is meant to examine the added-value in each school.

In-Service Training for the Secondary School Teachers

In China, generally speaking, qualified primary school teachers are defined by the Chinese officials as teachers with normal secondary education or above; qualified junior secondary school teachers are graduates from specialized higher institutes; and qualified senior secondary school teachers are graduates from higher academic universities (Hayhoe, 1984). Due to the Cultural Revolution and the rapid increase of the population of secondary school students (increased by 60 million between 1965 and 1977), "[U]sing a teacher-student ratio of 1 to 30, the number of teachers should have increased by 2 million. However, higher teacher-training institutes were only able to turn out 210,000 graduates in the same period" (Lo, 1984, p. 175). According to the Chinese official magazine *Renmin Jiaoyu* (1981, p. 41), only 47% of primary school teachers, 10% of the junior secondary school teachers, and 50% of the senior secondary school teachers were qualified in 1980. The new education policy then emphasized qualifying by means of in-service training. To ensure the quality and standards of education and teaching, the state set relevant academic qualification requirements and criteria for professional certificate assessment for primary and secondary school teachers. Those teachers who failed to get higher educational diplomas from qualifying in-service training could not go on teaching in secondary schools. The number of such unqualified teachers was large.

The teachers' colleges and universities in China were unable to meet the training needs. Distance education through radios and satellite TV networks then played a central role in teacher education and development in China. It enabled millions of teachers to get in-service training without leaving their schools. After 18 years (1979-1997), the Chinese Radio Television University (CRTVU) graduates numbered 1.93 million, which accounts for 14% of the total number of graduates from all forms of regular and adult colleges across China during the same period (Sun, 1998). All over China, 20 million teachers and headmasters have received continuing education and in-service training through CRTVU (Yi & Xiang, 1997). In September 1997, the then Director (now Minister) of the Chinese Education Committee highly praised the CRTVU by saying "China is a poor country running the largest educational system in the world. Within its educational system, the most advantageous, the most cost-effective, the largest areas-covered educational form is the CRTVU. It has contributed greatly to Chinese education" (Yun, 1997, p. 1). At present, television-based teacher education offers all courses covering the 12 specialties of secondary and higher teacher education. It also delivers exemplary classes by excellent primary and secondary school teachers and training courses for school managerial personnel. When teachers successfully complete training, the state recognizes their qualifications and confers the appropriate status. Large numbers of secondary school teachers benefited from distance education. Such in-service training leads not only to their academic promotion but also to their financial promotion. Nowadays, the CSEC (1997) notes:

> There are 2273 in-service training institutions in China, among which 35 are provincial educational colleges (mainly for senior secondary school teacher training). 207 prefectual or municipal educational colleges (mainly for junior secondary school teacher training) and 2031 county in-service training schools (mainly for primary school teacher training). Meanwhile general teacher training schools, distance education through radio and satellite TV networks, and self-study examinations also play an active part in in-service teacher training. For a long period, teacher training has adhered to the following principles: spare time study, self-study, short-term training, tutorial among students of different levels, teaching according to specific needs and a combination of learning and practice and pursuit of efficiency. (p. 71)

CSEC (1997) acknowledges that, through training, the professional capabilities of primary and secondary teachers and principals have been improved markedly and fundamental changes have taken place in the overall academic qualifications of the teaching staff.

In Belgium, teachers who teach kindergarten, primary school, and lower secondary school must graduate from teacher college (three years). Teachers who teach upper secondary schools must graduate from universities (four years plus extra teacher training for half a year or one year). Given this requirement and the smaller population, the in-service teacher training task is much lighter than that in China. In-service training in Belgium is considered as a long-term process and a part of continuing education designed to professionalize teachers, to improve the quality and effectiveness of education systems, to promote the mastery of technical and scientific advances, and to anticipate changes.

In Belgium, teachers have the right to pursue in-service training, but there is no legal obligation for them to do so. Participating in in–service training does not lead to financial or career advantages. Traveling expenses and other expenses resulting from participation in in-service training programs may be reimbursed. We summarize the main features of in-service training in Belgium in Table 2, based on the information of "The Education Information Network in the European Union" [EURYDICE] (1995, pp. 13-19).

Table 2: *Main Features of In-service Training in Belgium*

Structure & responsible bodies	Type of organization	Main training establishment	Voluntary training	% of the education budget spent on in-service training (per year)

* government
* training
  network
	Centralized then de-centralized by network	* self-training
		  and in-service
		  training centers
		* Higher
		  institutes of
		  teacher training
		* Universities
			right to 10 days	around 0.12%
				
				funds are distributed through educational networks

*   Source: EURYDICE (1995)

Regarding trainers and methods in Belgium, mostly, the trainers are full-time staff, university teaching staff, and experts. The methods include lectures, study trips abroad, seminars, practical placements, and summer university courses. We attended some English in-service training activities in Belgium: for instance, once a week (mostly in the evenings) there was an activity organized by the English teacher training center. Most of the training activities were highly interactive. The participants were prepared discussion partners; they shared a common background of knowledge or experiences. There was peer-teaching, learning by doing, demonstrations on how to teach listening, reading, speaking, and writing by outstanding teachers. Trainees benefited a lot from such activities.

It seems as if the most welcome and effective structure was the "sandwich" model in which theory and practice were combined. The sandwich model offers the materials that teachers can take home and apply immediately in their teaching. The participants received theoretical training followed by specific assignments for practice in class during the first sessions. Later sessions were devoted to group discussions on the problems or advantages generated from applying the theories into practice. Besides seminars, English teachers in Belgium had opportunities to participate in the activities organised by the VVLE (Flemish Association for English Teachers), like tours of the English Teaching Theatre, Word and Action (Instant Theatre), other English-speaking performers, and a well-prepared annual two-week excursion for Flemish English teachers to the United Kingdom (Goethals, 1997).

There is also another kind of exchange program, namely, the tradition of a European Week. During this week, each of the 12 member states sends one teacher and two students to a Belgian institution (change yearly). "The European week is focused on a central theme like comparing teacher training education. During this week schools are visited and ideas are exchanged. There are also students of polytechnics involved in several projects with schools in Antwerp (in Belgium) in which they give courses to those pupils in England" (Bhesena & Edelenbos, forthcoming).

A CASE STUDY – DIFFERENCES AT THE SCHOOL LEVEL

In the first part of the chapter, we described some characteristics of the educational system in China and Belgium. In this part, our focus turns to the school level. A school, like every individual, has personalities of its own. To a certain degree, the personalities of a school are its unique culture.

Many researchers (Cheng, 1996b; Fullan, 1982; Hargreaves, 1999; Stoll & Fink, 1996) declare that school cultures play a powerful role in changing the schools. Organizational culture is a key factor in understanding the school process or studying school effectiveness (Cheng, 1996b). It is often assumed that organizational culture is a dominant factor affecting members' job attitudes and productivity and that strong organizational culture can promise high satisfaction, high commitment, and high performance of members. Inevitably, organizational culture is believed to contribute substantially to organizational effectiveness in general and school effectiveness in particular (Cheng, 1993).

School Culture

Firestone and Corbett (1995) describes school culture as a widely shared understanding of "what is" and "what ought to be," symbolized in the acts of students, teachers, and administrators, as well as in the school's artifacts, like billboards, wall charts, documents, awards, and use of space. The shared understanding and beliefs are the result of a long period of daily interactions among teachers, school leaders, other staff members, and students. However, school culture cannot exist in vacuum and is inseparable from its embedded national culture. A national culture is like the roots of a tree while school cultures are like different branches or leaves of this tree. Although every single leaf differs, they all manifest from the same roots and they all share the same genes (values) from their own national culture tree (Sun et al., 2000).

Moreover, school culture consists of different layers. Its surface layer is termed as the school climate (Sun et al., 1999). Climate is a set of overt, perceptible, and behavioral norms but culture may be multi-level, including implicit assumptions, beliefs, and values and also explicit behavioral norms. It will be very difficult, if not impossible, to access the deeper levels of culture without knowing the climate. Therefore, the climate research can be employed to explore the overt and superficial level of culture (Cheng, 1996b).

In school effectiveness research, climate factors have been incorporated in effectiveness models (Creemers, 1994). Teaching cannot be effective without a co-operative, positive class climate and an orderly, peaceful, encouraging school climate. Concerning school climate, Creemers and Reezigt (1999) propose the following set of indicators:

- the physical environment of the school (school buildings, corridors, canteens, school yard, and playground);

- the social system (relationships and interactions among school members; rules and agreements concerning behaviour towards each other; between school and parents; and between school and external agencies);

- an orderly school environment;

- the expectations for teacher behavior and student outcomes.

Based on the above mentioned literature, we present in this part a picture by describing the "personalities" of Sancta Mariainstituut and compare them with that of secondary schools in China. We focus on the school climate, the physical environment, the rules and agreements concerning behavior toward students and an orderly, peaceful, well-organized school environment.

The school, Sancta Mariainstituut (SM), is a middle-sized, inner-city school with a nursery, a primary school, and a junior and senior secondary school. It is a Flemish free school located in Leuven, Belgium. It was founded by nuns in 1872 for the education of poor girls. Only 18 years ago, it started to enroll boy students. Table 3 records the number of its pupils and teachers as in March 1997.

The government pays the teachers' salaries. Each year, an average wise of 140 students graduate from the SM higher secondary school, each school year's failure rate is around 6%; however, by the sixth year, only 2 or 3 students failed.

An Orderly, Peaceful School Environment

An orderly, peaceful school environment is a positive factor in running a school successfully. Visiting SM, we were impressed by how the school tried to ensure an orderly, peaceful, and quiet learning environment through strict door and record-keeping systems.

In China, schools have door-keepers but they are usually retired elderly people. In fact, the function of many school door-keepers is like the "ear of a deaf person" – the outside form is perfect with no actual ability at all as everyone can easily pass through.

The door of SM is closed. There is a door-bell and a reception near the door where the secretary sits. Talking with her, we got to know the strict door system of SM. The side-door for the students opens every morning from 8:15

to 8:20, then closes. If the students come after 8:20, they must go the front door, push the door-bell, then come in. They are also requested to fill a form for late-comers. In this way, the school door secretary knows very well how many students and who are late for their classes every day. She sends their names to the teacher who is in charge of the students' files, who informs the student's parents. School-parent contact occurs frequently in SM.

Table 3: *The Number of Students and Teachers in the Sancta Mariainstituut School*

Schools	Nursery	Primary school	Secondary school	Total
Students	115	171	685	971
Teachers	6	10	35*	51*
Other staff members				7**

* 35 is the number of full time secondary school teachers and the number of part time secondary school teachers is around 55-60. Accordingly, 51 is the total number of full time teachers in SM.
** Among the seven staff members of the school, one is the school headmaster, five are full time secretaries or working staff (36 hours), and two part time workers (18 hours).

Since the lunch break is very short (55 minutes), all the students are requested to eat inside the school *eetzaal* (canteen) except three kinds of students: the final year students, those who live in Leuven, and the students who are over 18 years old. The school distributes to each student a yellow card with his/her photo on it. Every day when they leave the school for lunch, they must leave their yellow-cards with the door secretary where they can be retrieved upon their return.

Whenever visitors come, they must push the door-bell and go to the secretary first. The dutiful woman will check if they have an appointment or not. She can inform the person they want to visit or politely tell the visitors to wait. The strict door system keeps SM in an orderly, peaceful, and well-organized atmosphere. Moreover, it guarantees, to a certain degree, the time the students spend at school and time for learning.

The Daily Activities, Textbooks, and PMS on Campus

No Uni-edited Textbooks But a Textbook-rental System
In Chinese secondary schools, "[I]nstructional plans and curriculum are centrally decided by the CSEC and textbooks are nationally standardized" (Thogersen, 1990). Teachers must use *tongbian jiaocai* (uni-edited textbooks) except university teachers. One reason for this is the national entrance

examinations are based on *tongbian jiaocai*, another is that textbooks are considered to be so important that they can shape students' morality and personalities, by influencing their thinking. So the CSEC needs to "unify" them. Although the textbooks are printed every year, the contents remain the same for several years. At a time schools order the textbooks before the new school year starts and students buy them at full price. Fortunately, the price of the textbooks is much cheaper than the price of the textbooks in Belgium. Chinese teachers dislike students using second-hand textbooks. Few textbook-rental systems which are very common in schools in Belgium exist in Chinese secondary schools.

Contrary to the Chinese system, the decentralized education system in Belgium offers schools more autonomy: textbooks can be chosen by schools and even by teachers. There are no uni-edited textbooks or unified national tests in Belgium. Taking English textbooks as an example, in the Flemish schools, around 28% of the teachers used the British publications and the rest use the Belgian textbooks. The Belgian publishers' strongest point is their understanding of the local needs and curriculum requirements and their implicit or explicit contrastive approaches (Goethals, 1997). Anyhow, the textbooks used in SM were decided by the teaching group. Once the textbooks have been chosen, they are used for four years. SM buys textbooks for the students and the students pay 1/4 of the cost. The next year's students pay a second quarter, and so on. Of course, students are obliged to maintain the textbooks well; otherwise, the following year's students cannot use them.

Here, a special mention must be made of: the great influence the Belgian publishers have on the content of the textbooks. They are the real "powerhouse behind" in textbooks' content and editing. This is quite different from the situation in China where publishers have little say in the content of the textbooks. Belgium publishers re-construct the national curriculum guidelines; they organize each textbook's content writing, editing, publishing, and selling. They provide very detailed handbooks for teachers including the correct answers to exercises, teaching approaches, and particular methodologies including questions to be asked in class and even how to teach (by a plan on the disk) the class when teachers are inspected.

Such detailed prescriptive textbooks have a great impact on teachers. In Belgian schools, "[M]ost teachers say that they are influenced more by their books than by the national curriculum and they take it for granted that the books conform to policy and guidelines" (Bhesena & Edelenbos, forthcoming).

Different Daily Activities and Time Schedule

In Chinese secondary schools, there are usually seven or eight classes a day. Classes start at 8:00 am (in some areas, 7:30 a.m.). In many schools, there is a 30 minutes self-study in the classroom before 8:00 a.m. Some schools have a student teacher system, during this 30 minutes, the student teacher can teach the whole class to read English or other foreign languages. Each class lasts 45 minutes. After the second class in the morning, there is a ten-minute break. The whole school assembles to do *zaocao* (the morning exercises). In some schools, they do "eye exercises" every day, a set of movements devised by doctors and set to music. When the fourth or the fifth class ends, it is around Noon. Most students go home for lunch. Those students whose homes are not close enough go to the students dining hall where they can buy hot dishes for lunch. Lunch break lasts two hours or even two and a half hours. In summer time, most students take a nap at noon. In the afternoon, there are three or four classes. The school ends around 5:00 to 5:30 p.m. (depending on different areas). In China, the two "magic" weapons that are believed to improve performance in unified examinations are more exercises (including homework) and more pre-examinations. Therefore, most secondary schools then have *wanzi xi* (evening classes for doing homework) for 2 or 3 hours. Teachers will be there if the students need help or coaching. In most secondary schools, the final year students are obliged to attend *wanzi xi* because of the pressure of the national entrance examinations for higher education. Normally, students need to pay extra money for *wanzi xi*. So Chinese students, especially the higher secondary school students, study all day long. For them, no weekends and no holidays occur. They are burdened with homework. The great pressures of the national entrance examinations leave little room for free time.

The class schedule in SM is more tight in the daytime but it has no classes in the evening. Classes start at 8:20 a.m. and each class lasts 50 minutes. There are seven or eight classes a day. After the second class, there is 15 minutes break. The fourth class ends at 11:55 a.m. and from 11:55 a.m. to 12:45 p.m. is lunch time. Most students eat the food they have brought from home at the school *eetzaal*. The students have no time to take a nap; that is probably the reason why people in the West like coffee so much. Most afternoon classes start at 12:45 p.m. and finish at 3:25 p.m. Some end at 4:15 p.m. In this case, teachers and students in SM can go home around 4:30 p.m. There are no evening classes in SM.

PMS on Campus

Like all the schools in Belgium, SM has the PMS system. A woman from a PMS center works in SM. She has her own office and telephone. She works three days a week at this school and she is always busy at her work. Students like her so much that they address her directly by her first name. Whenever they have problems in their learning, behavior, emotions with their teachers, classmates, friends, or families, they can talk to her and she tries to help them solve the problems. She also provides the students with information or advice concerning opportunities in studies, training, and employment.

School Culture and the Physical Environment

The school culture pervading SM is strikingly different from school culture in China. First, the different school culture is reflected in the campus surroundings. In China, with the large student population, most secondary schools are bigger in area and number of students. The local government offers all public schools free land for school buildings, including the sports ground, student dormitories, and teachers' apartment buildings. Many schools even have school factories and school farm fields. On the campus, many trees, flowers, and grasses are grown. But inside the school buildings, there are almost no flowers, plants, or ornaments. Instead, schools have loudspeakers, school doctors, school badges, school wall-newspapers; some of them have school uniforms and the students are obliged to wear them. During the school year, every Monday morning there is a national flag-raising ceremony. The whole school gathers together to salute while the Chinese national flag is hoisted. Generally speaking, an overall impression of the Chinese schools would be large, spacious, serious, and noisy.

At SM, its school-culture starts on the red wall of its building along the street. Two big letters "SM" are striking near its front door. Its school-culture pervades at the entrance way where a large well-shaped potted landscape with yellow spring flowers and little green trees expressing welcome. (We were informed that it changes every month with different styles and has been created by fine-arts teachers.) Above, four pencil drawings on the right side wall and three colorful paintings on the left side tell the school history. A colorful map of Leuven indicates the location of SM. Flowers, paintings, and plants are interspersed in the school corridors or classrooms, creating a homely warm environment which strongly reflects Western culture and is surprisingly different from Chinese schools.

Second, school culture is also reflected by class size and the relationships between teachers and students, and among students. Contrary to the big classes in China, classes in SM are rather small, less than 20 students in each class. It creates more opportunities for teacher-student interactions and for the teacher to show an interest in every student. Moreover, SM teachers are expected to address their students by their first names whenever they call them. Every year, graduation is celebrated with a reception of the students with teachers and parents attending. The school orchestra performs and there are speeches. Drinks and snacks are offered by the school at the occasion of this reception. This family-like, easy-going relationship improves on the "cat and mouse" like teacher-student relationship found in many Chinese schools.

In Chinese schools, teachers address their students by their full names, while students can never address their teachers by their full names. If they do so, not only will the teacher be offended but the students will also be considered impolite. Whenever they address their teachers, they must put the title ahead of the teacher's name, for instance, "Teacher Li," "Headteacher Wang," "Dean Fan," and so on. In most cases, when the job and work are respectable, the title of that profession is addressed together with that person's family name to show respect. In schools, the roles of parent-child in family are replaced by the roles of teacher-student (Sun et al., 1999). Teachers have 'absolute' authority in the classrooms and students are seldom encouraged to challenge or question their teachers. Since their childhood, Chinese children are taught that they should obey their teachers. Competition is a strong feature of the relationship between the Chinese students. The national university entrance examinations are the key source of such competition, as universities admit very few secondary school graduates: for example, "in 1986 is 3.92%, 1987 is 4%, in 1988 is 3.74% " (Thogersen, 1990, p. 55). "Forcing 1,000 troops and 10,000 horses across a one-plank bridge" is a vivid metaphor of the competition to enter universities. In a competitive Chinese school system, students learn to compete with each other despite the virtues of co-operation and mutual help being exhorted by teachers and textbooks.

Third, the different school culture is also reflected within the social school activities. In China, many secondary schools and even some primary schools invite soldiers to come to the schools to train the students. This is termed "learning from the army." Schools also organize trips of *chunyou* (Spring Outing) and *qiuyou* (Autumn Outing), visiting museums, parks, exhibitions, and fairs of science and technology.

SM also organizes trips to visit parks and museums too. In addition, an interesting inter-cultural exchange program is organized: every March or April, the final year students visit a foreign country for one week (e.g., Prague, the capital city of Czech Republic) and Prague students return to visit SM and Belgium for one week in October. During the Prague trip, SM buys some works of art, such as paintings. Then, they organize a yearly exhibition to sell them to build up a school social fund. With this social-fund, SM can aid financially the students from poor families and do many other things for the students.

DISCUSSION

Every educational system wants to improve the quality of its schools, but the way different countries attempt to accomplish it may differ. The different educational policies and systems in China and Belgium reveal different values, different cultures, and different social contexts. It is difficult to tell which educational system is better since each system is growing on the tree rooted in its own soil (embedded in its own national context). This does not mean it is impossible to improve or better a particular educational system by "transplanting" knowledge and successful experience and findings from one culture to another, from one country to another. Such transplanting, however, must be applicable, adaptable, and suitable for the contextual reality of the respective country. Among our findings in this chapter, many can be adapted for use in Chinese schools: for example, the close school-parent contact, teachers addressing the given name of every student, the textbook-rental system, the PMS student caring system, the Sandwich Model for teacher training, to mention just a few.

We do not need a unified world culture but rather a pluricultural world, one with an international mind. We need to assimilate experience from other nations. Also, teachers need to bring students to discover this rapidly changing world and to learn from the strong points of other countries. This is a great challenge faced by teacher education and development. In order to make our schools effective, secondary schools in different countries need to learn from each other and enrich themselves with what they can learn from others. For this purpose, we suggest the following four recommendations for Chinese education and teacher education development in China.

More Funds for Chinese Education and Equity Education

Since making good schools and equity education for all children are the two essential issues for Chinese education in the 21st century, we need equivalent policies, strategies, and initiatives to ensure these two essential issues. Putting more funds into Chinese education is a very crucial step. First of all, Chinese education urgently needs more funds so as to provide those possibilities for quality education: to provide more pre-service and in-service teacher training opportunities; to lessen the inequities between urban and rural teachers and students; to better the conditions of the school buildings; to build up an encouraging and powerful learning environment with the necessary equipment and materials in schools; and to equip teachers colleges and secondary schools with computers. This last point is to improve computer literacy among the future teachers. Chinese teachers need to learn how to use the new information technologies so as to utilize these technologies in improving the effectiveness of their teaching.

Second, the student/teacher ratio in Chinese secondary schools is over twice than that in Belgium. However, the Chinese teachers' salary is only 1/4 or 1/5 of the Belgian teachers'. If Chinese teachers have to work very hard for a low salary, the attractiveness of teaching as a job will be diminished. Teachers are the shapers of a nation's future. To attract and retain competent and suitable people in the occupation of teaching, there are the needs to raise the teachers' salaries and to offer them improved working conditions, parity, and further training. In addition, there is an urgent need to better the rural schools conditions so as to provide equal opportunities for all children. China cannot successfully modernize itself if the majority of its population has received only five years' education, no matter how well some key school students perform in international competitions (Sun, 1997). Hannum's study (1999) discovers that policy changes designed to promote efficiency and quality do not necessarily promote equity, and may in fact exert the opposite influence. Ensuring adequate attention to emerging equity issues in China and other nations undergoing competitiveness-driven reforms is thus an essential direction for further research.

The Needs of Research on School Effectiveness and Cost Effectiveness

More funds should definitely be put into Chinese education, how can these limited funds wisely be used? This calls for research on cost-effectiveness (CE) and school effectiveness (SE). SE research findings tell us whether changes in inputs to schools can be successfully converted into improvement of education outcomes inevitably depends on an effective school process including management and instructional processes. According to Cheng (1996b), without considering the whole school when assessing possible improvements, the change of individual school practices through input intervention may become fragmentary, superficial, and ineffective.

China is a large country with the largest population, but its economic position indicates that China is unable to offer the ample educational funding as the advanced countries do. With the little money in its pocket and many "mouths" wanting feeding, what should China do? How to spend the least money to achieve the most effective results in Chinese education becomes more and more important. This falls under the scope of SE and CE research. CE does not only refer to the input of money and the effective output. It covers a much wider scope: for example, the input of human resources (teachers) and the outcome of the students; the input of time and the outcome of the students (see Scheerens & Bosker, 1997); the input of teachers' pre-service and in-service training and the output of the quality of the teachers, etc. The same applies to selecting resource types in education policy-making, including human resources, equipment and facilities resources, accommodation or space resources, and monetary resources. The government needs to watch closely how the schools use the resources (Cheng, 1996a, p. 55).

International Exchange Programs and Training Teachers in a Future-oriented and World-oriented Way

China needs to open wider not only its doors but also its windows to the outside world and tries to benefit from international exchange programs for teacher training. In Europe, exchanging students to study in different countries is one effective approach. For example, students from Belgium may go to the United Kingdom to study for three months and vice versa. In recent years, these international exchange programs have expanded not only to all the countries within the European Commission but also to the countries like Japan, Russia, Romania, the United States, Canada, New Zealand, etc. Such international student exchange programs result in positive development for teacher education and development. For instance, many teachers were the benefiters of the international student exchange program: they had the opportunity to study in foreign countries while they were students. Some attend international seminars for European teachers. All these activities enable them to build up partnerships and enlarge networks with their "foreign peers" abroad. Nowadays, these programs do not only concentrate on the exchange of students but on the exchange of teachers as well. For example, all schools in Belgium are well informed about the possibilities to participate in teacher exchange projects. Schools that are connected to the Internet have extra means to enter into international contacts. It is wise for the Chinese educational system to open its doors and windows wider and to join these international mutual-beneficial programs especially for teacher education and development.

Teacher education needs to train future teachers in a more effective, future-oriented and world-oriented way. Secondary schools are training students for the future, not for the past. According to Mayer (1996), during the 20th century, the role of teachers have changed from "dispensers of rewards and punishments" (1900s-1950s), to "dispense of knowledge" (1960s-1970s), and to "cognitive guides" (1980s-1990s). However, the prevailing teaching approach in China is still "spoon-feeding" (teacher-centered). Although we cannot say that it is totally wrong within the constraints of the Chinese context (e.g., big classes, poor teaching conditions, and large power distance in culture), the questions remain: How can the Chinese combine the strengths of constructive learning with the strengths of direct instruction? How can teacher education train future teachers in a more effective, future-oriented and world-oriented way? Indeed, Cheng (1996b) has noted:

> With very different contextual and historical constrains, obviously the tradition
> of research in China may be different from Western societies. How to further
> develop its research tradition with integration of the advance in other countries
> to meet the urgent needs of current educational reforms should be a major
> concern in the research agenda in the coming years. (p. 189)

The Relationship Between Theory and Practice

Teachers, no matter in China or in Belgium, often complain about the discrepancies between what higher education offers them in the teacher training courses and what is needed in the classroom teaching. Universities pay scarce attention to the needs of future teachers and the requirements they face. Therefore, many graduates join the teaching profession without knowing whether they will be able to cope with their future students. This practice shock is normal for any new teacher, even the talented ones. However, this shock could be reduced if universities do more to prepare future teachers for the reality of teaching in the classroom. In short, teacher education development may become more effective if it focuses more on learning by participating in the real classroom teaching under the guidance of good, proper theories. Effective teacher education and development requires a thorough integration of the both.

ACKNOWLEDGEMENTS

We would like to thank the editors of this book for their encouragement and all their efforts. If there are any errors, they are all ours. We would like to express a special debt of gratitude to Prof. Bert Creemers for his insightful suggestions on revising this manuscript. We would like to thank SM school in Leuven, Belgium, especially Mrs. Wellens and Mr. Willy Lennens. Our thanks also go to Prof. dr. J. Van Damme of University of Leuven for organizing the visit, to Mr. Erik de Gelder for kindly offering the useful information.

REFERENCES

Bhesena, U., & Edelenbos, P. (forthcoming). *National policies on foreign language teaching within a European Community Framework.*

Brown, H. O. (1981). Recent policy towards rural education in the People's Republic of China. *Hong Kong Journal of Public Administration, 3*(2), 171.

Cheng, Y. C. (1993). Profiles of organisational culture and effective schools. *School Effectiveness and School Improvement, 4*(2), 85-110.

Cheng, Y. C. (1996a). *School effectiveness & school-based management - A mechanism for development.* London: The Falmer Press.

Cheng, Y. C. (1996b). *The pursuit of school effectiveness research management and policy.* Hong Kong: Hong Kong Institute of Educational Research, the Chinese University of Hong Kong.

Creemers, B. P. M. (1994). *The effective classroom.* London: Cassell.

Creemers, B. P. M., & Reezigt. (1999). The role of school and classroom climate in elementary school learning environments. In H. J. Freiberg (Ed.), *School climate: Measuring, improving and sustaining healthy learning environments* (pp. 30-48). Hampshire: Falmer.

China State Education Commission [CSEC]. (1986). *Secondary school education in China.* Beijing: Author.

CSEC. (1995). *Educational law of the People's Republic of China, State Education*

Commission of the P. R. China. Beijing:Author.

CSEC. (1997). *Education in China*. Beijing: Author.

Damme, J. van. (1990). Comprehensive secondary education and middle schools in Belgium. In B. P. M. Creemers (Ed.), *Development in middle school education*. Groningen: GION.

Delors, J. (1996). *Learning the treasure within*. Paris: UNESCO Publishing.

Edwards, G. M. (1996). *1996 Britannica Book of the year*. Chicago: Encyclopaedia Britannica. Inc.

EURYDICE. (1995). *In-service training of teachers in the European Union & the EFTA/EEA Countries*. Brussels: Author.

Firestone, W. A., & Corbett, H. D. (1995). Planned organisational change. In Boyan (Ed.), *Handbook of research of educational administration*. London: Longman.

Flemish Government. (2000, November 17). Information and communication technology in education [online]. Available: http://www.ond.vlaanderen.be/ict. (2000)

Fullan, M. (1982). *The meaning of educational change*. New York: OISE/Teachers' Press.

Goethals, M. (1997). English in Flanders (Belgium). *World English, 16*(1).

Hannum, E. (1999). Political change and the urban-rural gap in basic education in China, 1949-1990. *Comparative Education Review, 43*(2), 193-211.

Hargreaves, D. (1999). Helping practitioners explore their school's culture. In J. Prosser (ed.), *School Culture* (pp. 48-66). London: Paul Chapman Publishing.

Hayhoe, R. (1984). *Contemporary Chinese education*. London: Croom Helm.

Heynemann, S. P., & Loxley, W. A. (1983). The effect of primary school quality on academic achievement across twenty-nine high and low income countries. *American Journal of Sociology, 88*(6), 1162-1194.

Lo, B. L. C. (1984). Teacher education in the Eighties. In Hayhoe (ed.), *Contemporary Chinese Education*. London: Croom Helm.

Luyn, F-J. van. (2000, March 28). Chinese scholier wordt get van zijn huiswerk [Chinese students get mad of their homework]. *New Rotterdam Daily [NRC]*, p. 5.

Maclean, R. (1999). Developments in teacher education in Asia and the Pacific: Issues and prospects towards the 21st century. In Y. C. Cheng (ed.), *Asia-Pacific Journal of Teacher Education & Development, 2*(1), 87-94.

Mayer, R. E. (1996). History of instructional psychology. In De Corte & F. Weinert, (Eds.), *International encyclopaedia of developmental and instructional psychology (2nd ed.)*. Oxford: Pergamon.

Ministerie van Onderwijs. (1997). *The salaries in Flemish primary and secondary education*. Unpublished document for internal use. Brussels: Author

Ministerie van Onderwijs. (1988). *Educational developments in Belgium*. Brussels: Author.

Ministerie van de Vlaamse Gemeenschap. (1991). *Education in Belgium: The diverging paths*. Brussel-Bruxelles-Eupen: Author.

Ministerie van de Vlaamse Gemeenschap. (1996). *Education in Flanders*. Brussels: Author.

Renmin Jiaoyu. (1981). Renmin Jiaoyu. Vol. 1, January 1981. Beijng: Author.

Reynolds, D. (2000). School effectiveness: The international dimension. In C. Teddilie & D. Reynolds (Eds.). *The international handbook of school effectiveness research*. London: Falmer Press.

Scheerens, J., & Bosker, R. (1997). *The foundations of school effectiveness*. Oxford: Pergamon Press.

Stoll, L., & Fink, D. (1996). *Changing our schools*. Buckingham, Philadelphia: Open University Press.

Sun, H. C., Vandenberghe, V., Creemers, B. P. M., & Jong, R. de. (1999). *A university president's suicide related to educational innovations*. Paper accepted for ICSEI 1999, Trinity University, San Antonio, the United States.

Sun, H. C. (1997). *Comparative study of primary education in China and Belgium*. Unpublished master course paper, University of Leuven-PED, Leuven.

Sun, H. C. (1998). *Distance education for socially disadvantaged women in China*. Unpublished master's thesis, University of Leuven, Leuven.

Sun, H. C., Creemers, B. P. M., & Jong, de. R. (2000). *The culture of higher education in its national context: A case study*. Paper presented at the European Conference on Educational Research 2000, Edinburgh, the United Kingdom.

The World Bank. (1995). *World development report 1995*. Oxford University.

Thogersen, S. (1990). *Secondary education in China after Mao: Reform and social conflict*. Demark: University of Aarhus.

UNESCO. (2000). *World data on education*. Paris: Author.

Yi, M., & Xiang, Q. (1997). *Dianda jigou gaige de tantao*. Beijing: Zhongguo Dianda Jiaoyu, 7, p. 29.

Yun, X. (1997). *Guojia jiaowei dangzu shuji Chen Zhili shicha dianjiao dalou*. Beijing: Zhongguo Dianda Jiaoyu, 9.

Zhou, N. Z. (1995). *Social change and educational development*. Hong Kong: University of Hong Kong.

Zhongguo Jiaoyu Bao. (1988, August 18). *Zhongguo Jiaoyu Bao* [The Education Newspaper of China]. Beijing: Author.

Appendix One: *Syllabi in Junior and Senior Secondary Education in China* (CSEC, 1986)

Subject	Junior secondary school Grade			Senior secondary school Grade			Total class hours
	1	2	3	1	2	3	
Political and Ideological edu	2	2	2	2	2	2	384
Chinese language	6	6	6	5	4	4	1000
Mathematics	5	6	6	5	5	5	1026
Foreign language	5	5	5	5	5	4	932
Physics		2	3	4	3	4	500
Chemistry			3	3	3	3	372
History	3	2		3			266
Geography	3	2			2		234
Biology	2	2				2	192
Physiology & hygiene			2				64
Physical education	2	2	2	2	2	2	384
Music	1	1	1				100
Fine arts	1	1	1				100
Weekly required course hours	*30*	*31*	*31*	*29*	*26*	*26*	*5554*
Elective course hours					4	24	240
Job training		2 weeks*			2 weeks*		576

Notes: Each period lasts 45 minutes in Chinese secondary schools.
* job training hour calculation is based on 4 classes daily for both junior and senior schools

Appendix Two: *The Syllabus of the 1ˢᵗ year "A" in Flemish Secondary Schools in Belgium* (Damme, 1990)

Language community	Dutch speaking		French speaking	
School system	State	Catholic	State	Catholic
Religion/ethics	2	2	2	2
Mother language	4	5	5	5
Second language	3	4	4	3
Third language	3	-	-	-
Mathematics	5	4	4	4
Biology/sciences	1	2	2	2
Geography	2	2	2	3*
History	2	1	2	
Music	1	1	2	1
Plastic arts	2	1	2	1
Technology	2	3	-	2
Physical education	3	2	3	3
Latin	-	2	-	2
Total	30	29	28	28
Electives	2**	-	6***	-
Complementary activities****	-	3	-	4
Remedial teaching	0-2	0-2	0-2	0-2

Note: Each period lasts 50 minutes in secondary schools in Belgium.
*   study of the environment (integrating several subjects)
**   Latin or technology or science
*** Latin and/or Mother language and/or economics and/or technology
****for example, sport, arts and crafts

Chapter 17

Professional Development, Management Training, and School Improvement: An Experience of Innovation

Ken FOSTER

Faculty of Cultural, Legal and Social Studies
University of Central Lancashire, United Kingdom

This chapter explores the relationship between school management training and school improvement and is informed in part by the outcomes of an action research case study. The focus is on the professional development of teachers in the context of an innovative management training strategy developed by a large Local Education Authority (LEA) in the North West of England. The action research dimension of the program involves LEA advisers, teachers (including headteachers and deputy headteachers), and university tutors working collaboratively to promote teacher development and to monitor progress of the scheme.

The strategy adopted is intended to demonstrate how those involved with professional development work need to respond to a range of challenging encounters. This includes the practical management of local schemes, engagement with theory and research, and the broader context of educational policy. Simmons, Konecki, Crowell, and Gates-Duffield (1999) aptly describes these circumstances in an account of the work of tutors in Professional Development Schools (PDSs) in the United States. Three metaphors are proposed for theories-in-action in school and university sites in Michigan. There are "dream keepers" who help to keep the vision of PDSs in sight, the "weavers," often university co-ordinators, who strive to hold together the contribution of their reform teams, and "shape-shifters" who are constantly engaged in taking on new roles in order to sustain the collaborative effort. The components of this PDS strategy aptly describe the work of the partners involved in the project featured in this account.

The starting point is a brief overview of the policy context and sources of influence on the professional development of teachers. This is followed by a discussion of school improvement literature, identifying links with school management and leadership. Understanding of leadership is then further explored, noting in particular the political influences which are likely to shape teachers' responses to leadership roles. At this point, an overview and critique of the National Professional Qualification for Headship (NPQH) is presented. This government sponsored project provides an example of system level opportunities which may, or may not, accord with more localized initiatives focused on leadership and management training. This is followed by an account of the Lancashire Education Management Program (LEMP), outlining its main features and the responses from teachers in relation to the available postgraduate awards in educational management within the scheme. Next is a review of the approach to action research adopted for the project, focusing on the nature of role relationships and the nature of collaboration in this context. These discussions lead into a consideration of the future professional development needs of school leaders, taking into account current experience of management and leadership training and the state of play evident in the literature. Finally, an attempt is made to outline some possible implications for those involved in the development of leadership programs.

THE POLICY CONTEXT

The Department for Education and Employment (DfEE) has played a central role in determining strategies for training and continuing professional development, including the recently launched NPQH. This particular government-sponsored award for aspiring headteachers raises questions concerning the status of other existing management training schemes and awards and how they might articulate with these new national mandatory requirements.

The advent of NPQH also reflects the well-documented trend in the education system of England and Wales towards increased central control, coupled with de-centralized responsibilities for school management. Gewirtz (1997) refers to this trend as part of the "post-welfarist education policy complex (PWEPC)" and identifies the characteristics of this context in the following way:

> The PWEPC is comprised of a number of elements which combine to exert greater control over schools, teachers and their work: the abolition of secondary picketing and of teachers' negotiating rights and the imposition of new teaching contracts and new pay and promotional structures; the national curriculum and

national testing, performance tables; parental choice and competition; local management of schools; per capita funding; the new inspection system; and changes in the provision of teacher training. The complex is permeated by a utilitarian discourse of efficiency, effectiveness, performance and productivity. All of these elements combine to constrain schools and teachers whilst increasing central control over the school system. (pp. 220-21)

The DfEE has played a central role in determining the way teachers are to be prepared for a supportive role in this policy complex. With this in mind, the NPQH scheme has become part of an overall strategy for training and continuing professional development that now includes newly qualified teachers, advanced skills teachers, subject leaders, headteachers, and Special Needs Co-ordinators.

These initiatives all have an impact on local provision aimed at meeting teachers' professional development needs. Increasingly, the national agenda has embraced requirements for training, especially through nationally prescribed funding dedicated to raising standards in schools. NPQH developments are closely linked to the establishment of a National College for School Leadership and have paved the way in terms of forging agreement on national standards for headship. Local training schemes have had to adapt their programs and recruitment strategies in order to ensure continuity and progression for teachers, enabling them to advance from local to national forms of accreditation.

SCHOOL MANAGEMENT AND SCHOOL IMPROVEMENT

Much of the recent literature on school improvement draws attention to the significance of management activity and the form it takes as a key to change. Hopkins (1996) identifies three dimensions of management arrangements that form the basis for realization of school policy. These are "frameworks," "roles and responsibilities," and "ways of working." Hopkins is concerned to explore 'the structure-and-culture complex that underpins school organization." He distinguishes between maintenance and development as different but essentially complementary aspects of the management of change. The cultural conditions necessary for school improvement are those which sustain an open and democratic approach to management. As Hopkins (1996) states,

The types of cultures most supportive of school improvement efforts appear to be those that are collaborative, have high expectations for both students and staff, exhibit a consensus on values (or an ability to deal effectively with differences), support an orderly and secure environment, and encourage teachers to assume a variety of leadership roles. (p. 43)

MacGilchrist, Myers, and Reed (1997) endorse the significance of school culture and consider it to be "the deciding factor when it comes to a school's state of readiness and its capacity to improve" (MacGilchrist et al., 1997, p. 11). Alongside organizational arrangements and professional relationships sustained by a shared sense of purpose, favorable school cultures provide support and encouragement for teachers' professional development on a collegial basis.

In similar vein, a number of school improvement authors have identified key factors which embrace both cultural and structural aspects of school management. These include, for example, opportunities for leadership roles (Hopkins, Ainscow, & West, 1994) with leadership functions dispersed throughout the school (Bush, 1996; Fidler, 1997; Hopkins, 1996; Hopkins et al., 1994) and linked to a philosophy of ownership of school management and decision-making (Ribbins & Burridge, 1994). Such strategies are also equated with open management and shared vision and goals for the school (Hopkins et al., 1994; Ribbins & Burridge, 1994; Sammons et al., 1994) and the integration of professional development with school improvement strategies (Stoll, 1996).

Gray, Hopkins, Reynolds, Wilcox, Farrell, and Jesson (1999) survey school improvement research during the 1990s and identifies some of the key factors that may be taken as "guides for development, rather than blueprints." These include reference to leadership provided by the headteacher but also include strategies for involving staff in decision-making, thus broadening the way in which leadership may be exercised. Gray et al. (1999) comments on organizational leadership in the following terms:

> The fostering of organizational cohesion through planning and co-ordination of school activities, through ensuring a degree of ownership of the school by the staff and through the flow of information through the school in ways which facilitate staff involvement ... As part of its approach the school is likely to support development planning and forms of professional development which involve utilizing members of staff as 'experts' who can support both their own and colleague's needs for professional development. (pp. 28-9)

A similar argument is presented by Dimmock (2000), who makes a case for the development of learning-centered leadership in schools where student learning outcomes are part of a core technology. In this context, leadership is organization-wide with both teacher leadership and student leadership being as important as the leadership exercised by the principal. Dimmock's (2000) view of leadership is outlined below.

> Leadership is not therefore seen as a zero-sum concept with all of it vested in the person of the principal. Rather, part of the principal's exercise of leadership is the empowerment of leadership in others. Thus leadership in the learning-centered school is seen as a nested concept, the lowest level of which applies to students, the next layer to teachers, another layer to senior teachers, then deputy principals and finally, the overarching layer, to the principal. (pp. 251)

Although these views may be considered entirely plausible and sound commonsense, it is also necessary to maintain a critical stance towards the school improvement literature, especially when the focus is on internal structures and processes. Accomplishing more effective approaches may not be as easy as we are sometimes led to believe. Thrupp (1999), having reviewed a series of leading authors associated with improvement research, concludes that the "school mix" or social class composition of a school's intake tends to be marginalized in many accounts. Thrupp (1999) suggests that the social mix is, in part, excluded from improvement research "through notions of school culture which emphasise the organizational, management and instructional dimensions of schooling at the expense of the culture of students and the community" (pp. 177-178).

A case is made for a broader more inclusive approach which acknowledges the influence of student cultures on school leadership.

> This is not to argue that the various attempts by improvers to sum up different types of school and teacher culture might not be useful in some respects. However they do fail to consider the impact of students and their cultures, either individually or collectively, on school organization and management and instruction. As a result they do not acknowledge the reciprocal, negotiated nature of schooling and therefore tend to attribute school processes to staff rather than students. (Thrupp, 1999, pp. 178)

Commentaries of this kind support the case for an informed approach to professional development, one which recognizes the limitations to knowledge and understanding and the need to be sceptical of claims.

Professional development in the educational management field also demands a critical stance towards the ideology and social control elements implicit in managerialist approaches (Ball, 1994; Grace, 1995; Inglis, 1989; Woods & Jeffrey, 1996). This is referred to by Bottery (1994) as "institutional isomorphism," whereby practices in profit-making organizations may be taken on unquestioningly by those who are non-profit-making, such as schools. Recognizing these differences in terms of the range of constituencies and goals to be addressed in education, relative to other types of organization, is probably the most challenging aspect of any professional development program, but especially so in educational management. Ideally, the purpose of such activity should be to promote a critical stance in relation to the limitations of a competitive, market approach to schooling, and a management style based on business values.

CONCEPTIONS OF SCHOOL LEADERSHIP

Bolman and Deal (1991) suggest that leadership can only be understood in relation to context and the interactions with others of those who attempt to lead. The forms that leadership may take are always likely to be constrained by the micro-politics of institutions. In this context, the claims and counter-claims of those who wish to influence the action may render "leadership" a diffuse and elusive term, not easy to acquire or live with.

Fidler (1997), too, broadens our understanding of leadership requirements in the school and, by implication, the needs of teachers in relation to professional development and management training. He suggests that preparation for headship has emphasized structural and human relations approaches with less concern for the symbolic and political aspects of leadership. As Fidler (1997) puts it,

> When diverse aspects and expectations are present the political arts of advocacy and coalition building are likely to be particularly needed. When the future is less predictable and those in organizations need to believe in what they do, the symbolic acts of vision building and inspiration are also likely to be indispensable. (p. 35)

Such observations suggest that professional development for management purposes has to be premised on a holistic approach taking into account meta-competences and those qualities of school leadership that are not easily specifiable or measurable. It is a matter of engaging with practical circumstances in such a way that enables teachers to respond to the increasingly diverse demands of schooling. As Osterman and Kottkamp (1994) observe, learning to manage involves cognitive, emotional, and social dimensions; to this needs to be added the idea of intellectual endeavour that seeks to improve and transform educational practice. It could be argued that this is a minimum requirement if there is to be a purchase on a style of professional development for teachers that is future-oriented. At its best management education should promote and facilitate changes in management policy within the school, possibly anticipating the kinds of changes suggested by Davies (1990) whereby the emphasis on "leadership" and "headship" becomes progressively replaced by federalism, power-sharing and new forms of organizational responsiveness.

Certainly there are signs of a paradigm shift in perceptions of leadership as a more diverse series of management roles become available for teachers. These include such tangible aspects of school management as curricular or instructional leadership, and special educational needs. There are also qualitative dimensions which may inform a variety of functional roles, including moral leadership, visionary leadership and professional leadership. Learning about and adapting to these changes may be necessary if schools are to engage with and promote their improvement. In this respect, for example, Glatter (1997) argues that it is essential for educational managers to understand the influence of contextual factors and the impact of national policies on institutional practice. The determinants of school improvement and school effectiveness are not easily agreed upon, and we need to recognize that approaches to school management have to aspire beyond the technocratic and mechanistic in order to interrogate the extent to which schools do make a difference.

There is, at the very least, a need to ensure that professional development enables teachers to aspire beyond the functional level of analysis to interpret and critically evaluate their role as managers. Even at this level of operation there is likely to be some conflict of interest between the academic knowledge base of management theory and research and the practical concerns of teachers in schools and classrooms. Much of this tension can also be traced to the spread of economic utility in the education system which, according to Hyland

(1994), has led to "a narrowing of academic focus et all levels of the profession." Hyland considers that the establishment of the Teacher Training Agency (TTA) was part of the continued move to de-professionalize and de-skill the teaching role. The pressures on teachers to take on the trappings of managerialism are still very considerable. The demands of local management of schools (LMS), open enrolment, formula funding and marketing, formal requirements for assessment, and client accountability all conspire to preclude informed debate about alternative ways to manage the school.

Whitty (1999) considers this issue of professionalism in teaching in the context of "a marketized civil society" accompanied by a shift to "regulated autonomy." As Whitty (1999) points out, this involves,

> ... a move away from the notion that the teaching profession should have a professional mandate to act on behalf of the state in the best interests of its citizens to a view that teachers (and other professions) need to be subjected to the rigours of the market and/or greater control and surveillance on the part of the re-formed state. (p. 3)

Whitty also forecasts possible future trends for the profession.

> One reading of the dominant tendency is that it is preparing the leading cadres of the profession for leadership in the new marketized culture of schooling, while others have to be prevented from perpetuating an outmoded social service version of professionalism even if they cannot be won to the new agenda. In these circumstances, one would expect that new teachers would be given a rather restricted version of professionalism/professionality, but also opportunities to demonstrate their potential to join the leading cadres. (P.3)

These observations provide further insights concerning the political nature of the context within which teachers may have to work. Such circumstances are likely to influence their reponses to professional development opportunities as well as to the specific demands of school leadership. On this basis, it seems reasonable to argue that this turbulent state of affairs, and the contradictions in the professional mandate, alluded to by Whitty, should be subject to assessment by teachers at some point within their professional development programs. School leaders need encouragement and support to confront those political conditions that determine the forms school leadership may take.

THE NATIONAL QUALIFICATION FOR HEADSHIP

The following brief review of NPQH provides an example of national policy which has been influential in promoting debate about training for school leadership. It is a significant element of the policy context which has had considerable impact on local provision. The initial paragraphs, below, describe some of the main features of the scheme for those readers who may not be familiar with developments in the United Kingdom. This is followed by a short, critical assessment of the attempt to re-structure training for school leadership.

In readiness for the start of NPQH in 1998, TTA devised a series of standards for headship based on extensive consultation with LEAs, higher education institutions, OFSTED, and other agencies. The aim was to establish a national professional framework of standards, associated with the role of headteacher, grouped around five main areas. These became Core Purpose of Headship; Key Outcomes of Headship; Professional Knowledge and Understanding; Skills and Attributes; and Key Areas of Headship.

Each of these areas is further subdivided so that, for example, Knowledge and Understanding has 13 elements, including effective teaching and assessment methods, leadership styles, employment law, and equal opportunities legislation. Skills and Attributes include a list of 40 items under four broad headings associated with leadership, decision-making, communication, and self-management. Key Areas of Headship are identified as strategic direction and development of the school; Teaching and learning; Leading and managing staff; Efficient and effective deployment of staff and resources; and Accountability.

The definition of the Core Purpose of Headship gives some indication of the management style of NPQH and its strong links with standards and school improvement: "To provide professional leadership for a school which secures its success and improvement, ensuring high quality education for all its pupils and improved standards of achievement" (TTA, National Standards for Headteachers, 1998, May, p. 4).

This core purpose is expanded on in the following extract,

> The headteacher is the leading professional in the school. Working with the

governing body, the headteacher must provide vision, leadership and direction for the school and ensure that it is managed and organised to meet its aims. With the governing body, the headteacher is responsible for the continuous improvement in the quality of education; for raising standards; for ensuring equality of opportunity for all; for the development of policies and practices; and for ensuring that resources are efficiently and effectively used to achieve the schools aims. (TTA, National Standards for Headteachers, 1998, May, p. 4)

THE LANGUAGE OF HEADSHIP

There is no doubt that the outline of standards and the proposed requirements for training and assessment are very thorough and comprehensive. They are also representative in terms of current legislation and policy on school management and accountability. This representativeness is apparent in the language used to portray the characteristics of headship. There are typical references to "efficient" and "effective" methods, to "accountability," "high standards," "targets for improvement," "increasing teachers' effectiveness," and securing school improvement." The headteacher's brief is underlined by the use of active descriptors, such as "create and implement," "create and maintain," "lead by example," "ensure that," "monitor, evaluate and review," "maximise the contribution," and "determine, organize and implement."

Such documentation appears to represent what Gewirtz (1997) refers to as the "articulated unity" of post-welfare education policy. As Gewirtz notes, "… there is a growing preoccupation with target-setting and performance monitoring in order to improve league-table performance and align school activities more closely with the requirements of OFSTED" (pp. 221-222).

In similar vein, Mahony and Hextall (1997) observe how the TTA conceives the role of the head using a mixture of direct control, based on "old managerialism," and people-centered management based on 'new managerialsim." This, too, supports the argument that NPQH standards are a reflection of officially sponsored ideas and terminology evident in recent developments associated with school management training. The TTA, through a series of planning and consultation processes, has managed to gauge with some precision the currency of a particular model of headship, one which commands support from key players in the education management field. This point is acknowledged by Bolam (1997), who suggests that the NPQH principles and framework appear to be broadly acceptable to professional associations, LEAs, schools, and higher education institutions. The appeal of the scheme resides in its practical focus and its concern with school improvement.

Although such observations may be taken as signalling positive benefits for education, there may also be a need for caution in terms of access and delivery. As Mahony and Hextall point out, it is possible to construe these developments as representing consensus on a relatively narrow front. Those who are supportive of the NPQH framework and who share its assumptions about the nature of headship and school management may serve to select and sponsor those candidates who, likewise, subscribe to the model and are "people like us." (Mahony & Hextall, 1997, p. 5). Mahony and Hextall are concerned that this approach to management training may lead to "structural discrimination" (p. 5), particularly in relation to race and gender bias, but also in terms of limiting the prospects for critical debate. They note, for example, that the TTA seem to have imposed limitations on the use of contemporary management theory "… which often promotes as good practice the need for creative thinking and defiance of authority" (Mahony & Hextall, 1997, p. 7).

The main thrust of the argument presented here is that the TTA initiatives constitute a political steer on the agenda of management training. This steer is reinforced by the selective use of a managerialist discourse which gains power from its capacity to represent the interests of those who have access to a particular corpus of knowledge. This is not unlike the situation described by Mills (1976) with reference to the links between vocabularies of motive and systems of action. The TTA's choice of vocabulary is such that it accords with much that is spoken of in the public domain at the present time and, in Mill's terms, may serve to integrate actions on an unquestioned basis.

The reservations expressed by Mahony and Hextall demonstrate how the advent of NPQH has prompted extensive debate about educational leadership and about how leadership skills are acquired and assessed. These issues will be returned to later in the chapter. In the next section, discussion is focused on the development of local provision for school leadership and management training.

A FLEXIBLE AND INNOVATIVE APPROACH TO SCHOOL MANAGEMENT TRAINING

The LEMP was developed as a Partnership Scheme involving LEA and the University of Central Lancashire. The purpose of the scheme was to encourage a focus on management development in primary and secondary schools based on a series of management standards originally devised by the National Foundation for Educational Research (NFER) School Management South Project (Earley, 1992). The intention was to break away from more traditional modes of management training and to place emphasis on school-based activity. Teachers are encouraged to identify key dimensions of their roles as managers in relation to *managing people, learning, resources, and policy,* and to provide evidence of their success as school leaders. Within the program, there are opportunities to obtain a series of staged awards, including a Postgraduate Certificate and Postgraduate Diploma in Educational Management with the possibility of progression to a Masters Degree in Strategic Leadership in Education. The framework of standards provides a series of learning goals and is used as a means to structure a portfolio of evidence. There is also a requirement to provide a written commentary, interpreting, and critically evaluating management tasks and the challenges of becoming a more effective manager.

The Lancashire scheme is a radical departure from earlier in-service models where taught courses might be the norm. Delivery of the program is accomplished by a core team of inspector-advisers, supported by experienced headteachers as external consultants. Mentoring and day-to-day guidance on the practical aspects of school management is provided by senior staff in schools. University tutors provide support on portfolio construction and advice on matters relating to assessment and progression. This is collaborative, off-campus work which ensures a school focus, coupled with the added bonus of networking between local groups of schools. Regular meetings are held so that teachers can check their progress and seek advice on drawing together evidence of their competence as managers and school leaders. Responsibility for the success of the scheme also rests in considerable measure upon the willingness of schools to be proactive, developing their own policy on management training, incorporating the program into their organization and promoting a sense of ownership.

Coping With the Challenges of Work-based Skills Development

Levels of success within the scheme are variable. In some schools teamwork, inspired by a committed headteacher has ensured full support for a group of candidates. This is an ideal setting for professional development providing both expert guidance and peer support. In other situations, teachers may experience some degree of isolation and are more dependent on support and encouragement from outside the school. The ideal of teamwork, though recognized by many teachers, is not easily realized given the considerable demands on schools determined by the requirements to meet national standards. Even so, adapting to these circumstances and providing leadership which facilitates the achievement of officially prescribed outcomes can be a valuable means to achieve the management standards of the scheme. In this respect, the project serves to forge links between a school's development plan and the national educational agenda.

Unfortunately, the current policy context with its managerialist tendencies also works against consideration of the academic knowledge base of management theory and research. Similarly, it is difficult to promote critical assessment of values and issues in education and to develop an awareness of the moral and ethical dimensions of leadership. Although these aspects are addressed within the Lancashire scheme, they are particularly challenging in a work-based context. To establish links between practical action and theoretical concerns is an advanced skill which does not accord readily with the pressured environment of the school manager.

Accommodating such problems is a priority for those wishing to promote continuing professional development for teachers. To meet the challenge, the Lancashire scheme has taken a long-term view providing opportunities for advancing levels of understanding on an incremental basis. Work undertaken for the Postgraduate Diploma, for example, provides a broad-based foundation for further study. Key dimensions of management activity are reviewed and reflected on as a preliminary step towards a more ambitious exploration of management processes within the masters program. At each stage it is recognized that existing models of effectiveness and school improvement may not provide a ready means to initiate change, that no two schools are likely to be the same (MacGilchrist et al., 1997), and that there is a constant need to question the validity of management-oriented variables in terms of their purchase on teachers' work (Riddell, Brown, & Duffield, 1998).

The MA in Strategic Leadership in Education is entirely school-focused with a requirement that candidates plan for and manage change in their own school. Typical examples of projects include a whole school approach to the development of numeracy skills in a secondary school, turning a primary school round in response to a critical OFSTED report, developing a school-centered approach to target-setting, and integrating the work of school governors with the day-to-day concerns of a primary school. Such projects have in common a concern to embrace whole school development issues, to link ideas about school improvement to other research and theoretical inquiry. They also take account of the values and ethics which underpin management activity.

Teachers' Responses to the Management of Change

A series of interviews with MA candidates revealed the way in which understanding of the management of change had been informed by the work undertaken for their projects. The following list identifies some of the key points discussed.

- Teachers on the scheme were attracted to the program because of its practical orientation and the way it presented an opportunity to bring about change in the school.

- Leadership and control of key activities in school presented a dilemma in terms of allowing others to take the initiative, especially when reservations were held concerning the likely success of what was being proposed. One deputy headteacher, for example, determined to let other teachers "try something out" even though she had doubts about the prospects of success. In another school difficulties were encountered in gaining commitment and sustained interest from staff in relation to delivering the change strategy.

- Where other teachers (colleagues) were involved in Inservice Education for Teachers (INSET) work supporting the project, their preference was for practical, classroom-focused activity. This was explained by one candidate as being a consequence of the current climate in which teachers considered themselves accountable for results.

- Changing cultures can be a challenge and not all teachers will be supportive of change. One noticeable consequence of obtaining data on teaching styles, for example, was the prospect of drawing attention to limitations or weaknesses in practice, or to preferences that ran counter to the philosophy of the intended change.

- Working on school-based strategies (in relation to target-setting) helped build teachers' confidence in their own skills and to challenge the imposition of targets by others who were external to the school.

- Qualitative judgements, based on numerous interactions in the classroom and staff room, challenged the idea of a controlled and systematic approach to evaluation. As one candidate put it these informal evaluations seemed inevitable and were "based on your interpretations of what's going on."

- The boundaries of a change project were not easily determined and controlled. Strategies for change often became linked with other concerns in the school.

The change projects represented here displayed the characteristics identified by Glatter (1997) in his discussion of leadership and ambiguity. Drawing on the work of Bolman and Deal (1991), Glatter (1997) points out that leadership is about interactive relationships and "the art of managing dilemmas" (p. 189). Similarly, the teachers' accounts in this sample were concerned with implementation skills, first and foremost, though our discussions also addressed ethics and values and the development of a "wider social, analytical and professional understanding" (Glatter, 1997, p. 190).

In all instances, the projects featured strategic dimensions of school management that were clearly linked to the "education policy context" referred to earlier above. Given the nature of late 20th Century schooling in the UK, this is probably inevitable, though it would be inaccurate to claim that this work was informed exclusively by a managerialist perspective. Candidates were clearly aware of the requirements of their role as a school manager and as a facilitator of change geared to national requirements.

Equally they voiced awareness of the limitations to externally imposed measures for improving standards and frequently drew attention to the sophisticated nature of teaching and learning which defied mechanistic forms of control. Most importantly, each project provided evidence of actions, of ideas being implemented, and of endeavours to bring about strategic change. This was complemented by reflections on theoretical aspects of strategic leadership and school improvement and insights related to action research.

In the next section, attention is given to the methodological aspects of action research within the Lancashire scheme. This includes an assessment of the emergent collaborative structures, linking the contributions of participants who represent the interests of the LEA, the schools, and the university.

ACTION RESEARCH AND COLLABORATION

Lomax (1994) defines action research as "an intervention in practice to bring about improvement." This is considered to be linked to professional goals and a moral commitment to transform "routine everyday practice." Similarly, Easterby-Smith, Thorpe, and Lowe (1994) equate action research with the desire to learn about an organization through attempting to change it. Ideally, those who are most likely to be affected by the changes should be the ones actively involved in the research process. This emphasis on organizational contexts and the idea of promoting change becomes a critical determinant in relation to the character of action research projects. It shapes the kind of role that may be adopted by researchers and raises questions about the relationship between the researcher and the researched. In particular, there is a need to consider the form that collaboration of key participants may take. As Lomax points out, this is likely to be influenced by the tensions and constraints evident in the research context and will involve researchers in seeking "to relate their own value stance to that of other professionals and wider policies and practices" (Lomax, 1994, pp. 161).

In the case of the Lancashire project, the terms of collaboration were formally identified in a protocol agreement, though this was essentially concerned with delivery of a program rather than with proposals for research. Even so, the values and expectations of the participants are evident in such documentation and provided a starting point for the negotiation of subsequent working arrangements. All the participants became involved in a process of defining and re-defining roles for themselves and each other, often seeking and defending clarification in relation to institutionally-specific criteria. A key dimension of such defining activity for LEA advisers, external consultants and university tutors, involved reference to existing commitments and priorities. Each group was concerned to be involved with the project but this had to involve a realistic appraisal of what might be possible in relation to other dimensions of their job role.   The Lancashire Management Development Service (LMDS), for example, had other projects in hand associated with management development and training. They had a range of consultancy links with schools and other types of organization and had to cope with the demands of working as members of OfSTED inspection teams. University tutors were involved in a range of undergraduate and postgraduate courses, with administrative and teaching duties, and were also committed to other activities within the University, including their own research.

Johnston and Kerper (1996) report on a similar school-university project in Ohio State. They comment on the way existing hierarchies and institutional roles set limits to the form that collaboration might take. A note of realism is added by the acknowledgement that the "inherently political nature of our roles" needed to be "appreciated, critiqued, and integrated into our collaborative relations" (Johnston & Kerper, 1996, p. 21).

The collaborative structure, established for purposes of promoting management training and professional development for teachers, did provide a potential basis for a critical community in which self-monitoring and innovative team work were to the fore. The work of this group has so far focused on practical concerns, rather than terms of reference for action research, but there are noticeable parallels. Group meetings have adapted to circumstances and formulated changes in the interests of establishing a workable scheme. This has entailed seeking means to encourage teachers to participate and to accept a form of professional development that is radically different to other conventional modes of delivery. Such activity has meant, in Lomax' terms, grappling with "the intransigence of context" in order to make things work. The accommodations made are characteristic of practical action needed in the given context and constitute a latent source of data for future research.   Although some of the uncertainties identified by Johnston and Kerper (1996) were experienced by the Lancashire group, there was professional support for the process of collaboration within our respective institutions. It is also of note to record that key aspects of our official roles helped gain recognition for the project, legitimating its acceptance by staff in schools as a means to enhance professional development.

STAKEHOLDERS' RESPONSE TO THE NATIONAL AGENDA

Whatever the nature of this potential, it is also necessary to acknowledge the broader constraints which hedge in the project on virtually every side. These concern the local and regional circumstances of school administration and the way these are influenced by national policy. LMDS and University staff are also involved in Central Government training initiatives, including NPQH, and local responses to professional development needs are caught up in a super-ordinate framework of professional development requirements. Local concerns have become linked with those of other providing institutions and concern is voiced about the uncertain future of in-service education and of the system of university awards currently in place. Although an action research project may have a selective focus on the interests of a small number of schools it cannot afford to ignore the likely effects of national policy in this instance.

Contextualizing of a problem in this way is not new; it has frequently been acknowledged in the field of educational evaluation. Weiss (1986), for example, raises questions about the prospects and limitations of the stakeholder approach to evaluation, drawing attention to the distinction between research and the accommodations pursued by decision-makers. As Weiss (1986) notes, "[W]hile evidence of program effectiveness is important it probably never will be the sole determinant - or even the most powerful determinant - of political choice" (p. 193). Then, involvement of the stakeholders can serve to democratize the evaluation processes, increasing their knowledge base and the prospects of more informed engagement with future policy decisions at the national level.

The extent to which activity of this kind may lead to "critical transformation" (Carr, 1989) or even "collaborative resonance" (Cochran-Smith, 1992) may have its limitations. Sultana (1995) points to the weakness of localized projects that, by utilizing spaces "created by the predominantly political forces of the time, have grave political and strategic implications." There is the danger of taking-for-granted and leaving un-challenged the "ideological and political grounds provided by the wider institutional framework" (Sultana, 1995, p. 137). This point is taken up by Hargreaves (1995) in his assessment of collaborative work with teachers. To offset some of the perceived disadvantages it is suggested that such activity needs to be "inspected repeatedly" so that there is a sustained dialogue focused on the educational and social benefits of the program.

COLLABORATION AND THE POTENTIAL OF NETWORKING

Hargreaves equates some forms of collaboration with his idea of "contrived collegiality" (Hargreaves, 1991, 1994), whereby project members are caught up in administrative devices not of their own making "with little time or incentive to collaborate on their own initiative" (Hargreaves, 1995, p. 155). Hargreaves is also adept at describing the conditions of the postmodern organization, drawing upon Toffler's (1990) metaphor of the "moving mosaic" and his multi-dimensional view of power. In ideal terms, this may be seen as conducive to "organizational learning" (Senge, 1990) and in the context of education an opening up of the prospects for networking of teachers focused on their professional development needs and interests. Hargreaves (1995) describes such trends in the following way:

> Beyond schools themselves, there are trends in staff development towards establishing professional networks where teachers are connected by electronic mail and satellite TV and can meet in smaller, interconnected sites. These networks are neither course-based in universities or school districts nor site-based in individual schools, but incorporate, extend beyond and interconnect both of these more conventional patterns. (pp. 162)

The Lancashire scheme featured in the research under review has set up a similar networking arrangement to the one described above, though perhaps not quite as ambitious. It is served by an electronic mail conferencing system which links teachers in schools with the University and the Lancashire Management Development Service. Its prime purpose is to give teachers access to tutorial guidance and to link with other teachers in the scheme for additional support and exchange of ideas related to their school-based projects. In terms of the broader aims of action research, this particular use of technology can serve to promote critical consciousness, in relation to the nature of management issues, and political awareness of those contexts and processes that set limits to what we might, otherwise, hope to accomplish.

There is good reason to encourage collaboration and action research as a means to promote a sense of identity and moral purpose for members of the teaching force. With this in mind, Hargreaves elevates the idea of collaboration to the status of a "metaparadigm of educational and organizational change in the postmodern age," seeing it "as an articulating and integrating principle of action, planning, culture, development, organization and research." Collaboration is seen "as a productive response to a world in which problems are unpredictable, solutions are unclear, and demands and expectations are intensifying" (Hargreaves, 1995, pp. 150-151).

Collaboration is considered to embody principles such as provision of care and moral support for teachers. It can promote certainty based on collective professional wisdom in particular educational situations and communities, and an increased capacity for reflection based on feedback, evaluation and enquiry. Hargreaves also outlines the principle of political assertiveness which is particularly apt in relation to current developments in educational management.

> Collaboration, in its strongest forms, enables teachers to interact more confidently and assertively with their surrounding systems and with the multiplicity of reasonable and unreasonable innovations and reforms that come to them. It strengthens the confidence to adopt externally introduced innovations, the wisdom to delay them and the moral fortitude to resist them, where appropriate. (Hargreaves, 1995, pp. 153)

There is also a particular methodological advantage of collaboration which involves stakeholders who have differing roles and commitments outside the school, as in the case of the Lancashire project. Unlike teacher collaboration in the school context this provides a broader framework and range of perspectives for purposes of validation and critical debate. Such arrangements have the potential to strike a balance in relation to insider and outsider views of management activities, providing in Hammersley's terms a "judicious combination of involvement and estrangement" (Hammersley, 1993, p. 219). There is an important strategic dimension to action research in the management field which requires all participants to be conversant with current political reforms and initiatives. It is increasingly the case that central policy-makers exert their influence over the management of schools and over the professional development of teachers. In these circumstances, there is a need to sustain as clear a vision as possible of the relationship between "inside" and "outside" activity. Given the increased complexity and rapidity of educational change in the new Millennium, a holistic approach based on informed collaboration would seem essential.

The challenges this presents are clearly identified by Johnston and Kerper

(1996) when they acknowledge the interdependency of parity and power in collaborative ventures. They suggest that rather than give up power it is preferable to recognize "the personal and political character of the self and of relationships" and to work towards putting such power to good use.

> There are many personal and public agendas in a collaborative project, and at times certain capabilities are more important for some goals than for others ... Parity, from our present perspective, is not always about being the same, that is, having the same power, status or influence. Our differences must constantly be negotiated as we learn to trust in these variations and appreciate their separate and uneven contribution to the ongoing conversation and "untidiness" of collaborative work. Parity is now a more complex concept that stretches our imaginations and personal relationships. (Johnston & Kerper, 1996, p. 8)

Such arguments are instructive in relation to forming expectations about collaborative work in action research. They suggest that such projects need to examine very carefully existing arrangements for co-operation and to see these as the basis for further development. The distinction between research and everyday practical action may be rarely clear-cut. The intention in the Lancashire scheme is to build on the potential energy of a collaborative group that is already in place. It has institutional support and a clear purpose already formulated and operational. Plans for action research need to be articulated in such a way that they complement and enhance existing arrangements, raising the general level of impact, strengthening existing allegiances with schools, and making more widely known the potential benefits of the work of the group.

THE FUTURE PROFESSIONAL DEVELOPMENT NEEDS OF TEACHERS AS SCHOOL LEADERS

The above review of a local initiative has taken account of the national scene and the way this may condition what happens in schools. The remainder of this chapter broadens out the discussion to consider the future prospects for professional development in relation to changes in the school system and in approaches to school management in particular.

In the very near future, teachers will be subject to pull and push factors in a changing mosaic of professional demands, many of which have already been charted in some detail, for example, by Hargreaves (1994) and Dalin and Rust

(1996). The multi-dimensional character of schooling will present major challenges for governments intent on controlling the "outputs" of the system while at the same time, making allowance for such changes. There will be a greater need than ever before to safeguard the professional autonomy of teachers and, in particular, to develop more sophisticated modes of professional development and school leadership. It may be necessary to further intellectualize our understanding of teaching and learning "variables," to question more rigorously what it takes to manage a school effectively and challenge some of those taken-for-granted assumptions which abound in managerialist jargon. This would include, for example, addressing the basic mismatch between proposals made for improving schools, by those in key positions in the public domain, and the increasingly sophisticated analysis of school improvement and effectiveness provided by leading researchers (Gray et al., 1996; Slee, Weiner, & Tomlinson, 1998; Stoll & Myers, 1998).

Whatever the outcomes of these debates, teachers will need to have the ability to respond quickly to feedback and to take into account new data; on this basis, the key skills will be those of "implementation management" and "coping behaviour" (Louis & Miles, 1991).   Such descriptors which attempt to summarize the dynamic and responsive aspects of school management are likely to be increasingly to the fore (see, also, for example, Blase & Anderson, 1995; Hargreaves, 1997; Fidler, 1997). They signal the need for qualitative judgements that are situation-specific. They are needed both to inform the focus of professional development and, more importantly, to enable teachers to aspire beyond the mere functional prescriptions of state control.   In the management field, these changes have already been anticipated by a number of authors (Bhindi & Duignan, 1997; Caldwell, 1997; Davies, 1997; Diggins, 1997; Fullan, 1993; Handy & Aitken, 1986; Hargreaves, 1994).

Changing Conceptions of Leadership

Bhindi and Duignan suggest that there is "disquiet about excessive managerialism" and outline alternative approaches in which leadership as stewardship becomes something that has to be earned. It is observed that there is "a major paradigm shift" occurring in which organizations will be more inclined to place relationships, values, and ethics at the center of their affairs. The following extract makes clear what the authors have in mind.

Leaders earn their allegiance through authentic actions and interactions in trusting relationships, and through the shaping of organizational structures, processes and practices that enshrine authentic values and standards. Such leaders help nurture, inspire and empower others. They encourage sharing and partnership based on the recognition of mutuality and interdependence in relationships. (Bhindi & Duignan, 1997, p. 119)

Other authors, too, are challenging existing conceptions of leadership (and, by implication, "headship") and are pressing for a radical change in focus in terms of educational processes, including the changing of "mind sets," the establishment of schools as learning organizations and the re-conceptualization of leadership. West-Burnham (1997), somewhat in accord with Bhindi and Duignan (1997), proposes some alternative key concepts for leadership as follows: intellectualism; artistry; spirituality; moral confidence; subsidiarity; and emotional intelligence.

In discussing the nature of subsidiarity, for example, West-Burnham (1997) challenges the capacity of headship founded on notions of hierarchy and delegation to be able to cope with rapid change; a culture of subsidiarity, on the other hand, is based on trust and the *surrender of power,* such that the central idea becomes "not to manage but rather to enable, facilitate, interpret, create meaning and to develop trust" (West-Burnham, 1997, p. 242).

Dimmock (2000) further extends these ideas by adopting Boisot's (1995) typology of strategic leadership (following Caldwell, 1998a, 1998b), distinguishing between, for example, "strategic planning," which is effective in "more predictable environments" and "strategic intent" as the means to cope with a greater degree of turbulence. Strategic intent operates on the basis of "direct, intuitive understanding of what is occuring" and enables schools "to make timely and effective reponses to changing conditions" (Dimmock, 2000, p. 262).

As far as the management of schools is concerned, such observations as these suggest that radical measures may be needed in order to anticipate and keep pace with change. A more determined focus on those principles which encourage professional growth and autonomy for all teachers would seem desirable, coupled with a more serious concern for an inquiry-oriented approach to what constitutes effective leadership.

The arguments put forward by Blase and Anderson (1995) concerning the limitations to facilitative leadership in schools give some indication of the challenges ahead. Following Starratt (1991), they suggest that the ethic of critique is not only concerned with critiquing technicist approaches to teaching, learning, and assessment, but also issues concerning equality, the common good, and human civil rights. Implementation of national standards, such as those ordained by NPQH, for example, are unlikely to promote such critique and may leave untouched the bureaucratic institutions candidates work in. The prospects for change will be locked out.

An exclusively prescribed national model is probably the wrong model for the 21st Century for, as Blase and Anderson put it, "[I]nstitutions that silence the voices of teachers and students are deprived of the input they need to be effective" (Blase & Anderson, 1995, p. 146).

More importantly, a focus on management training for aspiring headteachers of the kind offered by NPQH will do little to democratize the workplace for all teachers. A greater emphasis on the management development needs of a broader range of candidates would seem better suited to the nature of schools as they currently exist, let alone the form they may take in the near future.

School Leaders Responding to Change

The action research outlined in this chapter demonstrates how leadership skills may be developed in context, without abandoning the intellectual challenges presented by theory and research. The collaborative approach also indicates how expertise can be usefully brought together in a way that sustains dialogue about effective leadership and strategic change. Above all the spirit and purpose of such an approach sustains control at the local level and equates professional development with personal interests and commitment.

Barnett's (1997) reference to meta-abilities and processes of professional reconstruction is relevant in this context. What is needed "… are generic human capacities, capable of handling and deploying knowledge in pressing pragmatic situations" (Barnett, 1997, p. 35). For teachers, advisers and university tutors alike, these are major challenges in a venture such as the Lancashire Educational Management Program, located, as it is, within a changing school system and in circumstances where there is increased government intervention and control of professional development. The circumstances described here are precisely those referred to by Riley and MacBeath (1998) in their challenging review of the relationship between school leadership and effective schools. They describe the way in which school leaders have to respond to the inner life of the school as well as the demands of external constituencies. This model of leadership is described in the following terms.

> It acknowledges that school leaders have to manage contested notions about achievement and cope with multiple interests and demands. It rests on uncertainty, as well as certainty, and is rooted in a deep understanding of context – national, local and school-based. It is because of this complexity that no single recipe will work. (Riley & MacBeath, 1998, p. 148)

There is no doubt that collaborating institutions will need to assess the market situation in relation to the provision of continuing professional development for teachers and take account of the national agenda in order to establish the best way to serve the needs of teachers in schools. There is also a pressing need for dialogue and negotiation in order to ensure a dynamic response and a means to give teachers as leaders continuing access to the meta-discourse of educational change. In the words of MacGilchrist et al. (1997), it is a matter of helping schools to be "intelligent" organizations whose core characteristics include high quality leadership and management, informed by a commitment to change for the benefit of their pupils.

RECOMMENDATIONS AND CONCLUSION

The following recommendations are proposed as a means to inform policy on the future professional development of teachers in the field of school management and leadership. They have been formulated on the basis of the above discussion and experience of co-ordinating local provision for teachers in the North West of England. It is proposed that such schemes should aim to,

- Take into account the nature of knowledge and capability relevant to the professional development of school leaders. This includes identifying and mapping skills and types of evidence that are in accord with the developmental needs of schools.

- Promote the intellectual capability of school leaders, especially in relation to their understanding of leadership skills, contexts, and processes. This could include the leadership dimensions identified by Dimmock (2000), including educational, technological, structural, moral, cultural, human resources, political, strategic, and transformational.

- Take account of the social mix of a school and its influence on approaches to school improvement. This would include the significance of social class in relation to educational attainment (Gibson & Asthana, 1998; Riddell et al., 1998). There is, for example, a rich tradition in ethnographic research concerned with subcultural variations in response to schooling (see the review by Woods, 1990). This approach would be in accord with Lauder et al.'s proposals (1998) concerning contextual models of effective schools.

- Recognize and adapt to sector-specific differences in schools and tailor professional development in a way that gives recognition to the developmental phases of schools and their capacity to encompass self-management or more radical forms of re-structuring (Caldwell, 1997; Dalin, 1993; Leithwood et al., 1994).

- Develop an informed approach to school leadership and school improvement. This could follow the recommendations of Dimmock (2000) and include reference to the research literature on school effectiveness, effective teaching and learning, and features of organizational cultures.

- Encourage teachers to undertake action research projects in their own schools in order to bring about change focused on school-centered priorities. This has the advantage of ensuring engagement with colleagues and is an opportunity to rehearse leadership skills and to disseminate elements of informed practice to other staff in the school. Ideally, this should be developed within partnerships, involving school leaders, universities, and local education authorities. On this basis, action research would serve to link theory and practice and forge an alliance between leadership training and school improvement.

- Challenge the capacity of management theories to inform practice and to be an exact science (Bolam, 1997). This involves exploring and contesting the relationship between pure and applied knowledge as a means to establish what might constitute exemplary professional activity.

It is important to acknowledge that in the context of the United Kingdom, the strength of these recommendations needs to be assessed in relation to the policy context alluded to at the beginning of this chapter. Making progress in these terms may not be simply a matter of relying on good will and professional integrity. Some formal recognition of a federal component to professional development may be needed, linking schools, LEAs, higher education institutions and other partners within a constitutional framework. The DfEE consultation paper on professional development in support of teaching and learning (DfEE, 2000) provides some grounds for being optimistic about future partnerships. This consultation paper includes reference to the Lancashire LEA Accreditation Ladder, of which the scheme described in this chapter forms a major part, as a model of good practice. Within this policy context, frameworks are closely associated with proposals for performance management in schools, but it is clear that this will also involve considerable support for professional development as outlined in the extract below.

> Lancashire offers a competence-based accreditation ladder to its aspiring school managers that tracks a teacher's progression into management responsibilities. The program identifies professional development targets within the context of the wider needs of the school and the teacher's current role and responsibilities. The process deliberately introduces a wide range of learning opportunities that includes job enrichment as a part of the needs identification process. (DfEE, 2000, section 19, p. 8)

The paper also makes reference to the work of Hay McBer on models of effective teaching, including Advanced Skills Teachers and headteachers. This is envisaged as providing elements of a framework for teacher development that is likely to be sustained by building on the best tradition of partnerships between schools, universities, and local education authorities (DfEE, 2000, section 47, p. 16).

Such proposals, though welcome, are likely to present challenges in terms of partnership responses to the official agenda. These represent changing terms of reference with higher education institutions, for example, needing to relinquish some of their defining power and interest in order to take on board new and dynamic conceptions of school leadership. In particular, the grounds and criteria for making judgements about professional competence or capability may have to be substantially transformed in order for such partnerships to be effective. This would be essential in order to provide the flexibility required for professional learning as a lifelong process for, in Eraut's (1994) terms the framework would need to be "coherent and continuous, quite independently of any qualification acquired en route" (Eraut, 1994, p. 218).

Such responsiveness would also include taking account of changing definitions of roles, responsibilities, and competence.

In addition to the development of national frameworks based on consultation and agreed standards, there is a need for policy-makers to work in harmony with existing providers, giving support to local initiatives. The system should be sufficiently open to allow school leaders to be pro-active as managers. It would also be beneficial to consider means to sustain teacher education and professional development in the context of collaborative networks, forming alliances with schools, local authorities, universities and other stakeholders. These networks could function at local and regional levels serving to co-ordinate professional development for school leadership within an agreed constitutional framework of standards and progression opportunities. It is also distinctly possible that such developments would complement schools' involvement in initial teacher training, including its school-based variants, especially in relation to the management and leadership requirements of this provision.

An important dimension of this activity would involve those in senior leadership positions in schools creating opportunities for all staff to develop their leadership skills. The aim would be to establish an ethos and culture in the school that is supportive of continuing professional development fully integrated with the management of change and school improvement initiatives.

Taylor (1997) considers partnership approaches to professional development and the role of educators as facilitators. It is pointed out that this will signify a key role for the users of professional services and will involve "a collaborative or user-led vision ... where power is shifted from professionals to communities" (Taylor, 1997, p. 173). The changes likely to be expected of teachers, including headteachers, will require proactive innovation in equal measure from those responsible for co-ordinating professional development. Future planning will need to anticipate some of those more advanced conceptions of leadership reviewed above in order to ensure an authentic and effective response.

REFERENCES

Ball, S. (1994). *Education Reform: A critical and post-structural approach.* Buckingham, Philadelphia: Open University Press.

Barnett, R. (1997). *The limits of competence: Knowledge, higher education and society.* Buckingham: SRHE/Open University Press.

Bhindi, N., & Duignan, P. (1997). Leadership for a new century: Authenticity, intentionally, spirituality and sensibility. *Educational Management and Administration, 25*(2), 117-132.

Blase, J., & Anderson, G. (1995). *The micropolitics of educational leadership.* London: Cassell.

Boisot, M. (1995). Preparing for turbulence: The changing relationship between strategy and management development in the learning organization. In B. Garrat, (Ed.), *Developing Strategic Thought: Rediscovering the Art of Direction-Giving.* London: McGraw-Hill.

Bolam, R. (1997). Management development for headteachers: Retrospect and prospect. *Educational Management and Administration, 25*(3), 265-283.

Bolman, L., & Deal, T. (1991). *Reframing organizations: Artistry, choice and leadership.* San Francisco: Jossey-Bass.

Bottery, M. (1994). Management codes. *Educational Studies, 20*(3), 329-343.

Bush, T. (1996). School autonomy and school improvement. In J. Gray et al. (Eds.), *Merging traditions: The future of research on school effectiveness and school improvement.* London: Cassell.

Caldwell, B. (1997). A gestalt for the reengineering of school education for the knowledge society. *School Leadership and Management, 17*(2), 201-215.

Caldwell, B. (1998a). *Beyond the self-managing school.* London: Falmer Press.

Caldwell, B. (1998b). *Leadership in the creation of world class schools: Beyond the self-managing school.* Paper presented at the Leadership for Quality Schooling Conference, Hong Kong.

Carr, W. (1989). Action research: Ten years on. *Journal of Curriculum Studies, 21*(1), 85-90.

Cochran-Smith, M. (1992). Learning to teach against the grain. *Harvard Educational Review, 61*(3), 279-310.

Dalin, P. (1993). *Changing the school culture.* London: Falmer Press.

Dalin, P., & Rust, V. (1996). *Towards schooling for the twenty-first century.* Lewes: Falmer Press.

Davies, B. (1997). Reengineering the political/educational system. *School Leadership and Management, 17*(2), 173-185.

Davies, L. (1990). *Equity and efficiency? School management in an international context.* Lewes: Falmer Press.

DfEE. (2000). *Professional development: support for teaching and learning* (Ref: DfEE 0008/2000). UK: Author.

Diggins P. (1997). Reflections on leadership characteristics necessary to develop and sustain learning school communities. *School Leadership and Management, 17*(3), 413-425.

Dimmock, C. (2000). *Designing the learning-centered school: A cross-cultural perspective.* London; New York: Falmer Press.

Earley, P. (1992). *The school management competencies project.* Crawley School: Management South.

Eraut, M. (1994). *Developing professional knowledge and competence.* London; New York: Falmer Press.

Easterby-Smith, M., Thorpe, R., & Lowe, A. (1994). The Philosophy of research design. In N. Bennett, R. Glatter, & R. Levacic (Eds.), *Improving educational management through research and consultancy.* London: Paul Chapman/Open University Press.

Fidler, B. (1997). School leadership: Some key ideas. *School Leadership and Management, 17*(1), 23-37.

Fullan, M. (1993). *Change forces: Probing the depths of educational reform.* London: Falmer Press.

Gewirtz, S. (1997). Post-welfarism and the reconstruction of teachers' work in the UK. *Journal of Education Policy, 12*(4), 217-231.

Gibson, A., & Asthana, S. (1998). School performance, school effectiveness and the 1997 white paper. *Oxford Review of Education, 24*(2), 195-210.

Glatter, R. (1997). Context and capability in educational management. *Educational Management and Administration, 25*(2), 181-192.

Grace, G. (1995). *School leadership: Beyond education management.* Lewes: Falmer Press.

Gray, J. et al. (1996). *Merging traditions: The future of research on school effectiveness and school improvement.* London: Cassell.

Gray, J., Hopkins, D., Reynolds, D., Wilcox, B., Farrell, S., & Jesson, D. (1999). *Improving schools: Performance and potential.* Buckingham: Open University Press.

Hammersley, M. (1993). On the teacher as researcher. In M. Hammersley (Ed.), *Educational research: Current issues.* London: Paul Chapman/Open University Press.

Handy, C., & Aitken, R. (1986). *Understanding schools as organizations.* London: Penguin Books.

Hargreaves, A. (1991). A contrived collegiality: The micro-politics of teacher collaboration. In J. Blase (Ed.), *The politics of life in schools.* Thousand Oaks, California: Sage.

Hargreaves, A. (1994). *Changing teachers, changing times: Teachers' work and culture in the postmodern age.* Lewes: Falmer Press.

Hargreaves, A. (1995). Beyond collaboration: Critical teacher development in the postmodern age. In J. Smyth (Ed.), *Critical discourses on teacher development.* London: Cassell.

Hargreaves, D. H. (1997). A road to the learning society. *School Leadership and Management, 17*(1), 9-21.

Hopkins, D. (1996). Towards a theory for school improvement. In J. Gray et al. (Eds.),

Merging traditions: The future of research on school effectiveness and school improvement. London: Cassell.

Hopkins, D., Ainscow, M., & West, M. (1994). *School improvement in an era of change.* London: Cassell.

Hyland. (1994). *Competence, education and NVQ's: Dissenting perspectives.* London: Cassell.

Inglis, F. (1989). Managerialism and morality: The corporate and the republic school. In Carr, W. (ed.), *Quality in teaching: Arguments for a reflective profession.* Lewes: Falmer Press.

Johnston, M., & Kerper, R. (1996). Positioning ourselves: Parity and power in collaborative work. *Curriculum Inquiry, 26*(1), 5-24.

Lauder, H., Jamieson, I., & Wikeley, F. (1998). Models of effective schools: Limits and capabilities. In R. Slee & G. Weiner (Eds.), *School effectiveness for whom? Challenges to the school effectiveness and school improvement movements.* London; New York: Falmer Press.

Leithwood, K., Begley, P., & Cousins, J. (1994). *Developing expert leadership for future schools.* London: Falmer Press.

Lomax, P. (1994). Action research for managing change. In N. Bennett, R. Glatter & R. Levacic (Eds.), *Improving educational management through research and consultancy.* London: Paul Chapman/Open University Press.

Louis, K., & Miles, M. (1991). Managing reform: Lessons for urban high schools. *School Effectiveness and School Improvement, 2*(2), 75-96.

MacGilchrist, B., Myers, K., & Reed, J. (1997). *The intelligent school.* London: Paul Chapman.

Mahony, P., Hextall, I. (1997, September). *Social justice and the reconstruction of teaching.* Paper presented at the British Educational Research Association (BERA) Conference.

Mills, C. W. (1976). Situated actions and vocabularies of motive. In B. Cosin et al. (Eds.), *School and Society.* London: Routledge/Kegan Paul.

Osterman, K., & Kottkamp, R. (1994). Rethinking professional development. In N. Bennett, R. Glatter & R. Levacic (Eds.), *Improving educational management through research and consultancy.* London: Paul Chapman/Open University Press.

Ribbins, P., & Burridge, E. (1994). *Improving education: Promoting quality in schools.* London: Cassell.

Riddell, S., Brown, S., & Duffield, J. (1998). The utility of qualitative research for influencing policy and practice on school effectiveness. In R. Slee et al. (Eds.), *School effectiveness for whom? Challenges to the school effectiveness and school improvement movements.* London: Falmer Press.

Riley, K., & MacBeath, J. (1998). Effective leaders and effective schools. In J. Macbeath (Ed.), *Effective school leadership: Responding to change.* London: Paul Chapman.

Sammons, P., Hillman, J., & Mortimore, P. (1994). *Key characteristics of effective schools: A review of school effectiveness research.* London: Office for Standards in Education.

Senge, P. (1990). *The fifth discipline.* New York: Doubleday.

Simmons, J., Konecki, L., Crowell, R., & Gates-Duffield, P. (1999). Dream keepers, weavers, and shape-shifters: emerging roles of pds university coordinators in educational reform. In D. Byrd & D. McIntyre (Eds.), *Research on professional development schools. Teacher Education Yearbook VII.* Thousands Oaks, California: Corwin Press.

Slee, R., Weiner, G., & Tomlinson, S. (1998). *School effectiveness for whom? Challenges to the school effectiveness and school improvement movement.* London: Falmer Press.

Starratt, R. (1991). Building an ethical school: A theory for practice in educational leadership. *Educational Administration Quarterly, 27*(2), 185-202.

Stoll, L. (1996). Linking school effectiveness and school improvement: issues and possibilities. In J. Gray et al. (Eds.), *Merging traditions: The future of research on school effectiveness and school improvement.* London: Falmer Press.

Stoll, L., & Myers, K. (1998). *No quick fixes: Perspectives on schools in difficulty.* London: Falmer Press.

Sultana, R. (1995). From critical education to a critical practice of teaching. In J. Smyth (Ed.), *Critical discourses on teacher development.* London: Cassell.

Taylor, I. (1997). *Developing learning in professional education.* Buckingham: SRHE/Open University Press.

Teacher Training Agency (TTA). (1998). National Standards for Headteachers. London: Author.

Thrupp, M. (1999). *Schools making a difference: Let's be realistic.* Buckingham: Open University Press.

Toffler, A. (1990). *Powershift.* London: Bantam Books.

Weiss, C. (1986). Toward the future of stakeholder. Approaches in evaluation. In House, E. (Ed.). *New directions in educational evaluation.* Lewes: Falmer Press.

West-Burnham, J. (1997). Leadership for Learning – reengineering "mind sets". *School Leadership and Management, 17*(2), 231-244.

Whitty, G. (1999). *Teacher professionalism in new times.* Paper presented at the Annual Conference of the Standing Committee for the Education and Training of Teachers (SCETT), Teacher Professionalism and the State in the 21st Century, Dunchurch, Rugby.

Woods, P. (1990). *The happiest days? How pupils cope with school.* London; NewYork: Falmer Press.

Woods, P., & Jeffrey, R. (1996). A new professional discourse? Adjusting to managerialism. In P. Woods (Ed.), *Contemporary issues in teaching and learning.* London: Routledge/Open University Press.

Chapter 18

Educator Attachment for Professional Development: A Hong Kong Experience

Angela Hing Man MOK-CHEUNG and Alice Wai Kwan CHOW

School of Languages in Education
The Hong Kong Institute of Education, Hong Kong

The education system in Hong Kong has been under intense and comprehensive review since the hand-over of sovereignty from Britain to the People's Republic of China in 1997. Reforms of a massive scale at all levels of schooling have been proposed, and are currently being debated (Education Commission, 1999a). The aims of the reforms are to prepare pupils to deal with the challenges of a rapidly expanding and changing knowledge base (Education Commission, 1999b; Tung, 1999; Wong, 2000). Sizeable consultation documents have been published exploring different aspects of education reforms, such as on the quality of education and information technology in education (Education and Manpower Bureau, 1998) and the school curriculum (Curriculum Development Council, 1999). The notion of lifelong learning is extensively advocated to enable pupils to develop the orientation and an ever-improving capability to meet with such challenges. This concept of continuing knowledge upgrading and skills revitalization is especially essential to invigorating the education faculty of higher education institutions (HEI), whose members have always been regarded as theorists operating in "ivory towers" (Warshaw, 1986) or "crystal palace" (Russell, 1992).

In many other countries, one of the central arguments upon which the broad education reform agenda is based is that school reform is dependent on the reform of teacher preparation (Knowles & Coles, 1998). Teacher education should therefore be redesigned to strengthen its knowledge base and its connection to both practice and theory (Goodlad, 1990; Zeichner, 1993). Knowles & Cole (1998) argue that teacher education professors should situate themselves at the heart of the teacher education reform agendas. The following quote from the Holmes group report (1995) best illustrates such a position:

The education school should cease to act as a silent agent in the preservation of the status quo .... Those who prepare teachers ... continue to dwell in a bygone era, using outmoded conceptions of professional work to guide their preparation. (p. 8)

Teacher educators are always criticized as being remote from practice (Darling-Hammond, 1999). Oftentimes, they are repeatedly asked the same questions. "When did you last teach in a school?", "Have you taught in a ghetto school?", "How much do you know about the adolescent culture of the 1990s?" While such questions may appear superficial to those who maintain that the detached and contemplative environment of teacher education institution is conducive to improving the quality of teacher education, the criticism, in some cases, is clearly justified (Hansgen, 1983). Indeed, it is rare to find education professors returning to an elementary or secondary classroom to teach a number of lessons for a semester or two in order to keep abreast of the current conditions in schools. Hansgen (1983) attributes this phenomenon to increasing institutional demands on teacher educators, the reality of "publish or perish" (Russell & Korthagen, 1995), and a lack of recognition given for such kind of work by the teacher education institutions.

To address the above criticism, various attempts have been undertaken in the past years albeit taking place slowly. To help education professors to strengthen and validate their professional knowledge base, renew their skills and reinstate their credibility with professionals and beginning teachers, back-to-school schemes have been taking shape in various forms over the years. Some were held in the mode of institute-school staff development collaborative projects, and others through legislative mandate (Corbitt, 1993; Hansgen, 1983; Hudson-Ross & McWhorter, 1995; Stahl, 1987). For instance, the California state legislation passed an education reform bill that requires all professors who teach methods courses to return to the elementary or secondary classroom once every three years (Warshaw, 1986).

Stahl (1987) proposed mandating a "Back to the Trenches" scheme with the purposes of giving teacher educators first-hand observation of the changes in the demographics and abilities of the student population, the everyday activities and current attitudes of the teaching force, and the school environment as a whole. Through such a scheme, teacher educators are provided with an opportunity to develop practical insights into new pedagogical theories, to field test curricular projects, and to conduct applied research.

Job exchange projects such as "A Clinical Professorship" program tried out at Denison University (Hansgen, 1983), the "Synergy Project" (Hudson-Ross & McWhorter, 1995), and "Professor-In-Residence" program (Simpson, 1997) enable both education professors and school teachers to benefit from a fresh perspective and a dose of reality to each through mutual sharing of ideas and experiences. Moving each day from teacher education institution to school and back, participating teacher educators become more keenly aware of the differences in the two cultural settings, which have quite different characteristics and basic values (Russell, 1992). Teacher education programs are subsequently enriched and made more relevant for education students in light of the "reality checks" that participating education faculty members conduct in the "field."

Amidst the changes in teacher education world wide, The Hong Kong Institute of Education (HKIEd), a newly established teacher education institution which started its operation in 1995, has been initiating innovations to enhance the professional development of its academic staff. The Lecturer Attachment Scheme (LAS) is one of the innovations introduced in 1997 aiming to develop continual professional growth in the lecturers and a more genuine institute-school staff collaboration in improving teaching and learning within schools at the same time. As mentioned in the beginning of this section, Hong Kong is undergoing massive educational overhaul, and teachers are one of the key players contributing to the success of education reforms. Teacher educators are thus faced with the new challenges of assisting and supporting school teachers to understand and actuate the reforms. LAS is one approach to develop school-based collaborative learning, both for the educator and the teacher. Through LAS, on the one hand, the HKIEd teacher educators can verify their theoretical knowledge and renew their practical teaching skills in context, while school teachers can update their knowledge and reflect upon their practice. This kind of school-based learning for both parties is achievable and beneficial (Goodlad, 1993; Hunkins, Wiseman, & Williams, 1995), and is viewed as a worthwhile practice for staff development.

As faculty members of the HKIEd's English Department, we had participated in LAS. This chapter shall report our back-to-school teaching experience, and discuss the implications of this scheme for site-based continuing teacher education. We believe that the chapter contributes significantly to the literature on the professional development of teacher educators that is scant and meager (Knowles & Cole, 1998; Webber, 1990). We also attempt to further discuss and outline the place of LAS in supporting curriculum change and teacher development.

BACKGROUND

The academic staff of HKIED is composed teacher educators transferred from the former Colleges of Education and new recruits from all over the world with a wide range of experience and expertise. Some are expert teacher educators with an international background and perspective, but lacking in local teaching experience. There are staff members who have either primary or secondary teaching experience but would be required to teach the programs of the other level in which they have no teaching experience. Thus, it seems to be beneficial to all concerned to provide an avenue for the lecturing staff to get into the local schools, to gain first-hand teaching experience in local settings as part of an institute-initiated staff development program. LAS was thus formulated and introduced in 1997 and started its operation in February 1998.

Launched for three years now, LAS has since then been an on-going initiative to provide opportunities for HKIEd academic staff to update their school teaching experience in the local context. Moreover, through this scheme, it is anticipated that the Institute will build up collaborative relationships with schools for developing school-based staff development activities and research.

LAS has been presented as a three-stage activity within the Institute. Before the attachment to chosen primary schools, seminars are arranged on a range of relevant topics such as "the Hong Kong primary school context," "the primary school curriculum in Hong Kong," and "conducting research in classrooms and primary schools." Experienced local primary teachers and principals are invited to participate in the seminars. The attachment lasts for a period of two weeks within the academic year in local primary schools, with participating lecturers teaching the subjects of their choice. Besides teaching, during the attachment period, the lecturers may initiate any activities that enhance the professional development of both the lecturers and the school teachers. They also can explore possible opportunities for future staff development and research collaborations.

After the attachment period, lecturers are required to submit a brief report on their observations and reflection. Post-LAS seminars are organized for lecturers to share their experiences, through which it is hoped that other colleagues will gain insights from their peers' experience.

Anderson and Cheung (1999) reported the effectiveness of this scheme, focusing on two areas: in updating the lecturers' teaching experience in the primary school; and in creating new opportunities for establishing productive collaborative relationships with schools in areas like staff development and research. The evaluation was based on the school attachment reports submitted by a total of 73 teaching staff (from 12 departments) who were attached to 39 primary schools. Major findings include significant personal satisfaction from the attachment. They contend that the level of satisfaction was associated with the development of new perspectives of putting theories into practices and the updating of professional experience. Other findings comprise personal gains in teaching skills and the opportunities for intensive staff development activities in schools. The latter refers to lecturers conducting site-based staff development programs tailored to meet the needs of the schools, such as lesson observation with follow-up discussion, and specific forums on topics of subject teaching. There were drawbacks of this Scheme, one of which, for example, is that the attachment period only lasts for two weeks and time is a great constraint. The lecturer has to get into a new culture of operation and at the same time, meeting the expectation and other demands of the teachers in the attached school.

Like many of our colleagues in the Institute, we found it beneficial to enroll in LAS and enrich ourselves with the experience. What follows is our account: we will first present our attachment experience with critical reflection, and then discuss the implications for in-service teacher education.

THE PRIMARY SCHOOL ATTACHMENT

Since the implementation of LAS in 1997, the Institute's lecturers, especially those who are experienced in secondary teaching, like ourselves, are very much aware of the need to join such a scheme for a couple of obvious reasons. On the one hand, it enables us to be qualified for teaching the newly accredited B.Ed. Primary program which requires all its program lecturing staff to have local primary teaching experience. On the other hand, as educators, we strive for a wide range of teaching experiences, both local and recent, in order to broaden our knowledge base, revitalize our skills, and inform our practices. All these in turn will help improve the content and delivery of our teacher preparation curriculum.

In addition to our personal professional development, we would also like to forge a longer-term partnership with the attachment school for future projects which may be mutually beneficial. To capitalize on this Attachment Scheme as a good opportunity for initiating a collaborative project with a suitable school, we opted to approach a particular primary school rather than letting the Institute make the necessary placement arrangement. The reasons were quite apparent. We would like to be able to work with a school that would grant us autonomy in selecting our teaching approach and developing relevant curriculum materials, and we anticipated follow-up collaboration with the school. With the above purposes in mind, we embarked on our attachment.

Gaining Access

A school matching our criteria was identified to be our LAS school. The principal of the school was fairly new to her school and she was starting her second year of service there. She was keen on establishing a strong link with the Institute which is the only teacher education institute in Hong Kong and is reputable for its primary teacher education. She also saw it as an avenue for staff development for the English Panel of her school. To us, this school was a desirable choice. One the one hand, we could get the full support from the principal. On the other, we would be granted the opportunity to assist the school in meeting part of its staff development agenda, especially for its English panel. We also hoped that such kind of relationship could be extended into a collaborative project.

Details of the attachment arrangement were agreed upon in the beginning of the academic year of 1998/99. Numerous phone contacts were made between the lecturer co-ordinator and the school principal. The English Panel teachers were consulted and they agreed to participate in it. We visited the school for the first time during the latter part of their first term and had an informal meeting with the principal, the vice-principal, the English subject panel chairperson, a senior teacher who was in charge of the reading scheme, and two teachers who agreed to work with the lecturers. We elaborated on the aims of our attachment and underscored the possibilities of longer term partnership in staff development activities such as providing workshops for their English teachers regarding the current English Language teaching (ELT) approach adopted in the newly launched English syllabus. We indicated our intention of learning more about primary level teaching and trying out what we believed to be "good" teaching. The teachers expressed strong confidence in our ability to practice and demonstrate effective and exemplary instructional skills and strategies in our teaching that they requested video-taping all our lessons. We agreed to their request but reiterated that our taped lessons might be examples of what-not-to-do in class.

In order to enhance understanding, discussion, and the exchange of ideas, we invited the two teachers whose classes we would take up to come and sit in our lessons as much as they could and the other English teachers were also invited to come and observe our lessons. We reckoned that such arrangements would inform the teachers of our practice and, as a result, it would bring about dialogues and the exchange of ideas.

Preparation

One of the outcomes of the meeting was that we scheduled to observe two lessons conducted by the two English teachers who agreed to work with us in LAS. The main reason for the lesson observation was that we wanted to know the pupils' standard and the patterns of communication between the English teachers and the pupils. We identified a day convenient to us all, and we sat in a P.3 and a P.5 class, the classes we were to take over from the teachers.

The two teachers impressed us as very experienced, and both lessons went very smoothly. One major difference was that the P.5 teacher Lilian used English as the only medium of instruction whereas the P.3 teacher Yvonne used a mixed code, with isolated English words and chunks of Cantonese substitutes and translations. We immediately asked ourselves whether the teachers' choice of the instructional medium was largely determined by the level of English proficiency of the pupils or by teacher beliefs. We were somehow convinced that it was the belief of the teachers that shaped their practice. Our conviction in "teaching English through English" would be one of the challenges we faced in taking up the classes and perhaps addressing the issue of classroom English at primary levels.

It should be noted that in Hong Kong, despite British ruling for one and a half centuries, Chinese, or Cantonese more specifically, is the language used predominately in the society. Cantonese is a Chinese dialect spoken in the southern part of China and is the mother tongue of Hong Kong people. For government and government subsidized primary schools, Cantonese is the medium of instruction (MoI) and the written Chinese is standard Chinese. Only a handful of private funded primary schools adopt English as the MoI. Cantonese is used extensively in schools and, in general, pupils do not have a lot of chances to be exposed to the use of English. Despite the fact that English language teacher educators advocating the use of English in English lessons this may not necessarily happen in the classroom. Teachers may not be convinced and they may have many different reasons for not adopting English in teaching English. Given the relatively low English standards of primary pupils, teachers perceive it difficult to adopt the English-only instruction. We felt that it is a very good opportunity for us to experiment with English medium instruction and discuss its feasibility with the teachers.

Other challenges included adapting the textbook materials to make them coherent and well-connected. This is one of the areas that teachers often complained about. Textbook materials are usually perceived as very fragmented, with many mechanical, unrelated, and form-focused exercises. We would like to demonstrate our approach of material adaptation, making the best use of textbook materials, and at the same time taking care of the standards and interests of pupils. There were two other areas for us to work on during our attachment as a result of our discussions in the meeting. They were the use of "Big Books" in teaching reading and the use of information technology (IT) and computer in ELT.

We went away with the textbooks and their teaching schedule, and started planning for our "teaching practice" in the primary classroom for the first time ever. We evaluated the P.3 and P.5 textbook units we were to teach and attempted to outline the theme and focus. "Big books" would be incorporated in our teaching as this had been seen as one of our expert areas which teachers liked to explore.

REFLECTING ON THE EXPERIENCE: LECTURERS' PERSPECTIVES

Our experience with actual primary teaching is limited though our exposure to primary teaching is extensive. We have been teaching primary pre-service and in-service teachers and supervising them in their teaching practice. Moreover, we have been conducting research projects in primary schools. However, to observe other teachers teach as outsiders is very different from becoming insiders and participating in the planning and teaching process and we found our experience very illuminating.

The first thing that struck us as former secondary school teachers was the mindless and mechanical choral reading aloud in the Hong Kong primary classroom, which had become pervasive and uninspired, especially in a reading comprehension where the main focus was on the construction of meaning.

Towards the end of the first reading lesson, when all the reading activities were completed, we read the whole text once to the pupils, expecting them to listen quietly to our reading. Without exception, every little mouth opened and read after the teacher throughout though they had been asked only to listen carefully. Perhaps they just would not believe what they had heard and that we could not have finished the lesson without asking them to read after us! Our observation in other lessons added to our belief that they had formed the habit of repeating after the teacher, mindlessly perhaps a lot of the times.

The next interesting observation relates to homework. As a rule, teachers assign written homework after every lesson. We were reminded by both P.3 and P.5 pupils who invariably whispered to our ears after each lesson pointing out that we had forgotten to give them homework! We had considered asking them to do some reading at home as homework; however, neither the pupils nor the teachers perceived it in the same way. They seemed to consider only paper and pencil work as homework.

One issue regarding classroom language use is how much English should be used in class. English is a foreign language to the pupils and in general there is no need for them to use any English outside the classroom. Whether only English should be used in the English language classroom is something not all teachers agree on. They may not believe that their pupils have the ability to survive let alone learn through English in the classroom. What teachers find most indisputable is that it just seems to be too time consuming to use all English, the kind of English that can be understood by the pupils.

We, however, believe in supporting and helping the pupils to learn through English and were ready to demonstrate using all English in both classes. It was somewhat quite threatening to the pupils in the first couple of lessons in both classes, especially the P.3's. As soon as we started talking and "teaching" all in English, there was low but disturbing "ruffles" from the pupils, who made disconcerting remarks such as "Vow she used all English"; "I don't understand what she said"; and "What did she say?"

The pupils seemed to be well settled in with us after the first two lessons. They began to get used to the classroom routines we set, but it was not until group activities were assigned that we observed, again, unease and uncertainty arose from among the pupils. It was highly probable that they were not used to the type of activities we introduced, and that our instructions which were solely in English was not understood by all, especially the P.3s. We did reflect on whether the use of the mother tongue at "critical" time should help reduce the pupils' worries and economize time and extra effort. The debate on this issue of course is not as simple as it appears and we are still pondering.

We also found that we had "prepared" more than enough for our lessons, in part due to our inexperience in adjusting our planning to the level of primary pupils and their pace of learning. One of the compounding factors was that routines such as getting into lines between breaks, before the school begins and ends, which are particularly important in primary schools as a form of discipline training took up much of the class time, leaving virtually very little time for follow-up activities to extend pupils' language use.

Moreover, regarding language use and the choice of instructional medium in the classroom, we observed that we tended to use vocabulary or expressions too difficult for the pupils, which again, was due to possibly our inexperience in primary teaching, and which necessitated a much longer attachment and practice period to get our orientation right.

In sum, we felt that the gap was attributed mainly to the differences in operational cultures between the primary school and the teacher education institution. Our perception of learning and homework differs considerably from the teachers'. Moreover, our background in secondary teaching also contributed to the disparity in our perceptions regarding teaching and learning. Such issues are complex and intertwined and will be further explored in the discussion part.

REFLECTING ON THE EXPERIENCE: TEACHERS' PERSPECTIVE

It was helpful and useful for the two regular teachers, Lilian and Yvonne, to sit in our class most of time. They might help with some group activities and locating stuff from their classroom cabinets. Their presence was particularly important as they shared with us their observations and perspectives of our teaching and pupil response and performance. They were also very well informed of the approach we adopted and the process of our teaching.

A discussion took place towards the end of the two-week attachment involving the two English teachers of P.3 and P.5 and the school principal. We had a very open discussion regarding the standards of the pupil, constraints within the school system, and our own strength and weaknesses. Both parties felt that the attachment was very useful in helping all of us understand more about the classroom situations.

The two teachers agreed to be interviewed by a research assistant regarding their perspectives and comments on our attachment. The following is a summary of their views on our attachment.

Our attachment was perceived as important in enabling us as teacher educators to gain primary teaching experience, which would in turn help us in our teaching and curriculum planning at the Institute. Two particular issues related to teaching were raised by the teachers. One was the medium of instruction and the other was our classroom teaching activities.

Lilian thought that the P.3 pupils were at times confused by our English-only instructions. Though the interactive activities we used were good, the pupils found them unfamiliar and thus could not benefit fully from them. She then concluded that our methods were beneficial only to pupils with good English standards.

Yvonne commented on the use of English as the medium of instruction in our teaching. Though she was told by her P.3 pupils that they did not understand all of what we said, she was very surprised to see many of her pupils actively volunteering and attempting to answer our questions in the lessons. She thought that the pupils were very happy in our class:

Sometimes I watched at the back and I remembered that they were not so attentive in my lessons. There were some children who sat in the front who were not very smart. In fact, they were quite weak. But they always raised their hands and were very attentive during the lecturers' lessons. They also laughed. I talked to them afterwards and asked why they were so happy. They were very attentive because it was new and refreshing. The lecturers' preparation was very good and the pupils' involvement and engagement were greater. Sometimes the kids might not really understand, but they felt this teacher did not know them so there were no labeling effects and they raised their hands. It was felt OK to give the wrong answer. So they were very motivated to raise their hands. I found that many of them who raised their hands were the weaker ones. I think it is quite good.

The two teachers also commented favorably on the material adaptation approach and were appreciative of the worksheets we designed, which were creative and interesting. However, the two teachers expressed doubts about their feasibility given the time constraint and the heavy workload they had in a school year. A quote from Yvonne best demonstrate the teachers' concern:

I remember in the first lesson they already had three or four worksheets. How can we do that? We have the workload of the whole term .... What they did was very idealistic. If we would have more resources it would be very nice. For example, the worksheets are already made, or we can prepare them in advance in the summer and plan what to do in each class. Then it would be different. But we cannot do that in the summer.

The teachers, however, acknowledged that such activities did bring about lively atmosphere and arouse interest of the pupils. Lilian pointed out that the prescribed workbooks were not directly related to the main coursebook, which implied teachers having to spend class time on teaching the workbook materials in addition to covering the coursebook. Our attempt at material adaptation and selection in order to make our teaching coherent was considered a 'problem' by the teachers who were concerned about challenges from parents regarding coursebook materials which were not dealt with. The issue of public accountability, especially to parents, was clearly a cause for concern for the two teachers. This also illustrated one of the dissimilarities in the work culture between school teachers and teacher educators.

Nevertheless, the teachers were very appreciative of the enthusiasm and seriousness we brought to our teaching. While commending on the approaches we adopted, they were critical of our limited practical experience in the primary school setting which resulted in insufficient attention paid to areas which they deemed significant. Their overall comments on us were we had more time, more resources; however, we did not know the pupils well enough.

In sum, the gap of different cultures of teaching and learning reflects persistently in the teachers in judging our approach and teaching in the classroom. However, it was fruitful in enhancing both the teachers' and our reflection on the medium of instruction for English teaching in the classroom. More discussion of the above will be followed up in the next part.

DISCUSSION

In the light of our attachment experience, we would like to analyze and review what we gained and learned from our teaching and then discuss the implications for teacher education

Broadening Knowledge Base and Re-living Teaching Practice Experience

As teacher educators with a background in secondary English language education, we found working in the primary classroom both challenging and rewarding. Through reflecting on our teaching while in action as well as afterwards, we came to a much deeper understanding of the marked differences between primary and secondary school pupils in terms of their learning needs and behavior which correspond with the developmental stages they are in. While secondary school pupils especially those at senior levels are capable of handling abstract structural analysis of the language, primary pupils learn best through concrete and contextualized use of the language.

We also experienced the same kind of struggles and frustration student teachers undergo during their teaching practice and the adjustments they have to make while developing a temporary relationship with the pupils, coping with a tight teaching schedule, and handling teaching materials and homework which they neither regard as worthwhile nor have much control over. Student teachers operate in a borrowed place at a borrowed time. Not only are they expected to be able to pitch their teaching at the level of pupils of which they have limited knowledge, they have to fit in with the culture of the school and perform in accordance with its requirements and practice. The Attachment

Experience heightened our understanding of the learning that student teachers are expected to accomplish during their student teaching, and our awareness of the process of socialization that they invariably go through as they learn the "trade" of the profession.

Bridging the Credibility Gap

In terms of professional credibility, the success we achieved in trying out task-based learning during our attachment was a testimony to our fundamental beliefs in communicative language learning. It was also our attempt to bridge the gap between the realities of "practice" and the ideals of "theory". With the insights we gained from the Attachment, we were able to inspire our student teachers and in-service teachers at the Institute with anecdotes of our attachment experience, especially on issues relating to classroom language and integrated learning. We could easily cite examples to demonstrate how we were able to create an English speaking environment and utilize resources creatively and purposefully to enhance language development. It was no longer possible for them to criticize us as "unrealistic and uniformed."

Validating Knowledge Base Through Reality Checks

Through field testing what we perceived to be "good" ELT at the attachment school, the value of the approach we espoused were further confirmed by the teachers. We planned our lessons with the aim of promoting an integrated use of the language. With such a purpose in mind, we selected, resequenced, and modified the prescribed materials to make them coherent and purposeful. This had been explained to the teachers whom we worked with, but not to the pupils, which understandably caused confusions and anxiety in them who were used to being taught the coursebook from cover to cover. Nonetheless, our attempt to enhance pupil learning through a creative but well-considered adaptation of coursebook materials, embracing a student-centered orientation, was given due recognition by both teachers. Another "new" element we brought into the classroom was the use of "Big books" a part we perceive as an integral part of the English curriculum supporting pupils' second language development, which was also well received by the teachers.

Differences in Work Culture

Having been operating within a relatively autonomous environment of the

Institute, we as teacher educators have more freedom, to a certain extent, over the content and mode of delivery of the curriculum. We are more concerned about improving schools for tomorrow's world, through experimenting with a range of approaches and materials whereas school teachers are more concerned about covering the syllabus "now" so that they can report marks to pupils and parents at regular intervals. The root of the disparity lies in the tension between "quality" and "quantity" which was best illustrated by the concluding remarks of the teachers, who hailed our approach as being creative and interesting. They detected obvious qualities in the strategies we adopted but were still "overpowered" by the "culture" of "cover and report" and the quantity context of the school, an issue well documented (Russell, 1992). It would be fruitful for both the school teachers and teacher educators to discuss and sort out the different views, with an attempt to maintain the desirable quantity of work to assist learning, but without compromising the quality of it.

Professional Growth of Both Parties

LAS engendered professional benefits to both parties, the teacher educators and teachers, in classroom teaching, planning, and materials development. It is particularly useful for us as teacher educators to learn from within. Throughout the process, we all reflected on and discussed issues of concern to classroom practitioners. As advocated by Simpson (1997), the "Professor-In-Residence" program enables the mutual understanding and sharing of ideas in teaching between teacher educators and classroom teachers. With the busy life of teachers, on-site teacher development can alleviate the demands of teacher time and effort. Moreover, such kind of professional support rendered within the work context of the teachers is highly relevant and meaningful to them. To the teacher educators, besides updating their teaching in the field, they can have their theories verified and innovations tested.

IMPLICATIONS

To conclude, the above discussions elucidate the two levels of significance of LAS: one centering on the knowledge and skill renewal endeavors of teacher educators, which extended to the professional development of school teachers; the other accentuating a wider perspective of in-service teacher education model, establishing a direction for collaborative learning. The potential strength behind this kind of link or activity is enormous. While updating his/her field experience, the lecturer works with the teachers on-site assisting the latter in resolving identified issues of concern, which can be mutually beneficial to the practitioners in school and lecturers in higher institution. This is an avenue for teacher education institutions to establish close links with schools. Besides catering for the professional learning and development of both the lecturers and the school teachers, the interface between schools and institutes as established through LAS can be further developed into a closer relationship of collaboration and further development for the betterment of pupil learning. As Knowles and Coles (1998) contend that teacher educators should be at the heart of the education reform working with teachers, LAS is therefore a possible mode to be further developed into a model of school-based or site-based teacher in-service education program that starts off with a period of attachment and continues with collaborative projects.

Sankey (1996) discusses the feasibility of adopting the model of school-based teacher training for pre-service teaching education. He elaborates in detail different aspects of the school-based approach. He asserts that "school-based" training is "a way of re-conceptualising the purpose, content and style of teacher training courses" (p. 68). He emphasizes the notion of "interactive theory and practice" which maintains that theory is an integral part of practice and is generated and verified from practice. It is therefore essential that student teachers should learn within the school setting. His discussion can well be extended to the in-service teacher programs given that teachers' initial training in the last couple of decades or before did not prepare them for the current educational innovations that are very demanding on the learning and improvement of teachers in order to implement changes. As such, this kind of school-based or site-based collaborative model could link educators, viewed as the theorists, from higher institutions with the teachers, the practitioners, into new forms of collaborative partnership. This is also well supported by Kennedy (1992) who argues that teachers are "practitioners, not theoreticians." He cautions that any innovation that does not take this point into account "is doomed to fail."

Cheng (1998) explores teacher effectiveness in the changing era of technology, economic, and social-political globalization. Rapid changes are in place in the Asia as well as in the Western countries in the nineties and the new millennium. Cheng contends:

> In such a fast changing era, schools and teachers have to face numerous new problems, uncertainties, and challenges rising from their internal and external

environments.... In the 21st century, schools become very crucial to supporting the rapid developments of individuals and in local communities, societies, and international relations and are expected to perform a wide range of new structural, social, political, cultural, and educational functions.

In this connection, teachers in the era of rapid change are often required to take up expanded roles and responsibilities, including curriculum developer, new teacher mentor, staff development facilitator, action researcher, pre-service teacher educator, team leader, decision maker, member of management board, etc. (p. 1)

The new roles mentioned above require teacher knowledge and competence that teachers may not possess from their early teacher training courses. The new education reforms proposed in our society demand life-long learning of the individual and the teacher will need to learn and update the relevant knowledge. In the same article, Cheng discusses the multi-models of teacher effectiveness. One of the models he elaborates is the Continuous Learning Model which requires teachers to have "the necessary knowledge and competence to analyze and reflect on environmental changes and develop appropriate strategies to make continuous improvement and development" and he states that it is useful to understand how teachers can conduct action learning in their daily work process, how they can benefit more from external and school-based staff development. This approach complements and supports what Kennedy (1992) and Sankey (1996) advocate.

Thus, the collaborative efforts of university staff and local teachers explored in this chapter for education innovations can be seen as the "right" match, with an external party from the outside who possesses the knowledge and theories and the teacher practitioner from the inside who can work closely with the educator on issues of concern. Models of in-service programs capitalizing on the strengths of the two parties may be an effective means to enhance implementation of education innovations. LAS in this respect can be regarded as the preparation or bridge to effective in-service teacher development.

Tsui and Cheng (1999) further explore the framework of curriculum effectiveness. They discuss the inter-relation of different levels of curriculum making which includes the societal level, the school (institutional) level, the classroom (teacher) level, and the student level. They then outline a framework of curriculum effectiveness which is a multi-level and developmental processes at work. Regarding classroom/teacher level, they pose a number of questions related to the individual teacher's competence required for implementing the classroom-based curriculum. They raise key questions such as what kind of teacher competence, the consistence between teacher competence and classroom-based curriculum, and the match between teacher competence and classroom-based curriculum and school environment. These are very important issues to be explored and LAS would be a practical means to cater for research agendas.

CONCLUSION

Our Attachment carried a dual purpose, one for our own professional development and the other to establish a longer-term relationship with the attachment school and subsequently we developed a collaborative school-based curriculum project with the school. By the end of the attachment period, both parties felt that we could work together for future collaborative projects. We had an initial agreement that we would go back and work with the English teachers near the end of the school year on a school-based curriculum project. The first phase would include offering workshops to the English Panel on task-based teaching/learning approach, a direction advocated in the new primary English syllabus. The second phase of this project would be a follow through of the implementation and evaluation of their school-based curriculum developed by the English Panel. We identified the focus of the workshops with the teachers during the first phase and tentatively agreed on the time we would go back to the school, with two other "experts" from the Institute to form a team of four to provide staff development workshops. Through the workshops, we identified the area for curriculum development for English language teaching in their school.

This school-based curriculum project took place immediately after our attachment period and extended to the following academic year. Details of this project are reported and discussed by Wong and Pang (1999). The central point here is to give emphasis to the fact that because of our attachment through LAS, we established mutual understanding and trust, from which enhanced fruitful outcomes of the collaboration derived.

HKIEd LAS was launched with the aim of enabling lecturers to obtain up-to-date local school teaching experiences and as a kind of internal staff development program. Through our Attachment experience, we felt that the aim has been achieved to a large extent. Our knowledge base has been broadened and theories validated. It seems professional development did not transpire exclusively to the Institute lecturers; it in fact was extended to the school teachers. Sitting in the classrooms of the lecturers, the two teachers had the opportunities of examining classroom teaching/learning from a different angle and perspective. The opportunities also enabled them to reflect on their own teaching and raise questions for their further development.

This kind of learning together is beneficial to educational innovations, especially school-based activities. Through such kind of partnership, both parties can have a common ground to see issues within the school or classroom situations. As a result, practical insights can be developed into new pedagogical theories (Stahl 1987) and these theories can be verified on site.

In sum, this kind of partnership is more desirable than the traditional relationship whereby education faculty or institution staff enjoyed a "higher" and more privileged position and are assumed to be more knowledgeable. Their usual roles include visiting schools to conduct teaching practice supervision or to assist with curriculum or staff development. This status sometimes can be problematic and the school practitioners may rely too much on the "expert" advice and as a result diminishing the contributions and on-site knowledge of the teachers. A more genuine partnership is therefore more advantageous especially from a shared view of problems and a joint pursuit of solutions (Kwo, 1998).

In the present climate of education reform in Hong Kong and elsewhere, life-long learning is given the strongest impetus. As pointed out in the beginning of this chapter, the Hong Kong Government is determined to embark on massive scale of educational reform on all levels of the education system. LAS is a viable alternative to equip teacher educators with practical insights derived from practicing at the front-line and partnerships with schools, through which the learning and development of both parties would be enhanced. This kind of partnerships contribute significantly to education innovations, especially those involving curriculum changes, without which there is bound to be a mismatch between curriculum intentions and classroom realities for any curriculum innovation (Corbitt, 1993; Clark, Scarino, & Brownell, 1994).

The present HKIEd LAS takes place in a period of two weeks and Anderson and Cheung (1999) recommend that the period of attachment be extended to a longer period of time so that the experience can be more sustained and comprehensive.

We acknowledge the merit of this recommendation judging from the experience we had. We felt that two weeks were not adequate for us to improve our teaching skills on the primary level, and neither were we able to explore in depth the other aspects of the primary school teaching and operation given the short duration of attachment. We may be somehow superficial in some of our observations. Taking into consideration of our work load in the Institute, a longer block of time for the attachment may not be feasible. Thus, a more flexible scheme can be built in to extend the attachment with follow up visits or extended teaching period. Such arrangement can ensure more in-depth understanding of the school teaching and operation and as a result, more appropriate on-site collaborative projects.

Future studies of LAS should investigate whether the length of the attachment makes a difference, what enhances lecturer and teacher learning and collaboration, and whether the attachment and collaboration enhance school reform and student learning. Moreover, LAS can be further developed in a two-phase operation. The first phase would be the attachment period for the educator to experience/revive the back-to-school teaching. This first phase can also include at the same time trying out new ideas or methodologies. Building on the first phase relationship, agendas for the second phase can be identified if both parties find it worth working together on issues of common interests.

The second phase of this LAS developed into a school-based curriculum renewal initiative. The authors of this chapter and two lecturers who are primary teaching "experts" formed a team to support the school in a curriculum development project. Starting off with an area of concern in the English teachers' practice, 11 English teachers (out of a Panel of 15) were involved in an English subject curriculum development project for their P.5 and P.6 pupils. The project was reported in a conference paper, entitled "The interface between theory and practice: The role of teacher educators and teachers in a school-based teacher development initiative" (Wong and Pang, 1999). In this paper, a Framework for School-based Teacher Development was presented. The paper described and discussed the project which adopted the Framework comprising a four-stage development. After identifying and agreeing on the language teaching problem, Stage 1 consisted of analyzing further the situation and planned the relevant actions. Stage 2 saw the teachers and researchers negotiated and defined the objectives, after which they designed the teaching and learning activities. Teachers and researchers were at work in different roles and met as planned to finalize the activities. The planned activities were then implemented as indicated in Stage 3 and evaluation was done in the final stage to inform both parties the outcomes of the activities and whether modification was necessary for future implementation. The following figure summarizes the actions and happenings using the Framework.

Morris (1996) discusses the change strategies in education initiatives. He contends that of the three types of strategies, namely, problem-solving, conceptual changes and agents of authority or power over others, in a highly centralized educational system such as Hong Kong, the last one usually predominates. Teachers as the implementers of the curriculum rarely are involved in the planning and decision-making processes. The main weakness or problem of this is that there is seldom a sense of "ownership" from the side of the teacher and whether the intended curriculum is implemented is always doubtful. The collaborative approach adopted in the teacher development framework (Figure 1) can alleviate the problem and can involve the teachers in the whole process. Apart from the implementation of the intended curriculum, one of the most important outcomes of this approach is teacher learning and teacher development. As Wong and Pang (1999) point out, there are concerns in this approach. They include the difficulties of having disparity of teacher involvement, and addressing the diverse needs of different teachers. The

Figure 1: *School-based Language Teacher Development Framework (from Wong and Pang, 1999)*

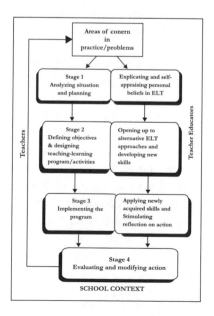

framework can be further refined to address the more practical operational issues in future studies.

With further refinement, research agendas raised by Tsui and Cheng (1999) can be worked out to investigate different aspects of teacher curriculum making. As discussed in the earlier section, teacher effectiveness in the changing era has to be looked at in the relevant contexts. Teacher learning and development would be a necessary condition to meet the present educational challenges. Tsui and Cheng's (1999) framework illustrates the macro level of looking at teacher knowledge and competence. LAS, modified into a two-phase operation, will bring about the practical aspects including the findings of teacher learning and competence and, at the same time, support curriculum initiatives. Findings of further studies using the framework would be valuable in outlining the operational aspects of the framework.

Given curriculum reform is happening in Hong Kong on all levels, different forms of Institute-school partnership can be further promoted through the LAS mode. Such partnership can open up avenues for an interflow of expertise, skills, and perspective which contributes directly to the success of education innovations in a practical and effective manner. However, the mode of operation should take under school-based approach which would enable genuine collaboration of university lecturers and school teachers. With their expertise in theory and knowledge gained from research, the lecturers can work closely with the teachers in planning and refining curriculum which at the same time can be tried out and verified by the teachers in school sites.

The school-based teacher development framework presented can be adopted as the second phase of LAS if the educator and the school see the potential of working and collaborating on issues of mutual interests. This two-phase approach can support the real needs of teachers and at the same time satisfy the demand on teacher educators doing relevant and meaningful research to support education innovations. If the success of school reform is dependent upon the reform of teacher preparation (Knowles & Coles, 1998), policy-makers both on the government level and from within education institutions may need to study closely the feasibility of making learning and development activities mandatory for all, including teacher educators and school teachers. A refined form of LAS based on the above discussion may be one of the appropriate and effective alternatives to support education reform and improvement.

REFERENCES

Anderson, R., & Cheung, F. W. M. (1999). *Enhancing institute-school partnership: Lecturer-school attachment in Hong Kong.* Paper presented at the International Conference on Teacher Education, Hong Kong Institute of Education.

Cheng, Y. C. (1998). The pursuit of a new knowledge base for teacher education and development in the new century. *Asia-Pacific Journal of Teacher Education and Development, 1*(1), 1-15.

Clark, J. L., Scarino, A., & Brownell, J. A. (1994). *Improving the quality of learning: A framework for target-oriented curriculum renewal in Hong Kong.* Hong Kong: Institute of Language in Education.

Corbitt, E. R. (1993, March 11-13). Hand in hand: Supporting change through practitioner-college partnerships. In D. Montgomery (Ed.), *Rural America: Where all innovations begin. Conference Proceedings* (pp. 299-307). Savannah, GA.

Curriculum Development Council. (1999). *Holistic review of the Hong Kong school curriculum: Proposed reforms. Consultative document.* Hong Kong: Author.

Darling-Hammond, L. (1999). The case for university – based teacher education. In A. R. Robert (Ed.), *The role of university in the preparation of teachers.* London: Falmer Press.

Education Commission. (1999a). *Review of education system: Framework for education reform: Learning for life.* Hong Kong: Government Printer.

Education Commission. (1999b). *Review of academic system. Aims of education: Consultation document / Education Commission.* Hong Kong: Government Printer.

Education and Manpower Bureau. (1998). *Information technology for quality education. 5-year strategy 1998/99 to 2002/03. Consultation document.* Hong Kong: Government Printer.

Goodlad, J. (1990). *Teachers for our nation's schools.* San Francisco, CA: Jossey-Bass.

Goodlad, J. I. (1993). School-university partnerships and partner school. *Educational Policy, 7*(1), 24-39.

Hansgen, R. (1983). A clinical professorship. *Action in teacher education, 5*(1-2), 21-24.

Holmes Group (1995). *Tomorrow's schools of education.* East Lansing, MI: The Holmes Group.

Hudson-Ross, S., & McWhorter, P. (1995). Going back/looking in: A teacher educator and a high school teacher explore beginning teaching together. *English Journal, 84*(2), 46-54.

Hunkins, F. P., Wiseman, D. L., & Williams, R. C. (1995). Supporting collaborative inquiry. In R. T. Osguthorpe, R. C. Harris, M. C. Harris & B. Sharon (Eds.), *Partnership schools: Centers for educational renewal.* San Francisco: Jossey-Bass.

Kennedy, K. J. (1992). School-based curriculum development as a policy option for the 1990s: An australian perspective. *Journal of Curriculum and Supervision, 7*(2), 180-195.

Knowles, J. G., & Coles, A. L. (1998). Setting and defining the context. In C. L. Ardra, E. Rosebud & J. G. Knowles (Eds.), *The heart of the matter: Teacher educators and teacher education reform.* California: Caddo Gap Press.

Kwo, O. (Ed.). (1998). *Professional learning together: Building a collaborative culture in teaching practicum supervision.* Hong Kong: INSTEP, Faculty of Education, Hong Kong University.

Morris, P. (1996). *The Hong Kong school curriculum: Development, issues and policies* (2nd ed.). Hong Kong: Hong Kong University Press.

Orstein, A. C. (1967). Why ghetto school teachers fail. *Kappa Delta Pi record,* Winter, 99-101.

Russell, T. (1992, April 20-24). *A teacher educator and his pupils reflect on teaching high school physics.* Paper presented at the Annual Meeting of the American Educational Research Association, San Francisco, CA.

Russell, T., & Korthagen, F. (Eds.). (1995). *Teachers who teach teachers: Reflections on teacher education.* London: Falmer Presss

Sankey, D. (1996). Beyond the ideology of school-based teacher training. *Journal of Primary Education, 6*(1-2), 67-77.

Simpson, F. M. (1997, July 9-13). *Professor-in-residence: Redefining the work of teacher educators.* Paper presented at the China-U.S. Conference on Education, Beijing. (ERIC Document Reproduction Service No. ED 425 412)

Stahl, N. A. (1987). Back to the trenches, you pedagogical dogs! *Georgia Journal of Reading, Fall,* 2-6.

Tsui, K. T. & Cheng, Y. C. (1999). A framework of curriculum effectiveness: Development and research. In Y. C. Cheng, K. W. Chow & K. T. Tsui (Eds.), *School curriculum change and development in Hong Kong.* Hong Kong: The Hong Kong Institution of Education.

Tung, C. W. (1999). *Policy address 1999. Quality education: Policy objective for education and manpower bureau.* Hong Kong: Printing Department.

Warshaw, M. (1986). Return from the tower. *Phi Delta Kappan, Sept, 68,* 67-69.

Weber, S. J. (1990). The teacher educator's experience: Cultural generality and duality of commitment. *Curriculum Inquiry, 20*(2), 141-159.

Wong, J. W. P. (2000*). Meeting the education needs of Hong Kong in the new millennium.* Paper presented at International Congress for School Effectivenss and Improvement, The Hong Kong Institute of Education.

Wong, W., & Pang, M. (1999). The interface between theory and practice: The role of teacher educators and teachers in a school-based teacher development initiative. Paper presented at AARE-NZARE Conference 1999, Australia.

Zeichner, K. (1993, February). Traditions practice in US preservice teacher education programs. *Teaching and Teacher Education, 9*(1), 1-13.

Chapter 19

Enhancing Reflective and Critical Thinking Skills: Semantic Mapping as A Strategy in Teacher Education

Audrey Swee Eng LIM, Doris Pui Wah CHAN-CHENG, Michelle Mei Seung LAM, and So Fong NGAN

The School of Early Childhood Education
The Hong Kong Institute of Education, Hong Kong

The aim of this chapter is to report and analyze an essential issue in early childhood teacher education in Hong Kong in an era where concerns are on the quality of teacher education and the emphasis is on developing critical and reflective thinking in teachers. The brief review of relevant literature focuses on how researchers and practitioners address this issue of developing teachers who are able to engage in critical and reflective thinking, with specific emphasis on a recent initiative – the use of semantic mapping strategies as a tool for developing critical and reflective thinking in pre-school teachers. It documents the findings of an exploratory study applying the use of semantic mapping strategies to assess understanding of three components of a module "Further Studies in Kindergarten Curriculum" in in-service student-teachers undertaking a Certificate in Kindergarten Education (Chinese) Course at the Hong Kong Institute of Education. Implications are drawn from this study for researchers and practitioners in the field of early childhood education to make use of semantic maps as viable tools for diagnostic, instructional, assessment, and research purposes.

A crucial factor influencing the success of teachers, whether elementary, secondary, or pre-primary teachers, is their ability to engage in critical and reflective thinking. Thus, a challenge facing teacher-educators in the new millennium is how best they can facilitate these skills in the student-teachers that will enable them to become more effective and efficient teachers. In order to achieve this objective, various initiatives need to be taken in aspects that will make a difference. As teacher-educators, attention should be focused on the best way to introduce new ideas, facts, and skills based on what they already know, helping them revise what they already know in the light of new information, as well as helping them represent the new structure of what they know in a way that integrates these ideas, facts, and skills (Clarke, 1990). Based on research and sound cognitive theory, this focus will influence the way teacher-educators teach and the way they expect their students to learn, as well as the way they evaluate learning.

A technique that has become popular in teaching is "semantic mapping," variously referred to as "concept mapping," "knowledge mapping," "word webbing," "networking," "clustering," "mind-maps," "think-links," "idea branches," "structured overviews," "graphic organisers," "semantic networking," or "plot maps" (Buzan, 1974; Clarke, 1990; Fisher, 1995; Heimlich & Pittelman, 1986; Novak, 1998; Novak & Gowin, 1984; Schwartz & Parks, 1994). These terms refer to a strategy of portraying graphically and visually a relationship of concepts or ideas. Semantic mapping has recently emerged as a technique that allows students "... to see the structure of their prior knowledge, plan for the addition of new information, guide inquiry from what is known toward what is not, and encourage the recognition of relationships in the content areas" (Clarke, 1990, p. 166). Fisher (1995, p. 63) has made the distinction between "thinking map" and "concept maps." Thinking maps refer to graphic and visual structures in which words and ideas are merely listed as in brainstorming whereas concept maps illustrate the relationships among words and ideas. In this chapter, the term "semantic mapping" was used synonymously with "concept mapping," "cognitive mapping" or "mind mapping" and no distinctions were made between "thinking maps" or "concept maps."

THE CONTEXTS AND RELATED ISSUES

Program Description

The Certificate in Kindergarten Education Course (Chinese) (CE [KG]) is a 60 credit-point professional upgrading program for qualified experienced kindergarten teachers. (Each credit-point is equivalent to 15 contact hours.) It is an in-service teacher education course which provides holders of the Qualified Kindergarten Teacher (QKT) qualification a means of furthering their professional and academic development. (The QKT course is a 30 credit-point course.) The CE (KG) course has a modular structure and its content is arranged in five domains, including Professional Studies, Curriculum Studies, Subject Studies, General Education, and Field

Experience. Modules in the Professional Studies domain are designed to further students' understanding of the theoretical bases of early childhood education. The Curriculum Studies modules introduce the basic theories in early childhood curriculum, various approaches to teaching and provide a framework for further understanding of the preschool curriculum. The Subject Studies modules provide students with broad-based academic discipline knowledge essential for their development into informed and educated professionals. It also supports both curriculum design and teaching at the kindergarten level. The General Education domain is designed to enhance students' personal development. Field Experience is an integral part of the curriculum in the two-year CE (KG) course. It provides an avenue for students to apply theory to practice. It also *emphasizes the development of critical and reflective thinking in practice* through a number of components including Supervised Teaching, Practicum Workshops, Peer Support and Educational Visits (School of Early Childhood Education, Course Document: Two-year Mixed-mode Certificate in Kindergarten Education Course (Chinese), 1998, p. 1).

The module "Further Studies in Kindergarten Curriculum" is a six credit-point module categorized under the domain of Professional Studies and the sub-domain of Teaching and Learning. This module comprises six components of Language, Mathematics and Science, Social Studies, Art, Music, and Physical Education, each of one credit-point. The study to be reported here was undertaken with student-teachers of the CE (KG) cohort of 1997-1999 while they were in their second year and first semester of study. During that semester, three components of the module were taught, including Social Studies, Mathematics and Science, and Art. Each of these components were taught in five sessions, with each session lasting three hours.

Before the beginning of the semester, the module convenors in charge of each of the components of the module "Further Studies in Kindergarten Curriculum" met to discuss the mode of evaluation of these components. The main responsibilities of the module convenors include coordinating the teaching team's effort to maintain consistency in the delivery of the teaching and evaluation of the module and generally, ensuring the smooth running of the lecture/tutorial sessions. They decided, as a team, to integrate the assessment of the three components and to make use of semantic mapping as an assessment mode. The assessment read as follows:

a. Individual students are required to draw a semantic map (one for each of the areas) to demonstrate their understanding of the kindergarten curriculum in relation to each of the other areas.

b. Based on these semantic maps, students are required to critically examine and evaluate the curriculum in their own kindergartens and devise a plan to improve their existing curriculum. They should also state the reasons for and benefits of such changes (of about 1,500 words).

Rationale for Using Semantic Mapping in Student-teachers

There were several factors influencing the module convenors' decision to use semantic mapping as a means of assessment of student-teachers' understanding. One of the considerations was that the module or components of the module "Further Studies in Kindergarten Curriculum" should facilitate "the development of critical and reflective thinking" in student-teachers. Another issue influencing the decision to make use of an integrated mode of assessment is the need to reduce the assessment load. Thus, the use of semantic mapping as an assessment mode serves dual purposes. It has also been considered to be the "most powerful tool for capturing knowledge held by an individual or group of individuals" (Novak, 1998, p. 101). Another important factor affecting this decision is the need for the integration of subject areas, a common practice in early childhood education.

The manifestation of an integrated early childhood curriculum takes many forms, one of which is the use of concept webs in a spiral thematic curriculum. The main sources of semantic webbing and the integration of webbed concepts in the early childhood curriculum derive from the work of Bruner, Biber, and Levin (see Workman & Anziano, 1994 for a review of these sources). In summary, Bruner's work provides us with an understanding of how a particular concept web lends itself to a spiral process while Biber's work provides a basis for the integration of various concept webs. Biber also suggested a curriculum approach in which cognitive, affective, and social processes are all interdependent. In a spiral curriculum, a concept is introduced in a simple form early and in more complex form later. Levin's work adds the dimension of the "interaction of concept webs" (Workman & Anziano, 1994, p. 96).

The rationale for the use of concept webs in the early childhood curriculum is based on four main principles. First, concept webs provide a means for writing down the spiral curriculum. Second, they assure that both teachers and children see relationships. Third, concept webbing incorporates the advantages of thematic planning while eliminating the disadvantages of units of study. And fourth, webbing provides flexibility and the ability to document emergent curriculum.

Since many of the student-teachers are themselves principals or senior teachers of their own preschools or kindergartens, they were expected to plan curricula. Thematic webs were the most common format used for planning the content of the early childhood curricula. Common themes such as Spring, Transportation, or Food may recur from the nursery level to the higher grade levels K1 (three- to four-year-olds) or K2 (four- to five-year-olds) and so on. Thus, the themes may be repeated using content appropriate to the grade level in what may be termed a spiral thematic curriculum. The use of concept webs or semantic mapping as an assessment mode was, therefore, a valid means of evaluating student-teachers' knowledge of the early childhood curriculum since its application in practice was functional for the student-teachers. However, as a means of assessment, it was a mode which might be considered "untraditional." The most common modes used in both the QKT and CE (KG) course were tests, examinations, essays, or projects. The main disadvantage of essays is that they are time-consuming for student-teachers to write as well as time-consuming to read and evaluate. Yet, they do not assess directly their ability to see relations between ideas or reflect how they perceive the structure of a large topic. Concept maps, in contrast, could reveal a complex structure of ideas about sophisticated concepts or multiple links between concepts. Thus, besides being a valid assessment tool, concept maps are also useful as a means of probing student-teachers' understanding, whether of a limited aspect of a topic, or their ability to relate distinct topics, or their ability to identify key concepts or changes in perceptions of relations between concepts (White & Gunstone, 1992).

Benefits of Concept Maps as a Learning Tool

According to Connelly, Claudinin, and He (1997), one of the main ways of improve education through research is to study the construction and expression of the knowledge held by teachers. It has recently become commonplace to believe that what teachers know and how they express their knowledge is central to student learning. In the study being described in this chapter, the investigation focused on the notion of making explicit the embedded knowledge held by the student-teachers and, in so doing, helped both the teacher-educators and student-teachers understand the construction and expression of the knowledge. In this way, the teacher-educators hoped to achieve their objective of facilitating critical/reflective thinking in the module "Further Studies in Kindergarten Curriculum" of the Certificate in Kindergarten Teachers In-service Course. By requiring the use of semantic maps instead of essays, previously employed as an assessment mode in the module, student-teachers' knowledge of each of the components of Social studies, Mathematics and Science, and Art was made visible during the learning process. Concept maps had the advantage over essays of demonstrating the student-teachers' ability to see the relationships between and among concepts/ideas and their ability to organize the structure of this knowledge. These skills were especially important when they are required to integrate multiple subject areas such as Social Studies, Mathematics and Science, and Art. As semantic maps are useful artifactual tools for tapping embedded knowledge and for demonstrating how the knowledge is expressed and integrated, student-teachers' semantic maps were used as a means not only to provide insights into their "baseline" knowledge of each of the subject areas, but also to probe their understanding of the construction and expression of their own knowledge. The semantic maps served as tools by which student-teachers demonstrated their own thinking and derived meaning from them. They were also visible tools by which they could reflect on their thinking. At the same time, they were the tools by which the teacher-educators could gain insights into the student-teachers' understanding, and their skills in relating different subject areas.

REVIEW OF RELEVANT LITERATURE

The primary focus of this chapter is on the use of semantic maps as a means of facilitating critical and reflective thinking, and thus the review of relevant literature touches on what has been done by researchers who have used them for three interrelated functions encompassing the full spectrum of educational applications: as instructional tools; as evaluation tools; and as research tools. The following paragraphs highlight the literature review of studies carried out which have used semantic maps as instructional tools, as a means of evaluating understanding or as a means of demonstrating that semantic maps were viable as tools for research. In some cases, these three main applications of semantic mapping have overlapped.

A meta-analysis (Horton et al., 1993) of studies which investigated the effectiveness of concept mapping as an instructional tool yielded 19 studies. There were three criteria for the inclusion of the studies in the meta-analysis. Only studies which occurred in actual classrooms and which used concept mapping as an instructional tool were considered. Furthermore, the studies that compared quantitative measures of outcomes for treatment classes using concept mapping, with outcomes for classes using some alternative instructional method as a control were included. Also, the report had to provide sufficient data for the calculation of an effect size. The studies analyzed included two involving elementary grade students, two which involved middle school students, nine which involved high school students, and the remaining six which involved college students as subjects. In terms of content focus, nearly all involved science content; only two involved non-science subject content. The meta-analysis is cited here to illustrate that very few studies focusing on concept mapping as an instructional tool actually involved preschool/kindergarten teachers as subjects.

Instructional strategies using semantic maps include those prepared by students and those prepared by the teacher. A distinction between these two types of activities emphasizes that strategies using teacher-prepared maps are essentially product-centered while student concept mapping approaches are more process-oriented (Cliburn, 1990). The findings of the meta-analysis (Horton et al., 1993) demonstrated that student-prepared concept maps were the most common in the studies examined. Student-prepared maps were used in 79% (15 out of 19) of the studies included in the meta-analysis. Of these 19 studies, three involved teacher-prepared maps and only one involved both students and teachers preparing the maps. The majority of the studies examined focused on science content; only two used non-science subject areas. More recent work using student-made maps include Arnaudin, Mintzes, Dunn, and Shafer (1984); Ault (1985); and Ost (1987). The most explicit forms of instructional schemes involving students' mapping activities are reflected in Novak and Gowin's (1984) work.

The use of concepts maps as evidence of students' thought processes is an approach developed by Novak (1980). The rationale underlying this strategy is that concept maps portray students' current perceptions and misconceptions. By developing concept maps, students create their own unique set of meanings. The map forces them to explore the ideas and think about their interrelationships. Concept maps were, therefore, powerful tools for reflecting thinking, but also for helping students develop an understanding of their own thinking and helping teachers gain insights into students' thinking and understanding of subject matter content and inter-relationships among content areas. As such, semantic mapping is a viable means of assessing students' thinking and understanding. If semantic mapping is a valid tool for instruction and assessment, its use as a research tool could also be exploited.

The use of concept mapping as a research and evaluation tool in science education originated from the work of Novak (1972) and his graduate students at Cornell University (Rowell, 1978). It was originally applied as a means of exploring meaningful learning through audio-tutorial instruction in science at the elementary school level. Since then, concept mapping has been employed by many teachers at all levels as a diagnostic tool, as an assessment tool, for instructional design and curriculum development, and more recently as an aid to helping students "learn how to learn" (Novak, 1990).

Most studies done using concept mapping in assessment have compared student maps to teacher-constructed ideal maps (Diekhoff & Diekhoff, 1982; Novak & Gowin, 1984), rather than describing changes in the structure and content of the maps. Some studies (Heinze-Fry & Novak, 1990; Novak & Gowin, 1984) have used quantitative scores derived from maps to indicate conceptual growth of knowledge. Theoretical constructs such as differentiation and hierarchical organization have been used to demonstrate a growth of understanding in a particular subject area (Novak & Gowin, 1984). A study done by Beyerbach and Smith (1990), however, described changes in the content and organization of the maps, which is the focus of analysis in the investigation discussed in this chapter. In Beyerbach and Smith's study, early childhood majors in their senior year of study (in the first class of the year) were asked to construct concept maps following a two-step procedure. The two steps involved "brainstorming" of categories and subcategories related to effective teaching and then arranging these concepts in a hierarchical order from super-ordinate to ordinate. Subsequently in the second semester, students were asked to construct and continually update a concept map for the topic of "effective teaching" using the "Learning Tool" computerized program. Changes in the organization and content of the concept maps reflected the prospective teachers' thinking. Additionally, each pre-service teacher's reflective journals were analyzed to provide insights into their evolving beliefs about teaching and learning. Thus, the study by Beyerbach and Smith (1990) assesses pre-service teachers' thinking about effective teaching by analyzing their concepts to describe their evolving constructions of knowledge in a particular subject, and by this means to promote reflection.

The strategy in which pre- and post-maps were constructed by undergraduate teachers was also applied in a study by Beyerbach (1988). Changes in these teachers' thinking about teacher planning were described based on content analysis of the maps. The students also discussed their pre- and post-maps in an essay completed immediately after the post-mapping. The instructors were also interviewed several times about their intentions to guide students' thinking and their observations of changes in the maps.

RESEARCH PROBLEMS

The small-scale investigation documented in this chapter addresses the problem: how can teacher-educators facilitate student-teachers' reflective and critical thinking through the use of semantic mapping strategies. The review of literature suggested several questions that could be answered in the documentation process described in this chapter.

1. What do student-teachers' "first" maps (drawn before a series of taught sessions) reveal concerning what they know about the three components of Social Studies, Mathematics and Science, and Art? (A related question should be: "What do the semantic maps drawn by student-teachers at the beginning of a unit of teaching illustrate regarding their prior/existing knowledge, including gaps in their knowledge, and misconceptions they may have?")

2. Do the semantic maps drawn by the student-teachers at the end of a series of taught sessions in the three components of social Studies, Mathematics and Science, and Art become more enhanced in quality in terms of their structure and content?

3. Do student-teachers find semantic mapping useful as a strategy in developing concept webs in the early childhood curriculum?

The first two questions provide the researchers with means to achieving the goal of the study, "Using semantic mapping to facilitate critical/reflective thinking'. The third question directly addresses this ultimate goal.

Implications can be drawn from this process of documentation of the "first" and "second" maps and a comparison of these maps in terms of their structure and content, together with student-teachers' own views, to provide insights on the usefulness of semantic mapping as a strategy for facilitating the development of reflective and critical thinking skills in student-teachers.

Addressing the first question, if student-teachers' semantic maps drawn at the beginning of a series of taught sessions do reveal their "baseline" knowledge, prior/existing knowledge, including gaps in their knowledge, and misconceptions they may have, it would mean that these maps could provide a valid diagnostic tool for the teacher-educator. Applied systematically, the teacher-educator could gain valuable information about student-teachers already know as a basis for further developing their knowledge, that is, semantic mapping could be employed as an instructional tool. Addressing the second question would mean that semantic maps could be used as artifacts for detailed analysis of development in student-teachers' understanding of subject-specific knowledge. Findings from such analyses would provide a basis for the use of semantic maps as valid assessment and research tools. The documentation of these artifacts of learning together with the feedback of the student-teachers during the interviews concerning the usefulness of semantic mapping strategies described in this chapter could provide useful insights on the use of semantic maps as a tool for planning a spiral thematic curriculum, which is a common practice in early childhood education.

METHODOLOGY

For the above purposes, student teachers were asked to construct a concept map before a series of lessons at the start and at the end of each component of the module "Further Studies in Kindergarten Curriculum." When each of the subject areas (Social Studies, Mathematics and Science, and Art) had been taught, each student-teacher had in hand three semantic maps. They were then asked to relate the subject areas to the context of their early childhood curriculum, i.e., they were required to devise the final concept map comprising the subject areas covered, in connection with a theme. In this way, the graphic representation helped to make explicit the knowledge during their own learning process and allowed student-teachers as well as teacher-educators to track through the process and probe this understanding.

Furthermore, interviews with a random sample of nine student-teachers were conducted to find out their views on whether semantic maps helped them understand the subject matter and whether they were helpful in the design of thematic webs, as well as whether they should be used as a means of assessment in the module. These interviews served to triangulate the use of the semantic maps as a means of making explicit the student-teachers' understanding of the subject content and the teacher-educators' probing of this understanding using semantic maps as tools in the process. These interviews identified data to address Research Question 3.

Documentation Process

The documentation process of the study is depicted in Figure 1.

Sample

A total sample of 58 Year Two student-teachers (from two classes) attending the Certificate of Kindergarten Education (Chinese) Course (1997-1999) at The Hong Kong Institute of Education participated in the study. This represented about two-thirds of the cohort which were taught by three of the investigators of this study. A total of 160 samples of semantic maps were collected from these student-teachers at the beginning and at the end of the components (Social Studies, Mathematics and Science, and Art) of the module "Further Studies in Kindergarten Curriculum."

Data Collection

Before beginning a series of taught sessions, student-teachers were asked to draw concept maps (referred to as "first maps") to reflect their understanding of the subject matter content of each of the components. After a series of four or five taught sessions, the student-teachers were again asked to draw concept maps (referred to as "second maps"). A total of 73 first maps and 87 second maps were analyzed according to the criteria outlined in the next section. The 73 "first" maps came from one class of the student-teachers who contributed 29 maps for the Art component and 29 for the Social Studies component. The remaining 15 first maps came from the other class (approximately 50% of the class) who contributed maps for the Mathematics and Science component). 87 "second" maps came from the same two classes of student-teachers sampled whose "first" maps were analyzed. In addition, the "second" maps included those drawn by 14 other student-teachers in the second class whose "first"

Mathematics and Science maps were not included in the analysis (see Table 1).

Figure 1: *A Semantic Map of the Documentation Process of the Study*

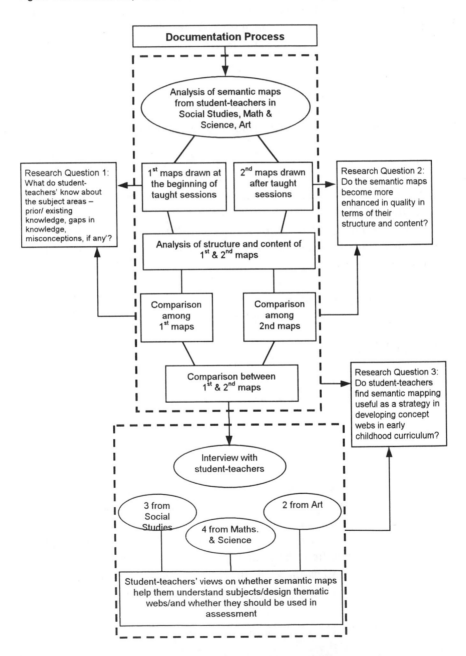

(This explains the discrepancy in the number of "first" and "second" maps as well as the discrepancy between the number of student-teachers and the number of maps sampled.) Subsequently, a random selection of two to four (two from the Art component, three from Social Studies, and four from Mathematics and Science) student-teachers were interviewed personally by the teacher-educator (investigator) who had taught the class.

Table 1: *Number of "First" and "Second" Maps by Class and Subject Component*

	Art	Maths & science	Social Studies	Total "first" maps
"First" Maps				
Class 1	29	15	0	44
Class 2	0	0	29	29
Total	29	15	29	73
"Second" Maps				
	Art	Maths & Science	Social Studies	Total "second" maps
Class 1	29	29	0	58
Class 2	0	0	29	29
Total	29	29	29	87

Scoring of the Semantic Maps

A procedure for scoring suggested by Novak and Gowin (1984), based on three principles of Ausubel's (1986) cognitive learning theory, may be used. This procedure involves the three features of hierarchical structure incorporating the idea of subsumption; progressive differentiation, and integrative reconciliation. In other words, concept maps may be evaluated based on how new information has been related to and subsumed under more general concepts. Concepts maps may be judged by the extent to which concepts have been linked together to form propositions. Another important feature of concept maps is the way new relationships are perceived between related sets of propositional concepts.

The criteria for assessing individual semantic maps were arrived at based on a review of relevant literature (Fisher, 1995; Novak, 1998). Levels of explanation outlined by Fisher (1995, p. 61) were considered, including "labeling" (where no explanation is given); "enumerating" (odd facts are given); "making a link"(contiguous ideas are paired up); and "identifying concepts belonging to a pattern or hierarchy of concepts as relating to other patterns of concepts." In addition to the above features, characteristics considered by Novak (1998, p. 192) were also incorporated: creativity in the organization of the map, inclusion of important, relevant concepts to be added to the map, salient cross-links indicating relationships between concepts in different sections of the map. The criteria used in the study were the level of clarity, relevance, integration, organization, and creativity. Each of the maps were evaluated on each of the criteria up to a maximum of three marks.

The aspect of "clarity" refers to the clarity of the content knowledge reflected in the semantic maps drawn by the student-teachers. It also refers to the quality of the maps in terms of the clarity of structure of the maps for representing content knowledge: in other words, to what extent does the map clearly present the links, and cross-links between concepts? The second criterion, "relevance" reflects on the appropriateness of the content knowledge (concepts) expressed in the map as related to the subject areas (Social Studies, Mathematics and Science, Art) and the specific "theme" of the individual map. Both "integration" and "organization" refer to the overall quality of the maps in reflecting the complexity of relationships (subsumption; progressive differentiation and/or integrative reconciliation) among the concepts/propositions depicted in the map. Finally, the criterion "creativity" assesses the extent to which the student-teacher has used creative ideas (creative structures) to represent content (subject matter knowledge/content).

The student-teachers' maps were originally scored according to the five criteria of clarity, relevance, integration, organization, and creativity. For each criterion, marks were awarded based on degree/extent to which the maps demonstrated each of the characteristics being assessed. However, the scores for the individual maps will not be reported in this study as the investigators were more interested in providing a general description of the type of structures used and what the content of the maps involved rather than assigning quantitative scores to the maps. Thus, for the purpose of the study, student-teachers' maps for each of the components (Social Studies, Mathematics and Science, and Art) were compared in terms of structure and content in the following ways: comparison among the "first" maps of each component to obtain a general idea of the structure and content of the maps; comparison among the "second" maps within the component in terms of structure and content; comparison between the "first" and "second" maps also in terms of structure and content.

A holistic method, as suggested by Rafferty and Fleschner (1993), of assessing the semantic maps was used. For example, semantic maps were judged to be "simple" (i.e. a semantic web created from a simple idea or concept) or judged to "hierarchical" (i.e. containing concepts organized into a hierarchy) (Fisher, 1995, p. 68). Semantic maps may be organized in a "linear" arrangement, in a geometric form or in any other "free flowing organic" structure (Fisher, 1995, p. 69).

The decision to use the holistic method of scoring the maps is premised on the assumption that the maps drawn "before" and "after" maps could provide a formative assessment tool to check on learning in progress or summatively to evaluate depth and breadth of understanding (Rafferty and Fleschner, 1993). The concept maps, by virtue of the fact that they display what student-teachers know or do not know as well as what they understand about the connections/relationships between concepts, are a viable method for assessing knowledge.

In the study, the maps were analyzed for their content in terms of concept, representational and propositional knowledge. (Ausubel, Novak, and Hanesan [1978] refer to "concept learning," "representational learning" and "proposition learning.") For example, concepts portrayed in a map drawn for the Mathematics and Science component may include aspects such as "Number" or "Flotation." Other terms may appear in such a map to represent the concept of "Number," such as "One-to-one correspondence," "Rote counting," etc. "Propositional knowledge" includes words/logical connectives to express how a group of concepts are related to one another. The structure of a map is inextricately related to the content portrayed in the map. Together, analysis of the content and the structure of the map provides insights into the knowledge/understanding of the student-teacher who has drawn the map. The semantic map demonstrates what he or she has identified as the important concepts, their attributes, their associations with meaningful concepts and the relationships between and among the group of concepts. Thus, the more he or she knows about a concept, the more enriched the web of understanding becomes. It is logical to assume that maps containing more rich information and demonstrating more complex relationships among concepts do show deeper understanding.

Interviews of Individual Student-teachers

Interviews (mostly one-to-one) were conducted with two to four student-teachers per component. The lecturer-investigator asked the following questions: Do semantic maps help you understand the specific subject? How do they help you? How do they help you to design the thematic web? Do you think we should continue using semantic maps as an assessment mode in the component of the module "Further Studies in Kindergarten Curriculum?"

It was hoped that these questions would probe the student-teachers' views on the experience and to ascertain whether they had benefited from applying the strategy.

FINDINGS

In this section, qualitative data from analysis of the student-teachers' "first" maps for each of the components of Social Studies, Mathematics and Science, and Art are presented, followed by qualitative data from analysis of the "second" maps. Following this is a comparison of the "first" and "second" maps to highlight the development of their knowledge in the three subject components. Finally, the data from the personal interviews with student-teachers are discussed.

Figure 2, 3, and 4 are examples of maps constructed by students at the beginning of the taught sessions. These examples are presented for the purposes of demonstrating the structure and content of the "first" maps. They are not meant to portray typical or average subjects of any group but are tangible exemplars for illustrative purposes.

Overall, the first maps were simple in structure. There was little variation in the organization format used in the maps: most of them were in the form of a web. The number of branchings and hierarchies were also limited. Concept connections were more linear. There was very little integration of concepts as revealed by the number of cross-links between concepts. In terms of content, they contained few basic concepts and relationships related to the knowledge domain of Social Studies, Mathematics and Science, and Art. In general, the majority of the propositions employed by student-teachers in the first maps was valid. However, the first maps revealed a limited range of subject-specific and super-ordinate concepts which were used to organize the knowledge structure. There were fewer specific examples of concepts or teaching strategies. A review of the semantic maps drawn by the student-teachers at the beginning of the components suggests a strong emphasis on concepts that may be considered to be common knowledge. There was very little integration of concepts (see Figure 2, 3, and 4).

Figure 5, 6 and 7 are examples of maps constructed by students at the end of the series of taught sessions. Again these are tangible exemplars (by no means typical or average subjects of any group) but are presented for the purposes of demonstrating the more complex structure and detail in content of the second maps. They are not meant to portray subjects of any group but are tangible exemplars for illustrative purposes.

Figure 2: *"First" Map Drawn by Student-teacher for the Social Studies Component*

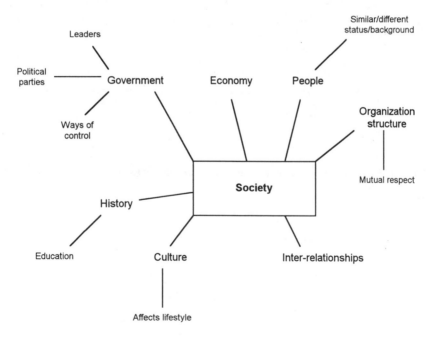

Figure 3: *"First" Map Drawn by Student-teacher for the Mathematics and Science Component*

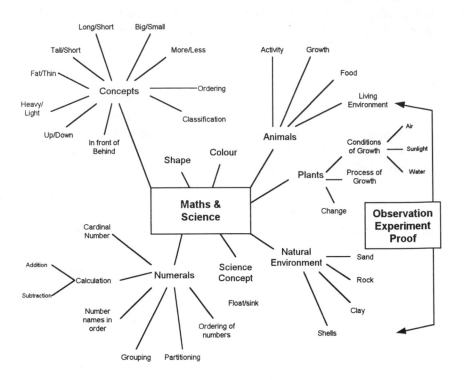

Figure 4: *"First" Map Drawn by Student-teacher for the Art Component*

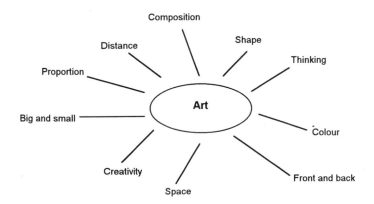

Table 2: *Analysis of "First" Maps for the Components of Social Studies, Mathematics and Science, and Art*

Components	Structure	Content
Social Studies (n=29)	• They varied from simple to detailed/complex. • There were similar patterns (usually in the shape of a sun with rays radiating from the centre).	• Picture relating the subject to people • Some included major aspects of Social studies such as historical, geographical, environmental. Political, and economic. • The maps were drawn from the perspective of an adult. • No interrelated/hierarchical concepts were shown.
Mathematics and Science (n=29)	• Most of the maps were in the form of a spider web. • Only a few were presented in a networking format. • Various shapes were used (rectangles, circles) with lines linking the key concepts. • Most of them were limited to one level. • Only a few (20%) depicted two or three levels: Key concepts were organized in categories and in a hierarchical structure.	• A list of loosely-related Maths concepts were included: shapes, comparison, ordering, time, number, space, computation, big/small, many/few, etc. • In terms of Science concepts, about 50% of the student-teachers included scientific inquiry skills partially or loosely into their maps. • A few listed developing logical thinking and problem-solving skills. • No cross-linking of key concepts.
Art (n=15)	• Most of the maps were very simple. • 53% of the maps had one level; 20% had two levels; three had three levels; one had four levels. • Very few of the uni-level maps showed relations between and among concepts presented. • For maps showing two to four levels, key concepts were organized in a hierarchical structure. • Most of the maps were loosely organized and not well developed. • The items in the maps were listed as in brainstorming, involving little or no detailed thinking. • Most of the maps were in the form of spider webs; only one was presented linearly and very few maps were organized in a networking format. • Regular shapes such as rectangles, circles were used to indicate key concepts and lines used to link the items and represent the path of thinking.	• All items in the maps could be categorized into nine items, e.g., activities/forms (such as printing, drawing, collage, etc.); knowledge about art (such as color, lines, space and structure, etc); skills of art (such as drawing, cut and paste, etc.); functions of art; value of art in education (such as to release emotions, to enhance aesthetic development); expression; appreciation; creativity, materials. • (Most common item: color) • The three most common items were value of art in education, knowledge of art, and creativity. • Most of the students mentioned the value of art (fine motor development, emotional release). • Only 33% mentioned aesthetic development, which is the most important in art education. • Most of the student-teachers mentioned the aims and content of an art curriculum but some focused on the names of the art activities.

Figure 5: *"Second" Map Drawn by Student-teacher for the Social Studies Component*

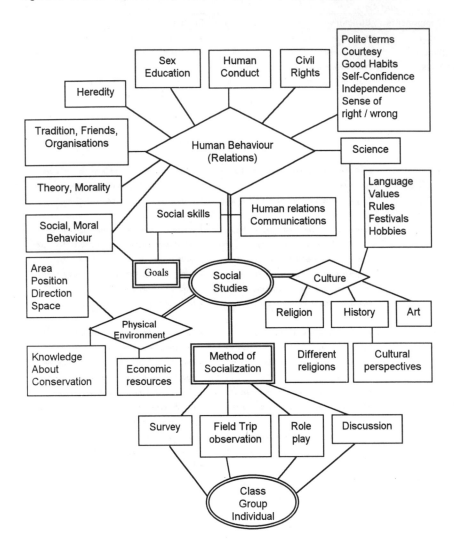

Figure 6: "Second" Map Drawn by Student-teacher for the Mathematics and Science Component

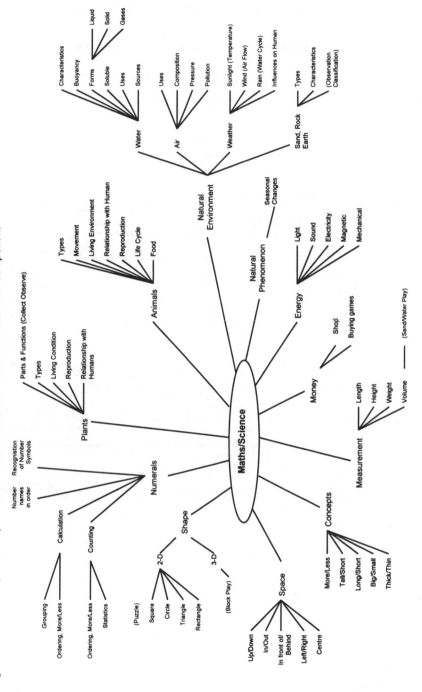

Figure 7: *"Second" Map Drawn by Student-teacher for the Art Component*

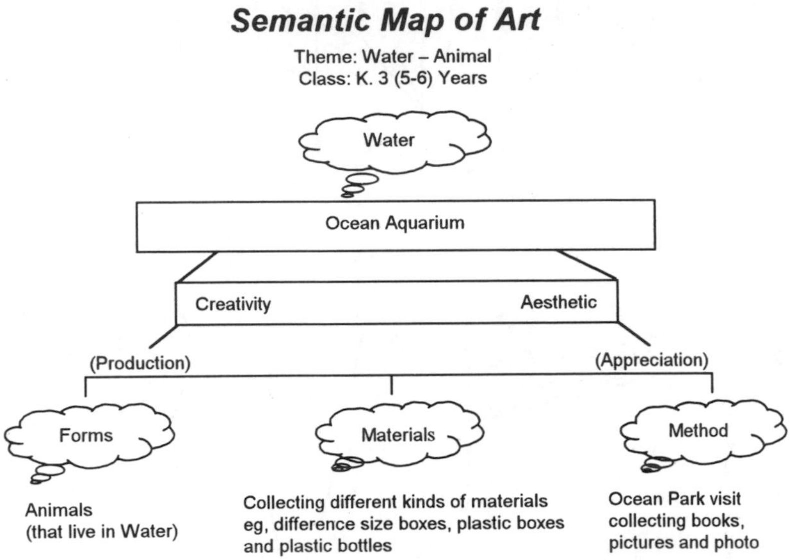

Semantic Map of Art

Theme: Water – Animal
Class: K. 3 (5-6) Years

Water

Ocean Aquarium

Creativity   Aesthetic

(Production)   (Appreciation)

Forms   Materials   Method

Animals   Collecting different kinds of materials   Ocean Park visit
(that live in Water)   eg, difference size boxes, plastic boxes   collecting books,
                         and plastic bottles   pictures and photo

Bas-relief fish	Different colours, shape of fishes scissors and colour	Shape, line
Shark	Different size boxes, cartridge paper, water colour and pastel paper	Shape, composition
Fish fossil	1. Sand paper-frottage, paper crayon and water 2. comflour or play dough	Line, shape, composition of the craft
Competition of sea animal design	Craft-paper cups, paper plates, plastic bottles, crepe and cartridge paper Model-big boxes, paper blocks, Lego and blocks	Shape, colour Space, composition
Aquarium design	Table, chair, cupboard and shelf	Space, composition
Sea animal poster design	Paper, water colour, water colour pen, pastel colour and crayon	Colour, line
Invitation card	Different sized paper, different shape design	Shape, colour
Entrance	Different sized paper, different shape design	Shape, colour
Octopus mobile	Different size paper cups and coloured cotton thread	Shape, colour

Table 3: *Analysis of "Second" Maps for the Components of Social Studies, Mathematics and Science, and Art*

Components	Structure	Content
Social Studies (n=29)	• There was a variety in the format of the maps: some used a cyclic form while others used webs in the shape of squares and some used a hierarchical structure. • There were different ways of categorizing concepts.	• Concepts were categorized in terms of their nature and relations; the concepts were also extended. • There was greater complexity of content reflected in the maps. • There was integration of concepts, e.g., according to knowledge of social aspects, skills, attitudes, or according to social activities or lecture topics taught in the component.
Mathematics and Science (n=29)	• Most of the maps were presented in a networking format. • The rest were presented in the form of a spider web, grouping in sets (Venn diagrams), sequencing and tree shapes. • Various shapes were used (rectangles, circles) with lines linking the key concepts. (Some used color as well). • Most of the maps were more complex: Key concepts were organized in a hierarchical structure (with two to four layers) • Some of them were still being presented at one level which resembled brainstorming of concepts related to a them. • Only some had cross-links among key concepts.	• Most of the maps listed concepts in a hierarchical structure and included specific curriculum concepts, and illustrations of a teaching/activity strategy including process skills and examples of activities. • Some maps followed the sequence from activities to key concepts while others proceeded from key concepts to activities. • Some of the maps still reflected a single perspective from the curriculum content of Mathematics and Science, but they were richer in content and more specific. Most of the concepts were related to the theme.
Art (n=29)	• All the maps were more complex and more detailed (having at least three levels) • Most of the maps were organized in a hierarchical structure in a vertical direction. • There was a higher frequency of networking and hierarchical structures. • Very few had cross relations. • Different shapes such as regular shapes (e.g., circles, rectangles) or irregular shapes were used to indicate the main concept. • Lines and arrows were used to show the path of thinking and to indicate the relation between concepts. • Most of them had clear relations within levels.	• All of them included the items "activities of art"; "knowledge about art" and "materials" • Most of them included the items "process of activities," "teaching strategies," and "objectives of art." • Some of them mentioned appreciation activities. • Some examples of concepts and levels include: from theme to sub-theme to forms /activities of art to content to materials of art to objectives of the activities; or from theme to activities to forms/activities of art to materials of art to objectives of the activities.

In general, the "second" maps were more complex than the "first" maps. There was a greater variety of visual arrangements used in the maps: although some still used the web format, which is the most commonly used pattern in the first maps, many used other formats, such as tree diagrams, Venn diagrams (grouping in sets), and networking. The number of branchings and hierarchies were also extensive. Concept connections were more hierarchical. There was more integration of concepts as revealed by the increased number of cross-links between concepts. In terms of content, they contained greater numbers of basic concepts and relationships related to the knowledge domain of Social Studies, Mathematics and Science, and Art. In general, the majority of the propositions employed by student-teachers in the second maps was valid. In addition, the range of subject-specific and super-ordinate concepts used to organize the knowledge structure was more extensive. There were more examples of specific concepts or teaching strategies. The "second" maps were also more integrated and better presented.

Findings from Interviews with Student-teachers

As mentioned, the questions posted to student-teachers in the interviews were "Do semantic maps help you understand the specific subject?"; "How do they help you?"; "How do they help you to design the thematic web?: and "Do you think we should continue using semantic maps as an assessment mode in the component of the module 'Further Studies in Kindergarten Curriculum'?" The responses to the first two questions are summarized in Table 4.

In general, all subjects interviewed agreed that semantic maps helped them understand the different components of Social Studies, Mathematics and Science, and Art. The responses may be categorized into various areas which they indicated semantic mapping strategies were useful. From the responses, it appeared that semantic mapping facilitated thinking, the organization of key concepts/ideas, brainstorming strategies, convergence of key concepts, and ease of "reading" and memory (see Table 4).

Four of the student-teachers interviewed mentioned that semantic mapping facilitated their thinking by helping them make sense of their own learning, clarifying their thoughts, helping them think more clearly or fostering understanding of their own knowledge/thinking. Two students mentioned that semantic maps also served to help them understand the direction of their own thinking. They facilitated thinking in greater detail (two students). They also

Table 4: *Summary of Responses to the Questions "Do semantic maps help you understand the specific subject?" and "How do they help you?"*

	SS1	SS2	SS3	MS 1	MS 2	MS 3	MS 4	A1	A2
Facilitating thinking									
• Make sense of learning/Clarify thoughts/Think more clearly/ Understand own knowledge/ thinking	/						/	/	/
• Understand direction of own thinking	/						/		
• Think in greater detail								/	/
• Easy to identify the main points in the maps								/	/
• Go beyond usual pattern of thinking		/							
Facilitating organization/ linking of key concepts/ ideas									
• Help in organizing the key concepts (into categories); (see interrelationships); grouping the ideas; linking key concepts in hierarchical form	/	/	/		/			/	/
• Useful in organizing ideas in sequence								/	/
• Identify links and extend beyond points more easily			/						
• Easy to obtain a holistic view of the relationships			/						
Facilitating "brainstorming" of ideas									
• Help in thinking of more possibilities	/	/	/						
• Useful tools in (Facilitates) brainstorming	/	/	/					/	/
• Transfer of strategy of brainstorming to other assignments			/						
Facilitating "convergence" on key concepts									
• Help in converging on key concepts within the theme	/	/	/						
• Minimizes diverse interpretations			/						
Facilitating ease of "reading" and memory									
• Easy to read the map (content of) because of visual and graphical representation	/	/	/				/	/	/
• Easy to remember (key words) (because of graphic form/visual images)	/	/	/	/	/				

made it easy to identify key points (two students), and encouraged them to go beyond their usual pattern of thinking (one student).

A total of ten responses related to semantic maps facilitating the organization/linking of key concepts/ideas. Among these responses, six referred to semantic maps fostering the organization of key concepts (into categories), helping them see interrelationships, group the ideas or link key concepts in hierarchical form. Two of the responses related to organizing ideas in sequence. One response has to do with identifying links and extending beyond points more easily and one response referred to the ease with which a holistic view of relationships could be obtained by means of semantic maps.

As many responses related to facilitating "brainstorming" of ideas. These included three responses which mentioned that semantic maps helped them think of more possibilities; five responses which referred semantic maps to as useful tools in brainstorming; and one response related to the transfer of "brainstorming" strategies to other assignments.

Four of the responses of student-teachers mentioned that semantic maps facilitated the "convergence" on key concepts. Of these, three responses referred specifically to "converging on key concepts within a theme." Only one response made reference to minimizing diverse interpretations.

Twelve of the student-teachers' responses could be categorized under the term "Facilitating ease of 'reading' and memory." Six student-teachers mentioned that the visual and graphic representation made it easy to read the maps and the content thereof. Six of the responses made reference to the fact that the graphic form/visual images actually made it easier to remember key words in the maps.

Table 5 summarizes the responses of the student-teachers to the question "How do (semantic maps) help you design the thematic web?" The analysis of responses may be categorized as follows: those regarding facilitating thinking from a thematic perspective and those regarding facilitating lesson planning and curriculum planning.

A total of seven responses could be categorized under the heading "Facilitating thinking from a thematic perspective." Of these responses, four referred to semantic maps as a means of synthesizing understanding of specific subjects from a thematic perspective or the synthesis of key concepts

Table 5: *Summary of Responses to the Question "How do they help you to design the thematic web?"*

Responses	SS1	SS2	SS3	MS 1	MS 2	MS 3	MS 4	A1	A2
Facilitating thinking from a thematic perspective									
• Think clearly of the key concepts within the theme/Derive subject content from theme				/		/			
• Synthesize understanding of specific subject from a thematic perspective/ Synthesize key concepts of a subject	/	/	/		/				
• Offers an alternative thinking strategy		/							
Facilitating lesson planning									
• Guide to achieving objectives of the activities						/			
• Makes it easier/quicker to design/plan a lesson/Improve design of lesson plan (in width and depth)	/	/							/
• School has adopted the strategy in lesson planning	/		/	/	/	/			
Facilitates curriculum planning									
• Transfer of strategy of brainstorming to planning in kindergarten			/						
• Use in planning kindergarten curriculum					/				
• Identify whether planning is comprehensive or not/More comprehensive planning/organization of teaching content of the theme	/	/	/	/	/	/	/		
• Easy to check if key points are missing/Convenient to add missing points	/	/	/			/			
• Present outline of subject content clearly					/				
• Help communicate more effectively with colleagues				/	/	/	/		
• Go beyond teaching kits						/			

of a subject. Two of the student-teachers mentioned that semantic maps helped them think clearly of the key concepts within the theme or to derive subject content from the theme. Only one response related to semantic maps as an alternative thinking strategy.

Semantic mapping strategies also helped student-teachers by facilitating lesson planning. For instance, three of them mentioned that semantic maps made it easier/quicker to design/plan a lesson or improve the design of a lesson plan (in terms of its width and depth). One student-teacher said that it could be used as a guide to find out whether the objectives of the activities designed had been achieved. An important indication of the usefulness of semantic maps is the fact that five out of the nine student-teachers interviewed emphasized that their own kindergartens had adopted the strategy in lesson planning.

Semantic mapping strategies also facilitated planning at yet another level, that of curriculum planning. Of the 19 responses categorized, seven of them related to identifying whether or not planning is comprehensive, or whether it is more comprehensive when compared to other means. Four responses were categorized under each of the following: "Easy to check if key points are missing/Convenient to add missing points" and "Help communicate more effectively with colleagues." One response was recorded for each of these categories: "Transfer of brainstorming to planning in kindergarten"; "Use in planning kindergarten curriculum"; "Present outline of subject content clearly"; and "Go beyond teaching kits."

Responses to the question, "Do you think we should continue using semantic maps as an assessment mode in the components of the module 'Further studies in Kindergarten Curriculum'?" are discussed below.

All the student-teachers interviewed expressed that they valued the experience and agreed that it was worthwhile as an assessment mode. However, some of the students (MS1, MS2, MS3, and MS4) expressed that there was a need to guide/teach them to use semantic mapping strategies. A student-teacher (MS1) expressed that she felt "insecure" when devising semantic maps; and another student-teacher (A1) stated that she did not know how to begin drawing the maps. As another student-teacher (MS2) stated that they "need to learn this kind of thinking strategy" and, in fact, she attributed success in the use of semantic mapping to the individual's "thinking style/learning strategy.

Another subject (A2) also expressed a similar view: that it was necessary 'to introduce the maps in more concrete ways." They needed a better understanding of subject knowledge and expected more input in terms of how to construct semantic maps. For instance, they may require guidance in how to create a hierarchy in the map (MS1). The student-teachers identified as subjects of the Art component had the following responses: "the criteria for assessment of the maps (A1) should be made clear" and fear of "taking the wrong direction in thinking" (A2). These remarks were made by student-teachers during the interviews which occurred at the end of the module. However, they expressed their concerns regarding the use of semantic mapping as an assessment mode. This was the element that was new to the student-teachers. Previous cohorts of student-teachers had been assessed by means of the traditional modes – essays, tests or examinations. From the moment the student-teachers were informed about the mode of assessment to be used at the beginning of each component, they had approached the teacher-educator who was teaching that component for clarification of the criteria for assessment of the semantic maps and strategies to use in the drawing of the maps. In fact, the teacher-educators had anticipated these problems and had interspersed the teaching of subject content with teaching of semantic mapping strategies. Indeed, the teacher-educators benefited tremendously from the experience gained from teaching this cohort of student-teachers and the strategies for handling their "fears" and concerns. In retrospect, the feedback informed the next round of teaching where the teacher-educator-investigators were involved.

LIMITATIONS

There are several methodological limitations of the study. Although the data is not limited by the sample size of the subjects or the number of semantic maps used for analysis, the research investigation is seriously limited by the method of scoring applied to the individual maps and the holistic nature of the scoring method used.

Originally, the teacher-educators had used a method of scoring the maps based on five the criteria of clarity, relevance, integration, organization, and creativity. To recall, the aspect of "clarity" refers to clarity of both content knowledge and representation of this knowledge (quality of the map in terms of the clarity of structure for representing content knowledge: clarity of presentation of the links, and cross-links between concepts). The second criterion, "relevance" refers to the appropriateness of the content knowledge (concepts/aspects/strategies) expressed in the map. The overall quality of the map is assessed in the criteria of "integration" and "organization" which reflect the complexity of relationships (subsumption; progressive different-tiation and/or integrative reconciliation) among the concepts/aspects/propositions depicted in the map. The final criterion of "creativity" assesses the extent to which the student-teacher has used creative ideas (creative structures) to represent content (subject matter knowledge/content).

For each of these criteria, the teacher-educator had awarded a mark of 0-3 according to the degree to which the characteristic was present. However, for the purposes of the study, these individual scores were not reported as the teacher-educator researchers were more interested in obtaining an overall picture of the content depicted in the semantic maps and the structure of the maps used to represent the content. Neither did the researchers make any attempts to correlate these scores with assessment of the content and structure of the maps obtained by the holistic/global method employed in the study.

Although, the researchers based the criteria for assessment on a review of relevant literature, there is a need to carry out more research to evaluate the validity of these aspects in reflecting content and structure of the maps. Assuming that these are valid constructs of assessment, the researchers would suggest that the individual scores of the maps be used as a means to evaluate content and structure. In fact, in order to ensure greater consistency in assessment, the following grade descriptors would be suggested. The suggested grade descriptors for assessment are as follows:

A: Excellent. The map demonstrates very clear and relevant concepts/aspects/strategies which are very well integrated and organized. A high degree of creativity is demonstrated in the representation of the concepts/aspects/strategies displayed in the map.

B: Very Good. The map demonstrates clear and relevant concepts/aspects/strategies which are well integrated and organized. There is creativity in the representation of the concepts/aspects/strategies displayed in the map.

C: Good. The map demonstrates clear and relevant concepts/aspects/strategies which may not be well integrated and organized. There is little creativity in the representation of the concepts/aspects/strategies displayed in the map.

D: Pass. The concepts/aspects/strategies displayed in the map may not be clear or relevant and there are minor flaws in their integration and organization of the map. There is little creativity in the representation of the concepts/aspects/strategies displayed in the map.

E: Fail. Many of the concepts/aspects/strategies displayed in the map are unclear or irrelevant and there are major flaws in the integration and organization of the map. There is no creativity in the representation of the concepts/aspects/strategies displayed in the map.

The method of evaluating the maps employed in this study involved analysis of the content and structure of the maps on a holistic/global basis. The structure of a map may be judged to be simple or complex. In addition, the format/pattern used for representing content would be noted. For instance, webs, tree diagrams, Venn diagrams (grouping in sets), network diagrams, cycle format, or other shapes were used. Concepts/aspects could be presented in a hierarchical manner and various levels of a hierarchy may be employed. In terms of the content, the researchers were interested in the concepts presented in the maps (whether they referred to content knowledge or curriculum strategies/activities).

This method where a comparison was made between the first maps drawn by the student-teachers at the beginning of each component and the maps they drew after a series of taught sessions ("second" maps) would have yielded more conclusive results if the researchers had used a more objective means of scoring the maps. As a holistic means of scoring was adopted, this gave rise to a certain degree of subjectivity in the evaluation of the structure and content of the semantic maps produced by the student-teachers.

Using a holistic scoring method for evaluating the semantic maps has also placed a limitation on the extent to which the investigators could assess progress or change in student-teachers' understanding about each the subject areas (components) of Social Studies, Mathematics and Science, and Art, and their ability to integrate the content of these components over the course of the module "Further Studies in Kindergarten Curriculum."

The fact that the "first" maps were not used for diagnostic purposes, as suggested by Clarke (1990) gave rise to another limitation. Analysis of the "first" maps did provide the teacher–educators with a general idea of the "model" the student-teachers were using to think about the subject area content. The "first" maps helped the teacher-educators identify some of the baseline information their student-teachers had within the subject area, including the gaps that could be filled, as well as their misconceptions, if any. At best, it was only possible to provide a global description of the characteristics of their "first" maps in terms of structure and content. A more detailed analysis of the features of the first maps would have provided more concrete information regarding their prior knowledge and the gaps and misconceptions so that this information could be better utilized to inform teaching. Furthermore, analysis of the semantic maps before beginning the taught sessions would have yielded more specific data about student-teachers' existing concepts which could be elaborated.

The process of using semantic maps as a means of organizing content information to be taught in the classrooms within the units was not systematically documented. Thus, it was not possible to study the process by which the teacher-educators actually guided and facilitated the student-teachers' critical and reflective thinking.

IMPLICATIONS FOR RESEARCHERS AND TEACHER-EDUCATORS

The strategy used in the study where student-teachers were required to draw semantic maps before the beginning of a series of taught sessions would have been more effective if the teacher-educators had analyzed the maps before actually teaching the sessions. In this way, the teacher-educators could have used the "first" maps for diagnostic purposes: to obtain valuable information regarding student-teachers' baseline knowledge of the subject area; the gaps that exist in their knowledge; the misconceptions that needed to be corrected; and the existing concepts that should be elaborated through exposure to additional information.

Increased rigor in the scoring of the semantic maps could be achieved by means of a points system of scoring the structure and content of the semantic maps. A method of scoring used by Novak and Gowin (1984) and modified by Markham, Mintzes, and Jones (1994) could be used for scoring the concept maps. In the scoring method, points were given for the number of concepts, relationships, branchings, hierarchies, crosslinks, and examples represented in each map. These aspects were taken to indicate various constructs such as "extent of knowledge" (number of concepts and relationships), "progressive differentiation" (branching), knowledge subsumption (hierarchies), "knowledge integration" (crosslinks), and "specificity of knowledge" (examples) (Markham, Mintzes & Jones, 1994). In the study reported here, these aspects were subsumed in the holistic method of evaluating the maps but were not explicitly used to derive quantitative scores. By assigning quantitative scores to each of these aspects, it is hoped that the aspects of content and structure could be assessed more objectively to provide quantitative data to lend support to the qualitative data obtained in this study. Such data would provide a more specific and accurate picture of the structural complexity and concept hierarchy of student-teachers' knowledge.

SUMMARY AND CONCLUSION

The results of the semantic mapping procedure and the interviews converged on some specific findings. From the semantic mapping procedure, the main findings are summarized in the following paragraphs.

The holistic method of analyzing the structure and content of the first maps yield the following data. Structurally, the first maps were more simple, with fewer branchings, cross-links, and hierarchical levels. Linear connections of concepts were more common. The content analysis of these maps indicated that concepts commonly associated with the subject component and valid propositions were presented, though little integration of these concepts/propositions was evident. However, the range of subject-specific and superordinate concepts was limited. Fewer examples, whether of concepts or teaching strategies, were included.

In contrast, the second maps were structurally more complex. More varied visual/graphic arrangements were employed including webs, tree diagrams, Venn diagrams, and networking. More branchings, cross-links, and hierarchies were evident. There was more extensive content knowledge (as indicated by the number of concepts and relationships). More subject-specific knowledge was displayed (judging from number of examples provided), and there was greater integration of knowledge (as indicated by the number of crosslinks, branchings, and hierarchies). The second maps were also better presented visually.

From the interview data, two themes emerged as important considerations. First, semantic mapping did facilitate thinking, organization of concepts/ideas, and convergent (focusing on key concepts, subject-specific knowledge), as well as divergent thinking (through "brainstorming") and facilitated memory of content and easy "reading" of the maps. And second, semantic mapping also facilitated thinking from a thematic perspective as well as lesson and curriculum planning.

However, the data from the personal interviews also revealed some inherent problems in the use of semantic mapping strategies. These problems were related to the lack of familiarity with the technique and, perhaps, a lack of practice in using the strategy. The responses point to a need to guide student-teachers in constructing semantic maps as well as more input in terms of subject knowledge and interrelationships among key subject-specific concepts. Another issue raised is related to the use of semantic mapping as an assessment mode. There is a need to convey to student-teachers the criteria for assessment.

Within the limitations of the exploratory investigation, it was possible to obtain a very general overall idea of the student-teachers' baseline knowledge from the semantic maps drawn at the beginning of the unit of teaching. The teacher-educators were able to gauge what was common knowledge among the student-teachers in the class, as well as indications of the gaps in their knowledge and some misconceptions they may have. The holistic scoring method employed in the study enabled the teacher-educators to analyze the structure and content of the student-teachers' semantic "first" maps in order to obtain insights about their knowledge structure:

1. What is the extent of their subject-specific knowledge? (What are some of the key concepts/ideas associated with the subject area? Are they valid? What examples can they provide to illustrate these key concept/ideas?)

2. How are these key concepts/ideas linked or integrated? (Are there limited/numerous branchings, cross-links, hierarchies [linear or networked]?)

Regarding the second question – "Do the semantic maps drawn by the student-teachers at the end of a series of taught sessions in the three components of Social Studies, Mathematics and Science, and Art become more complex in terms of their structure and content?" – the findings from the analysis of the second maps and the comparison of their structural and content features with those of the first maps indicated some changes in structural complexity and concept hierarchy of the student-teachers' subject-specific knowledge. The analysis indicated an increase in the extent of knowledge in the subjects under study, and their ability to demonstrate greater knowledge integration and differentiation. Semantic maps, by virtue of their visual/graphic nature, permitted both teacher-educators and student-teachers to see at a glance the representational configurations of their knowledge base and to analyze the changes in these representations as reflections of their knowledge. Semantic maps are excellent for illuminating their understanding and in fact, serve as documents of their thinking processes. As artifacts of this thinking, semantic maps provide a viable tool for the assessment of student-teachers' knowledge structure.

To the extent that this study has provided insights into student-teachers' initial knowledge base and the "second" maps do indicate greater complexity in terms of structure and content, the objectives of this study (as reflected in the first two questions asked) have been achieved. However, the effectiveness of this investigation and documentation could have been enhanced if quantitative data could have been obtained by means of a points-system of scoring, such as the one suggested by Markham, Mintzes, and Jones (1994), in addition to the holistic method of scoring adopted in this study. These quantitative data would support the qualitative data provided by the holistic scoring method used. The potential of semantic maps as a means of facilitating the development of critical and reflective thinking skills could be further augmented and the purpose of semantic maps as diagnostic, instructional, assessment, and research tools could be further explored.

The data from interviews with the student-teachers demonstrated that they found semantic mapping to be a useful strategy in practical terms, and could be applied specifically for facilitating their own thinking, integrating different subject areas, lesson, and curriculum planning. In summary, the documentation process described in this chapter has been well worthwhile, even though it is time-consuming. It has provided both student-teachers and teacher-educators with insights into how semantic mapping strategies could be applied to facilitating the development of reflective and critical thinking in student-teachers. Their application in curriculum planning in early childhood education could be further exploited.

REFERENCES

Arnaudin, M. W., Mintzes, J. J., Dunn, C. S., & Shafer, T. S. (1984). Concept mapping in college science teaching. *Journal of College Science Teaching. 14*(2), 117-121.

Ault, C. R., Jr. (1985). Concept mapping as a study strategy in Earth Science. *Journal of College Science Teaching, 15*(1), 38-44.

Ausubel, D. P. (1968). *Educational psychology: A cognitive view.* New York: Rinehart, & Winston.

Ausubel, D. P., Novak, J. D., & Hanesan, H. (1978). *Educational psychology: A cognitive view.* New York: Rinehart, & Winston.

Beyerbach, B. A. (1988). Developing a technical vocabulary on teacher planning: Preservice teachers' concept maps. *Teaching & Teacher Education, 4*(4), 339-347.

Beyerbach, B. A., & Smith, J. M. (1990). Using a computerized concept mapping program to assess preservice teachers' thinking about effective teaching. *Journal of Research in Science Teaching, 27*(10), 961-967.

Buzan, T. (1974). *Use your head.* London, England: BBC Publications.

Connely, F. M., Claudinin, D. J., & He, M. H. (1997). Teachers' personal practical knowledge on the professional knowledge landscape. *Teaching and Teacher Education, 13*, 665-674.

Clarke, J. H. (1990). *Patterns of thinking: Integrating learning skills in content teaching.* Masschusetts: Allyn and Bacon.

Cliburn, J. W. (1990). Concept maps to promote meaningful learning. *Journal of College Science Teaching, 19*(4), 212-217.

Ost, D. H., (1987). The evolution of a Biology curriculum. *The American Biology Teacher, 49*, 153-156.

Dieknoff, G. M., & Diekhoff, K. B. (1982). Cognitive maps as a tool in communicating structural knowledge. *Educational Technology, 22*(4), 28-30.

Fisher, R. (1995). *Teaching children to learn.* Chelteham: Stanley Thornes.

Heimlich, J. E., & Pittelman, S. D. (1986). *Semantic mapping: Classroom applications.* Newark, DE: International Reading Association.

Heinze-Fry, J. A., & Novak, J. D. (1990). Concept mapping brings long-term movement toward meaningful learning. *Science Education, 74*(4), 451-472.

Horton, P., McConney, A. A., Gallo, M., Woods, A. L., Senn, G. J., & Hamelin, D. (1993). An investigation of the effectiveness of concept mapping as an instructional tool. *Science Education, 77*(1), 95-111.

Markham, K. M., Mintzes, J. J., & Jones, M. G. (1994). The concept map as a research and evaluation tool: Further evidence of validity. *Journal of Research in Science teaching, 31*(1), 91-101.

Novak, J. D. (1972). Audio-tutorial techniques for individualized science instruction in the elementary school. In H. Triezenberg (Ed.), *Individualized science: Like it is* (pp. 14-30). Washington, DC: National Science Teachers Association.

Novak, J. D. (1980). Meaningful reception learning as a basis for rational thinking. In A. E. Lawson (Ed.), *1980 Association for the Education of Teachers in Science Yearbook: The psychology of teaching for thinking and creativity*, (pp. 191-224). US: Ohio. (ERIC Document Reproduction Service No. ED 184 894).

Novak, J. D. (1990). *Learning how to learn*. Cambridge, England: Cambridge University Press.

Novak, J. D. (1998). *Learning, creating, and using knowledge: Concepts maps as facilitative tools in schools and corporations*. Mahwah, NJ: Lawrence Erlbaum.

Novak, J. D., & Gowin, D. B. (1984). *Learning how to learn*. Cambridge, Great Britain: Cambridge University Press.

Rafferty, C. D., & Fleschner, L. K. (1993). Concept mapping: A viable alternative to objective and essay exams. *Reading Research and Instruction, 32*(2), 25-34.

Rowell, R. (1978). *Concept mapping: Evaluation of children's science concepts following audio-instruction.* Unpublished doctoral dissertation, Cornell University.

Schwartz, R., & Parks, S. (1994). *Infusing the teaching of critical and creative thinking into elementary instruction*. Pacific Grove, CA: Critical Thinking Press.

White, R., & Gunstone, R. (1992). *Probing understanding*. London, United Kingdom: Palmer Press.

Workman, S. H., & Anziano, M. C. (1994). Extending children's ideas: Concepts webs and early childhood curriculum. *Day Care and Early Childhood, 21*(3), 23-28.

Chapter 20

Tertiary Learning: The Case of Student Teachers in Self-research

Victor FORRESTER

The School of Languages in Education
The Hong Kong Institute of Education, Hong Kong

The central theme of this chapter, that of helping tertiary level students obtain the maximum benefit from their advanced studies, is predicated on a view of curriculum as being evolving, essentially developmental in nature. This view recognizes that education involves change, that change is essentially unpredictable, and that students' respond to change in unpredictable ways reflecting their essential individuality. Attempts to imbue stability to the learning process are well documented in the literature of curriculum development both globally (Beane, 1995; Doll, 1993; Tyler, 1949) and recurrently in the context of Asia, (Biggs & Moore, 1993; Biggs & Watkins, 1995; Ellis, 1997, 1992; Nunan, 1992; Nunan & Lamb, 1996). Such attempts however have themselves been subjected to fruitful critiques (Pinar & Reynolds, 1992; Reynolds, 1987; Sears & Marshall 1990), critiques which serve to remind us that the curriculum is essentially a contestable arena. Where the focus is on education, and in particular teacher education, as opposed to subject mastery, the curriculum can justifiably take, as its locus, our understanding of the *learning process*. Rather than seeking a curriculum that sets the goal of Subject mastery, there are valid contexts in which the goal is to understand the learning process.

One such context comprises the recently established Hong Kong Institute of Education (HKIEd) with its major role as teacher-trainer for the Hong Kong School system. Following a decade of constant economic growth in Hong Kong (1987-97), the Hong Kong Government addressed the issue of upgrading school education by expanding the opportunities for a graduate teaching profession (Hong Kong Special Administrative Region Government, 1997). Facilitating this move, five former Colleges of Education were combined and upgraded to form the degree awarding HKIEd. The accreditation process for these new degree programs focused attention on pedagogy and the curriculum, an evolution reported elsewhere (Forrester 1994, 1998). The teaching of the new degree programs now focuses attention on the relationship between pedagogy and student learning. It is the relationship between pedagogy and student learning that this chapter now explores.

To explore the relationship between pedagogy and tertiary student learning, this chapter reports a series of student-based self-research tasks in the form of two critiques. The first critique considers a series of student-based research in terms of its *results*. This first critique presents a contextual demographic framework that here serves to highlight the perceptions held by students moving from secondary to tertiary education at HKIEd. The relationship between student perceptions and attributions is then explored to generate a hypothesis about these students' learning needs. The second critique then considers self-research as a *learning process*. In this second critique, the pedagogic implications of student-based self-research are considered: specifically the pedagogic implications of Task Based Learning and its potential for enhancing language learning.

The rationale for presenting a demographic study in tandem with reporting of series of student-based self-research tasks lies in making real the wisdom that "we do research with people, not on people" (Reason, 1981, p. 115, original underlining). Following Reason's advocacy of a new research paradigm, a demographic study here serves to locate but not proscribe students within an informing context. Awareness of this context enriches an interpretation of these students' self-research results.

Extending Reason's advocacy that "we do research with people" (ibid.) forms a rationale for employing student-based self-research. By employing student-based self-research two enriching benefits accrue. First, the research focus is enriched by the insights of the research subjects. Second, the process of doing "research with people" who are in teacher education enables the pedagogical implications to emerge of self-research as a *learning* process.

Limitations abound to the practical implementation of Reason's research paradigm (see Reason, 1994). Central to these limitations is the descriptor "participatory research" (Reason, 1994, p. 1). To have students participated in self-research at once enriches but also "contaminates" – raising quasi-scientific concerns about reliability, validity, and interpretation. Although it is beyond this chapter to explore such issues here, there are articulate voices which suggest that by nature *human* inquiry is unscientific and that, like its subject *human,* inquiry is not susceptible to controlled experimentation (see Reason, 1994; Tarnas, 1991).

The first critique now follows in which a series of student-based research is considered in terms of its *results,* prefaced here by first the findings of a demographic survey. Framing this first critique is the over-arching question of "Which factors affect students' learning?"

WHICH FACTORS AFFECT STUDENTS' LEARNING?

Following the early work of Turner-Smith (1981), students at Hong Kong's tertiary institutions have been the subject of demographic surveys (Chinese University, 1986-1999; Colleges of Education, 1985; Hong Kong Institute of Education 1999; Polytechnic University, 1986-99; University of Hong Kong, 1985-99).

The HKIEd Survey

The demographics reported here differ for their focus is on revealing factors which affect student learning. The students, whose demographics inform this study, comprise the 1998-99 cohort enrolled in the first year of study on the Bachelor of Education program offered by HKIEd. Enrolment into this program is selective: HKIEd selects students according to academic attainment and individual screening-interviews; the students select HKIEd according to vocational interest and competition for places in other tertiary Institutions. This dual selection process engenders a student cohort that is qualified for a tertiary education though not necessarily one devoted to teacher training.

This cohort (n = 106) completed individual demographic questionnaires within the first week of their first Semester. The summary results are displayed in Table 1.

Findings

The demographic features in Table 1 are arrayed in two layers: first, their demographic *foreground* and, secondly, their demographic *background.* Considering the demographic *foreground*: the 1998-99 cohort comprises 106 students with a gender ratio of 6.5 Females to every 1 Male student. For this cohort tertiary learning takes place in a distinctly female learning environment.

The cohort's median age is 19 years, place of birth for the majority is Hong Kong and only 2 students are married. In terms of maturation and Life experience, the cohort's demographic *foreground* is reasonably uniform.

Table 1: *Students' Demography*

A Demographic Profile of the B.Ed 1998-99 cohort	
Foreground	n = 106 students
Ratio:	Female 6.5 : Male 1
Median Age:	19 years
Born in Hong Kong:	88%
Married:	2
Background	
• Parents' Education:	Post Secondary: 10%
• Home Size:	44% 40-60sq m
	24% 20-39sq m
• Home Study Facilities:	36% have own room & desk
	41% Share room & No desk
• Student Travel Time to HKIEd:	50% = 90-120 minutes
	31% = 60-90 minutes
• Strongest reason for Living-on-Campus:	57% to save travel time
• Family Income:	44% less than HK$19,000
	(= HK Graduate Teacher's salary)
• Seeking Part-time work:	85%
	Reason: 50% to cover basic living expenses

Considering the demographic *background*, the majority of these students are "family front-runners" in terms of education at tertiary level – of their parents, only 10% have any experience of post-secondary education. The 1998-99 cohort comprised home-based students;[1] accordingly home living conditions are relevant to this study. Typical of Hong Kong, home size is tight: 44% live in homes of 40-60 square meters; 24% live in homes of 20-39 square meters. Within these constrained living conditions, a third (36%) of these students report having their own room and their own desk. However, 41% of these students report having not only to share a room but also having no desk. From this home environment, these students travel to the HKIEd campus: a time consuming experience. For half of the B.Ed. cohort, this daily travel takes between one and a half hours to two hours for a single journey. For an additional third of this cohort, the daily travel takes between one hour to one and a half hours for a single journey. It is hardly surprising that the reason given for wishing to "Live-on Campus" was to save travel time (57%). Family incomes – reported before the 1999-2000 "economic downturn" – show 44% of these students reporting total family incomes of less than HK$19,000. In contrast a 1998 Graduate Teacher salary is HKHK$21,000.[2] The attitude of such families to the potential salary commanded by a "graduate teacher" can be imagined. However, such longer-term financial goals are mediated by more immediate concerns: 85% of these students report being actively seeking part-time work; the reason given by 50% is their need to cover basic living expenses.

This review of these students' demographics reveals a demographic *foreground* that in terms of maturation and life experience is reasonably uniform. One distinctive feature is that for this cohort, tertiary learning takes place in a distinctly female learning environment. This cohort's demographic *background* reveals congested family households offering unsatisfactory home-study facilities combined with long travel-times. Low family incomes may place a teacher's salary as a desirable end-goal; however, a more immediate impact is to drive these students to actively seek part-time work.

Implications for Policy-makers

The demographic review raise several features of direct relevance to those involved in teacher training policy. This section now reviews some of these implications.

The first feature is that currently teacher training taking place within a distinctly female learning environment. The implications for policy-makers include considerations of stereo-typing, narrowed educational focus, work-force demographics, and "top-down" management.

Stereo-typing is both the purpose and bete-noir of a learning environment – good teaching is frequently seen as "good modeling." However within an educational environment which recognizes that good teaching involves change, the definition of "good modeling" may not be synonymous with "stereo-typing." A teacher training environment which appears to be distinctly "female" is one which may challenge the true implementation of educational change. For those involved in educational policy-making, the implementation of effective educational change may be seen as having its grassroots in the demographics of the teacher training environment.

A narrowed educational focus is Janus-headed: one perspective sees the learning process as being discriminating, allowing for prioritization and sequencing; the other perspective sees a constricted learning horizon which dis-empowers the learner's natural pace and appetite for acquiring knowledge. Learning which takes place within a distinctly female environment accordingly has strengths but also weaknesses, particularly in not exposing training-teachers to the full spectrum of learning potentials. Those involved in creating an educational policy which addresses the full spectrum of a truly comprehensive education may consider teacher training as a lens that can focus but also limit.

Work-force demographics in education are numerically dominated by females. The implications here for those involved in education policy-making are as simple and as complex as assuming that in the learning process the messenger is distinct from the message. Where the distinction between messenger (here the teacher) and the message (here the curriculum) is at best uncertain, those involved in creating an educational policy will recognize the interpretative force of work-force demographics on the effective implementation of educational policy.

Work-force demographics in education may be numerically dominated by females; yet, this need not imply a democratic distribution within the management of education. Where learning takes place within a distinctly female environment but authority is exercised within a distinctly masculine environment, this "lesson" escapes the attention of few students. Equally apparent to students are learning environments which advocate a "joy in learning" yet proscribe the what, how, and when of learning. These two samples serve here to illustrate the derailing effects on policy where education is perceived as being managed from the top-down. For those involved in creating effective educational policy, work-force demographics has a significant influence.

Having considered the demographic feature of teacher training taking place within a distinctly female learning environment, the second demographic feature – a background of poverty – is now reviewed in terms of its implications for educational policy.

This cohort's demographic *background* reveals congested family households offering unsatisfactory home-study facilities combined with long travel-times. Low family incomes may place a teacher's salary as a desirable end-goal; however, a more immediate impact is to drive these students to actively seek part-time work. This demographic pattern – a reductive approach to learning – has policy implications.

Where policy makes education compulsory, it is reasonable to expect this policy should also make education accessible. Where students are compelled to seek part-time work, to study in unsatisfactory home-surroundings, and to travel for excessive lengths of time, the access to teacher education can be questioned. The provision of grants/loans and student hostels[3] is a matter of education policy – the levels of provision serving as markers of a communities commitment to compulsory, universal, and/or comprehensive education.

A reductive approach to learning has another implication for education policy which go beyond the above concerns with economic support. This second implication refers to education as a tool for societal change. Where education empowers societal movement, education policy can be viewed as a tool for societal change. The demographics detailed above indicate that a family's income may be doubled by the salary of one family member becoming a graduate teacher. This realization places teacher training under social pressures which need have little to do with becoming an effective educator. For those involved in educational policy, compliance for socio-economic reasons amongst even the freshest teacher-trainees may feature in making education "reform" a "paper-dragon."

Implications for Pedagogy

The implications of these demographics for those involved in education policy are shown by the above examples to be considerable. The implications of these demographics for those involved in teacher education are equally significant. The following section now considers some of the implications of these demographics for those involved in the pedagogy of teacher education.

The first feature is that currently the pedagogy of teacher education takes place within a distinctly female learning environment. Two causes for this female-dominant environment can be examined here.

The first cause for teacher education taking place within a distinctly female learning environment is linked to a school examination system in which the majority of "marginal-pass" pupils are female. The demographics outlined above indicate that teacher education attracts "marginal-pass" pupils who have been unsuccessful in gaining admittance to other degree programs. The majority of these pupils are female. The pedagogic implications here include a teaching style and an examination system which dis-favors female pupils. In terms of teacher education, clearly to repeat the pedagogy of the past is to entrench further the results of this education. From this logic, the pedagogy of teacher education by definition needs to be "revolutionary."

A second cause for teacher education taking place within a distinctly female learning environment is linked to a benevolent myopia. In countries that espouse the principle of democracy, turn-taking between female and male students appears to be fair and equitable. Where there is a perceived "minority" grouping (here of male students), such turn-taking seems equitable in terms of encouraging a minority. In terms of teacher education, clearly to repeat the pedagogy of the past is to entrench further the results of this benevolent myopia. From this logic, once again the pedagogy of teacher education by definition needs be "revolutionary."

Having argued for teacher education to be "revolutionary" it is meet here to highlight some of its "revolutionary" characteristics. Firstly, it is helpful to recall that the source for the "revolutionary" characteristics of teacher education lies in the teacher-trainees demographics – specifically, here the demographics of teacher education taking place within a distinctly female learning environment and within the challenges of a background of poverty. For teacher education to effectively "revolt" against these specifics requires not so much pedagogic skill – the traits which make any good teacher's teaching "engaging" – rather what is significant here are pedagogic insights. These insights center on teacher-trainees being both the product and reformers of their own education system. To centralize teacher-trainees, to draw from them their insights and self-reflections, to debate with them the value of educational "change" and to analyze with them the practical results of implementing educational change is "revolutionary" only where teacher training has previously been seen as an induction process, a way of molding individuals to a standardized mean.

The pedagogy of teacher education, as suggested above, can be a distinctive marker of the function of teacher education. However, the pedagogy of teacher education must also address other dimensions that affect student learning. Demographics form one dimension of the factors that affect students' learning. The particular demographics outlined above indicate the potential for *background* poverty to become a circle of poverty. However, in economically and socially open societies, individual endeavor may challenge the poverty circle. The level of interaction between demographics and individual enterprise is reflected in individual perceptions. It is appropriate now to move from considering cohort demographics to consider a second dimension of the factors that affect students' learning. This second dimension comprises an investigation of student perceptions.

Student Perceptions: Moving from Secondary to Tertiary Education

Role perceptions of post-secondary students reported elsewhere (Cheng, 1997; Chow & Lou, 1992; Tse & Chung, 1995) point to a congruence between environment, personality and tertiary "success." It is perhaps unsurprising that in Hong Kong, "successful" secondary students tend to become "successful Tertiary students." However, not all enrollees for teacher training are "successful" secondary school students. Where reports consider "less successful" secondary students the results are more revealing. "Less successful' Hong Kong secondary students face a complex array of challenges including the grasping the role of independent study, monitoring their own learning and actively developing their own potential (MacLennan, 1995). What such studies serve to illustrate is that when moving from secondary to tertiary education it is the "less successful" students who face a complex of challenges. Adding to this complexity is the pivotal role of student perceptions. This pivotal role of student perceptions can be decisive leading to an overall decline in attitudes toward the learning situation (Crew, 1994). To investigate the complex challenges facing "less successful" secondary students requires a research approach which will address both the complex of challenges and the pivotal role of student perceptions. The following now reports just such a multi-dimensional research approach.

To investigate student perceptions of moving from secondary to tertiary education a variety of methodologies was adopted. Following input sessions on research methods, 60% of the cohort (n = 106) elected to research the topic "*Moving from Secondary to Tertiary education.*" Groups, with two to four each, students adopted a variety of research methodologies – direct interviews (audio/video recorded), telephone surveys (audio recorded), and questionnaires. The sample populations included HKIEd and senior level secondary school students – peers on the B.Ed. program, first, second and third year students on the Certificate program and senior level secondary school students. Sampling throughout was convenience-based. Given the context it is perhaps not surprising that all the research groups adopted a rather narrow definition of *"Tertiary education"* as being a student at HKIEd. Research reports were first presented by each group at the International Conference of Teacher Education held in Hong Kong on 22-24 February 1999, and included an account of the methodology, a critique of its limitations, and discussion of the results. Table 2 displays in rank-order the topics reported as being significant for students *"Moving from Secondary to Tertiary education."*

Findings

As shown in Table 2, financial concerns dominated these students' findings. The cost of fees and travel and living expenses ranked foremost for these students whose family background (see Table 1) tends towards encouraging their 18-plus year olds towards a degree of financial self-dependency.

Time management for these students is a major burden in respect to their dependency on public transport. Daily travel time for many exceeds four hours. Having no control over these four hours, combined with the need to additionally manage study and paid-work time places these students in conditions which have been described elsewhere as "learned helplessness" (Galloway, 1998). Lacking control over daily basics provides a daily experience of "helplessness" which cumulatively consolidates into a "learned" experience. As has been shown elsewhere, such "learned helplessness" tends to spread beyond immediate experience, to mould generic learning attitudes (Galloway, 1998).

Table 2: *Ranking of the Topics*

Rank-ordered: Most Significant > Less Significant
• gender differences (to making friends/to studying/ to new environment)
• time management (travel/study/curricula activities/paid work)
• social (dating/ making new friends/relations with staff)
• initial attitudes (to joining HKIEd/becoming a teacher)
• environmental (campus facilities/accommodation)
• financial (income/expenses)

Social changes are particularly significant for 18-plus year olds, offering both a "fresh start" and a sense of "isolation." Such ambivalent feelings are reflected in these students' results where some students embrace, others reject the ideal of "dating," welcome and complain about having to find "new friends." Their relations with lecturing staff reflects this ambivalence – some groups reported student complaints that compared with secondary, their tertiary learning is less staff-friendly.

Environmental factors (apart from travel time) are generally positively reported. A new purpose-built campus and open access to information technology (IT) are clearly welcomed. Requests for enhanced food outlets, shopping, and Student Residences are common. Interestingly, such environmental comments tend to be reported in terms of "doing OK" rather than "are OK." Throughout the reporting, there is a sense of evolution rather than arrival, of things progressing towards rather than being acceptable.

Reported gender differences were marked. HKIEd males reported feeling confident both in terms of "making new friends" and adjusting to the "new environment." HKIEd females reported the opposite, feeling initially challenged by having to make new friends, travelling to and from this new environment. Notably, females reported greater ease adjusting to "studying." Such gender stereotypical reporting is perhaps not unexpected given the demographics reported in Table 1.

Reported initial attitudes to joining the HKIEd were uniform: beneath a thin surface of enthusiasm, lurked a strong feeling of having arrived here by "failing" to gain admission to a "proper university." This negative perception pervaded attitudes to "becoming a teacher" which reportedly was commonly characterized as being a profession of "last resort."

Individually or combined the above factors – financial concerns, "learned helplessness," social isolation, an environment that is perceived as "just OK," gender stereotyping, and negative views on becoming a teacher – do not constitute a fertile ground for academic pursuits. These reported negative factors support the reported demographics of poverty in identifying dimensions that would appear to work *against* quality tertiary learning. These two dimensions – first student demographics, second their perceptions of "Moving from Secondary to Tertiary Education" – certainly present an intriguing challenge to attaining a quality tertiary education defined in the HKIEd's vision statement as "Optimizing each child's potential through the shared joy of learning."

To further investigate how students perceive their tertiary learning experience, a second group of the B.Ed cohort researched the gender realities of the classroom situation – *"Who gets attention in the HKIEd classroom?"*

Gendered-Classroom-Attention

The methodology for researching the gender realities of the classroom - *"Who gets attention in the HKIEd classroom?"* – replicates research reported elsewhere (Forrester, 1997). Three student groups, (with a total of 24 students) monitored nine convenience-sampled two-hour lectures. All nine lectures occurred during the mid-semester, across three subject areas, and involved "normal" classroom teaching. Observers were class-attendees, with sample observations taken in rotation at set times against a set checklist. Observations were logged of both student and lecturer attention giving. Raw results were then calibrated to reflect the actual student gender-ratio of each class.

An analysis of the observation results reveals that lecturer attention-giving uniformly ignores the gender ratio – resulting in lecturers giving 500% more attention to male students. This discrepancy is not explained by student behavior, for observed student attention-giving by both female and male students is balanced. An explanation for this disturbing result may lie in a form of overt "democracy" that favors addressing female and male students in turn. The classroom reality, however, is that there are more female than male students (mean of observed classes: five females to one male student). By addressing female and male students in turn, the overt "democratic" turn taking favors male students.

The gendered classroom research replicates a methodology reported elsewhere (Forrester, 1997). Although the results obtained here support this earlier work, of significance here is to note how the student-observers received these results. On reviewing their first observation results, these student-observers at first thought the evidence should be *denied.* When reviewing their second observation results, these student-observers viewed the evidence with *scepticism.* Even when reviewing their third observation results, these student-observers viewed the evidence with *caution.*

An explanation for these responses lies in follow-up discussion that drew from these students' self-reflections on their prior education experience. Firstly, these students noted that in co-education classrooms, teacher "turn-taking" was the norm. Secondly, that these students felt dis-empowered in terms of influencing a teacher's routine. What this follow-up discussion reveals is the connection between long-term experience and students' current perceptions. In this instance, a long-term experience of gendered-classroom behavior directs these students to perceive its manifestation at the tertiary level with denial, skepticism, and caution. Where a basic human right to equal treatment is perceived with denial, skepticism, and caution creates a challenging context to attaining a quality tertiary education, a challenge acutely contrary to the vision of a "*shared* joy of learning, a critical component of the HKIEd motto."

To further investigate how students perceive their tertiary learning experience, a third group of the B.Ed cohort researched the realities of their own learning by investigating the research question "*How do I learn?*"

How Do I Learn?

The methodology for researching "*How do I learn?*" required pairs of students (2 x 10: pop. = 20) to "mirror" their partner's classroom behavior. In this study, 10 pairs, total 20 students, were formed. Then, firstly, each student observed classroom learning characteristics using a standardized notation. Secondly, they wrote a "report" summarizing their observations. And thirdly, they exchanged reports which they read and then added written responses in the form of self-reflection. This sequence of observation, reporting, and self-reflection was repeated twice, to mitigate the "experiment-effect," and empower self-change. The students' written self-reflections were then analyzed in terms of response-types.

Results of the response-type analysis reveal individual differences and prior learning habits – response-types formed a spectrum of learning profiles from the "stuck" student who denies anything can be improved to the "moving" student who embarks on self-change. The majority (74%) reported learning profiles that were, at least initially, "stuck."

In terms of revealing student perceptions, these results suggest that students moving from secondary to tertiary education are, at least initially, cautious. That students who have provided evidence of academic attainment should also show caution perhaps reveals something about their underlying perceptions of education. It is pertinent here to recall the impact of prior learning on student responses to the research into classroom gendered-attention. Student responses revealed perceptions of denial, skepticism, and caution stemming from the influence of prior learning.

Summary: Which Factors Affect Students' Learning?

The demographic data supports a view of these students as, first, learning within a distinctly female environment and, second, being challenged to convert a circle of poverty into a spiral of improvement. Student perspectives would support this challenging view: evidence of gendered-classroom bias is perceived with denial, distrust, and at best caution; moving from secondary to tertiary is perceived solely in pragmatic and negative terms. The impact of these factors on students' learning is crystallized in their approach to learning and, in the majority of cases, learning is perceived with caution.

The implications of these findings for those involved in education policy-making cited considerations of stereo-typing, narrowed educational focus, work-force demographics, and "top-down" management. These considerations were shown to be significant in terms of the even the freshest teacher-trainees forestalling educational initiatives and rendering educational policy into a "paper-dragon."

The implications for those involved in the pedagogy of teacher training cited recognition that the pedagogy of teacher education by definition is "revolutionary," for teacher-trainees are both the product and reformers of their own education system. To effect this "revolution" requires a pedagogy that centralizes teacher-trainees, draws from them their insights and self-reflections, debates with them the value of educational "change," and analyzes with them the practical results of implementing educational change. Such a "revolution," however, is diluted by pedagogy also addressing other factors affecting student learning – specifically how students perceived their learning. Student perceptions have been shown to be conservative. From this conclusion, the pedagogic challenge of teacher training lies in addressing a student body whose perceptions are essentially conservative.

Before proceeding to further explore these student perceptions and then their impact on the pedagogy of teacher training, certain cautions are to be recognized. In brief, numerous cautions limit the reliability and ability to generalize from these conclusions viz. concerns over the impact of context on research methodologies, sampling, and participant-researchers. The defining context here is of one student cohort starting out on one tertiary degree program. This context defines researchers as conscripts in that their research output is to satisfy the requirements of an academic module. The context also defines available/convenience sampling and renders data analysis/reporting open to bias skewing. The ability to generalize from these results is suspect as no provision is made to establish if groups represent the cohort and if this cohort represents other students moving from secondary to tertiary education. Acknowledging these cautions against the ability to generalize, the rationale remains true that, at sample level, this data serves as exemplars of these students reported perceptions. As exemplars of reported perceptions, it is now possible to advance this research by exploring what these reported perceptions reveal about student *attribution*.

The following section now critiques what these reported perceptions reveal about student *attribution* and what impact such perceptions/attributions have both on student learning and the pedagogy of teacher training.

A Critique of Student Perspectives as Exemplars of Student Attribution

The relationship between one's perspective and one's attribution is debated elsewhere (Weiner, 1986, 1992). The relevance of this debate here lies in understanding the *impact* of student perspectives on their learning. The research results reported above may indicate that these students have a deep conservatism based on learnt dis-empowerment.[4] Such perspectives should be depressing in many contexts, particularly so where the context involves student teachers learning what to teach another generation of students. The impact of perceptions on attributions can be seen as central to determining whether students learn in a repetitive circle or a creative spiral.

The demographic results indicate that these students have a social background characterized as a circle of poverty, mitigating against academic pursuits. Yet, the historical evidence of Hong Kong is that such circumstances (and worse) fail to entrap. Rather than embracing the static nature of "learned-helplessness," the historical evidence of Hong Kong infers a growth built on pragmatics. In individual terms, what cannot be changed is subsumed and what can be changed is tackled. An exemplar of such pragmatics is to be detected in the reported rank ordering of topics of concern to students moving from secondary to tertiary education (see Table 2). The most commonly perceived concern (Table 2) is "financial (income/expenses)," a perception significantly attributed not with helplessness nor physical hardship but with personal enterprise[5]. Here, the perception may be negative, but the attribution is pragmatic. This pattern is also noted in the last concern (Table 2) listed as "initial attitudes." Here, the perception is again negative, but the attribution "to joining the HKIEd/becoming a teacher" identifies concerns over which they have little control: i.e., the students were being "sandwiched" between "minimal" academic results denying "university" acceptance and family demographics whose income will nearly double on their becoming a graduate teacher. From these observations, it is possible to hypothesize that pragmatic students award high priority to perceptions when the attribute is within their control and low priority to perceptions to which they attribute little control.

Exploring the hypothesis that pragmatic students prioritize perceptions to which they attribute being within their control, two scenarios readily follow. Where education is a "challenge" (Beane, 1995; Doll, 1993), pragmatic students will set the pragmatic goal of attaining grades at a "pass" rather than at the higher-risk "excellent" level. Where education is a "challenge," pragmatic students will voice course evaluations in pragmatic terms (I passed, ergo this course is good). Such a scenario presents students as being passive and appreciative. Where the aim of education is cited as "optimizing . . . potential through ... the joy of learning"[6] pragmatic students may become disorientated by "fuzzy objectives" and complain of assessment bias (I passed but I don't understand why). Such a scenario presents students as being unthinking and difficult.

These two scenarios present intriguing pedagogic challenges. Where education is a "challenge," pedagogy faces students' apparent "passivity." Where education is cited as "optimizing ... potential through ... the joy of learning," pedagogy faces students' apparent inability to "think." To effectively address these two pedagogic challenges – of the "passive" or "unthinking" student – requires cognition of their underlying causes. The first cause lies in the hypothesis that pragmatic students prioritize perceptions to which they attribute being within their control; the second cause is the underlying Aim of education. The contention here is that simply to extol students to "be active, not passive" or to "think for yourself" is futile for it fails to address the underlying causes. However, to create a learning context in which pragmatic students experience "control" will address these underlying causes. From this line of argument, the pedagogic challenge lies in creating learning contexts within which pragmatic students can experience "control."

The following section now explores one exemplar of a learning context within which pragmatic students can experience "control." The exemplar here is that of self-research. In self-research, the individual is both researcher and subject of research joint roles that award self-control – an attribute pragmatic students have been shown to prioritize. Two perspectives of self-research as a *learning process* are explored: the first perspective is of self-research as a variant of Task-based learning, the second perspective is of self-research as a pedagogical strategy to provide learning opportunities.

SELF-RESEARCH AS A VARIANT OF TASK-BASED LEARNING

Task-based learning, by its very nature, is context-specific (Willis, 1996), as reflected in Table 3.

Table 3: *The Context-specific Nature of Task-based Learning*

Task Initiator and Facilitator	Task-based Learner
Pre-Task:	
The Teacher	*Students*
Introduces and defines the topic	Prepares for the task individually
Ensures students understand task instruction	
May display other students doing the same	
or Similar task	
Task Cycle:	
Task:	
The Teacher	*Students*
Teacher acts as monitor and encourages students	Students do task
Planning	
The Teacher	*Students*
Ensures purpose of report is clear	Prepare to report to class
Helps rehearse	Rehearse
Report	
The Teacher	*Students*
Acts as chairperson and provides feedback	Present reports to class

Table 3 presents the context-specific nature of Task-based learning: the Teacher as task initiator (Pre-Task) then as facilitator (Task Cycle), and the context as bounded-language-learning (the stress on "understand task instruction," individual student work, teacher as "monitor," ensuring "purpose of report is clear," "acts as chairperson," "provides feedback"). Task-based learning in the context of Hong Kong has by necessity expanded the bounds of the Willis (1996) model – at the Hong Kong University, the teaching of medical nurses introduces a humane, responsive context; at the Hong Kong Polytechnic University the teaching of engineers imposes a respect of time-cost management. At HKIEd, the defining context is one of teacher training.

Within the context of teacher training, the "product" of a self-research task can be considered to extend beyond its reported results to embrace the participant's *learning experience.* Reflecting the essential individuality of thelearning experience, the self-research tasks reported here offered certain "freedoms." These "freedoms" included, first, a *choice* of tasks ranging from structured-replication to open-methodology; second, either pair, small group or large-group work; third to "learn" from real contexts with "live" subjects; and fourth open-ended results. A discussion of these four "freedoms" now follows.

The first "freedom" provided a *choice* from three tasks across the spectrum from structured-replication to open-methodology. This element of task-level choice addresses incoming students' range of self-confidence and their willingness to take learning "risks." With a cohort size of 106 students, a spectrum of learning "risk taking" may be predicted, and this prediction in part is supported by the results shown in Table 4.

The results recorded in Table 4 indicate that the most popular choice 60% of cohort, i.e., 63 students presented a "High" risk-level. This "High" risk-level refers to the "open" methodology which required students to develop and trial their own research methodology. In contrast, the "medium" and "low" risk-levels – where appropriate, methodologies were provided – proved less popular, 20 and 23 students respectively (a total 40% of cohort). The indication here is that when offered educational choices pragmatic students are willing to elect for "high-risk" learning.

Table 4 also displays a second "freedom" that of electing to work in pair, small group, or large-groups. The results indicate that these students prefer to work in small groups (only 21% elected to work in large groups). This result raises the question of why do some students elect to work in large groups? Analysis of video data showing these large groups at work reveals three categories of body language: first, the "leaders"; second, the "followers"; and third, students clearly "out-of-group." Detailed analysis identifies the ratio of "out-of-group" students to the combined "leaders"/"followers" as 11:12 (total 23) revealing that social dilemma, of (here female) students yet to adapt to the new social environment of first-year tertiary studies. Clearly incoming students vary in the time they need to become socially integrated. Task-based learning built exclusively on small group work may falter by ignoring such student needs.

The third "freedom" allowed students to "learn" from real contexts with "live" subjects. This "freedom" reverberates throughout the raison d'être of task-based learning with its underlying principle of "learning from Life." For post-secondary students (19-plus years old) the cultural context of Hong Kong is not noted for being adolescent-centered, nor is the Hong Kong secondary learning context noted for being student-centered. In contrast, the center of teacher training is the student as a learner and as a training-teacher. The transition from secondary to tertiary learning present circumstances that combine to form a potent motivation. This potent motivation stems from tapping the natural self-interest of being aged 19-plus years, the prestige role-playing of "being a researcher", the authority of "becoming a teacher" and the novelty of accessing not "acquired" but self-knowledge. When this combination of self-interest, prestige, authority, and novelty is focused on researching real contexts with "live" subjects, research judgments and interpretative insights can prove incisive.

Table 4: *Task-types and Student Preference*

Risk Level	Methodology	Grouping	Student Preference	Percentage
"High":	Open	group size of 2/3/4	(63 students, 58F:5M)	60%
"Medium":	Semi-structured	pair work	(20 students, 14F:6M)	19%
"Low":	Replication	3 large groups	(23 students, all female)	21%

Adding to the above potent combination is the fourth "freedom" of open-ended-results. Rather than contriving to meet or replicate a set "learning-agenda," self-research tasks provided "learning-freedom" in which what students discovered was less important than their ability to question their research methodology. From the outset, students were clearly aware that the questioning of their methodology was paramount, and this questioning was to be grounded on their own experience.

Having explored four "freedoms" and their impact on pragmatic students, it is perhaps inconceivable that pragmatic students will not equally be sensitive to that classic yoke on "learning" the need for assessment. The students whose self-research is reported here were working on a task they knew would be assessed. The impact of assessment is well documented (Shohamy, 1999). However, it has also been argued that assessment is not separate but rather a part of the learning process (Biggs & Watkins, 1995). Developing from work with constructive-alignment, in which both the teaching aims and learning assessment are brought together the form of assessment facing these self-researchers comprised two key characteristics: firstly, assessment descriptors were provided at the outset; and secondly, these self-researchers were required also to be self-graders.

Assessment descriptors were issued along with the self-research task options. Developing on Biggs and Watson's (1993) concept of constructive alignment here the teaching aims and assessment descriptors were collapsed by providing students with specific assessment "goal-posts" and giving them the "freedom" to find their individual ways in which to provide evidence for their own target grade.

A weakness with Biggs and Watson's (1993) constructive alignment lies in its implementation stage. Assessment descriptors are open to interpretation. Where the lecturer is the sole-marker the lecturer remains the assessment "gate-keeper." To address this weakness student self-grading was adopted. Based on the evidence submitted and the set assessment descriptors, each student self-graded. Self-grading and evidence was then presented to the lecturer as second-marker. Where a grade was questioned, a third, independent marker adjudicated. This assessment process proved a powerful learning instrument for both students and lecturers, shifting as it does the student/lecturer relationship from receiver/giver to a somewhat more equitable, learning partnership.

In sum, task-based learning – reported here in the context of teacher training – has been expanded well beyond the Willis (1996) model of bounded-language-learning. Certainly, the essential core remains true to the task-based learning ethos of "learning by doing." However, as reported above, this ethos can adapt to embrace both a spectrum of learning levels, a spectrum of task-based groupings, an over-riding focus on both the student as research-subject and as research-evaluator and finally an assessment procedure that empowers an equitable, learning partnership between faculty and students.

SELF-RESEARCH AS A MODEL OF EFFECTIVE LANGUAGE LEARNING

Having considered above the first perspective of self-research as a variant of task-based learning, a second perspective, self-research as a strategy for providing learning opportunities, is to be examined here. This examination considers language acquisition from five perspectives. These five perspectives consider good language learning as a developmental process (Ellis, 1997), a process of negotiation (Esch, 1997), a decision-making process (Nunan, 1991), a meaning-focused activity (Kumaravadivelu, 1993), and a non-linear process (Joseph & Taylor, 1990; Mulcahy, Peat, Andrews, Darko-Yeboah, Marfo, & Cho, 1991).

The first perspective views language learning as a developmental process. Essentially, two strands of language learning have engaged the interest of linguists and researchers: first, its occurrence as a pre-ordained, pre-specified sequence; and second, as a developmental, organic process that follows an agenda. Empirical evidence tends to lend credence to the latter during which errors are not necessarily the result of bad learning, but are part of the natural process of interlanguage (Elliot, 1983; Foster, 1999). The self-research task reported in this chapter provided students with three options ranging from replication, semi-open to open methodology where students tried various approaches to achieve set objectives. The underlying message here is that errors made in the process are not just tolerated but recognized as an integral part of language acquisition, acting as a springboard to move learning forward. Enhancing this message is the dynamic interplay between empathy and the lowered inhibition of the students. This interplay mobilizes the students' linguistic resources in two domains – cognitive (e.g., how to present their findings) and affective (e.g. surged confidence through presentation of the research at the 1999 International Teacher and Education Conference).

The second perspective views language learning as a process of negotiation. The self-researches reported here give leeway to students to negotiate learning routes. In more specific terms, *what* they do and *how* they proceed are primarily at the discretion of the students with the teacher as a facilitator. For instance, the self-research topic *"Moving from Secondary to Tertiary Education"* required students to report their findings and to provide a critique of their research methodology. These requirements necessitated a critical examination of the linguistic forms (genre and register) and an application of verbal and non-communication skills (to solicit views and share feelings). These students were also empowered to select *how best* to exploit the research context and *when* to terminate an approach perceived to be less profitable – determinant ingredients for successful learning (Esch, 1997). This ability to exercise control and to negotiate has been shown to be central to effecting deep change in learning (Sadovnik, 1995).

The third perspective sees language learning as a decision-making process. Rubin and Thompson (Nunan, 1991) characterize efficient language learners as those who, among others, "... make their own opportunities, and find strategies for getting practice in using the language inside and outside the classroom; use mnemonics; are creative and experiment with language" (Nunan, 1991, p. 171).

How to help students evolve towards this ideal learner is not immediately clear. From the literature on different learners and learning styles (Cotton, 1995; Tennant, 1988), the crux of the issue appears to reside in the depth of participant involvement. The depth of participation attained in the self-research reported here include developed study skills, an ability to pursue learning *outside* class (in a non-conventional setting), and to negotiate a learning agreement with themselves and others.

The fourth perspective views language learning as a meaning-focused activity. Meaning-focused activities are defined as those in which "[L]earners are preoccupied with the process of understanding, extending or conveying meaning" (Kumaravadivelu, 1993, p. 78). On meaningful engagement, Marton and Booth (1997) make a pertinent observation: (making) "[N]ovel utterances in accordance with the rules of grammar and the conventions of lexical occurrence is the most essential and the most difficult Problem for the learner" (p. 66).

To make "novel utterances" may be an essential measure of language development but to do so, learners need multiple opportunities to discover the regularities and irregularities of the language system to develop and extend their potential to decode others' meaning. In the self-research tasks reported here, the didactic elements[7] do not necessarily conflict with the meaning-focused principle for modeling and rehearsal, but when accompanied by *meaningful* connections, create a satisfactory condition for augmenting knowledge (Evans, 1991). This positive view of didactic elements, such as modeling and rehearsal, recognizes that instruction can lead to development (Shannon, 1994). The determining factor here is context, for here the self-research is determined by the participants. Even when the problem seems to assessment-based, the motivating drive behind it embodies choice, power, and collaboration with an empathetic partner, thus minimizing anxiety found to be associated with negative "backwash" (Biggs & Watkins, 1993). Adding to these positive elements is the multiple roles required of these students[8] of which permits meaningful transaction to be conducted rehearsing a panoply of strategies across linguistic, academic, and affective domains (Kelly, 1996).

The fifth perspective views language learning as a non-linear process. This view recognizes that language learning involves social competence – language helps share feelings, establish relations, as negotiate meaning (Mulcahy et al., 1991). Focusing on this social role, "language is not an organism or a passive reflection, but a social institution deeply implicated in culture, in society, in political relations at every level" (Joseph & Taylor, 1990, p.163). With this focus, language is used for meaning negotiation. Language development does not or need not proceed in neat steps for language learners may choose to abandon or adopt specific approaches or strategies without detriment to the learners' progress.

Language learning has been examined from five perspectives. These five perspectives on language learning serve to indicate here that any one exclusive language learning approach is contestable and that language development is context defined. This discussion has also revealed that self-research provides multiple, non-exclusive approaches to language learning with these approaches operating within clearly defined contexts. Accordingly, this discussion supports the view that self-research is a model of effective language learning.

CONCLUSION

This chapter has offered two critiques of a series of student-based self-research tasks. This first critique considered research in terms of its *results*. The results revealed a conceptualizing demographic framework consisting of learning taking place within a distinctly feminine environment and a circle of poverty. Implications for those involved in policy-making were then explored, citing the impact of stereo-typing, narrowed educational focus, work-force demographics, and "top-down" management. These implications were shown to be significant in terms of the even the freshest teacher-trainees forestalling educational initiatives and rendering educational policy into a "paper-dragon." For those involved in the pedagogy of teacher training, the implications cited recognition that the pedagogy of teacher education is by definition "revolutionary." The pedagogic challenge lay in making this "revolution" not cyclical but into a spiral of improvement. To explore this pedagogic challenge, student learning perceptions and student attributions were then examined – specifically of students moving from secondary to tertiary education at HKIEd. These students' learning perceptions were shown to be conservative. Their attributions were to accord high priority when perceiving to be "in control" and low priority when perceiving little control. This relationship between student perceptions and attributions generated a hypothesis: that pragmatic students prioritize perceptions whose attribution is within their control. This hypothesis was then shown to be stable across two diverse aims of education – one aim being that students should face a "challenge," the second Aim being to experience "the joy of learning." Pedagogic implications of this hypothesis were then explored, positing a solution of creating learning contexts within which pragmatic students can experience "control."

A second critique considered student-based self-self-research as a *learning process*. This learning process was explored first as a variant of Task-based learning, revealing self-research to be multi-leveled for it embraces a spectrum of learning levels, a spectrum of student groupings, a view of the student as both research-subject and research-evaluator, and finally an assessment procedure that empowers a balanced, equitable partnership between faculty members and students. A second exploration considered the learning potential of student-based self-research within a specific context – here of language learning. This second exploration revealed self-research to offer an enriching language potential with an ability to provide multiple, non-exclusive approaches to language learning within clearly defined contexts. Of specific interest was the appeal of self-research as satisfying the needs of both subject knowledge, "revolutionary" learning and the attributes/perceptions of incoming teacher-trainees to HKIEd.

Conclusions drawn for this database are limited by two concerns. Firstly, there is concern about the impact of context on research methodologies, sampling, and participant-researchers. And secondly, there is concern about the ability to generalize from results which are context specific. These two concerns go to the heart of Reason's (1994) advocacy of a new research paradigm – by definition *human* inquiry is not scientific. To address concerns of reliability and the ability to generalize requires further inquiry within other *human* contexts.

The hypothesis that pragmatic students prioritize learning that they attribute to be within their control requires further development. Are pragmatic students a distinguishable subset? Is the pragmatism identified here a function of age or society, or both?

The policy implications sound alarmist. The claims that teacher-trainees may forestall educational initiatives and render educational policy into a "paper-dragon" requires further investigation.

The pedagogical claims for student-based self-research as a *learning process* require trials within other contexts – could secondary/primary level students benefit from self-research? Is there a threshold limitation set by language or by research design? The pedagogical implications center on a view that effective learning involves (pragmatic) students feeling in "control" – does such a view disturb societal and cultural norms?

What remains intriguing from this investigation into tertiary student learning is the revelation of a complex of factors which connect learning with teaching and educational policy-making. At the macro-level of policy-making, this complex of factors reveals an individual's and society's views on education. For those involved in teacher education, such indicators can acutely define the reality of "teacher education."

NOTES

[1] Student Hostel accommodation became available from 1999 onwards.

[2] Since April 2000, the salary has been reduced to HK$ 17,000..

[3] At HKIEd, both are made available from 1999 onwards.

[4] The indicators are as follows: moving from secondary to tertiary is perceived solely in pragmatic and negative terms; evidence of gendered-classroom bias is perceived, in the majority of cases, with caution.

[5] As Table 1 indicates: 85% are seeking part-time work.

[6] The HKIEd Vision Statement is "Optimizing each child's potential through the shared joy of learning and teaching."

[7] For example, teacher gives Problem instructions, helps rehearse, and offers corrective feedback.

[8] For example, student as learner, and/or researcher, presenter; teacher as facilitator,

listener, and/or co-presenter.

REFERENCES

Beane, J. A. (Ed.). (1995). *Toward a coherent curriculum.* V.A. USA: Association for Supervision and Curriculum Development.

Biggs, J. B., & Moore, P. J. (1993). *The process of learning.* New York: Prentice Hall.

Biggs, J. B., & Watkins, D. A. (1993). *Learning and teaching in Hong Kong: What is and what might be.* Hong Kong: University of Hong Kong, Faculty of Education.

Biggs, J. B., & Watkins, D. A. (1995). *Classroom learning: Educational psychology for the Asian teacher.* New York: Prentice Hall.

Cheng, M. H. (1997, March 24-28). *Perception of teacher competence: From student to teacher.* Paper presented at the Annual Meeting of the American Educational Research Association, Chicago, IL.

Chow, B. C., & Lou, L. (1992). A comparison of role perceptions of a successful physical educator among physical education majors and established physical educators in Hong Kong. *Education Journal, 20*(1), 65-73.

Colleges of Education, Research Co-ordination Committee. (1985). *Colleges of Education student profile survey.* Hong Kong: Author.

Cotton, J. (1995). *The theory of learners.* London: Kogan Page.

Crew, V. (1994, December). *When does a carrot become a stick? changing attitudes and English.* Paper presented at the International Language in Education Conference.

Doll, W. E. (1993). *A post-modern perspective on curriculum.* New York: Teachers College Press.

Elliot, A. B. (1983). *Errors in English.* Singapore: Singapore University Press.

Ellis, R. (1997). *SLA research and language teaching.* Oxford: Oxford University Press.

Ellis, R. (1992). *Second language acquisition & language pedagogy.* Clevedon, England: Multilingual Matters.

Esch, E. M. (1997). Learner training for autonomous language learning. In P. Benson & P. Voller (Eds.), *Autonomy and independence in language learning* (pp. 164 – 175). London: Longman.

Evans, G. (1991). Student control over learning. In J. B. Biggs, (Ed.), *Teaching for learning: The view from cognitive psychology* (pp. 51 – 70). Hawthorn: ACER.

Forrester, V. (1994). *Our starting point.* Hong Kong: Hong Kong Institute of Education.

Forrester, V. (1997). The challenge of gender-bias reform: A case study of teacher trainees in Hong Kong. *Asian Journal of English Language Teaching, 7,* 113-120.

Forrester, V. (1998). Not remedial English rather English in the liberal arts. *ACUCA Exchange, VIII*(1), 156-180.

Foster, P. (1999). Problem-based learning and pedagogy. *ELT Journal, 53*(1), 69-70.

Galloway, D. (1998). *Motivating the difficult to teach.* Harlow: Longman.

Hong Kong Special Administrative Region Government. (1997). *Chief Executive's policy address.* [Online]. Available: http://www.info.gov.hk/pa97/english/paindex.htm.

Joseph, J. E., & Taylor, T. J. (Eds.). (1990). *Ideologies of language.* London: Routledge.

Kelly, R. (1996). Language counselling for learning autonomy: the skilled helper in self-access language learning. In R. Pemberton, E. Li, W. Or, & H. D. Pierson (Eds.), *Taking control: autonomy in language learning* (pp. 93-113). Hong Kong: Hong Kong University Press.

Kumaravadivelu, B. (1993). The name of the problem and the problem of naming: methodological aspects of problem-based pedagogy. In G. Crookes & S. M. Gass (Eds.), *Problems in a pedagogical context: Integrating theory and practice* (pp. 69-96). Clevedon: Multilingual Matters.

MacLennan, C. (1995, June 5-7). Student teachers and curriculum change. Paper presented at *International Conference on Teacher Education in the Asian Region.*

Marton, F. & Booth, S. (1997) *Learning and awareness.* Mahwah, NJ: L. Erlbaum Associates.

Mulcahy, R., Peat D., Andrews J., Darko-Yeboah J., Marfo K., & Cho, S. (1991). Cognitive strategy-based instruction. In J. B. Biggs (Ed.), *Teaching for learning: the view from cognitive psychology* (pp. 195-214). Hawthorn : ACER.

Nunan. D. (1992). *Collaborative language learning and teaching.* Cambridge: Cambridge University Press.

Nunan, D. (1991). *Language teaching methodology.* London: Prentice Hall.

Nunan. D., & Lamb, C. (1996). *The self-directed teacher: Managing the learning process.* Cambridge; New York: Cambridge University Press.

Nunan. D., & Bailey, K. M. (1996). *Voices from the language classroom: Qualitative research in second language education.* Cambridge: Cambridge University Press.

Office of Student Affairs, Chinese University of Hong Kong. (1998). *A profile of new students.* Hong Kong: Author.

Office of Student Affairs, University of Hong Kong. (1998). *A profile of new students.* Hong Kong: Author.

Pinar, W. F., & Reynolds, W. M. (1992). *Understanding curriculum as phenomenological and deconstructed text.* New York: Teachers College Press.

Reason, P. editor (1994) *Participation in human inquiry.* London: Sage Publications.

Reason, P. editor (1981) *Human inquiry.* New York: Wiley & Sons.

Reynolds, W. (1987). *Implications of effective teacher research: Madeline Hunter's seven steps to educational paradise.* Chapter presented at the AERA Conference, Washington, D.C.

Sadovnik, A. R. (Ed.). (1995). *Knowledge and pedagogy: the sociology of Basil Bernstein.* Norwood, NJ: Ablex Pub. Corp.

Sears, J. T., & Marshall., J. D. (Ed.). (1990). *Teaching and thinking about curriculum: Critical inquiries.* New York: Teachers College Press.

Shannon, S. M. (1994). Introduction. In R. M. Barasch & J. C. Vaughan (Eds.), *Beyond the Monitor Model* (pp. 7-20). Boston: Heinle & Heinle.

Shohamy, E. (2000). *Issues in benchmarking*. Hong Kong: Hong Kong Institute of Education.

Student Affairs Office, Hong Kong Institute of Education. (1999). *A profile of year one full-time Students*. Hong Kong: Author.

Student Affairs Office, Polytechnic University. (1998). *A Profile of new students*. Hong Kong: Author.

Tarnas. R. (1991). *The passion of the western mind: Understanding the ideas that have shaped our world view.* New York: Ballantine.

Tennant, M. (1988). *Psychology and adult learning*. London: Routledge.

Tse, K., & Chung, C. (1995). The relationship between personality-environment congruency and teaching performance in student teachers. *Education Journal, 23*(1), 69-81.

Turner-Smith, R. F. (1981). *Study patterns and attitudes of first year students*. Hong Kong: Chinese University of Hong Kong.

Tyler, R. W. (1949). *Basic principles of curriculum and instruction, syllabus for Education.* Chicago: University of Chicago.

Weiner, B. (1992). *Human motivation: Metaphors, theories and research*. London: Sage.

Weiner, B. (1986). *An attributional theory of motivation and emotion*. New York: Springer-Verlag.

Willis, J. (1996). *A framework for task-based learning*. Harlow, England: Longman.